Seventh Edition **7**

Criminal
INVESTIGATION

A Method for Reconstructing the Past

James W. **Osterburg** / Richard H. **Ward**
University of Illinois / University of New Haven

ELSEVIER

AMSTERDAM • BOSTON • HEIDELBERG • LONDON
NEW YORK • OXFORD • PARIS • SAN DIEGO
SAN FRANCISCO • SINGAPORE • SYDNEY • TOKYO
Anderson Publishing is an imprint of Elsevier

Acquiring Editor: Shirley Decker-Lucke
Development Editor: Ellen S. Boyne
Project Manager: Laura Jackson
Designer: Tin Box Studio

Anderson Publishing is an imprint of Elsevier
225 Wyman Street, Waltham, MA 02451, USA

Library of Congress Cataloging-in-Publication Data
Application submitted

British Library Cataloguing-in-Publication Data
A catalogue record for this book is available from the British Library

ISBN: 978-1-4557-3138-1

For information on all Anderson publications
visit our website at http://store.elsevier.com

Printed in the United States of America
14 15 16 17 18   10 9 8 7 6 5 4 3 2 1

There is no accepted test of civilization. It is not wealth, or the degree of comfort, or the average duration of life, or the increase of knowledge. All such tests would be disputed. In default of any other measure, may it not be suggested that as good a measure as any is the degree to which justice is carried out, the degree to which men are sensitive to wrongdoing and desirous to right it?

Sir John Macdonell. *Historical Trials.* London: Oxford University Press, 1927, 148.

To Julia, wife and life-long companion since high school days, mother of our children, and early copy editor of this book. She made it readable by refusing to type any paragraph she could not understand. She is missed, having battled and was felled by ovarian cancer. In loving memory of a remarkable woman—Julia Mary Osterburg.

—Jim Osterburg

To the many students, friends, and colleagues who have enriched my life. To my wife, Michelle, and our daughter, Michelle Sophia, my appreciation and love for understanding the many hours in my den pursuing new ideas and new horizons. And to our grandchildren, Declan and Keeley, their parents, Juli and Jon, and our daughter, Jeanne. Finally, to our editor, Ellen Boyne, who has been there since the first edition of this text in 1992.

—Dick Ward

In memory of friends and colleagues who have passed along the way, and to those who serve in law enforcement and the military at home and on distant shores.

—DW and JO

CONTENTS

PART C
FOLLOW-UP MEASURES: REAPING INFORMATION

15 Crime and Constitutional Law: The Foundations of Criminal Investigation

16 Evidence and Effective Testimony

Dedication

In the history of a field of study, landmark events chronicle the stages of its progress toward a discipline. We have chosen to commemorate a number of events in the evolution of criminal justice beginning with the establishment of university programs in the early 1940s, the roles played by those police departments that took the lead in recognizing the value of education and the importance of professionalization in law enforcement, the impetus of the federal government in providing funds for research and development in the 1960s and 1970s, and the leadership provided by local, state and federal officials who fostered change.

Well before the designation of our field as criminal justice, a few universities were prodded by a progressive police chief to set up departments centered largely on the study of the police. Leading the way were the Departments of Police Administration at Indiana University, Michigan State University, Washington State University, the (now defunct) School of Criminology at the University of California, Berkeley, John Jay College of Criminal Justice, and Sam Houston State University in Texas. The uneasy alliance between some in academia and criminal justice took many years to overcome, but today there are more than 1,000 college-level programs in the field, strong testimony to the many faculties who have contributed to the development of education and research.

Dr. Donald H. Riddle (1921–1999) was a distinguished leader and innovator in the field of criminal justice education. When President of John Jay University, he was once asked "How do you educate the police?" His answer, "Like everyone else," became legendary and helped set the direction for curriculum and research in the field. His vision and understanding of the special mission of an urban university was realized during his tenure as Chancellor of the University of Illinois at Chicago. His wisdom and dedication to higher education and the field of criminal justice were an inspiration to faculty and students. The authors were privileged to know Don Riddle as a friend and mentor and are honored to dedicate this book to his memory.

Dr. Gordon Misner (1927–2006), a pioneer in criminal justice education, is remembered as a good friend and mentor of Richard H. Ward. His contributions to the investigative function and to his many students are recalled in this dedication.

We also honor (former) Dean Victor Strecher and the faculty of the School of Criminal Justice at Sam Houston State University for securing the funding for the first endowed chair in criminal justice—the George J. Beto Chair.

James W. Osterburg
Richard H. Ward

In Memoriam: James W. Osterburg

The passage of Jim Osterburg in November 2012, as we completed work on this edition of the text, marks the end of an era in which Jim's distinguished career spanned almost eight decades and saw what might be described as a revolution in criminal justice and crime investigation. Jim retired as a First Grade Detective in the New York City Police Department and was one of a few early forensic scientists who helped establish the discipline as an area of higher education within the field of criminal justice. Jim served as chair of the Department of Forensic Studies at Indiana University, and later as Chair of the Department of Criminal Justice at the University of Illinois at Chicago. He was the author of numerous articles and books, and our association as coauthor and editor with him began with the first edition of the book in 1992. His ongoing involvement and participation over the years are examples of Jim's dedication to the study of criminal investigation and his contributions to a science and research methodology.

Jim was a dedicated family person, and the loss of his wife, Julia, who helped with earlier drafts of this text, was a great loss. He was very proud of his four sons and his grandchildren. Despite his many awards and honors, Jim was also a person who did not seek recognition, and spent most of his life seeking answers to what he referred to as "the unanswered questions." He will be missed, but he will also be remembered for his many contributions to the pursuit of justice.

Richard H. Ward
Ellen S. Boyne, Editor

Acknowledgments

Maureen Aceto	Administrative Assistant to Richard H. Ward
James Adkins	Chief, Brooksville Fire Department (Brooksville, FL)
Mike Ahearn	Assistant Director (retired), U.S. Postal Inspection Service
Ahmet Akici	Superintendent, Turkish National Police
James Albrecht	Captain, New York Police Department (retired)
Michael Bozeman	Sergeant (retired), Houston Police Department Homicide Division
Kathy Brown	Consultant
Jeff Builta	Defense Intelligence Agency, Department of Defense
Matt Casey	Deputy Superintendent (retired), Chicago Police Department
Tae J. Chung	Consultant, Republic of Korea
John Conley	Special Agent (retired), FBI Academy (Quantico, VA)
Thomas Constantine	Director (retired), Drug Enforcement Administration
John Decarlo	Former Chief, Branford, CT, Police Department and Associate Professor, University of New Haven
John DeHaan	Program Manager, Bureau of Forensic Services, Department of Justice, State of California; author of *Kirk's Fire Investigation*
Rolando del Carmen	Distinguished and Regents Professor, College of Criminal Justice, Sam Houston State University
Duayne J. Dillon	Assistant Sheriff and Chief Executive Officer (retired), Sheriff's Department, Contra Costa County, CA; founder and former Director, Criminalistics Laboratory, Contra Costa County, CA
James Dozier	Associate Professor, Sam Houston State University
William Dyson	Supervisory Special Agent and Head of Joint FBI Terrorist Task Force in Chicago (retired)
Dean Esserman	Chief, New Haven Police Department
Michael Fain	Director, Collections, Institute for the Study of Violent Groups, University of New Haven
Evginiya Fedotova	Research Assistant. University of New Haven
Michael Figorito	Director, Police Research, Institute for the Study of Violent Groups, University of New Haven

Robert Gaensslen	Professor of Forensic Science, University of Illinois at Chicago (retired)
Archie Generoso	Chief of Detectives, New Haven Police Department
Tony Grubisic	Federal Bureau of Investigation
Chris Hale	Assistant Professor, Sam Houston State University
Marshall J. Hartman	Public Defender, Lake County, IL
Howard Henderson	Assistant Professor, Sam Houston State University
Josh Hill	Consultant
Sean Hill	Consultant
Cindy Moors-Hill	Consultant
Terry Hillard	Superintendent (retired), Chicago Police Department
Sorin Iliescu	Chair, Fire Science Department, University of New Haven
Michael Jenkins	Assistant Professor, University of New Haven
Wayne A. Kerstetter	Professor of Criminal Justice (retired), University of Illinois at Chicago
Kathleen Kiernan	Assistant Director (retired), Bureau of Alcohol, Tobacco, Firearms, and Explosives; Founder and CEO, Kiernan Group Holdings.
Keith Killacky	Associate Professor of Criminal Justice, St. Louis University; Federal Bureau of Investigation (retired)
Joseph King	Associate Professor, John Jay College of Criminal Justice
Henry C. Lee	Professor, University of New Haven
John J. Lentini	Fire Investigation Chemist, Applied Technical Services (Marietta, GA)
Charles Lieberman	New York City Police Department
Thomas Linkowski	Deputy Chief, Evanston Fire Department (Evanston, IL)
Cali Luco	Research Associate, Yale University School of Medicine
Daniel Mabrey	Assistant Dean and Assistant Professor, Executive Director of the Institute for the Study of Violent Groups, University of New Haven
Herbert L. MacDonell	Director, Laboratory of Forensic Science, Corning, NY; Adjunct Professor, Corning Community College, Corning, NY
Debra Malinowski	Police Officer, Los Angeles Police Department
Sean Malinowski	Captain, Los Angeles Police Department
Michael D. Maltz	Professor of Criminal Justice and Professor of Information and Decision Sciences (retired), University of Illinois at Chicago
Virginia Maxwell	Associate Dean, University of New Haven
Jian Ming Mei	Associate Professor, Chinese People's Public Security University
Jason Moore	Federal Bureau of Investigation
Nathan Moran	Professor and Chair, Midwestern State University

Richard Mugno	Security Consultant
John Murray	Sergeant (retired), Chicago Police Department
Richard A. Myren	Professor Emeritus, School of Justice, American University; Founding Dean, School of Criminal Justice, SUNY at Albany
Aziz Osman	Superintendent, Turkish National Police
Will Oliver	Professor, Sam Houston State University
John O'Neill	Federal Bureau of Investigation (deceased)
Joseph L. Peterson	Professor of Criminal Justice, School of Criminal Justice and Criminalistics, California State University
Frank Pierczynski	Sergeant (retired), Chicago Police Department
John E. Pless	Culbertson Professor of Pathology and Professor of Pathology, School of Medicine, Indiana University
Michael A. Prieto	Director, American Institute of Applied Sciences (Syracuse, NY)
Rachel Putorti	Research Assistant, 7th Edition
Charles Ramsey	Former Chief of Police, Philadelphia (PA) Police Department
Fred Rice	Superintendent (deceased), Chicago Police Department;
Jack Ridges	Sergeant (retired), Central Homicide Evaluation and Support Squad, Chicago Police Department
Benjamin Riley	Department of Defense
Matt Rodriguez	Superintendent (retired), Chicago Police Department
Dennis Rowe	Chief Superintendent (deceased), Metropolitan Police, London
Joseph Ryan	Professor and Chair, Pace University
Anthony Schembri	International Police Consultant
Chris Sedelmier	Associate Professor, University of New Haven
Joseph D. Serio	Author of *Investigating the Russian Mafia*
Robert "Jerry" Simandl	Detective, Gang Unit, Chicago Police Department
Savannah Smith	Research Assistant, New Haven Police Department
Darrel Stephens	Chief of Police (retired), Charlotte, NC
Mark J. Stolorow	Manager, Forensic Sciences, Cellmark Diagnostics; former Director, Research and Development, Illinois State Police, Bureau of Forensic Science
Tim Stone	Federal Bureau of Investigation
William Tafoya	Federal Bureau of Investigation (retired); Professor, University of New Haven
Vince Webb	Dean and Director, Sam Houston State University, Criminal Justice Center

Jeffery D. Wells	Professor of Justice Sciences, University of Alabama at Birmingham
Carl Williams	Assistant Commissioner, Jamaica Constabulary
Ed Worthington	Federal Bureau of Investigation (retired)
Steve Young	Assistant Professor, Criminal Justice Center, Sam Houston State University
Joe Zhou	Lawyer, Vice President, Hope Technology, Shanghai, China

A special note of thanks to the University of New Haven and its President, Dr. Steven Kaplan, and to Sam Houston State University, where much of the early planning and organization of the recent editions was undertaken, and to Harold Smith, a friend and colleague who passed away during the preparation of an earlier edition. Our appreciation extends also to the many faculty and trainers who use this text in their classes and have taken time to offer their suggestions over the years. Their contributions have been important to the longevity of the book.

Over the years a great many others have offered their advice or otherwise helped to improve the quality of the work; they are:

Hasan Arslan	Assistant Professor, Pace University
Mary Bartucci	Administrative Secretary (retired), Office of the Vice Chancellor for Special Programs, University of Illinois at Chicago
Frank Bolz	Commander (retired), Hostage Negotiation Team, New York Police Department
André Bossard	Former Executive Director, INTERPOL (Paris)
Tony Bouza	Chief (retired), Minneapolis Police Department
Harriet Brewster	Director, Graphic Arts, Criminal Justice Center, Sam Houston State University
Kathy Brown	Assistant Professor, University of New Haven
Jane Buckwalter	Illinois Criminal Justice Information Authority (retired) and former Associate Vice Chancellor, University of Illinois at Chicago
Stan Delaney	Vice Chancellor for Administration (retired), University of Illinois at Chicago
Jerry L. Dowling	Professor (retired), College of Criminal Justice, Sam Houston State University
Mario Gaboury	Dean, Henry C. Lee College of Criminal Justice and Forensic Sciences, University of New Haven
Mark Galazka	Graduate Assistant
Randy Garner	Professor, Sam Houston State University
Evynne Graveline	Former Graduate Assistant to Richard H. Ward
Wu Han	Professor, East China Institute of Politics and Law (Shanghai)

Josh Hill	Institute for the Study of Violent Groups
John Hitzeman	Director, Information Technology, Institute for the Study of Violent Groups, University of New Haven
Joyce Hornback	Editor
Wayne Johnson	Chief Investigator (retired), Chicago Crime Commission
Wes Johnson	Doctoral Program Director, School of Criminal Justice, University of Southern Mississippi
Robert Keppel	Professor, University of New Haven
Bruce Lewis	Chief of Police, Northwestern University
Ray Liu	Professor of Forensic Sciences, University of Alabama at Birmingham
Vesna Markovic	Director, Institute for the Study of Violent Groups; Assistant Professor, University of New Haven
Peter Massey	Assistant Professor and Criminalist, Henry C. Lee College of Criminal Justice and Forensic Sciences, University of New Haven
Janice May	Author
Peter May	Author
Debra McCall	Executive Assistant to Richard H. Ward (1999–2006), Criminal Justice Center, Sam Houston State University
Richard Natoli	Professor of Criminal Justice, Massasoit Community College
Bette Naysmith	Chair, Committee on Ritual Abuse, Cult Awareness Network
William Norton	Director, School of Public Service, University of New Haven
Harry O'Reilly	Detective Sergeant (retired), New York Police Department
Tim Palmbach	Chair, Department of Forensic Science, University of New Haven
Carlo Pecori	Director, Institute for the Study of Violent Groups
Dave Peters	Deputy Chief, University of Illinois Police Department
Mitchell Roth	Professor, Sam Houston State University
Prapon Sahapattara	Colonel, Royal Thai Police
Gene Scaramella	Chicago Police Department (retired)
David Schroeder	Assistant Dean, University of New Haven
Larry St. Regis	Department of Public Safety, Sunnyvale California
Jay Stahle	Network Administrator, University of New Haven
Victor Strecher	Professor and former Dean, College of Criminal Justice, Sam Houston State University (retired)
John Truitt	Criminal Justice Consultant

Marie Tyse	Chief of Police (retired), University of Illinois at Chicago
Bruce Varga	Assistant Professor of Fire Science, University of New Haven
Rafal Wasniak	Major, Polish National Police
Rita Watkins	Director, Law Enforcement Management Institute, Sam Houston State University
Dave Webb	Associate Director, Law Enforcement Management Institute, Sam Houston State University
Hubert Williams	President, Police Foundation
Angelica Zdonek	Research Assistant, 7th Edition

Several firms that market equipment used in law enforcement generously provided illustrative material. Our thanks to John Carrington of Sirchie Finger Print Laboratories; Elliot L. Parker of Instant Image Systems; Doug Peavey of Lynn Peavey Company; Michael A. Prieto of the American Institute of Applied Sciences; Robert Smith of UNISYS Corporation; James D. Werner of Cellmark Diagnostics and Mike Carpenter of the Siemens Group.

Permission was granted to use material that first appeared in the publications of Clark Boardman Co., Ltd.; the *Journal of Police Science and Administration* (International Association of Chiefs of Police); and the National Center for Missing and Exploited Children. We thank Judge William S. Sessions, former Director of the Federal Bureau of Investigation, for permission to reprint "FBI Suggestions for Packaging Physical Evidence" in earlier editions of this text.

The collections of several libraries were available. We thank the staffs of the University of Illinois at Chicago; Sam Houston State University; University of New Haven; Northwestern University; University of Alabama, Birmingham; University of South Florida; Pasco-Hernando Community College; Lykes Memorial (Hernando) County Library; and Evanston Public Library. Many members of the Institute for the Study of Violent Groups (ISVG) were also helpful in a number of ways. Special thanks also to Provost David Dauwalder, University of New Haven, a friend and colleague.

Our editor, Ellen S. Boyne, has been with us since the beginning and the first edition in 1992. Her patience and fine editorial hand through numerous and major changes in both organization and content, as well as her suggestions, have been an important part of the success this book has enjoyed. We are truly indebted to her.

Cheerful editorial assistance and encouragement were provided by past and present colleagues from Anderson Publishing, LexisNexis, and Elsevier: William L. Simon, Vice President, Anderson Publishing (retired); and Kelly Grondin, Director, Criminal Justice, LexisNexis. They have been most patient and helpful in bringing this book to print. We also wish to acknowledge the suggestions made by Professors Larry Miller of East Tennessee State University, Larry Myers of Western Carolina University, and David L. Carter of Michigan State University.

Although we received numerous suggestions and acted upon most of them, we rejected some; in the final analysis, therefore, the text is our responsibility and not that of any of the readers listed above.

JWO
RHW

Online Instructor and Student Resources

Thank you for selecting Anderson Publishing's *Criminal Investigation: A Method for Reconstructing the Past*. To complement the learning experience, we have provided a number of online tools to accompany this edition. Two distinct packages of interactive resources are available: one for instructors and one for students.

Please consult your local sales representative with any additional questions. You may also e-mail the Academic Sales Team at textbook@elsevier.com.

FOR THE INSTRUCTOR

Qualified adopters and instructors can access valuable material for free by registering at: http://textbooks.elsevier.com/web/manuals.aspx?isbn=9781455731381

- **Test Bank** Compose, customize, and deliver exams using unique questions created for *Criminal Investigation: A Method for Reconstructing the Past,* 7th ed.

- **PowerPoint Lecture Slides** Reinforce key topics with PowerPoint slides. Each book chapter has its own dedicated slide show.

- **Lesson Plans** Design your course around customized lesson plans. Each lesson plan contains content synopses, key terms, and other aids designed to spur class discussion.

FOR THE STUDENT

Students can access all the resources below by simply following this link: http://booksite.elsevier.com/9781455731381

- **Self-Assessment Question Bank** Enhance review and study sessions with the help of this online self-quizzing asset. Each question is presented in an interactive format that allows for immediate feedback.

- **Case Studies** Apply what is on the page to the world beyond with the help of topic-specific case studies, each designed to turn theory into practice and followed by interactive scenario-based questions that allow for immediate feedback.

- **Additional Resources** Consult an assortment of dynamic resources extending the discussion of topics covered in the text.

Preface

In this seventh edition of this book, we adhere to the principles of the first edition to provide a fundamental text on criminal investigation. Much has changed over the years in the field of criminal investigation, the law, and in society. Each edition has changed significantly to stay abreast of the many developments, and this edition marks yet another major revision of the book's structure and content. Issues affecting law enforcement display a combination of traditional concepts and terminology, and the emergence of new forms of crime and criminal activity. Cybercrime, global crime, terrorism, violent gang activity, complex fraud scandals, and enterprise crime are but a few of the issues that have taken new form in the criminal justice process. Indeed, the scope of the information and data has grown to the point that no single text can cover the field of criminal investigation. With this in mind, the seventh edition has been designed to enable instructors to emphasize those sections of the book that may be more relevant to their geographic location, of particular interest to students studying in specialized areas, or where the expertise of the instructor may go beyond the fundamentals of a particular type of investigation. Of particular note is the establishment of web site containing ancillary materials that will be of interest to readers.

Another goal is to help the general reader understand how detective work should be performed, and, most important, to demystify the investigative process. To the extent that criminal investigation is perceived as part and parcel of a more universal kind of inquiry, we will have succeeded. Human beings, it must be agreed, have always acknowledged their need to understand the past. In the study of ancient history, this understanding relies largely on what records survive from that era; in criminal investigation, on the other hand, reconstructing a past event (i.e., a crime) is based on evidence developed by the forensic laboratory, from questioning people, and from examining records.

There are numerous reminders throughout the text that criminal investigation must be conducted within the framework of our democratic system. Hence, those U.S. Supreme Court decisions that affect the investigative function are quoted extensively. They reveal the inherent tension created by the state's obligation to enforce the law while protecting a citizen's rights under the Constitution. In addition, the Court's carefully crafted opinions expose the student to legal reasoning at its best. Although courses in criminal procedure are covered in the criminal justice curricula, we believe that issues that have been or will be brought before the court are better comprehended when there is an awareness of law enforcement's perspective as well as that of the civil libertarian's.

Whatever may be the need for information, it is fairly obvious that the ability to conduct any type of inquiry can be honed by studying the investigative process. Perhaps one of the most important changes in American life has been the expansive range of information available through technology, research, and social media. Ultimately, the investigator relies upon three sources of information—physical evidence, people, and records. The manner in which this information is collected, compiled, and analyzed by the investigator involves much more than a vocational or training emphasis, and relies in great measure on the educational processes that emphasize knowledge, abstract reasoning, intellectual curiosity, and a philosophy based on searching for the truth. Undoubtedly, one of the major events since earlier editions of this book has been a report by the National Academy of Sciences: *Strengthening Forensic Science in the United States: A Path Forward.* This report identifies many of the problems associated with forensic examinations and laboratories in many parts of the United States, and offers a set of recommendations, many of which have become hotly debated topics within the forensic science and law enforcement communities. This is discussed more fully in Chapter 2, and the complete recommendations of this report are included in the ancillary web site.

Over the years this text has had wide appeal. Its heuristic approach to the investigative function serves to enlighten the average reader and the law enforcement investigator. But in today's world it will also serve many other kinds of investigators, including for example public prosecutors, defense attorneys, public defenders, medical examiners, fraud examiners, insurance investigators, private investigators, the media's investigative reporters, and the criminal investigation arms of the military. Each year we find new forms of investigative specialization, especially at the federal level where most federal departments now have some form of investigative unit.

The authors have reorganized parts of the text based on the suggestions of colleagues and in an effort to better accommodate the text for a quarter or semester course of study. It is now divided into three sections. The first discusses the basics of criminal investigation. The second illustrates their application to many of the major felonies. Instructors and students are given several kinds of specialized investigations and topics to choose from in the remaining section. We believe that dividing the material in this fashion has not only preserved the text's comprehensiveness, but has also rendered the material eminently more teachable. The first two sections constitute the heart of the investigative process; the last offers enrichment on special topics—to be savored as time and desire permit. Several new chapters have been added on the Influence and Impact of Technology in keeping with the growing emphasis in this area on the investigative process. The authors express their appreciation to Professor Tim Palmbach, Chair, Department of Forensic Science, and Associate Dean and Professor Virginia Maxwell, University of New Haven, for their assistance with Chapter 2, and Assistant Professor Peter Massey (UNH) for his assistance with Chapter 3.

The authors thank the many users who have commented on the readability of our text, and trust that the new material is of similar quality. Suggestions from instructors and students alike are most welcome and can be addressed by e-mail to rward@newhaven.edu.

Section I

THE FOUNDATION AND PRINCIPLES OF CRIMINAL INVESTIGATION

Conceptually, it is often difficult to know where you are going if you don't know where you've been. Like most disciplines, criminal investigation is based on a foundation of knowledge gathered over time. This historical body of knowledge also provides the framework for understanding where mistakes have been made and how new ideas and innovative advances contribute to success, and to some degree for helping to chart future directions. In this regard, the evolutionary aspects of crime investigation borrow from the past as a means of adapting to change, whether it is in tradecraft, legal decisions, or technology. This section on criminal investigation comprises three parts: the first emphasizes the uses that can be made of the basic sources of information; the second is concerned with the role of the investigator and problems associated with obtaining information; and the third focuses on the kinds of follow-through activities necessary for capitalizing on the efforts described in the first two parts. Considered together, these three parts form the foundation and principles of criminal investigation.

Part A

SOURCES AND USES
OF INFORMATION

Part A begins with a discussion of the detective's role and responsibilities and the personal attributes that are required for success. A brief history of criminal investigation follows (touching on a sometimes less-than-honorable past). Part A concludes with a review of the trends and future developments that are likely to occur.

The three principal sources of information in criminal investigation (physical evidence, people, and records) are studied first from the standpoint of what information may be obtained and why it can be of help. Then, because understanding physical evidence—its development, interpretation, and investigative use—is fundamental, some familiarity with criminalistics is recommended. The crime scene—its limits, the purpose for a search, legal constraints on the discovery of physical evidence— are presented next. Finally, the other appropriate sources of information are considered: people (criminals, victims, witnesses, and friends), records (public and private), and new forms of social media (such as Facebook, LinkedIn, blogs, and Twitter).

Given the impact of a rapidly changing society in such areas as technology, transportation, communication, and globalization, the task of the criminal investigator has become more complex. In addition to terrorism and urban violence, there has been a greater focus on corporate crime, serial murder, and technological crime. The result has been a greater need for investigators who are not only familiar with basics but who have the ability to "think outside the box."

CHAPTER 1

THE INVESTIGATOR
Responsibilities and Attributes; Origins and Trends

The role and responsibilities of the criminal investigator have changed dramatically over the past 20 years, largely as a result of changes in social perceptions, culture, technology, the law, the media, and new forms of communication—such as the Internet, cellular telephones, imaging, and social media. Perhaps most important has been the changing role of the investigator as a specialist, educated and trained to be knowledgeable about complex systems, societal differences, and organizational theory.

This chapter addresses the general framework associated with being a criminal investigator: the functional aspects of the job, necessary skills, tools of the trade, and the criteria necessary for success in what can be a challenging and rewarding career. Like most professional occupations, criminal investigation encompasses a historical framework that continues to evolve through new techniques and technology, as well as research. Thus, a brief description of the history of investigating crime is included in this chapter. Although much has changed in the way criminal investigations are conducted, the one thing that has not changed radically over time has been the definition of criminal investigation.

CRIMINAL INVESTIGATION DEFINED

The investigation of crime encompasses "the collection of information and evidence for identifying, apprehending, and convicting suspected offenders,"[1] or in the words of Professor Ralph Turner, a pioneer in the field, "the reconstruction of a past event."[2] In essence, the responsibilities of the investigator include the following:

1. Determine whether a crime has been committed.

2. Decide if the crime was committed within the investigator's jurisdiction.

3. Discover all facts pertaining to the complaint.
    a. Gather and preserve physical evidence.
    b. Develop and follow up all clues.

4. Recover stolen property.

5. Identify the perpetrator or eliminate a suspect as the perpetrator.

6.   Locate and apprehend the perpetrator.

7.   Aid in the prosecution of the offender by providing evidence of guilt that is admissible in court.

8.   Testify effectively as a witness in court.

The date and time when each responsibility was carried out should be recorded. Being unable to answer confidently "when" a task was carried out affords defense counsel the opportunity to cast doubt on the investigator's capability. If a witness repeatedly responds to the question "At what time did you do_____?" with "I don't remember" or "as best as I can recall," defense counsel will use this technique to impugn a witness's competence.

Determine if a Crime Has Been Committed

Determining whether a crime has been committed necessitates an understanding of the criminal law and the elements of each criminal act. For this reason the investigator should have in his or her possession copies of the penal and case law of the state or jurisdiction. The jurisdiction of federal investigators may be broader in some cases, but it is limited by legislation, and state and local investigators should be familiar with the crimes over which federal statutes may apply.

The availability of legal documents and texts on-line or as downloads makes it possible for an investigator to have the penal law and criminal code at hand immediately. Ideally, an investigator should have digital copies of the various legal texts on a personal computer, making it easy to identify and answer questions. In more complex cases, such as cybercrime or fraud, the investigator may contact the state prosecutor, district attorney, or U.S. attorney. In rare cases in which it is determined that a crime has not been committed, or where the issue is one for a civil court, law enforcement personnel do not have responsibility.

Verify Jurisdiction

If a crime is not within the investigator's jurisdiction, there is no responsibility for its investigation, but the complainant may need to be referred to the proper authority. Occasionally a crime is committed on the border line of two jurisdictions or involves more than one jurisdiction. If a case has the potential for publicity, affords the chance to make a "good arrest," or is inherently interesting or important, an investigator will probably seek to retain authority over it and remain involved; otherwise, he or she may talk the other jurisdiction into accepting it.

When two investigators have concurrent jurisdiction, the issue of who will handle the case can become complicated. Cases involving cross-border fraud, Internet crime, illegal immigration, drug trafficking, terrorism, and other multiple-jurisdiction criminal activity may involve joint investigative activities, and may require clarification by legal authority (such as a U.S. attorney or local prosecuting authority—district, city, or county attorney). In other cases, such as serial murder involving multiple jurisdictions, the place where the suspect is apprehended (for the crime in that jurisdiction) will usually have the right to prosecute. In those cases in which there may be federal as well as state jurisdiction (such as bank robbery), the U.S. attorney has the first right of refusal, and relatively minor cases may be prosecuted at a local level.

Discover All Facts and Collect Physical Evidence

The facts available to the first officer to arrive at a crime scene are provided by observation, and by the victim or complainant and any eyewitness(es). Except in departments with programs in place for managing criminal investigations (see Chapter 13), they will be communicated to the detective dispatched to investigate the crime. He or she may decide to verify and pursue all of them, or to home in on specific details. At the outset, the investigator should develop a preliminary record that addresses the following points:

- When?
- Where?
- Who?
- What?
- How?
- Why?

In addition, the detective will collect any physical evidence, or arrange for its collection (prefer ably by an evidence technician) and examination in the appropriate crime laboratory. Of particular importance are observation and a mental image of the scene, the victim or witnesses, or suspect if on the scene. Depending on the kind of information provided, immediate follow-up might be required or the investigator may have to await laboratory results. In either event, it is essential at this point to follow through on any clue that holds promise for the identification of the perpetrator, and promptly exploit it (see Figure 1.1).

Keeping in mind that information and records may be called into question during a later court case, the investigator must take care to prepare a comprehensive record of the crime scene, using

Courtesy, Peter Massey, Department of Forensic Sciences, University of New Haven

Figure 1.1
A crime scene presents many questions.

notes, photographs, sketches, and in some cases video and voice recording. Care must be taken not to rely on memory, which has shown to be notoriously unreliable in many cases. Statements of victims, witnesses, and suspects should be recorded accurately and verbatim where possible.

In longer investigations, the use of records or other forms of information is more likely to contribute to the solution. If the victim furnishes the suspect's name to the detective, the case may be solved promptly. Then the chief problem is proving that the particular individual did in fact commit the crime. If the identity of the perpetrator must be developed, the effort required is much greater and, for certain crimes, often not successful. When it is, there comes a point not unlike that reached in solving a jigsaw puzzle: when the crucial piece is found, those remaining quickly fall into place.

Recover Stolen Property

The description and identification of stolen property are important aspects of an investigation, and may later be critical in establishing ownership. Stolen property may turn up at a pawn shop, in the hands of secondhand dealers, or for sale on the Internet. The ability to establish makes and models, serial numbers, or other distinguishing characteristics of an item can contribute to a successful investigation. Pawn shops, flea markets, and Internet sites are common locations for stolen property to be sold or advertised, and the investigator should be familiar with record keeping and the various types of locations where evidence or property may turn up (see Figure 1.2).

Identify the Perpetrator

Identifying the perpetrator is, of course, the primary goal of a criminal investigation, but the ability to bring a suspect to justice also depends on the evidence necessary for conviction. This may take

Courtesy, Ellen S. Boyne

Figure 1.2
Police often check pawn shops for stolen property, which may be sold or advertised there.

many forms, including physical evidence linking the suspect to the scene (fingerprints, blood, DNA, toolmarks); possession of evidence from the scene (property, fibers, hair); physical identification (tattoos, deformities, physical descriptors); and eyewitness descriptions, which, incidentally, have proven to be highly unreliable when the suspect is not known to victims or witnesses. *Modus operandi*, or method of operation, is also an important consideration. Unfortunately, it is not unusual for a police officer to make assumptions on the basis of the way a person looks or acts, based on race, language, mode of dress, or "signs of guilt."

In addition to the identification of the perpetrator from records, physical evidence, and eyewitnesses, the value of motive must be examined. Certain crimes, such as burglary, robbery, and rape, seem to have a universal motive; others, such as homicide, arson, and assault, have what might be called "particularized motives," because they often relate victim to criminal. Once established, it would be practical to develop a short list of persons who might have a particularized motive; then, if the investigator considers who had the opportunity and the temperament to carry out the crime, one or perhaps a few suspects may remain on the list. When physical evidence is available, as it often is in these crimes, this extends the possibility of a solution beyond what can be accomplished by interrogation alone.

Locate and Apprehend the Perpetrator

When people who know the perpetrator are unwilling or unable to provide an address or a clue to his or her whereabouts (should the suspect be elusive or have escaped), records or other forms of information may provide the answer as to a person's whereabouts. (See Chapters 5 and 7, which discuss the value and utilization of records and other forms of information.) When the suspect is located, apprehension may present difficulties. If it does, a raid may be called for. Planning and staging a raid require coordination, but this is essentially a police function rather than an investigative one. Owing, however, to several raids that received worldwide attention and, to some extent, had a deleterious impact on all law enforcement agencies, it is important to consider these events.

Aid the Prosecution by Providing Evidence of Guilt Admissible in Court

Largely as a result of plea bargaining, only a few cases that are investigated and solved eventually go to trial, but the detective **must** operate on the assumption that each will be tried. This necessitates that investigators follow correct procedures in conducting the investigation, and not assume that the perpetrator will plead guilty and plea bargain, or assume that other evidence will carry the case.

Because such a large number of cases are plea-bargained, the number of times an investigator may actually testify in a trial may be quite low. Problems concerning physical evidence can arise needlessly when it is presumed that a case will involve plea bargaining. One example is of a major city detective who had handled 75 burglary cases and none had gone to trial (each defendant having pleaded guilty to a reduced charge). Based on this experience, and because the suspect had confessed verbally, the detective believed that it was but a needless exercise to submit the physical evidence to the laboratory. Unfortunately, the prisoner was allowed to be placed in a police station cell wearing the incriminating evidence; once there, he ripped incriminating crepe shoe soles into pieces and flushed them down the toilet. He then repudiated the confession and demanded a trial.

Testify Effectively as a Witness in Court

Although few people are comfortable when called to the witness stand, the experienced investigator who has testified often can appear jaded. Yet testimony is effective only when it is credible. When sincerity, knowledge of the facts, and impartiality are projected, credibility is established. In all events, it is helpful that the investigator be familiar with the rules of evidence and the pitfalls of cross-examination (see Chapter 16).

ATTRIBUTES DESIRABLE IN AN INVESTIGATOR

Abilities and Skills

The attributes that enable a person to be an accomplished investigator are many (see Table 1.1), including three important areas:

1.   the ability, both physical and mental, to conduct an inquiry

2.   the knowledge and training necessary to handle complex investigations

3.   those skills necessary to reach the intended objectives.

Qualifications of Mind, Personality, Attitude, and Knowledge

The following list of traits, which are desirable and help to qualify an individual for investigative work, was developed through classroom discussions (including many detectives who were students) and by conferring with police administrators interested in the topic of qualifications.

1.   Intelligence and reasoning ability.
     An above-average score on an accepted intelligence test.
     Ability to analyze and interrelate a large number of facts.
     Ability to use advanced computer programs related to investigation.

2.   Curiosity and imagination.
     Taking nothing for granted.
     Skepticism of the obvious.
     A sense of the unusual: anything out of place or not in keeping with the norm.
     An inquisitive mind.
     A suspicious nature with respect to the behavior of people.
     A sense of awareness.
     Insight.
     A flair for detective work.

3.   Observation and memory.
     All five senses are intact and functioning.
     The investigator is alert and attentive.

Table 1.1
Role and Responsibilities of a Crime Scene Specialist

ABILITIES	RELATED SKILLS
Conduct a proper crime scene search for physical evidence.	Know how to recognize, collect, and preserve physical evidence. Know the varieties of *modus operandi*. Be familiar with contemporary collection and recording techniques.
Question complainants, witnesses, and suspects.	Know how to use interviewing techniques. Know interrogation methods. Have a knowledge of local street jargon, and if pertinent, any foreign language spoken in the community. Be sensitive to the constitutional and civil rights of all: rich or poor, witness or suspect. Have a developed sense of mind-set.
Develop and follow up clues.	Know sources of records and how to check them. Know how to cultivate and use informants. Know how to conduct surveillances. Know how to check pawn shops, secondhand dealers, Internet sites, and the like.
Prepare written reports of case activity as it develops.	Have knowledge and skill in English, and a second language when possible.
Obtain legal search warrants based on evidence of probable cause.	Know how to use departmental and court forms to secure a search warrant.
Conduct raids, possibly under adverse conditions.	Know the techniques of cover and concealment.
Act with initiative, as the fluidity of the (raid) situation demands.	Acquire skill in silent communication. Use teamwork—within and between agencies.
Apprehend violators in a lawful manner.	Acquire a working knowledge of applicable laws, departmental rules, and regulations. Know about the use of handcuffs and the various types of firearms and other weapons that may be used, especially with regard to legal restrictions. Know proper search and seizure techniques and electronic intercept procedures used for suspects, houses, and automobiles.
Assist prosecuting attorney in presentation to the grand jury or trial court.	Know how to prepare clear, comprehensive reports. Know how to serve subpoenas, when necessary. Know how to have witnesses available or willing to appear on notice.
Appear as a witness in court.	Testify effectively in court. Know how to serve subpoenas, when necessary. Know how to have witnesses available or willing to appear on notice.

4. Knowledge of life and people.

    Includes all strata of society; especially necessary to deal with the heterogeneous population of large cities.

    Also helpful: common sense, an outgoing personality, a spirit of cooperativeness, emotional stability, and some acting ability for role-playing.

5. Possession of technical "know-how."

    Implies training and knowledge of statutory and case law, as well as in the recognition, collection, preservation, and investigative value of physical evidence.

    It is important to be widely read and willing to keep up with current research and writing in the field.

6. Perseverance, "stick-to-itiveness," and energy.

    Many who wish to become detectives believe the job involves a glamorous life style, but the ability to be indefatigable, survive boredom, and keep energy in reserve to carry on, is more realistic.

7. Ability to recognize and control bias and prejudice in one's self and on the job.

    Owing to bias and prejudice, for example, there may be a preconceived idea as to the perpetrator. Other truths may be ignored, such as: a chronic complainant can have a legitimate grievance; a prostitute can be raped; etc.

8. Sensitivity to people's feelings; acts with discretion and tact; respects a confidence.

9. The honesty and courage to withstand temptation and corruption, or pressure from supervisors or others to solve the case.

10. When testifying, is not overzealous and does not commit perjury.

11. Miscellaneous characteristics:

    Physically fit appearance, report-writing skills, awareness of good public relations as a future source of cooperation and information.

Some police administrators believe that the traditional means of selecting detectives—written and oral examinations—have proved to be unsatisfactory:

> Prepared written examinations have not proved predictive in the selection of outstanding candidates for the position of investigator. ... No theoretical foundation exists for the oral board portion of the current testing process, other than a belief in its content validity.[3]

In recent years written and oral testing has been used largely to eliminate individuals who do not have the basic skills or demeanor to manage an investigation. Because the investigative field has become more specialized, individuals with particular skills, such as forensic accounting, sex crime investigations, undercover work, particular language skills, or information technology, may have an advantage, as the selection of investigators may be more focused on particular attributes of applicants.

A number of federal and local agencies have taken to hiring specialized types of investigators. For example, the FBI hires individuals specifically for their skills in computer and social media technology, surveillance, and language, as well as crime scene processing.

It is suggested that future performance can be gauged by an individual's "past work product." Further, good prospects must be recruited—not merely be a fallout of the hiring process. Selection should include such considerations as: computer literacy, superior analytical capability, and good communication and reading skills.[4] Another prerequisite is education.

> ... [The] most important requirement is education. Study after study produces the same conclusions: that college educated people make better law enforcement officers.[5]

The National Institute of Justice published the results of a more comprehensive study of the detective selection process. In the foreword, James K. Stewart wrote:

> ... managers and line personnel alike could identify some officers who were much better investigators than others. Studies bear out their observation: a small proportion of officers in any department is responsible for the majority of cases that successfully result in convictions.[6]

The concept of "past work product" is again endorsed as a predictor of success, yet criminal justice researchers have paid scant attention to the problem of detective selection, despite the impact of crime on the quality of life in communities across the nation.

ORIGINS OF CRIMINAL INVESTIGATION

The concept of criminal investigation can be traced back thousands of years, to early times in China and other parts of Asia, as well as the Middle East, where agents of government used a great many legal, as well as illegal approaches (most notably torture) as a means of identifying transgressors of public order.

From a Western perspective, the Industrial Revolution in Europe drew many from the peasant classes in the countryside to larger towns and cities, resulting in burgeoning crime waves, forcing governments to move beyond the traditional night watches and use of the military to maintain order.[7] In England, the so-called "thief catchers" were frequently drawn from elements of the underworld. The rank and file of the recruits constituted a distinct breed, but two clear-cut differences in motivation set some apart from others. Hirelings, with mercenary motives, would play both sides of the street; social climbers would incriminate their confederates in order to move into respectable society.

An example of the former may be found in eighteenth-century England where Jonathan Wild personified the old saying, "Set a thief to catch a thief" (see Figure 1.3). Wild was well-acquainted with London's riffraff, having operated a brothel that served as headquarters for the gang of thieves and cutthroats under his tight control. Simultaneously, he was the public servant doing undercover work for the authorities. A rogue on the grand scale, Wild was both law enforcer and law breaker. He soon realized, however, that there was more profit to be made arranging for the return of stolen goods than for its disposal at the stiff discounts taken by the fence. Therefore, throughout the period he worked for the authorities, he was actually a receiver of stolen goods posing as the recoverer of lost property—the middle man exacting his cut while protecting the criminals in his employ. Even today, there are resemblances between his fictitious "Lost Property Office" and the "no questions asked" practices of individuals (even of some insurance companies) when stolen property, such as valuable jewelry and priceless paintings, is ransomed.

The earliest police in England worked only at night. First known as the "Watch of London," and later as the "Old Charleys," they were paid by the inhabitants in the vicinity of the watchman's

en.wikipedia.org

Figure 1.3
Ticket to the hanging of "thief taker" Jonathan Wild.

box from which they regularly made the rounds of their beat. These parish constables had been appointed in 1253; they lasted until 1829 in London. In 1748, novelist Henry Fielding (who wrote about Wild's exploits in a genial, tolerant vein) accepted an appointment as a London magistrate. Taking his call to the bar seriously, Fielding was promptly embroiled in the sorry state of England's penal codes and its administration of justice (see Figure 1.4).

The new magistrate tried to deal with the rising crime rate by enlarging the scope of the government's crime-fighting methods and assigning to his court a few parish constables, who had been accustomed to night-watchman duties, to perform some criminal investigative functions. They came to be successful "thief-takers," owing to the use of informants and their close ties with the underworld. First called "Mr. Fielding's People," they later came to be known as the "Bow Street Runners" (see Figure 1.5). Unofficial and unpaid, the constables wore no uniforms and

were ranked directly under the magistrate, who had to fight for their fair share of the reward moneys for apprehending criminals.

When the public finally became aware of their goings-on, the Bow Street Runners were perceived as thief-takers of the Jonathan Wild mold. Inevitably, abuses followed hard upon their close ties with the underworld, resulting in widespread criticism and loss of public trust. Then, around 1790, a staff of trained detectives was established, known as the "Runners." Officially recognized and paid, they were plainclothesmen who wore no uniforms and coexisted with the constables until the passage of the Metropolitan Police Act in 1829. The constables were replaced by a professional police force of 1,000 men, the "Runners" lasting another 10 years until the passage of the Metropolitan Police Act and Metropolitan Police Courts Act of 1839.[8] The members of this first professional force, organized by Sir Robert Peel, Britain's Home Secretary

en.Wikipedia.com

Figure 1.4
Henry Fielding, Chief Magistrate in London, was instrumental in founding what some have called London's first police force: the Bow Street Runners.

Metropolitan Police, New Scotland Yard, London

Figure 1.5
One of "Mr. Fielding's People," who came after the "Old Charleys," and were later known as the "Bow Street Runners." They covered all of London, yet were never greater than 10 in number.

(see Figure 1.6), were called the "Peelers"; later, and up until the present, they became known as the "Bobbies."

About a decade later, a small number of full-time plain-clothes officers had become an integral part of the new force. Because it was quartered in the Scotland Yard, an ancient structure that once protected Scottish kings and royal visitors, the police force in general and the detective force in particular were dubbed with that name.

In the early nineteenth century, French authorities also sought out convicted criminals to do undercover work. A notorious example of the thief-turned-informer, Eugène François Vidocq, quickly set an enviable arrest and conviction record for the Paris police (see Figure 1.7). Throughout 1812 the high crime rate in Paris continued and Vidocq's suggestion to establish a plainclothes bureau was finally adopted. The Brigade de la Sûreté, created by the Ministry of Police, would function in all of the city's districts and report directly to the Prefect (the head of the Paris police force). Then Vidocq, the thief-turned-informer-turned-detective, became chief of this cohort of ex-convicts.

Meanwhile, in the United States, Thomas Byrnes was appointed detective bureau chief for the New York Police

en.wikipedia.com

Figure 1.6
Sir Robert Peel organized a professional police force initially referred to as "Peelers"; they later came to be known as "Bobbies."

en.wikipedia.org

Figure 1.7
Eugène François Vidocq quickly set an enviable arrest and conviction record for the Paris police.

Department. His stewardship in 1880 exemplifies this gradual shift in direction—from one who consorted with criminals to one who was first and foremost a policeman. But just as the Bow Street Runners' close ties with the underworld were unethical, so were Byrnes's. With his coterie of informers, and his system of singling out which criminals to prosecute and which to tolerate—a system almost as corrupt as that of Jonathan Wild (who actually set up, or framed, his own confederates)—this chief of detectives, like Wild, gave the impression that crime was under control. One of Theodore Roosevelt's first acts upon assuming the post of President of the Board of Police Commissioners in 1895 was to force Byrnes out.

Because federal laws also needed to be enforced, the Department of Justice was created by Congress in 1870. The investigative forces of the federal government consisted largely of the Treasury Department's Secret Service and Bureau of Customs, together with the U.S. Postal Inspection Service. All were essentially ad hoc agencies with restricted jurisdictions. The next year, limited funds were appropriated for the newly formed Department of Justice; its mandate, the detection and prosecution of federal crimes. As investigators it employed part-time outsiders, some Pinkerton detectives, paid informers, political patronage workers, and occasionally agents borrowed from the Secret Service and other units. This practice continued for 30 years, until the administration of President Theodore Roosevelt in 1901. Among the many concerns of this conservationist, activist, reformer president were the "public be damned" attitude of big business and its flouting of the Sherman Antitrust Act. The effort to make it subservient to law and government was evident from the angry force of Roosevelt's speeches about the large-scale thefts of public lands in the western states; he was advancing the new idea that natural resources should be held in trust. Subsequently, two politicians (a senator and a congressman, both from Oregon) were convicted for "conspiracy to defraud the United States out of public lands." A historic investigation, it was accomplished with borrowed Secret Service agents. Roosevelt's administration called the attention of Congress to the fact that the Department of Justice had no permanent detective force under its direct control, stating:

> … it seems obvious that the Department … ought to have a means of … enforcement subject to its own call; a Department of Justice with no force of permanent police in any form under its control is assuredly not fully equipped for its work."[9]

Not only did Congress ignore the request, it retaliated by initiating an inquiry into the Justice Department's habit of employing the investigative forces of other federal agencies. Indeed, just before adjournment, Congress amended an appropriation bill to expressly forbid the department's use of Secret Service or other agents. Roosevelt's response to the challenge was characteristically quick. Rather than accede to a continual hamstringing of the new department, his attorney general established an investigative unit within the Department of Justice soon after Congress adjourned. Named "The Bureau of Investigation" a short time later, the unit was to report only to the attorney general.

Two of the men who directed this unit formerly had been in command of the Secret Service. President Harding's appointee, the director since 1921, was replaced by another former Secret Service head, William J. Burns. Burns, however, was responsible for bringing Gaston B. Means, a man of unsavory reputation, into the Bureau. It was not long before the new agent was suspended for such unethical deals as selling departmental reports to underworld figures and offering to fix federal cases.

The Attorney General suspended Means; quietly, Burns brought him back, ostensibly because of Means's underworld contacts. Under such stewardship, needless to say, the prestige of the Bureau declined; it sank even further when Harding's attorney general used the agency to frame a senator. This scandal, among the many others in Harding's administration, brought about the appointment of a new attorney general when, upon the sudden death of the president in 1923, Calvin Coolidge was catapulted into office.

President Coolidge did not equivocate about replacing Harding's corrupt cabinet members. The first decision of Harlan Fiske Stone, the new attorney general (later chief justice of the Supreme Court,) was to demand Burns's resignation and offer the directorship to a 29-year-old attorney in the Justice Department. J. Edgar Hoover (see Figure 1.8) accepted the post, but only under certain conditions. The first applied to the Bureau's personnel practice: it must be divorced from politics, cease to be a catch-all for political hacks, and base appointments on merit. The director's authority was the subject of his second condition: he must have full control over hiring and firing (with promotion solely on proven ability), and be responsible only to the attorney general. Appointed to clean up the scandals, Stone not only agreed, he asserted that J. Edgar Hoover would not be allowed to take the job under any other conditions.

Figure 1.8
J. Edgar Hoover, first director of the Federal Bureau of Investigation (FBI), stands next to a sculpture of himself. The sculpture was presented to him on the 40th anniversary as director of the FBI.

AP Photo

The sweeping powers given the new director brought a radical improvement in personnel quality. Although such sweeping authority was certainly necessary to effect change, the seeds of disaster accompanied it nonetheless. As Lord Acton's aphorism aptly warns, "Power tends to corrupt, and absolute power corrupts absolutely." It should not be unexpected, therefore, that absolute power corrupted once more. Toward the close of Hoover's distinguished 48-year regime, some investigative practices were viewed critically, first by a Senate committee, and then by the press. What should be surprising is that the far greater excesses proposed were not countenanced. Indeed, they were rejected by the Director.[10]

Of all the executive departments of government, those having the power to investigate crime represent a potential threat to freedom. In a democracy, therefore, civilian supervision of the exercise of such power is crucial.

Shift in Investigative Methods

When formally organized police departments came into being in response to crime conditions, the use of informers as the main staple in the investigative cupboard was supplemented by the use

Figure 1.9
Sir Francis Galton wrote about the technique identifying common patterns in fingerprints and devising a classification system.

of interrogation, though the methods permitted to secure confessions varied widely from country to country. In the United States in 1931, the Wickersham Commission (appointed by President Herbert Hoover) employed the term "third degree" to characterize the extraction of confessions accompanied by brute force. It was, said the report, a widespread, almost universal police practice. Then the Supreme Court began to apply the provisions of the Bill of Rights to the states. Its judicial decisions, together with the potential offered by the application of science to the examination of physical evidence, brought an end to brutal methods of interrogation.

Europe was well ahead of the States in recognizing that potential. In 1893, Hans Gross, an Austrian who might be called the father of forensic investigation, wrote a monumental treatise so advanced for its time that it was unmatched for decades. *Handbuch fur Untersuchungsrichter* when translated became *Criminal Investigation*. At about the same time in England, Sir Francis Galton's landmark book, *Fingerprints*, was published (in 1892). See Figure 1.9. It led to the identification of criminals based on fingerprint evidence found at the crime scene. The marks or visible evidence left on an object by a person's fingers had long been observed, but such observations lacked any understanding of the intrinsic value of a human fingerprint. A somewhat similar situation prevailed with respect to bloodstain evidence. For a long time it could not be proved that a suspected stain was in fact blood; when it could, its presence would be explained by alleging the source to be that of a chicken or other animal. Prior to 1901, such allegations could neither be proved nor disproved; then, a German, Paul Uhlenhuth, discovered the precipitin test for distinguishing human blood from animal blood. In the field of firearms identification, it was not until 1923 that Calvin Goddard, an American, developed (with others) the comparison microscope; it helped to determine whether a particular gun fired a bullet or cartridge found at a crime scene.

These scientific developments, when applied to the examination of physical evidence, pointed to the need for properly equipped crime laboratories. In 1910 the first police laboratory was established by Edmond Locard in Lyon, France. In the United States it ultimately led, in the mid-1920s to early 1930s, to the installation of crime laboratories in a few of the larger cities. In Washington, DC, one was established in the Bureau of Investigation (renamed the Federal Bureau of Investigation in 1935). The expansion of crime laboratories proceeded slowly: by 1968, there still were none within the borders of 17 (mostly western) states. The availability of Law Enforcement Assistance Administration (LEAA) funds, however, soon permitted each state to install a crime laboratory. In California, a university program in criminalistics (a term coined by Hans Gross), coupled with strong support from the law enforcement community, led to the greatest proliferation of county laboratories in this country. With his research contributions and leadership of the program at the University of California, Professor Paul L. Kirk must be viewed as one of the few major figures in the field of criminalistics. In the Midwest, another major figure, Professor Ralph F. Turner, integrated criminalistics with the teaching of criminal investigation at Michigan State University's strong police/law enforcement program, turning out criminalists to serve that area of the country.

In the 1970s, research was undertaken that examined the proficiency of crime laboratories in the United States in examining common types of physical evidence: bloodstains, bullets and cartridge cases, controlled substances, latent fingerprints, hair, glass, paint, and other types of evidence. Many laboratories did not perform well; they made errors in identifying substances and in determining if two or more objects/evidence shared a common origin. This research continues to this day (Collaborative Testing Services), and proficiency testing has become an integral part of most crime laboratory quality assurance procedures. It is one way in which laboratories attempt to ensure their examiners' routine work is of the highest quality. Most laboratories in the nation seek to meet accreditation standards that are sponsored by the American Society of Crime Laboratory Directors (ASCLD).

Although the nation's crime laboratories have made dramatic improvements over the years, problems persist. Many of the problems are the result of laboratories being placed within law enforcement organizations that either do not devote adequate resources to these enterprises or pressure scientists to provide them with results that match their conclusions. Laboratories must have the resources to examine evidence in a timely manner and to hire personnel that possess the equipment, training, and research opportunities to ensure quality scientific work. Even though the science is progressing, there are still individuals within certain laboratories who lack proper scientific credentials. Laboratories must also be independent operations that are allowed to pursue investigations of evidence without interference and are free to report results—even if they show a prime suspect is uninvolved in the crime. There have been many instances brought to the public's attention in recent years in which forensic examiners have been too eager to assist police investigators and have cut corners or compromised high scientific standards.

Forensic medicine, the other main branch of forensic science, developed outside the control of police agencies. For this reason and because it otherwise contributes to the general well-being, forensic medicine evolved sooner and grew more quickly, remaining well ahead of criminalistics. This was the state of affairs until the 1960s when both branches benefited from the infusion of federal funds. Just the same, forensic medicine and its subdivisions are largely, but not exclusively, concerned with homicide; their use within the totality of criminal investigation is more limited than is that of criminalistics. Owing to the importance attached to homicide, however, forensic medicine is of vital significance to the criminal investigator.

The field of forensic medicine has evolved through ongoing research and by the move away from the "coroner" system that involved autopsies conducted by medical doctors with little experience in handling suspicious deaths. Today, most medical examiners are schooled in pathology and devote their full time to the profession.

More recently, the field of forensic nursing has emerged as an important tool, especially in the area of sexual assault cases. It should be noted that an increasing number of nursing practitioners with a background in forensics are employed in emergency room settings. "Forensic nursing is an area of clinical expertise that has evolved into a significant independent nursing specialty. Its development reflects a response designed to fulfil a societal need: The growing public health problem of societal violence."[11]

TRENDS IN INVESTIGATION

The influences of developments in transportation (the automobile), communications (telephone, radio, computers), and forensic science changed the practice of criminal investigation over the past century. The rapid pace of more recent modifications in virtually all aspects of American society have contributed directly to the many changes in law enforcement, not the least of which have been in the area of investigating crime. It has been more than 40 years since publication of the President's Crime Commission Report in 1968, and the infusion of billions of federal, state, and local funds to the criminal justice system. Policing has changed dramatically, due in no small part to higher education, training, and research. Improved management, salaries, and professionalism have characterized much of the past two decades. At the same time, criticism of investigative practices by the courts, legislators, and the public has also increased over the years, perhaps largely due to expanded media coverage, the influence of social media, and a public consumed by many different perceptions, misperceptions, and conceptions, frequently drawn from popular television shows and movies. But one must also recognize that the police and detectives are under a microscope of public opinion, and mistakes are made.

The following chapters address the many aspects of conducting a criminal investigation, but it is important to recognize that as society changes it is incumbent on the investigator to stay abreast of the many changes taking place in the world that have an impact on policing. Sophisticated information systems have become prevalent and their implications are driving both reform and change in the investigative process.

Although basic technology is now commonly used in police work, law enforcement is woefully far behind in developing and using much more sophisticated forms of technology and, in many cases, lacking in helping find new ways to utilize the technology developed for other disciplines to aid in investigations. All too often it is the criminal who is "teaching" law enforcement how to use technology, but when discovered it may be too late. Part D in this book addresses many of the new and emerging forms of technology available or being developed, as well as some of the types of crimes that have been spawned by sophisticated electronic information systems, data manipulation, cyber crime, digital breakthroughs, and social media. On the brighter side, technology has also helped the detective by providing clues and identifying potential suspects, and by making it possible to prepare reports quickly, better use physical evidence and better prepare a case for presentation in court. Present technology allows for the transfer of photographs, fingerprints, and other forms of visual information through networks. iPad technology is opening further models that can serve to enhance the investigative function. Cell phone technology extends the capabilities, and digital cameras and visual technology coupled with a wide array of software and so-called apps, or applications, are changing the way today's detectives work. Technology makes it possible for an investigator to carry an iPad, "notebook" or hand-held computer containing thousands of pages of information, images, and artificial intelligence programs. For example, "mug shot" presentations can now be utilized in the field, though be aware that ongoing research has questioned the way in which photo lineups are conducted. Photos can also be shared between organizations and police departments instantaneously. Despite the promise, in many law enforcement agencies, the reality is far from perfection.

On the international level, the need for enhanced information technology systems increases as the world becomes smaller owing to rapid global travel. Computerized databases are critical in combating terrorism and fraud. INTERPOL, the International Criminal Police Organization, acknowledged this by significantly upgrading its computer systems. The United Nations also views the goal of worldwide computerization as crucial. Indeed, large criminal syndicates and those involved in "enterprise crime" are in many respects much further ahead in their use of information technology than are many law enforcement agencies. The use of artificial intelligence is also being adapted to criminal investigation.

The scrutiny of the criminal investigation process by police administrators, researchers, and scholars has also been important. Today, many of the major changes in crime investigation have come through research conducted by universities, private laboratories, and government-sponsored projects. As many retired investigators took up careers in the academic community, closer dialogue between practitioners, academics, and researchers has proven beneficial. Research across the spectrum of the behavioral and information sciences holds great promise for improvement in the investigative function.

NOTES

1   Elinor Ostrum, Roger B. Parks, and Gordon P. Whitaker, *Patterns of Metropolitan Policing* (Cambridge, MA: Ballinger, 1978), 131.

2   Ralph F. Turner, personal communication, 1987.

3   Frank Adams, "Selecting Successful Investigative Candidates," *The Police Chief*, 61:7, 12–14 (July 1994), 12.

4   Ibid., 12, 14.

5   Ibid., 14.

6   Bernard Cohen and Jan Chalken, *Investigators Who Perform Well* (Washington, DC: U.S. Department of Justice, September 1987), iii.

7   Henry Fielding, *Jonathan Wild*, ed. by David Nokes (New York: Penguin Books, 1982), 8.

8   R.L. Jones, "Back to the Bow Street Runners," *Police Journal*, 63:3 (1990), 246–248.

9   D. Whitehead, *The FBI Story* (New York: Random House, 1956), 19.

10 W.C. Sullivan with Bill Brown, *The Bureau: My Thirty Years in Hoover's FBI* (New York: Norton, 1979), 205–217, 251–257.

11 Rita M. Hammer, Barbara Moynihan, and Elaine M. Pagliaro. *Forensic Nursing: A Handbook for Practice*, 2nd ed. (Boston: Jones and Bartlett Learning, 2013), xiii.

DISCUSSION QUESTIONS

1. What are the responsibilities of the investigator? Identify the eight points listed in the text.

2. Explain what is meant by jurisdiction. What is the difference between local and federal jurisdiction? What is meant by joint jurisdiction?

3. What are the six key points an investigator should address?

4. List five of the major changes that have taken place in policing and criminal investigation over the last 100 years.

SUPPLEMENTAL READINGS

Berman, J. S. (1987). *Police administration and progressive reform: Theodore Roosevelt as police commissioner of New York*. Westport, CT: Greenwood Press.

Defoe, D. (1982). *Introduction and notes to "The True and Genuine Account of the Life and Actions of the Late Jonathan Wild."* In David Nokes (Ed.), *Jonathan Wild*, by Henry Fielding, (pp. 225–227). New York: Penguin Books.

Edwards, S. (1977). *The Vidocq dossier: The story of the world's first detective*. Boston: Houghton-Mifflin.

Ericson, R. V. (1984). *Making crime: A study of detective work*. Toronto: Butterworth.

Hopkins, E. J. (1931). *Our lawless police*. New York: Viking Press. New York: Da Capo Press, 1971.

Joy, P. A., & McMunigal, K. (2006). Ethics. *Criminal Justice, 20*(4), 50–52.

Mones, P. (1995). *Stalking justice: The dramatic true story of the detective who first used DNA testing to catch a serial killer*. New York: Pocket Books.

National Commission on Law Observance and Enforcement. *Report on lawlessness in law enforcement*. Washington, DC: U.S. Government Printing Office. [Report No. 11 of the Wickersham Commission appointed by President Herbert Hoover in 1929.]

Roth, M. P. (2010). *Crime and punishment: A history of the criminal justice system* (2nd ed.). Belmont, CA: Wadsworth.

Thorwald, J. (1965). *The century of the detective*. New York: Harcourt, Brace & World.

CHAPTER 2

PHYSICAL EVIDENCE

Development, Interpretation, Investigative Value*

FORENSIC SCIENCE

The word *forensic* is derived from the Latin *forensis*, meaning "forum." A town square or marketplace in ancient cities, the forum was the arena of discussion and disputation in judicial and other public matters. As society became more complex, disputes were argued and settled in formally organized courts. Today, the term *forensic* still applies to and is used in courts of law or public discussion and debate. *Forensics*, an all-encompassing term in criminal justice, also includes the relatively new fields of forensic accounting, forensic engineering, and forensic nursing, all of which characterize the scientific examination of evidence. Owing largely to television shows and motion pictures, the term is now generic and part of the vocabulary of the average person—and, therefore, jurors. At least two major branches of forensic science are recognized, the most obvious being criminalistics and forensic medicine (see Table 2.1). Each has several subdivisions. The less obvious branches of forensic medicine, forensic accounting and forensic engineering will be discussed later in this and subsequent chapters.

The purpose of this chapter is to further the reader's understanding of the principles involved in converting physical clues into evidence that has investigative or probative value—or both. The work of forensic laboratories is treated later in the chapter. Discussed later are the most common kinds of clue materials to be found at crime scenes (in terms of the information provided by the investigator if they are examined by a forensic scientist). DNA analysis, having obtained major acceptance in the criminal justice system, is treated at some length.

Criminalistics: The Development and Interpretation of Physical Evidence

Criminalistics, the branch of forensic science concerned with the recording, scientific examination, and interpretation of the minute details to be found in physical evidence, is directed toward the following ends:

1. To identify a substance, object, or instrument.

2. To establish a connection between physical evidence, the victim, the suspect, and potential crime scenes.

---

* The authors would like to express their appreciation to professors Virginia Maxwell and Tim Palmbach for their review and comments on this chapter.

Table 2.1
Types of Evidence Examination

CRIMINALISTICS	FORENSIC MEDICINE
Drug Analysis/Toxicology	Anthropology
Instrumental Chemistry	Serology
Firearms and Toolmarks	Toxicology
Questioned Documents	Odontology
Fingerprints/Footprints/Lip Prints	Psychiatry
Photography	
Forensic Biology/DNA (deoxyribonucleic acid)	
Trace Evidence	
Imprint Evidence	
Digital Evidence	
Crime Scene Reconstruction	

3.   To reconstruct how a crime was committed and what happened at the time it was being committed. To get at the details regarding the analysis of bloodstain patterns (distribution, location, size, and shape) or to determine the trajectory of a bullet and gun-to-target range, training and experience is a must.

4.   To protect the innocent by developing evidence that may exonerate a suspect.

5.   To provide expert testimony in court.

Occasionally, those minute details are visible to the naked eye; more often, scientific instruments must be used to make them so. In either circumstance, they must be evaluated and interpreted by the criminalist as to their investigative significance for the detective and their probative significance for the jury (or judge in a nonjury trial).

The Federal Bureau of Investigation maintains one of the largest forensic science laboratories in the world, providing assistance to local law enforcement on request in most types of crimes, the exception being property crime that is only handled in very special instances. Table 2.2 illustrates the types of forensic investigations that the laboratory handles.

Report of the National Academy of Sciences

At the end of 2005 the United States Congress passed the Science, State, Justice, Commerce, and Related Agencies Appropriation Act of 2006, which authorized the National Academy of Sciences to conduct a study of forensic science.[1] This legislation, based on a Senate report, directed the Attorney General to provide funding to establish an independent Forensic Science Committee consisting of: members of the forensics community representing operational crime laboratories, medical examiners, and coroners; legal experts; and other scientists as determined appropriate.[2]

The Senate Report, released in 2008, instructed and charged the committee with the following responsibilities:

1.   assess the present and future resource needs of the forensic science community, to include state and local crime labs, medical examiners, and coroners;

Table 2.2
FBI Types of Evidence Examinations

Abrasives	Ink
Adhesives	Latent Prints
Anthropology	Lubricants
Arson	Metallurgy
Audio	Missing Persons
Bank Security Dyes	Paint
Building Materials	Pepper Spray or Foam
Bullet Jacket Alloys	Pharmaceuticals
Caulk	Polymers
Chemical Unknowns	Product Tampering
Computers	Questioned Documents
Controlled Substances	Racketeering Records
Cordage	Rope
Crime Scene Surveys	Safe Insulation
Documentation and Reconstruction	Sealants
Cryptanalysis	Serial Numbers
Demonstrative Evidence	Shoe Prints
Disaster Squad	Soil
DNA	Special Event and
Electronic Devices	Situational Awareness
Explosives	Support
Explosive Residue	Tape
Feathers	Tire Treads
Firearms	Toolmarks
Forensic Facial Imaging	Toxicology
Glass	Video
Hair	Weapons of Mass Destruction
Image Analysis	Wood

Source: Federal Bureau of Investigation: FBI Handbook of Crime Scene Forensics

2. make recommendations for maximizing the use of forensic technologies and techniques to solve crimes, investigate deaths, and protect the public;

3. identify potential scientific advances that may assist law enforcement in using forensic technologies and techniques to protect the public;

4. make recommendations for programs that will increase the number of qualified forensic scientists and medical examiners available to work in public crime laboratories;

5. disseminate best practices and guidelines concerning the collection and analysis of forensic evidence to help ensure quality and consistency in the use of forensic technologies and techniques to solve crimes, investigate deaths, and protect the public;

6. examine the role of the forensic community in the homeland security mission;

7.   [examine] interoperability of Automated Fingerprint Information Systems [AFIS]; and

8.   examine additional issues pertaining to forensic science as determined by the Committee.[3]

The study was conducted through committee hearings and deliberations and represented the most comprehensive national study of forensic science ever undertaken in the United States. The summary report indicated that the following issues were addressed:

a.   the fundamentals of the scientific method as applied to forensic practice—hypothesis genera-tion and testing, falsifiability and replication, and peer review of scientific publications;

b.   the assessment of forensic methods and technologies—the collection and analysis of forensic data; accuracy and error rates of forensic analyses; sources of potential bias and human error in interpretation by forensic experts; and proficiency testing of forensic experts;

c.   infrastructure and needs for basic research and technology assessment in forensic science;

d.   current training and education in forensic science;

e.   the structure and operation of forensic science laboratories;

f.   the structure and operation of the coroner and medical examiner systems;

g.   budget, future needs, and priorities of the forensic science community and the coroner and medical examiner systems;

h.   the accreditation, certification, and licensing of forensic science operations, medical death investigation systems, and scientists;

i.   Scientific Working Groups (SWGs) and their practices;

j.   forensic science practices—pattern/experience evidence
   • fingerprints (including the interoperability of AFIS)
   • firearms examination
   • toolmarks
   • bite marks
   • impressions (tires, footwear)
   • bloodstain pattern analysis
   • handwriting
   • hair
   • analytical evidence
   • DNA
   • coatings (e.g., paint)
   • chemicals (including drugs)
   • materials (including fibers)
   • fluids
   • serology
   • fire and explosive analysis
   • digital evidence;

k.   the effectiveness of coroner systems as compared with medical examiner systems;

l.   the use of forensic evidence in criminal and civil litigation—
   • the collection and flow of evidence from crime scenes to courtrooms
   • the manner in which forensic practitioners testify in court
   • cases involving the misinterpretation of forensic evidence

- the adversarial system in criminal and civil litigation
- lawyers' use and misuse of forensic evidence
- judges' handling of forensic evidence;

m. forensic practice and projects at various federal agencies, including NIST, the FBI, DHS, U.S. Secret Service, NIJ, DEA, and DOD;

n. forensic practice in state and local agencies;

o. nontraditional forensic service providers; and

p. the forensic science community in the United Kingdom.[4]

The final report consists of 13 recommendations, based on expert testimony and other materials including representation from: "federal agency officials; academics and research scholars; private consultants; federal, state, and local law enforcement officials; scientists; medical examiners; a coroner; crime laboratory officials from the public and private sectors; independent investigators; defense attorneys; forensic science practitioners; and leadership of professional and standard setting organizations."[5] The recommendations of the Commission appear on the companion site for this book.

Critical Thinking Question

One of the more controversial recommendations of the report by the National Academy of Sciences is that jurisdiction of crime laboratories should be removed from law enforcement agencies (Recommendation 13). Would this be a good idea? What prompted the Commission to make this recommendation? Discuss the pros and cons.

A copy of the report, "Strengthening Forensic Science in the United States: A Path Forward," should be read by all those involved in or interested in the field of forensic science. It can be obtained from the National Academy of Sciences (search at http://www.nap.edu). In many ways this report represents not only a critical analysis of the forensic science field, but a reasoned approach to fixing the problems associated with the collection and examination of physical evidence. Further, it raises the question whether or not crime laboratories should be located within law enforcement agencies, especially at the local level. Undoubtedly, this is a controversial subject worthy of debate. Perhaps more striking is the fact that in 2012 virtually none of the recommendations have been enacted under federal law.

Basic Concepts—Details in Physical Evidence

What are They?

The *details* that may be found in physical evidence are best illustrated by examples from actual cases and some by line drawings (see Figures 2.1–2.7). With evidence such as fingerprints, these details are given specific names (e.g., ridge ending, bifurcation, short ridge); with bullets, cartridge castings, or toolmarks, a more general descriptive term is used—*striations*. Essentially a series of roughly parallel lines of varying width, depth, and separation, striations are scratch

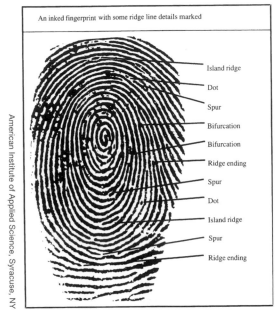

An inked fingerprint with some ridge line details marked

Island ridge
Dot
Spur
Bifurcation
Bifurcation
Ridge ending
Spur
Dot
Island ridge
Spur
Ridge ending

American Institute of Applied Science, Syracuse, NY

Figure 2.1
An inked fingerprint with some ridge line details marked.

Types of individual characteristics	Illustration of individual characteristics
Ending ridge	
Fork (bifurcation)	
Island ridge or short ridge	
Dot	
Bridge	
Spur	
Eye (island)	
Double bifurcation	
Trifurcation	

American Institute of Applied Science, Syracuse, NY

Figure 2.2
Examples of individual characteristics (Galton minutiae or ridge line details) used to individualize a fingerprint—latent or inked.

marks caused by irregularities or a lack of microfine smoothness on the barrel of a gun, head of a firing pin, or working face or edge of a tool. DNA analysis has advanced considerably in recent years and has proven to be a major factor in investigations. Digital imaging, used almost exclusively in fingerprint analyses to identify suspects from huge databases today, provides the capability to search on single digits (fingerprints). This technology has now been adopted in all states. With evidence like paint, hair, grease, and glass, the chemical composition (qualitative and quantitative) provides the significant details. Particularly important are those chemical elements present in trace amounts resulting from accidental impurities, secondary transfer, or environmental conditions.

Morphology

With some types of evidence, the general term *morphology* describes the structure and shape (or form)—hence, the details. Figure 2.5 illustrates the morphology of a screwdriver, the tip of which was broken during the commission of a burglary. In the examination of an undergarment for a suspected seminal stain, the presence of at least one intact spermatozoon, identifiable under the microscope by its structure and form, helps to corroborate a charge of rape. In addition, the jigsaw-puzzle fit of several pieces of evidence—for example, the glass fragments of a broken automobile headlight (or radiator grill) in a hit-and-run homicide—illustrates morphological details effectively put to work in criminalistics (see Figure 2.6). Figure 2.7 is another illustration of the morphological linking of crime scene evidence to a suspected source.

Figure 2.3
Striations and bar code patterns. Such details are used to analyze, compare, and identify some kinds of physical evidence from a crime scene (Q) with physical evidence from a suspect (K).
A. Striations left by a tool used as a jimmy on a safe. **B.** Striations on the breech face of a revolver left on the head of a cartridge fired in a suspect's weapon (K). The vertical dividing line in the middle separates images K and Q as seen in the comparison microscope. **C.** Line bar code pattern or spectrogram of the chemical element iron. Each metal trace impurity in a clue material provides a different spectrogram when analyzed by the spectrograph. **D.** A DNA bar code pattern revealed through analysis of biological specimens.

K (known)
Q (questioned)

A.
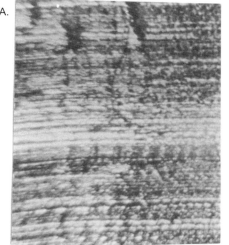

C.
D.

B.

Figure 2.3D, Courtesy, Mark D. Stolorow, Cellmark Diagnostics, Germantown, MD

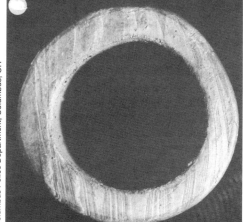

Columbus Police Department, Columbus, OH

Figure 2.4
Toolmark striations left by a knife on the end(s) of a hose that was connected to an illicit still.

Santa Ana Police Department, Santa Ana, CA

Figure 2.5
The irregularity in shape of the broken tip of a screwdriver is a morphological detail used to link a jimmy impression left on a doorjamb at the scene of a burglary to a suspect's screwdriver.

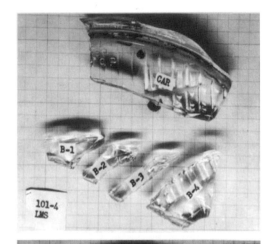

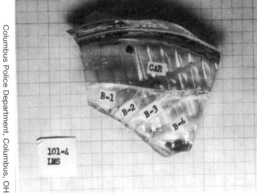

Columbus Police Department, Columbus, OH

Figure 2.6
The morphological or jigsaw puzzle fit of the crime scene glass lens fragments (B-1 through B-4) with a piece of headlight lens removed from a car suspected in a hit-and-run case.

New York City Police Department

Figure 2.7
A photomacrograph depicting the morphological detail and consequently a physical match between a piece of automobile grill (bottom) with a piece of metal found at the scene of a hit-and-run accident.

How are they Developed?

The means now at the disposal of the criminalist to make visible the forensic details in physical evidence include the altering of contrast and the use of optical and analytical instruments.

Contrast

The most common way to bring out details is by altering contrast. One method uses black or white powder to process a crime scene for fingerprints. With the possible exception of small children, people seldom leave visible fingerprints after touching an object; therefore, the indistinct image or latent print must be converted to one that can be seen. This is achieved by "dusting" it with black or white fingerprint powder, the color of the object dictating the choice of powder: on a white kitchen appliance, black powder; on a green bottle, white powder. The latent fingerprint developed by dusting will contrast with the object on which it is located. Current techniques utilize fluorescent powders or dyes used in conjunction with alternate light sources.

Photography is another well-known means of enhancing contrast. The type of film (emulsion) and developer, illumination (oblique lighting and filters), enlarger, and photographic paper can all affect contrast. The criminalist is generally concerned with increasing contrast, but occasionally it must be reduced. If so, the process is reversed and many of the same means that enhance contrast are then employed to decrease it. With the advent of digital enhancements, common software programs are capable of performing a wide variety of contrast and layer enhancements.

Optical Instruments

Invaluable optical devices, the microscope and camera, make details visible that are difficult, or even impossible, to see with the unaided eye. Mere enlargement, however, is not enough: there must be enlargement with resolution. This term describes the ability of a microscope or camera lens to separate what, to the unaided eye, appears to be one object (or point) into two or more objects (or points), and thus yield details not perceptible in any other way. It might be easier to understand this concept if the reader imagines he or she is looking down a railroad track. At some distant spot the rails will appear to converge. With binoculars, however, this spot can be separated into two objects (the rails), the lenses having given an enlarged image with resolution.

It is possible to have enlargement or magnification without resolution. For example, in the enlargement of a fingerprint negative made with a fingerprint camera, no details other than those present in the negative can be reproduced. The term 1 to 1 (1:1) describes the size of the image produced on a negative by the fingerprint camera lens. If larger than life-size—2 to 1 or greater—it is termed a photomacrograph (not to be confused with a photomicrograph, i.e., a photograph of an object as seen in the eyepiece of a microscope). Both photomacrographs and photomicrographs furnish resolution of details, and though the practical limit of photomacrography is about 25 to 1, it is still a powerful tool in the hands of the criminalist. Much physical evidence, fortunately, yields the necessary details at magnifications between 2× and 10×. An alternate light source (ALS) is an instrument that allows investigators to examine a crime scene or evidence with light of varying wavelengths. ALS units are very effective at finding biological fluids and various other trace materials. In recent years these units have become portable and affordable, allowing both labs and crime scene units daily access to them.

Analytical Instruments

The need for quality control in World War II weapons production brought unique scientific analytical instruments (heretofore found only in isolated university laboratories) to the commercial arena. Coupled with the vast financial support given to science after the war, this development greatly enhanced the capabilities of forensic laboratories to examine evidentiary materials. Samples considerably smaller than those required by traditional wet chemistry—with its emphasis on test tubes, beakers, and flasks—could now be analyzed. Available clue material at a crime scene being limited, such instrumentation was particularly suited to the needs of the criminal investigator. Today, the problem of the small-sized specimen is mitigated owing to the development and availability of:

Spectrophotometers
  Ultraviolet
  Visible
  Infrared
  Atomic Absorption (AA)
Emission Spectrograph
  Laser Excitation Method
  Inductively Coupled Plasma (ICP) Spectrometry
Mass Spectrograph (MS)
X-ray Diffraction (XRD)
Scanning Electron Microscope/Energy
  Dispersive X-Ray (SEM/EDX)
Chromatography
Liquid Chromatography (LC)
  Gas Chromatography (GC)
  Gas Liquid Chromatography (GLC)
  Thin Layer Chromatography (TLC)
  Electrophoresis
Capillary Electrophoresis

The mere mention of such instruments makes them seem formidable and intimidating, but the criminal investigator need not understand how they work; after all, tuning a radio hardly requires a grasp of physics and electronics. It is sufficient to know their capabilities: that analytical instruments can furnish essential qualitative and/or quantitative details about a substance. Interpreting the investigative and probative value of this information is another role the criminalist ultimately fills for the detective, jury, and judge.

There are two major classes of instruments—destructive and nondestructive. The destructive class consumes the sample during analysis; the nondestructive does not alter the sample, leaving it available for further instrumental analysis or for presentation as evidence in court. If applicable, nondestructive methods should be tried first. For each instrument, Table 2.3 summarizes the type

Table 2.3
Instrumental Methods: Type of Sample—How Effected and Information Acquired

INSTRUMENT	TYPE OF SUBSTANCE	EFFECT ON SAMPLE	INFORMATION Qualitative	Quantitative
SPECTROPHOTOMETERS				
Infrared (IR)	Organic compounds	Nondestructive	Yes	Difficult
Visible	Organic compounds, inorganic elements	Nondestructive	No	Yes
Ultraviolet (UV)	Organic compounds, inorganic elements	Nondestructive	No	Yes
Atomic Absorption (AA)	Inorganic elements	Destructive	No	Yes
SPECTROGRAPH				
Arc excitation	Inorganic elements	Destructive	Yes	Yes
Laser excitation	Inorganic elements	Destructive	Yes	Semi-quantitative
Mass	Organic compounds	Destructive	Yes	Difficult
X-RAY DIFFRACTION	Cyrstalline substances (organic and inorganic)	Nondestructive	Yes	No
NEUTRON ACTIVATION (NAA)	Inorganic elements	Nondestructive	Yes	Yes
SCANNING ELECTRON MICROSCOPE (SEM)	Organic compounds, inorganic elements	Nondestructive	NA	NA
SEM coupled to an X-ray dispersive analyzer (EDX)	Inorganic elements	Nondestructive	Yes	Difficult
CHROMATOGRAPHY				
Gas-liquid (GLC)	Organic compounds	Nondestructive	Yes	Yes
Thin Layer (TLC)	Organic compounds	Nondestructive	Yes	Difficult
Electrophoresis	Organic (large biomolecules)	Nondestructive	Yes	Difficult

of clue material that can be analyzed, whether or not it is destroyed by the method, and what kind of information can result. Advances in technology have expanded the list of nondestructive samples and require ever smaller samples.

Perhaps the terms *organic* and *inorganic* in Table 2.3 need review. An organic substance is one that contains carbon; all other substances are inorganic. Table 2.4 lists clue materials in accordance with this chemical dichotomy. Because there are more than 90 chemical elements besides carbon, it may surprise the reader to learn that organic substances are far more common than inorganic. Materials comprising a mixture rather than a single chemical substance are listed in both categories.

The instruments of most significant value are the gas chromatograph in combination with the mass spectrometer (GC/MS), the scanning electron microscope (SEM), capillary electrophoresis for DNA analysis, and Fourier transform infrared spectroscopy (FTIR). Many listed in Table 2.3 are costly; only large forensic laboratories are likely to have all of them. Once acquired, their operation

Table 2.4
Some Examples of Clue Materials Characterized as Organic or Inorganic Substances

ORGANIC
Petroleum products (arson accelerants)
Gunpowder and gunshot residue
Controlled substances and other drugs:
Heroin, morphine, cocaine, and so on
Marijuana
LSD and other hallucinogens
Phenobarbital and other barbiturates
Benzedrine and other amphetamines
Valium and other tranquilizers
Ethyl alcohol
Explosives
Hair and polymer fibers (e.g., nylon, Dacron)
Paint (some constituents)
Dyes in gasoline, cosmetics, and some inks
Poisons (e.g., digitalis, strychnine)
Biological fluids (e.g., proteins and enzymes)

INORGANIC
Dirt
Gunpowder and gunshot residue (e.g., lead, antimony, and barium)
Hair (trace elements)
Poisons (e.g., arsenic, mercury)
Paint (some constituents)
Glass (e.g., windows, automobile headlights)

may have some handicaps, for evidentiary material must be in an acceptable form. Nevertheless, there are great advantages attached to these advanced analytical methods:

1.   The sample may often be preserved for future use as evidence, many of these instruments being nondestructive.

2.   A permanent record is obtained for presentation in court, in the form of a photograph, chart on graph paper, or computer printout.

3.   Personal error is minimized; one analyst's results can be checked by another.

4.   A smaller amount of clue material is required than for wet chemistry.

5.   Often more definitive results are obtained than from classical methods of analysis.

6.   The information (or details) provided by one instrument supplements rather than duplicates what is provided by another instrument.

7.   The instrument and techniques apply to the evidence. It is not the nature of the crime that counts; it is the nature of the evidence.

Basic Concepts—Identification and Identity

Identification, a significant term in criminalistics, describes the classification process by which an entity is placed in a predefined, limited, or restricted class. For example, if the entity is a packet of white powder, the crime laboratory report on such evidence seized in a narcotics arrest might read: "The powdered substance submitted in Case 123 contains heroin." Two other examples: If the physical evidence is a typed ransom note, the laboratory might inform the investigator that of all cameras, the one used was in the Canon PowerShot class; if a bullet (perhaps in a homicide case before a weapon is recovered), the finding might be that it was fired from a .25 caliber automatic pistol with a left twist and six lands.

In a rape case, the crime laboratory report might state that the fiber found beneath the victim's fingernail is a naturally occurring filament that has a very specific definition for fibers (distinct from a synthetic) in the class of human hair. However unequivocal this identification, it has not established that the physical evidence originated from one singular origin exclusive of all others. When it does, an identity has been established. However, this could never be accomplished through microscopic examination alone. DNA technology is opening up new possibilities in this important aspect of the criminalist's work. An identity, therefore, extends the classification process to the point at which the entity is in a class by itself—a class of one. It has been individualized—effected by comparing physical evidence discovered at the crime scene with apparently similar evidence obtained from a suspect (or defendant). The following will illustrate:

•   The partial fingerprint found at the crime scene matches the inked impression of the right ring finger of the suspect (or defendant).

•   The .25 caliber bullet retrieved by the medical examiner from the deceased's body was fired from a Beretta .25 caliber automatic pistol (Serial #01234C) found in the possession of the suspect (or defendant).

A criminalist's finding that a unique connection existed between the victim or crime scene and the suspect prompted Paul L. Kirk, a major figure in the field, to define criminalistics as "the science of individualization."[6] Taken together, the details that uniquely characterize the entity—that is, put it in a class of one (by itself) and thereby establish an identity—are called individual characteristics. When a sufficient number of individual characteristics in the crime scene evidence and a specimen

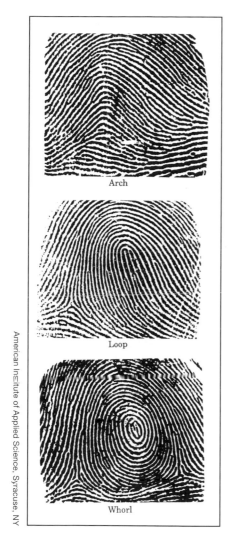

Figure 2.8
Basic fingerprint patterns: arches, loops, and whorls.

of known origin (the exemplar obtained from a suspect) can be matched, the criminalist is said to have developed associative evidence and established an identity.

Figures 2.1 and 2.2 indicate the points of identity (Galton details) that an expert uses to establish and demonstrate that a latent crime scene fingerprint and an inked record print were made by the same finger—and no other finger in the world. The general patterns of fingerprints (whorls, loops, arches) are shown in Figure 2.8; all fingerprints are divided into the three major groups. Called class characteristics, each can be subdivided further: loops into ulnar and radial; arches into plain and tented; whorls into six subgroups. Because a fingerprint falls into one or the other, these subcategories are also class characteristics.

Another illustration: the class characteristics of rubber shoe heels may include the name of the manufacturer, the decorative pattern, and the heel size. The individual characteristics found in or on a heel (or tool) are those cuts, nicks, and gouges acquired through wear (Figures 2.9 and 2.10).

There are rare occasions when an imprint (sole, heel) is so unusual that its class characteristic renders it of probative value in and of itself. To illustrate, a bloody heel print (see Figure 2.11) was found on the walkway of murder victim Nicole Simpson's condominium. Its distinctive pattern, an S-like waffle design, was not in the FBI's computerized shoe print library or in any other country's file (Japan excepted). In due course, FBI agent William Bodziak determined that it was designed for Bruno Magli shoes. Being an expensive Italian brand and a model marketed for only two years in but 40 locations in the United States and Puerto Rico, the number sold was limited. Likewise, the number of potential suspects was limited to a crime scene print estimated to be size 12: at most, 9 percent of the United States population wears size 12 shoes.

Digital imaging and color can frequently provide additional data that heretofore had been lost in black-and-white photography.

Class characteristics come into play when it is impossible to link a suspect directly to the crime scene or other physical evidence, and is thus circumstantial. For example, recovery of a pistol in possession of a suspect that can be shown to have the same characteristics as a bullet recovered from the victim has probative value that, while not conclusive, along with other evidence can prove valuable. Therefore, a class characteristic can have probative value and be utilized as evidence even though it is not conclusive proof of a suspect's involvement in the crime. (It is conclusive when class characteristics are not the same, and an exclusion is concluded.)

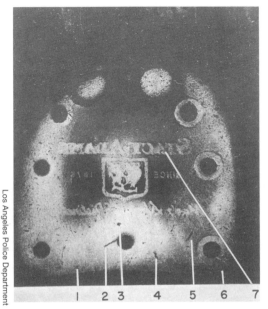

Los Angeles Police Department

Figure 2.9
Impression found at a crime scene. The nicks, cuts, and gouges—the details that individualize this heel—are marked.

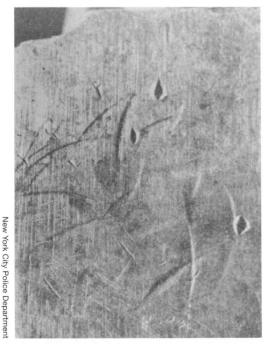

New York City Police Department

Figure 2.10
Face of hammer head damaged by misuse. Nicks and gouges present, as well as the shape (morphology) of the upper edge, provide a basis for establishing an identity.

So long as a Bruno Magli shoe was never recovered, there is no way of knowing whether the apparent individual characteristics in Figure 2.11 are "real." If they are real (that is, not altered because of the concrete surface on which it was found or by other factors), then a criminalist could have compared a suspect shoe (had there been one) with the crime scene imprint.

Unfortunately, the science of criminalistics has not yet evolved to the point at which it is always possible to establish an identity. Consider the following statements in regard to bloodstain and pubic hair evidence. Each illustrates a comparison that has greater probative value than a mere identification, but less than a conclusion of an identity.

- This reddish brown stain on the suspect's underwear contains group AB blood of human origin.

- Approximately 5 percent or less of humanity has AB blood (groups A, O, B, and AB being class characteristics). If a stain is AB, approximately 95 percent of the population is thereby eliminated as being suspect.

- The strand lodged beneath the rape victim's fingernail matches in all observable details the pubic hair specimen obtained from the suspect.

- The Scientific Working Group on Comparative Analysis recommends that statements on all hair reports include a qualifying statement that the sample could be linked to more than one individual. This last statement is open to misinterpretation. Does it mean that the strand is from the defendant (suspect)? It might seem so to some. However, the informed defense attorney, prepared to cross-examine rigorously, should not allow a jury to make this mistake. Until recently, this was an accurate statement and if asked by defense counsel a criminalist would explain and interpret what it meant—that it could be, but is not necessarily, the defendant's hair. The development of DNA short-tandem repeat (STR) technology now permits hair to be individualized.

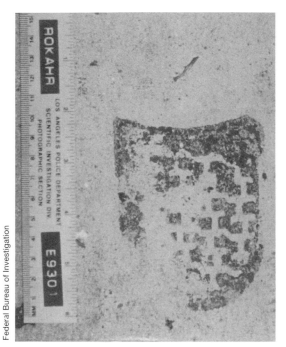

Federal Bureau of Investigation

Figure 2.11
Bloody heel print found on the walkway outside of Nicole Brown Simpson's condominium.

Table 2.5 summarizes class and individual characteristics in various types of evidence. If the individual characteristics are the same, and are found in sufficient number each at the same location, then two specimens under comparison may be judged an identity. What constitutes a sufficient number is a judgment call, an integral part of the criminalist's work.

The Role of the Crime Laboratory

The definition of criminalistics (given earlier) can be expanded by illustrating what the laboratory does to assist the detective: namely, establish an element of the crime, link the crime scene or victim to the criminal, and reconstruct the crime. For example, heroin is proscribed by law, and alcohol is regulated. If the pertinent law is to apply, their presence in seized evidence must be established. The concept of identification is involved and chemistry is needed to effect the determination. The presence of heroin or alcohol is an element of the crime.

Associative evidence, a nonlegal term, describes the aspect of laboratory work involving the concept of identity (i.e., linking a subject to the crime scene or victim—such as by a fingerprint). The most effective means of developing associative evidence are instrumental chemistry, photomacrography, microscopy, other optical methods, and morphology.

Finally, the reconstruction of a crime has long been of interest to detectives. The FBI Behavioral Science Unit uses the principles of psychology to reconstruct the criminal act. *Psychological profiling* (see Chapter 4) provides investigative leads by evaluating intangible evidence such as emotions apparently underlying a criminal act, a rapist's remarks to the victim, or interviews of witnesses.[7]

Throughout the years considerable debate has occurred in the courts when statements of identity or "matches" have been preferred. These debates are frequently associated with identification or pattern disciplines such as fingerprints, questioned documents, firearms evidence, imprints, bite marks, and bloodstain pattern analysis. The forensic sciences report, *Strengthening Forensic Science in the United States: A Path Forward*, stated, "it is clear that change and advancement, both systemic and scientific, are needed in a number of forensic science disciplines—to ensure reliability of the disciplines, establish enforceable standards and promote better practices and their consistent application," and many of the recommendations focused on issues of identification.[8]

With so many advances in crime scene technology and laboratory analysis, crime scene reconstruction has developed into an applied science that follows the guidelines of scientific method. Thus, crime scene reconstruction has developed into a discipline reliable, scientifically defensible, and able to meet scientific admissibility standards.

Table 2.5
Class and Individual Characteristics in Various Types of Evidence

TYPE OF EVIDENCE	CHARACTERISTICS		
	CLASS	INDIVIDUAL	
	Example	Example	Visual Appearance
Fingerprints	arches loops whorls	ridge ending, bifurcation, short ridge, enclosure, dot, bridge, spur, trifurcation	see Figs. 2.1 and 2.2 for class characteristics
Bullets and Cartridges	caliber; number of lands and grooves; direction of twist or rifling	scratch marks or striations in the lands and grooves; casing head, firing pin	see Fig. 2.3B
Handwriting	school of handwriting; hand printing; cursive printing	any deviation from the model letters of the system used to teach handwriting, i.e., peculiarities of letter formation	$\mathcal{R}$ for R $\mathcal{Y}$ for g
Shoe impressions	heel design; sole design; manufacturer's name	gouges, cuts and other marks acquired accidentally through wear	see Fig. 2.9
Tool impressions	hammer screwdriver jimmy cutting devices	nicks, dents, broken edges, and other damage from misuse or abuse; striations are left by some tools when drawn across a suitable surface	see Figs. 2.3A, 2.4, 2.5, and 2.10

Are the Facts Consistent with the Story?

A crime is reconstructed for other equally important reasons: for example, to check details provided by a suspect or witness against those disclosed by the crime scene examination. The laws of physics are helpful here: a bullet travels in a straight line (unless it ricochets off a solid object); therefore, by sighting from the point of impact (on a wall) through the bullet hole (in a window shade or sofa), it is possible to decide whether the shot indeed came from the location claimed by a witness (or suspect).

Just as the laws of physics (and chemistry) apply when determining the distance between victim and gun muzzle at time of firing, or whether the weapon had a hair trigger, so too must spattered blood from a gunshot (or bludgeoned) victim obey the laws of momentum, gravity, and surface tension. Accordingly, the inductive method (i.e., moving from the specific to the general) can determine where the criminal stood to fire the shot (or deliver the blows). Reconstruction also can find out: Was the window of a burglarized warehouse broken from the outside to gain entrance or from the inside to conceal employee theft? Was the driver killed when his motorcycle smashed into the telephone pole or was he the victim of a hate crime—beaten to death, and the cycle subsequently damaged (by running over it with an automobile) to simulate the effects of striking the pole? Scientific reconstruction can provide answers to these and similar questions on how a crime or event occurred. (See Chapter 14 for a more detailed discussion of reconstructing the past.)

Any significant discrepancy between an individual's statement and the physical evidence will raise suspicion if not explained satisfactorily. Is a suspect trying to cover up? Is a witness trying to mislead? Whatever the logical follow-up steps entail, the outcome can either be more incriminating or it may diminish initial suspicions; therefore, the development of inculpatory evidence or exculpatory evidence that protects the innocent is another reason for undertaking crime reconstruction. The cause of justice is served by permitting the statements of complainants and witnesses to be proved or challenged, corroborated or refuted.

Time: The question of whether a suspect had sufficient time to commit the crime is occasionally of investigative and prosecutorial interest. When the window of opportunity is quite narrow, a defendant's lawyer is likely to argue that there was insufficient time. If there apparently would not have been enough time to carry out the crime, the police must exercise caution and weigh all the circumstances. For example, if a victim has been seriously assaulted (skull crushed, large bones broken, body mutilated), the interval between the time when the report came in and when the suspect was last seen can be crucial. If that interval is too short, it should create doubt in the minds of the police. It also may very well create doubt in the minds of the jury. Physical evidence, the testimony of witnesses, and the opinion of a forensic pathologist can provide answers to the "time" issue.

The time required for blood to dry can also be a crucial factor in a case. Because blood can seep through a metal watchband or the weave of a garment's fabric, the question is: how much time would elapse before an impression (of watchband or fabric) is left dried on the skin of the deceased? In one homicide case, the watch worn by the (suspect's) murdered wife had been removed, presumably by the intruder the husband claimed to be the killer; on the dead woman's wrist the dried-blood impression of the metal watchband was clearly visible. Investigators did not think it feasible for an intruder-turned-killer to wait around for the blood to dry before removing the watch. On the other hand, they reasoned, the killer's attempt to divert suspicion required time to concoct a story and set the scene by removing the watch to suggest a motive of burglary.

Induce an Admission or Confession

A necessary condition for obtaining a confession is for the person to believe incriminating evidence exists. This condition having been met, the guilty may either be sufficiently troubled to make an admission against interest ("I own the gun but I did not use it") or confess ("Yes, I did it"). Evidence clearly indicating involvement in a crime induces an inner turmoil that seeks relief. An innocent person, however, would not usually feel pressure arising from self-generated guilt, there being no guilt to build up, even when there appears to be incriminating physical evidence. With no need for relief, confession by the innocent is unlikely.

Protect the Innocent

Though the crime laboratory is more often involved in developing evidence to establish guilt, an equally consequential aspect of its work is the protection of the innocent. Physical evidence that discloses unbiased facts that are not subject to the distortions of perception or memory can weaken an apparently strong case. Should those facts be in conflict (e.g., if the white powder does not contain heroin; if the suspected weapon did not fire the fatal shot; if the stain was not human blood; or if the available light or vantage point made it impossible for the witness to have observed what was claimed), then the innocent person may be protected—provided the crime scene search for physical evidence is diligent and knowledgeable.

In this regard, lack of diligence is the most troubling aspect. As research indicates, physical evidence is invariably undercollected and underutilized at crime scenes, despite its availability.[9] Because a democratic society prizes individual freedom, the price is continual vigilance—a citizenry watchful for any abuses of power by the state. Accordingly, if a fair chance to limit that power is lost when physical evidence that might have exculpated a suspect went uncollected or unused, not only is the suspect harmed, but the government is as well. A double blow is dealt: the first tarnishes democracy; the second adversely affects a department's reputation. The latter result may be intangible, but the former can, over time, be calamitous.

Provide Expert Testimony in Court

For cases that go to trial, a criminalist's ultimate task is the presentation of laboratory findings to the jury. To do this, the criminalist must first be qualified as an expert. At each and every trial, either the judge qualifies proposed experts, or their qualifications are stipulated to by defense counsel and accepted by the judge. It is necessary to demonstrate to the court that the "expert" possesses specialized, relevant knowledge ordinarily not expected of the average layperson. Such knowledge can be acquired through any combination of education and practical experience, and augmented through a study of books and journals in the field. Writing, research, and active membership in pertinent professional organizations are expected of most experts if they are to be considered current in the field.

The effective expert is able to describe his or her work and its significance to the jury in plain, everyday language. A faculty for putting scientific concepts into lay terms cannot be overrated; neither can the ability to remain cool under cross-examination. These attributes, inherent for some people, must be acquired by others through experience and hard work. Yet, diligence in recognizing and collecting physical evidence, and competence in the laboratory, are of no avail if the results are not readily perceived by the jury—if credibility is damaged by defense counsel's success in rattling the expert, causing testimony to be modified or weakened.

In the O.J. Simpson case in 1994, a pair of socks became a critical aspect of cross-examination of the evidence and their collection and examination. For further information on this case see the companion web site for this book.

FORENSIC MEDICINE: INVESTIGATIVE VALUE

Forensic medicine is also referred to as *legal medicine* or *medical jurisprudence*. The branch of medicine offering training in the study of diseases and trauma (their causes and consequences) is pathology.

Forensic pathology goes beyond the normal concern with disease, to the study of the causes of death—whether from natural, accidental, or criminal agency. Forensic medicine—including forensic pathology, toxicology, forensic odontology, and forensic psychiatry—contributes not only to homicide investigation, but to other kinds of criminal investigation, in the following ways.

Forensic Pathology

1. Establish the cause and manner of death—natural, suicide, accident, homicide.

2. Establish the time of death.

3. Indicate the type of instrument used to commit the homicide.

4. Indicate whether injuries to the body were postmortem or antemortem.

5. Establish the identity of the victim.

6. Determine the age of the victim.

7. Determine the sex, height, weight, and age of mutilated or decomposed bodies and skeletons.

8. Determine virginity, defloration, pregnancy and delivery, sodomy.

Toxicology

Toxicology is the study of poisons: their origins and properties, their identification by chemical analysis, their action upon humans and animals, and the treatment of the conditions they produce. Most crucial to the criminal investigator is the toxicologist's work of identifying a poison; then, there is the significant issue of quantity: was there or was there not a lethal amount present? The detection of poison may also allow the pathologist to exclude all other causes of death.

Forensic Odontology

Forensic odontology is the study of teeth, dentures, and bite marks for the following purposes:

1. To connect a bite mark to a particular person.

2. To identify an individual through an examination of fillings, missing teeth, and root canal work. If a silver amalgam or other type of metal restoration is present, X-rays can be compared.

3. To identify a person, a dentist, or a laboratory through information on a denture or partial denture.

4. To estimate a person's age.

Forensic Psychiatry

Forensic psychiatry, the study of a criminal's mental state and probable intent, is applicable to three areas of criminal justice: law enforcement, the courts, and the correctional system. Unfortunately for our purposes, it offers less assistance to the criminal investigator than to other actors in the criminal justice field.

Law Enforcement

With a skyjacker, terrorist, or barricaded malefactor who perhaps has taken hostages, a psychiatrist's evaluation of the criminal's mental state and probable intent can be useful in formulating plans to deal with the situation. In other cases, where the manner of death is in doubt, the likelihood of accident or suicide must be considered. To provide answers to the latter possibility, a technique called *psychological autopsy* was developed in Los Angeles in the 1950s. Working in concert, a team of specialists and nonspecialists might include: the pathologist who performed the medical autopsy; a psychiatrist; a social worker; the deceased's family, friends, and acquaintances; as well as the criminal investigator. Each member of the team discusses, from his or her own perspective, what is known about the deceased. Then the team arrives at a consensus (a psychological autopsy) as to whether or not death was by suicide.

A police department is occasionally confronted with a series of heinous crimes committed against prostitutes or the homeless, or such well-defined targets as utility companies subjected to sporadic bombings. An unusual investigative technique that has had some success is an "open letter" appeal printed on the front page of a newspaper, or read over television and radio. The intention is to frame an irresistible plea for the offender to seek help by surrendering to a well-known newspaper columnist or TV reporter; in return, the interests of the offender will be protected. Profiting from insights provided by psychiatrists, psychologists, and other behavioral scientists, the famous cases of the Unabomber (Ted Kaczynski) in the period between 1978 and 1995 as well as the "Skid Row Slasher" (Vaughn Greenwood) in the 1970s in Los Angeles were solved in this fashion.

The Courts

Forensic psychiatry is more often employed in the courtroom than anywhere else in the criminal justice system. It offers expert testimony on the following issues:

1. Did the accused's state of mind at the time of the offense comport with the definition of insanity used in the jurisdiction in which the crime was committed? Legal insanity is established by applying one of the following tests:

    The M'Naghten Rule[10]

    This rule is the common law test for criminal responsibility. It provides for an acquittal by reason of insanity if the accused did not know the difference between right and wrong at the time of the act or did not understand the nature of the act because of impaired reasoning and/or mental disease.

    The Concept of Irresistible Impulse[11]

    An irresistible impulse is one in which the individual knew the act to be wrong but was unable to resist the psychological forces driving him to commit the forbidden act.

    The Concept of Diminished Responsibility[12]

    Diminished responsibility or diminished capacity involves mental impairment to the extent that it prevented the individual from acting with premeditation and deliberation.

    The American Law Institute Test[13]

    A person is not responsible for criminal conduct if, at the time of such conduct, as a result of a mental disease or defect, he or she lacks substantial capacity to appreciate the wrongfulness of his or her conduct or to conform his or her conduct to the requirements of the law.

2. Does the accused understand the nature and purpose of the proceedings against him or her, and assist in his or her own defense?

3. Did the accused have the capacity to pursue deliberately the criminal course of action? What was his or her state of mind? Was there intent to commit the act?

4. Was the defendant capable of intelligently waiving constitutional rights?

5. Was the defendant's confession made voluntarily?

6. Is a witness competent to testify?

The Correctional System

Although the potential contribution of psychiatry to correctional administration is fairly obvious, it has never received commensurate funding. As long as society talks about prisoner rehabilitation but practices warehousing, this should not be surprising. The parolee returned to the community with prospects no better than before incarceration will almost certainly resume a delinquent lifestyle, and again become a police problem. Once criminal justice operates like a system whose components function compatibly, perhaps society will begin to act more sensibly toward preventing crime. Preparing prisoners to cope with a return to society will require a heavy monetary outlay for social workers, psychiatrists, and educators. In calculating the cost–benefit of such a policy, the actual dollar cost may be seen in a different light if the loss of life, property, and peace of mind for the population in general are taken into account.

CLUE MATERIALS AS INFORMATION SOURCES

Physical evidence may be removed from or brought to and left at the crime scene. In either event, such an occurrence is seldom deliberate, but rather a natural consequence of committing the crime. A shoe impression left by a burglar on breaking into a house through the backyard unavoidably remains in receptive soil. In an assault with a knife, the victim's blood can drop on the shoes or spurt on the criminal's clothing. Other possibilities include handwriting; teeth marks; finger, palm, foot, and even ear prints; wearing apparel (glove, shoe, heel) impressions; or traces of a distinctive weave in cloth or stitching pattern made by a sewing machine. Impressions of a victim's clothing fabric have been found on the hood or fender of an automobile suspected of being involved in a hit-and-run case.

Other sources of physical evidence are the instruments used to commit the crime: for example, jimmies, metal cutters, axes, and hammers to gain access; firearms and knives to threaten a victim; shovels to bury a body; a kidnapper's note; metal punches to open a safe. All are examples of what to look for at the crime scene.

Familiarity with actual crime scene evidence is a prerequisite for the recognition of clues. For example, Figure 2.12 is a partial heel mark found on the back of one of the office file papers scattered by a safe burglar. Is it worth preserving? Can such a poor impression link the criminal to the crime scene? Can it be developed into associative evidence? The criminalist can answer each question with an emphatic "Yes!"

To learn how such a decision is made, and to acquire a familiarity with other crime scene evidence, see the companion website for this book.

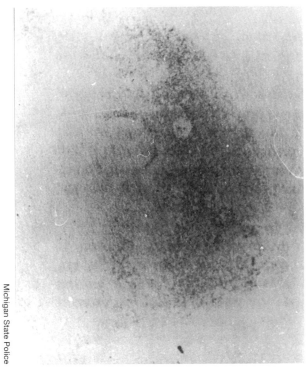

Michigan State Police

Figure 2.12
An indistinct, partial heel print left at the scene of a burglary. It was compared and identified as made by the shoe of a suspect.

Information of investigative or probative value may often be developed by the laboratory when any of the following common clue materials are encountered:

- Fingerprints
- Documents
- Firearms
- Glass
- Blood
- Trace evidence
- Semen, other biological materials

Fingerprints, Lip Prints, and Ear Prints

A person reporting a crime—especially a burglary—expects the police to find fingerprints of the offender(s). Few detectives share this unrealistic expectation; most recognize that even if fingerprints are not always left by a criminal, the crime scene should still be examined for them.

Fingerprints, lip prints, and ear prints are addressed in this section. What are they? How are they developed and preserved? When was the print made? Are there different kinds of print experts? What is the probative value of a single, partial fingerprint? What is the difference between fingerprints, lip prints, and ear prints.

What are fingerprints? The friction ridges on the hands (fingers and palms) and feet (toes, soles, and heels), which facilitate gripping an object and the sense of touch, form on the fetus before birth. They do not change during life. The prints of either the hands or feet can be a means of identifying an individual, but only the fingers are used routinely. Extensive files are maintained for this purpose.

A fingerprint is an impression of the friction ridges on the skin of the fingers. In leaving an impression, an outline of the ridges is transferred and duplicated by the deposit of perspiration and other substances on the object handled. If the impression is not visible, which is most often the case, it must be made visible. To do so, certain conditions must prevail as to the fingers themselves and the surface with which they come in contact (see Latent Fingerprints later in the chapter). The friction ridges must contain either a substance already present on the fingers or one purposely rolled on (for example, the printer's ink used by the police). Printer's ink can register each finger in the proper order on a fingerprint card, producing a set of record fingerprints (see Figure 2.13). Later, these prints become the exemplars needed by the fingerprint expert or through the use of technology to identify (individualize) prints found at the scene of a crime. When touching an object or surface and thereby depositing some natural or environmentally acquired material, the impression is usually an invisible or *latent* print ("latent" from the Latin for "hidden"). This

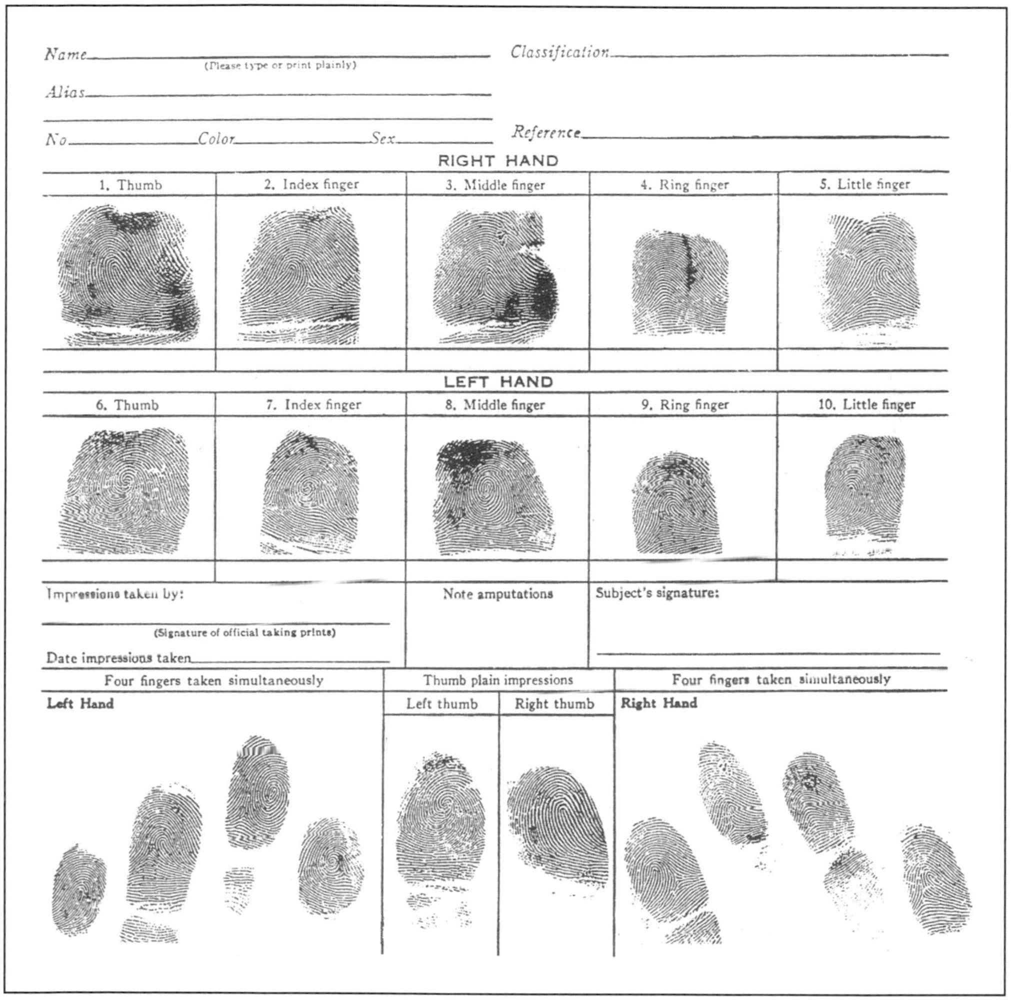

American Institute of Applied Science, Syracuse, NY

Figure 2.13
Set of record fingerprints.

necessitates that something be done to make it visible; called "developing the print," it is the result of processing the crime scene for fingerprints. It is quite possible to handle an object (for example, a gun) and leave no latent fingerprint on it; it also is possible to leave a partial impression (often the case) or a smudged and blurred print in which no useful ridge line details remain (see Figure 2.14).

Lip prints bear characteristics similar to those of fingerprints, although they are used almost exclusively in cases where a suspect has been identified for comparison purposes. Although their use is rare, it should be noted that lip prints can be obtained from a drinking glass, envelopes, and from lipstick imprints, to name a few examples.

Ear prints are rarely used and, unlike the use of ridge impressions, the configuration of the ear can be used as a comparative sample where the ear print was left at the scene. Examples of this include an ear print in blood or dust on the floor as a result of a fight between the suspect and the victim; an impression

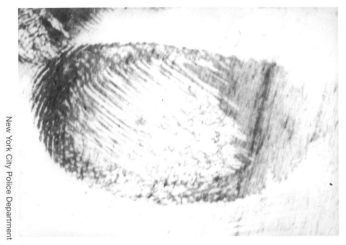

New York City Police Department

Figure 2.14
A smudged (blurred) fingerprint impression. Note lack of ridge line detail—making identification impossible.

left on a non-porous object, such as a briefcase on which a subject laid. Because these types of impressions are rare, the rest of this chapter focuses on finger and palm prints.

Latent Fingerprints— Constituents and Their Sources

The two kinds of sources for the material on the fingers that produces latent fingerprints are natural and environmental.

Natural Sources

Natural materials are perspiration and the residue left by the evaporation of its water content, and sebum—a semifluid, fatty substance secreted by sebaceous glands at the base of the hair follicles. Although perspiration is about 99 percent water, it also contains some dissolved solids that are the byproducts of food metabolism: organic compounds (amino acids, urea, and lipids—fats, oils, waxes) and an inorganic compound (table salt). The presence of some vitamins in perspiration makes development by lasers feasible.

Environmental Sources

In the course of daily living, the hands touch and thereby pick up foreign matter from the environment such as: dust, soot, cooking oils, kitchen grease, and hair preparations, as well as pollen and other plant particulate matter.

Latent Fingerprints—Controlling Factors

Whether a latent impression is left depends on physiology (does the person perspire?) and what substances are present on the fingers, the nature of the surface touched, and the manner in which it was touched; and such environmental factors as temperature and humidity.

Surface

A latent print requires a suitable surface for it to be registered. The surface needs to be relatively smooth. Smooth surfaces can be either porous or nonporous, and determination of that factor will dictate the best course to pursue for latent print development. Rough surfaces are unsuitable because the friction ridge lines will be recorded only partially on their flat, high spots, and completely lost in their troughs and valleys (although attempts to develop latents on leather have been successful). When called to the scene of a burglary, evidence technicians would not be surprised to find that the safe they are expected to process for fingerprints has a crinkled surface that will not take a fingerprint. (Perhaps a case of form preceding rather than following function?) Human skin (dead or alive) and the sticky side of adhesive tape are two surfaces that are tractable to the development of prints, but with some difficulty. There are chemical and other means available to attempt to process these and other such unusual surfaces, although not always with success.

Finger Pressure

A fingerprint requires firm but not heavy pressure; otherwise, ridges will be flattened and the details distorted or not registered at all. Moreover, if a good print rather than a smudged one is to be left behind, the fingers must not be pulled or slipped across the surface, but lifted in a perpendicular motion. Needless to say, criminals seldom satisfy these conditions. Latent prints of the perpetrator are not found as often as most crime victims believe; one or more of the necessary conditions—a deposit on the fingers, suitable surface, or correct pressure—is usually missing.

Other Kinds of Fingerprints

A few fingerprints found at the crime scene are visible (patent) owing to the (largely environmental) substances present on the fingers. They also can be on partially dried, tacky paint, or even on a bar of butter, cream cheese, or chocolate that a burglar may remove from the refrigerator. In burglary cases in which access was through a window, they may be found in soft window putty. In assault cases, they may be found on adhesive tape that had been left on a finger for several days (for example, a Band-Aid dislodged in a struggle), or on tape removed from a bound victim or an explosive device. If the impression is three-dimensional, it is called a *plastic* print. Plastic prints are encountered far less than other visible prints, but all visible prints combined are far less common than latent prints.

How are Latent Fingerprints Made Visible?

The means available for developing latent fingerprints run the gamut from powders to chemical methods to different kinds of exposure to a light source.

Powders

The most common practice is to "dust" an object or crime scene with fingerprint powder. The color of the powder is selected to provide contrast between the developed print and its background: black powder on light-colored backgrounds, white powder on dark. Other colors are available and sometimes used, but white and black are customary. Fingerprint powders are designed to cling to natural and/or environmental source material; this makes the development of fingerprints possible. The powders must not cling to the background; the friction ridge lines should remain clearly delineated. In processing an object, powders are applied with an ostrich feather, a camel hair or nylon brush, or an atomizer. Herbert L. MacDonell invented the Magna-Brush and a magnetic powder.

His method develops and preserves ridge line details better than any other mechanical means. In all dusting attempts, however, great care must be taken not to distort or destroy those details by using too much powder or by brushing too vigorously.

Investigators can learn to process a crime scene with fingerprint powder. More technically difficult methods require an evidence technician or criminalist; they rely on specific kinds of light energy in the form of lasers or alternative light sources (ALSs), or involve a chemical reaction with a component of the residue left after an object has been touched. Brief descriptions of a few of these methods follow.

Chemical Methods

Several methods employ specific chemicals to process an object. The most common are: iodine, ninhydrin, silver nitrate, or cyanoacrylate esters. The process involves fuming, spraying, brushing, or dipping the object in a solution of the chemical.

Ninhydrin: Ninhydrin, an organic chemical, reacts with amino acids and other products of protein metabolism to yield purple-colored fingerprints. It takes from one to three days for a print to be developed fully, but this can be hastened with controlled heat and humidity. The relatively stable prints will last many months, possibly years; like iodine prints, they can be "fixed" chemically and, of course, photographed. Ninhydrin is particularly useful in developing prints on paper, including cardboard. It is not useful on paper money; because it is handled so often, the entire bill turns purple. Ninhydrin is very sensitive and can bring up old prints; however, others of recent origin may be partially superimposed on them, producing a dual impression of no value.

Cyanoacrylate Fuming: The cyanoacrylate fuming method came about in the 1950s by chance, when cyanoacrylate esters (resins) were first discovered as a means for bonding plastics and metals. To the surprise of observers, fingerprints were often seen on the bonded objects. In 1978 Japan's National Police were first to employ the method in criminal investigations and, through contacts with the U.S. Army crime laboratory in the Far East, brought their observations to the attention of law enforcement in the United States. The first source of cyanoacrylate esters was an adhesive called "Super Glue," and the method is still referred to as the superglue procedure. Marketed directly to law enforcement as a volatile liquid, it is now used (in an enclosed space) to fume an object for latent fingerprints, detecting them on such nonporous surfaces as glass, gun metal, plastic steering wheels, and other plastic objects—such as the packages in which street narcotics are sold. The resulting impression is white in color; it should be photographed or dusted with powder and lifted. Although employed largely in the laboratory, fuming an automobile or a room is safe if special circumstances dictate and precautions are taken. It should also be noted that cyanoacrylate fumes interfere with the examination of the following biological materials: blood, semen, and hair. Such evidence, therefore, should be collected or examined beforehand. However, recent techniques have been developed to recover DNA from cyanoacrylate prints. Additionally, fluorescent dyes can be utilized to enhance the image.

Alternate Light Sources (ALSs)

There are many newer methods that utilize fluorescent powders or dyes in conjunction with superglue fuming. These methods require the use of an alternate light source and can present some photographic challenges. Additionally, the use of superglue to develop latent prints on human skin has shown some degree of success, particularly if done soon after death.

Department of Forensic Science, University of New Haven

Figure 2.15
"Alternate light source" technology can be used in a variety of settings to identify latent images.

There are several wavelengths of light within the electromagnetic spectrum that can be utilized to develop latent prints. Some of the methods, such as an argon laser or the reflected ultraviolet light imaging system, work with the natural fluorescence of a latent print. Other methods use dyes or powders in conjunction with a specific wavelength of light. When viewed with the proper goggles or barrier filter the latent print is clearly visible. See Figure 2.15.

Ultraviolet Rays: Sunlight consists of the many colors in a rainbow; collectively, these colors constitute the visible spectrum. Just beyond the visible spectrum lies the ultraviolet (UV) region. Though imperceptible to the human eye, UV light can be produced by commercially available lamps. It is of interest here because certain substances respond to UV, including some materials found in the residue left on an object after it was handled. Substances that absorb ultraviolet radiation, and instantaneously re-emit it in the visible region of the spectrum, are said to fluoresce—they can be seen by the naked eye. Not all fingerprints fluoresce naturally; dusting with fluorescent powder can enhance ridge line details (when viewed in UV light in a darkened room). The use of these powders is most appropriate when a multicolored background must be examined, black or white powder alone producing insufficient contrast to make the ridge lines clear. The investigator will not often run across fingerprints that necessitate development by fluorescent powders.

Laser Radiation: Laser detection of fingerprints was first accomplished in the mid-1970s. Riboflavin and a few other vitamins are the organic solids in perspiration that can be detected by lasers. The vitamin molecules absorb the laser illumination, re-emitting it almost immediately at a wavelength different from the incident laser light. Called luminescence, this phenomenon is akin to fluorescence. The inherent luminescence of fingerprints can be enhanced by dusting them with luminescent material or by using chemicals that react with fingerprint residue to form compounds that luminesce.

Surfaces normally regarded as unsuitable for registering a fingerprint, such as live human skin and paper toweling, may sometimes display the ridge lines of a print when illuminated by a laser. Not durable on skin, they must be looked for without delay. When a laser is employed, it should be utilized before regular dusting or any chemical method is tried.

Preserving Fingerprint Evidence

Basically, there are two means of preserving fingerprint evidence if the object bearing the print cannot be moved or protected: photographing and "lifting." Photography, the most common method, is preferred, especially from a legal viewpoint. Whether visible naturally or made so by dusting or other means, the print should be photographed life-size (1 to 1). A high-resolution digital fingerprint camera is generally used to photograph fingerprints at the crime scene. The advantage of this is the ability to study the photo to ensure that it has value for analysis. A special fingerprint camera used in the laboratory is especially useful for photographing fingerprints on movable objects. Care should be taken to photograph the print at the scene, where possible, to establish location. Anyone who is steady of hand and able to push a button and count to 10 can, with a minimum of training, produce consistently reliable photographs of latent prints. A one-inch scale and the date and initials of the investigator or evidence technician should be included, particularly if a fingerprint camera is not used.

Sometimes a fingerprint is hard to photograph because of its location—for example, on the side of a filing cabinet that is close to a wall and too heavy to move. In these situations, it can be "lifted" using a special cellophane transparent tape or other commercially available lifter. This lift may be accomplished with ease on a flat surface, but a print on a curved surface presents some difficulty. The use of clear, stretchable bookbinding tape, which conforms to the shape of the object and does not distort the print, will minimize or eliminate the problem.

It is important to keep careful notes describing the object and the location of the print. A photograph has the advantage of recording an object's background, serving to establish the source (which seldom can be done from a lift). A photograph would preclude a defense attorney's challenging the source of the print or claiming it was lifted while the defendant was in custody. The prudent investigator will attempt to preserve all objects bearing a fingerprint and, if possible, photograph the print in situ (in its original location) before lifting.

The defense of Count Alfred de Marigny, indicted for the murder of Sir Harry Oaks in a famous homicide case in the Bahamas, rested largely on the source of a latent fingerprint. Although the print was identified as that of de Marigny, defense counsel brought out the fact that it (allegedly lifted from a moveable Chinese screen at the crime scene, the victim's bedroom) was not photographed *in situ* because a fingerprint camera was not available. On examining the background of the lifted print, an investigator for the defense noted the presence of circular marks that could not be duplicated on lifts taken from any part of the Chinese screen. The defense made another telling point: there was no need to lift the developed print; the lightweight screen could have been carried to a place to be photographed. Largely because of the suspicious circumstances under which the latent print was allegedly obtained, the case was lost.[14] The lesson for the evidence technician and the investigator is that developed latent prints should be photographed first, then lifted. Many departments ignore this admonition, perhaps for reasons of economy. Should they have jurisdiction over an important case and the identity of a lifted fingerprint becomes an issue at trial, the price paid for a damaged reputation as a competent law enforcement agency may be far greater than the money saved by not providing film for the evidence technician to record the latent print properly.

How is a Fingerprint Classified and Identified?

Fingerprint bureaus were established about three decades before crime laboratories; hence, historically, the identification of a latent print was often not considered the responsibility of the crime laboratory. Because the fingerprint personnel of the past were not trained in science, such identification work traditionally had not been thought of as a criminalist's work. Fortunately, James F. Cowger helped to correct this in 1983 with his book, *Friction Ridge Skin*, which emphasized the basis on which a fingerprint identity is established. It avoids the complicated, arbitrary rules for building fingerprint classification schemes, with the exception of those rules necessary to understand why some inked record prints are rejected by the FBI.

How fingerprints are classified and filed is not given an extended explanation in this text because:

1. The field investigator generally does not possess the know-how to classify a set of fingerprints, and only a general understanding is required to answer a complainant's questions.

2. Unless utilized on a regular basis, classification rules beyond the few described are arbitrary and soon forgotten. In addition, because fingerprint files grow in size, so does the need to define more subtypes. As this need is met, variations will be found between agencies, there being no single authority for the introduction of new rules. Classification schemes thus require a text of their own.

3. The use of Automated Fingerprint Identification Systems (AFISs) is now available to local agencies through state and federal organizations.

4. New forms of image-related technology, including photography and digital imaging, are furthering forensic investigative techniques.

Ridge Line Details

Different features of the friction ridge lines are significant in the classification and the individualization of fingerprints. Classification details are largely concerned with line patterns, whereas individualization (comparison) details focus on deviations from a straight or curved continuous ridge line. To the criminalist, ridge line patterns represent *class characteristics*; ridge line deviation details, *individual characteristics*. Those interested in learning more about classification are referred to the book's ancillary website.

Identifying a Latent Fingerprint. A latent fingerprint cannot be identified unless one of known origin is available for comparison (see Figure 2.16). For this, fingerprint exemplars must be acquired. The sources through which known fingerprints are secured and the way the comparison is made are discussed below.

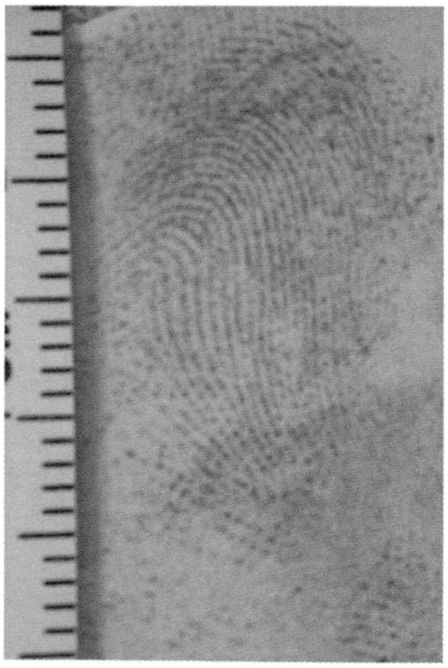

Courtesy, Peter Massey, Department of Forensic Sciences, University of New Haven.

Figure 2.16
A latent print. Note the ruler used to determine size of print. Are there enough points available for identification?

—Fingerprint Exemplars: Sources

The three sources providing the exemplars needed for comparison with a latent print are: (1) police fingerprint files, (2) a set of prints taken from a suspect who has no arrest or fingerprint record, and (3) a set of prints taken from each person who frequents the area in which the latent print was found. The last set, called *elimination prints*, is used to determine whether the latent print is that of a stranger or someone who is customarily present. An unidentified latent print found on an object or in places that a stranger would be unable to justify is potentially valuable evidence.

—Comparison of a Latent with a Known Fingerprint

The first step toward identifying a latent fingerprint is to scrutinize it for any discernible class characteristics in order to eliminate comparison prints that are not of the same pattern type. The next task is to find a cluster of individual characteristics—two or three points bunched together. This grouping is chosen as a landmark to be searched for in the known comparison print. If a corresponding cluster is not noted, the known print is eliminated. If one is noted, the third step is to examine the latent for the next point of identification closest to the landmark cluster; then compare it to the known print to see if that characteristic is present in the same location, based on ridge counting. If it is, the latent is further examined for yet another individual characteristic, and the known is checked to see if there is a match. When all points of identification in each print are of the same type (bifurcation, dot, etc.) in the same unit relationship (same location), and no inexplicable differences are noted in either print, a conclusion that both impressions were made by the same person may be warranted.

—Number of Points Necessary for an Identification

The question of how many individual characteristics are needed for "a conclusion of an identity" (in the language of criminalistics) or "an identification" (in the language of latent print examiners) has not been definitively settled. Among European countries, the minimum number of points is set in France at 17, in England at 16, and in Spain at 10 to 12. In the United States at one time, 12 was a common number. Nevertheless, in 1973 following a three-year study, the International Association for Identification (IAI) pronounced: "… no valid basis exists at this time for requiring that a pre-determined number of friction ridge characteristics must be present in two impressions in order to establish a positive identification."[15]

See Figures 2.17 and 2.18.

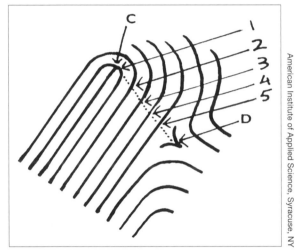

Figure 2.17
Loop pattern with a ridge count—from core (C) to delta (D)—of five.

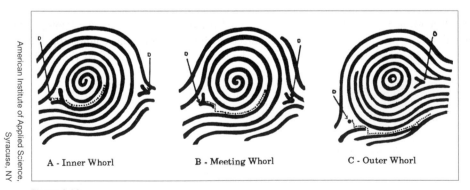

Figure 2.18
Three kinds of whorls as determined by ridge tracing from the left delta to the right delta. "D" points to the two deltas. The dotted line is adjacent to the traced ridge.

Automated Fingerprint Identification Systems (AFISs)

Automated Fingerprint Identification Systems (AFIS) have become commonplace and are now available in most large city police departments as well as state crime laboratories and federal agencies. The development of biometric single-digit collection systems being used by the military offers a number of other future possibilities for law enforcement, including rapid identification of suspects.

Automated fingerprint identification systems (AFISs) scan suspect images with the recorded fingerprints of individuals whose records are in a computerized system using an algorithm that has a high degree of accuracy. Suspect images, which may be no more than a single print, may be collected from a crime scene or from other evidence in an investigation. Where there is a "match," the two images are examined by a fingerprint examiner, who makes the final determination as to whether there is or is not a match.

The FBI created an Integrated Automated Fingerprint Identification System (IAFIS) that went online in 1999. Since then, its use has grown to the point where in 2011 more than 97 percent of submissions were received electronically.[16]

Evidentiary Value

When the friction ridge lines of a fingerprint are properly examined, and an identity between the latent print and a known print can be shown, there is irrefutable evidence that the identified individual made the latent print. This is true whatever the source—finger, palm, or foot. Its value lies in the connection established between the crime scene (or victim) and the identified individual. A defense attorney confronted with such convincing evidence has little chance of disputing it as long as investigators have seen to it that the evidence was legally collected and preserved. Occasionally, however, defendants will either assert that they were at the crime scene at some earlier time or that they had previously handled the object in question. In some cases the question of how long a latent print lasts has been raised.

Determining the age of a latent fingerprint is almost impossible, unless there are other factors, such as when the object or location containing the print can be shown to have a time associated with it.

There is no reason to believe that a latent print will improve over time; sooner or later it will deteriorate, depending on its environment. In a protected environment it is likely to last longer than when exposed to rain, sun, dust, and wind. If the object bearing the print—e.g., counter top, kitchen appliance, or window—receives frequent cleaning, the last time it was cleaned fixes the maximum possible age of the latent print. To evaluate the feasibility of its having lasted for the period claimed, the conditions prevailing during the interval the print was supposedly present must be ascertained. If time permits, a criminalist can be asked to place a print on a surface similar to the one bearing the incriminating print to determine empirically whether a useful latent of a particular age can last and ultimately be developed.

In checking out the explanation of the presence of such a print, the investigator need not rely entirely on forensic considerations. For example, does a code mark on a soda can indicate when and if that can was distributed in the area? If brought in from elsewhere, from where? In general, the investigator must check all the circumstances that either support or contradict any and all such explanations, keeping in mind the equally important task of protecting the innocent.

Levels of Expertise

To make fingerprints serviceable in the criminal justice system, several kinds of expertise are required. First are the inked record prints made of arrestees for police files or, when no file record print exists, taken expressly for comparison with a latent impression. Making a set of acceptable record prints is easily learned and relatively simple; even so, it entails a modicum of expertise. Otherwise, the prints may be rejected as "unclassifiable" by the FBI.

Special training is required to classify a set of inked fingerprints. After several years of experience, a "classifier" may be selected for training as a "latent print examiner." The two tasks are quite different, and experience alone is not sufficient. Yet apprenticeship, long abandoned by the learned professions, is still the mode for creating a "fingerprint identification expert." As pointed out earlier in this chapter, establishing a fingerprint identity is a criminalistics problem, and some criminalists are now performing this work.

Processing a crime scene for fingerprints requires training. The necessary skills for the use of powders can be mastered quickly. Chemical methods and laser radiation, however, require more formal education in science—especially in chemistry and physics (Figure 2.19).

Expert testimony in court is required of the following people:

AP Photo/Keith Srakocic

Figure 2.19
A piece of paper containing latent fingerprints is adjusted in front of filtered green xenon light used to highlight chemical images captured on a digital camera at the ChemIcon Inc. lab in Pittsburgh.

1.   The evidence technician (or investigator) who developed the latent impression.

2.   The file supervisor or detective who can vouch for the authenticity of the known fingerprint record used to identify the defendant.

3.   The expert (a latent print examiner) who can prove the source of the latent print (i.e., to whom it belongs).

Probative Value

A single, partial, latent fingerprint identified as that of a defendant—absent any other evidence—is sufficient proof to convict the accused. It must be shown, however, that the defendant's print was present under circumstances that exclude any reasonable possibility consistent with innocence. Accordingly, the prosecution may have to prove that any object bearing the latent print was inaccessible to the accused. If the defendant had legitimate access to the location before (and reasonably close to when) the crime was committed, the value of the fingerprint evidence is largely negated.

Firearms

Whenever a firearm is discharged in the commission of a crime, physical evidence is likely to be available. The investigator will have several questions to ask concerning its investigative worth:

1. Can the crime scene bullet or cartridge casing be linked to a suspected weapon (if one is located)?

2. Relative to the gun and its mechanical condition:
   a. What is a correct description of the weapon?
   b. Is it capable of firing a cartridge?
   c. Is there evidence of the bullet's trajectory that will permit a determination of the line of fire?
   d. Can the weapon be discharged accidentally?
   e. What is the trigger pull?
   f. Can the serial number (if removed) be restored?

3. What was the muzzle-to-victim (or shooting) distance at the time the weapon was discharged?

4. Is there gunpowder evidence on the firing hand, indicating that it had recently discharged a firearm?

5. Was the weapon recently fired? How many shots?

6. Can the type of gun be determined from an examination of the class characteristics of a bullet or cartridge recovered at the crime scene?

Crime Scene Bullet or Cartridge and Suspected Weapon

Linking a suspected weapon, when one is recovered, to a crime scene bullet or cartridge has both investigative and probative value. The owner or person in possession of the weapon has some explaining to do—certainly to a jury—if put on trial. The owner might have loaned it to another person; if so, that person's name must be disclosed and the alibi checked.

Establishing that a particular weapon fired a bullet is determined by using an instrument designed for this purpose. A comparison microscope is used to compare toolmarks as well as bullets and cartridges (see Figure 2.20).

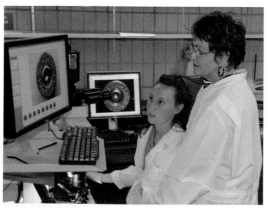

Department of Forensic Sciences, University of New Haven

Figure 2.20
Comparative analysis of shell casings and bullets can be made using a comparison microscope with a digital camera attachment.

Make and Mechanical Condition of Gun

Several matters concerning the make and mechanical condition of a firearm arise when a detective prepares a report or needs information to reconstruct the crime:

1. What is the proper description of the weapon?

2. Is it in working order?

3. Can the trajectory of the bullet be established?

4. Can the weapon be accidentally discharged?

5. Does it have a hair trigger?

Description of a Weapon

It is widely assumed that because police officers carry guns, they are familiar with weapons in general. For many officers nothing is further from the truth. As President Kennedy's assassination illustrates, the correct description of a firearm is best left to the firearms examiner because an incorrect description creates difficulties. Initially, a deputy sheriff reported that the rifle discovered on the sixth floor of the book depository building in Dallas was a 7.65 mm German Mauser; later, it was accurately described as a Mannlicher-Carcano 6.5 mm Italian carbine. In this case, a result of the confusion ensuing from the incorrect identification of the weapon was the credence it gave to a conspiracy theory. See Figures 2.21 and 2.22.

Figure 2.21
Derringer and revolvers.

Operating Condition of a Weapon

Is a particular gun capable of firing a cartridge? This determination is made simply by loading the weapon with proper cartridge and attempting to fire it in an appropriate place such as a range or other facility in which thorough safety precautions have been taken. Then, by firing into cotton, oiled waste, or a water recovery tank, the test bullet can be retrieved for examination under the comparison microscope. If a bullet is found at a crime scene, it can be compared with bullets and cartridges from these test firings, and with evidence on file from other apparently unrelated crimes.

Bullet Trajectory

If there are two or more holes made by one bullet, it may be feasible to determine the line of fire and the firing position of the shooter. Such determinations are made by sighting through the holes and using a laser light (or at night, by directing the beam of a flashlight through them) to trace the line of flight back to the source. The line of fire cannot be established with accuracy, however, when a bullet is diverted from a straight line by an object that causes it to ricochet, or because of a mechanical defect in the weapon.

Figure 2.22
Semi-automatic pistols.

Accidental Discharge

Whether a gun is defective or was accidentally discharged because it was tampered with should be determined solely by someone thoroughly familiar with guns and their mechanisms. Reputable manufacturers are quite reliable, and their products rarely go off by chance. However, the "Saturday-Night Special" and the zip gun are particularly dangerous; if dropped, they can be set off. Official concern over the question of accidental discharge is yet another illustration of the need to reconstruct the event under investigation.

Trigger Pull

A gun is said to have a hair trigger when the force required to pull it is less than that normally set by the factory. For a .38 caliber revolver, a hair trigger pull would be 2.5 pounds to 3.5 pounds with the hammer uncocked, i.e., double action. Trigger pull can be determined by using a spring scale (tension method), or by adding weights to a pan scale hooked over the trigger until the hammer falls (inertia method).

Restoration of Serial Numbers

The serial numbers on a weapon are useful in proving ownership or in tracing a gun from the time of its manufacture. By filing, grinding, punching, or drilling, serial numbers in metal can be obliterated. It should be noted that there are other stolen items such as typewriters, automobile engines, and cameras that also may have their serial numbers altered or obliterated.

An etching process can often restore the original numbers or marks. After the area has been cleaned and polished, a suitable reagent is chosen (depending on the metal: steel, copper, aluminum, or brass) and applied with a cotton swab. Because the original stamping process sets up a strain in the metal by compressing the area beneath the stamp, the etching rate for the metal under pressure and that not so compressed is not the same. This differential causes the original numbers to be restored.

The etching process requires great care and patience; it can take from a few minutes to several hours—even days. During this time the numbers may not appear simultaneously, and the criminalist's attention to reconstituting them must be continuous. Because they may suddenly appear then disappear (usually forever), it is imperative that the details be photographed quickly.

Shooting Distance

The question of the distance between the muzzle of the gun and the victim at the time of the shooting can be significant. The following situations will illustrate:

1. When suicide or foul play is a possibility.

2. In a claim of self-defense or other allegation.

3. Where poor lighting conditions make the victim's recognition of the perpetrator questionable.

With regard to suicide, it is clearly impossible to shoot oneself if the trigger is out of reach. When the firing distance is very small (as in a contact wound) or when it is measured in inches, probative support is given a claim of self-defense. Firing distance is also important when victim recognition is the issue. In New York City—where not many harbor waterfront homicides are brought to trial—one such case was influenced by the criminalist's testimony that the shooting distance was less than six inches. This apparently convinced the jury that the victim's dying declaration identifying an old friend as the killer was believable although the illumination was very poor at the time.

The basis for the determination of shooting distance is found in the smoke halo and powder pattern of the burned, partially burned, and unburned powder particles blown from the muzzle of a gun when fired (see Figure 2.23). Should the victim have been wearing dark clothing, however, a powder pattern may not be discernible. Several technical procedures can be used to make such details visible:

- Contrast photography

- Infrared photography

- Soft X-rays (produced by a low-voltage X-ray tube)

- Modified Greiss test

- Sodium rhodizionate test

Powder Traces on Gun Hand

In addition to powder residue from the muzzle, powder is blown out laterally in the area of the revolver's cylinder or, when an automatic pistol is fired, during the ejection of the cartridge casing. One of the first tests proposed to detect such traces on the hand that fired the gun, the dermal nitrate or paraffin test, has since proved unreliable and lost credibility. A person can fire a gun yet have no detectable traces on the hand, or not fire a gun and have traces of a nitrate present from a source other than gunpowder.

Previously, *neutron activation analysis* (NAA) was used to detect the metal residue (barium and antimony) that comes from the primer of the cartridge. Although residue levels are substantially reduced by wiping or washing the hands with soap, the sensitivity of NAA is so great that even minute traces are readily detected. Current methods involve the use of a scanning electron microscope with energy dispersive X-ray (SEM/EDX), inductively coupled plasma (ISP) spectroscopy. SEM/EDX analysis is the only method that can conclusively identify gunshot residue.

Weapon Recently Fired?—How Many Shots?

The question of whether a gun was recently fired cannot be decisively answered. The best that can be said is that the gun was fired since it was last cleaned. This determination is easily made by running a cleaning patch through the barrel of the weapon. The information provided, however, does not reveal whether the gun has been fired recently.

If cartridge casings are recovered at the crime scene or bullet holes are found, the minimum number of shots fired may be ascertained. This can sometimes be useful in checking out descriptions of the event.

Type and Model of Weapon Used

Following the commission of a crime in which a gun was discharged, notifying area police forces about the type of weapon sought could be productive. Many police officers believe that the crime laboratory can pinpoint the weapon by examining the spent bullet or cartridge casing. It may be

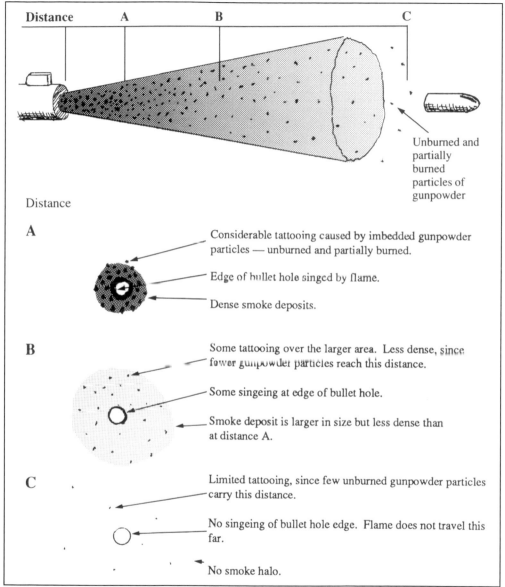

Distance   A   B   C

Unburned and partially burned particles of gunpowder

Distance

A

Considerable tattooing caused by imbedded gunpowder particles — unburned and partially burned.

Edge of bullet hole singed by flame.

Dense smoke deposits.

B

Some tattooing over the larger area. Less dense, since fewer gunpowder particles reach this distance.

Some singeing at edge of bullet hole.

Smoke deposit is larger in size but less dense than at distance A.

C

Limited tattooing, since few unburned gunpowder particles carry this distance.

No singeing of bullet hole edge. Flame does not travel this far.

No smoke halo.

Prepared by Jerzy J. Hoga, graphic designer.

Figure 2.23
Patterns of the smoke halo and gunpowder particles blown out of muzzle upon discharge of a firearm.

feasible to determine caliber this way, but it is seldom possible to identify a specific manufacturer or model. Elimination is a more viable procedure. If a bullet has a left twist to the rifling, then any gun with a right twist would be eliminated automatically based on class characteristics.

Cartridge casings are more useful for identifying the weapon: their shape and size reveal type (revolver or automatic pistol) and caliber. The absence of cartridge casings at the crime scene indicates that a revolver was probably used, since an automatic ejects its casing with each shot fired. The offender, however, may have had the presence of mind to retrieve the ejected cartridge cases, not necessarily to have it appear that a revolver was used, but to eliminate the prospects of the weapon being linked to the crime scene.

Blood

Blood is a common clue material in many of the more serious crimes against a person: homicide, felonious assault, robbery, and rape. Occasionally, it is available in crimes against property. When breaking and entering, a burglar may cut himself or herself—the odds increasing in proportion to the haste or carelessness typical in a crime like automobile larceny. Although fresh blood is easy to discern, its appearance can be altered even after a short time by sunlight, heat, airborne bacteria, age, and other factors; then it is difficult to recognize. Blood that was removed by washing or covered with paint might go unnoticed unless suspicion of such a circumstance is aroused. Fortunately, very sensitive, simple field tests using a chemical reagent permit detection of the slightest residues. Called *presumptive tests*, they are not specific for blood, are only preliminary, and are of little value for court purposes. Still, they have great investigative potential and can be performed at the crime scene. The following are several field color tests presumptive for blood:

- Leuco-Malachite Green Test
- Reduced Phenolphthalein Test
- Luminol Test
- Tetramethyl Benzidine Test

Other tests performed on suspected stains can yield additional information. For example, Hematrace can be used for blood grouping or to determine whether the blood is human. In addition, DNA tests became a reality in 1989. Most of these tests are usually not possible in the field; they call for laboratory equipment and carefully controlled conditions. When the amount of clue material is limited, it is best not to expend it by field testing. The degree of investigative value for each of the examinations on a suspected bloodstain varies.

Investigative Uses

From the viewpoint of the investigator, the concern is not with how blood tests are performed but with the investigative prospects they hold. The following practical results have been achieved through the examination of suspected bloodstains:

- The crime scene has been located
- The crime weapon has been identified
- A link has been established between criminal and victim—or, one or both of them has been connected to the crime scene
- A reconstruction of the crime (how it was committed) has been accomplished
- An alibi has been corroborated or disproved
- A suspect has made an admission or a confession during an interrogation after having been informed of blood test results

Locate the Crime Scene

In homicide cases, a body is sometimes discovered at a location other than where the assault occurred. In the meantime, of course, if the primary crime scene can be found, the investigation has taken a step forward. Moving the body suggests a deliberate attempt by the criminal to dissociate himself or herself from the killing. It is often apparent from the nature of the injuries that a significant quantity of blood is likely to be present at the crime scene, making it equally likely that the criminal will take countermeasures to forestall discovery of that site. This, however, is not easy to do, because the guilty person is hindered by internal pressures to avoid exposure.

Here are a few circumstances that have alerted investigators and aroused their suspicion that blood might have been present:

- In an otherwise grubby home, the kitchen floor had been immaculately cleaned

- Only one wall of a living room had been freshly painted

- A rug was missing from a floor that obviously had been previously covered (judging by a color difference in the varnish at the room's borders and the lack of scratch marks in the middle)

- A bedspread could not be located, nor its whereabouts satisfactorily explained

- The seat covers of an automobile had been removed, though reported to have been in good condition the day before the crime

- A few tons of coal had been moved within a coal bin (shoveled to another side and away from where it would normally be), making it inconvenient to use

- Ketchup had been smeared over the kitchen floor and rubbed into the carpet

In such circumstances when a positive preliminary blood test is obtained despite an effort to cover it up, the clue must be followed up. Although not admissible as evidence in court, preliminary blood tests have significant investigative value. Additional information can become available when the original crime scene is located.

Identify the Weapon or Instrument

Although the law does not require that a weapon be produced as evidence in court, an intensive search is generally made to recover it. The impact on the jury is considerable if an unusually terrifying instrument was wielded to wound or injure. On observing the injuries on the victim's body, the pathologist—and in many cases the detective—may be able to arrive at some conclusion with respect to the type of weapon; obviously, the search is more likely to be successful when one knows what to look for.

The presence of blood on a hammer or other bludgeon, knife, ice pick, heavy boot, or spike heel can expose it as the likely assault weapon. Most weapons seem to present difficulties regarding removal of all residual traces. This is often true despite precautions taken by the perpetrator soon after committing the crime. Careful washing of cutting or stabbing instruments, on the other hand, is quite effective; if done thoroughly, even the most sensitive reagent fails to detect blood. Fortunately, most criminals are satisfied if their weapon appears free of visible traces of blood; hence, there is always the chance that invisible traces remain. For example, a boot thought to be implicated in a stomping homicide may retain traces of blood on its welt or on the side or inside of the shoelace. Therefore, even when no signs of blood are apparent, it will profit the conscientious investigator to submit a suspected weapon to the crime laboratory.

Develop Associative Evidence

Relating the criminal to the victim—or either of them to the crime scene—through the discovery and grouping of a bloodstain or through DNA content are examples of associative evidence. It is not unusual to find the victim's blood on the perpetrator's clothing or body, or alternatively, the criminal's blood at the crime scene. There are a few cases on record in which a trail of the perpetrator's blood was tracked from the crime scene back to the perpetrator's house. Usually, however, the identity of the suspect is gradually disclosed through normal investigative techniques. Then the crime laboratory's ability is called on to process the physical evidence. Two extreme investigative possibilities for blood are represented in the following examples:

1. No test other than normal visual observation—tracking a trail of blood—is required.

2. Significant investigative results are provided when the bloodstain can be analyzed for DNA.

    Identifying the source, especially of animal blood, can be significant in some circumstances.

Reconstruct How the Crime was Committed

Reconstructing the crime, an increasingly important laboratory function, can be accomplished through the study of blood groups and bloodstain patterns. One of the authors is familiar with a case of a double homicide by a third person. Despite the perpetrator's attempt to have it appear that a duel with carving knives had taken place, the homicide was reconstructed in the crime laboratory by the blood grouping of stains found throughout the apartment. The apparent duelists obviously dead, this strategy might have been successful and the case closed had the unusual distribution of blood in widely separated areas not aroused the suspicion of the investigator. Blood was found on the back of the entrance door to the apartment, on the inside of the bathroom door, on the telephone ripped from the wall, and on a window shade (normally open, but closed when the crime was discovered).

The samples were sufficient in quantity for grouping purposes, and two different blood groups were present. The laboratory ascertained the specific objects each victim had touched and, through a reconstruction of how the crime was committed, was able to explain the wide distribution of blood. It became clear that the criminal had been unable to deal lethally with two victims at the same time. When switching from one to the other, he would find the first attempting to escape or call for help. The bloody doors, the ripped telephone wire, and the closed window shade testified to the killer's resolve to prevent such attempts. Although the perpetrator was ultimately apprehended by conventional techniques, his confession was corroborated by the crime laboratory's blood grouping, which reconstructed how the crime was committed. In many jurisdictions, corroboration of a confession is a requisite in more serious crimes. Corroboration through independent evidence is desirable in all crimes. Sometimes blood examinations have this potential.

In a monograph on the interpretation of bloodstain patterns, MacDonell describes how knowledge of the flight characteristics and the stain patterns of spattered blood can be employed to determine several things:

1. The distance between the surface bearing the stain and the origin of the blood at the time it was shed;

2. The point(s) of origin of the blood;

3. The type of impacting object (bludgeon or gunshot) that produced the bloodstains, and the direction of its force;

4. The movement and direction of the person(s) and/or object(s) during the shedding of blood;

5. The number of blows or shots; with arterial gushing, the number of heartbeats;

6. The position(s) of the victim and/or object(s) during the shedding of blood;

7. The movement of the victim and/or object(s) following the shedding of blood.[17]

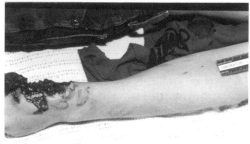

Herbert L. MacDonell, Laboratory of Forensic Science, Corning, NY

Figure 2.24

Blood spatter on arm (to the left of ruler) shows directionality to be from right to left. These small stains establish that the arm origin of spatter was not from the thumb but from the other area of damage (or impact), i.e., the chin.

In one case, MacDonell's expertise was called on to examine blood spatter stains on the clothing of an individual who claimed he found the victim in a pool of blood and dragged the body to get help, thereby causing the stains. MacDonell, however, testified that the blood pattern on the defendant's clothing could not have resulted as described—that is, from mere contact with the victim. It could only have been produced by blood spattering with great velocity, as from a beating or stabbing.[18] See Figure 2.24.

Corroborate or Disprove an Alibi

Suspects finding it somewhat disconcerting when a bloodstain is discovered in their home or automobile, or on their clothing, often proffer an explanation for its presence. Typical alibis include: a recent visit to the butcher shop, a cookout, a hunting trip, or a nosebleed. They may be proved or disproved in the laboratory by determining the origin of a stain (animal, human, or both), or its DNA content. Simplistic excuses that wine, ketchup, or iron are the cause can be readily checked in the field by one of the preliminary catalytic color tests (such as the Leuco-Malachite Green Test).

Interrogate a Suspect

The average suspect does not know the difference between a blood examination that is no more than an investigative technique and one with genuine evidentiary value. One of the prerequisites of effective interrogation is met when suspects understand that evidence exists that can be used against them; at least they must believe it is available. To invoke this belief, a color test (such as the Leuco-Malachite Green Test) performed in the presence of the suspect on a stain that seems to be implicative can be effective. If the other conditions necessary for a confession are satisfied (see Chapter 11), a formal declaration of guilt can result.

Evidentiary Value

A laboratory finding that a suspicious stain contains blood of human origin may work against a defendant on trial, and laboratory testimony on its blood group will carry greater weight. A determination, therefore, that incriminating stains on the suspect's clothing are of the same group as the victim's (and different from the suspect's) represents a contribution to the evidence that few juries would ignore. This also applies to a determination resulting from DNA analysis. Any explanation of why the same DNA or blood group as the victim's should have been found on the defendant must satisfy the jury. Should it fail to, the consequences are apt to be grave when the jury deliberates on the evidence.

Semen, other Biological Material, and DNA Profiling

DNA (deoxyribonucleic acid) technology is a relative newcomer to serving the needs of law enforcement. Developed in the 1970s as a tool for the molecular biologist, and coming as a surprise spin-off from gene splicing, it was first applied to forensic matters in 1985. Not since Neutron Activation Analysis (NAA) was viewed as a godsend in the late 1940s has a promising new method for the examination of physical evidence caused such a stir in the world of forensic scientists, prosecutors, and defense attorneys. Particularly in rape cases, prosecutors see the possibility of presenting positive DNA (semen) results as associative evidence or proof that the defendant's ejaculate was present at the crime scene or on the victim's clothing or body. The linkage of suspect to crime scene has strong probative value and is likely to be persuasive to a jury. Defense attorneys are also tantalized by the prospect that DNA findings may (and can) eliminate their client as a rape suspect, or free him or her should he or she have been convicted and the test not done originally. Similarly, interest is aroused because other kinds of biological evidence are suitable for DNA analysis: blood (if white cells are present), hair (if the root is present), saliva, skin (if nucleated epithelial cells are present), bone, teeth, urine, feces, or stamps or sealed envelopes that were licked. Similarly, dandruff, chewing gum, razor blades, facial tissues, eyeglasses, and wristwatch bands also can yield DNA results. Most biological evidence (to be examined for DNA) is best preserved when kept dry and cold to prevent bacterial growth and the degradation of the DNA. Each item of evidence should be stored, after drying, in paper envelopes or paper bags while assiduously maintaining the chain of custody.

DNA analysis (profiling) is regarded by some in law enforcement as the greatest breakthrough since the advent of fingerprinting and the computer. Today, the courts in all 50 states allow DNA test results to be admitted as evidence since the practice's first appeal in a Florida criminal case. Of the first 54 cases handled by the FBI Laboratory, 29 suspects were linked to the crime through a comparison of DNA profiles obtained from the suspect's specimen and the biological crime scene specimen. Fourteen suspects were cleared when DNA results did not match.

DNA profiling would, therefore, appear to be a powerful forensic tool for protecting the innocent. And yet it could be used maliciously to do just the opposite: namely, frame a victim. Specimens of hair, blood, and semen could be procured (though not without some difficulty), then placed at a crime scene to incriminate the "patsy" selected to take the "fall." Great care must therefore be taken to gather evidence independent of DNA results to corroborate that the suspect did, in fact, commit the crime or at least had the opportunity and compelling motive to do so.

DNA—What is it?

A naturally occurring substance, and the principal component of cellular chromosomes, DNA is responsible for the hereditary (genetic) characteristics in all life forms. It is a large, heavy macromolecule consisting of two strands coiled about each other—like a spiral staircase—forming DNA into the structure of a double helix. The steps in the staircase are composed of four nitrogenous bases known as adenine, guanine, cytosine, and thymine—each represented respectively by A, G, C, and T. Only when A is paired with T, or G with C, can a step be built in the staircase. In nature, when a sugar (deoxyribose) is linked to a phosphate group and to one of the four nitrogenous bases (A, G, C, T), the resultant molecule is called nucleotide.

The number of arrangements for nucleotides is almost infinite, the human genetic code comprising three billion combinations. For example, base pairings in a nucleotide and its two-strand structure can be depicted for one possible fragment of the DNA code as follows:

$$\text{-A-G-T-T-C-A-G-G-G-T-C-C-A-}$$
$$\text{| | | | | | | | | | | | |}$$
$$\text{-T-C-A-A-G-T-C-C-C-A-G-G-T-}$$

Within a human cell, each of the 46 chromosomes (23 from each parent) has a DNA structure built from the randomly alternating base pairings:

The vast majority of the 3 billion nucleotides are shared in common by all human beings. Only a small portion is sufficiently variable in base pairing sequence to permit discriminating one individual from another through the variations of genetic material at the molecular level.

DNA—How is it Analyzed?

Certain nucleotide combinations, however, repeat themselves at random intervals throughout the length of the DNA chain. The sequence is called a *restriction site*, the term coming from the naturally occurring restriction enzymes obtained from certain bacteria. Restriction enzymes can be purified for use in fragmenting DNA after it is extracted from the specimen (Step 1 in Figure 2.25); they act like chemical scissors, cutting or breaking the DNA chain at its restriction sites (Step 2 in Figure 2.25). The resultant fragments, varying in length and weight, are separated by gel electrophoresis (Step 3 in Figure 2.25). The double-stranded DNA fragments are further broken apart (denatured by heat or chemical means), resulting in single-stranded fragments. These single strands can be joined together again under certain conditions to reform the original double-stranded DNA. The process of recombining single DNA strands to form a double strand is called hybridization (Step 4 in Figure 2.25). It is possible to hybridize (combine) the denatured single strands of DNA obtained from the questioned biological evidence with other single (complementary) strands obtained through laboratory recombinant techniques. If the complementary strands (or probes) are tagged (by incorporating radioactive phosphorous into the DNA molecule), the resulting hybrid is detected by using X-ray film (Step 5 in Figure 2.25). The process is repeated with a known sample obtained from the suspect or victim. Laboratory-tagged single-stranded DNA molecules are again used to detect any complementary single strands of DNA obtained by denaturing the known sample. The labeled (or tagged) molecules used for this purpose are called probes.

There are several methods available for DNA profiling. They differ from each other in the amount of sample required for analysis. The accuracy of the results is dependent on the quantity and quality of the sample. The laboratory-made probes used to identify the DNA denatured fragments obtained from the crime scene evidence also differ significantly. Restriction Fragment Length Polymorphism (RFLP) analysis, the earliest known technique (Steps 3 through 7 in Figure 2.25),

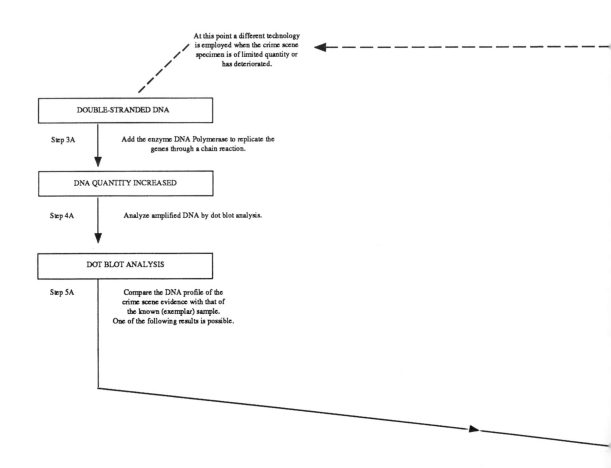

At this point a different technology
is employed when the crime scene
specimen is of limited quantity or
has deteriorated.

DOUBLE-STRANDED DNA

Step 3A   Add the enzyme DNA Polymerase to replicate the
               genes through a chain reaction.

DNA QUANTITY INCREASED

Step 4A   Analyze amplified DNA by dot blot analysis.

DOT BLOT ANALYSIS

Step 5A   Compare the DNA profile of the
               crime scene evidence with that of
               the known (exemplar) sample.
               One of the following results is possible.

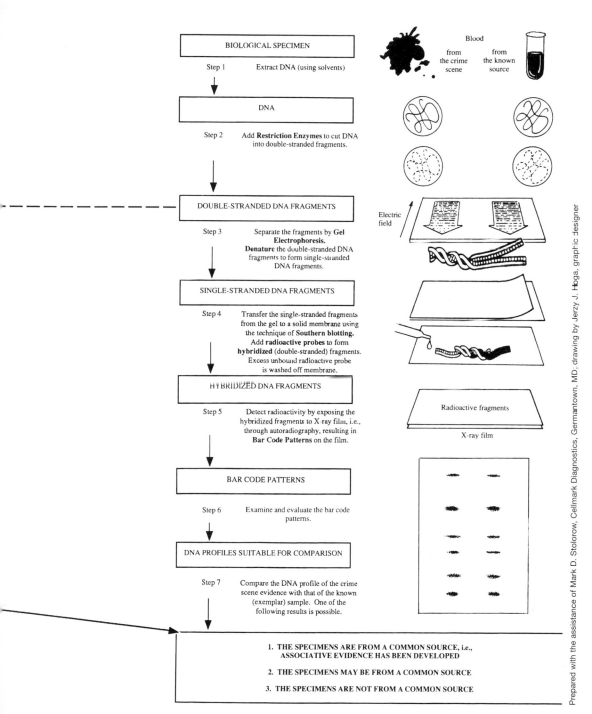

Figure 2.25
Schematic outline for the analysis of DNA.

Prepared with the assistance of Mark D. Stolorow, Cellmark Diagnostics, Germantown, MD; drawing by Jerzy J. Hoga, graphic designer

involves either of two kinds of probes. Originally called Jeffreys probes and White probes (named after the scientists who developed them), they are now better characterized as multilocus and single-locus probes. A multilocus probe (MLP) can, in one test, simultaneously bind many DNA fragments from many different chromosomes; this process is a multilocus probe test. A single-locus probe (SLP) test, on the other hand, identifies a fragment whose sequence appears only once in a chromosome. (However, several single-locus tests can be performed using different probes.) At the beginning of DNA testing for forensic purposes, only the SLP method was used in North America; both were used in Europe. Of the two, the MLP is less costly and does not require as much time because only one test need be made. A drawback of both methods is the requirement that the DNA sample be of high molecular weight, i.e., a sample that has not begun to deteriorate or decompose in stages—resulting in lower molecular weights. Because heat, bacteria, and moisture can cause it to decompose, the preservation of DNA evidence is critical.

Fortunately, another procedure is useful when a crime scene specimen has undergone some deterioration, is of insufficient molecular weight, or was limited in quantity to begin with. This procedure involves a chain reaction that amplifies certain (target) DNA sequences in the specimen. To accomplish this, the enzyme DNA polymerase is used, and the procedure is known as the polymerase chain reaction (PCR), or alternatively, the gene amplification technique (Steps 3A through 5A in Figure 2.25). Although the time needed to complete a PCR procedure is measured in hours, it takes additional time to complete any of the several identification methods that must then be used.

Newer DNA Technology

A newer approach to DNA analysis involves *short tandem repeats* (STRs). Individually, STRs are less discriminating, but when multiple ones are examined, the combined probability can equal that of RFLP results. Similarly, Y-chromosome DNA typing is currently being used as yet another form of STR analysis.[19] This technology could help identify males involved in sexual assault cases, as heretofore it was the victim's word versus the accused individual's word as to whether he assaulted the victim. Chromosome STRs (see below) are increasingly accepted because of their value in the investigation of sexual crimes. At the cutting edge of DNA technology is the study of *single nucleotide polymorphism* (SNP) sites, with the future prospect of their use as an additional kind of DNA evidence.

Another development enhancing the value of DNA as evidence is the utilization of a different DNA that is also found in body cells: *mitochondrial DNA* (mtDNA). The more familiar DNA, found only in the nucleus of the cell, is properly designated as nDNA.

Short Tandem Repeats (STRs)

The DNA molecule is chemically stable, long-living, and quite resistant to environmental factors. Although preserved by desiccation or cold storage, it can be degraded by enzyme action (cellular or bacterial) when damp; then, it separates into fragments with far fewer base pairs than are present in intact DNA, which has 3 billion base pairs.

The greater the DNA degradation, the more likely the survival of only the shortest fragments. Such small DNA fragments are still useful for analyzing old specimens and crime scene evidence. Short Tandem Repeat (STR) defines a small region (locus) in which different numbers of tandemly repeated core DNA sequences, two to eight base pairs in length, are found. STRs are favored because of the ease with which they amplify by the polymerase (PCR) chain reaction. STR markers have a number of repeats that vary considerably among individuals, thus making them useful for identification. With one nanogram (1 ng) of DNA sample, matching probabilities of one in a billion or more is possible. Moreover, the results can be obtained in a few hours, compared to the days or weeks required by RFLP. In part, this is the result of automating the analysis of STRs. In addition, with STR methods, owing to the use of PCR chain reaction, both the quantity and quality of the crime scene DNA can be small (0.1 to 1 ng) and highly degraded, yet it is possible to obtain distinctive discrimination between unrelated or even closely related individuals, except identical twins. The DNA database now being compiled uses 13 core STR loci in the DNA molecule (see CODIS below). The "core" STR loci referred to is the use of the same DNA regions for typing, used by forensic science laboratories in the United States, in cooperation with the FBI in CODIS. With this uniformity of procedure, they can exchange and compare case work and database typing information. By selecting 13 loci, the power of discrimination rivals that of RFLP analysis, which is expensive and requires considerably more time and DNA to complete. STR markers are now also used for paternity testing. Similarly, STR typing is employed to identify human remains in cases of mass disasters, including high-temperature fires and airplane crashes in which the victims are subjected to obdurate water damage.

Mitochondrial DNA

The cell is the basic building block of all living things. Although it contains many components, two are of interest from a DNA standpoint: the *nucleus* and the *mitochondrion*. The nucleus is the source of the DNA (more properly nDNA) that is commonly tested for. The mitochondrion is a specialized part of the cell, the function of which is to produce energy for the body by using the food digested. It too has a DNA molecule, mitochondrial DNA (mtDNA), which is relatively small (about 17,000 base pairs) compared to the 3 billion base pairs in nDNA. Although mtDNA offers much less discriminatory information than nDNA, the hundreds or thousands of mitochondria per cell (compared to one nucleus per cell) make it much easier to extract mtDNA from biological specimens. Thus, a very small sample or one that is old and badly degraded may not be suitable for nDNA analysis, yet could be fit for mtDNA analysis of mitochondrial DNA. Moreover, mtDNA can often be recovered from samples that will not yield much nDNA, such as hair shafts, saliva, and skeletal remains.

Unlike nDNA (which is inherited from both parents), mtDNA is passed only through the mother. This fact, coupled with the fact that mtDNA is recoverable from ancient bones, has led to the solution of some interesting historical questions. For instance, were the bodies buried in an unmarked grave those of the Romanov family, the Russian royal family believed to be shot more than 70 years ago at the start of the Russian Revolution? Typing revealed that the mtDNA sequences obtained from the Romanov descendants matched that extracted from the bones believed to be those of the royal family. The counterpart to mtDNA being passed only through the female line in the family is the Y chromosome, which is passed only through the male line of the family.

DNA—Investigative Use

DNA tests for forensic evidence were first performed in the United States by commercial laboratories. In 1989 the FBI laboratory began to offer them for law enforcement purposes. Since then the agency has received many thousands of submissions of evidence from federal, state, and local law enforcement agencies.

DNA results are obtained in about seventy-five percent of cases studied. DNA testing eliminates the suspect in about one-third of these cases. ... [There] are numerous criminal cases in which the defendant pleads guilty in the face of compelling DNA evidence.[20]

To push the potential of DNA even further and use it to generate investigative leads, the FBI Laboratory's Combined DNA Index System (CODIS) blends forensic science and computer technology to create an effective tool for solving violent crimes. CODIS enables federal, state, and local crime labs to exchange and compare DNA profiles electronically, thereby linking crimes to each other and convicted offenders. All DNA files originate at the local level, then flow to state and national levels.[21] Oftentimes, DNA obtained from a crime scene is less than ideal. Exposure to water and enzymes, both commonly found in nature, can fracture the DNA molecule. Such degraded DNA was difficult to analyze until PCR methods and STR typing became possible. Now less than 1 nanogram (1 ng) can be analyzed, whereas 100 ng were required when the RFLP method was the only way possible. Such sensitivity (1 ng analysis) has a price, however, in the form of potential contamination in the collection, transportation, and analysis of biological evidence. When DNA testing was first employed, it took from six to eight weeks to reach a result. Improvement in methods over the past 20 years has reduced the time to a few hours—and with greater discrimination as to the DNA source. If a match between crime scene sample and a suspect's DNA is realized, the DNA profile is then compared with population databases. A report stating the probability of a random match is then calculated, if a match is determined. So-called "touch analysis," in which samples drawn from a location where a subject has touched an object, can now be identified, and DNA can also be used to determine whether a sample is from a male or a female.

A population database is a collection of DNA profiles of unrelated individuals from a particular ethnic group, for example, Caucasians and African Americans. A random match probability is the chance a randomly selected individual from a particular population will have an identical STR profile at the DNA marker tested. A large DNA-sequence database, known as GenBank, is maintained at the U.S. National Institute of Health and contains more than 125 billion nucleotide bases and 135 million sequences.[22]

Ever since the first United States case was solved by searching a convicted offender's DNA records—a 1991 Minnesota rape-homicide—CODIS has solved "otherwise unsolvable violent crimes" with increasing frequency.[23] When all 13 CODIS loci are tested, the average random-match probability (assuming unrelated individuals) is rarer than one in a trillion.

In 1993, crime laboratories in the United States had collected 142,000 samples and analyzed more than 7,000. As of April 2012, the National DNA Index System (NDIS) contained 10,718,700 offender profiles and almost 400,000 forensic profiles, and the CODIS system had provided 178,300 hits in more than 171,000 investigations.[24]

Moreover, all 50 states passed legislation requiring convicted offenders to provide samples for DNA databases.[25] In the United States thus far, DNA samples are for the most part analyzed in cases involving sexual assault and homicide, whereas in the UK, evidence obtained in burglary cases is also analyzed. Even in the 1990s, the British were getting between 300 and 500 "hits" weekly, largely for burglary. These include crime-scene-to-crime-scene hits (in CODIS, the Forensic Index), but also convicted-offender-to-crime-scene matches (in CODIS, the Convicted Offender Index).[26] A significant number of released prisoners are convicted again within a short time for committing the same or another crime. Both the Forensic Casework Index and the Convicted Offender Index (COI), especially as they grow in size, assist in clearing crimes that otherwise would not have been solved. The COI is compiled using liquid blood samples, thereby enhancing the ability to automate the DNA typing procedure.

The development and use of a DNA database embraces three elements: (a) the collection of specimens from known individuals, (b) analyzing these specimens and entering their DNA profiles in a computer database, and (c) the comparison of the crime scene DNA profile with the known profiles recorded in the computer database. Each of the 50 states has passed legislation establishing a DNA database for their state. To be included in the national CODIS database, all 13 STR markers (at least 10 for degraded DNA samples) must be submitted to the national file. This file contains no case-related information. When a CODIS "hit"—that is, a potential match between two or more DNA profiles—is established, the laboratories originating the matching profiles get together to confirm or challenge the match. After qualified DNA analysts have validated the match, a further exchange of information between the criminal investigators is the next logical step.

There are several problems associated with the development of DNA databases for law enforcement:

1. Incarcerated felons resist providing blood or saliva samples for they are aware that their DNA can be used to match it to unsolved crimes or to identify them if they commit additional crimes in the future.

2. Crime scene samples may be a mixture of DNA from two or more individuals, thereby making the interpretation of the DNA results more difficult.

3. Quality assurance guidelines must be rigorously followed and regulated by carrying out periodic proficiency tests of analysts.

4. The matter of privacy is of some interest. Thus, information in the DNA database must be solely for law enforcement needs, that is, to be used only for human identity testing and not for any generic medical assessment. Only the crime laboratory submitting the DNA data should retain the capability to link DNA results to a known person. Any unauthorized disclosure of DNA database information for other than law enforcement purposes must be sternly penalized.

DNA Results—Evidence and Proof

The probe patterns obtained from crime scene biological evidence and those from the suspect's known biological sample must match if an identity is to be established (Steps 5A and 7 in Figure 2.25). When there are no matching patterns, the suspect clearly is not the source of the crime scene evidence.

Proponents of the Jeffreys method use the term *DNA fingerprinting* to describe the results obtained through MLP testing. To approach the same certainty, the SLP procedure must employ several single-locus probes. However, there were some in the forensic science community who shared the belief that DNA profiling offered a promise rather than a realization of the individualization of some biological evidence.

In 1988 the FBI undertook an ambitious research program to perfect the method used in its laboratory, and to establish its scientific validity and reliability.[27] It is important to recognize that DNA test patterns depend on the restriction enzyme(s) and probe(s) employed. Different enzyme/probe combinations will produce different DNA patterns. Standardization of DNA technology, therefore, is important when the results are to be used as evidence in a court of law. The ultimate goal of the FBI is to ensure that DNA-based evidence withstands the inevitable challenges.

Another aspect of the need and importance of standardization for DNA testing methods relates to the desirability of creating a DNA file (or database) comparable to that of a fingerprint file. DNA technology was in its infancy in the late 1980s, and it was probably premature to start compiling such a database on a wide scale. But, as a means of tying together apparently unrelated rapes or homicides—establishing that they are the work of one person (a serial murderer, for example)—DNA has an important immediate contribution to make.

Those who use the term "fingerprinting" to imply certitude regarding DNA profiling inevitably invite comparison. Identical twins yield identical DNA profiles that cannot be distinguished from one another; however, with their real fingerprints, there is no problem. In addition to theoretical *(a priori)* reasons for believing fingerprints are unique, there is considerable empirical *(a posteriori)* evidence to confirm the absolute nature of fingerprint identification. Except for identical twins, there is good theoretical reason to support individualization by DNA testing. However, until the necessary database and file are fully constructed and tested, it is premature to rank DNA profiling with the certainty of an identity established by matching a good, usable latent print with a known print.

Newer forensic examination methods have given rise to a similar set of concerns among those interested in evidence and proof. Yale H. Caplan, co-editor of *Academic News*, in a column on professional issues in forensic science, wrote:

> With the use of a new technology, the interpretation of the results becomes critical. Serious consequences may result if the expert overinterprets or overextends the technology. This occurred in the application of neutron activation analysis (NAA) to hair examinations; result, NAA is no longer utilized for this purpose. ... It is incredibly powerful to be able to state in a courtroom that a bloodstain came from a particular person to the exclusion of everyone else in the world. It is hoped that such statements can be backed up by a valid statistical base and that such studies have been verified by peer review.[28]

Caplan further stated:

> In this early stage in the application of DNA probe technology to forensic cases, it is vital that the laboratories conducting such tests employ stringent quality control in their procedures. The experts testifying should be conservative in their use of statistics. The greater concern is the manner in which this technology will be transferred from the few highly specialized laboratories performing this test today to crime laboratories throughout the country. This will require extensive training and must include stringent quality control, certification and proficiency testing.[29]

Documents

The examination of the handwriting, printing, or typewriting on a document (in addition to the paper itself) affords opportunities to develop useful information.

Handwriting and Hand-Printing Examinations

Questions that should be asked include:

1. Did the suspect write, print, or sign the document? This question arises with kidnap ransom notes, anonymous letters, and signatures that are questioned.

2. Is the document genuine? This question arises with receipts and bills, suicide notes, letters, diaries, and wills suspected of being forgeries.

3. Are there any additions or deletions? If so, were they made at the time of original preparation or at a different time? These questions arise in forgery cases.

4. Was the document written or printed by one or more than one person? This is usually a civil rather than a criminal matter.

Typewriting and Computer Printing Examinations

The availability of typewriters makes their use very likely when a document is employed in the commission of a crime. However, typewriters have become almost extinct in the United States, giving rise to the prevalence of computer-generated documents. Where a typewriter is used in kidnap and ransom notes, threatening letters, forged documents, and bank robber notes, the following questions should be considered:

1. Can the make and perhaps the model of the typewriter be identified? This information limits the inquiry to those who have such an instrument available.

2. Can it be shown that a specific machine typed the questioned document? If so, associative evidence has been developed.

3. Were any additions or changes made by a typewriter other than the one used to type the original document? This question is more often raised in civil matters.

4. Was the typewriter manufactured after the ascribed date of the document? Again, this usually (but not exclusively) involves a civil rather than a criminal matter.

The rapid increase in the use of computer-generated documents on printers has had an impact on document examination. Carbon copies are virtually extinct, and the use of color copy machines has also contributed to changes in the way documents are examined. For this reason, the type and manufacturer of the printer, and paper and ink examinations have become very important. Although traditional examination of documents has changed, modern techniques have contributed to new methods using more advanced technology that shows promise for criminal investigation.

The Siemens Group research on a number of image-related subjects, including handwriting and type fonts, shows great promise for questioned document examinations. The development of algorithms that measure such attributes as angle, size, and spacing in written communication has proven itself in postal and other forms of print analysis.

Paper and other Examinations

Investigators are often familiar with the potential value of handwriting and print evidence yet they are frequently unaware of new methods of analysis and other information that could be developed by further examination of the document. With regard to the paper used, one should consider:

1. Can a sheet of paper, which was directly beneath another at the time of the writing, be used to restore the original writing, if the top sheet was not recovered? In one case, a patrol officer stopped a vehicle, but before approaching the driver, wrote the license number on his paper pad. The driver

shot and killed the officer as he approached, then went to the patrol car and tore off the incriminating top page. The pad was brought to the laboratory, where the indented writing was made visible and photographed by means of sidewise (oblique) illumination, which provided the needed contrast. With the license number known, the killer's apprehension resulted.

Fish, Jacqueline T., Larry S. Miller, and Michael C. Braswell, *Crime Scene Investigation*, 2nd ed. Boston: Elsevier/Anderson Publishing, 2011.

Figure 2.26
The top signature is genuine. The bottom signature is a freehand simulation. Note the differences in line quality, spacing between letters, and variation of pressure pattern. The top signature looks smoothly executed while the bottom signature appears drawn.

2. Can writing that has been obliterated by covering it with scratch marks be restored? In a conspiracy case, the obliterated name of a hotel, the telephone and room numbers, and alias of its occupant were revealed by means of infrared photography. A red-ink pen had been used to scratch out the writing.

3. Can a mechanical or chemical erasure be restored? These and other alterations are found on affidavits, ballots, checks, and receipts.

4. Was one piece of paper torn from another? A jigsaw-puzzle-like reassembly of the evidence answers this question.

5. What company manufactured the paper? When was it manufactured? Such information is often involved with civil matters, but sometimes it bears on the crime of forgery.

Further, where the writing appears on a wall or other object, the use of digital imaging by photographing the writing or marking can be used to develop comparative analysis with a suspect's handwriting, use of particular words or images, and spacing characteristics that link the suspect to the crime. See Figure 2.26.

Glass

Window glass broken during the commission of a crime retains details in its cracks that permit the event to be reconstructed. For example, it might be important to determine whether the glass was broken from the outside or inside. Determining whether a bullet (or other breaking force) came from the outside or the inside of a dwelling can be crucial; sometimes it can reverse the direction of an investigation. For example, a visiting child was shot dead while seated at a table having lunch. An aunt, an uncle, and two nephews were in the apartment at the time; all said a sniper's bullet had been the cause of death. Examination of the window, however, disclosed that the breaking force had come from the inside (see Figure 2.27). Then, by separating and reinterrogating the witnesses, the actual events were revealed: toying with an unfamiliar gun, the aunt had accidentally killed the child; to account for the tragedy to the mother, the uncle broke the window from the inside with a ball-peen hammer and concocted the sniper story.

Figure 2.27
A. Sash of broken window removed from its frame.
B. Same window, but the piece in the 7 o'clock position has been removed for an examination of its radial and spiral cracks.
C. A photomacrograph of a radial edge of B, depicting its rib marks. See Figures 2.29 and 2.30 to determine direction of force.

Direction of Break

The details needed by a detective (or criminalist) to determine where the breaking force was applied to a pane of glass are developed as follows:

1. To obtain the required details, a piece of the broken window is used.

2. The inside and outside surfaces of the piece must be identified. If a piece of the broken pane can be removed from the window, the respective sides should be carefully marked with gummed labels. The outside surface of a window is generally dirtier and streaked by rain, and often has paint or putty serving as a tell-tale sign indicating that it was on the outside.

3. One edge of a crack in the broken piece of glass must be examined for its rib marks (see Figure 2.27C). It is customary to examine the edge of a radial crack, but examining the edge of a spiral crack may work, if the examination is restricted to the spiral crack innermost to the original impact hole and the examiner is certain which edge—radial or spiral—is being studied. This visual examination involves scrutinizing the edge for the rib mark pattern. There are two types: in one pattern, the rib marks run perpendicular to the right side of the glass; in the other, they run to the left side (see Figure 2.28).

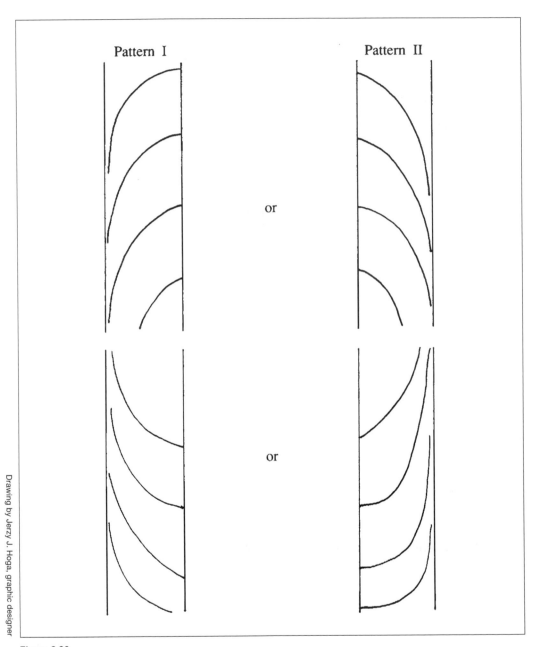

Figure 2.28
Types of rib mark patterns that may be seen on the edge of a glass crack.

Should the rib mark pattern be difficult to see, the illumination may need to be subdued. This can be done simply by turning one's back to the light, or by viewing the edge beneath a table and gently turning or rocking the glass until the light reveals the rib mark pattern. Figure 2.29 is a worksheet that facilitates the recording of the observation and provides other details necessary to arrive at a conclusion. The interpretation of the recorded details is illustrated in Figure 2.30.

**STEPWISE
DIRECTIONS**

1. Indicate type of edge: Radial ☐   or Spiral ☐

2. Indicate outside and inside surfaces by labeling each side:

   Outside surface is labeled: ....
   Inside surface is labeled: ....

3. Draw in the space below the type of pattern observed when the edge of the glass crack is examined in subdued light:

   SIDE A   **SIDE B**

3. See Figure 2.30 for interpretation of these data.

Drawing by Jerzy J. Hoga, graphic designer

Figure 2.29
Worksheet for the examination of a glass crack: gathering the data necessary to determine the direction of the breaking force.

Which Bullet Hole was Made First?

When two bullets are fired through opposite sides of a window, the crucial question can be: which bullet hole was made first? A reconstruction can resolve which person fired first so a claim of self-defense can be checked.

The determination is very simply made. In Figure 2.31, it is possible to determine that the bullet on the right was fired last because its cracks were stopped by the cracks made by the bullet on the

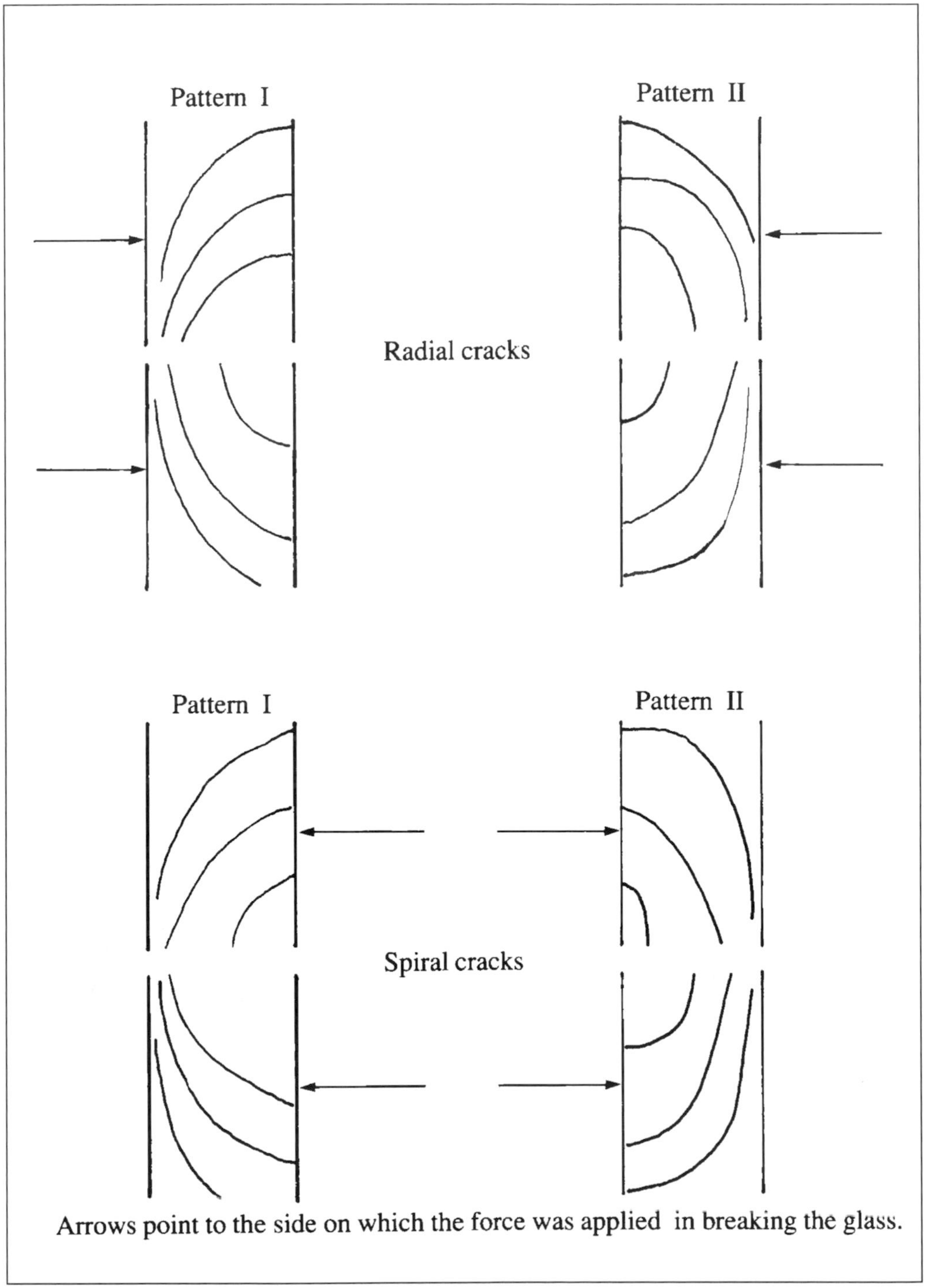

Pattern I

Pattern II

Radial cracks

Pattern I

Pattern II

Spiral cracks

Arrows point to the side on which the force was applied in breaking the glass.

Drawing by Jerzy J. Hoga, graphic designer

Figure 2.30
Interpretation of rib mark patterns.

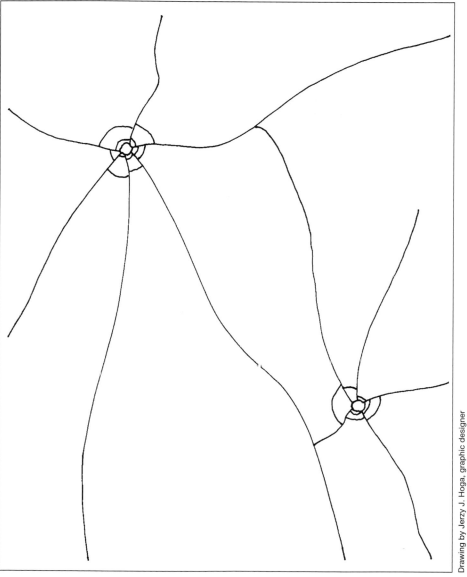

Drawing by Jerzy J. Hoga, graphic designer

Figure 2.31
Two bullet holes in a window made at different times. Hole in lower right was made after that of upper left.

left. Crack lines represent the transmission and dissipation of energy. Energy can be transmitted through a solid, but upon reaching a break, cannot go beyond it. Thus, the bullet hole cracks on the left were not stopped by those of the right, because the right cracks were not there when the left cracks were made.

Trace Evidence

It is a common belief that an offender's whereabouts can be tracked through trace evidence. Although this is usually not the case, such evidence can be of help to the investigator in other ways. *Trace evidence* is a criminalistics term; it describes physical evidence so small (in size or forensic details) that an examination usually requires either a stereomicroscope, a polarized light microscope, or both. It is not practical to list every conceivable trace material to be found at a crime scene. Based on routine case work experience, however, Nicholas Petraco has categorized the most commonly encountered types as either fibrous substances or particulate matter.[30] Fibrous substances include: hair (human or animal); plant fibers (sisal in cordage or rope, linen, and cotton); mineral fibers (asbestos, glass wool); and synthetic fibers (nylon, rayon, and Dacron in fabrics and carpeting). Particulate matter includes: building material, safe insulation, paint chips, metal filings or shavings, soil, seeds, pollen, wood chips (or splinters or sawdust), and cosmetics—to name some of the more obvious kinds. Because trace evidence can be minuscule, it is located and collected by means of: (1) a vacuum cleaner, (2) adhesive tape, or (3) by shaking it loose over a large, clean, white sheet of paper (see Chapter 3).

Petraco notes that human hair and other fiber evidence are frequently encountered at the scenes of violent crimes such as homicide and robbery; particulate matter is often available in burglary cases; and human hair is discovered in just under 75 percent of those cases in which trace evidence was present.[31] More significant is the "regularity with which the various forms of trace evidence occur, rather than the fact that one form occurs more or less frequently than another."[32] The most common source of trace evidence is the crime scene, then the victim's home or business, followed by the victim's body and the clothing of the suspect and victim. The least productive source is "things"—vehicles, hats, furniture, and bludgeons (such as baseball bats or pipes).[33] Petraco finds disturbing

> ... the low percent occurrence of fibers and particulate matter for the category of rape and sex crimes. One possible explanation for this unexpected finding might be the prevalent use of commercially available rape kits for collecting evidence in these cases. The prepared kits usually concentrate on the collection of physiological fluids and hair specimens, while giving little attention to the collection of fibers and particulate matter.[34]

In a later paper, Petraco states that trace evidence can be used to:

1. Reconstruct the event.

2. Associate people, places, and things involved with the event.

3. Surmise (with some accuracy) the occupations of the principals in the case.

4. Describe the environment or location involved in the event. Then, armed with such information, use it to establish probable cause for a warrant to search a home, vehicle, garage or other area specified on the basis of the trace evidence found.[35]

Petraco makes a shrewd observation: "All this is achieved without the aid of an eyewitness. It is a powerful source of information indeed, and one that is barely utilized in our criminal justice system."[36]

A number of agencies at the public and private level maintain databases on any number of products that may assist the investigator, including tire tread comparisons, paint compositions, firearm comparisons, and handwriting, to name a few.

CONCLUSION

Of the common clue materials, fingerprints, firearms evidence, and blood are encountered far more often than documents, glass, or biological material (including semen). Trace evidence is present at many crime scenes, but is frequently overlooked despite its considerable potential. In varying degrees, therefore, each clue material can serve to link an offender to the crime scene or victim. If an investigator is to recognize, collect, and preserve such evidence, there must be an appreciation of the needs of—and the means used by—the forensic laboratory to make that linkage.

NOTES

[1] P.L. No. 109_108, 119 Stat. 2290 (2005), and H.R. Rep. No. 109_272, at 121 (2005) (Conf. Rep.).

[2] S.Rep. No. 109_88, at 46 (2005).

[3] Ibid., 1, 2.

[4] National Research Council, Committee on Identifying the Needs of the Forensic Sciences Community, *Strengthening Forensic Science in the United States: A Path Forward* (Washington, DC: National Research Council, 2009), 2–3.

[5] Ibid., 3.

[6] P.E. Kirk, "The Ontogeny of Criminalistics," *Journal of Criminal Law, Criminology, and Police Science*, 54 (1963), 236.

[7] Joseph M. Rynearson and William J. Chisum, *Evidence and Crime Scene Reconstruction*, 3rd ed. (Redding, CA: National Crime Investigation and Training, 1993); Henry C. Lee, *Crime Scene Investigation* (Taoyuan, Taiwan, Republic of China: Central Police Agency, 1994), Chapter 10.

[8] National Research Council, *Strengthening Forensic Science in the United States: A Path Forward*, 2009.

[9] B. Parker and J.L. Peterson, *Physical Evidence Utilization in the Administration of Criminal Justice* (Washington, DC: U.S. Department of Justice, 1972).

[10] *The Queen v. M'Naghten*, 8 Eng. Rep. 718, 10 Cl. & Fin. 200 (1843).

[11] *Commonwealth v. Rogers*, 7 Metc. 500 (1844).

[12] Homicide Act, 5 & 6 Eliz. II C. II. Sec.2 (1957).

[13] American Law Institute, Model Penal Code, Section 401(1) 1962.

[14] Frank Smyth and Myles Ludwig, *The Detectives: Crime and Detection in Fact and Fiction* (Philadelphia: J.B. Lippincott, 1978), 25–26.

[15] Paul D. McCann. "Report of the Standardization Committee of the International Association for Identification," *Identification News*, 23:8 (Aug. 1973), 13–14.

[16] http://www.fbi.gov/about-us/cjis/fingerprints_biometrics/iafis/iafis_facts

[17] H.L. MacDonell, *Bloodstain Pattern Interpretation* (Corning, NY: Laboratory of Forensic Science, 1982).

[18] *State v. Hall*, 297 N.W.2d 80 (Iowa 1980).

[19]   F.C. Delfin, B.J. Madrid, M.P. Tan, and M.C.A. de Ungria, "Y-STR Analysis for Detection and Objective Confirmation of Child Sexual Abuse," *International Journal of Legal Medicine*, 119:3 (2005), 158. C. Duverneuil Sibille, G.L. de la Grandmaison, K. Guerrouache, F. Teissiere, M. Durigon, and P. de Mazancourt, "Y-STR DNA_Amplification as Biological Evidence in Sexually Assaulted Female Victims with No Cytological Detection of Spermatozoa," *Forensic Science International*, 125:2–3 (2002), 212.

[20]   John R. Brown, "DNA Analysis: A Significant Tool for Law Enforcement," *The Police Chief*, 61:3, 51–52 (Mar. 1994), 51.

[21]   Originally found at http://www.fbi.gov/bq/lab/codis/program.htm

[22]   http://www.ncbi.nlm.nih.gov/genbank/

[23]   John W. Hicks, "DNA Profiling: A Tool for Law Enforcement," *FBI Law Enforcement Bulletin*, 57:8 (Aug. 1988), 3.

[24]   http://www.fbi.gov/about-us/lab/codis/ndis-statistics

[25]   4th Annual CODIS User Group Meeting, Nov. 1998, Arlington, VA; originally found at http://www.fbi.gov/bq/lab/codis/clickmap.htm

[26]   Barry Scheck, "Getting Smart About DNA," *Newsweek*, (Nov. 16, 1998), 69.

[27]   Butler, John M., *Forensic DNA Typing* (San Diego: Academic Press, 2001), 62.

[28]   Yale H. Caplan, "Current Issues in Forensic Science: DNA Probe Technology in Forensic Serology: Statistics, Quality Control and Interpretation," [American Academy of Forensic Science] *Academy News* 18:6 (Nov. 1988), 23.

[29]   Ibid., 11.

[30]   N. Petraco, "The Occurrence of Trace Evidence in One Examiner's Casework," *Journal of Forensic Sciences*, 30:2 (1985), 486.

[31]   Ibid., 487–490.

[32]   Ibid., 487–488.

[33]   Ibid., 492 (Table 7).

[34]   Ibid., 487.

[35]   N. Petraco, "Trace Evidence—The Invisible Witness," *Journal of Forensic Sciences*, 31:1 (1986), 321, 327.

[36]   N. Petraco, loc. cit. (1985), 493.

DISCUSSION QUESTIONS

1. *Criminalistics* and *forensic medicine* are two major branches of forensic science. List at least five types of examinations listed under the table in the text.

2. Criminalistics is the branch of forensic science concerned with the recording, scientific examination, and interpretation of minute details, directed toward what ends?

3. List at least 10 types of evidence examinations conducted by the FBI.

4. The 2008 Report of the National Academy of Sciences released a report on forensic science in the United States. Discuss the major findings of this report.

5. What is the difference between the terms *organic* and *inorganic*?

6. What scientific instruments are of most value in conducting forensic examinations?

7. What is meant by associative evidence?

8. What is the role of *forensic pathology*?

9. What are some of the common forensic clue materials that may be found at a crime scene?

10. What are some of the common methods of recovering latent fingerprints?

11. What is an Automated Fingerprint Identification System (AFIS)?

12. What types of physical evidence might be valuable in investigations involving firearms?

13. MacDonnell addresses the interpretation of bloodstain patterns. How can these patterns be used?

14. What is DNA (deoxyribonucleic acid) technology and how is it used in criminal investigations?

15. What is CODIS, and how is it used?

SUPPLEMENTAL READINGS

Beavan, C. (2001). *Fingerprints: The origins of crime detection and the murder case that launched forensic science.* New York: Hyperion.

Bergslien, E. (2012). *An introduction to forensic geosciences.* Hoboken, NJ: Wiley Blackwell

Bodziak, W. J. (2000). *Footwear impression evidence: Detection, recovery, and examination* (2nd ed.). Boca Raton, FL: CRC Press.

Bodziak, W. J. (2008). *Tire tread and tire track examination: Recovery and forensic examination.* Boca Raton, FL: CRC Press.

Bowers, C. M. (2010). *Forensic dental evidence: An investigator's handbook* (2nd ed.). Boston: Elsevier/Academic Press.

Buckleton, J., Triggs, C. M., & Walsh, S. J. (2004). *Forensic DNA evidence interpretation.* Boca Raton, FL: CRC Press.

Caddy, B. (Ed.). (2001). *Forensic examination of glass and paint: Analysis and interpretation.* New York: Taylor & Francis.

Champod, C., Lennard, C., Margot, P., & Stoilovic, M. (2004). *Fingerprints and other ridge skin impressions.* Boca Raton, FL: CRC Press.

Chisum, W. J., & Turvey, B. E. (2010). *Crime reconstruction* (2nd ed.). Boston: Elsevier/Academic Press.

Cowger, J. F. (1992). *Friction ridge skin: Comparison and identification of fingerprints.* Boca Raton, FL: CRC Press.

Di Maio, V. J. M. (1999). *Gunshot wounds: Practical aspects of firearms, ballistics, and forensic techniques* (2nd ed.). Boca Raton, FL: CRC Press.

Di Maio, V. J. M., & Di Maio, D. (2001). *Forensic pathology* (2nd ed.). Boca Raton, FL: CRC Press.

Ellen, D. (2006). *Scientific examination of documents: Methods and techniques* (3rd ed.). Boca Raton, FL: CRC Press.

Erickson, E. (2014). *Criminalistics laboratory manual: The basics of forensic investigation.* Boston: Elsevier/Anderson Publishing.

Fish, J. T., Miller, L. S., & Braswell, M. C. (2010). *Crime scene investigation* (2nd ed.). Boston: Elsevier/Anderson Publishing.

Federal Bureau of Investigation. *FBI handbook of crime scene forensics.*

Harralson, H., & Miller, L. (2013). *Developments in handwriting and signature identification in the digital age.* Boston: Elsevier/Anderson Publishing.

Houck, M. M., & Siegel, J. A. (2011). *Fundamentals of forensic science* (2nd ed.). Oxford, UK: Elsevier/Academic Press.

Huber, R. A., & Headrick, A. M. (1999). *Handwriting identification: Facts and fundamentals.* Boca Raton, FL: CRC Press.

James, S. H., & Nordby, J. J. (2005). *Forensic science: An introduction to scientific and investigative techniques.* Boca Raton, FL: CRC Press.

Lee, H., & Labriola, J. (2001). *Famous crimes revisited: From Sacco-Vanzetti to O.J. Simpson.* Southbury, CT: Publishing Directions.

Lee, H. C., Palmbach, T., & Miller, M. T. (2001). *Henry Lee's crime scene handbook.* San Diego: Academic.

Lee, H., & O'Neill, T. W. (2002). *Cracking cases: The science of solving cases.* New York: Prometheus Books.

Leo, W. (2005). *Fingerprint identification.* San Clemente, CA: LawTech.

Ludas, M. (2005). *Fingerprint & impression analysis workbook.* San Clemente, CA: LawTech.

Miller, L. S., & McEvoy, R. T., Jr. (2010). *Police photography* (6th ed.). Boston: Elsevier/Anderson Publishing.

Osterburg, J. W. (1982). *The crime laboratory: Case studies of scientific investigation* (2nd ed.). New York: Clark Boardman.

Physicians' Desk Reference 2013, (67th ed.). Montvale, NJ: PDR Network, 2013.

Redsicker, D. R. (2001). *The practical methodology of forensic photography* (2nd ed.). Boca Raton, FL: CRC Press.

Robinson, E. (2012). *Introduction to crime scene photography.* Boston: Elsevier/Academic Press.

Saferstein, R. (2007). *Criminalistics: An introduction to forensic science* (9th ed.). Upper Saddle River, NJ: Pearson Prentice Hall.

Senn, D. R., & Stimson, P. G. (Eds.). (2010). *Forensic dentistry* (2nd ed.). Boca Raton, FL: CRC Press.

Shaler, R. (2002). Modern forensic biology. In R. Saferstein (Ed.), *Forensic science handbook*, (2nd ed.). Upper Saddle River, NJ: Prentice Hall.

Stauffer, E., & Bonfanti, M. (2006). *Forensic investigation of stolen-recovered and other crime-related vehicles.* Boston: Elsevier/Academic Press.

Thornton, J. (2002). Forensic paint examination. In R. Saferstein (Ed.), *Forensic science handbook* (2nd ed.). Upper Saddle River, NJ: Prentice Hall.

Woodward, J. D., Orlans, N. M., & Higgins, P. T. (2003). *Biometrics: identity assurance in the information age.* New York: McGraw-Hill/Osborne.

Wright, J. D. (2008). *Hair and fibers.* Armonk, NY: Sharpe Focus.

CHAPTER 3

THE CRIME SCENE

Discovery, Preservation, Collection, and Transmission of Evidence*

DEFINING THE LIMITS OF THE CRIME SCENE

The crime scene encompasses all areas over which the actors—victim, criminal, and eyewitness—move during the commission of a crime. Usually it is one readily defined area of limited size, but sometimes it comprises several sites. A case example of the latter is to be found in the abduction of a bank manager as he left for work one morning. The car that conveyed him to the bank, the vault and other areas in the bank, the vicinity of the place in the woods where he was found tied to a tree—each site is a part of the crime scene. Another example is a homicide in which the murder is committed in one place and the body is dumped or buried in another.

Although the precise boundary lines of a crime scene are most often well-defined, sometimes they can be in dispute. Consider for example the 911 attacks on the World Trade Center and the Pentagon. Was this one crime that originated at the airport from which the flights originated, or three separate crime scenes where three planes struck their targets, and one fell when passengers attacked the perpetrators, or does the crime scene originate where the attackers last met together to plan the attack? Although the question is moot, investigations involved the collection of evidence from many locations. In a bank robbery, for example, the crime scene may involve more than the scene in which the robbery took place. In the world of cyberspace, the crime scene may be less obvious, and may involve multiple sites and multiple victims. For example, in cases involving child pornography distributed over the Internet, there may be several crime scenes: a crime scene in which children were victimized and photographed, a location where the photographs or images were later distributed (for sale or otherwise) on the Internet or by mail, and a buyer or user who may also be liable if a law is violated. Other examples may involve identity theft or fraud involving multiple locations and victims.

It is clear from the preceding cases that the crime scene must be conceptualized. Once its position and boundaries are defined, the scene must then be made secure, the physical evidence discovered, documented, and collected, and the crime reconstructed (if needed). In all cases it means excluding reporters, government officials, even superior police officers who are not directly involved in the investigation; not to mention local residents and curiosity seekers. In an ambush investigation it is important to establish where the perpetrator was concealed and to record details of activity within

---

* The authors would like to express their appreciation to Prof. Peter Massey, University of New Haven, for his review and comments on this chapter.

Figure 3.1
Scene of the crash of Pan Am Flight 103 in Lockerbie, Scotland. Crucial fragmentary evidence was recognized and collected in an area about 25 miles away from Lockerbie. At the time, the Pan Am Flight 103 evidence scene was the largest crime scene ever (more than 800 square miles) that needed to be searched.

that area. Afterward, it can be searched for other physical evidence, such as spent cartridges, food containers, or discarded cigarettes and matches. The in-flight bombing of Pan Am Flight 103 over Lockerbie, Scotland, gave new meaning to the concept of the limits of a crime scene. Fragments of physical evidence—plane parts, bomb bits, personal belongings, body parts—were scattered over 800 square miles of countryside (see Figure 3.1). The painstaking recovery of four million pieces of physical evidence attests to the diligence and thoroughness of the effort to solve the case.

In cases involving cybercrime, the evidence may lie in a computer, or in some cases on disks or "jump" drives, as well as hard copies of materials, such as e-mails between individuals. In most cases, evidence recovery will require the assistance of experts. Nevertheless, it is important that the investigator recognize the broad dimensions of such cases and be familiar with the *modus operandi* of this type of criminal activity.

THE CRIME SCENE AS AN EVIDENCE SOURCE

An offender brings physical evidence to the crime scene: in burglary cases, tools needed to break into the premises or a safe; in robbery or homicide cases, a weapon used to threaten, assault, or kill; in arson cases, a container of flammable fluid; in technology-related cases, a hard drive or the messages on a smart phone. During the commission of a crime, an offender may inadvertently leave evidence behind (*in situ*): fingerprints, toolmarks, shoe prints, blood-spatter patterns, spent bullets, fired cartridge casings. Other physical evidence can by its very nature be unavoidably left behind: in kidnapping cases, the ransom note; in bank robbery cases, the note handed to the teller. For instance, it may be left on a computer or as an indentation of a note pad. In one homicide case, the suspect's name first emerged in a message left on the deceased's answering machine.[1] The caller asked that a meeting be set up at a specific time in the owner's home, and when the latter was found dead there and time of death was determined to be an hour or two after the proposed meeting, this crucial piece of information had to be followed up. In this instance, it was—with success.

When searching the crime scene (and afterward), an investigator's observations and interviews might develop intangible evidence. For example, the emotional factors involved in motivating and carrying out a homicide become manifest as intangible evidence through an assessment of such observations as: grossly excessive stab wounds, bones unnecessarily broken, parts of the body cut out or cut off, or the choice and kind of lethal weapon employed. A shrewd appraisal of intangible evidence (as in psychological profiling) can provide leads to possible perpetrators. Interviewing also can be used to develop intangible evidence. Witnesses or victims may report on the language used during the commission of the crime. How exactly did the robber convey intentions and demands? What did the rapist say, before, during, and after the assault? Because such commands and comments are elements of the perpetrator's *modus operandi*, they have investigative and probative value.

The CSI Effect

Television programs focusing on crime scene investigation (CSI) are among the most popular. From a forensic scientist's perspective, or more correctly, a criminalist's viewpoint, such shows have been both meaningful and detrimental. They have alerted the public that forensic science exists and should be employed on their behalf. Unfortunately, these shows have also led many members of the public to believe they are knowledgeable about crime scene evidence and what should be collected, rather than leaving it to the CSI or criminalist to decide. Thus, sometimes the so-called evidence pointed out by the complainant and reluctantly collected by the crime scene investigator merely covers the analyst's lab work space with mostly irrelevant clue material. For example, a smudged fingerprint or a shoe impression with no details with which to compare the suspect's finger or shoe are often collected merely to satisfy the "expert" complainant.

OPPORTUNITY FOR DISCOVERY

The crime scene provides the major opportunity to locate physical evidence. The initial response should be regarded as the only chance to recognize, record, and collect physical evidence. The investigator must make the most of it. This search, however, must be conducted properly and lawfully, or the evidence will be suppressed in the course of a trial. Police should not relinquish control over the scene and its environs until all evidence has been discovered, documented and collected. If it must be gone over again later, legal difficulties may be created because pertinent evidence was not recognized or collected initially.

In 1984, the U.S. Supreme Court in *Michigan v. Clifford* reversed a decision based on evidence obtained by investigators who entered the scene of a suspected arson five hours after the blaze had been extinguished.[2] Another case, *Michigan v. Tyler*, also illustrates the need to collect evidence without unnecessary delay, otherwise a warrant must be obtained.[3] In the *Tyler* arson case there were three searches. The first was within one and a half hours after the fire; the second, four hours later (dense smoke having caused the delay); but the third was made three weeks later. Evidence from the first two was held admissible, but the evidence seized in the third attempt was not, because no emergency validated the warrantless search. The court found that investigators were able to stay inside the building after the fire was exhausted, but are required to obtain a warrant to conduct a search for evidence of crime not related to the cause of fire. Courts have consistently followed precedent from the *Tyler* case, including the case of *United States v. Mitchell*, in which firefighters entered a building 12 hours after the fire was exhausted to continue looking for evidence on how the fire started. The detectives were not able to continue the search immediately after the fire because of adverse conditions of the scene. All evidence retrieved during the second search was admissible as evidence.[4] Delayed or late attempts are legal if the permission of the owner or occupant of the premises is obtained, preferably in writing. Figure 3.2 is a consent form for this purpose.

In *Mincey v. Arizona*, involving the homicide of a narcotics officer, the identity of the offender (Mincey) was known from the outset.[5] Investigators took four days to search his apartment, and the evidence they discovered led to a conviction. On appeal, the Court noted that no occupant of the premises had summoned police and that the search continued for four days. It held, therefore, that no justification for the warrantless search existed under the Fourth Amendment. Police officers are able to search a home when exigent circumstances exist, such as the case in *United States v. Richardson*, in which a 911 call was made to report a homicide victim in the basement of Richardson's residence. A similar call was made approximately one week before, and no evidence of homicide was found. When police investigated this call, with no warrant, they found evidence and charged Richardson with unlawful possession of a firearm and possession with intent to distribute cocaine. No homicide victim or evidence of a homicide was found. Richardson appealed on the notion that the 911 call did not suffice for exigent circumstances; the court rejected the claim.[6]

An extended discussion of the need to comply with the search requirements of the Fourth Amendment can be found in an *FBI Law Enforcement Bulletin* article.[7] Its author, Special Agent Kimberly Crawford, points out that the Supreme Court, in *Katz v. United States*, created the presumption that all searches conducted without warrants are unreasonable. Accordingly, a valid search warrant must be secured before any crime scene search is undertaken; that is, unless it falls under the exceptions allowed by the Court (consent-to-search or emergency situations).

A consent to search must be given voluntarily by a person reasonably believed to have control over and legal access to the premises.[8]

There are two kinds of emergency situations:

1. Those involving an attempt or opportunity to carry off or destroy evidence. To support this contention, belief must meet the standard of probable cause.

2. Those involving threats to safety or life. In these cases, a lower level of proof—reasonable suspicion—is acceptable.

In an emergency situation, a warrantless search is lawful, but it must not go beyond the limits of the emergency; thus, a general exploratory search of the premises cannot be conducted lawfully.

Crawford offers an example of a crime scene search for evidence that exceeded the scope of the emergency.[9] In this case, a 14-year-old kidnap victim, upon being liberated by police officers, told them where the kidnapper kept his guns and ammunition. Beyond retrieving the weapons from a closet, no further search of the apartment was made. On appeal, it was held that the emergency situation ("exigent circumstances," in the Court's language) justified entry into the apartment, but the emergency ended when it was determined that neither the defendant nor anyone else was in the apartment. Entering the closet to locate the weapons exceeded the scope of the emergency search. The evidence, therefore, was not admissible. Because the 14-year-old victim did not have control over the apartment, the consent exception was not applicable.

In recent years, the use of roadblocks by police departments to gain information on recently committed crimes and to prevent drunk driving has increased considerably. In *Illinois v. Lidster*,

State of _____

County of _____

I, _____ , hereby permit

(name of searcher) _____ of the

(name of agency or dept.) _____

to search my * _____

located at _____ _____ _____

described as ** _____ _

    I authorize them to process, collect, and take *any* relevant object including, *but not limited to,* latent fingerprints, hairs, fiber, blood, tracks, impressions, clothing, criminal instruments, contraband, and fruits of a crime.

    I further authorize the making of photographs, videotapes, and sketches of the area being searched.

    I understand that I have the right to refuse such consent.

I freely and voluntarily give this consent this _____ day of _____, 19_____.

Witnessed

_____

    (name)   (date)

* Entire home; basement only, if one or more rooms, specify which; garage; locker; automobile or truck; and so on.

** Single family house; condominium, apartment number; a four-door sedan (make and model); mobile home; and so on.

Figure 3.2
Consent-to-search form.

a roadblock was set up to elicit information about a fatal hit-and-run accident that occurred one week before at the same location at about the same time. As Lidster approached the roadblock, his vehicle swerved, almost hitting an officer. When an officer noticed the smell of alcohol on Lidster's breath, a field sobriety test was performed, which Lidster failed. Lidster was cited for driving under the influence of alcohol (DUI), which he appealed. The Supreme Court found that the roadblock did not violate Lidster's Fourth Amendment rights against unreasonable search and seizure because its purpose was not for crime control but rather to gain public information to solve a crime.[10]

Historically, police officers were required to knock and announce themselves and wait a reasonable amount of time before entering a home to serve a search warrant. The consequences for not abiding by these requirements was losing all evidence under the exclusionary rule guidelines. The Supreme Court decided in *Hudson v. Michigan* that the evidence found in such searches would have been discovered anyway, and that all evidence should be admissible in court. The understanding is that the "reasonable wait time" was ambiguous and the proper consequence of not meeting this requirement should not be the loss of all evidence found in the search.[11]

PURPOSE OF SEARCH

To understand the numerous precepts imposed on police behavior at a crime scene, one must be aware of the reasons for conducting a search. The most common reason is to develop associative evidence; that is, to find evidence that could link a suspect to the crime or the victim. Should some linkage be developed, its probative strength can range from an intimation of who may have been involved up to actual proof of something (as when a fingerprint is developed at the scene). Accordingly, nothing at the crime scene should be touched or stepped on.

Another purpose for the crime scene search is to seek answers to: What happened? How, when, and where did it happen? In a homicide the forensic pathologist is usually able to provide answers after the autopsy, and sometimes (in other kinds of cases) answers are obvious even to the detective. When they are not, however, it is essential that nothing be moved or altered. Then, at least some of the questions may be satisfied when a reconstruction of the crime is attempted. In all events, before the criminalist can collect associative evidence or undertake a reconstruction, the scene must first be carefully recorded and photographed.

The police sometimes have other reasons for making a crime scene search: (1) to recognize evidence from which a psychological profile may be developed, and from which, conceivably, a motive may be determined (i.e., why the crime was committed); (2) to identify an object the use or purpose of which is not readily apparent or is foreign to the scene, thereby calling for efforts to trace ownership—through a serial number (as with Lee Harvey Oswald's rifle in the John F. Kennedy assassination) or by locating its source, through point of sale (as in an item of clothing bought in the Pan Am Flight 103 bombing case) or manufacturer; or (3) to recognize a perpetrator's *modus operandi* (MO). In a burglary, for example, the use of a push drill to make a hole in the top sash of the bottom half of a window (to insert a wire and open the catch) is sufficiently unusual to be viewed as the MO of that criminal. Pooling clues from several burglaries with the same tell-tale marks increases the chances of a suspect's apprehension.

ARRIVAL OF THE FIRST POLICE OFFICER

When the criminal has not been caught red-handed and has fled the scene before the first officer arrives (which is what generally happens), several responsibilities devolve upon the first officer on the scene:

1. To call for medical aid for the injured. In those cases in which a person is seriously injured, the steps (below) may be deferred until this is attended to. Medical personnel should be admonished not to step on footprints or other clues, and not to move anything beyond what is required to assist the injured. They should be instructed to carry a victim out on a stretcher. This is preferred because a wheeler or cart makes it difficult to avoid disturbing blood spatters, foot or shoe impressions, or other evidence on the floor or pathways to and from the scene.

2. To ascertain any facts pertinent to the criminal(s) that should be immediately transmitted to the patrol force—personal description, make and model of vehicle used, direction fled from scene.

3. To isolate the crime scene (and if necessary, its environs). To limit access to those with responsibility for its examination and processing, and to establish a crime scene log.

4. To detain and separate any eyewitnesses so they cannot discuss their individual observations with each other.

5. To continue to protect the scene until the officer who is to be responsible for the continuing investigation arrives. This authority is determined by departmental policy.

The time of any significant subsequent action (as well as its nature, the reasons for taking it, and people involved) should be carefully noted and recorded. Not doing so permits defense counsel to create the impression that an investigator is lazy, not thorough, or incompetent. Being well-informed on the rules of evidence, attorneys often attack the collection and handling of physical evidence at the crime scene. Their aim is often to have it ruled inadmissible should there have been any procedural lapse. In the Nicole Brown Simpson/Ronald Goldman double-murder case, for example, investigators left the original scene early on, only to run into what they believed to be a second crime scene. As a consequence, the protection of the original scene, the reasons for leaving it, and the processing of both scenes for physical evidence became matters of intense interest to the defense. In such cases it is crucial that the investigator take good notes in a timely fashion, recording the investigative actions taken and the reasons why.

ARRIVAL OF THE INVESTIGATOR

On arrival at the crime scene, the investigator must note the following details to write a report and, possibly much later, to answer questions by defense counsel at trial:

1. Who made the notification; the time of arrival; and how long it took to respond.

2. The weather conditions and visibility.

3. The names of persons at the scene; in particular, the names of those who already went through the scene or any part of it.

4. The facts of the case as ascertained by the first officer(s) at the scene.

5. Subsequent actions on taking responsibility for the crime scene from the uniformed officer who was in charge up to that point.

OTHER SOURCES OF PHYSICAL EVIDENCE

In addition to the crime scene, there are several other possible sources of physical evidence:

1. The clothing and body of the victim (if not at the crime scene).

2. The suspect: the body, clothing, weapon, automobile, house, garage, or other area or article under his or her control.

3. Electronic evidence that may be stored on a movable device.

4. Receipts or bills for purchases of materials, such as a weapon, map or tools, used during the commission or planning of the crime.

5. Photographs that the suspect or victim may have taken.

Whatever the source—crime scene, victim, or suspect—the basic precepts governing the discovery, preservation, and collection of physical evidence apply equally.

DISCOVERY OF PHYSICAL EVIDENCE

Barry Fisher, the Crime Laboratory Director of the Los Angeles County Sheriff's Department, and author of the landmark text on crime scene investigation notes:

> Forensic scientists, crime scene specialists, and latent print experts are the individuals whose jobs apply science and technology to the solution of criminal acts. They shoulder an important role in the criminal justice system. Their skill and knowledge in the criminal investigation may establish the innocence or guilt of a defendant. Professional ethics and integrity are important to their work (p. 15).[12]

It should be noted, however, that before any physical evidence can be collected and transported, it must first be recognized as such. Recognition is a routine matter when clue materials are familiar, like bullets, cartridge casings, toolmarks, and blood. When materials are unfamiliar, recognition depends on the investigator's education, training, and imagination. Large police departments today have technicians and scientific equipment available for collecting and preserving physical evidence. In small departments the investigator shoulders this responsibility, responding to the extent possible with skills acquired through training, self-study, and experience on the job.

For readers who are looking for vicarious hands-on experience, there are several books and publications that are illustrated with police photographs (one-to-one or photomacrograph) of evidence discovered at the crime scene, together with those of a known comparison specimen (exemplar) obtained from the suspect (see Figures 3.3 and 3.4). By comparing the two pieces of evidence, the reader determines

Herbert MacDonell, Laboratory of Forensic Sciences, Corning, NY

Figure 3.3
Impression in wood.

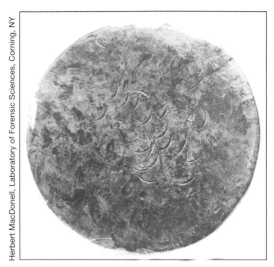

Herbert MacDonell, Laboratory of Forensic Sciences, Corning, NY

Figure 3.4
Hammer face is reproduced to permit a direct comparison with Figure 3.3. These pieces of potential evidence can be compared to determine whether a common origin exists.

whether an identity exists. For many of the case examples, solutions arrived at by the criminalist who worked on the investigation are provided. When the exercises are mastered, the details upon which an identity depends will be recognized. The trainee will appreciate what specific aspects of physical evidence covered in the exercises need protection when being collected and transmitted to the laboratory. In addition, he or she will better understand the principles underlying the various protocols for handling of physical evidence. For those already in law enforcement, a local laboratory may be able to provide photographs of crime scene evidence and known comparison samples. It is important to recognize that advances in technology have made comparative analysis of toolmarks, cartridges, photo images, and other materials much more reliable, and particularly valuable in court presentations.

Overview, Walk-through, and Search

The process of discovery begins after the complainant (and often before an eyewitness, if any) has been questioned. When information is not otherwise available, the investigator's experience with that type of crime is put to use in forming a general impression of what happened and where to look for physical evidence. The search should include:

1. The most probable access and escape routes. When fleeing the scene, some criminals deliberately discard a weapon or burglar's tools, or on occasion, the proceeds of the crime.

2. Any area where the perpetrator waited before committing the crime. Burglars often gain entrance to a building just before closing time, then wait until it has been vacated. Killers or robbers also wait in ambush for their victims. In these areas, such clues as used matches, burned cigarettes, spent cartridge casings, food containers, etc., may be found.

3. The point and method of entry to the premises.

4. The route used within the premises where signs of the perpetrator's activity—such as objects that have been moved or places broken into—are apparent.

5. Any objects that seem to have received the attention of the criminal, such as a safe, a lockbox, a jewelry box, or a file cabinet.

6. Some unusual places where evidence might be discovered:
    A. refrigerator
        a. half-eaten food (this actually happens)
        b. latent fingerprints on handle

     B.   bathroom
         a.   toilet seat—fingerprints—hairs
         b.   trash can
     C.   computer, smart phone, or social media sites
     D.   videotapes or other storage devices

A walk-through of the crime scene is first undertaken to observe the actual physical evidence and to ascertain which locations and articles require processing: namely, dusting for fingerprints or photographing blood-spatter details or toolmarks. If an outdoor search must be made during the hours of darkness, the scene should be protected and searched again in daylight. Under these circumstances, the first search should be confined to the fairly obvious and to what could be of immediate value in identifying or apprehending the perpetrator. Priority must be given to evidence that has a short life and is easily destroyed unless prompt action is taken to preserve and protect it. Whether indoors or out, sufficient illumination is crucial: it will help to prevent the mistake of walking on or missing evidence that cannot be seen.

The preliminary walk-through process helps to define the boundaries of the areas to be examined. Regardless of the search pattern employed, it must be systematic and thorough. When the area is large, a piecemeal probing of small sections (or strips) is effective. However, this task can be shortened. In a homicide committed in a sand pit, in which the victim's skull was fractured, the search for the missing weapon could start where the body was found. A better idea, however, would be to divide the area surrounding the sand pit area into a large grid. Those cells in the grid along the possible escape route (which, owing to foliage, offered a place to discard and conceal the weapon) might be searched after the sand pit area. If unsuccessful, the search could be directed to other cells in the grid and, upon completion, the entire process reviewed to make certain none were overlooked.

RECORDING CONDITIONS AND EVIDENCE FOUND AT THE CRIME SCENE

For a number of reasons, it is essential upon arrival to record the investigative evidence or clue materials that were noted during the search of the crime scene:

1. Some investigators use a tape, digital recorder, or cell phone camera for dictating or photographing observations and other information.

2. Writing an official report of the day's activities provides a record of information that will be useful later for jogging the memory and assuring accuracy.

3. Details that the criminalist can use for reconstructing the crime or developing associative evidence will be available.

4. As an investigation progresses and the suspect or witness makes statements, some aspects of the crime scene that did not initially appear significant can become important. A record made before anything was disturbed will permit such a reevaluation.

5. Records are useful in preparing for the interrogation of a suspect.

6. Defense attorneys, legitimately, will be curious about where and when the evidence was found and by whom. The investigator's preparation for cross-examination should begin at this early stage, not delayed until the trial date is set.

7. The effectiveness of courtroom testimony is enhanced when more than mere memory is available to recall events.

AP Photo/Butch Dill

Figure 3.5
Agents from the Bureau of Alcohol, Tobacco, Firearms, and Explosives (ATF) mark tire tracks on a road leaving the Galilee Baptist Church, which was destroyed by arson. The church is located off a dirt road, allowing investigators to get tire tracks from the mud.

Methods of recording the situation, conditions, and physical evidence found at the crime scene include: notes, video recording, photographs, and sketches. Other methods used by some agencies require audio or video recording equipment. Each method has a distinct value in that it supplements the others; in general, however, all four should be used to document the crime scene.

Notes

Recording the activities upon the arrival of the first officer and investigator at the scene is best accomplished with notes kept on a chronological basis. Many believe that a separate notebook should be utilized for each major case to log the arrivals, departures, and assignments of assisting personnel, as well as the directions given to evidence technicians for processing the scene. It facilitates having material pertinent to the case at hand. If the notes are needed to refresh the investigator's memory when testifying, or should the court grant defense permission to examine them, then only the applicable jottings are open to inspection. This also ensures that all information—confidential and otherwise, or pertaining to other cases—is revealed.

Some people believe a bound notebook is best because it makes it difficult to change facts as first recorded should there be an attempt later to challenge the veracity of the officer. For the same reason, ink is preferable for crime scene notes. Should a correction be necessary, it is admissible to draw a line through the original notes and initial the alteration. Regardless of what form they take, the notes may become part of the *res gestae*, a record of what was said or done by the complainant, witness, or suspect in the first moments of the investigation. *Res gestae* (statements or acts), being an exception to the hearsay rule, may be admitted as evidence for consideration by a jury.

Videography

The video recording of a crime scene is an essential component of crime scene documentation. The video is used to establish the overall layout of the crime scene and the orientation or relationship of the evidence therein. It also provides depth perspective that is not available in photographs. Video is not utilized for documenting specific items of evidence. That is reserved for photographs.

Photographs

Photography is a key component of any police department's inventory of tools. Larry Miller, a former crime scene investigator, identifies the following uses of different types of photography:

- Identification files
- Communications and microfilm files
- Evidence
- Offender detection
- Court exhibits
- Reproduction and copying
- Personnel training
- Crime and fire prevention
- Public relations[13]

Two kinds of photographs are taken at the crime scene. The first is intended to record the overall scene: the approach to the premises used by the criminal, the point of entrance, the pathway through the premises, the various rooms the criminal entered, and the location of any physical evidence (see Figure 3.6). The second kind records details needed by the criminalist to reconstruct the crime or establish an identity. They are preserved by life-size or one-to-one photographs (of fingerprints, blood spatter patterns, toolmarks). In all instances of evidence in which a possible comparison might be required, such as fingerprints, footwear impressions, tire impressions, blood spatter patterns, and toolmarks, the use of a scale is imperative. The investigator must make sure that the image taken is of evidence quality, which means any photograph in which a scale is utilized is taken at a 90-degree angle relative to the scale, the scale and items of evidence are clearly readable and in focus, and the proper lighting is utilized. The introduction of the video camcorder and digital

Miller, Larry S., and Richard J. McEvoy Jr., *Police Photography*, 6th ed. Boston: Elsevier/Anderson Publishing, 2011.

Figure 3.6
A photograph of a crime scene. The square in the forefront was included in the photograph to aid in perspective and mapping.

camera with a power zoom lens and macro capability has simplified both the taking of record pictures and the preservation of evidence details by photograph. On the other hand, the ability to alter or retouch a photo is much easier in a digital format than in traditional photography using film; this is something that should be considered by the investigator and the photo lab. The original image should always be archived, and it is suggested that departments utilizing digital cameras establish Standard Operating Procedures for their use.

Sketches

The advantage of a sketch is that it includes only essential details; in addition, it best indicates distances or spatial relationships between items of evidence, indoors or out. There are two kinds: rough and finished. The rough sketch, a relatively crude, free-hand representation of all essential information, including measurements, is made at the crime scene (see Figure 3.7). Because there is great variation in individual sketching ability, changes are often needed in tracing outlines. It is best to use pencil for this task. The finished sketch is more precise: its lines are clean and straight and its lettering is either typeset or typewritten. Usually prepared later when time is available, it uses information from the rough sketch, notes, and photographs taken at the crime scene. Computer Aided Design (CAD) systems are now often available in crime laboratories and can be of great assistance in preparing complicated exhibits.

When the distances in the finished sketch are precise and proportional, it is termed a *scale drawing* (see Figure 3.8). Scale drawings can be helpful in court to demonstrate exact distances. For example, in a case involving an unsuccessful attempt to choke the victim, the issue of manslaughter versus murder came up at trial. The jury had to decide whether the time it took for the killer to run down a hallway to the kitchen for a knife and return to the bedroom to finish the job was sufficient to constitute premeditation. A scale drawing would help in making this determination.

Commercially available CAD systems and crime scene sketch kits provide several templates: some for house furnishings, others for store and office layouts, and so on. Computerized systems (such as Compu-Scene, by Allied Security Innovations, Inc.) are also available. In addition to routine drawing materials, a 100-foot steel tape and two people are needed to make the measurement. Each person must verify the distance between the item (the physical evidence) and a fixed object (a wall, boulder, house, telephone pole, or tree). Indoor measurements (from item of evidence to wall) are made along the shortest perpendicular lines, with at least two such right-angle measurements required to locate it. Each measurement is best made to the nearest walls not parallel to each other. This is known as the rectangular method for measuring an object (see Figure 3.9). Another method (the triangulation method) is employed outdoors, the measurements being made from two fixed objects such as the corner of a house, a telephone pole, fence post, or tree (see Figure 3.10). If the direction and angle (obtained from a compass) are known for each measurement, the location of the object or item of evidence can be established (see Figure 3.11). Even when the angles are unknown, if each distance is considered the radius of a circle, the two circles can intersect at two points only, and the evidence will be located at but one of these two points. In addition to "flat scene" diagrams, more sophisticated systems make it possible to prepare various three-dimensional or other images from different perspectives. A third method of taking measurements at a crime scene is the baseline method. The baseline method utilizes two tape measures to establish right

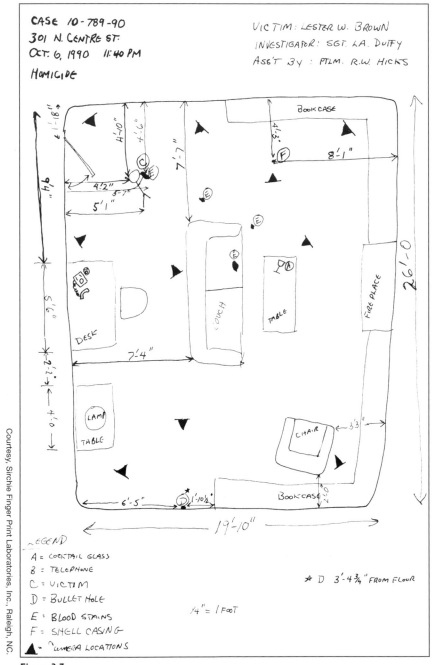

Figure 3.7
Rough sketch of a homicide crime scene.

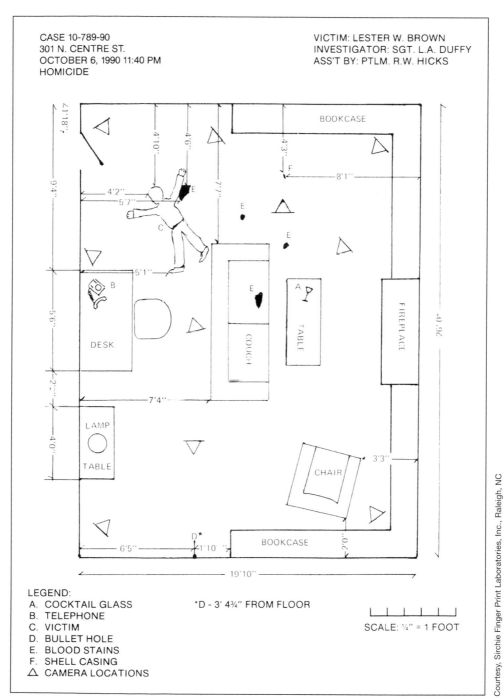

Figure 3.8
Finished sketch and scale drawing of same scene as Figure 3.7.

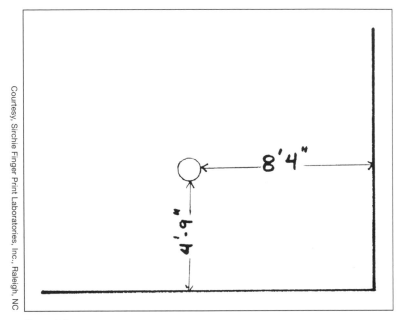

Figure 3.9
Coordinate method for locating an object.

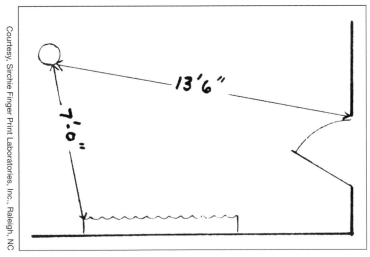

Figure 3.10
Triangulation method for locating an object.

angles to each item of evidence. The placing of one tape measure along a baseline of the room or area to be measured and then measuring off that baseline perpendicularly to the item of evidence creates the rectangular measurements needed for reconstruction. See Figure 3.12 for a detailed sketch prepared by a crime scene technician.

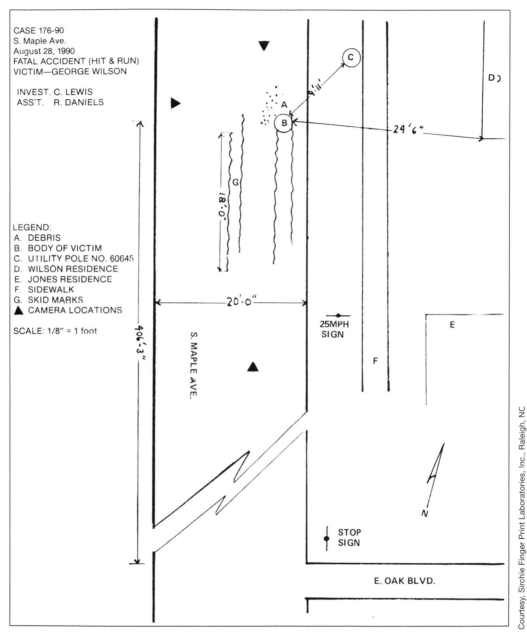

CASE 176-90
S. Maple Ave.
August 28, 1990
FATAL ACCIDENT (HIT & RUN)
VICTIM—GEORGE WILSON

INVEST. C. LEWIS
ASS'T.   R. DANIELS

LEGEND:
A. DEBRIS
B. BODY OF VICTIM
C. UTILITY POLE NO. 60645
D. WILSON RESIDENCE
E. JONES RESIDENCE
F. SIDEWALK
G. SKID MARKS
▲ CAMERA LOCATIONS

SCALE: 1/8" = 1 foot

S. MAPLE AVE.

25MPH
SIGN

STOP
SIGN

E. OAK BLVD.

Courtesy, Sirchie Finger Print Laboratories, Inc., Raleigh, NC

Figure 3.11
Finished sketch and scale drawing of a homicide that took place outdoors.

Exact measurements are important for two reasons: one, to reconstruct the crime—namely, to check the account given by a suspect or witness; and two, to give clear-cut, precise answers to defense counsel's questions, and ensure that counsel is provided no opportunity to impugn the investigator's competence or confidence. It is very important to place all evidence seized at the crime scene on the crime scene sketch.

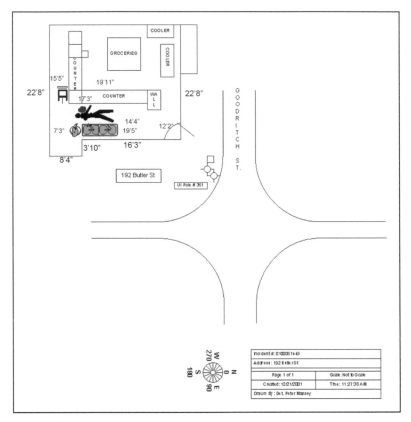

Figure 3.12
A detailed sketch prepared by a crime scene technician.

COLLECTION AND PRESERVATION

When each item of physical evidence has been properly recorded, it must then be collected separately and preserved for examination in the laboratory and eventually in court. The requirements of both scientist and lawyer therefore must be kept in mind. Because improperly collected or preserved evidence will fail to meet the tests defense counsel can apply in court, legal requirements will be considered first.

Preservation—Legal Requirements

The same information used by the criminalist to reconstruct the crime serves to answer defense counsel's questions at trial. For example, the distribution pattern of spent cartridges ejected from an automatic pistol may allow the criminalist to determine where the shooter stood when firing the weapon, and defense counsel will certainly ask how he or she knows the exact position of each cartridge. An admissible set of photographs and a sketch can defuse this challenge. Other tests lawyers can apply in attempting to exclude evidence involve the certainty of the identification (of the cartridges in this example) and the issue of continuity of possession—the chain of custody of each item of evidence.

Identification

To be admissible in court, an item of evidence must be shown to be identical with that discovered at the crime scene or secured at the time of arrest. Thus, any alleged marijuana cigarettes found in the defendant's possession on arrest or bullets removed from the bedroom mattress after a homicide must be shown to be the cigarettes or the bullets acquired originally. To make identifications with certainty and thereby preclude a successful challenge, some method of marking each item of evidence must be devised, the marks serving to connect each bit of evidence to both investigator and defendant or scene. If possible, they should include the date and location of the acquisition of the evidence. Attempting to squeeze this information onto a small item would be impractical, but an envelope, bottle, or other container provides an enlarged labeling surface. For biological evidence, paper bags, envelopes, or boxes are the preferred method. Plastic containers are preferred for non-biological evidence and arson evidence, because this material is less likely to break or contaminate the evidence. Any container must be sealed and initialed on the seal. In cases involving computers or other storage devices, special handling may be required, and care must be taken not to alter or destroy data. For this reason, an expert in this area should be consulted. The Federal Bureau of Investigation has established specialized units in major cities to assist local law enforcement in cases involving computers and other electronic storage devices.

An all-in-one evidence tag/label is available that can be used for the identification of many kinds of evidence. Printed on heavy-duty stock, it can be either threaded using tamper-proof ties through a pre-punched hole to form an evidence tag or made into an adhesive-backed evidence label by peeling off the protective backing (see Figure 3.13).

In large police departments the storage and retrieval of evidence from the property clerk or evidence custodian is somewhat complicated. For simplification, a voucher number system may be utilized to account for the evidence. Some large departments use a computer to inventory and track evidence as it is examined within the laboratory. This has little to do with the identification of the original evidence by the detective; rather, it is related to the other legal requirement: chain of custody.

Courtesy, Lynn Peavey Co., Lenexa, KS

Figure 3.13
An all-in-one evidence tag/label. It is supplied with tamper-proof ties for tagging and peel-off backing with a permanent adhesive to make it into a label.

Continuity of Possession/Chain of Custody

Evidence must be continuously accounted for from the time of its discovery until it is presented in court. Anyone who had it in their possession, even momentarily, may be called upon to testify as to when, where, and from whom it was received; what (if anything) was done to it; to whom it was surrendered, and at what time and date. The greater the number of people handling the evidence, the greater the potential for conflict in, or contradiction of, their testimony. Any disruption in the chain of custody may cause evidence to be inadmissible. Even if it is admitted, a disruption can weaken or destroy its probative value. Accordingly, the rule is to have the least possible number of persons handle evidence. If at all practical, the investigator should personally deliver evidence to the laboratory. If the facility is far away, the use of the U.S. Post Office (Registered), United Parcel Service or Fed Ex (Acknowledgment of Delivery) is permissible. Their signed receipts usually suffice to satisfy the court. The court appearance of a postal or delivery clerk is not usually required.

Police departments normally specify how physical evidence should be marked, transported, and stored. These procedures are not specified here, as they vary from department to department, but the general considerations can be met in a number of ways. Any practice that ignores them can create major problems regarding the admissibility of evidence in court. If investigators do not comprehend the legal aspects intrinsic to the preservation of physical evidence, they become vulnerable to attack by defense counsel. Further, failure to be familiar with different types of examination or the limitations of instrumentation can prove disastrous on the witness stand.

Preservation—Scientific Requirements and Means

Scientific Requirements

The criminalist also has scientific requirements for the preservation of evidence, the primary one being that there be no alteration in its inherent quality or composition. Sometimes, deterioration may occur in such biological materials as blood, semen, and vomit before the investigator arrives at the scene. Any change after that must be minimized by taking proper precautions promptly. Physical evidence may undergo change in the following ways:

1.   Loss by leakage (of a powder) from an opening in the seam of an envelope, or by evaporation (of a volatile liquid) from an improperly stoppered container.

2.   Decomposition through exposure to light, heat, or bacteria; for example, direct exposure to summer sun can alter a bloodstain in a very short time. It may not be recognized.

3.   Intermingling of evidence from various sources and locations in a common container. In a sex crime, the suspect's and victim's underwear should not be placed in the same bag. Such commingling, surprisingly, is not uncommon.

4.   Alteration by the unwitting addition of a fresh fold or crease in a document, or a tear or cut in a garment. For example, hospital personnel, in haste to remove clothing, have cut right through the powder mark on the victim's shirt (see Figure 3.14). They also have disposed of such clothing. If it has any potential as evidence, immediate measures must be taken to retrieve it.

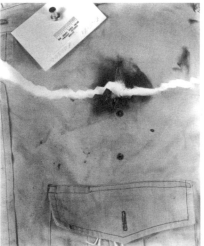

Courtesy, New Jersey State Police

Figure 3.14
Powder mark on victim's shirt cut through by hospital personnel unmindful of its potential evidentiary value.

5.   Contamination, bacterial or chemical, resulting from the use of unclean containers.

6.   Alteration of data on computers or electronic storage devices.

A few precautions can minimize or eliminate these problems:

1.   Use only fresh, clean containers. For powders, utilize a druggist fold, which is then placed into a secondary container like an envelope.

2.   Use leak-proof, sealable containers.

3.   Uphold the integrity of each item of evidence by using separate containers.

4.   Keep evidence away from direct sunlight and heat. Refrigerate biological evidence (such as whole blood, urine, and sex crime kits) when not being transported.

5.   Deliver evidence as quickly as possible to the laboratory.

6.   Handle evidence as little as possible.

7.   Do not attempt to access or remove computer files without competent assistance.

Biological specimens, particularly blood and semen stains, are best preserved by permitting them to dry at room temperature, away from direct sunlight. No air currents (e.g., from a fan) or heat (e.g., from a blow dryer) should be directed at them.[14]

Collection—Scientific Requirements and Means

Scientific Requirements

It was pointed out earlier that the comparison and interpretation of details in physical evidence—especially the development of associative evidence—is a major activity for the criminalist. As part of this process, the criminalist requires that a specimen from the suspect be checked against the evidence from the crime scene. Therefore, an inked set of the suspect's fingerprints must be at hand for comparison with a latent print found at the scene, or a bullet fired from the suspected weapon or cartridge case at the scene must be available to link the crime scene bullet or cartridge to a certain weapon. Generally, comparison specimens of known origin (exemplars) must be collected and made available to criminalists. Three considerations should govern the collection:

1.   Whenever possible, variables must be controlled.

2.   Background material must be collected.

3.   The quantity of the sample must be sufficient.

Control of Variables

It is fundamental to scientific experimentation that, where feasible, all variables except one be controlled during the test. Because controlling the variables is not always possible in criminalistics, all variables that can possibly be eliminated should be. Thus, when collecting handwriting specimens for comparison with a forged check, variables to be scrutinized for possible elimination include: the size, color, and printing on the check; and the type of writing instrument (by employing the same type—ballpoint pen, pencil, marker, etc.—used in the original forgery). Similarly, when examining a firearm, the same ammunition used in the commission of the crime, if available, should be employed in the test firing. The aim in controlling variables is to have the evidence specimen duplicated to the fullest extent possible in the exemplar.

Background Material

A material that has been bloodstained or has had paint transferred to it (in a hit-and-run accident, for instance) contains valuable physical evidence. Something, however, may have been present on the material prior to the crime that could interfere with the tests that the criminalist performs. For this reason, an unstained sample that is quite close to the stained area should be collected. A bloodstained mattress, for instance, can yield misleading results if perspiration or saliva was already on the ticking when the crime was committed. By testing an unstained sample of the ticking, DNA can be discovered and dealt with by a serologist. Another example: When a bicycle is struck by an automobile, each vehicle's paint can be transferred to the other. To evaluate the spectrograms of each paint, a specimen of the original paint on each vehicle must be taken from a spot near the collision-transfer point. These specimens, like the unstained ticking, constitute the background samples.

Sample Sufficiency

It is accurate to say that most investigators do not collect comparison samples of adequate size or quantity. This may partly be a result of misunderstanding, for the sensitivity of modern instrumental methods of analysis has certainly been exaggerated. Still, it is better that samples be too large rather than too small. The investigator or evidence technician, naturally, is limited to what is available at the crime scene. In general, this factor does not pertain to the known specimen (exemplar), which usually is large. As a result, the criminalist is able to establish the conditions and method of examination before comparing the crime scene evidence with it.

Means

Various tools are required to separate and remove material from its setting when collecting physical evidence at the crime scene. Special means are employed to gather trace evidence. Similarly, an assortment of containers is needed to isolate and protect each material.

Tools

In general, tools that cut, grip, or force are needed for the collection of physical evidence. If using for biological evidence, they must be cleaned prior to every use or, if disposable, thrown away. They can be classified as follows:

1. Cutting Implements
    Scissors—compound-action metal snips or shears
    Saws for wood and metal
    Scalpels and razors
    Chisels for wood and metal
    Knives
    Drills with assorted bits
    Axes
    Files

2.   Gripping Devices
   Assorted wrenches
   Assorted pliers
   Tweezers—straight and angled

3.   Forcing or Prying Tools
   Screwdrivers—various sizes of regular and Phillips-head types
   Hammers—claw, ball-peen, chipping, mallet
   Crowbars

Containers

All items listed below are available in most communities. They are best collected in advance, in anticipation of future need:

1.	Bags	paper, plastic
2.	Boxes	pill (drug store type), shoe, large cartons
3.	Envelopes	assorted sizes and types; mail, brown manila with metal clasp, plastic.
4.	Other containers	
	Plastic	used by druggists to dispense tablets and capsules; or used to store or freeze foods.
	Glass	bottles with stoppers, Mason jars with lids
	Cans	with tight covers

Expansion envelopes; heat-sealable, extra-strength polyethylene bags; and other items for the collection of crime scene evidence are available from police equipment specialists such as Sirchie Finger Print Laboratories, Lynn Peavey Company, Ames Safety Envelope Company, and Kinderprint Company (see Figures 3.15–3.18).

Collection—Special Considerations

In addition to the routine collection of physical evidence, today's investigator should not overlook the possibility of trace evidence, and also must keep in mind the hazard imposed by HIV-infected blood.

Trace Evidence

Trace evidence, a type of physical evidence distinguished mainly because of its small size, calls for special methods. Some techniques for discovering and gathering trace evidence are: adhesion to tape, shaking, sweeping, and vacuuming. A specialized vacuum cleaner with good suction, equipped with a special attachment to hold filter paper in place, can be used to trap the debris as a deposit on the paper. Each item of evidence processed requires a fresh filter. Particulate matter and fibers (on clothing, automobile rug, bed sheet, blanket, etc.) are dislodged by vigorous shaking over a clean white sheet of paper laid on a large table. The adhesion technique involves pressing a three- or four-inch piece of transparent tape on the evidence to be examined; with the tape placed sticky side down on a glass slide, the debris adhering to it can be studied directly under the microscope. A stereomicroscope is employed to sort out the fibers or particles obtained from vacuuming or shaking; a polarized light microscope is used for comparison and identification.

Figure 3.15
Kraft bags.

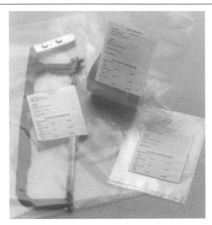

Figure 3.16
Heat-sealable, clear polyethylene bags.

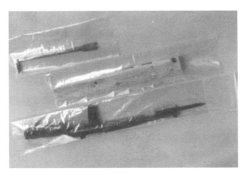

Figure 3.17
Evidence bags for rifles or other long items.

Figure 3.18
Clear evidence jars with tight-fitting screw-on caps.

Courtesy, Lynn Peavey Co., Lenexa, KS

Detective Nicholas Petraco (New York Police Department), who specializes in trace evidence examination, believes that even in this day of highly advanced laboratory instrumentation "the microscope, especially the polarized microscope, is the most important and versatile instrument available to the criminalist for the study of trace evidential materials."[15] He cites several cases that were solved because of the "vital role that the microscope and trace evidence played."[16]

AIDS and Hepatitis C as a Concern for Crime Scene Investigators

The potential of Acquired Immune Deficiency Syndrome (AIDS) as a serious hazard to the health of those charged with collecting physical evidence at scenes of violent crimes has been acknowledged.[17] Hepatitis C has also been identified as a serious concern. A research paper by D.B. Kennedy and others points to the special vulnerability of crime scene investigators:

> [For] ... unlike the doctor, nurse, or health worker who most often works in a controlled environment, the criminal investigator may be confronted with less manageable conditions.[18]

... using conventional methods such as latex gloves for protection against the potential risk of AIDS or other infectious diseases may not be adequate at every crime scene ... While the human skin and protective garments are barriers to exposure to the AIDS virus, there are objects and conditions present at a crime scene which may, through abrasion, puncturing, or cutting action, provide an avenue for transmission and infection.[19]

The authors raise the following problem:

... If investigators believe they are not properly protected from the AIDS virus, they may limit their evidentiary searches, consciously or unconsciously, to only those scenarios they believe to be "safe." Physical evidence may only be cursorily dealt with, hunches may not be followed up, and officers may avoid specialized forensic assignments. If evidence of poor quality must be relied upon by the courts, the truly guilty may not be convicted. Worse yet, the innocent may fail to be exonerated.[20]

They conclude with some recommendations, to wit:

... Notwithstanding these clear concerns for the AIDS problem in general and their own safety in particular, the vast majority of crime scene investigators and evidence technicians report that the quality of their work is not adversely affected. While policy makers at all levels of the criminal justice system may be pleased by the perseverance of forensic line officers, it is clear that their efforts must be supported by stronger departmental measures if they are to continue effectively in their work. At the very least, clear guidelines that incorporate the latest information on AIDS prevention should be developed and publicized. The feasibility of issuing various support equipment, such as specialized clothing, also needs to be explored.[21]

TRANSMISSION OF EVIDENCE TO THE LABORATORY

Delivering physical evidence to the laboratory is best done in person for legal and scientific reasons. In the case that this is not possible, the U.S. Postal Service, United Parcel Service (UPS), or FedEx can be used to deliver the packaged evidence. Proper packing, wrapping, and sealing are extremely important when evidence is to be shipped. With this in mind, the FBI has prepared a helpful set of explicit recommendations and instructions, which are available at their web site.

This text thus far has treated investigations as though the detective and his or her partner are conducting the crime scene search by themselves. However, when a high-profile case, a large crime scene, or multiple scenes are involved, a more elaborate evidence collection process is desirable. To this end, the FBI has published a booklet with the aim of ensuring that search efforts are conducted in an organized and methodical fashion.[22] It describes the duties and responsibilities of the response team, which includes: a team leader, a photographer and photographic log recorder, an evidence recorder/custodian, and specialists (e.g., bomb expert, geologist, etc.). Other issues treated include: organization and basic stages in a search operation, documentation procedures, and equipment recommendations.

While largely concerned with how to conduct a search, the booklet also warns the user of the pitfalls involved in blindly following their recommendations. Considering the gravity of high-profile crimes, the booklet's suggestions help investigators recall things to do that can be overlooked in the heat of the moment.

FINDING PHYSICAL EVIDENCE BY CANVASSING

Canvassing is employed most often to search out witnesses who do not know they have useful information about a crime under investigation. It is also used to track down the source of crime scene evidence. For example, interviewing neighbors or companions of suspects may produce writing samples, trace evidence, or DNA samples from where the suspect visited or was in contact.

CONCLUSION

The crime scene, in most cases, is a critical aspect of the investigation. Unfortunately, the expanding use of crime scene technicians frequently results in the patrol officer, or perhaps the first investigator on the scene, to forgo any crime scene work. Although the first officer on the scene may not be expected to conduct an in-depth examination, such as lifting latent prints, it is incumbent upon him or her to conduct preliminary crime scene activities, such as making a rough sketch, looking for evidence that may deteriorate or succumb to weather conditions if outside, or identifying evidence that may not be visible. In some cases it may be some time before a crime scene unit responds, or is perhaps reassigned to a more serious crime. For this reason, knowledge of crime scene activities is an important aspect of the investigative function.

In the following chapter, the importance of people—be they victims, witnesses, or individuals—who can provide information about the case is addressed.

NOTES

[1]   Shannon Tangonan, "Accused Levin Killers Due to Be Arraigned," *USA Today*, (June 9, 1997), 9A.

[2]   *Michigan v. Clifford*, 464 U.S. 1 (1983).

[3]   *Michigan v. Tyler*, 436 U.S. 499 (1978).

[4]   *United States v. Mitchell*, 85F.3d 800 (1st Cir. 1996).

[5]   *Mincey v. Arizona*, 437 U.S. 385 (1978).

[6]   *United States v. Richardson*, 208F.3d 626 (7th Cir. 2000).

[7]   Kimberly A. Crawford, "Crime Scene Searches: The Need for Fourth Amendment Compliance," *FBI Law Enforcement Bulletin*, 68:1 (1999), 26–31.

[8]   *Illinois v. Rodriquez*, 497 U.S. 177 (1990).

[9]   Crawford, op. cit., 29.

[10]   *Illinois v. Lidster*, 540 U.S. 419 (2004).

[11]   *Hudson v. Michigan*, 547 U.S. 586 (2006).

[12]   Richard F. Fox and Carl L. Cunningham, *Crime Scene Search and Physical Evidence Handbook*, reprint (Washington, DC: U.S. Government Printing Office, 1973), iii.

13   Larry S. Miller and Richard McEvoy Jr, *Police Photography*, 6th ed. (Boston: Elsevier/Anderson Publishing, 2010), 4–5.

14   For more information, see http://www.fbi.gov/hq/lab/pdf/Evidence%20Reference%20Guide.pdf

15   Nicholas Petraco, "Trace Evidence—The Invisible Witness," *Journal of Forensic Sciences*, 31:1 (1986), 321–327.

16   Ibid., 321–327.

17   D.B. Kennedy, R.J. Homant, and G.L. Emery, "AIDS Concerns Among Crime Scene Investigators," *Journal of Police Science and Administration*, 17:1 (1990), 12–18.

18   Ibid., 13.

19   Ibid., 14.

20   Ibid.

21   Ibid., 18.

22   Federal Bureau of Investigation. *Suggested Guidelines for Establishing Evidence Response Teams*. (Washington, DC: Department of Justice, no date).

IMPORTANT CASES

Hudson v. Michigan (2006)
Illinois v. Lidster (2004)
Katz v. United States (1967)
Michigan v. Clifford (1983)
Michigan v. Tyler (1978)
Mincey v. Arizona (1978)
United States v. Mitchell (1996)
United States v. Richardson (2000)

DISCUSSION QUESTIONS

1.   What is the definition of a crime scene?

2.   What are some of the purposes for conducting a crime scene search?

3.   In addition to the crime scene, there are several other possible sources of physical evidence. What are they?

4.   What are some of the methods of recording the situation, conditions, and physical evidence found at the crime scene?

5.   What are the two types of photographs taken at a crime scene?

6.   What is the purpose of a crime scene sketch?

7.   How should physical evidence be transmitted to the crime lab?

SUPPLEMENTAL READINGS

Adams, T. F., Caddell, A. G., & Krutsinger, J. L. (2004). *Crime scene investigation* (2nd ed.). Upper Saddle River, NJ: Prentice Hall.

Bevel, T., & Gardiner, R. M. (2008). *Blood stain pattern analysis with an introduction to crime scene reconstruction, 3rd ed. (Practical Aspects of Criminal & Forensic Investigations).* Boca Raton, FL: CRC Press.

Bodziak, W. J. (2000). *Footwear impression evidence: Detection, recover, and examination* (2nd ed.). Boca Raton, FL: CRC Press.

Cowger, J. F. (1992). *Friction ridge skin: Comparison and identification of fingerprints.* Boca Raton, FL: CRC Press.

Davis, R. (2005). *Evidence collection and presentation.* San Clemente, CA: LawTech.

DeForest, P. R., Gaensslen, R. E., & Lee, H. C. (1995). *Forensic science: An introduction to criminalistics* (2nd ed.). New York: McGraw-Hill.

Eckert, W. G., & James, S. H. (1998). *Interpretation of bloodstain evidence at crime scenes* (2nd ed.). Boca Raton, FL: CRC Press.

Fisher, B. A. J. (2004). *Techniques of crime scene investigation* (7th ed.). Boca Raton, FL: CRC Press.

Fox, R. H., & Cunningham, C. L. (1992). *Crime scene search and physical evidence handbook.* Boulder, CO: Paladin Press.

Gardner, R. M. (2011). *Practical crime scene processing and investigation* (2nd ed.). Boca Raton, FL: Taylor & Francis.

Goodall, J., & Hawks, C. (2005). *Crime scene documentation.* San Clemente, CA: LawTech.

Hawthorne, M. R. (1999). *First unit responder: A guide to physical evidence collection for patrol officers.* Boca Raton, FL: CRC Press.

James, S. H., Kish, P. E., & Sutton, T. P. (2005). *Principles of bloodstain pattern analysis: Theory and practice.* Boca Raton, FL: CRC Press.

Lee, H. C. (1994). *Crime scene investigation.* Taoyuan, Taiwan (Republic of China): Central Police University Press.

Lee, H. C., & Gaensslen, R. F. (Eds.). (2001). *Advances in fingerprint technology* (2nd ed.). Boca Raton, FL: CRC Press.

Lewis, J. M. A. (2005). *Criminalistics for crime scene investigators.* San Clemente, CA: LawTech.

McDonald, P. (1992). *Tire print identification: Practical aspects of criminal forensic investigation.* Boca Raton, FL: CRC Press.

Miller, L. S., & McEvoy, R., Jr. (2010). *Police photography* (6th ed.). Boston: Elsevier/Anderson Publishing.

Miller, L. S., & Whitehead, J. T. (2010). *Report writing for criminal justice professionals* (4th ed.). Boston: Elsevier/Anderson Publishing.

Moody, K. J., & Grant, P. M. (2005). *Nuclear forensic analysis.* Boca Raton, FL: CRC Press.

Nordby, J. J., James, S. H., & Bell, S. (2009). *Forensic science: An introduction to scientific and investigative techniques* (3rd ed.). Boca Raton, FL: CRC Press.

Osterburg, J. W. (1982). *The crime laboratory: Case studies of scientific investigation* (2nd ed.). Eagan, MN: West Group.

Pederson, D. (2000). Down on the body farm. *Newsweek*, October 23, 50–52.

Petraco, N., & Sherman, H. (2006). *Illustrated guide to crime scene investigation*. Boca Raton, FL: CRC Press.

Redsicker, D. R. (2001). *The practical methodology of forensic photography* (2nd ed.). Boca Raton, FL: CRC Press.

Rynearson, J. M. (2002). *Evidence and crime scene reconstruction* (6th ed.). Redding, CA: National Crime Investigation and Training.

Safferstein, R. (2003). *Criminalistics: An introduction to forensic science* (8th ed.). Englewood Cliffs, NJ: Prentice Hall.

Staggs, S. (2005). *Crime scene photography*. San Clemente, CA: LawTech.

U.S. Department of Justice (2012). *Handbook of forensic services*. Quantico, VA: Federal Bureau of Investigation.

U.S. Department of Justice. (2000). *Crime scene investigation: A guide for law enforcement*. Washington, D.C.

CHAPTER 4

PEOPLE AS A SOURCE OF INFORMATION

Individually and collectively, people possess a wide spectrum of information about other people. Through social media they also share personal information and that of family and friends. Today corporations, businesses, and data collection agencies also amass a wealth of information about people. Of potential value to the criminal investigator, this information can range from what a victim plainly knows to what an eyewitness chances to see or hear prior to or during the commission of a crime. This is firsthand knowledge. People also accumulate a quantity of secondhand knowledge during the course of daily life—from intimate and casual relationships, remarks overheard, or quarrels witnessed. It may involve physical evidence such as a threatening note, or something that comes into the hands of a victim or witness by coincidence—a bullet, or an instrument used in the crime (e.g., a baseball bat or piece of pipe). Whatever the form, it is the detective's task either to find those who have such knowledge or evidence, or to persuade people to come forward and volunteer what they know. Victims and eyewitnesses are the most obvious sources of information. Others of potential value are relatives and acquaintances of the suspect, informants, and the perpetrator (when apprehended).

This chapter addresses the kinds of information that can be obtained from people by means of interviewing, psychological profiling, surveillance, lineups, neighborhood canvasses, interrogation, hypnosis, and nonverbal clues. The use of records and files appears in the next chapter.

THE CRIMINAL

Mind, body, words, actions—all can serve to betray the identity of the offender through a consideration of motive, the physical evidence brought to or taken from the crime scene, or the method of committing the crime. In one sense, this restates Hans Gross's thesis that:

> ... criminal investigation consist[s] of two parts; one, the utilization by police officers of all available knowledge and information concerning the psychology, motivation, and character of the criminal before, during, and after the commission of a crime; and two, the application of all useful technological and scientific information to solve a crime and support the allegations in the courtroom.[1]

Motive

From the standpoint of motive, crime may be divided into two classes. In the first class, crimes such as robbery, rape, and burglary may have a universal motive which is—in and of itself—of little value in furthering the investigation. Those in the second class, such as homicide, arson, and assault, are more likely to have a particularized motive; when one is discovered, the connection between victim and criminal may be deduced. (The high clearance rate for homicide is based in part on this logic.)

Investigative experience is helpful in ferreting out the motive for a crime. In some cases, motive may be learned through adroit interviewing. In others, however, it is implied—when it can be determined who might benefit from committing the crime. Occasionally, a victim is able to suggest the names of suspects and their motives. When several individuals have motive, their number can be pared down by ascertaining who had the opportunity of time and place, and who among them had the enterprise. This sifting process allows investigators to channel their efforts into those aspects of the inquiry most likely to produce evidence of the offender's involvement.

There is another important reason for establishing motive—even when it is not helpful in suggesting possible suspects. Though not an element of any crime, a jury is more likely to be convinced of a defendant's guilt if a motive for committing the crime can be shown.

Modus Operandi (MO)

An offender's pattern of operation (method of preparing for and committing a crime) is called the *modus operandi* or MO (discussed in detail in Chapter 5). When collected, stored, and classified, MO information can assist in the identification and apprehension of a perpetrator. It also can be useful in devising strategies for deterring crime.

The computer and other forms of information technology have greatly expanded the investigator's ability to utilize MO information in helping to identify suspects, link crimes, and provide temporal and visualization models that serve as leads. Recent research at the Institute for the Study of Violent Groups (ISVG) at the University of New Haven has proven the value of including minutia or detailed variables in helping to identify suspects or groups through the use of statistical probability, analytics, and visualization models. These advanced techniques are being used increasingly by law enforcement analysts.

Identification

Ideally, MO characteristics can identify an offender. When an individual has an arrest record and a unique MO is on file, an identification may occur if the MO is used again and recognized. In general, however, MO characteristics are not sufficiently unique for this purpose. Just the same, MO can lead to the identification of an offender when a string of crimes is recognized as having a common perpetrator and the respective clues are pooled and used inductively. The pooled information also can send the investigator to search records, set up a surveillance, or seek out an informant.

Apprehension

An analysis of the pattern of operation (or MO) may provide the basis for a plan to apprehend an offender. The general aim is to discover possible targets and place them under a fixed surveillance, frequently using cameras in place of traditional human stakeouts. Wireless technology has greatly enhanced the ability to monitor more than one location at a time. (See Part D on technology.) Though this may constitute a considerable commitment of staff and resources, under the right circumstances, the prospects are good.

MO data make another highly useful contribution to the cause of justice when a run of crimes appears to have been solved, yet the convicted person still claims innocence. Should those crimes continue after the individual has been imprisoned, and if they are characterized by the same MO (especially a somewhat unusual one), it is an indication that an innocent person may have been wronged. The case should then be thoroughly reviewed to settle the matter.

When MO analysis indicates that a previously crime-free area is beset by a series of crimes, implementation of more intensive visible patrol during the relevant period may bring about an abatement of the activity. An apprehension may also be a consequence of preventive patrol and intelligence-led policing strategies.

Psychological Profiling

Occasionally, a psychiatrist or psychologist is invited to make an assessment of a crime that is presenting difficulties. When the specialists are asked "Who would do a thing like this?," their answers may provide direction to the investigation or limit the number of suspects. This procedure, confined to crimes of brutality or those in which strong emotions were manifest, has been employed more frequently in investigations. Psychological assessment of a crime is called profiling and is not to be confused with racial profiling; its purpose is to recognize and interpret visible contextual evidence at the scene as indicative of the personality type of the perpetrator. According to the FBI:

> The officer must bear in mind that the profile is not an exact science and a suspect who fits the description is not automatically guilty. The use of profiling does not replace sound investigative procedures. ...
>
> The entire basis for a good profile is a good crime scene examination and adequate interviews of victims and witnesses. ...
>
> The victim is one of the most important aspects of the psychological profile. In cases involving a surviving victim, particularly a rape victim, the perpetrator's exact conversation with the victim is of utmost importance and can play a very large role in the construction of an accurate profile.
>
> The profile is not all inclusive and does not always provide the same information from one profile to another. It is based on what was or was not left at the crime scene. Since the amount of psychological evidence varies, as does physical evidence, the profile may also vary.
>
> It is most important that this investigative technique be confined chiefly to crimes against the person where the motive is lacking and where there is sufficient data to recognize the presence of psychopathology at the crime scene. ... It should be understood that analysis is for lead value only.[2]

If a potential suspect emerges as a result of profiling or routine investigation, the information may be of help during interrogation. One of the necessary conditions for confession is a feeling of guilt, and the insight gained from profiling may provide an understanding of what will and will not provoke such a feeling. This permits the avoidance of some areas of a suspect's behavior in an interrogative session and the more vigorous pursuit of other areas.

BOX 4.1 TYPES OF PROFILE INFORMATION

1. The perpetrator's race
2. Sex
3. Age range
4. Marital status
5. General employment
6. Reaction to questioning by police
7. Degree of sexual maturity
8. Whether the individual might strike again
9. The possibility that he or she has committed a similar offense in the past
10. Possible police record
11. Geographic background, based on accents or language, including slang
12. Specific characteristics of the crime

Although forensic psychological profiling has a long history as a method by which investigators formed conclusions or theories based upon the actions of the offender, it is only in the past 20 or 30 years that a more scientific approach has been adapted to the term. The formation of the Behavioral Science Unit in 1972 at the FBI Academy in Quantico, Virginia was a major step forward in advancing the notion that psychological profiling can be an important tool in crime investigation. See Box 4.1.

Clues from Evidence Brought to Crime Scene

Physical evidence brought to the crime scene by a criminal may yield a clue to his or her identity. Determining the intended use of a particular object wielded as a murder weapon has investigative value (see discussion in Chapter 5). The potential value of other foreign objects (a wallet, letter, or receipt) accidentally dropped or left at the scene hardly needs discussing. Suffice it to say such clues are not always apparent. Uncovering them calls for thoroughness; for example, an evidence technician discovered a dry cleaner's tag in a waste basket after homicide detectives had "searched" the room. This clue led to the identification of the offender.

Trampled vegetation, tracks in mud or snow, or any other visible evidence of the route taken to or from the scene, may be important—especially if the route is not one most people would choose. When no plausible reason can be inferred for not taking the most likely route (too many possible witnesses who might be encountered, for example), consideration must then be given to why the less likely one was chosen. Is it in the direction (especially in remote areas) of the offender's house? Would it lead to where a vehicle might be parked and not be noticed? Is there an attraction nearby (for example, an amusement park set up temporarily in some vacant space) that could provide a cover and explain the suspect's presence in the area? When any reason for the choice becomes apparent, investigative efforts can then be focused on this insight to see if additional leads can be developed.

Confessions and Admissions

A suspect is often interrogated in the latter stages of an investigation, primarily to ascertain what happened, and why, from the suspect's own mouth. The ultimate result may be a written, signed confession. A less conclusive result, a statement that stops short of a confession yet admits to facts from which guilt might be inferred, is called an *admission*. Such a statement has probative value; coupled with independent, corroborative physical evidence or testimony, an admission against interest may be sufficient to meet the reasonable doubt criterion the law imposes on a jury. (The reasons why a person may confess to a crime are discussed in Chapter 10.)

THE VICTIM

A victim is at the same time a witness and—like any other witness—is able to provide information. By virtue of being a victim, an additional contribution can be made, sometimes by suggesting the name of a suspect and sometimes by speculating about why he or she was the target. Underlying this input is motive. Even though a victim is not always aware of those who were motivated to commit the crime, such suggestions and speculations may give direction to the investigator's efforts. If blood or hair is found at the crime scene or on the victim's clothing, its potential as associative evidence should be exploited. (The discussion on "Witnesses" in the following section is equally applicable to the victim as a source of information.)

WITNESSES

The Five Senses

A visual observation is the most frequent source of information contributed by a witness. The next is auditory in nature: the witness hears something said or someone speaking. Sources that are less frequent, but important at times, include: smell (e.g., the use of dogs to sniff out the presence of narcotics), touch (e.g., by a blindfolded rape victim), and taste (e.g., an odd or "off" flavor in food as in poisonings). In a series of rapes, several victims recognized the odor of home furnace heating oil in the rapist's automobile and on his clothing. Several victims described his car, and this led to a survey of parking areas adjacent to heating oil delivery companies. The victims also recalled a particular decal on the car's windshield. These visual and olfactory clues, together with an intensified, thorough investigative effort, pointed to a suspect who was later identified by each of the victims in separate lineups.

> **The Five Senses**
>
> Hearing
> Sight
> Smell
> Touch
> Taste

A visual observation contributed important information to the solution of a bombing case. A woman glancing out her window at the street noted six men and five women, dressed as joggers, grouped around a Volkswagen van. What caught her attention and aroused her suspicions was the strange sight of cigarettes in the mouths of joggers. Her call to the police led to the capture of Puerto Rican nationalists wanted for bombings on the island and in the United States. The recognition "that something is not right" is an ingredient of investigative mind-set; fortunately, it is not limited to detectives.

It is through eyewitnesses that the investigator may secure answers to the six questions of *who, what, where, when, why,* and *how.* They can make major contributions to the investigation of an event when the perpetrator, vehicle, or both are accurately described, and everything that happened is recalled in exact detail. More often than not, though, eyewitnesses are unable to meet these high standards.

Describing the Perpetrator

To some degree, an eyewitness or victim may be able to describe the perpetrator to police. This description can then be transmitted in three ways to other law enforcement personnel (or the public at large) for assistance in apprehending the offender:

1. A verbal description *(portrait parlé)* of the perpetrator's physical characteristics and clothing is taken, and then printed;

2. A likeness of the perceived image is captured by a police artist (the variety of feature nuances is almost infinite);

3. A likeness of the perceived image is captured by mechanical means such as Identi-Kit or Penry Photo-Fit (a choice of features is offered: forehead, hairline, eyebrows, chin, ears, eyes, nose, and mouth). Or, a computer can be used to compose a likeness of an offender; the variety of feature nuances is comparable to that which the police artist is able to capture.

   Whether hand-drawn or obtained by mechanical means, these images can be electronically transmitted to other law enforcement agencies.

Describing Vehicles or Weapons

Unfortunately, witnesses are often unable to provide a serviceable description of a vehicle or weapon used in the commission of a crime. Accurate information would permit police to alert officers on patrol about what to look for. Once such property is located, it should be placed in protective custody until examined for fingerprints or other trace evidence.

Vehicles

The following information may be provided by witnesses:

• Kind of vehicle	automobile, pickup truck, motorcycle, bicycle, etc.
• Color of vehicle	white, red, two-tone—gray on top, blue on bottom, etc.
• Body style	2-door, 4-door, SUV, panel truck, etc.
• Make or manufacturer	Chevrolet, Ford, Chrysler, Honda, Volkswagen, Toyota, etc.
• Model	Camaro, Mustang, PT Cruiser, Jetta, Camry, etc.
• License plate	the state; the number (or a part of the number)
• Distinguishing features	bumper stickers, vanity plates, wheel covers, customizing

Weapons

The information obtained from witnesses is generally sketchy with respect to a weapon used in a crime, but some people may be able to provide the following details:

- Kind   Gun, knife, hatchet, club, etc.
- Color   Shiny, black, olive green, dull gray, etc.
- Type   Gun (revolver, automatic, shotgun, rifle); knife (hunting, carving, pocket, kitchen), etc.
- Length   Gun (short or long barrel); knife (long or short blade), etc.
- Caliber (of gun) .22, .38, .45, .357 Magnum, large bore, small bore, etc.

Persons Acquainted with the Suspect

Relatives, friends, and business associates usually know a great deal about an individual. Not only are they familiar with the person's lifestyle and activities, but also with his or her thoughts and opinions. Some of this knowledge can be useful to the detective; even what seems to be worthless can turn out to be helpful. What a person eats on a given day can even be important. In a burglary case, a suspect under surveillance was reported to have just had a big steak for dinner. From another source it had already been learned that the burglar made a habit of eating a hearty steak dinner before going to "work." Surveillance was difficult because he was wary, and considerable resources in vehicles and personnel had to be assigned. Armed with the knowledge of the suspect's habit, the wherewithal could be assembled quickly and utilized efficiently.

Informants

Witnesses are informants in the strictest sense. Others provide information about criminal activity in the area for venal reasons. For instance, before a case has been fully made against him or her, a fence, suspect, or felon engaging in plea bargaining may offer to provide information about a major crime or a series of lesser crimes. For such proposals to be acceptable, explicit information must be supplied. Hence, even though who, what, where, when, why, and how are handed up on a platter, as it were, the investigator should obtain other, independent evidence if the assertions are to be proved and have credibility in court. (The motivation and usefulness of informants are treated at greater length in Chapter 7.)

Follow-Up Activities

Regardless of the source of information, in order to bring about an arrest and prove guilt, it is the detective who must do the follow-up. The investigative potential of some follow-up activities is treated below.

Surveillance

Surveillance may be described as the unobtrusive observation of a person, place, or thing. A "person" is usually a suspect or the relative or friend of a suspect. Anyone, however, is a potential subject of surveillance—provided it is reasonable to expect that their activities would furnish significant information in a criminal investigation. A "place" might be a drug store or liquor store, supermarket, bank, or any other locus in which transactions are largely in cash, or where contraband such as narcotics is available. For the investigator, any place may become sufficiently interesting to be put under surveillance. A "thing" worthy of surveillance might include the ransom dropped at a designated spot, an automobile, or the fruits or instruments of a crime that were hidden for later recovery. In the last named circumstance, other investigative measures would have to be employed first if the perpetrator is to be caught in the act of recovering what was hidden. The increasing use of social media whereby police can "track" the movement or actions of suspects by monitoring "tweets," "blogs" or Facebook communications has proven valuable. However, other forms of monitoring suspects, such as the use of GPS (Global Positioning Systems) on vehicles without a search warrant was deemed unconstitutional in the 2012 case of *United States v. Jones*, although this decision has led to further questions regarding admissibility by the Supreme Court.[3] See Chapter 8.

Surveillance has a dual function in police work: one is investigative; the other, preventive. The specific objectives are:

1. To locate a suspect.

2. To obtain detailed information about the nature and scope of an individual's activities as they relate to suspected criminality.

3. To prevent the commission of crimes such as arson or robbery, which may put lives in jeopardy.

4. To apprehend immediately those who commit a crime while under surveillance (in a burglary for instance, the arrest is made as the perpetrators emerge from the building they broke into).

There is a temptation to discuss surveillance as though it were an independent investigative technique, but this is seldom true. On the contrary, facts acquired through interviewing, interrogation, informants, and legitimate wiretapping or monitoring often supplement and confirm those developed through traditional surveillance methods.

Locating Suspect

Suspects who have absented themselves from their normal haunts present a problem for the detective. Given the gregarious nature of the human being, surveilling a relative or close friend may quickly lead to the subject's whereabouts—except in cases where extreme measures are taken (e.g., flight from the jurisdiction). Sometimes a hobby or favorite activity can help to locate a suspect who, for example, follows the horses from track to track, loves deep sea fishing, or frequents pornography shops.

Determining Activities of Suspect

An investigator needs details on the nature and scope of a suspect's activities for the following reasons:

1. To identify a suspect's associates; and to infer from their observed behavior (individual or group) any criminal intentions or plans.

2. To obtain evidence necessary to establish probable cause for a search warrant or an arrest.

3. To obtain information useful for interrogating a suspect.

4. To establish patterns of travel and behavior of a suspect.

5. As a means of later establishing the truthfulness of a suspect's statements.

Concluding Existence of Probable Cause for Search Warrant—Based on Behavior of Suspect

There may come a point in an investigation when it no longer seems likely that sufficient evidence will be produced to establish guilt beyond a reasonable doubt. By utilizing professional judgment and other sources (such as informants), the investigator may have grounds for believing the individual is engaging in criminal acts. Under such circumstances, suspect and associates should be put under surveillance. If a professional criminal is involved, considerable staff and equipment will be required. With some luck there will be a speedy, satisfactory outcome, but probably days, weeks, or even months will go by before results are achieved.

If contraband (such as alcohol or narcotics) is suspected, or stolen cars are involved, surveillance may permit observations to support an application for a search warrant. When the observations are correctly interpreted by the investigator, the search should uncover the necessary evidence in most situations.

Obtaining Information for Interrogation

M.W. Horowitz has analyzed the requisite conditions for obtaining a confession (see Chapter 10). Two of them may be assisted by information obtained through surveillance. They require the suspect to believe that:

1. Evidence is available against them;

2. Forces hostile to their interests are being employed with maximum effort; meanwhile, friendly forces are being kept to a minimum.

A thorough surveillance or interview of the suspect's family and friends puts detailed, personal facts at the disposal of the investigator. This, if skillfully utilized, can prove to be invaluable. By disclosing an inconsequential detail at the proper moment during an interrogation, a suspect's life appears to be an open book. After a few repetitions of this methodology and, having met the conditions outlined by Horowitz (i.e., accusation, available evidence, friendly and hostile forces, guilt feelings), an admission or confession may result. To corroborate the confession, a diligent check on the admitted details must follow. For an innocent person, of course, guilty knowledge is not coupled with the other conditions described by Horowitz; therefore, a confession is not likely.

Judging when to invest significant surveillance resources, and at what stage in the investigative process, depends on other priority needs, the personnel available, and additional developments in the case. The economist's notion of a "trade-off" can be of help in arriving at a decision to continue or discontinue a surveillance.

Lineup (Identification Parade)

After a suspect has been apprehended, a lineup is assembled for the purpose of having the perpetrator correctly identified by those who witnessed the crime. At the same time, it is employed to protect the innocent, a correct identification eliminating an individual otherwise thought to be a suspect. A properly conducted lineup also serves to support an eyewitness concerned about making a mistake or the ability to make an identification. And, just as a perpetrator who is given a fair lineup is less likely to harbor a grudge, so will an eyewitness testify more effectively when confidence in the identification was based on and tested by the proper procedure (see Chapters 9 and 10). In recent years eyewitness identifications have come under severe criticism by researchers and the courts, resulting in legislation in several states to further define the methodology used in securing eyewitness testimony.

Neighborhood Canvass

When all clues have been followed up without avail and a case holds little hope of solution, a canvass of the area might be productive. The British use the term *intensive inquiry* for seeking information by canvass. Law enforcement procedures in Great Britain and the United States justify neighborhood canvasses for two reasons: one, there is the possibility that someone saw or heard something that was not reported—perhaps because its importance is not realized until an inquiring officer knocks at the door; and two, there is the likelihood of a shock to the security of a criminal. Believing that he or she managed to leave the crime scene undetected, a guilty person could be unnerved by a sudden confrontation with an investigator. Because neighborhood surveillance is conducted without publicity, the customary mode in cities, the culpable may jump to the wrong conclusions and either confess or betray their involvement by their responses to questions. See Figure 4.1.

AP Photo/Elaine Thompson

Figure 4.1
Seattle SWAT police canvass a neighborhood with search dogs near a home where a suspect in the slaying of four police officers gunned down a day earlier was believed to have been.

Questioning People: Proposed Refinements

In seeking information from people, an investigator should be aware of two difficulties that may not immediately be recognized or comprehended. One is presented by those who are willing to talk, but cannot recall (in whole or in part) what was observed, or those who do not remember anything beyond the information already provided. The second difficulty is presented by those who refuse to talk, or do talk yet withhold what might be of use, or attempt to misdirect the investigator by providing time-consuming and ultimately unproductive leads.

Among the old and new methods proposed to remedy these difficulties and elicit useful information are: lie detection (by traditional polygraph and the voice stress analyzer), hypnosis, nonverbal communication signals, and the behavioral analysis interview (see Chapter 6). To be effective, the results obtained from any of these methods should be followed up and buttressed by independent evidence.

Soliciting information by using the media should not be overlooked. Theodore John "Ted" Kaczynski, the Unabomber, was apprehended because his brother recognized the "manifesto" he wrote, which was publicized by the FBI in *The New York Times*.

Lie Detection by Polygraph

The polygraph or lie detector is a mechanical device designed to ascertain whether a subject is telling the truth (Figure 4.2). It records any changes in blood pressure and pulse, breathing rate, and the electrical conductance of the skin, known as GSR (galvanic skin response). For control purposes, neutral questions like "What is your name?" are interspersed with critical questions such as "Did you kill Mary Smith?" The instrument is based on the idea that ordinarily a person is under stress when telling a lie; therefore physiological responses to psychological stimuli (the questions) are produced that can be detected and measured. They may be interpreted to mean that the subject is telling the truth, that he or she is lying, or the result may be inconclusive.

The polygraph's principal contribution to criminal investigation is that it frequently leads to a confession. It is not uncommon for confessions to be obtained from suspects when it is suggested that they take a lie detector test. At other times, people will steadfastly deny involvement until just before the test is to be administered. Confessions also occur during testing, but more often take place afterward when the visible results (a series of graphs) are shown and discussed with the suspect. Most important, the test may protect the innocent person who asserts having no knowledge of the crime under investigation.

Polygraph admissibility is an ongoing controversy in the United States. Currently results of polygraph tests are not allowed as the sole establisher of an individual's guilt or innocence. However, polygraphs are admissible in some jurisdictions to provide background on confessions and when the defendant volunteered such examination. There are several leading cases that address the concerns of polygraph admissibility in the courts.[4]

In *Frye v. United States* (1923), the Court established that for scientific evidence to be admitted into court, it "must be sufficiently established to have gained general acceptance in the particular field in which it belongs." Although the scientific evidence used in *Frye* dealt with the polygraph, this became the landmark case for most courts and jurisdictions for all scientific evidence and became known as the "*Frye* standard."[5] However, in *Daubert v. Merrell Dow Pharmaceuticals, Inc.* (1993), the *Frye* standard was abandoned in favor of the holding that an "expert's testimony both rests on a

Figure 4.2
A police officer assigned to criminal investigations with the Harrisonburg Police Department studies the readouts on a computer monitor during a demonstration test with the Lafayette LX 4000 polygraph.

reliable foundation and is relevant to the task at hand." This two-pronged standard requires the trial judge to determine if scientific evidence is both relevant to the case and reliable. Daubert quickly became the new standard, and many courts continue to adopt it.[6]

In *United States v. Scheffer*, which involved a defendant's right to present polygraph evidence in military courts, the defendant appealed his denial on the basis that the military's *per se* rule excluding polygraph evidence violated his Fifth and Sixth Amendment rights to present a defense. The Supreme Court held that the *per se* rule was not in violation of his rights because there are validity issues within the field on polygraphs: "Although the degree of reliability of polygraph evidence may depend upon a variety of identifiable factors, there is simply no way to know in a particular case whether a polygraph examiner's conclusion is accurate, because certain doubts and uncertainties plague even the best polygraph exams."[7]

There are three general standards for polygraph admissibility in most state and federal courts. The first standard, *per se* exclusion, does not allow polygraph tests in the court for any reason. Courts that use this standard usually rely on the *Frye* standard or another precedent that questions polygraph reliability. The second standard allows polygraphs to be admitted into evidence, but with stipulation of the parties involved. These courts rely on court precedent and statute for standard, although it has been argued that stipulation does not address or resolve reliability concerns. The last type of polygraph admissibility standard is based on discretionary admission. This standard does not require stipulation and is used in only several jurisdictions. New Mexico has the most liberal use of this standard, and admits polygraph evidence if the following criteria are met: (1) the operator is qualified, (2) the testing procedures were reliable, and (3) the test of the particular subject was valid.[8] Until issues of reliability and validity are resolved, the controversy surrounding polygraph testing will continue.

> In 2003, at the request of the Department of Energy, a Committee to Review the Scientific Evidence on the Polygraph submitted its report, which states that the usefulness of polygraph test results depends on the context of the test and the consequences that follow its use. Validity is not something that courts can assess in a vacuum. The wisdom of applying any science depends on both the test itself and the application contemplated.[9]
>
> Polygraph examinations may have utility to the extent that they can elicit admissions and confessions, deter undesired activity, and instill public confidence. However, such utility is separate from polygraph validity. There is substantial anecdotal evidence that admissions and confessions occur in polygraph examinations, but no direct scientific evidence assessing the utility of the polygraph.[10]

A secondary, though far less frequent, contribution of a polygraph test is the emergence of follow-up leads; the whereabouts of stolen property, a weapon, or a person may be determined from the reactions to direct questions about them. In addition, any inconsistencies in prior statements and explanations given to police by the suspect can be verified or challenged. Statements likely to be untruthful must be followed up by checking them against the facts as determined from the physical evidence.

When there are numerous suspects in a case, the polygraph is occasionally employed to separate the unlikely ones; however, some polygraphers regard this as a misuse. Most often, the polygraph is employed in an investigation that is already developed to a point at which its test results may resolve an issue or produce further leads. In either situation, the investigator must furnish the polygraph examiner with investigative information to permit the construction of fruitful questions. Despite the claims for lie detection, it should be noted that its acceptance as an investigative tool is not universal. About 10 countries accept it; Britain's Scotland Yard does not.

Lie Detection by Voice Stress Analysis

Several names have been given to instruments designed in the early 1970s to detect voice changes in people who are upset or under stress. Among the so-called voice polygraphs are the Psychological Stress Evaluator (PSE), the Mark II Voice Analyzer, the Hagoth voice stress analyzer, and the Computerized Voice Stress Analyzer (CVSA). In certain circumstances, it is possible to use *voice stress analysis* even when an individual is unwilling to take the voice polygraph test, because attachments to the body need not be made as with the traditional polygraph. The value of voice stress analysis for the investigator is claimed by proponents to equal that of the traditional polygraph, but criticism of its scientific basis has developed.

The findings suggest that when a speaker is under stress, his or her voice characteristics change. Changes in pitch, glottal source factors, duration, intensity, and spectral structure from the vocal tract are all influenced in different ways by the presence of speaker stress. Results also suggest that the features upon which commercial voice stress analyzers are based can at times reflect changes in the speech production system that occur when a speaker is under stress. However, as is the case with speaker control of pitch, a variety of factors could influence the presence or absence of the microtremors that are claimed to exist in our muscle control during speech production. It is clearly unlikely that a single measure, such as that based on the CVSA, could be universally successful in assessing stress (such as that which might be experienced during the act of deception). However, it is not inconceivable that under extreme levels of stress, the muscle control of the speaker will be affected, including muscles associated with speech production. The level and degree to which this change in muscle control imparts less or more fluctuations in the speech signal cannot be conclusively determined, because even if these tremors exist, their influence will most certainly be speaker-dependent.[11] Before widespread support and acceptance can be achieved, additional objective testing and investigative usage is necessary.

A comparison of the Computer Voice Stress Analyzer (CVSA) with traditional polygraphy reveals several interesting facts:

1. Both the polygraph and CVSA are in use today.
2. Either machine may be effective in measuring exactly what it was designed to measure.
3. The operation of either device is an "art": it depends on skill, technique, and experience.
4. For legal and ethical reasons, permission (granted by the subject) is required before any test is run on either instrument.[12]

Many traditional polygraphers are critical of CVSA. There is a dearth of "scientifically valid, objective research," and a reliance on only one input (i.e., "microtremors" in the human voice). The polygraph, they point out, can measure several physiological inputs: blood pressure and pulse, breathing rate, and GSR. All the same, CVSA is popular in many law enforcement agencies at the local, state, and federal levels as well as with the U.S. military. Apparently it has flourished because it seems to work "especially in child molester and rape cases ... (with) a high confession rate."[13]

Unlike the polygraph, which must be physically connected to the subject, CVSA merely tape-records the questioning session. This can be done at the subject's home, detention facility, or hospital room. The advantages of portability and flexibility are important considerations in an investigation. Advances in technology have allowed CVSA to be used alongside computer analysis to immediately evaluate a subject's speech.[14]

A 1996 Department of Defense Polygraph Institute study of the CVSA found that the device performs no better than chance in detecting deception. In other words, guessing or flipping a coin would be as accurate as the test. Based on this study, the Department of Defense, the Central Intelligence Agency, and the Federal Bureau of Investigation do not use voice stress tests.[15]

Hypnosis

Hypnosis is a method of eliciting information from victims and witnesses (and sometimes suspects) who are willing to be put into a sleep-like state in which they respond to questions about an event they have observed. Under hypnosis, such details as license plate numbers, the make or color of a car, the race of an offender, parts of conversations (including places and names incidentally referred to therein), and other details of the crime may be recalled. Facial characteristics for the police artist also may be provided under hypnosis, even though not recalled when the victim or witness is questioned under normal conditions. In traumatic, emotionally charged events like murder, rape, or kidnapping, repression of the conscious memory may be undone in the hypnotic state, and information obtained that was not forthcoming during a normal interview.

There are, of course, fundamental legal questions concerning the use of hypnosis. For example, are the results of having a witness's memory refreshed by hypnosis admissible as evidence in court? This was addressed by a Michigan appellate court and the Arizona Supreme Court.[16] A basic point at issue was whether the witness's testimony was a true recollection of the event, or one implanted unwittingly or deliberately by the hypnotist. Stated another way: could such testimony be "tainted" as the court declared, and therefore, constitute inadmissible evidence?

Until 1980, courts held that hypnosis did not render the testimony tainted or the witness incompetent. The shift in judicial attitude, first manifested in 1980, is best illustrated by quoting from two decisions:

> Although we perceive that hypnosis is a useful tool in the investigative stage, we do not feel the state of the science (or art) has been shown to be such as to admit testimony which may have been developed as a result of hypnosis. A witness who has been under hypnosis, as in the case here, should not be allowed to testify when there is a question that the testimony may have been produced by that hypnosis.[17]

The second decision states:

> The determination of the guilt or innocence of an accused should not depend on the unknown consequences of a procedure concededly used for the purpose of changing in some way a

witness' memory. Therefore, until hypnosis gains general acceptance in the fields of medicine and psychiatry as a method by which memories are accurately improved without undue
danger of distortion, delusion, or fantasy, we feel that testimony of witnesses which has been
tainted by hypnosis should be excluded in criminal cases.[18]

Another legal question raised is whether hypnosis can be used to determine the state of mind of a
defendant before or during the commission of a crime.[19] Although such a determination is important
to prosecutors when trying a case, using hypnosis for this purpose provokes yet another issue: Is the
defendant denied a basic right to confront and cross-examine a hostile witness who was previously
hypnotized? Effective cross-examination is prevented when there is no recollection of questions asked,
answers given, or even the subject matter. Thus, the details elicited under hypnosis cannot be probed
under cross-examination because the witness is technically unaware of them.[20]

There are several tests employed by different jurisdictions regarding the admissibility of hypnotically refreshed testimony of witnesses. The landmark case for these standards is *State v. Hurd*,
in which six rules were enacted:

1. The hypnotic session should be conducted by a licensed psychiatrist or psychologist trained
   in the use of hypnosis.

2. The qualified professional conducting the hypnotic session should be independent of and not
   responsible to the prosecutor, investigator, or the defense.

3. Any information given to the hypnotist by law enforcement personnel prior to the hypnotic
   session must be in written form so that subsequently the extent of the information the subject
   received from the hypnotist may be determined.

4. Before induction of hypnosis, the hypnotist should obtain from the subject a detailed description of the facts as the subject remembers them, carefully avoiding adding any new elements
   to the witness' description of the events.

5. All contacts between the hypnotist and the subject should be recorded so that a permanent
   record is available for comparison and study to establish that the witness has not received
   information or suggestion which might later be reported as having been first described by
   the subject during hypnosis. Videotape should be employed if possible, but should not be
   mandatory.

6. Only the hypnotist and the subject should be present during any phase of the hypnotic session,
   including the pre-hypnotic testing and posthypnotic interview.[21]

A little later, in *Zani v. State*,[22] the court allowed hypnosis if it neither rendered witnesses'
posthypnotic memory untrustworthy nor substantially impaired the ability of the opponent to test
witnesses' recall by cross-examination. The standard examines the totality of circumstances.

One of the most significant cases regarding hypnotically refreshed witness testimony is *Rock
v. Arkansas* (1987), in which the Supreme Court overturned Arkansas' inadmissible *per se* rule. The
defendant was charged with shooting and killing her husband after an argument. The argument
escalated into a physical altercation and the husband was shot to death. After the defendant underwent
two sessions of hypnosis, she recalled additional details of the event, which expert witnesses corroborated. She stated that during the altercation, she grabbed a gun and when she pointed it at her
husband her finger was not on the trigger; he hit her arm to release the firearm and the gun misfired,
hitting and killing him. Expert witnesses testified that the gun was broken and prone to misfiring
when hit or dropped. The court denied any statements or details after her hypnosis session, following

the state's inadmissible *per se* rule regarding hypnotically refreshed witness testimony. The Supreme Court in *Rock v. Arkansas* reversed this decision, stating that:

> The more traditional means of assessing accuracy of testimony also remain applicable in the case of a previously hypnotized defendant. Certain information recalled as a result of hypnosis may be verified as highly accurate by corroborating evidence. Cross-examination, even in the face of a confident defendant, is an effective tool for revealing inconsistencies. Moreover, a jury can be educated to the risks of hypnosis through expert testimony and cautionary instructions. Indeed, it is probably to a defendant's advantage to establish carefully the extent of his memory prior to hypnosis, in order to minimize the decrease in credibility the procedure might introduce. We are not now prepared to endorse without qualifications the use of hypnosis as an investigative tool; scientific understanding of the phenomenon and of the means to control the effects of hypnosis is still in its infancy. Arkansas, however, has not justified the exclusion of all of a defendant's testimony that the defendant is unable to prove to be the product of prehypnosis memory."[23]

Additional cases having an impact on the admissibility of hypnosis results in courts include *Mancuso v. Olivarez* (2002), *People v. Sutton* (2004), *State v. Broadway* (1999), *Nolan v. State* (2006), and *State v. Medrano* (2004).[24]

Nonverbal Communication

Communication between people is not limited to the spoken or written word. Thoughts and feelings not stated openly may be expressed unconsciously through nonverbal behavior. Nonverbal methods may also be employed to change another person's unfavorable opinion to a favorable one. Generally, people use both verbal and nonverbal methods simultaneously.

> Nonverbal communication tends to be nonrational in that the response is direct and immediate, circumventing the conscious deliberative process. Nonverbal messages tend to follow a stimulus-response pattern without any intervening conscious decision-making process we call thinking. For these reasons nonverbal communication is less conscious than verbal, but it may be the more powerful force in face-to-face interaction. ...[25]

There are many modes of nonverbal communication, including kinesics, paralinguistics, and proxemics. *Kinesics*, the study of the use of body movement and posture to convey meaning, is most important for the investigator. Serving to a lesser extent is *paralinguistics*, the study of the variations in the quality of the voice (its pitch or intonation, its loudness or softness) and the effect of these variations on the meaning conveyed. *Proxemics* pertains to the physical distance individuals put between themselves and others, as well as to the space a person occupies (in particular, the placement and use of the limbs). Nonverbal signals are referred to as "leakage" by psychologists who study the phenomenon.

Nonverbal Communications

Kinesics—Eye, hand, fast movements, facial expression, body posture
Paralinguistics—voice intonation, changes in verbal expressions
Proxemics—Posture and body movements

Kinesics

Eye, hand, leg, and foot movement; facial expression; and body posture provide valuable cues to the investigator. In the practical application of kinesics, most people focus on the eyes and face for indications that a verbal statement is or is not in accord with the speaker's innermost thoughts and feelings. It also may be evidenced by constant crossing and recrossing of the legs, foot tapping, or finger drumming—all of which belie verbal denials of culpability or involvement.

Paralinguistics

It is possible to give a resounding "no" that, by its loudness, means "no" emphatically; or, through varying the pitch in the voice, to intone a "no" that means "maybe." Through intonation, "no" can also either ask a question or express disbelief. Similar paralinguistic clues may be communicated during an interview or interrogation by replies spoken in a low voice when the previous volume was normal, or (toward the end of the session) by those spoken in a dispirited tone. These cues may signal that the person is about to "break" and make a confession.

Proxemics

An individual at ease may sit with legs apart and arms at the sides. However, if questioning becomes unnerving, the subject may shift to a protective posture by crossing the legs and folding the arms across the chest. Another proxemic clue is made manifest by any movement or action taken by the subject to increase the distance between him or her and the questioner.

The Value of Nonverbal Signals

In order to obtain the most benefit from nonverbal leakage, a base line needs to be established for the nonverbal clues normally employed by the subject. This is best done by first engaging in non-threatening conversation and looking for signs (or lack thereof) of the nonverbal clues basic to the individual's makeup. Later, when the stress of official questioning (especially that of interrogation) is felt by the subject, any new nonverbal clue or sign of increase in frequency or intensity is meaningful. The subject should be in plain view, not seated in front of a desk or allowed to have a throw pillow or other object on the lap that masks the hands.

During an interview (and particularly during an interrogation), the detective must be alert to the nonverbal clues suspects may emit. Indeed, when offenders are interrogated, they will subtly try (initially at least) to induce a belief in their innocence. Through eye contact they may attempt to demonstrate sincerity; through other body and facial expressions they may show concern for the victim or surprise and shock at a question that implies involvement. By means of such role-playing, they hope to convince the investigator that the police are on the wrong track. In so doing, the guilty person must resort to lying. When contradictions are exposed by other evidence and pointed out, the symptoms of lying conveyed through body language can sometimes be observed.

At the appropriate point, the detective is at liberty to employ nonverbal behavior consciously to communicate with the suspect. Facial expressions (raised eyebrow, beady stare, smirk) or other body movements (hand gestures, head shaking, rolling of the eyes) will convey disbelief in the explanation that a suspect is providing.

In addition to serving as a kind of lie detector, nonverbal signals can provide follow-up clues. In summary, nonverbal signals may serve to expose a deception, eliminate fruitless effort, or suggest possible leads for further investigation.

CONCLUSION

People are at the core of any criminal investigation, and the successful investigator will continue to improve upon his or her verbal and cognitive skills. This involves much more than experience, for the amount of research on the psychology of individuals and groups is increasing dramatically. Of particular importance is the investigator's personal understanding of his or her own biases, traits, and nonverbal clues, all of which come into play in working with people from all walks of life. Part B and the following chapters address the use of records, interviewing, the use of informants, surveillance, and interrogation in much more detail.

NOTES

[1] R.F. Turner, "Hans Gross: The Model of the Detective," in *Pioneers in Policing*, edited by P.J. Stead. (Montclair, NJ: Patterson Smith, 1977), 148–158.

[2] R.L. Ault and J.T. Reese. "Profiling: A Psychological Assessment of Crime," *FBI Law Enforcement Bulletin*, 49:3 (March 1980), 22–25.

[3] *United States v. Jones*, 565 US ___, 132 S.Ct. 945 (2012).

[4] For a more detailed discussion on court precedents on polygraph admissibility, refer to Paul C. Giannelli, "Forensic Science: Polygraph Evidence: Part II," *Criminal Law Bulletin*, 30 (1994), 366.

[5] *Frye v. United States*, 293 F. 1013 (App. D.C. 1923).

[6] *Daubert v. Merrell Dow Pharmaceuticals, Inc.*, 509 U.S. 579 (1993).

[7] *United States v. Scheffer,* 523 U.S. 303 (1998).

[8] *State v. Dorsey*, 88 N.M. 184 (1975).

[9] Committee to Review the Scientific Evidence on the Polygraph. *The Polygraph and Lie Detection* (Washington, DC: The National Academies Press, 2003), 204.

[10] Ibid., 214.

[11] Ibid., 71.

[12] A.W. Whitworth. "Polygraph or CVSA: What's the Truth About Deception Analysis?" *Law and Order*, 41:11, 29–31 (Nov. 1993), 30.

[13] Ibid., 31.

[14] Ibid.

[15] Margie Wylie. "Police Use of Voice Stress Analysis Generates Controversy." Newhouse News Service, 2001. See: http://www.polygraph.com.au/pdf/police_use_of_voice_stress_analysis _generates_ controversy.pdf

[16] *People v. Tait*, 297 N.W.2d 853 (Mich. App. 1980); *State v. Mena*, 624P.2d 1274 (Arizona 1980).

[17] *State v. La Mountain*, 611 P.2d 551 (Arizona 1980).

[18] *State v. Mena*, supra note 15.

[19] M. Reiser, "Hypnosis and Its Uses in Law Enforcement," *Police Journal* (Brit.), 51 (1978), 24–33.

[20]   B.L. Diamond, "Inherent Problems in the Use of Pretrial Hypnosis on a Prospective Witness," *California Law Review*, 68 (1980), 313.

[21]   *State v. Hurd*, 86 N.J. 525 (1981); *Moore v. Morton*, 255 F.3d 95 (2001); *State v. Moore*, 188 N.J. 182 (2006).

[22]   *Zani v. State*, 758 S.W.2d 333 (Tex. Cr. App. 1988).

[23]   *Rock v. Arkansas*, 483 U.S. 44 (1987), 4.

[24]   *Mancuso v. Olivarez*, 282 F.3d 728 (9th Cir. 2002); *People v. Sutton*, 349 Ill. App.3d 608 (1st Dist. 2004); *State v. Broadway*, 753 So.2d 801 (La. 1999); *Nolan v. State*, 132 P.3d. 564 (Nev. 2006); and *State v. Medrano*, 127 S.W.3d 781 (Tex. Crim. App. 2004).

[25]   Raymond L. Gorden, *Interviewing: Strategy, Techniques and Tactics*, 4th ed. (Chicago: Dorsey Press, 1987).

IMPORTANT CASES

Daubert v. Merrell Dow Pharmaceuticals, Inc. (1993)
Frye v. United States (1923)
Mancuso v. Olivarez (2002)
Moore v. Morton (2001)
Nolan v. State (2006)
People v. Sutton (2004)
People v. Tait (1980)
Rock v. Arkansas (1987)
State v. Broadway (1999)
State v. Dorsey (1978)
State v. Hurd (1981)
State v. Medrano (2004)
State v. Moore (2006)
State v. Mountain (1980)
United States v. Jones (2012)
United States v. Scheffer (1998)
Zani v. State (1987)

DISCUSSION QUESTIONS

1.   What is meant by *modus operandi*?

2.   What is meant by psychological profiling?

3.   In addition to a visual description of the perpetrator, victims and witnesses may provide other information based upon what senses?

4.   What are the primary objectives of surveillance?

5.   What is a "lineup," and how is it used?

6.   What is a polygraph, and how is it used in investigations?

7.   How is hypnosis used in investigations?

8.   What is meant by nonverbal communication? What are kinesics, proxemics, and paralinguistics?

SUPPLEMENTAL READINGS

Alison, L. (2011). *The forensic psychologist's casebook: Psychological profiling and criminal investigation.* Portland, OR: Willan.

Anon. Offender profiles: A multidisciplinary approach. *FBI Law Enforcement Bulletin, 49*(9), 16–20.

Ekman, P., & Friesen, M. V. (1969). Leakage and clues to deception. *Psychiatry, 32,* 88–106.

Faigin, G. (2008). *The artist's complete guide to facial expression.* New York: Watson-Guptill.

Federal Bureau of Investigation. *FBI handbook of crime scene forensics.* New York: Skyhorse.

Gibson, L. (2008). *Forensic art essentials: A manual for law enforcement artists.* New York: Elsevier.

Granhag, P. A., & Strömwall, L. A. (2004). *The detection of deception in forensic contexts.* New York: Cambridge University Press.

Hess, J. E. (2010). *Interviewing and interrogation for law enforcement* (2nd ed.). New Providence, NJ: LexisNexis Matthew Bender.

Inbau, F. E. (1985). *Criminal investigation and confessions* (3rd ed.). Baltimore: Williams & Wilkins.

Macdonald, J. M., & Michaud, D. L. (1992). rev. & enl. ed.. *Criminal interrogation.* Denver: Apache Press.

Morris, D. (1994). *Bodytalk: A world guide to human gestures.* London: Cape.

Nizer, L. (1979). *How to tell a liar: Reflections without mirrors.* New York: Berkley.

Rabon, D. (2005). *Interviewing and interrogation.* Durham, NC: Carolina Academic Press.

Reid, J. E., & Inbau, F. E. (1977). *Truth and deception: The polygraph (Lie Detector) technique* (2nd ed.). Baltimore: Williams & Williams.

Turvey, B. E. (2011). *Criminal profiling: An introduction to behavioral evidence analysis* (4th ed.). Burlington, MA: Academic Press.

Walters, S. B. (2003). *Principles of kinesic interview and interrogation* (2nd ed.). Boca Raton, FL: CRC Press.

Zulawski, D. E., & Wicklander, D. E. (Eds.). (2001). *Practical aspects of interview and interrogation* (2nd ed.). Boca Raton, FL: CRC Press.

Part B

SEEKING AND OBTAINING INFORMATION: PEOPLE AND RECORDS

The acquisition of facts requires specialized procedures. Doctors, mechanics, detectives—all have methods for obtaining the information necessary to deal with the particular issue confronting them, and have innumerable technical and scientific instruments at their disposal. Although relatively few diagnostic tools address the needs of criminal investigators, change is bringing new technology, and there is no doubt that the future will bring new tools to the investigative function. However, change within the law enforcement environment frequently follows change in the private sector, as well as among criminal elements. Today's sophisticated criminals are well versed in the use of technology, and investigators must be resourceful, and call on diverse, special capabilities—wider in range and more difficult to apply. In short, though detective work is not easy, the task is greatly assisted by the ability to interview people, cultivate and deal with informants, and learn to adapt in a changing world. Nowhere is this more important than in the ability to collect and analyze records and information, and draw upon interpersonal skills to interview and interrogate.

Part B covers some of the methods detectives employ to elicit facts from people and gather information from records.

CHAPTER 5

RECORDS AND FILES

Investigative Uses and Sources

RECORDS AS INVESTIGATIVE AIDS

From the day of birth, and actually one might argue from the day of conception, a person, at least in most developed societies, becomes part of an ongoing system of records that usually begins with a birth certificate. In most instances, an individual begins to develop a collection of records, both official and unofficial, ranging from medical history; education records; driver's license; insurance; purchases (large and small); travel; and now Internet connections such as blogs, web sites, and social networking entities like Facebook, LinkedIn, and so on. Indeed, in today's technology-oriented society, most people can only begin to speculate just how much information about them is available through various types of records systems.

Recorded in one way or another, the trail of information is generally chronological, marked from earliest school days by intelligence and psychological test scores, teacher evaluations, and grades. It can be followed into adult life where business and personal dealings leave their own distinctive traces. Hence, just as school records can be used to locate a family, so can credit card purchases of goods and services account for a buyer's whereabouts and interests. And, because the stages of life from birth to death are for the most part duly noted by government and business, the patterns of human activity can be reconstructed through diligent, informed effort. The investigator, however, must have a reason to devote time and effort on the search for information. Generally, a criminal investigation is driven by the seriousness of a crime and its impact on the community, but it may be influenced by media or other pressures on the police to find a solution.

A mass of assorted material is on record for any one individual, and the investigator must have some appreciation of the existence and possible origins of what is sought. The wide variety of sources includes the records of: ownership of personal property (e.g., automobile, handgun, house); required licenses (e.g., driver, marriage, professional); business transactions (e.g., purchase or sale of property); utility services received (e.g., gas, electric, telephone); transportation (airline, car rental); and social networking (e.g., Facebook, LinkedIn). The following possibilities represent an overview of the kind of information that can be sought and uncovered through the study of records.

- Link a person to an object (such as a gun) through purchase or ownership

- Link one person to another (relatives through a marriage license, friends through social networking sites or telephone calls, or membership in an organization)

- Link a person to a location

- Trace a person's activities at particular times

- Discover information about an individual's lifestyle, personal behavior, or spending patterns or habits

> ### BOX 5.1 THE USE OF RECORDS
>
> - Follow up or provide additional leads
> - Identify the perpetrator
> - Trace and locate a suspect, criminal, or witness
> - Recover stolen or lost property
> - Ascertain facts about physical evidence—its source or ownership, for example
> - Identify friends and associates
> - Provide data for relational databases

Follow Up or Provide New Leads

Credit card and fraudulent check files are sources of stored information that can serve the purposes of law enforcement. License plate registration files for motor vehicles could be made more conducive to investigative purposes if application forms were to ask for vehicle color. Feasibly, the records of one agency of government (for example, the motor vehicle bureau) could at no additional cost be designed with another's needs (the police) in mind. Even such a modest innovation would require bureaucratic imagination and cooperation.

The pawnbroker file is a good example of how new leads may be supplied. In addition to the handwriting specimen provided by the required signature on the pawn slip, a personal description or photo of the individual who pledged the stolen goods is sometimes obtained. Occasionally, the alert pawnbroker makes a judgment call about the behavior of a customer or, recognizing that the articles were probably stolen, detains the customer on some pretext in order to telephone the local police.

The many directories compiled by Internet and telephone companies for public and intracompany use are especially helpful for follow-up purposes. They can be used to corroborate and augment incomplete information obtained verbally from people contacted during an investigation.

Identify the Perpetrator

The fingerprint record file, the criminal photograph file (sometimes called the "mug shot" file or "Rogues Gallery"), and the *modus operandi* (MO) file are all useful for identification purposes. Often housed in the same place, they supplement each other. Fingerprint files located in the Automated Fingerprint Identification System (AFIS) have revolutionized the ability to identify criminals on the basis of single-digit fingerprints. DNA files of individuals arrested and convicted for serious crimes also represent a major breakthrough in helping to identify suspects involved in past or future crimes. The FBI maintains a DNA file that includes records on serious offenders from all 50 states.

Biometrics, such as hand-held devices that can be used to digitally scan fingerprints and match the results against large databases, are being used by the military and being tested by law enforcement agencies nationwide. Such devices create digital images of fingerprints and wirelessly transfer them to a server, which is typically at an agency's headquarters, and then on to law enforcement agencies

Figure 5.1
A fingerprint, taken during a demonstration, is seen on the back of a wireless device called an IBIS (Integrated Biometric Identification System). The device can record a fingerprint in the field, and then have the fingerprint sent via a wireless connection to be checked against a database.

where algorithms match prints against records in databases. If there is a match, demographic information about the person is transferred back to the device's screen (see Figure 5.1). Retina scanners are also being used by the military for identification purposes, and are likely to be adaptable for law enforcement in the future. Portable DNA units are being tested and likely to be on the market in the near future.

Trace and Locate a Suspect, Criminal, or Witness

When the identity of a suspect, criminal, or witness is known, but he or she is absent from the usual places of abode, work, and recreation, the investigator is faced with the problem of tracing and locating that person. The investigative effort should be based on the knowledge that most people are to some extent gregarious and will tend to seek out familiar people and places. It is possible, for instance, to locate a particular individual through his or her child by arranging to be alerted to the transfer of any school records in the areas most frequented by that person. Placing relatives and friends of the fugitive under surveillance is another means to the same end. Because people generally require some continuity in their everyday business pursuits, the records of banks and public utilities are also quite useful.

Recover Stolen or Lost Property

The major problem in recovering stolen or lost property is making certain that the complainant's description of the property corresponds closely with the description recorded when it is located by police, either directly or through a pawn shop. This problem is readily solved by using carefully structured forms for pawnbrokers and secondhand dealers. Computers are also useful because their massive memory banks, and the application of "cloud computing" (resources delivered as a service over a network) facilitates the operation of comparative data banks over much wider geographical areas than was heretofore possible. When law enforcement computer systems are linked, a criminal crossing a state line or traveling hundreds of miles to pawn stolen articles can no longer avoid detection.

Ascertain Information Concerning Physical Evidence

Two distinctly different kinds of information are sought when physical evidence is discovered at a crime scene. The first has to do with tracing ownership of evidence like guns, poisons, and explosives.

Ownership can often be ascertained, as most states require records of such transactions. The rifle used to assassinate President Kennedy was traced to Lee Harvey Oswald through government records on the distribution and sale of firearms.

The second kind of information concerns the recognition and identification of physical evidence: what it is, what it is used for, and where it is manufactured and distributed. For example, trace evidence such as paint scrapings from an automobile may be used to identify the make and year of the vehicle, providing linking evidence to a vehicle used in the commission of a hit-and-run or other crime.

TYPES AND SOURCES OF RECORDED INFORMATION

Because the extent and scope of stored information is extraordinarily large, it is useful to generate a classification scheme. This will help the detective reach a record source quickly, follow up on a clue that came from an unexpected source, or develop a new clue. The following taxonomy ranks recorded information in proportion to its potential usefulness and availability:

- Law enforcement records
- Records of other governmental agencies
- Records of business organizations
  - Credit card records
  - Data bases such as Google and Wikipedia
  - Newspaper and magazine files
- Miscellaneous sources

Figure 5.2
Mike Fain is the Director of Collections for the Institute of Violent Groups, which maintains more than five million records on terrorist groups, including photos of individuals. This type of file is used by many police departments to link criminals to crimes.

Law Enforcement Records

The major sources of recorded information are the files maintained by government and business organizations. Within government, the agencies contacted most are those concerned with criminal justice. They, as well as some others not part of the criminal justice system, willingly provide information to the investigator. The remaining bureaucratic agencies, however, may not be very cooperative. The investigator will find them similar to business firms that do not necessarily make it an easy matter to extract information from their files. As a rule, problems arise when a detective does not, as a matter of right, have direct access to what is sought. That being so, the file keeper's cooperation must be secured. This chapter describes sources of information as well as methods that facilitate the acquisition of recorded information and make its investigative value more timely.

The files that yield the greatest amount of information and offer immediate access to the investigator are clearly those maintained for law enforcement.

Police files are often set up according to:

1. Type of offense
2. Name(s) of offender(s)
3. Name(s) of victim(s)
4. Location—where crime was committed
5. Date and time of occurrence
6. Relevant facts pertaining to the case
7. Disposition of case

This system may be adequate for many departments, but once set up, lethargy and lean budgets often prevent periodic updating. To be relevant, files must be culled regularly, and after some time, purged. Outdated records clearly do not meet the investigator's needs, as community crime patterns shift to reflect social and economic change. Two developments that have enhanced the investigative value of law enforcement records are the application of information science concepts to the storage and retrieval of information, and the more sophisticated use of records in crime pattern analysis. Police records can include:

*   DNA files
*   Fingerprint files
*   Arrest and conviction (rap sheet)
*   *Modus operandi*
*   Mug shot files ("Rogues Gallery")
*   "Stop and wanted" fugitives
*   Lost and stolen property
*   Pawnbrokers and secondhand dealers
*   Known habitual criminals
*   Receivers of stolen goods
*   Nicknames or aliases
*   Laundry and dry cleaner marks
*   Fraudulent checks and credit cards
*   Field contact reports

Penal records can include the following:

*   Regarding an inmate:
    Names of visitors
    Names of cellmates
    Names of other friends
    Places and periods of incarceration

Telephone and written communications
Probation and parole records

- Regarding the released offender:

Names of friends
Names of references for employment
Names of employers
Place(s) of residence
Name(s) of person(s) supervising release

Information Science

Today, almost all departments have some form of automated data processing; it is hard to imagine even the smallest departments without at least some kind of computer capability. With a computerized system, the magnitude of information collected and filed by police every day is accessible; their daily field contact reports can receive instantaneous cross-checks for correlations with crimes already in the computer. The following situation involving an unfamiliar car parked in a neighborhood illustrates how stored information can be utilized. An inhabitant of the neighborhood noting its presence there may call the police. Later, if a crime is reported and that person learns of it, he or she may inform the authorities about previous suspicions. Sometimes a license plate number will be supplied with such calls; more often only the color, make, or type (e.g., van, hatchback, SUV, four-door sedan) is observed. Then, if a patrol officer a few days later submits a report on a traffic infraction and the description of the vehicle involved—data readily accessed from the computer—even partly matches the report on the unfamiliar parked car, the investigator has a potential lead (the driver's or owner's name).

Data processing systems are not without problems. Difficulties arise when input depends on police officers filling out several page-long forms. Resenting the time required to complete them, many officers either fail to do so or are careless about verifying their facts. To cope with this problem, one large department altered its reporting format. They replaced the several separate forms for burglary, robbery, theft, sex offenses, and "miscellaneous" crimes with a single preliminary investigation form with a limited number of lines and boxes to be filled in, and ample space for a narrative report. Not only were department needs satisfied, so were the needs of its officers. In addition, the improvement made input more readily accessible from the computer. The use of drop-down menus, voice translation to print, and optical scanning systems can also aid in report preparation.

Crime Pattern Analysis

When a special unit is assigned to receive and analyze all available crime data, and to furnish or circulate the extracted information to operational units, the department is employing formal crime analysis. This is a good opportunity to apply information science to police operations, including criminal investigation. Most police departments engage in analysis to some degree.

Crime data are collected from internal and external sources. Internal sources include patrol, detective, communications, and special units; external sources include crime victims, the courts, correction agencies, and probation and parole departments. Other governmental agencies may contribute, as well as private organizations such as crime commissions and *ad hoc* groups.

The storage of data may be manual or electronic; its analysis will depend on the sophistication of personnel and equipment. Sophisticated software systems are changing the ways in which crime analysts can use relational data bases and analytics to provide real-time information for the investigator. Some of the possibilities include:

1. Pattern analysis.
2. Linking diagrams.
3. Temporal or time evaluations
4. Variable analysis.
5. Geospatial presentations.
6. Multi-dimensional images.
7. Crime and incident maps.
8. Individual relationships.

Modus Operandi

The identification of a suspect in a particular case is sometimes accomplished by examining how the crime was committed. Termed *modus operandi* (MO) by Llewelyn W. Atcherley in England, the concept was an early (1913) example of crime pattern analysis:

> ... if the methods of known criminals can be classified so that the *modus operandi* disclosed in a new crime can be compared with the methods disclosed in previous crimes, it may be possible to establish the identity of the person who commits the crime. This realization led to the formulation of the MO system which seeks to analyze according to a given formula the ingredients of a crime, and then, by systematic comparison with analyses of other crimes, to establish the identity of the criminal.[1]

The MO system meets with more success when some unusual mode of committing the offense is noted, or comparisons can be made of a large number of variables. For example, if a convicted child molester moves to a new neighborhood soon after being released and reverts to old habits, he or she may be recognized as a possible suspect if the geographical area covered is sufficiently large and the way the child is lured remains essentially the same. Such recognition would be an example of *linkage*—the production of a list of suspects based on MO. Linkage also occurs when a common offender is identified as the individual responsible for a series of crimes.

The ViCAP (Violent Criminal Apprehension Program) was set up by the FBI in 1985 to deal with serial murderers and other itinerant felons who commit violent crimes. In some respects it may be seen as an extension of the MO concept to the national level. The ViCAP program, which provides the necessary database software at no charge to state and local agencies, concentrates on cases involving several factors, including:

- solved or unsolved homicides or attempts, especially those that involve an abduction; are apparently random, motiveless, or sexually oriented; or are known or suspected to be part of a series;
- missing persons, where the circumstances indicate a strong possibility of foul play and the victim is still missing;

- unidentified dead bodies, where the manner of death is known or suspected to be homicide; and

- sexual assault cases

Information about cases involving the above criteria is inputted into a database and is checked against other cases involving similar patterns or MOs. ViCAP encourages coordination between agencies and allows participation between counties hundreds or thousands of miles apart.

The John Wayne Gacy case evidenced the crucial need for a procedure that would prevent a killer (in this case, of more than 30 adolescent boys within a three-year period) from falling between the cracks of the criminal justice system. When reporting the unexplained disappearances of their sons to police, some parents had voiced suspicions about Gacy. However, because each investigator had many other cases, and because the data system was unequal to the task, the offender–victim connection was not recognized. The suspect was ultimately apprehended by a department that followed up on the investigation. Had an area-wide computer system been operational, the missing persons thought to be victims of foul play would have been in its data bank, and the name of one suspect (recurring in several of the cases) would have emerged sooner. Some of the jurisdictions involved subsequently installed a computer with this capability.

Crime pattern analysis depends on the sophistication of equipment and personnel, but any system—manual or fully automated—ultimately relies on highly technical software and those who are properly trained to use the system. Curiosity, imagination, and a willingness to experiment and be objective when appraising results are vitally needed to raise performance above the mediocre-to-adequate level, which unfortunately is a hallmark. For crimes involving vehicles, the feature an eyewitness is most likely to observe is an automobile's color, yet, as noted earlier, many states fail to require automobile color on license plate applications. If accompanied by other information about the vehicle, this detail would reduce the number of suspected vehicles. In as much as the cost of acquiring and storing the data is negligible compared to the benefits to be derived in hit-and-run homicide investigations alone, it is hard to fathom why this obvious step has not been universally adopted. (See Chapters 11 and 12 for more detail on technological advances in criminal investigation.)

A research project on burglary and robbery in the New Haven and West Haven Police Departments focuses on further defining variables as a means of linking crimes and perpetrators. The project, supported by the College of Criminal Justice at the University of New Haven, goes a step further than traditional analytical techniques by using *modus operandi* and other pattern-based information in a relational database. Utilizing a sophisticated statistical and linking program, it has been possible to provide investigators with more detailed information on suspects and crime patterns.

Organization of a *Modus Operandi* File

To improve efficiency, many police departments have linked various files, such as the MO file, mug shot files (Rogues Gallery), parole and probation offenders, crime reports, and arrest data. The utility of the combined files rests to some degree upon the detective who interviews the complainant and eyewitnesses, and examines (or has a laboratory technician examine) the crime scene. Through these efforts it can be determined whether any feature, pattern, or trademark distinguishes the crime scene evidence or the behavior of the perpetrator. The advisability of assigning one specialist—or at most a few—to specific types of criminal activity has been demonstrated in larger departments, where teams or squads focus on subsets of property and violent crimes. Examples include homicide, robbery, burglary, sex crime, and cyber crime units.

Type of Crime: As stated previously, a logical starting point in building a classification scheme for MO would be by type of offense. With the exception of "professional" criminals who focus on large-scale activities, most street criminals, who tend to be younger, usually do not stick to one crime; they commit a variety of offenses, taking advantage of opportunities presented. Regardless of the type of crime, such criminals often employ the same or very similar MOs. For example, one offender ambushed his victims in apartment house hallways. If the victim was male, he would commit robbery; if female, he would stuff the washcloth he carried with him in her mouth, then rape and rob her. For taxonomy purposes, the distinctive features are apartment house hallways and the use of a washcloth. Robbery and rape are secondary variables for the purpose of MO.

Time, Day, and Location: The hour, the day (weekday, weekend, holiday), and the general area in which the crime was committed are other important aspects to be considered. Such information provides the basis on which a strategy for surveillance (including stakeouts and decoys) can be developed—or, should the criminal have been recognized from a broadcasted description, for putting a tail on the suspect. In addition, should an intended victim's suspicions have been aroused by a criminal's behavior and the incident is reported, police may be able to match that behavior to an MO in the file. With a description and name provided, patrol car officers or detectives in an unmarked car may spot the suspect "working" the neighborhood and subsequently catch him or her in the act.

Type of Property of Persons Targeted: The property and person(s) commonly attacked include: gasoline stations, taverns or package liquor stores, 24-hour convenience stores and restaurants, druggists and doctors, bank messengers, occupants of apartment buildings or private homes, and cab drivers. However, information on such attacks may be of transitory value in identifying the MO of someone just commencing a career in crime. The individual who starts by robbing a bar after first having a drink may then repeat this in another bar a half-hour later a mile or two away. The MO having become obvious, radio and patrol cars can be alerted to the perpetrator's description, type of car used, and possibly its license number; if this pattern continues, the robber might be caught committing or fleeing from a subsequent crime in another bar. With experience, however, the criminal may shift from bars to gasoline stations or liquor stores. Therefore, MO information based solely on type of target does not necessarily characterize the perpetrator for any considerable period of time.

What type of building was involved? Was it a loft, factory, condominium, single-family dwelling, or retail store? How was it entered? Did the burglar climb through a transom or exhaust fan opening, file through bars, cut through a roof, use a celluloid strip to slip the lock, or hide in a stairwell before closing time and then break in? These MOs are helpful in distinguishing burglars.

Sometimes the property damaged or taken, or the person attacked, will indicate motive. It is often possible to determine whether the crime was "fingered" (i.e., it was an "inside job" requiring private knowledge about the person or object of the crime). Experienced criminals hesitate to leave "scoring" to chance; they tend to seek assurances that any attempt will be worth their time, and not be a poor risk. The number of people privy to inside information being limited, this insight helps to channel investigative efforts.

Ruse Used by Perpetrator: Enterprising criminals may employ disguises that permit them to be in a locale without arousing suspicion. Accordingly, the following fairly common disguises warrant mention: house painter, telephone repair or store delivery worker, house-to-house sales representative, or police officer or detective. Many of these ruses (of dress and possibly equipment) can account for a criminal's presence in an area. Required "credentials" can be forged. Whatever the pattern, the stratagem for gaining entrance characterizes the offender. Recognizing it helps to reduce the number of potential suspects that must be pulled from the MO file.

Tale Used by Perpetrator: Closely related to the way perpetrators represent themselves is the tale they tell to gain entrance to—or account for their presence in—the area. To succeed, this recital must be consistent with the role they are playing; when used, it is another characteristic of MO.

Miscellaneous Idiosyncrasies: For reasons not fully understood, criminals will sometimes do something unusual, something not related to the crime particularly, and which—like a trademark—brands them. For example, one man intent on rape repeatedly selected a pedestrian who was out early and ran her down with his car, apparently by accident. Then, offering to rush her to the nearest hospital, he would proceed instead to a deserted place for the assault. Although the MO was soon recognized, he was able to commit several more rapes in the same fashion until enough information from the victims could be pieced together. The alarm sent out at that point had sufficient facts to enable a patrol officer or detective to identify the offender's car. Without this unusual MO, the connection between the rapes and vehicular accidents would not have been noted, nor would the assorted pieces of information from each victim have been assembled and directed toward apprehending one specific individual.

Peculiarities in MO are almost too numerous to mention. Examples include: the burglar who, in addition to the customary objects of the crime (e.g., money and jewelry), will always take food from the refrigerator; the robber who will offer the victim a cigarette; and the pyromaniac who will set two fires exactly six blocks apart on the first Friday of every month. Just as bizarre MOs can help to identify the criminal, so can unusual habits of dress: for instance, wearing a black beret in a neighborhood where such headgear is seldom seen. Again, before it is meaningful in a criminal investigation, odd behavior or dress must be observed, reported, and placed in the file.

Many departments today utilize field interview cards (FICs) or some version of a record of vehicle stops or interactions with the public. More recently this has been required in connection with the collection of racial profiling data. This information can also serve as a resource because, in most cases, the officer must explain why a stop was made, and also provide other types of information—such as time of day, registration number of vehicle, and names of those interviewed. This information can provide a valuable source of data for future reference if the data is recorded electronically.

Photographs

When a person is arrested for a serious crime, two photographs—one full face, one profile—should be taken in addition to a full-length photograph, mounted on a card or stored electronically, containing the MO, and filed according to a scheme developed to meet the needs of the particular department. To avoid viewer fatigue, the number of photographs shown to an eyewitness should be kept to a minimum. If the witness selects one that "resembles" the criminal, it is removed and returned covertly to the next group of photographs. If the eyewitness makes the same selection, greater reliance can be placed on the identification. This subject is covered in more detail in Chapter 9.

Geospatial Analysis

Geospatial analysis refers to the use of mapping technology to provide an array of information on the locations of specific events. In criminal investigation this approach can provide electronically developed maps that illustrate crimes by type, time of day, and relationship to other locations, such as roads or transit facilities, businesses, or drop-off points. For example, in the case of stolen vehicles, the location from which they were stolen and where they are recovered may prove important—especially

AP Photo/Alex Jones

Figure 5.3
An agent operates a computer displaying apprehensions in the Rio Grande Valley sector of Texas. Geographic Information Systems and other mapping programs can help law enforcement officials spot emerging trends in illegal activity.

in cases in which cars have been stripped and abandoned. A series of crimes close to highways or near rail stations may also provide information on the movement of perpetrators. When linked to addresses of suspects, the information can prove to be of immense value.

A *geographical information system* (GIS) is a system that captures, stores, analyzes, manages, and presents data that is linked to location (see Figure 5.3). Special reports and maps locating high criminal activity can be generated. Computer-generated maps can also provide investigators with an overall picture of the crimes that have occurred since they were last on duty. This facilitates the recognition of a pattern that may be attributable to a particular offender and the development of a strategy to apprehend the offender. Meanwhile, of course, the department's crime analysis unit will be looking for trends and crime patterns using data that cover a larger area than a local precinct or district.

The investigative value of geospatial analysis is only part of its usefulness in police work. Other benefits include managerial proactive resource allocation that can increase the productivity of a patrol officer at the beat (or "post") level and provide for a two-way exchange of information between the police department and community organizations.

Public and Private Organizations

Federal Government Agencies

There is a plethora of federal government agencies that can provide information helpful to investigations.

Department of Homeland Security. The mission of the Department of Homeland Security (DHS) is to lead the unified national effort to secure America. DHS will prevent and deter terrorist attacks and protect against and respond to threats and hazards to the nation. DHS will ensure safe and secure borders, welcome lawful immigrants and visitors, and promote the free flow of commerce.

Transportation Security Administration. The mission of the Transportation Security Administration (TSA) is to prevent terrorist attacks and to protect the U.S. transportation network.

Customs and Border Protection. Customs and Border Protection (CBP) safeguards the American homeland at and beyond our borders. CBP protects the American public against terrorists and the instruments of terror. They enforce the laws of the United States while fostering the nation's economic security through lawful international trade and travel.

Secret Service. The United States Secret Service is mandated by statute and executive order to carry out two significant missions: protection and criminal investigations. The Secret Service protects the President and Vice President, their families, heads of state, and other designated individuals; investigates threats against these protectees; protects the White House, Vice President's Residence, Foreign Missions, and other buildings within Washington, DC; and plans and implements security designs for designated National Special Security Events. The Secret Service also investigates violations of laws relating to counterfeiting of obligations and securities of the United States; financial crimes that include, but are not limited to, access device fraud, financial institution fraud, identity theft, computer fraud; and computer-based attacks on our nation's financial, banking, and telecommunications infrastructure.

Immigration and Customs Enforcement. The mission of Immigration and Customs Enforcement (ICE) is to protect America and uphold public safety. They fulfill this mission by identifying criminal activities and eliminating vulnerabilities that pose a threat to the nation's borders, as well as enforcing economic, transportation, and infrastructure security. By protecting national and border security, ICE seeks to eliminate the potential threat of terrorist acts against the United States.

U.S. Citizenship and Immigration Services. The mission of the U.S. Citizenship and Immigration Services is to secure America's promise as a nation of immigrants by providing accurate and useful information to customers, granting immigration and citizenship benefits, promoting an awareness and understanding of citizenship, and ensuring the integrity of the U.S. immigration system.

Federal Emergency Management Agency. The mission of the Federal Emergency Management Agency (FEMA) is to lead the effort to prepare the nation for all hazards and effectively manage federal response and recovery efforts following any national incident. FEMA also initiates proactive mitigation activities, trains first responders, and manages the National Flood Insurance Program.

Coast Guard. The Coast Guard is a military, multi-mission, maritime service and one of the nation's five Armed Services. Its mission is to protect the public, the environment, and U.S. economic interests—in the nation's ports and waterways, along the coast, on international waters, or in any maritime region as required to support national security.

Treasury Department. The mission of the Department of the Treasury is to promote the conditions for prosperity and stability in the United States and encourage prosperity and stability in the rest of the world.

Bureau of Alcohol, Tobacco, Firearms, and Explosives. The Bureau of Alcohol, Tobacco, Firearms, and Explosives (ATF) is a principal law enforcement agency within the United States Department of Justice dedicated to preventing terrorism, reducing violent crime, and protecting the nation. ATF agents perform the dual responsibilities of enforcing federal criminal laws and regulating the firearms and explosives industries. ATF is committed to working directly, and through partnerships, to investigate and reduce crime involving firearms and explosives, acts of arson, and illegal trafficking of alcohol and tobacco products.

Internal Revenue Service. The mission of the Internal Revenue Service is to provide America's taxpayers top-quality service by helping them understand and meet their tax responsibilities and by applying the tax law with integrity and fairness to all. Its role is to help the large majority of compliant taxpayers with the tax law, while ensuring that the minority who are unwilling to comply pay their fair share.

Department of Justice. The mission of the Department of Justice is to enforce the law and defend the interests of the United States according to the law; to ensure public safety against threats foreign and domestic; to provide federal leadership in preventing and controlling crime; to seek just punishment for those guilty of unlawful behavior; and to ensure fair and impartial administration of justice for all Americans.

Drug Enforcement Administration. The mission of the Drug Enforcement Administration (DEA) is to enforce the controlled substances laws and regulations of the United States and bring to the criminal and civil justice system of the United States, or any other competent jurisdiction, those organizations and principal members of organizations involved in the growing, manufacture, or distribution of controlled substances appearing in or destined for illicit traffic in the United States; and to recommend and support nonenforcement programs aimed at reducing the availability of illicit controlled substances on the domestic and international markets.

Federal Bureau of Investigation. The mission of the Federal Bureau of Investigation (FBI) is to uphold the law through the investigation of violations of federal criminal law; to protect the United States from foreign intelligence and terrorist activities; to provide leadership and law enforcement assistance to federal, state, local, and international agencies; and to perform these responsibilities in a manner that is responsive to the needs of the public and is faithful to the Constitution of the United States.

Federal Bureau of Prisons. The mission of the Federal Bureau of Prisons is to protect society by confining offenders in the controlled environments of prisons and community-based facilities that are safe, humane, cost-efficient, and appropriately secure, and that provide work and other self-improvement opportunities to assist offenders in becoming law-abiding citizens.

State Department. The mission of the State Department is to create a more secure, democratic, and prosperous world for the benefit of the American people and the international community.

Department of Transportation. The mission of the Department of Transportation is to serve the United States by ensuring a fast, safe, efficient, accessible, and convenient transportation system that meets our vital national interests and enhances the quality of life of the American people, today and into the future.

Postal Service. The United States Postal Service (USPS) receives, transmits, and delivers written and printed matter, parcels, and like materials throughout the United States, its territories, and possessions, and throughout the world. The postal service is sometimes overlooked as a possible aid in investigation, but with a court order, the Postal Service can maintain a "mail cover", which records the external information of letters or packages delivered to a particular person or address. USPS regulations constitute the sole authority and procedure for initiating, processing, placing, and using mail covers. Because the practice does not involve the reading of the mail but only information on the outside of the envelope or package, it has not been considered a violation of the Fourth Amendment.

State and Local Government Agencies

Under the federal system of government, the powers not delegated in the Constitution to the national government are retained by the states. Accordingly, most licensing and regulatory powers are exercised at the state and local levels. The process of granting or denying licenses and regulating business requires that information be provided; these documents are a resource the investigator might tap at the appropriate time. Some particularly useful sources are listed below for each level of government: state, county, and municipal.

State Police/Highway Patrol. State police agencies can provide information on traffic stops or violations, and in some states information on criminal investigation.

State Motor Vehicle Bureau. The information available from a driver's license application includes name, address, date of birth, sex, height, weight, color of eyes, sometimes the social security number, and a photograph; also, a handwriting specimen (the individual's signature). The bureau also maintains a Vehicle Identification Number (VIN) file.

State Department of Labor. The Department of Labor maintains names and addresses of persons who have sought employment as a day laborer, domestic, or hotel/restaurant employee.

State Department of Public Aid or Welfare. The Department of Public Aid and Welfare maintains names and addresses of applicants for and recipients of public aid.

Licensing Agencies. Alcohol and beverage control agencies can provide information on ownership and violations. Other state licensing and registration agencies, such as firearms control, welfare rolls, gambling sites, corporate registrations, and various permits, can also provide information on individuals and organizations.

Ad Hoc Agencies. An *ad hoc* or one-purpose agency is established to deal with a particularly vexatious problem, in connection, for instance, with a sport like horse racing or boxing, or with crime on the waterfront. (To wit, a compact between New York and New Jersey creating the New York Harbor Waterfront Commission dealt in a coordinated fashion with the numerous issues involved.) Because activities under the surveillance of an *ad hoc* agency usually entail the licensing of personnel, considerable information is available from licensee application forms. They are designed to elicit usable investigative information in anticipation of this need.

Among the records found at the county and municipal levels are birth certificates, marriage licenses, election and voting records, school records, library records, tax records, and property ownership records. These can provide valuable information such as names, addresses, telephone numbers, e-mail addresses, ages, employers, authenticated signatures (which may serve as an exemplar for a questioned document examiner), and more.

Business Organizations

It is not possible to exist in modern society without taking part in a certain amount of business dealings. People must find shelter, buy food, meet job-related demands, and take some recreation—all of which puts them on record. Indeed, given a list of checks written and credit card purchases made each month, an accurate socioeconomic picture can be reconstructed on an individual.

Business records, being numerous and widely distributed, are not readily available to the investigator. Indeed, if the search is likely to be protracted or costly, only a token effort, if any, may be undertaken by their custodians—who are not obliged to furnish what is sought. Lack of cooperation from businesses has historically been a problem, overcome usually by personal relationships between investigators and heads of security in large corporations. The situation has improved dramatically since the attacks on the World Trade Center and the Pentagon on September 11, 2001 ("9/11"), and cooperation in terrorist investigations has been much better. However, there is frequently a reluctance on the part of businesses to provide information on employees and customers unless there is a direct benefit to the business. Credit card companies work closely with fraud and identity theft investigators because it is in their best interest.

In some cases it may be necessary for the investigator to secure a search warrant. However, as noted earlier, much information can be obtained from the Internet. In addition to information on persons, it is possible to retrieve financial reports of corporations and corporate officers.

In order to acquire information from commercial establishments, the investigator must have a good idea of what the most common and useful business records are and be aware of other systematic compilations. When tackling the ways and means to access records and files, he or she must first know what exists.

Business organizations with records that are likely to provide investigative leads:

- Public utility companies
- Credit reporting agencies
- Insurance companies
- Labor unions
- Fraternal organizations
- Internet and cellular telephone companies

Public Utility Companies

As long as people must supply facts to obtain or transfer any utility service, there is a reservoir of useful information in utility company files. The files of telephone companies are particularly useful. For example, information can be obtained on cell phones, residential phones, and business phones: the telephone numbers called frequently by an individual; the unlisted numbers called; the long-distance numbers called (as well as the time and length of each call); the name of the subscriber for a particular number; and the numbers listed for a particular address.

The value of such information to the detective is apparent in the following example. In the case of the shooting of a well-known mobster in New York City, a search of the murdered man's overcoat pockets produced a slip of paper bearing a single telephone number. This evidence, obviously, was of interest to investigators; and yet, it would certainly have been unwise at that stage of the investigation to call the number directly. However, by knowing how to obtain the name of the subscriber discreetly and quickly, a potential source of information could be identified for follow-up. In similar cases, what the follow-up activity would entail depends on the needs of the particular situation. The circumstances may call for merely questioning the subscriber or a household member; it might mean placing one or several of them under surveillance; or, in order to clarify a partially developed detail, it might become necessary to use an informant or (where legal) a telephone surveillance or wiretap.

Credit Reporting Agencies

The extension of credit to a business or an individual requires assurances of the borrower's ability to repay the debt. This kind of information is compiled on a historical basis; it reveals the borrower's general reputation in the community. File-based credit reporting bureaus collect information from creditors on how bills were paid; investigative credit reporting bureaus gather information on an individual's lifestyle and reputation.

Although there are many local, file-based credit reporting companies, only a few are investigative credit reporting agencies that operate nationally. The three major national credit bureaus are: Experian, Equifax, and TransUnion. Hooper Holmes and Dun and Bradstreet are two major organizations that gather information on a business's corporate character, capital, and capacity to repay a loan. If a credit card was used, the whereabouts of a suspected serial murderer may be determined. The downfall of Ted Bundy, the notorious, multi-state serial killer, can be attributed in part to credit card records. For example, though he denied having been in Colorado, receipts for gasoline purchased by credit card led to Bundy's extradition to stand trial for murder in that state. In addition to credit activity records, even credit applications offer a variety of avenues to be pursued in the quest for recorded facts.

Insurance Companies

Most people are covered by one or more forms of insurance: life, health, accident, casualty, or fire. Regardless of the kind of insurance they sell, insurance companies share information quite freely in order to eliminate poor risks. They also exchange data with other sources such as motor vehicle and credit bureaus, social welfare agencies, and health services. As a consequence, insurance companies may possess more information than is contained in a client's initial application (considerable in itself). Pursuing this line of inquiry can serve a criminal investigator well.

Labor Unions

Millions of workers belong to labor unions in the United States. Not only must a union member's dues be paid on time in order for him or her to remain in good standing with the union, but in the case of closed shops it is necessary for continued employment. If the union is cooperative (and some are not), this dues-paying transaction can provide a means of locating an individual. In addition, labor union publications often contain photographs and news items covering members' activities.

Fraternal Organizations

Some organizations exist for fellowship (e.g., Elks, Moose, Odd Fellows); others have a religious base (e.g., Knights of Columbus, Masons, B'nai Brith) or were founded on pride of national origin (e.g., Ancient Order of Hibernians, Polish National Alliance, Dante Alighieri Society). The people in these organizations usually know each other better than do the members of professionally based organizations; hence, they may provide background material on an individual's vocational and avocational interests, hobbies, community activities, and close friends.

Miscellaneous Sources

The taxonomy (classification scheme) employed to outline record sources thus far has not included the more obscure repositories of information. Public and college libraries are available, of course, but the investigator also ought to be aware of sources that normally do not disclose information to the public. Sources often overlooked are Chambers of Commerce, Better Business Bureaus, and the morgue files of local newspapers.

The value of information stored in a reference library can be illustrated by the case of one college student found murdered on campus. The murder weapon was a fabricated piece of iron; there appeared to be a short handle at one end. No one was familiar with it, and the purpose for its manufacture could only be guessed. A visit to the university reference room, however, produced a list of trade associations that possibly could provide further insight. After several days of checking and telephoning, investigators located a company in a distant state that identified the piece of evidence as a furnace handle. It was not a familiar object because the company had foreseen a limited market and manufactured only a few such furnaces. A check of the university registry disclosed that a mere handful of students came from that distant state. After questioning them individually, the list was narrowed down to one suspect. When his car was found to have bloodstains on the door and the blood group matched that of the victim and differed from his own, the suspect confessed.

WHERE TO FIND RECORDS

There are innumerable Internet sources and books dedicated to unveiling records. They are of varying degrees of quality, but with perseverance, it is easier than ever to find what you need. The growing amount of information available through such search engines as Google makes it possible to search for individual names, groups, organizations, and specific topics. Search sites like Nexis.com provide a wealth of information, and search engines such as peekyou.com are designed to compile information about individuals. Social networking sites, such as MySpace, Facebook, and LinkedIn, are often valuable places to find details or information on acquaintances.

Several books have been published that give extensive coverage to the sources of information available in public and private systems. *Directories in Print* takes a general approach to other likely sources of business information and files.[2] Its purpose is to supply business and industry with lists of the many directories printed in the United States by business and reference book publishers, trade magazines, chambers of commerce, and federal, state, and city governmental agencies. Offering a means of locating the suppliers of products and services, the table of contents illustrates the extent of the areas and sources of information it can open up for the investigator. It includes descriptive listings in the following categories: General Business; Specific Industries and Lines of Business; Banking, Finance, Insurance, and Real Estate; Agriculture, Resource Industries, and the Environment; Law, Military, and Government; Science, Engineering, and Computer Science; Education; Information Sciences, Social Sciences, and Humanities; Biography; Arts and Entertainment; Public Affairs and Social Concerns; Health and Medicine; Religious, Ethnic, and Fraternal Affairs; Genealogical, Veterans, and Patriotic Affairs; Hobbies, Travel, and Leisure; and Sports and Outdoor Recreation.

The Encyclopedia of Associations[3] may be described as a basic guide to information on specific subjects. Unique in this respect, the associations and professional societies it catalogs serve as "switchboards" connecting those in need of information to highly qualified sources.

Other helpful books have been written to assist information searches. Joseph Culligan's reference manual, *You Can Find Anybody*,[4] lists a broad range of public record sources and how to use them to locate individuals. The book provides location and address information, and a detailed chapter on how to use the Internet to search for information. Another publication, *Confidential Information Sources: Public and Private*, was written by an information scientist with experience in security matters. It discusses a wide range of sources, including credit-reporting agencies, medical records, and student records.[5]

NOTES

[1]   Llewelyn W. Atcherley, *Modus Operandi: Criminal Investigation and Detection,* rev. ed., G.C. Vaughn, ed. (London: Her Majesty's Stationery Office, 1937), 4.

[2]   Gale Research, *Directories in Print,* 31st ed. (Detroit: Gale/Cengage, 2009).

[3]   Gale Research, *Encyclopedia of Associations: National Organizations of the U.S.,* 48th ed. (Detroit: Gale/Cengage, 2009).

[4]   Joseph J. Culligan, *You Can Find Anybody,* 2nd ed. (Austin, TX: Thomas Investigative Publications, 2006).

[5]   John M. Carroll, *Confidential Information Sources: Public and Private,* 2nd ed. (Boston: Butterworth-Heinemann, 1991).

DISCUSSION QUESTIONS

1.   What are some of the uses of records in an investigation?

2.   What are some of the types and sources of recorded information?

3.   The use of sophisticated relational databases and software combined with analytics can provide what types of information that may assist investigators?

4.   Numerous federal agencies maintain different types of databases that may be of value to the investigator. What are some of the agencies that can provide assistance?

5.   What state and local agencies can be of assistance in investigations?

6.   What private sector business organizations and associations can be of assistance in investigations?

SUPPLEMENTAL READINGS

Culligan, Joseph (2000). *You can find anybody* (2nd ed.). Austin, TX: Thomas Investigative Publications.

Gale Research (2013). *Directories in print* (35th ed.). Detroit: Gale/Cengage.

Gale Research (2013). *Encyclopedia of associations: National organizations of the U.S* (52nd ed.). Detroit: Gale/Cengage.

CHAPTER 6

INTERVIEWS
Obtaining Information from Witnesses

QUESTIONING PEOPLE

The investigator spends a great deal of professional time talking with people after a crime is committed. The victim and eyewitness(es) are first; next are those whose identities develop in the course of the investigation. Some people furnish complete and candid information, but some are less cooperative or will deliberately mislead authorities; others must be coaxed to come forward.

The terms used to describe the questioning process are *interrogation* and *interviewing*. Interrogation applies to a suspect and a suspect's family, friends, or associates—people who are likely to withhold information or be deceptive. Interviewing applies to victims or eyewitnesses who can reasonably be expected to disclose what they know. Hence, the guiding principles and techniques of interrogation (discussed in Chapter 10) differ considerably from those of interviewing.

> **Interrogation** applies to a suspect and a suspect's family, friends, or associates—people who are likely to withhold information or be deceptive.
>
> **Interviewing** applies to victims or eyewitnesses who can reasonably be expected to disclose what they know.

INTERVIEWING

There are few people who have neither been interviewed nor conducted an interview themselves. Whether formal or informal, it is the same process that is involved in job hunting, shopping, or talking over a child's progress with a teacher. Its purpose is the exchange of information. Investigators also are engaged in this exchange, and as practiced professionals they generally take in far more information than they give out. Seeking facts not divulged because there is little comprehension of their significance, the investigator needs to be intuitive, alert, and skillful—much more than a passive information-recorder. If interviewing at the crime scene is unavoidable and there is any chance that the suspect or accomplices are within hearing distance, absolute discretion is a must. The following questions—"five Ws and one H": Who?, What?, When?, Where?, Why?, and How?—should be regarded as the minimum to be covered in an interview.

Who: The question of who involves the name, address, sex, age, and occupation of the interviewee. Interviewees can be victims, witnesses, or others suggested by witnesses or friends of the victim. Who is the perpetrator? Who gains some advantage from committing the crime? The investigator taking information from a witness must make a point of verifying the name and address given. A driver's license or other identification can prevent a subpoena from being returned marked: "Addressee Unknown." It is not uncommon to lose a case because a witness could not be contacted; numerous cases have been lost for precisely that reason.

What: What was observed by the eyewitness? What was heard or learned through any of the other senses (smell, touch, taste)? What relationship exists or existed between victim and perpetrator? Between the complainant and witness? Between complainant and other witnesses? Between participants in the crime? What objects were moved, taken, or damaged?

When: When was the crime committed? When did the interviewee acquire this information? When did a suspect last see or talk to the victim?

Where: Where did the crime take place? Where did the interviewee observe, hear, or otherwise learn what he or she is reporting? Where did the interview take place?

Why: Why was the interviewee in a position to observe the incident? Why did the crime occur (possible motive)? Why was the victim, target, or object selected? Why was a particular object moved, taken, or damaged?

How: How was the crime consummated? How was it originally conceived?

Modus Operandi: As previously discussed, the manner in which a crime was committed can serve as the trademark or *modus operandi* (MO) of that criminal. For example, the language used to convey to the victim that a robbery is to take place differs among holdup perpetrators. In a sexual assault, a rapist's threats, demands, and remarks characterize him just as the means of breaking and entering—cutting a hole in the roof, breaking through a wall with a jack hammer, hiding in the stairwell until the building is closed, picking a lock—distinguish a burglar. Some aspects of MO must be sought at the crime scene; others are furnished by the complainant (and perhaps by witnesses) at the initial interview. As noted earlier, the well-maintained MO file can tie several crimes together through crime analysis, and it is through the interviewing process that the unique characteristics or variables are usually most apparent. Individual clues collected in each crime may not suffice, but a pool of clues from crimes sharing a common MO could suggest a strategy for identifying and apprehending the perpetrator. Even for crimes in which the victim may not be present, such as burglary, interviews can provide information that may only be obvious to the victim. For example, the movement of furniture or items, the presence of cigarettes, or perhaps the use of towels or discarded garbage may provide additional variables for the MO, or items for laboratory examination.

ACQUIRING THE FACTS

One method of acquiring the facts is to utilize a standardized form dealing with the significant details a complainant or witness may possess. Termed *complaint report* or *investigation report*, such forms are designed with questions framed to ensure that vital information is not overlooked. At the same time the forms are intended to ferret out facts that witnesses fail to volunteer because their potential value is unrealized. A note of caution:

> ... it is not true that more information necessarily is more productive. In some circumstances the use of precoded incident forms may be counterproductive.

... [Although] information is essential to apprehension and prosecution, [there are those who] are pessimistic about the way in which this notion has been implemented in some departments where investigating officers must wade through long, general lists of questions and precoded investigation forms. ... [It can be argued] that the key to enhanced productivity lies in collecting only that information likely to be useful in identifying and apprehending an offender.[1]

Thus, specialized forms need to be developed and tested. Their primary function is to minimize the amount of information collected and maximize its usefulness. If investigative efficiency is to be improved, applied research in this vein is essential. A simplified identification chart designed to focus a victim's or witness's immediate attention on a particular aspect of the crime or its perpetrator is needed. Also helpful would be a greater use by business establishments of a height line marker; placed on the exit doorjamb, it allows the height of the perpetrator passing through the door to be estimated.

A concept known as *Frame-by-Frame Analysis* (FFA) involves the detailed analysis of a victim or suspect's statement that focuses on very specific details. Savino and Turvey note that:

The best way to understand this particular method is by comparing it to a movie. If we watch a movie in real time we may understand what is going on, but we might not observe all of the details. However, if we run the same movie in slow motion, frame-by-frame, we may better recognize the details of the action as it occurs.[2]

Failing to heed the importance of recording details when handling interviews, though obvious, is one of the major mistakes made by investigators, and it is not unusual for an interviewer to screen out or fill in important points because of carelessness, preconceived notions, time constraints, or misperceptions. Consider, for example, watching a movie, and then seeing the movie a second or third time. How much information is added with each viewing?

Another important aspect of the interview is observation of the facial expressions of the interviewee. Gary Faigin has studied facial expressions in great detail. He notes that the slightest change in a person's facial movements may reveal lying, fear, anger, or a host of other subtle clues that can further the investigation. Is the subject being evasive, perhaps afraid or fearful, or maybe hiding something? If a subject has a tendency to avoid eye contact, what does that mean? Even further, what can a person's eyes reveal? Do they evince sadness, lack of interest, anger, or hostility? As Faigin notes, "The eyes and brow together are easily the most magnetic and compelling part of the face... We instinctively feel that the eyes provide our most direct link to the person within."[3]

Describing the Offender

The victim or eyewitness can make a major contribution by providing a good description of the perpetrator. Several procedures have been developed to accomplish this. The earliest, the *portrait parlé* (loosely translated, "verbal picture"), was suggested by Bertillon of the Sûreté. It was a supplement to his identification scheme, anthropometry (the recording of certain body measurements—especially bone length), which, despite his own fanatical opposition, was eventually dropped in favor of fingerprints. But *portrait parlé*, utilizing facial and bodily features to describe an individual, continues to this day.

Three other methods have emerged. In one, an artist draws a likeness of the person observed. People capable of this can be found in most communities; they may be on the staff in large police

Sirchie Finger Print Laboratories, Raleigh, NC

Figure 6.1
A few of the 193 forehead/hair styles available in the Photo-Fit female Caucasian front face kit.

departments. Another method employs a series of pre-drawn facial features—hairlines, mustaches, eyebrows, eyes, ears, noses, lips, chins, and so on. Choosing the one feature from each series most closely resembling the perpetrator's feature (see Figure 6.1), the eyewitness makes selections that form a composite picture of the perpetrator. Composite kits are commercially available. Identi-Kit is well known; other makes, such as the Penry Photo-Fit, are equally satisfactory (see Figure 6.2).

The third (and latest) method exploits the graphics capability of the computer. A number of software programs have been designed to produce images of suspects or wanted persons: Compu-Sketch and ComPHOTOfit.

Figure 6.2
A comparison of a Photo-Fit composite with a photograph of the same person.

Compu-Sketch, offered by Allied Security Innovations, Inc., evolved in conjunction with a California police officer, Tom Macris, who served for 12 years as sketch artist for the San Jose Police Department.[4] It has been described:

> [Compu-Sketch] combines and creates over 100,000 facial features by simply pressing a button; one feature quickly falls over another until the composite is complete. The positioning of features in their relation to each other is unlimited, while refinement of resultant images is by electronic "paint box" techniques. The product is printed out as a highly credible composite sketch for leaflets or wanted posters.
>
> At the system's heart is a comprehensive interview program. It provides maximum help to the witness to recall critical suspect features, while assuring completely unbiased answers with non-leading and non-suggestive queries. Incorporated into the computer program is the key interview process enabling the operator to assist the witness step-by-step with memory enhancement questions triggering other memory processes, with consistency from case to case and agency to agency.[5]

Some facial features available in the Compu-Sketch library are shown in Figure 6.3. ComPHOTOfit works with five features to draft the composite sketch, e.g., forehead, eyes, nose, mouth, and chin; a mustache, beard, eyeglasses, and headgear can be added if needed. ComPHOTOfit's developers claim that "the image generated is virtually photo quality after the image section lines of the component parts are blended out with a mouse, or moles and scars are 'painted' in."[6]

People normally see the features on a face in totality, unless one feature stands out. The totality (or gestalt) can be caught by the police artist, who offers the choice of an infinite number of facial features. Sirchie Finger Print Laboratories claims that more than 12 billion faces can be composed using the Photo-Fit system. If an artist's sketch or a composite picture is distributed, the likelihood of its utilization by the patrol force, community merchants, and the general public is greater than if a verbal description alone were circulated. When the general public must be looked to for help,

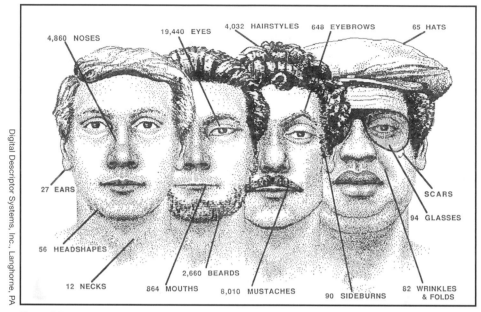

Digital Descriptor Systems, Inc., Langhorne, PA

Figure 6.3
Compu-Sketch feature library.

prospects for its involvement increase if resentment is felt about the crime, or if the request is a novelty. Of course, the ultimate result is an identification; short of that, productive results could include leads that send detectives in search of additional facts from a record file or another person.

Describing Stolen or Lost Property

The task of identifying stolen property arises when the stores of loot of a burglar or fence are located. Because theft is largely a means of acquiring cash by pawning or selling stolen goods, police monitoring of property sold to secondhand dealers or pledged as security in pawn shops can bring about its identification. For this to result, it must be described twice:

First: by the owner to the investigator handling the case

Second: by the pawnbroker or secondhand dealer to the stolen property bureau of a police department

Because it would practically take a miracle to bring owner/victim and pawnbroker reports together (filing dates can be 30 or more days apart), the information generated by each report must be similar. To achieve this, the Stolen/Lost Property Report Form is a requisite. In some jurisdictions the law stipulates that pawnshop owners file such forms; in others, their voluntary cooperation must be sought. Owing to the nature of this business, however, it is not uncommon for pawnbrokers to contact police when merchandise brought to them arouses suspicion. Whether filing is required by law or voluntary, both reports (owner/victim and pawnbroker) should ultimately come together in the stolen property bureau records, thereby helping to clear the case as well as facilitating a return of the stolen goods to their rightful owners.

A Stolen/Lost Property Report Form can be developed in accordance with the following (or similar) taxonomy:

KIND OF OBJECT	Camera, TV, stereo set, credit card, watch, binoculars, jewelry
NAME OF MANUFACTURER (OR OTHER SOURCE)	
MODEL NUMBER	
IDENTIFYING FEATURES	Serial number, initials, or other personal inscription
MATERIAL USED IN ITS CONSTRUCTION	Shiny chrome or dull black body of a camera; wood or plastic in a TV set; gold or silver in jewelry
PHYSICAL APPEARANCE	Size, shape (as of a diamond), condition (like new, scratched)
MARKINGS	In many cases an object may have markings or identifiable damage known to the victim

DEALING WITH THE RELUCTANT, FEARFUL, OR UNAWARE WITNESS

Securing Cooperation

It is a fact that many crimes occur in which no witnesses come forward. Several reasons account for this disinclination: a person may be concerned over loss of pay through court continuances, harbor a fear of the police, or dread the offender's retaliation. In addition, some people have information, but are unaware of its usefulness to the police. An effective way to secure cooperation is to set up a special 24-hour "hotline"; this allows witnesses to telephone police while remaining anonymous. Offering a reward is another time-honored formula. When the investigator learns the name of a potential witness who has not come forward, the rationale for this behavior must be ascertained. The means of dealing with this phenomenon vary with the reasons that foster it.

The growth of Crime Stoppers, local organizations of citizens that operate hotlines and offer rewards for information on crimes and criminals, has proven to be of assistance in investigations. Generally, an individual who provides information may remain anonymous, but in many cases the informant can be encouraged to come forward.

The Reluctant Witness

It does not require great imaginative ability to reassure the reluctant witness. Recognizing and realistically dealing with a legitimate complaint will usually suffice. For instance, many people are concerned about loss of pay when repeatedly called to court only to have the case continued (set for a later date). Should this be the basis for hesitancy, the investigator can arrange to have the witness placed on a telephone alert, to be called only when the case is actually on trial and the testimony wanted within an hour or so. In the course of duty, detectives continuously work out such arrangements.

The Fearful Witness

Witnesses who dread reprisal should their identity become known can be difficult to handle. For a key witness in an important case, protective custody (agreed to or imposed) may be required—a harsh measure that is seldom taken because it is hard on the individual and expensive for the state. A sympathetic attitude and a reliable appraisal of the danger (for example, by citing a witness's safety in the jurisdiction) may remove any remaining hesitancy. Just the same, there will be those who, for cultural or other reasons, cannot be persuaded to divulge what they know.

The witness who is reticent owing to fear of the police presents both short-term and long-term challenges. The short-term challenge is for the detective on the case to induce a person to divulge what he or she knows; the long-term challenge is for the department to surmount the misgivings that cause people to dread contact with the police. It may surprise many police officers to learn that law-abiding citizens fear them. In small communities with relatively homogenous populations, the degree of fear is not as great and usually is not manifest, but a latent fear may well exist.

In larger cities, and particularly in neighborhoods where there is gang activity, citizens may be reluctant to cooperate with police because they fear retaliation. In other instances there may be an "I don't want to get involved" attitude, or the belief that someone else will call the police or get involved. The classic case of citizen neglect occurred in New York City in 1964 when a young woman, Kitty Genovese, was accosted by an assailant at 3:30 in the morning. Her screams for help as she was stabbed repeatedly awakened many people, and the attacker fled, but returned 10 minutes later when no police cars responded and found his victim in a doorway a short distance away. Genovese continued to cry and scream for help, silenced by the attacker cutting her throat. Some 38 neighbors heard Kitty Genovese that night. Yet it was not until 3:55 A.M.—about 30 minutes after the first scream, by which time the killer had long departed—that one of them called the police. Thirty-eight people were at the scene, safe in their homes, with telephones available. Why the hesitation? Why was not one in this larger-than-average number of witnesses motivated by enlightened self-interest or plain civic duty to call the police? Queries by reporters reported a number of reasons, the most common being a reluctance to call because the police operators asked too many questions, putting them on the defensive. Ultimately, fear was a distinctive factor, and something that is all too common in many cities across the country.

Generating Long-Term Cooperation

The advent and frequently reluctant acceptance of community policing has served to improve relations between citizens and the police in many cities, but some would argue that citizens, especially in the inner cities, are still far removed from the police. Despite increased training and concerns about racial profiling, public cooperation leaves much to be desired in many communities.

Many departments have focused on victimology and have instituted victim-witness assistance units. In rape cases, for example, a female officer (who may be a trained social worker) responds to a reported rape scene. She supports the victim in a personal way throughout the questioning, then accompanies her to the hospital for medical examination, where physical evidence (semen, pubic hairs, blood) is acquired. Later, she provides follow-up counseling and sees the victim (now the witness) through the criminal justice process, explaining each step along the way—why it is necessary and what is next. A humanely treated victim is likely to be a willing witness, more so certainly than one who must—because official concern is focused only on the investigation—go over details of the ordeal while being inadvertently embarrassed by various male officers.

Some assistance programs concentrate on what is expected of the victim/witness when called to the stand. They supply transportation to court, child care, and a lounge or service center separated from the defendant. Some agencies even see to the repair of broken windows or damaged door locks in the home of a witness who has been threatened. For the witness or victim who feels intimidated, "hotline" telephones have been set up for advice, reassurance, and action.

The Unaware Witness

There are times when someone in the neighborhood sees the criminal on the way to or retreating from the crime scene. The observer could be sitting in a car, looking out a window, walking a dog, or driving a cab. Yet such observers are generally unaware of having seen anything that could be of value to the police. By revisiting the scene the following day or two, and exactly one week after the crime, the investigator may find a person who was passing when the crime was about to be (or was being) committed, or picked up information from others who wouldn't talk to the police. Follow-up interviewing by investigators, or working with patrol officers familiar with citizens, can frequently generate useful information. In a well-publicized crime, the observer may realize he or she has something to contribute and come forward. In a major case, broadcasting an appeal is sometimes effective, as are leaflets distributed in shopping and transportation centers.

Canvass

If the case warrants it after all other measures have failed, a neighborhood canvass may be undertaken to discover the offender or unaware witness. Expensive and time-consuming, a canvass requires careful administrative control to ensure that every person in the area is contacted and interviewed. Large cities pose the greatest number of problems in conducting a store-to-store, building-to-building, house-to-house canvass. But if the area can be reasonably well-defined, its size and number of inhabitants limited, and the search is marked by patience and thoroughness, the chances of success are enhanced.

In the United States, a canvass is often considered in cases of homicide. The tactic works for other crimes as well. It can be productive when based on the possibility that someone saw or heard something that he or she did not bother to report until confronted by the inquiries of a police officer knocking on the door. Then, there is always the chance that the officer will knock on the very door of the perpetrator, who will be exposed by the combined effect of surprise and guilty knowledge.

Indifferent Complainants

At times a complainant may display indifference or claim that he or she is too busy to be questioned. Since most victims are anxious to be helpful, such resistance raises the question: "Why?" Sometimes the answer can be found through a crime scene examination focused on how the crime was committed, e.g., through a reconstruction of the event. Re-examining the alleged facts and the physical evidence may reveal that the crime was simulated, and account for a complainant's reluctance to be interviewed and possibly exposed as the perpetrator. An interrogation then may have greater success. In addition, when evidence of a crime (a burglary, for instance) is recognized as having been simulated, Horowitz's condition that evidence be available against the individual is met. This factor can be effective when interrogating the complainant who is falsely claiming to have been the victim of a burglary. (See Chapter 10.)

BEHAVIORAL ANALYSIS INTERVIEWS

The Behavioral Analysis Interview (BAI) is an investigative technique that seeks to capitalize on the fact that a person being questioned unwittingly emits nonverbal signals. Called an interview, yet nearer to an interrogation in purpose, BAI can be likened to a bridge between the two. It also is described as an effective substitute when the polygraph is not available or acceptable for use.[7] So far, it has been of greatest help in private security work and for screening numbers of suspects when polygraph tests would be too time-consuming.

The objectives of the BAI technique include:

1. To develop investigative information, including statement inconsistencies or procedural/policy violations that may have contributed to the problem, as well as insight into the relevant activities of others;

2. To develop behavioral information indicative of the suspect's truthfulness or deception regarding the issue under investigation; and

3. To determine whether or not the person being interviewed did, in fact, commit the act that is under investigation.[8]

Behavior Analysis Interviews are based on the three levels of communication, including the verbal channel, paralinguistic channel, and the nonverbal channel. The most noticeable form of communication is verbal communication, in which word choice and arrangement are used. The paralinguistic channel involves the characteristics of speech that fall outside the spoken word, and nonverbal communication involves all nonverbal behavior, such as leg and arm movements, eye contact, and facial expressions.[9]

Based on an empirical study, the following symptoms are to be noted during the interview, because:

> … it was clear that the innocent suspects revealed their truthfulness by their behavior, and the guilty revealed their deception by their behavior.
>
> … truthful suspects were more at ease during the interview. They were able to sit comfortably without shifting while being questioned. These suspects were straightforward in their answers and looked at the interviewer with sincere eyes.
>
> The guilty suspects appeared to be more nervous and uneasy during the interview. Some acted resentful or aggressive. The guilty suspects were often evasive, would not look at the examiner, and moved around frequently during the interview.
>
> … It is important to note that the interviewer does not look for just one behavior symptom from the suspect. Rather, he is evaluating a cluster of behavior symptoms.[10]

To provoke a response, the person under suspicion is told that a specially trained interviewer will do the questioning and take fingerprints. If any other physical evidence has been found, this fact is also utilized; if, for instance, the evidence was a hair, the individual can be asked to provide a sample. The interviewer then begins with a review of some details of the crime, and watches for behavioral responses. Next, the person is turned over to another interviewer who has several prepared questions relevant to the crime; again, any behavioral reaction is noted. Finally, a third interviewer asks formulated questions based on previous responses, then terminates the session with the taking of fingerprints, watching all the while for any behavioral symptoms of guilt or innocence.

Sometimes a bait question is employed to draw the individual into modifying or even repudiating the original assertion of noninvolvement. An example: "Why would anyone say they saw you come out of the bar and go to the parking lot just before Joe was shot there?" A truthful response would be a direct denial such as "That can't be; I wasn't there" or "Whoever told you that is full of shit." A guilty response, based on the possibility that he or she was indeed seen in the lot, would either produce a denial—usually after some hesitation—or an admission that he or she was in the lot (but on another day), and a claim that the witness made a mistake as to when this occurred.

A response suggestive of guilt requires follow-up: by surveillance; perhaps seeking an informant; tracing the weapon used—if it was recovered; questioning associates; and so on. When and if further evidence is developed, a full-scale interrogation may be in order. Proponents claim that a professional BAI interviewer can "confidently eliminate over 80% of the innocent and can identify the guilty without the use of the polygraph technique."[11]

Hypnosis

The primary function of forensic hypnosis is that of an investigative tool. All information elicited should be independently verified as much as possible. Forensic hypnosis is used with the victim or a witness. It is not recommended for use with a suspect (remember: if you can lie when not in a "trance," you can lie when induced!). The following are some guidelines recommended for the hypno-investigator:

1. The hypno-investigator should not be involved in the direct investigation of the case.

2. Before hypnosis is induced, a written record should be made that includes a description of the subject matter and the information that was provided.

3. The session should be both videotaped and audiotaped.

4. There should be no "line-up" or mug shot viewing prior.

5. Explain hypnosis to the subject before the session.

6. After an introductory relaxation, the victim/witness should be allowed to give a verbatim account of the incident.

7. The session should be conducted in a comfortable, "homey" atmosphere that is soundproofed and free of distractions.

8. Only the hypnotist and victim/witness should be allowed in the session, unless the hypnotist determines that it is necessary for a parent/guardian, case investigator, or police artist to be present.

Hypnosis, when properly used, can be a valuable tool for the investigator. Hypnosis is no longer considered to be "black magic voodoo witchcraft" but a positive and reliable information-gathering, crime-solving tool for the twenty-first-century criminal investigator.[12] The use of hypnosis by law enforcement as a means of interviewing has met with some criticism. Two concerns are expressed: (1) in some crimes the victim suffers severe psychological trauma, and reliving the experience through hypnosis could make it worse; and (2) "facts" may be implanted to cue or lead the witness under hypnosis, he or she being suggestible in this condition. To avoid criticism while retaining the benefits of hypnosis, the FBI has established elaborate guidelines for its use as an investigative tool.

> The FBI's policy basically states that the FBI is to use hypnosis only in selected cases. This would include bank robbery, where force is used or a large amount of money is involved, kidnapping, extortion, and crimes of violence which occur where the FBI has jurisdiction. Hypnosis is confined to use with key witnesses or victims of crimes only. No one who has the potential of becoming a suspect or subject in a case is to be hypnotized for any reason. For the sake of brevity, the term "witness" will be used in this article as a substitute for "witness/ victim." The FBI uses only highly qualified hypnotists to do the actual induction. The use of hypnosis must be discussed with the U.S. attorney and his permission obtained. The U.S. attorney must then obtain written permission from the Assistant Attorney General of the Criminal Division, U.S. Department of Justice. The current policy also states that no Agent may participate in a hypnotic interview without written permission from the Attorney General. Further, the hypnotic interview must be recorded in its entirety, either by audio or videotape, with video the preferred method.
>
> The guidelines specify the use of a psychiatrist, psychologist, physician, or dentist who is qualified as a hypnotist. The use of a qualified health professional provides additional protection for the witness, the cost of which is minimal. Agents have used the services of professionals who have given generously of their time, or who have charged only a modest fee for the sessions, because of their desire to help in what is for some a new area of hypnosis. Furthermore, the FBI has found that this added protection has not restricted Agents in their use of hypnosis.[13]

The FBI has utilized hypnosis in numerous cases; in many of these investigations, additional intelligence was obtained. Some was relevant and produced immediate results (e.g., an accurate sketch drawn from the witness's recall), but some is still open to question because the imprecise nature of hypnosis-based information makes corroboration difficult.

Often overlooked as a member of the investigation "team," sketch artists have sometimes proved invaluable in hypnosis sessions. Several cases in which the FBI was involved were resolved dramatically because artists provided satisfactory composite sketches of suspects. An FBI artist will travel to various field offices to work with the witness, coordinator, and doctor to produce composite drawings of suspects. Outside artists should be familiarized with the FBI guidelines and the use of hypnosis in aiding recall.

The Future of Hypnosis

Hypnosis continues to be a minor tool in the investigator's repertory. Nevertheless, it can be an effective one. Not only will it save many work hours, the potential also exists for its use by investigators themselves to enhance their own recall of events or details.

The team approach has proved valuable to the FBI. Introducing a "doctor-patient" relationship into an investigation, it ensures additional protection for witness and victim, while minimizing the hazards (potential and real) of hypnosis. Most important, the team approach helps to offset doubts about professionalism. There may well be a few individuals in law enforcement whose techniques are unscrupulous, but the same might be said of the health professions, both mental and physical. Law enforcement agencies may wish to consider some of the FBI's guidelines for improving an existing program or establishing the place of hypnosis in their departments.[14]

The National Board of Professional and Ethical Standards is one provider of Professional Board Certification and Teaching Credentials in hypnosis. Their Director of Ethics is a sitting police chief whose job it is to oversee the Ethics Committee for the organization and its members and students. The Board reminds users of hypnosis that the credibility of information obtained through hypnosis is enhanced when the facts disclosed are supported by independent evidence. It is important that such disclosures be followed up with additional investigative efforts involving other individuals, objects (physical evidence), and records to secure corroborative evidence.

EYEWITNESS EVIDENCE: THE ROLE OF PERCEPTION AND MEMORY

Most people have strong convictions about what they see with their own eyes, thus jurors tend to believe eyewitness testimony. However, experienced detectives have learned that eyewitnesses can be mistaken; indeed, it is not uncommon to find various eyewitness reports on an identical event to be incompatible. It is the task of the investigator to resolve such contradictions. One way is to reconstruct how the crime was committed (the use of physical evidence and the crime laboratory for this purpose are treated in Chapter 2). Another way to evaluate eyewitness reports is by understanding the psychological process involved: it begins with the original observation and proceeds to its retelling to the detective later and ultimate presentation to the court if the case goes to trial. A rather complicated process of observing and recalling, it can be divided into the following stages:

1. *Sensory input*: Information is encountered through visual observation or other senses, then encoded for storage in memory;

2. *Memory*: The storage and retention of what was observed and encoded;

3. *Retrieval*: The recovery of information through search of memory and its communication to others. The availability of cues to assist the search process is important at this stage.

Sensory Input

To understand how information is acquired, it is important to know the difference between perception and attention. Borrowing from Thomas Huxley's plain-talking style (which serves well for explaining the scientific method in Chapter 14) should be helpful. In one example, a person absorbed in reading hears a loud noise that seems to come from just outside the window. The reader, his or her attention diverted from the book, then interprets the meaning of the noise. Perception based on previous experience permits the likely cause to be determined. The sound could be of automobiles colliding, thunder, a scream, or a gunshot.

Now, consider a new baby asleep in its crib who is awakened by an identical noise. Though its attention would also be directed at the sound, having acquired no experience or knowledge in his or her brief life span, the baby is unable to interpret what the noise means. Like the reader, the baby's attention might be directed toward the sound; unlike the reader, however, the baby lacks any perception of its cause.

Perception is an important concept in comprehending the process of sensory input. Memory (essentially stored perceptions) and perception are intertwined, but for didactic reasons they are usually considered separate processes. To possess memory a person must have experiences. Something—a thought, emotion, object—must be comprehended through the mind or the senses. The person then perceives a new event in terms of experiences already stored up in memory and builds expectations and attitudes on them. So long as biases and stereotypes that can color expectations and attitudes are operative, perception may be faulty.

Perception can be considered the interpretation, classification, and conversion of sensory stimuli into a more durable configuration for memory. In other words, sensory input is assimilated to established knowledge stored in long-term memory. The discrete elements of an event are organized by the mind into meaningful categories, and stored. The aim is to assimilate the event, and then reconcile it with prior experience and knowledge so as to avoid any discrepancy between them—bringing both the perceived event and prior experience into harmony and making them compatible. The mind's need to effect such a reconciliation is, however, a possible source of error. Perception also can be affected by stress or arousal felt at the time cognizance was taken of the event. Thus, the perception of how long it took for a crime to be committed (or for the police to respond) is often much greater than the actual elapsed time. Other factors affecting perception include age, health, and gender.

Memory

What the witness to a crime sees is etched on the brain; and later, on request, it can be recollected precisely. This belief is pervasive—witnesses (particularly victims) often assert: "I'll never forget that face!" Common sense would seem to concur, yet clinical and laboratory experimentation demonstrate that memory is a complex phenomenon that cannot be explained with assumptions or beliefs. For example, common sense rejects the idea that sensory input received after an event can affect the memory of that event. Nonetheless, there is considerable empirical evidence that post-event information is indeed integrated with what already exists in memory. More recent research supports the theory that memory over time does change, and individuals are more likely to change details or forget certain aspects of what they witnessed. As a result, modifications may include: a change in the person's memory, enhancement of existing memory, or nonexistent details becoming embodied in the previous existing memory. Post-event information may arise from reading a newspaper article about it, from questions asked by an investigator or attorney, or from overhearing or talking about the event (particularly with other witnesses). The mind, therefore, is not like a videotape recorder that captures and retains what was seen (or heard) and remains unaffected by subsequent input.

Psychologists use the term *unconscious transference* to describe a witness's mistaken recollection about a crime—a recollection implicating an individual who was not involved. In one case, for instance, a young adult identified in a lineup (composed of several bank tellers) as the person who had robbed a bank was, in fact, an innocent depositor who had been in the bank the previous day. He was otherwise not connected with the institution, and certainly not with the robbery. This case illustrates the critical need to check out an accused person's explanation or alibi. Here, a review of the bank's deposit records would have challenged (and precluded) the lineup misidentification.

Information Retrieval

Two kinds of remembering are of interest to the detective: recall and recognition. In recall a previous event (e.g., a crime) is described verbally—in narrative form, in a *portrait parlé*, or to a police artist. In *recognition* there is an awareness that something was seen previously; some aspect of an event is remembered and selected from a group of similar items, persons, or photographs. This occurs when a mug shot is picked from the mug shot file or an individual is selected from a lineup. Generally, a person's ability with regard to recognition is better than it is for recall.

For retrieving information from a witness through an interview, a new technique, the result of psychological research into memory retrieval, is a major step forward. (See the section on The Cognitive Interview later in this chapter.)

WITNESS ERRORS

In addition to the possible errors associated with perception and memory, other sources of error include environmental conditions and personal factors.

Environmental Conditions

A person's ability to observe an event is limited by such factors as: the illumination of the scene, the distance of the observer from the scene, the noise level (if hearing is involved), and the weather (if the event occurred outdoors). If the evidence in a case depends largely on eyewitness testimony, it is desirable to verify whether environmental conditions existing at the time permitted such observations. Basic to the protection of the innocent, a verification can also deflect criticism by defense counsel and strengthen the confidence of the witness by establishing that there were no impediments to making the reported observations.

Personal Factors

Although sight and hearing most often provide the basis of witness testimony, any of the five senses can be involved. Again it is desirable to verify that the relevant sensory organs are or were not impaired. Taking this precaution enhances the credibility of the witness.

THE COGNITIVE INTERVIEW

In 1908 Harvard's Hugo Munsterberg (the first experimental psychologist in America) proved that although eyewitness testimony was remarkably faulty, it could be improved upon.[15] His effort was ignored by lawyers, judges, and law enforcement, and not until the 1970s would psychologists reexamine ways to improve eyewitness testimony. This kind of empirical research may have been further prompted by the RAND Corporation report noting that the single most important factor as to whether a case would be solved is the information provided by a witness or victim.[16]

This observation led R. Edward Geiselman and others to research the effectiveness of memory retrieval techniques; their program was labeled the *cognitive interview*.[17] Reminiscent of Munsterberg's earlier experiment, an incident was staged and 16 undergraduates became "eyewitnesses." Divided into two groups, only one group (the cognitive interview group) was given instruction in memory-retrieval techniques. It included four recommendations for completing the test booklet, which had an open-ended question and some pointed (short-answer) questions. The recommendations were:

> First, try to reinstate in your mind the context surrounding the incident. Think about what the room looked like and where you were sitting in the room. Think about how you were feeling at the time and think about your reactions to the incident.
>
> Second, some people hold back information because they are not quite sure about what they remember. Please do not edit anything out. Please write down everything, even things you think may not be important. Just be sure to indicate at the right how sure you are about each item.
>
> Third, it is natural to go through the incident from beginning to end, and that is probably what you should do at first. However, many people can come up with more information if they also go through events in reverse order. Or, you might start with the thing that impressed you the most and then go from there, proceeding both forward and backward in time.
>
> Fourth, try to adopt the perspective of others who were present during the incident. For example, try to place yourself in the experimenter's role and think about what she must have seen.[18]

The researchers concluded:

> The results of this study illustrate that the cognitive interview has substantial promise as a technique for the enhancement of eyewitness memory retrieval. The cognitive interview produced significantly more correct information without an accompanying increase in the amount of incorrect information. This advantage for subjects using the cognitive interview held for both an open-ended question and for pointed questions. Overall, 84 percent of the information generated with the cognitive interview was found to be accurate. Further, the confidence of the witnesses in their correct responses was enhanced with the cognitive interview, while confidence in their incorrect responses was not reliably affected. All but one of the subjects who received the cognitive interview reported that they found the methods to be useful.[19]

The next step for the Geiselman team was to compare the cognitive interview against hypnosis, another memory enhancement technique. Then both were matched against results obtained from a standard police interview.[20] This research revealed that both the cognitive and hypnosis procedures elicited a significantly greater number of correct items of information from the subjects than did the standard interview. This result, which held even for the most critical facts from the films, was most pronounced for crime scenarios in which the density of events was high. The number of incorrect items of information generated did not differ across the three interview conditions. The observed memory enhancement was interpreted in terms of the memory-guidance techniques common to both the cognitive and hypnosis interviews. Neither differential questioning time nor heightened subject or interviewer motivation could explain the results.[21] Three years later, Geiselman and Fisher reported on the effort to refine and revise the cognitive interview technique which, they stated, was based on four core principles: memory-event similarity, focused retrieval, extensive retrieval, and witness-compatible questioning.[22]

Memory-Event Similarity

Memory-event similarity involves an attempt to have the witness mentally recreate the environment surrounding the incident. A psychological environment similar to that which existed at the time of the crime is reproduced at the interview.

> The interviewer, therefore, should try to reinstate in the witness's mind the external (e.g., weather), emotional (e.g., feelings of fear), and cognitive (e.g., relevant thoughts) features that were experienced at the time the crime occurred.[23]

The witness is requested to think about the crime—the scene and what it looked like, where he or she was standing (or sitting), and the reaction to the crime at that time. This is a mental exercise; the witness is not physically placed at the scene. "In fact, if the crime scene has changed considerably, going back to the scene could conceivably interfere with the witness's recollection."[24]

Focused Retrieval

Because memory retrieval requires concentration, the interviewer helps witnesses to focus by refraining from asking too many short-answer, undirected, or irrelevant questions that tend to break concentration. Just as asking a series of questions can create a barrier that obstructs memory, so can interrupting the eyewitness who is responding to an open-ended question or providing a narrative description of the event. Another means of focusing memory retrieval is to have witnesses write everything down, even details they consider unimportant or about which they are unsure.

Extensive Retrieval

Memory retrieval is hard work, and witnesses are apt to terminate the effort after the first attempt. It is especially likely that the elderly will do so; they need to be encouraged to make other attempts. The usual mode is to begin at the beginning and continue chronologically to the end, but there are other ways. For example, witnesses can be asked to start with whatever detail is most indelibly inscribed in their memory, and from there, encouraged to go backward and forward. Another way is to reverse the order, urging witnesses to describe how the incident ended, and then proceed backward to the beginning.

Witness-Compatible Questioning

Just as the eyewitness is better able to retrieve memory when the environment surrounding the event is recreated, so are interviewers better able to ask questions if they can place themselves in the witness's frame of mind. The aim is to ask questions compatible with the situation in which the witness found himself or herself. To accomplish this, interviewers should try to place themselves in the witness' situation, and then frame questions on the basis of what was likely to have been observed at the time. This means adjusting to the witness's perspective rather than having the witness adjust to the investigator's. Geiselman and Fisher conclude by remarking:

> ... cognitive interviewing reliably enhances the completeness of a witness' recollection, and without increasing the number of incorrect or confabulated (replacing facts with fantasy) bits of information generated. ... The procedures are easy to learn and can be readily adopted in routine police interview procedures. In fact, the cognitive interview is in use as standard training at several police departments and other law enforcement agencies.[25]

CONCLUSION

Solid interviewing skills separate the novice from the professional; these are some of the most important skills in any police officer's personal profile. Cases are frequently made or lost, or even turned, by the manner in which an interview is conducted. One of the most commonly misused statements begins with, "You people..." or "In my experience..." In today's world, words mean a great deal to people, largely because advances in human communication and social media often create perceptions about law enforcement and police officers, not all of which is positive. Overcoming communication problems begins with a better understanding of the interviewing process.

NOTES

[1]   W.G. Skogan and G.E. Antunes, "Information, Apprehension, and Deterrence: Exploring the Limits of Police Productivity," *Journal of Criminal Justice,* 7 (1979), 234–235.

[2]   John O. Savino and Brent E. Turvey, *Rape Investigation Handbook*, 2nd ed. (Oxford, UK: Elsevier Science & Technology, 2011), 184.

[3]   Gary Faigin, *The Artist's Complete Guide to Facial Expression* (New York: Watson-Guptill, 1990), 64.

[4]   R. Bocklet. "Suspect Sketches Computerized for Faster Identification," *Law and Order,* 35:8 (Aug. 1987), 61–63.

[5]   Ibid., 62.

[6]   Ibid., 201.

[7]   D.E. Wicklander. "Behavioral Analysis," *Security World,* 17:3 (Mar. 1980), 41.

[8]   From the Reid Behavior Analysis Interview (BAI).

[9]   F.E. Inbau, J.E. Reid, J.P. Buckley, and B.C. Jayne, *Criminal Interrogation and Confessions,* 4th ed. (Sudbury, MA: Jones and Bartlett, 2004), 125.

[10] Wicklander, op. cit.

[11] Ibid., 61.

[12] E.G. Hall. "Watch Carefully Now: Solving Crime in the 21st Century," *Police,* (June 1999), 42–45.

[13] R.L. Ault. "Hypnosis: The FBI's Team Approach," *FBI Law Enforcement Bulletin,* 49:1 (Jan. 1980), 5–8. Available at: http://www.ncjrs.gov/App/Publications/abstract.aspx?ID = 64620

[14]   Ibid., 8.

[15]   Hugo Munsterberg, *On the Witness Stand* (Littleton, CO: Fred B. Rothman, 1981) [A reproduction of the original 1908 edition].

[16]   Peter Greenwood and Joan Petersilia, *The Criminal Investigation Process. Vol. III: Observations and Analysis* (Santa Monica, CA: RAND, 1975).

[17]   R. Edward Geiselman, R.P. Fisher, D.P. MacKinnon, and H.L. Holland, "Enhancement of Eyewitness Memory: An Empirical Evaluation of the Cognitive Interview," *Journal of Police Science and Administration,* 12:1 (1984), 74.

[18]   Ibid., 76.

[19]   Ibid., 79.

[20]   R. Edward Geiselman, R.P. Fisher, D.P. MacKinnon, and H.L. Holland, "Eyewitness Memory Enhancement in the Police Interview: Cognitive Retrieval Mnemonics Versus Hypnosis," *Journal of Applied Psychology,* 70:2 (1985), 401–412.

[21]   Ibid., 401.

[22]   R.E. Geiselman & R.P. Fisher. "The Cognitive Interview: An Innovative Technique for Questioning Witnesses of Crime," *Journal of Police and Criminal Psychology,* 4:2 (October 1988), 3.

[23]   Ibid.

[24]   Ibid.

[25]   Ibid., 4–5.

Discussion Questions

1.   What is the difference between interviews and interrogation?

2.   What are some of the principal aspects of interviewing?

3.   What is a common mistake investigators make when conducting interviews?

4.   What are some of the reasons that individuals refuse to cooperate in an interview?

5.   Why is neighborhood canvassing important in an investigation?

6.   What is a behavioral analysis interview?

7.   What are some of the issues related to eyewitness evidence?

Supplemental Readings

Bennett, M., John, E., & Hess, M. (Mar. 1991). Cognitive interviewing. *FBI Law Enforcement Bulletin 60(3)*, 8–12.

Ekman, P., & Wallace, V. F. (2003). *Unmasking the face*. Cambridge, MA: Malor Books.

Fast, J. (2002). *Body language*. New York: M: Evans and Company.

Fisher, R. P. (1992). *An R.E. Geiselman memory-enhancing technique for investigative interviewing: The cognitive interview.* Text. Ed. Springfield, IL: Charles C. Thomas.

Fisher, R. P., Falkner, K. L., Trevisan, M., & McCauley, M. R. (2000). Adapting the cognitive interview to enhance long-term recall of physical activities. *Journal of Applied Psychology, 85*, 180–189.

George, R., & Clifford, B. (1996). The cognitive interview—does it work? In G. Davies, S. Lloyd-Bostock, M. McMunan & C. Wilson (Eds.), *Psychology, law and criminal justice: International developments in research and practice* (pp. 146–154). New York: Walter de Gruyter.

Gordon, N. J., & William, L. (2011). Fleisher: *Effective interviewing and interrogation techniques* (3rd ed.). Boston: Elsevier/Academic Press.

Hess, J. (2011). *Interviewing and interrogation for law enforcement* (2nd ed.). Boston: Elsevier/Anderson Publishing.

Rabon, D., & Tanya, C. (2008). *Interviewing and interrogation.* Durham, NC: Carolina Academic Press.

Shearer, R. A. (2001). *Interviewing in criminal justice* (4th ed.). Acton, MA: Copley.

Spaulding, W. (1987). *Interviewing child victims of sexual exploitation.* Arlington, VA: National Center for Missing and Exploited Children.

Starrett, P. E., & Joseph, N. D. (2004). *Interview and interrogation with eyewitness evidence.* San Clemente, CA: LawTech.

Zulawski, D. E., & Wicklander, D. E. (Eds.). (2001). *Practical aspects of interview and Interrogation* (2nd ed.). Boca Raton, FL: CRC Press.

CHAPTER 7

INFORMANTS
Cultivation and Motivation

A BACKGROUND ON INFORMANTS

Anyone who discloses investigative information can be considered an informant. Today's journalists call their informants "sources". But whether the information is given to journalists or criminal investigators, when what is revealed is the result of a relatively close relationship between the informant and the one informed on, there is a certain repugnance attached to the activity. This is why unsavory names such as *stool pigeon, squealer, rat, fink, snitch, snout, informer*, and *agent provocateur* have been coined to describe those perceived as betrayers. And yet, no religious faith holds this practice—as old as civilization itself—to be morally wrong. Neither does the judiciary: as Judge Learned Hand writes, "Courts have countenanced informers from time immemorial."[1]

Hoffa v. United States can be considered one of the landmark cases involving police informants and the admissibility of their testimony in court. Notorious organized crime member James Hoffa was convicted of attempting to bribe members of a jury in a previous case. During the previous case, referred to as the "Test Fleet trial," Hoffa was staying in a local hotel in Nashville, Tennessee, and was in constant contact with several members of the Teamsters Union. One of these members made frequent trips to Nashville and would relay information discussed among Hoffa and his associates to a federal agent. This information was significant in the conviction of Hoffa and four of his associates for the attempted bribery of a jury member. Hoffa appealed his conviction to the Supreme Court; the issue in this case was:

> Whether evidence obtained by the Government by means of deceptively placing a secret informer in the quarters and councils of a defendant during one criminal trial so violates the defendant's Fourth, Fifth and Sixth Amendment rights that suppression of such evidence is required in a subsequent trial of the same defendant on a different charge.[2]

In response to this issue, the court denied Hoffa's claim of infringement on his constitutional rights, and made several significant findings relevant to future cases on informants. With regard to violations of Fourth Amendment rights, the court stated:

> In the present case, however, it is evident that no interest legitimately protected by the Fourth Amendment is involved. It is obvious that the petitioner was not relying on the security of his hotel suite when he made the incriminating statements to Partin or in Partin's presence. Partin did not enter the suite by force or by stealth. He was not a surreptitious eavesdropper. Partin was in the suite by invitation, and every conversation which he heard was either directed to

him or knowingly carried on in his presence. The petitioner, in a word, was not relying on the security of the hotel room; he was relying upon his misplaced confidence that Partin would not reveal his wrongdoing ... Neither this Court nor any member of it has ever expressed the view that the Fourth Amendment protects a wrongdoer's misplaced belief that a person to whom he voluntarily confides his wrongdoing will not reveal it."[3]

The court also found no support for Hoffa's allegation of Fifth Amendment violations, primarily because his statements were not a result of coercion or force. The court did not find any evidence of a Sixth Amendment violation, and Hoffa was not prevented from conferring with his counsel. Last, in regard to Hoffa's alleged due process violations, the court issued a strongly worded denial:

The argument boils down to a general attack upon the use of a government informer as 'a shabby thing in any case,' and to the claim that in the circumstances of this particular case the risk that Partin's testimony might be perjurious was very high. Insofar as the general attack upon the use of informers is based upon historic 'notions' of 'English-speaking peoples,' it is without historical foundation. In the words of Judge Learned Hand, 'Courts have countenanced the use of informers from time immemorial; in cases of conspiracy, or in other cases when the crime consists of preparing for another crime, it is usually necessary to rely upon them or upon accomplices because the criminals will almost certainly proceed covertly.'[4]

Alternatively, the dissenting opinion by Chief Justice Earl Warren stated:

At this late date in the annals of law enforcement, it seems to me that we cannot say either that every use of informers and undercover agents is proper or, on the other hand, that no uses are. There are some situations where the law could not adequately be enforced without the employment of some guile or misrepresentation of identity. A law enforcement officer performing his official duties cannot be required always to be in uniform or to wear his badge of authority on the lapel of his civilian clothing. Nor need he be required in all situations to proclaim himself an arm of the law. It blinks the realities of sophisticated, modern-day criminal activity and legitimate law enforcement practices to argue the contrary.[5]

In *Maine v. Moulton*, a case somewhat similar to *Hoffa*, the Court returned to the state's recruitment of an "insider" as an informant.[6] Colson, the informant and co-defendant with Moulton, was to learn of Moulton's threats and inchoate plans to murder a key prosecution witness (and other witnesses) in their upcoming trial. As the police wired his body with a transmitter, they warned Colson to "act natural," "not to attempt to question Moulton," and to "avoid trying to draw information out of Moulton."[7] Disregarding these admonitions and pretending memory lapse, Colson elicited incriminating facts concerning the event, as well as other joint criminal endeavors for which neither man had been indicted. On this evidence, additional felony charges were brought against Moulton, and he was convicted. He appealed on the ground that the admission into evidence of his statements to Colson violated his Sixth Amendment right to the assistance of counsel. In its decision affirming the conviction, the Court refers to and cites the Supreme Judicial Court of Maine, 481 A.2d 155 (1984):

... Regarding the admission of Moulton's recorded statements to Colson, the court agreed that there was "ample evidence" to support the trial court's finding that the police wired Colson for legitimate purposes, but held that "[r]eference to the State's legitimate motive may be relevant to, but cannot wholly refute, the alleged infringement of Moulton's right to counsel." Id., at 160... . the fact that at the time of the meeting Colson was "fully cooperating with the police and no longer stood in the same adversarial position as did Moulton," the (Maine Supreme) court held:

> When the police recommended the use of the body wire to Colson they intentionally created a situation that they knew, or should have known, was likely to result in Moulton's making incriminating statements during his meeting with Colson. The police's valid purpose in investigating threats against witnesses does not immunize the recordings of Moulton's incriminating statements from constitutional attack. Those statements may be admissible in the investigation or prosecution of charges for which, at the time the recordings were made, adversary proceedings had not yet commenced. But as to the charges for which Moulton's right to counsel had already attached, his incriminating statements should have been ruled inadmissible at trial, given the circumstances in which they were acquired. Id., at 161.[8]

In an early edition of *Constitutional Law*, John Klotter summarized the *Moulton* case as such:

> Succinctly, the rule in this case is that when a defendant has been formally charged with a crime and has retained counsel, incriminating statements made to an undercover informant, whose remarks prompted the statement, are not admissible.[9]

USEFULNESS

The reasons individuals furnish information to an investigator can be laudable as well as nefarious. Whatever the reason, an informant is one who furnishes intelligence that may:

1. Prevent a crime that is planned but not yet committed;
2. Uncover a crime that has been committed but has not been discovered or reported;
3. Identify the perpetrator of a crime;
4. Locate the perpetrator of a crime or help to locate stolen property;
5. Exonerate a suspect;
6. Lower morale among criminals through apprehension (unanticipated by those involved in unlawful activity).

How such different results can be achieved from information supplied by informants is best understood by considering the types of informants and their motivations. Table 7.1 summarizes this material.

TYPES OF INFORMANTS

There are many types of informants. There are informants who volunteer information and those who expect some form of payment (which need not be, but most often is money). Either type may act openly or upon the condition that their identity not be revealed. Others remain anonymous, furnishing information via telephone or mail. Some informants are generalists; others, specialists. Some function but once; others, continuously.

Table 7.1
Types of Informants; Information and Motivation

TYPE OF INFORMANT	OPEN		CONFIDENTIAL	
	Type of Information	Motivation	Type of Information	Motivation
VOLUNTEER	Observations of an eyewitness to a crime Facts on record or in a file Wife tells authorities about husband's gambling activities Income tax	Civic duty, vanity Official duty (one department to another) Monetary reward Revenge, gratitude	An investigator may receive, from time to time, details about almost any criminal activity Reports about vice activities Reports about suspicious behavior	Building a line of credit Friendship between informant and detective Fear, gratitude, civic duty Elimination of competition
PAID	Particulars about a specific crime or person Income tax matters	Monetary reward To make a "deal" with the police or prosecutor, i.e., plea bargaining Revenge, money from an informant fund	Income tax matters As above, information about almost any criminal activity	Monetary reward Payment from an informant fund Lenient treatment by authorities Revenge
ANONYMOUS	N/A	N/A	Precise information about a crime or its perpetrator Suspicious activities	Civic duty, fear, revenge, jealousy, repentance, gratitude Elimination of competition Money, reward

Municipal police departments and federal agencies hold different points of view with regard to informants. In police departments, each informant will usually work with a particular detective. When that officer is reassigned, retires, or dies, the informant frequently is lost to the department. In federal agencies, informants are seen as belonging to the agency and are passed along from one investigator to another. At that level, the administrative controls that exist for dealing with informants are generally more elaborate than at the local level, and funds are available to purchase information.

The kinds of investigative information made available by informants are dependent on various factors: the informant's relationship to the person or activity being reported on; where they live, work, or hang around; what opportunities exist to observe an individual's or group's behavior or activity;

and their motivation for providing the information. In other words, the contributory factors are opportunity and motivation.

At the outset it should be made clear that understanding the motives of informants is an important consideration for the investigator. All too often in an effort to build a case the investigator does not thoroughly question the informant or develop background as to the truthfulness of the individual and the information provided. Even citizens with what appears to be "no axe to grind" in providing information may have biases that are not readily apparent. Other individuals may be looking for attention or have conscious or subconscious feelings about a specific crime or suspect.

MOTIVES FOR INFORMING

Basic motives include fear, revenge, jealousy, repentance, gratitude, and concern with civic duty. Occasionally, individuals are prompted to act as an informant for venally self-serving and psychologically self-aggrandizing motives. An example of such mixed motivation is found in *The Informant*.[10] An engrossing tale of how a multi-motivated "insider," partly for psychological self-aggrandizement and partly for venal reasons, toppled his fellow corporate officers is superbly described in this book. A senior corporate insider looking to protect himself, but also out of civic duty, becomes an FBI informant. As the story unfolds, the agents recognize a shift in his motivation so that at the end, greed and betrayal emerge as motivating factors, while deceit and arrogance serve to meet deep psychological needs in carrying out his own agenda. Increasingly, the FBI agents are hard-pressed to control the destructive behavior of their informant while mindful that the case is threatened within by bureaucratic infighting about which branch of the Justice Department (the fraud division or the criminal division) was to prosecute and when it was to go to trial. The twists and turns encountered in this tale illustrate the difficulties that can arise in dealing with an informant who is disclosing a vast global conspiracy to fix commodity and other prices on the world market. Wearing a device to record the dialogue of the illegal meetings of top-level executives setting world market prices, the informant's recordings were viewed by investigators as almost too good to be true. However, government attorneys were less than pleased by them because the word "agreement" was not to be heard in the recordings although it was evident, on listening, that the conspirators were price-fixing. This points out the need to involve prosecutors early on, especially in complicated cases in which evidence is largely provided by an informant.

Self-Serving Reasons

Three kinds of self-serving (usually venal) motives are: cutting a deal, eliminating competition, and building a line of credit for future use.

Cutting a Deal

A deal is cut when a defendant agrees to impart what he or she knows about criminal activities in exchange for a promise (by a detective through a ranking departmental official) that a special recommendation for consideration will be made to a judge in a pending prosecution. By this means, informants may reduce or avoid altogether the punishment that would otherwise be expected on conviction. As a *quid pro quo* (something for something) arrangement, cutting a deal is in one sense a form of plea bargaining.

Elimination of Competition

In specialized crimes, particularly vice and narcotics (and, to some extent, arson and burglary), one lawbreaker may, most often anonymously, betray a rival to eliminate competition. This can occur when a new burglar invades the area and the rash of break-ins increases community pressure and police activity. By taking the competitor out of circulation, community anxiety will be kept at a level that does not provoke undue police response.

Building a Line of Credit

Uneasy pawnbrokers and secondhand dealers worry that police may one day discover stolen goods in their shops and accuse them of being receivers. Some will attempt to establish that they are not receivers by identifying those in the community who are fencing stolen goods, using this as a way to ingratiate themselves with authorities. For others on the fringe of the underworld, the ploy is to earn favors that could stay an arrest should they be apprehended for some law violation.

Mercenary Reasons

The old saying among investigators, "When the money ceases to clatter, the tongue stops the chatter," confirms what they well know: namely, that offering a reward for information is of fundamental importance. Merchants and farmers have long resorted to a bounty system; they will pay to find those responsible for stealing their merchandise or rustling their cattle. Law enforcement agencies budget ready monies (sometimes called "contingency funds") to buy information. The federal government is more lavish in this regard.

Self-Aggrandizement

Ordinary citizens as well as reformed criminals are motivated by vanity to provide information, believing it will win favorable attention from authorities. Employers, friends, and even the media in important cases may put them in the spotlight, making them instant celebrities. Because anonymity offers the best protection against retaliation, it is prudent that police safeguard such informants until public attention is directed elsewhere.

Emotions

Fear, revenge, jealousy, repentance, and gratitude are among the emotions that often induce people to divulge what otherwise would remain unrevealed. When the information concerns criminal activity, it usually constitutes a major break in an investigation.

Fear

Fear is a powerful inducement to becoming an informer; however, protection must be negotiated with authorities. It may be fear for one's self or fear for one's family being killed, tortured, or harmed in some fashion. Fear of imprisonment will cause some people to seek a trade-off: information for "nol-prossing" an indictment (i.e., convincing the prosecutor to agree not to proceed any further with the action; "nol-pros" is short for *nolle prosequi*). When a gang member takes to heavy drinking, becomes sexually involved, and rashly starts to tell a new partner everything—or displays conduct that otherwise seems to threaten the security of the group—he or she will be told in no uncertain terms to change, "or else." For more than a few, the reaction would be to inform on the gang's activities.

Revenge and Jealousy

A grudge based on a perception of unfair treatment can provoke a desire for revenge. However hackneyed the expression "Hell hath no fury like a woman scorned," it still seems to speak for the pain of rejection. Indeed, any pain or distress induced by another can result in jealousy and the need for revenge, and turn a person to informing. The need to get even is deep in the human psyche.

Repentance

Just as those who have "got religion" will be led by a need for forgiveness and reestablishment in the community to furnish what they would not have disclosed before, so will the outcast make amends by informing on confederates in past crimes. The approbation of newly acquired peers is an especially strong stimulus.

Gratitude

Gratitude is not usually a major factor in prompting an individual to furnish information, but it can be potent at times. Frequently the actions of a police officer or investigator in going out of their way to assist a citizen may result in a "return of the favor" by providing information. An investigator should recognize that every contact with another individual creates an opportunity, and the manner in which a citizen or colleague is spoken to or handled may well be the difference between receiving or being denied information.

Whistleblowers

Disaffected employees or individuals who believe that an organization or group is operating outside the law are often willing to serve as confidential informants to help gather information, or provide records of illegal activities. In such cases the investigator should be very familiar with the reasons an individual may be cooperating. They may be trying to cover up their own illegal activities; they may have a grudge against someone, perhaps because they were not promoted; or they may be trying to protect someone else in the company.

Nevertheless, whistleblowers have proven to be very helpful in developing a case, and the investigator, even if harboring suspicions, should not ignore allegations. One of the most effective means of "checking out" a whistleblower is to encourage them to provide details that can be checked, to maintain detailed records of allegations and when they were made, and as the investigation proceeds, to try to develop corroborating information or evidence.

Where the identity of an informant can be kept secret, the investigator is more likely to maintain an ongoing source.

Media Informants

Informants may not necessarily come forward to the police, but the information they provide to the media can prove useful in criminal investigations. Although reporters will not generally release the names of their informants, they are frequently willing to provide information to investigators. For this reason it is wise to maintain cordial relationships with reporters, recognizing that there is also the danger of becoming a confidential informant for a journalist.

Perhaps the most successful whistleblower was senior FBI official Mark Felt, known by the cover name of "Deep Throat," who leaked information to *Washington Post* reporters Robert Woodward and Carl Bernstein in the so-called Watergate scandal. Felt was not identified until 31 years after Nixon's resignation.

Civic Duty

A significant motivating factor for informing is a sense of good citizenship. When an eyewitness tells police of observations made while a crime was being committed, or of suspicious behavior noted, that person carries out a civic duty.

OPPORTUNITY

Two kinds of opportunity must prevail if an individual is to function as an informant: one is to acquire useful information; the other is to reveal it without exposure to retaliation. Before an individual can function as an informant, the opportunity must exist to observe through sight, sound, or even smell, taste, or touch. Most often, it is provided by chance; the rest of the time, by propinquity of relationship or location (kinship or proximity furnishing more than a few opportunities for acquiring what may later be disclosed). Anonymous and confidential informants needing assurance that their identities will not be revealed may still want to be able to collect a reward if one is offered. With these needs in mind, two mechanisms have been developed: a widely publicized special hotline telephone number and the anonymous tip. By calling police, the informant can claim the reward should the tip lead to an arrest and indictment. As noted earlier, civic associations, such as Crime Stoppers, represent a valuable tool.

CULTIVATION OF INFORMANTS

The combination of opportunity and motivation required for a person to serve as an informant need not be left to chance. The experienced detective will recognize or create the opportunity to develop informants through an intimate knowledge of the neighborhood and the character of its inhabitants. Timing can be critical: thus, a falling out among thieves or between lovers, or the decision of a law violator to rejoin the community of the law abiding can be propitious for cultivating informants. To capitalize on such openings as they occur, the detective must remain assigned to the same geographical area.

The itinerant nature of federal investigative assignments often forecloses the opportunities enjoyed by municipal, and to some extent, state investigators. This may partially account for the greater reliance at the federal level on money as the motivating factor in developing informants. See Box 7.1.

Box 7.1 Cultivating Informants

Certain occupations and persons who have informal associations with a large number of people are likely to be good informants. They include:

- Bartenders and waitresses
- Utility employees who have access to residences and businesses
- Postal carriers and delivery workers (e.g., UPS, Federal Express, DHL)
- Maintenance workers
- Service employees (such as licensing department personnel, clerks, meter readers)
- Credit card security investigators

DEALING WITH INFORMANTS

The following discussion is based on the collective experience of investigators in dealing with informants.

The Investigator–Informant Relationship

The relationship between investigator and informant can be fashioned in several ways. It might be a business arrangement in which the informant understands that the investigator associates with and employs him or her only to obtain information. The informant's motivation is often pecuniary, but another satisfaction such as revenge may serve as the inducement. A respectful relationship can be adopted with those motivated by vanity or civic duty. For the majority, a friendly relationship is probably the most useful. Although informants treated as equals may be eager to obtain the information needed, they nonetheless can be difficult to handle and may become a source of embarrassment. If the same results are otherwise achievable, informants should not be used.

Handling Informants

An informant who initially intends to furnish only limited information will often supply much more if properly handled. In light of this fact, the investigator should keep the following points in mind:

1. Meet the informant on neutral ground for the individual's protection and to preserve anonymity. Be careful to keep appointments.

2. Treat the informant fairly. Make promises with every intention of carrying them out; make none that cannot be fulfilled legally.

3. Treat the informant courteously. Never use offensive terms (such as fink, snitch, squealer, stoolie, double-crosser). Describing an informant as a "confidential source" or "special employee" is acceptable.

4. The value of appealing to the reason that motivated the informant should not be forgotten.

5. Newly recruited informants must be clued in with respect to the information sought and the target(s) to be aimed at and reported on. While admonishing them to exercise great care in doing so, investigators should encourage them to organize and develop subsources.

6. Informants must be taught what constitutes entrapment; in dealing with any person (including a suspect), they must avoid the possibility or even the appearance of entrapment.

7. The importance of maintaining their "cover" must be stressed; otherwise, they may compromise their own security or that of the investigation.

8. Never permit informants to take charge of the investigation—to "run the show." Tact is necessary to keep them in line when, intentionally or not, they attempt to direct any phase of the investigation. (This can occur when the informant begins to like the notion of playing detective).

9. An informant may not, in general, be permitted to commit a crime in return for information.

10. In all financial transactions the investigator must be scrupulously exact. Except where necessary to keep an informant interested, payment should not be made until the value of the information has been verified; also, proof of payment should be obtained, if possible.

11. Maintain a Confidential Informant File that is known to superiors.

Interviewing Informants

There is a technique for interviewing informants that is made clear by the following suggestions:

1. After allowing them to state what they wish to report, subtly press for details. Take notes or otherwise record the information as soon as possible after the interview.

2. Be tactful: accept any information offered at its face value. Expressing appreciation for valuable information is an inexpensive form of encouragement that will be well received by the informant. Do not belittle worthless information.

3. To check on the informant's reliability, ask for information that is already known. Take great care to frame the questions so that what is known is not divulged.

4. Do not reveal to informants how their information differs from other information (if it does).

5. Be sympathetic about any difficulties the informant may be experiencing in attempting to secure information.

6. Avoid asking questions that may be embarrassing or that pry into the informant's private affairs. Avoid arguments.

7. Maintain control of the interview. Do not allow it to wander too far afield. Keep the focus on what is sought.

Potential Problems and Precautions

The early years of detective work involved a close relationship between criminals and police. Because many informants still come from the underworld, the potential for corruption exists. This is especially true today in the enforcement of those victimless crimes in which considerable money can be made. Thus, a distinction is made between the general investigator and the investigator who is charged with a specific function, such as anti-corruption or licensing enforcement.

In recent years the use of informants in terrorist-related cases has become prevalent, and the testimony of the informant frequently forms the basis for an arrest as well as a conviction. Frequently, the informant provides information to avoid or lessen charges being brought against him or her. The defense will argue that the informant was pressured or threatened by the police, and that testimony should be excluded.

Similar situations arise in other criminal cases in which an individual who was a part of the crime provides information to lessen his or her sentence. In such cases, popular opinion frequently focuses on the actions of the police as being overbearing, manipulative, and threatening.

If an informant will be used in court to help establish a case, the investigator should make every effort to develop other evidence that supports the witness's statements. Examples might include wiretap recordings; individual actions of the other defendants, such as purchasing weapons or meeting separately with other suspects; or collected evidence of the suspect committing illegal acts.

AP Photo/Phil Coale

Figure 7.1
Margie Weiss, mother of Rachel Hoffman, waits for a news conference to start after the Florida House of Representatives passed "Rachel's Law," a confidential informants bill. The bill, named after Hoffman, who was killed in her role as a confidential informant for the Tallahassee Police Department, requires law enforcement to train informants, make sure they are fully aware of their rights, and allow them to seek legal counsel before agreeing to comply.

Similar Problems in Other Fields

It is illuminating to examine a similar problem in another field. In newspaper reporting, for instance, problems may arise when the identity of an informant (or "source") is not disclosed to the editor. When asked, reporters generally are required to divulge such information to their editor, but sometimes exceptions are made, as was the case in the so-called Watergate case.

Disclosure of a source of information becomes a matter of contention when a court or grand jury orders a news reporter to reveal the source. Because this issue is not covered by common law (as are privileged communications between attorney and client, for instance), it has come before state and federal courts with diverse results. For this reason, and in response to pleas from the journalistic profession, some state legislatures (but not the Congress) have passed laws to protect news reporters from being forced to divulge what they received in confidence.

GUIDELINES FOR THE USE OF INFORMANTS

The Attorney General of the United States issued a set of guidelines on the use of informants and confidential sources by the FBI. More extensively formulated than those issued publicly by the Home Secretary, it nonetheless covers much the same territory. For example, the introduction stated:

(1) The courts have recognized that the government's use of informants and confidential sources is lawful and often essential to the effectiveness of properly authorized law enforcement investigations. However, use of informants and confidential sources to assist in the investigation of criminal activity may involve an element of deception, intrusion into the privacy of individuals, or cooperation with persons whose reliability and motivation can be open to question. It is proper for the FBI to use informants and confidential sources in appropriate investigations, but special care must be taken to carefully evaluate and closely supervise their use, and to ensure that individual rights are not infringed and that the government itself does not become a violator of the law. Though informants and confidential sources are not employees of the FBI, their relationship to the FBI can impose a special responsibility on the FBI when the informant or confidential source engages in activity where he has received, or reasonably thinks he has received, encouragement or direction for that activity from the FBI.

(2) To implement these guidelines, the FBI shall issue detailed instructions to all Special Agents responsible for dealing with informants and confidential sources.[11]

The use of informants was then described under the following section:

General Authority

(1) An informant or confidential source may be asked to provide information already in his possession, to provide information which comes to his attention, or to affirmatively seek out information concerning criminal conduct or other subjects of authorized investigative activity. An informant or confidential source may also be asked to provide operational assistance to the FBI, including furnishing resources or facilities.

(2) The FBI may only use informants or confidential sources in furtherance of its authorized investigative activities and law enforcement responsibilities. Informants and confidential sources may not be used or encouraged to commit acts which the FBI could not authorize for its Special Agents.[12]

The guidelines also require that an informant or confidential source appear suitable for such a role. In making such a determination, the following factors should be weighed:

(a) the nature of the matter under investigation and the importance of the information or assistance being furnished;

(b) the seriousness of past and contemporaneous criminal activity of which the informant or confidential source may be suspected;

(c) the motivation of the informant or confidential source, including any consideration sought from the government for his cooperation;

(d) the likelihood that the information or assistance which an informant or confidential source could provide is not available in a timely and effective manner by less intrusive means;

(e) the informant's or confidential source's reliability and truthfulness, or the availability of means to verify information which he provides;

(f)   any record of conformance by the informant or confidential source to Bureau instructions and control in past operations: how closely the Bureau will be able to monitor and control the informant's or confidential source's activities insofar as he is acting on behalf of the Bureau;

(g)   the risk that use of informants or confidential sources in the particular investigation may intrude upon privileged communications, or inhibit the lawful association of individuals or expression of ideas; and

(h)   any risk that use of informants or confidential sources may compromise an investigation or subsequent prosecution, including court-ordered disclosures of identity which may require the government to move for dismissal of the criminal case.[13]

Regarding the participation of an informant or confidential source in an activity that would be criminal under state or federal law, the guidelines define it as "otherwise illegal activity." It is justified when the benefits to be obtained outweigh the risks and it is necessary:

(a)   to obtain information or evidence essential for the success of an investigation without such authorization [of otherwise illegal activity] or

(b)   to prevent death, serious bodily injury, or significant damage to property, and

(c)   if the need outweighs the seriousness of the conduct involved.[14]

Only designated supervisory FBI officials may authorize participation in otherwise criminal activity; and then only after a written finding that the above two conditions have been met. In other venues at the state and local level, most agencies have or should have written policies on informants.

> ### Important Court Cases Related to the Use of Informants
>
> *Aguilar v. Texas*
>
> *Draper v. United States*
>
> *Hoffa v. United States*
>
> *Illinois v. Gates*
>
> *Maine v. Moulton*
>
> *McCray v. Illinois*
>
> *Roviaro v. United States*
>
> *Shaw v. Illinois*
>
> *Smith v. Illinois*
>
> *Sorrels v. United States*
>
> *Spinelli v. United States*

LEGALITY OF EVIDENCE BASED ON INFORMANT-SUPPLIED INFORMATION

Legal issues can arise from the use of information furnished by an informant. Two issues have been raised by defense attorneys when evidence is seized or an arrest is made (with or without a warrant) on the basis of information supplied by an informant. One concerns the Fourth Amendment protection against unreasonable searches and seizures: based on an informant's tip, does probable cause exist to support an arrest or a seizure of evidence? The other concerns the Sixth Amendment right of a defendant to prepare a defense: must the identity of the informant be revealed, if sought for this purpose in a motion for a bill of particulars?

Probable Cause

The most difficult question regarding probable cause arises when the basis for establishing it depends on an unnamed informant's (hearsay) information. If a search warrant was approved by a judge, or the police made a warrantless search and arrest, will the evidence so obtained be suppressed on a defense attorney's motion? The objection rests on the propriety of using hearsay evidence to establish probable cause.

There are a number of Supreme Court decisions on this issue. In *Draper v. United States*, the Court specifically approved the use of an informant's hearsay information to make a warrantless arrest.[15] In *Aguilar v. Texas*, the Court reaffirmed previous decisions that the affidavit for an arrest warrant need not involve the personal, direct observation of the affiant, and that it may be based on hearsay information from an informant whose identity is not revealed.[16] The Court added, however, that the magistrate must be informed of the circumstances that caused the informant to conclude that a crime had, in fact, been committed. A few years later, in *Spinelli v. United States*, a two-pronged test was suggested to determine when an unnamed informant's information could be used to show probable cause.[17] The test would require: (1) that the informant be reliable, and (2) that the informant's information be credible.

After a decade and a half of experience with *Aguilar* and *Spinelli*, the Court abandoned them. Its next approach to evaluating an informant's hearsay evidence as a means of establishing probable cause was stated in *Illinois v. Gates*:

> ... we conclude that it is wiser to abandon the "two pronged test" established by our decisions in *Aguilar* and *Spinelli*. In its place we reaffirm the totality of the circumstances analysis that traditionally has informed probable cause determinations. The task of the issuing magistrate is simply to make a practical common-sense decision whether, given all the circumstances set forth in the affidavit before him, including the "veracity" and "basis of knowledge" of persons supplying hearsay information, there is a fair probability that contraband or evidence of a crime will be found in a particular place. And the duty of a reviewing court is simply to ensure that the magistrate had a "substantial basis for ... conclude [ing]" that probable cause existed.[18]

It is significant to note that in *Gates* an anonymous letter to police provided the basis for obtaining a search warrant. All of the facts (detailed travel plans of Sue Gates and Lance Gates to transport narcotics) alleged in the letter were verified through investigation, yet the Illinois Supreme Court sustained the trial court's suppression of the evidence. It reasoned that the letter failed both prongs of the *Spinelli* test. First, it provided no basis for determining the reliability and veracity of the informant. (Innocent people could well travel and behave as did the Gateses, without necessarily being involved in narcotics trafficking.) Second, the letter did not furnish the particulars (how the informant knew narcotics were actually present in the Gates household) that would allow a magistrate to make an informed decision concerning probable cause. In place of a detailed analysis to determine if the warrant affidavit met each prong, the Court reaffirmed a "totality of the circumstances analysis," thereby permitting the magistrate to intertwine the facts. Despite this revisionary attempt at clarification, an investigator would be well advised to bear the two-pronged test in mind, recognizing that if one prong is weak, the other must be strengthened in the affidavit.

Preservation of Confidentiality

The courts have consistently sided with the rights of individual informants to keep their identity confidential. Informants run a potential risk that harm will befall them or their families should their identities become known to the criminal or the criminal's associates. More than one has borne witness to the old proverb "Dead men tell no tales." In light of this possibility, they often seek assurances of anonymity. Such a promise can be made when an informant provides a lead that the investigator must follow up independently to obtain sufficient evidence for conviction. On the other hand, there are numerous reasons for a defense attorney to move for disclosure in preparing for, or in the midst of trial. Among them are:

1. To determine that the informant actually exists.

2. To determine the reliability of the informant.

3. To establish any differences between the police version of events and the informant's statements. (If the informant participated in the crime, is there a possibility of entrapment?)

4. To endeavor to have the charge dismissed by the court if the state refuses disclosure.

As to confidentiality, the Supreme Court decided in *Roviaro v. United States*:

> [A limitation on the applicability of the informer's privilege] arises from the fundamental requirements of fairness. Where the disclosure of an informer's identity, or of the content of his communication, is relevant and helpful to the defense of an accused, or is essential to a fair determination of a cause, the privilege must give way. In these situations, the trial court may require disclosure and, if the Government withholds the information, dismiss the action.[19]

At the same time the Court indicated that the rule regarding failure to disclose is not absolute with regard to reversible error.

> We believe that no fixed rule with respect to disclosure is justifiable. The problem is one that calls for balancing the public interest in protecting the flow of information against the individual's right to prepare his defense. Whether a proper balance renders nondisclosure erroneous must depend on the particular circumstances of each case, taking into consideration the crime charged, the possible defenses, the possible significance of the informer's testimony, and other relevant matters.[20]

A subsequent confidentiality case, *McCray v. Illinois*, involved an informant known by police to be reliable.[21] At a hearing to suppress, the defense requested but was denied the name and address of the informant. On conviction, the appeal was taken to the Supreme Court. Affirming the conviction, it held:

> When the issue is not guilt or innocence, but as here, the question of probable cause for an arrest or search, the Illinois Supreme Court has held that police officers need not invariably be required to disclose an informant's identity if the trial judge is convinced, by evidence submitted in open court and subject to cross-examination, that the officers did rely in good faith upon credible information supplied by a reliable informant.[22]

Elsewhere in the opinion, the Court went on to quote the New Jersey Supreme Court (*State v. Burnett*, 42 N.J. 377, 201 A.2d 39 (1974)):

> We must remember also that we are not dealing with the trial of the criminal charge itself. There the need for a truthful verdict outweighs society's need for the informer privilege.[23]

One year later, the Supreme Court accepted *Smith v. Illinois*,[24] which directly concerned an unnamed informant who testified at a trial (rather than a hearing to suppress). Asked to identify himself, the witness claiming to be the informant offered a fictitious name, and the trial judge denied a request for his true name. The Court reversed the conviction on Sixth Amendment grounds, stating that without knowing the identity of the informant, cross-examination could not be conducted effectively. In another Illinois case a year later (*Shaw v. Illinois*), the Court reversed the conviction on the basis of *Smith*.[25] The distinction in *Shaw* was that the informant gave his name but refused to reveal his address. Now, it would appear, an informant who testifies for the state must disclose both name and address if asked.

Entrapment

If grounds exist to support it, entrapment is another issue almost certain to be raised by a defense attorney. *Entrapment* may occur when a police officer (or an informant with official concurrence) beguiles an innocent person into committing a crime. This can be used as an affirmative defense for the accused; having committed an act that would otherwise be a crime, he or she is, by statute, not held accountable in this particular case. Entrapment is perpetrated when the following conditions are met:

1.   A law enforcement official (or a person cooperating with such an official);

2.   for the purpose of instituting a criminal prosecution;

3.   induces an individual;

4.   to engage in conduct that constitutes a criminal offense;

5.   by knowingly representing that such conduct is not prohibited by law; or prompting the individual who otherwise is not so inclined to act.

Sorrels v. United States was the first Supreme Court case that recognized entrapment as a viable defense. There are two tests that courts use to determine if a suspect has in fact been the victim of entrapment. The "objective" test focuses on the actions of the police; the "subjective" test focuses on the suspect's predisposition to commit crime.[26] The "subjective" test is used most often, and relies on characteristics of an individual's predisposition, such as arrest history.

Even if all of these enumerated conditions are unambiguously met, some ethical and legal questions still pertain. For example, as the U.S. Eastern District Court of New York states in the *United States v. Myers* case (Part V—"General Discussion of Basic Legal Concepts"):

> Whenever government agents, in carrying out their law enforcement functions, assist criminals or participate with them in their criminal activity, questions arise as to the propriety or legitimacy of the government's conduct and as to whether the law should punish a person for engaging in governmentally instigated criminal activity. The answers must draw on considerations of philosophy, psychology, statutory construction, constitutional law, practical needs of law enforcement, and even undifferentiated visceral feelings about right and wrong.
>
> Four Supreme Court decisions are central to the issue of entrapment. *Sorrells*, 287 U.S. 435; *Sherman* 356 U.S. 369; *Russell* 411 U.S. 423; *Hampton*, 425 U.S. 484, …
>
> Thus as the Court divided in Hampton, with Justice Stevens taking no part: three judges would make predisposition the only issue; three would eliminate predisposition entirely; and the decisive two concurring votes … indicate that predisposition is not only relevant but will be dispositive in all but the "rare" case where police over-involvement in the crime reaches "a demonstrable level of outrageousness."[27]

In other words, except when police encouragement and deception reaches a "demonstrable level of outrageousness" (i.e., conduct that grossly offends the sense of right and decency), an otherwise predisposed defendant can be convicted.

CONCLUSION

"Detectives are only as good as their informants" was a truism in law enforcement circles during the first half of the twentieth century. At that time, informant information ranged from a cautious hint to an almost completed case. Modern standards for permissible tactics are higher. As a result, extracting a confession after the perpetrator's name is supplied by an informant is no longer tolerated or considered adequate. Today, an informant's information provides direction for the detective that can shorten and strengthen an inquiry.

The opportunity to learn of a criminal's activities is never greater than when a close personal relationship between a criminal and an informant has fallen apart. The effective investigator is always cultivating potential informants and motivating them at the opportune moment to share what they know. Information obtained in this manner can represent an important breakthrough in an investigation by simplifying the task and improving the end product.

NOTES

[1] *United States v. Dennis*, 183 F.2d 201, 224 (2d Cir. 1950).

[2] *Hoffa v. United States*, 385 U.S. 293, 295–311 (1966).

[3] Ibid.

[4] Ibid.

[5] Ibid.

[6] *Maine v. Moulton*, 474 U.S. 159 (1985).

[7] Ibid., 165, 183.

[8] Ibid., 167-168.

[9] John C. Klotter and Jacqueline R. Kanovitz, *Constitutional Law*, 7th ed. (Cincinnati: Anderson, 1995), 426.

[10] Eichenwaldo, Kurt, *The Informant: A True Story* (New York: Broadway Books/Random House, 2000).

[11] Attorney General Benjamin Civiletti. "U.S. Attorney General's Guidelines on Criminal Investigations and Use of Informers," *Criminal Law Reporter* 28 (7 January 1981), 3032.

[12] Ibid.

[13] Ibid., 3033.

[14] *The Attorney General's Guidelines Regarding the Use of Confidential Informants*, May 30, 2002. Available at http://www.usdoj.gov/olp/dojguidelines.pdf

15   *Draper v. United States*, 358 U.S. 307 (1959).

16   *Aguilar v. Texas*, 378 U.S. 108 (1964).

17   *Spinelli v. United States*, 393 U.S. 410 (1969).

18   *Illinois v. Gates*, 462 U.S. 213 (1983). [Also see Kanovitz, *Constitutional Law*, 13th ed. (Boston: Elsevier/Anderson Publishing, 2013), Chapters 3 and 4.]

19   *Roviaro v. United States*, 353 U.S. 53, 58-61 (1957).

20   Ibid., 62.

21   *McCray v. Illinois*, 386 U.S. 300 (1967).

22   Ibid., 305.

23   Ibid., 307.

24   *Smith v. Illinois*, 390 U.S. 129 (1968).

25   *Shaw v. Illinois*, 394 U.S. 214 (1969).

26   *Sorrells v. United States*, 287 U.S. 435 (1932); *Sherman v. United States*, 356 U.S. 369 (1958); *United States v. Russell*, 411 U.S. 423 (1973).

27   *United States v. Myers*, 527 F. Supp. 1206 (E.D.N.Y. 1981).

IMPORTANT CASES

Aguilar v. Texas (1964)
Draper v. United States (1959)
Hoffa v. United States (1966)
Illinois v. Gates (1983)
Maine v. Moulton (1985)
McCray v. Illinois (1967)
Roviaro v. United States (1957)
Shaw v. Illinois (1969)
Smith v. Illinois (1968)
Sorrels v. United States (1932)
Spinelli v. United States (1969)
State v. Burnett (1974)
United States v. Dennis (1950)
United States v. Myers (1981)

DISCUSSION QUESTIONS

1. Identify the different types of informants

2. What are some of the reasons informants cooperate with law enforcement?

3. What are some of the potential problems and precautions an investigator must consider when working with informants?

4. What constitutes entrapment?

SUPPLEMENTAL READINGS

del Carmen, R. V., & Jeffery, T. W. (2012). *Briefs of leading cases in law enforcement* (8th ed.). Boston: Elsevier/Anderson Publishing.

Eichenwaldo, K. (2000). *The informant: A true story.* New York: Broadway Books/Random House.

Ingram, J. L. (2012). *Criminal evidence* (11th ed.). Boston: Elsevier/Anderson Publishing.

Kanovitz, Jacqueline R (2012). *Constitutional law* (13th ed.). Boston: Elsevier/Anderson Publishing.

Part C

FOLLOW-UP MEASURES: REAPING INFORMATION

Unfortunately, and for many reasons, investigators frequently fail to utilize information in the most effective or efficient manner. There is also a tendency for some investigators to either misread or misinterpret the vast amount of information that may be available in a case. In complex investigations there may be thousands of pages or even hundreds of boxes of data in a major case. The documents related to the JFK assassination fill a room, and the computer records and other data in the fraud case of stockbroker Bernard Madoff involve as much as a million documents, according to one investigator. Further, even where the information may be catalogued or recorded, its veracity may be in question.

When victim and eyewitness have been interviewed, laboratory findings reported, and records searched, the results must be assimilated, organized, and analyzed. They may be sufficient to identify and arrest the perpetrator or may suggest possible suspects to be investigated further. In either event, follow-up activity will depend on the facts on hand at that moment. If there is an eyewitness, an opportunity to scrutinize mug shots must be arranged without delay. If this is unproductive, an image of the offender should be developed by an artist, or from a composite image assembled with a facial-features kit or created by computer. Surveillance may be in order. When the end result is an arrest, additional action might require a lineup to see if a witness can make an identification. Finally, the suspect must be interrogated.

Understanding the theory underlying the methods provides a foundation. To become skilled in their use, on-the-job practice and experience are indispensable building blocks. (The police academy is well-suited to this purpose, as it can provide the requisite vicarious experience.)

Throughout an investigation the detective should be alert to potential clues that must be responded to and developed into evidence. This is a difficult process that calls for choices. In terms of resources and time, the choice must always be weighed against the likely yield of information—a *quasi*-cost/benefit consideration. The detective attuned to miscues and other unproductive leads conserves time and energy.

In summary, an alertness to unintentional hints, a healthy suspicion of everything said or observed, plus diligence, persistence, and thoroughness in follow-up efforts can serve as the cornerstone for promising, successful results.

CHAPTER 8

SURVEILLANCE
A Fact-Finding Tool—Legality and Practice

Conducting human surveillance is expensive. Indeed, to be successful, considerable resources in the form of work hours, equipment, and time (sometimes measured in months) must be invested. Given certain conditions, however, it may be the only means by which particular information can be obtained.

Advances in camera technology and digital storage have resulted in greater use of this technology for surveillance. In many ways, telescopic imaging and night vision equipment have improved to the point at which this form of surveillance can be better than natural visual efforts, and may also provide a record for later review. The drawback, of course, is the inability to follow a suspect. However, even this area is improving with the ability to "capture" a suspect on camera, and use this capability to "follow" the person as he or she moves from one location and camera to another.

Because surveillance requires a high degree of expertise, some larger police departments and federal agencies have established surveillance units. The FBI has non-agent surveillance teams in many cities, usually focusing on counter-intelligence or high-profile crimes. These teams are equipped with or have access to high-technology equipment as well as aircraft and unmarked vehicles.

The lore of surveillance is based for the most part on four perspectives. One view is the result of the "private eye's" experience in divorce cases, in which a relatively simple, one-on-one observation is feasible. Another is that of the "street smart" detective who learns from tailing professional criminals of the elaborate precautions they take to shake off the police. The third derives from the experience of investigators surveilling espionage agents who have been trained to detect and then lose anyone thought to be following them. The fourth involves technical surveillance practices. Increasingly, the use of electronic, video, and sophisticated monitoring technology has become more common in local law enforcement. These forms of surveillance, many used by federal agencies, as noted, enable investigators to monitor the movements or actions of suspects. In most cases, such action requires a court order. Because many of these techniques require a high degree of technical experience and skill, investigators will require additional training and support.

To understand the literature or participate in a surveillance operation, the reader should be conversant with the terms and jargon of the field. See Table 8.1.

KINDS OF SURVEILLANCE

Surveillance may be conducted from a stationary or fixed position, such as a parked van or a room facing the subject's residence or workplace, or by posing as a street vendor or utility worker. The aim is to allow the surveillant to remain inconspicuously in one locale. Occasionally a *fixed surveillance*

Table 8.1
Surveillance Terms to Know

Surveillance	the observation of a person, place, or thing, generally—but not necessarily—in an unobtrusive manner.
Electronic or technical surveillance	the use of any form of technological or computer equipment to monitor the movement or actions of a suspect.
Subject	the party under surveillance.
Surveillant	the person conducting the surveillance.
Tail	to follow and keep under surveillance; a surveillance.
Stakeout	also called a plant or fixed surveillance; here, the surveillant remains essentially in one position or locale. (The term is derived from the practice of tethering animals to a stake, allowing them a short radius in which to move.)
Undercover	an undercover agent who often gets to know or work alongside the subject. The term *roping* describes this situation, and the undercover agent is said to be *planted*.
Convoy	a countermeasure to detect a surveillance; a convoy, usually a person, is employed to determine whether a subject is under surveillance.
Shadow	to follow secretly; to place a person under surveillance.
Be made	to be detected or suspected of being a surveillant by the subject.
Burn the surveillance	when a surveillant's behavior causes the subject to surmise or know he or she is under surveillance.
Close surveillance	the subject is kept under constant surveillance. Also termed tight surveillance, the aim is not to lose the subject even at the risk of being "made." Example an arsonist (known through an informant or a wiretap) who sets out to burn an inhabited building.
Fixed surveillance	see Stakeout.
Moving surveillance	the surveillant moves about in order to follow the subject.
Loose surveillance	a cautious surveillance; also termed discreet surveillance because the loss of the subject is preferred over possible exposure. Example: obtaining information about a subject through tailing his or her associates when there is reason to believe the subject suspects there is a surveillance. Another example: a burglary gang "casing" banks to select their next job.
Open surveillance	a surveillance with little or no attempt at concealment; also termed rough surveillance, the subject is most likely aware of the surveillance, but must not be lost. Example: an important material witness who has been threatened refuses police protection.
Mustard plaster	a form of open surveillance; here, the subject is followed so closely that surveillant and subject are almost in lock step. It is tantamount to protective custody. See example for Open surveillance.
Plant	see Stakeout and Undercover.
Tailgating	a form of open surveillance in which the subject's vehicle is closely followed.
Mail cover	a method of tracking mail delivered to a particular person or address.

Table 8.1
(Continued)

Bugging	eavesdropping by electronic means, such as a hidden microphone or radio transmitter; bug: a device used for such eavesdropping.
GPS device	Global Positioning System device, a global navigation satellite system that provides reliable positioning, navigation, and timing services.
Pen register	a device that records all numbers dialed on a telephone; it is generally installed at the telephone company's central office.
Beeper	a battery-operated device that emits radio signals that permit it to be tracked (as it moves about) by a directional finder-receiver. Also called GPS device, beacon, transponder, and electronic tracking device.

is conducted openly; for instance, by posting a uniformed officer in front of a bank before business hours start.

More often, however, just as the subject moves about, so must the surveillant. Several means are employed in a *moving surveillance*. Surveillance can be conducted from a vehicle (automobile, bicycle, helicopter); on foot (walking, running), or even underwater (when the expertise of frogmen is required). *Electronic or technical surveillance* involves electronic eavesdropping devices (wiretaps, pen registers), electronic tracking devices (beepers and automobile GPS trackers), and assorted visual and infrared optical devices.

THE LEGALITY ISSUE

The issue of individual privacy (and possible harassment) has been invoked to confront the use of most forms of surveillance. Privacy and illegal search and seizure issues also have been used to confront the use of technical surveillance—employing as it does pen registers (to record all numbers dialed from a private phone) as well as wiretaps, electronic trackers (GPS devices), and telescopes or other optical devices (to listen, follow and record suspects, and peer into their homes or places of business). In 2012, the Supreme Court, in *United States v. Jones* held that police must obtain search warrants to utilize global tracking systems on vehicles.[1]

This decision was seen by some observers as the forerunner of the Court's move toward furthering restrictions under the Fourth Amendment on other forms of surveillance on electronic technology.

A Snoop Too Far?

New York City's counterterrorism unit came under fire in 2012 as a result of surveillance activities of Muslims outside the jurisdiction of the NYPD. Surveillance included the preparation of a report on Muslims in Newark that included "photographs of shops, restaurants and a school that are owned or frequented by Muslims." The report, prepared by the Intelligence Division, included information on Muslims on Long Island, a suburb of New York City. Information on Muslim college students was also collected, drawing criticism from civil rights groups. The police commissioner defended the Department's actions, noting, "If terrorists are not limited by borders and boundaries, we can't be either."

Source: *The Economist*, March 10, 2012, p. 44.

Fixed and Moving Surveillance

A major case dealing with these kinds of surveillance involves Sam Giancana, who was alleged to be the Mafia boss of the Chicago "family," when he brought a civil rights action.[2] Giancana claimed that the FBI had anywhere from three to five motor vehicles posted in a 24-hour close surveillance outside his residence, and that agents used binoculars to look into his home, and cameras with telescopic lenses to photograph people coming and going. He also claimed that he was closely followed into restaurants, stores, golf courses, and so on, and that the purpose of this was to embarrass, intimidate, and humiliate him in the eyes of his friends, neighbors, and associates.[3]

At the hearing for an injunction the judge stated:

> I suggest that the Bureau, and I think perhaps in order to give some force to it, that an injunction, a temporary injunction, be entered restraining the Bureau from having more than one car parked within a block of the plaintiff's house. This in no way is a restraining of having more than one car parked all over the neighborhood a block away. I feel that the parade of cars should be diminished to one car instead of three or four cars as the evidence heretofore indicates. I feel that one foursome should intervene between the plaintiff and his group, and those that are interested in determining what kind of game he is playing by following too closely.
>
> That I feel is as far as I can go without hampering the Bureau, and maybe that hampers them.[4]

Four days later the injunction was stayed. Later it was reversed on the ground that the federal district court judge lacked jurisdiction since Giancana had failed to allege damages of $10,000. On appeal, the Supreme Court denied certiorari, and there the matter ended.[5]

Electronic and Technical Surveillance and the USA PATRIOT Act

Technical and electronic surveillance involves the use of technology and visual enhancement devices to monitor suspects in the conduct of their daily affairs. Consequent legal issues are considered below.

Following the 9/11 attacks on the World Trade Center and the Pentagon, the U.S. Congress passed the Uniting and Strengthening America by Providing Appropriate Tools Required to Intercept and Obstruct Terrorism Act of 2001 (Public Law 107-56), known as the USA PATRIOT Act. This Act expanded the ability of law enforcement officials to conduct various types of surveillance in terrorism investigations. The impact of this development is covered more fully in Chapter 23.

The issue of electronic eavesdropping has become more complicated with the development of cell phones, text messaging, blogging, tweets, and other forms of direct and indirect communication using today's more sophisticated communications equipment. The Electronic Communications Privacy Act (ECPA) of 1986 expanded the powers of law enforcement to include Internet communication, and expanded the power of pen register use. The Federal Wiretap Act was initially enacted in 1968 under Title III of the Omnibus Crime Control Act, and was commonly referred to as the "Wiretap Act" or "Title III." In 1986, the federal statute was amended and is now the Electronic Communication Privacy Act (the "ECPA") (18 U.S.C.A. §§ 2510-3127). Although not technically correct, some courts and commentators continue to speak of the federal statute as "Title III." The ECPA amended the federal Wiretap Act to include cell phone conversations within the restrictions placed on wiretapping. The ECPA Amendments to the Wiretap Act now divide the Act into Titles I, II, and III. The former Title III is now Title I of the ECPA. Title I regulates the electronic surveillance of conversations (this could include e-mail conversations). Title II regulates access to e-mail, fax communications, and voicemail. Title III regulates call-tracing devices such as caller ID. Titles II and III are the most relevant to this chapter.[6]

Wiretapping

A 1928 Supreme Court decision concluded that wiretapping did not constitute unlawful search and seizure of messages passing over telephone wires and therefore did not come under the constitutional protection of the Fourth Amendment.[7] Undaunted, opponents turned to legislation. Their action to outlaw wiretapping is partially based on the *Olmstead v. United States* opinion written by Chief Justice Taft:

> Congress may of course protect the secrecy of telephone messages by making them, when intercepted, inadmissible in evidence in federal criminal trials, by direct legislation, and thus depart from the common law of evidence.[8]

Moving quickly on this suggestion, opponents thought they achieved relief through passage of the Federal Communications Act of 1934; Section 605 reads:

> ... [No] person not being authorized by the sender shall intercept any communication and divulge or publish the existence, contents, substance, purport, effect, or meaning of such intercepted communication to any person... .[9]

Subsequent Supreme Court decisions held that the wording of Section 605 covered federal and state officials as well as private persons, and applied to both interstate and intrastate transmissions. Wiretapping proponents were not to be undone. In reading Section 605, they noted that a telephone communication had to be intercepted and divulged to come under its provisions. Divulgence, they argued, meant disclosure to those outside of government; for instance, using it as evidence in court. They claimed further that a conversation between one investigator and another, or one between an investigator and a supervisor, did not constitute divulgence. Hence, so long as both requirements (interception and divulgence) had not been met, wiretapping did not take place. Because the Department of Justice supports this view, no prosecutions for wiretapping by government agents have been brought. In 1968, Congress partially abandoned Section 605 by passing the Omnibus Crime Control and Safe Streets Act. For the first time, law enforcement personnel were authorized to wiretap and conduct other kinds of electronic surveillance.[10]

Each state is free to enact measures against wiretapping stricter than those of the federal government. Because most states have done so, legality varies widely throughout the country. Some states have outlawed all wiretapping—whether by law enforcement or private citizens; others permit it to law enforcement personnel with court approval, but outlaw private wiretaps. Thus, when considering the use of wiretaps, it is particularly important for an investigator to ascertain its legal status in the jurisdiction involved.

Federal agents who rented an apartment next to a suspect and installed a microphone in the adjoining wall between the two apartments (without having to "penetrate or go physically into the other room") were found not to be in violation of the trespass rule.[11]

Mail Covers

One of the most effective tools in surveillance is the use of "mail covers." The Postal Inspection Service with the authority of a court order can copy the external writing or images addressed to a particular person or address to aid in an investigation. This procedure does not permit opening or using chemicals to see what is in the letter or package. (A possible exception is where drugs are being shipped by mail.) Knowing who is writing to or sending mail can provide important evidence during the course of an investigation.

Bugs, Pen Registers, Beepers

There are other ways to obtain investigative information in addition to wiretapping. They include: bugs to eavesdrop on private conversations, pen registers to record all numbers dialed, and beepers (GPS devices) attached—to a person, an automobile, or any wares being transported—to track the movement of a person or piece of merchandise. The Fourth Amendment's impact on these devices ranges from a total ban to outright approval.

Monitoring Conversations

Justice Tom C. Clark described eavesdropping as follows:

> At one time the eavesdropper listened by naked ear under the eaves of houses or their windows, or beyond their walls seeking after private discourse.[12]

Justice Hugo Black defined it another way:

> Perhaps as good a definition of eavesdropping as another is that it is listening secretly and sometimes "snoopily" to conversations and discussions believed to be private by those who engage in them. Eavesdroppers have always been deemed competent witnesses in English and American courts.[13]

It should be no surprise, however, that when it became possible to gather eavesdropping evidence through some kind of scientifically enhanced device, it would be challenged under the Fourth Amendment. When the first bugging case reached the Court in 1942, it was ruled that a detectaphone placed against a wall to listen to conversations in a neighboring office did not violate the amendment because there was no physical trespass upon the premises.[14] Two decades later, when a "spike mike" was inserted in an adjoining wall (making contact with a heating duct, "thus converting the [petitioner's] heating system into a conductor of sound"), the Court held it to be an intrusion of a constitutionally protected area—illegal search and seizure.[15] In another case of alleged trespass, the Court found no such transgression when, unknown to the suspect, a conversation inside his place of business was transmitted by one undercover agent "wired for sound" to another agent stationed outside to record it.[16]

Based on these cases, unless there is physical invasion of a constitutionally protected area, it would appear that electronic eavesdropping is permissible under the Fourth Amendment. But the *Katz v. United States* decision of 1967 alters this view.[17] In this case the suspect, placing a call from a public phone, had his conversation recorded by government investigators who had attached a listening device to the outside of the telephone booth. The Court held that the right to claim Fourth Amendment protection was not dependent upon a property right in the invaded place, but on a reasonable expectation of freedom from government intrusion.

> For the Fourth Amendment protects people, not places. What a person knowingly exposes to the public, even in his own home or office, is not a subject of a Fourth Amendment protection ... but what he seeks to preserve as private, even in an area accessible to the public, may be constitutionally protected.[18]

By adding the idea of privacy, the Court expanded the potential reach of the amendment. This will be clear when the use of a beeper for surveillance purposes is considered.

Katz is important because it also ventilates the Court's view on what legitimizes electronic surveillance.

> ... It is apparent that the agents in this case acted with restraint. Yet the inescapable fact is that this restraint was imposed by the agents themselves, not by a judicial officer. They were not required, before commencing the search, to present their estimate of probable cause for detached scrutiny by a neutral magistrate. They were not compelled, during the conduct of a search itself, to observe precise limits established in advance by a specific court order. Nor were they directed, after the search had been completed, to notify the authorizing magistrate in detail of all that had been seized. In the absence of such safeguards, this Court has never sustained a search upon the sole ground that officers reasonably expected to find evidence of a particular crime and voluntarily confined their activities to the least intrusive means consistent with that end. Searches conducted without warrants have been held unlawful "notwithstanding facts unquestionably showing probable cause," *Agnello v. United States*, 269 U.S. 20, 33 ... searches conducted outside the judicial process, without prior approval by judge or magistrate, are per se unreasonable under the Fourth Amendment—subject only to a few specifically established and well-delineated exceptions.[19]

Involving as it did a public telephone booth, *Katz* does not take up the issue of whether clandestine trespass to install a bug is permissible. This was resolved in 1979 by the Court in *Dalia v. United States*, when the constitutionality of Title III (Sections 2510–2520) of the Omnibus Crime Bill was challenged. (The former Title III permits courts to authorize electronic surveillance by government officers in specific situations.)[20] In the *Dalia* case, around midnight, FBI agents pried open an office window to install a bug in the ceiling; six weeks later, when they ceased the electronic surveillance, they reentered the office to remove the listening device. Partly on the basis of the overheard conversations, Dalia was convicted of receiving stolen goods. As framed by the Court the two issues were:

> ... First, may courts authorize electronic surveillance that requires covert entry into private premises for installation of the necessary equipment? Second, must authorization for such surveillance include a specific statement by the court that it approves of the covert entry?[21]

The first issue was disposed of:

> We make explicit, therefore, what has long been implicit in our decisions dealing with this subject: The Fourth Amendment does not prohibit *per se* a covert entry performed for the purpose of installing otherwise legal electronic bugging equipment.[22]

In resolving the second issue, however, the Court (going beyond the narrow issue posed) commented:

> The Fourth Amendment requires that search warrants be issued only "upon probable cause, supported by Oath or affirmation, and particularly describing the place to be searched, and the person or things to be seized." Finding these words to be "precise and clear" ... this Court has interpreted them to require only three things. First, warrants must be issued by neutral, disinterested magistrates ... Second, those seeking the warrant must demonstrate to the magistrate their probable cause to believe that "the evidence sought will aid in a particular apprehension or conviction" for a particular offense. ... Finally, "warrants must particularly describe the 'things to be seized'," as well as the place to be searched.[23]

These remarks are followed by the observation that:

> ... it is generally left to the discretion of the executing officers to determine the details of how best to proceed with the performance of a search authorized by warrant—subject of course to the general Fourth Amendment protection "against unreasonable searches and seizures."[24]

Finally, the Court settles the narrow issue posed:

> ... the Fourth Amendment does not require that a Title III electronic surveillance order include a specific authorization to enter covertly the premises described in the order.[25]

Monitoring Telephone Usage

It is obvious that telephones can be used to plan a crime, to help carry it out, and following its commission, to confer about avoiding detection or apprehension. It is also obvious that recorded information identifying who called whom would be of value to an investigator—especially if home phones are involved. The pen register, a telephone company device, is the least costly way to obtain such data. Generally but not necessarily installed at the utility's central offices, the pen register neither overhears conversations nor indicates whether a call was completed, but by monitoring the electrical impulses produced by rotary or push button phones, it records all numbers dialed.

What if a utility with the appropriate technical assistance and facilities refused to cooperate in the belief that government lacks authority to order an installation of the device? This question was joined and settled in 1977 when the Court held:

> ... The District Court had the power to authorize the installation of the pen registers under Federal Rule Crim. Proc. 41, that Rule being sufficiently flexible to include within its scope electronic intrusions authorized upon a finding of probable cause.[26]

It should be no surprise that the use of a pen register would also be contested on the ground that it constitutes a search and is thus subject to Fourth Amendment limitations that a warrant first be obtained. This issue was raised in *Smith v. Maryland*. The facts are fairly simple:

> The telephone company, at police request, installed at its central offices a pen register to record the numbers dialed from the telephone at petitioner's home.[27]

The Court went on to decide:

> We therefore conclude that petitioner in all probability entertained no actual expectation of privacy in the phone numbers he dialed, and that, even if he did, his expectation was not "legitimate." The installation and use of a pen register, consequently, was not a "search," and no warrant was required.[28]

The court has found that comments or discussion made within the jail, overheard by electronic monitor, are admissible in court: "Mr. Hinkston asserts that the statements he made while incarcerated had only a nominal probative value. We disagree. In fact, those statements were highly probative because they constituted admissions of his involvement in the murder and provided evidence of the circumstances surrounding the crime and his intent to kill the victim. Furthermore, the mere fact that his statements were incriminating does not render them unfairly prejudicial ... because 'any evidence that tends to establish the guilt of the defendant is inherently prejudicial.'" [29]

The Ohio Supreme Court ruled in late 2009 that police officers must obtain a search warrant before scouring the contents of a suspect's cell phone, unless their safety is in danger. The U.S. Supreme Court has not been faced with this issue as of the publication of this text, and the Ohio ruling appears to be the first time the issue reached a state high court. [30]

As will be seen shortly, the concept of "expectation of privacy" will be used to its fullest by the Court in cases involving GPS devices and plain view. Generally, the monitoring of cell phone and cell tower transmissions has been held to the same standards as land-line phones.

Monitoring Movement of Vehicles and Items of Commerce

The use of Global Positioning System (GPS) devices (sometimes referred to as beepers) to track the movement of contraband (items of commerce essential for criminal activity) in vehicles, or on persons suspected of or engaged in crime, can be of considerable help in an ongoing investigation. Of course, the GPS must be secreted in advance on the subject to be tracked if it is to be followed and traced to its ultimate destination. Tracking a drum containing an organic solvent or other chemical (which may be purchased legally and then used to manufacture contraband, such as a narcotic or a bomb) may lead to a clandestine laboratory or terrorist's arsenal. If a search warrant is obtained, evidence may then be secured from the premises. Again it should be obvious that defense counsel would contest the use of a beeper:

> The presence of a beeper in effect transforms private property into an instrument of surveil-lance, a surrogate police presence, a use unintended by the original owner. Moreover, the continuing presence of the beeper is not a mere technical trespass, but an extended physical intrusion: they continually broadcast the message, "Here I am." In sum these "uninvited shad-owers" pierce one's privacy of location and movement, as well as one's rights to protection of property against physical invasion.[31]

From another standpoint, law enforcement officials hold that the beeper merely facilitates surveillance: by substituting for the human eye, it reduces the danger of detection. Furthermore, it does not pinpoint location except when the receiver is very close; it would generally be too risky for an investigator to take up such a position.

In 1982 the Supreme Court addressed some of these issues for the first time in *United States v. Knotts*.[32] The facts of the case are as follows: A tracking device, or beeper, was installed in a five-gallon container of chloroform (a precursor chemical in the manufacture of illicit drugs), which was subsequently purchased by the suspect. Maintaining contact with visual surveillance and beeper signals, the officers following the transporting vehicle saw the container transferred to another automobile; again, it was tracked both visually and electronically. But during this part of the journey, the driver began to make evasive maneuvers, causing surveillants to call off their visual contact. At about the same time, the beeper signal was also lost. An hour or so later, with the aid of a monitoring device mounted in a helicopter, the beeper's approximate location was determined. Its resting place was next to a secluded cabin.

The officers secured a search warrant based on the foregoing experience and on additional information obtained after three more days of intermittent visual surveillance. Upon executing the warrant, they discovered a fully operable drug laboratory inside the cabin; outside, they found a chloroform container under a barrel. The defendant sought to suppress the evidence obtained from the *warrantless* monitoring of the beeper, but was denied. Later, his conviction for conspiring to manufacture a controlled substance and the imposed five-year prison sentence were appealed. When taken to the Supreme Court it ruled that:

> Monitoring the beeper signals did not invade any legitimate expectation of privacy on respon-dent's part, and thus there was neither a "search" nor a "seizure" within the contemplation of the Fourth Amendment. The beeper surveillance amounted principally to following an automobile on public streets and highways. A person traveling in an automobile on public thoroughfares has no reasonable expectation of privacy in his movements.[33]

Knotts appeared to be a victory for law enforcement, but it was a narrow one. The Court had approved the use of a beeper to monitor the movement of vehicles on public roads only. Before long, it again confronted the matter of beeper surveillance in *United States v. Karo*:[34]

> In this case, we are called upon to address two questions left unresolved in *Knotts*: (1) whether installation of a beeper in a container of chemicals with the consent of the original owner constitutes a search or seizure within the meaning of the Fourth Amendment when the container is delivered to a buyer having no knowledge of the presence of the beeper, and (2) whether monitoring of the beeper falls within the ambit of the Fourth Amendment when it reveals information that could not have been obtained through visual surveillance.[35]

The Court then ruled:

> We conclude that no Fourth Amendment interest of Karo or of any other respondent was infringed by the installation of the beeper. Rather, any impairment of privacy interests that may have occurred was occasioned by the monitoring of the beeper.[36]

The Court subsequently returned to the substance of the decision and declared:

> We also reject the Government's contention that it should be able to monitor beepers in private residences without a warrant if there is the requisite justification in the facts for believing that a crime is being or will be committed and that monitoring the beeper wherever it goes is likely to produce evidence of criminal activity. Warrantless searches are presumptively unreasonable. ... The primary reason for the warrant requirement is to interpose a "neutral and detached magistrate" between the citizen and "the officer engaged in the often competitive enterprise of ferreting out crime."[37]

Further along in *Karo*, another aspect of the warrant issue is treated:

> We are also unpersuaded by the argument that a warrant should not be required because of the difficulty in satisfying the particularity requirement of the Fourth Amendment. The Government contends that it would be impossible to describe the "place" to be searched, because the location of the place is precisely what is sought to be discovered through the search. ... However true that may be, it will still be possible to describe the object into which the beeper is to be placed, the circumstances that led agents to wish to install the beeper, and the length of time for which beeper surveillance is requested. In our view, this information will suffice to permit issuance of a warrant authorizing beeper installation and surveillance. In sum, we discern no reason for deviating from the general rule that a search of a house should be conducted pursuant to a warrant.[38]

The investigative practices permitted by *Knotts* and *Karo* were subsequently limited by the Electronic Communications Privacy Act. The statute requires police to obtain a prior court order; any evidence resulting from a violation of its provisions is not admissible in court. It further provides for criminal and civil penalties. [39]

As noted earlier, in *United States v. Jones*, the Supreme Court held that a search warrant must be secured to place a global positioning (GPS) device on a vehicle.

Visual and Sound Enhancement Devices

Other technical devices can be used to observe a subject, vehicle, or other object unobtrusively. Some are quite simple (a pair of binoculars, a camera, a telescope); others are more intricate (an infrared snooperscope) and/or expensive (a helicopter or an airplane). As should be expected, there have been constitutional challenges to their use. Though not unobtrusive, even a flashlight has been challenged, however, unsuccessfully.[40]

An early (1952) Supreme Court decision, one of the few to confront the use of visual enhancement devices, is *On Lee v. United States*:

> ... The use of bifocals, field glasses or the telescope to magnify the object of a witness' vision is not a forbidden search and seizure, even if they focus without his knowledge or consent upon what one supposes to be private indiscretions.[41]

In those early cases, the Court based its search and seizure decisions on a literal reading of the Fourth Amendment: "persons, housing, papers, and effects" are protected.[42] Thus, revenue officers who conducted a visual search without a warrant while trespassing on the defendant's land were not in violation because the amendment's protection "is not extended to open fields."[43] *Hester v. United States* (1924), the so-called "open fields case," established that places and property were protected. It then was but a short step for the Court to extend the area protected by including the immediate vicinity of the dwelling (the open space, courtyard, or curtilage within a common enclosure and belonging to it). In *Katz v. United States* (1967), the Court indeed altered and expanded the scope of the Fourth Amendment. It went beyond that of a "constitutionally protected area" to embrace the idea of "privacy."

> ... For the Fourth Amendment protects people, not places. What a person knowingly exposes to the public, even in his own home or office, is not a subject of Fourth Amendment protection ... but what he seeks to preserve as private, even in an area accessible to the public, may be constitutionally protected.[44]

Katz involved enhanced hearing, and questions involving enhanced observations soon arose. Would their use constitute a search requiring a warrant? Would the facts and circumstances (particularly in cases that entailed peering into premises) result in different judicial opinions as the

AP Photo/Mary Altaffer

Figure 8.1
The New York Police Department surveillance helicopter's cameras, including one for infrared photography, are mounted below the aircraft. The helicopter's arsenal of sophisticated surveillance and tracking equipment is powerful enough to stealthily read license plates—or even pedestrian's faces—from high above.

venue changed? Would the use of a visual enhancement device to observe an open public area require a search warrant? Because enhanced observations usually provide the evidence that is the basis for probable cause—a search warrant prerequisite—such questions are crucial.

Until 2012 no case had yet reached the Supreme Court (in which a written opinion is rendered), and relevant appellate court decisions must be consulted. Several post-*Katz* cases will illustrate. Before discussing them, it is important to note that "privacy" becomes qualified in these decisions. Appended to "expectation of privacy" are additional modifiers: justifiable, reasonable, legitimate. Many post-*Katz* cases involve the use of binoculars. In one, an FBI agent acting on a tip carried out the nighttime surveillance of a print shop suspected of turning out gambling forms for football games. Its high windows obstructing his view of the inside, the agent overcame the difficulty with a ladder, moving it some 30 to 35 feet from the building, well beyond the defendant's property. From this vantage, with the aid of binoculars, he could observe the print job. The Superior Court of Pennsylvania ruled:

> … [This] case presents the situation in which it was incumbent upon the suspect to preserve his privacy from visual observation. To do that the appellees had only to curtain the windows. Absent such obvious action, we cannot find that their expectation of privacy was justifiable or reasonable. The law will not shield criminal activity from visual observation when the actor shows such little regard for his privacy.[45]

When the case was taken to the Supreme Court, *certiorari* was denied.[46] In other lower court cases, however, visually enhanced observations and the circumstances surrounding them were viewed as searches within the purview of the Fourth Amendment. However, in *Ryburn v. Huff* in 2012, the Supreme Court held that in cases where there is an imminent threat of injury, officers may enter a home without a search warrant and without the permission of the occupants. In this case, which overturned a Ninth Circuit Court decision, the Court held that: "[I]t was objectionably reasonable for the officers to believe violence was imminent and they were justified in making warrantless entry into the home. However, it should be noted that in this case the officers did not undertake a search of the house after they entered, concluding that prior information based on a rumor that there was a weapon in the house was false."[47]

Therefore, until the Supreme Court speaks definitively, it would be productive to summarize the constitutional concerns of the various courts when analyzing visually enhanced surveillance. The issues of some importance are:

1. The nature of the area. (Surveilling through enhanced viewing "within an individual's home," using such artificial aids as a telescope, requires a search warrant.)[48]

2. The kind of precautions taken by the suspect to ensure privacy.[49]

3. Whether, after having first made the observations with the naked eye, an enhancement device is needed to avoid detection of the surveillance.[50]

4. Whether the investigator must do something unusual to make the observation, such as climb a fence to be high enough to view the activity, or use a telescope.[51]

5. The distance between the officer and the behavior or activity under observation.[52]

6. The level of sophistication of the viewing device.[53]

In 2001, in the case *Kyllo v. United States*, the court held that using a technological device to explore details of a home that would previously have been unknowable without physical intrusion is a search and is presumptively unreasonable without a warrant.[54]

In *United States v. Dunn* (1987), the Supreme Court reiterated that the area within the curtilage was protected by the Fourth Amendment.[55] In the *Dunn* case, drug enforcement agents crossed over the fence around the perimeter of a ranch, several interior barbed wire fences, and then a wooden fence, to look into a barn located 50 yards from a house. Observing what they took to be a drug laboratory, and confirming its presence twice more the next day, they secured a warrant and arrested Dunn. Subsequently convicted, he won an appeal claiming that the trial court's denial to suppress all evidence seized pursuant to the warrant was in error because the barn was within the curtilage of his home.

In resolving what is inside (and outside) that curtilage (and what, therefore, should be placed under the home's "umbrella" of protection), the Supreme Court suggested the following four factors be considered:

1. The proximity of the area to the home itself;

2. Whether the area is within the enclosure surrounding the home;

3. The nature of the uses to which an area is put;

4. The steps taken by the residents to protect the area from the observations of passersby.

Applying these criteria to *Dunn*, the Court found:

1. The barn's substantial distance from the fence surrounding the house (50 yards), and from the house itself (60 yards), supports no inference that it should be treated as an adjunct of the house;

2. The barn was not within the fence surrounding the house; it stands out as a distinct and separate portion of the ranch;

3. The barn was not being used for the intimate activities of the home;

4. Little had been done to protect the barn area from observation by those standing outside; ranch fences were the type to corral livestock, not ensure privacy.[56]

For these reasons the Supreme Court reversed the decision of the California Court of Appeals, agreeing with the trial judge who had denied a motion to suppress. In 1986 and again in 1989, the Court was engaged with the issue of surveillance (by means of an airplane or helicopter) to detect unlawful activity within the curtilage of a home; in one case (*California v. Ciraolo*), within the 2,000-acre "industrial curtilage" of a chemical manufacturing plant. In the *Ciraolo* investigation, police officers trained in the visual identification of marijuana were used. Based on an anonymous tip, they undertook in a private airplane at an altitude of 1,000 feet to detect with the naked eye (and photograph with a 35 mm. camera) marijuana allegedly growing in the defendant's backyard.[57] Based on the Fourth Amendment's protection of the curtilage, the defense attorney's motion to suppress the evidence was denied, and Ciraolo pleaded guilty. Agreeing that the backyard was part of the curtilage, the Court refused to require that a search warrant be obtained. It held:

> … any member of the public flying in this airspace who cared to glance down could have seen everything that the officers observed.[58]

In another (marijuana) curtilage case, *Florida v. Riley* (1989), the Supreme Court went beyond *Ciraolo* in approving surveillance from a police helicopter flying at a height of 400 feet.[59] Riley's greenhouse 20 feet behind his home carried a "Do Not Enter" sign. Enclosed on two sides, it was shielded from public view by his mobile home; on two other sides were trees and shrubbery; on top, two corrugated panels, constituting about 10 percent of its roof, were missing. Based on a tip and by means of a helicopter, police verified that marijuana was being grown in the greenhouse. Obtaining a warrant, police seized the marijuana, and Riley was eventually convicted. As the case worked its way up the appeals ladder, the motion to suppress the evidence was sustained, denied, sustained, and ultimately denied. Again, the Court allowed that, even though the greenhouse was within the curtilage, Riley's expectation of privacy was unrealistic. Furthermore, the Court concluded, the flight was permitted under FAA regulations. Police use helicopters in all 50 states, and since there was no physical intrusion of the greenhouse, the fly-by observation was not a search within the meaning of the Fourth Amendment.[60] *Riley* was a 5–4 decision. Some dissenting opinions were prophetic. Justice Brennan's was punctuated with a remembrance of George Orwell's *1984*:

> In the far distance a helicopter skimmed down between the roofs, hovering for an instant like a bluebottle, and darted away again with a curving flight. It was the Police Patrol, snooping into people's windows.[61]

It would be beneficial for the law enforcement profession to consider seriously and debate the Brennan citation, and meanwhile, confine this kind of surveillance to serious cases.

In *Dow Chemical v. United States* (1986), the Environmental Protection Agency (EPA) made aerial photographs of the 2,000 acres surrounding Dow's manufacturing plant. This action, taken without a search warrant, was in part based on the "open fields" doctrine.[62] Dow claimed the acreage to be within their "industrial curtilage" and under Fourth Amendment protection. The Court disagreed:

> … aerial photographs of petitioner's plant complex from an aircraft lawfully in public navigable airspace was not prohibited by the Fourth Amendment.
>
> … [and that] the open areas of an industrial plant complex … are not analogous to the "curtilage" of a dwelling… .[63]

In its 5–4 decision, the Court remarked in passing that only aerial photography and observation were involved. It went on to say, though, that had they made a physical entry, or used electronic eavesdropping or more sophisticated (satellite) cameras, a significant Fourth Amendment question might have been raised.

Enhanced sound techniques, using parabolic microphones as well as other sophisticated electronic listening devices, represent yet another surveillance tactic that is used largely by federal agencies. This technology has improved dramatically in recent years and can be used in a variety of surveillance settings. For example, using sound wave technology, it is possible to eavesdrop on persons within a building near glass windows.

PRACTICAL CONSIDERATIONS

Surveillance is seldom the task of one person. Vehicles equipped with direct intercommunication systems are generally essential. Less expensive equipment, such as infrared optical devices and high-quality binoculars, may suffice to locate suspects unobtrusively and to make a determination as to their (or an associate's) activities. These objectives, or a surveillance conducted to prevent a crime, may be realized without elaborate resources and staff. Although costly, sometimes a decision to invest whatever is necessary must be faced if an investigation is to progress. For the wary subject—the gang of interstate bank burglars, the espionage agent, or the terrorist—surveillance may require helicopters or even frogmen. Large departments will find it cost-effective in the long run to train a group of specialists who, when given ample opportunity to work together, will develop coordination. Because small departments are able to commit only modest resources, there is some argument for having surveillance specialists available at the state level. As many state and municipal governments lack the ability to mount an elaborate surveillance, cooperation at all administrative levels will be essential if funds, personnel, and equipment are to be readily available.

Such an arrangement may be feasible in some states. Accordingly, because most police agencies in the United States employ fewer than 20 officers, forming a task force with other departments is often the answer when resources for such operations are limited or nonexistent.[64]

Some attributes considered desirable when selecting individuals for a surveillance team:

- exceptional common sense and good judgment

- an ability to operate both independently and as a team member

- a proven track record as to dependability and presence of mind in times of high stress

- "street savvy," a "gift of the gab," extreme patience[65]

Tactics

Strategic considerations govern the use of surveillance in a particular case. Tactical concerns determine its execution. A major problem that soon intrudes is how to weigh the possible loss of contact with a subject against the risk of being detected or exposed. A quick, believable response is called for when a subject takes some action to determine whether there is indeed a surveillance. It is easier to drop surveillance before being confronted than to respond to a confrontation by convincing the subject that he or she is mistaken.

Loose Surveillance

Loose surveillance is used when the objective is to locate a suspect by tailing his or her relatives and friends. The surveillant exercises great caution while observing the subject, preferring to drop the tail rather than risk detection or exposure. Whether for espionage, burglary, or terrorism, this tactic applies when a group's activities are under scrutiny to determine their contacts and intentions.

Close Surveillance

The aim of *close surveillance* is to avoid losing the subject—even at the risk of detection or exposure. When the goal is to prevent a crime or learn more about the subject's contacts, it is acceptable procedure. A subject who is naive or lacks experience in crime may panic and reveal valuable clues when the fact of the surveillance is realized. This may force that person's hand. It is particularly useful on those who are only peripherally connected with the subject or the crime. When a subject's behavior signals suspicion of the tail, it is said to have been *burned*. When the objective is to prevent an assault or other crime against an individual, the term *mustard plaster* (a variety of open surveillance) describes the tactic.

Loose and close surveillance are the two extremes. When a loose tail is the prudent choice, there is always the possibility of losing the subject; with close surveillance, the chance of being burned. In practice, a balance is sought between "being made" or losing the subject.

Stop and Frisk

"Stop and frisk" is a procedure whereby a police officer may search an individual who is believed to be carrying a weapon based on observation, experience, and suspicion. It is a form of close surveillance that is frequently used to search gang members and organized crime figures who may be armed. It can also be used by detectives to make the subject aware that he or she is being watched in cases in which open or close surveillance is being undertaken. However, stop and frisk is also controversial. In New York in 2011, 685,000 people were searched under this procedure. Citizen complaints and a federal judge permitted a class action suit to proceed. The Police Commissioner implemented new procedures in 2012 that called for better training and supervision of such cases.[66]

Planning

Never to lose a subject or to arouse suspicion is impossible, of course. When confronted with either decision, any vacillation is an additional hazard. Investigative momentum will be squandered if plans are not made in anticipation of such contingencies. Should a subject be lost, a viable method of locating him or her is often by educated guess—people being creatures of habit, doing the same things at about the same time each day. Prior surveillance reports on the case also can furnish insight. If wiretapping is legal in the jurisdiction, taps will provide additional information about the subject's movements. Indeed, the guarded language criminals employ to confound the officers on the tap may only become intelligible through the study of surveillance reports. When two people agree over the telephone to meet at "the same place as last time," it is itself of little value. Hand-in-glove with the surveillance report, however, the designated place may become known to the investigator and the subject picked up again. Seldom employing one technique at a time, the successful practitioner is one who, like a fine cook, knows when to season the effort with the correct amounts of each.

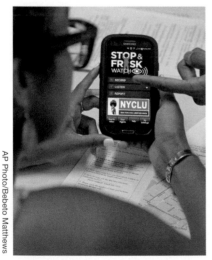

AP Photo/Bebeto Matthews

Figure 8.2
In this 2012 photo, a youth organizer with the community organization Make the Road reviews a phone app for monitoring police action. The app, called "Stop and Frisk Watch," was developed by the New York Civil Liberties Union for bystanders to monitor police during "stop and frisk" activity, a practice widely denounced by civil rights groups.

Preparation

The success of a surveillance depends on the degree of forethought and thoroughness given to the preliminary preparations. It is important to develop a plan of action for handling contingencies and to understand its objectives. Without such a plan, obvious, everyday matters—such as having a supply of coins and tokens available for transportation and telephone calls—can be overlooked. The major components of preliminary preparation are discussed next.

Familiarization

It is crucial that the surveillant(s) be certain of the identity of the subject, who should, if possible, be pointed out by one who knows him or her by sight. Though less satisfactory than direct "fingering," recent photographs are also acceptable. The surveillant must be familiar with details of the case, through discussion with others working on it and reading the previous surveillance reports. It is helpful to be familiar with the probable area of operations; for those working in unknown territory, preliminary inspections are worthwhile. Because many surveillances are conducted in cities (where most crimes occur) it is important to know about the type of people, the transportation facilities, street layout, public buildings, and other physical features. The investigator should be able to operate any technical equipment used. When teams of investigators are expected to work together, a briefing session is appropriate.

Equipment

It hardly needs to be said that all technical equipment be serviced, checked, and ready to operate. Department policy should cover who is authorized to operate technical equipment. Before evidence derived from such equipment can be offered in court, a foundation must be laid. Even for such a simple device as a tape recorder, the following considerations govern the matter:

- The recording device was capable of taping the conversation
- The operator was competent to operate the device
- The recording is authentic and correct
- Changes, additions, or deletions have not been made to the recording
- The recording has been preserved in a manner satisfactory to the court
- The speakers are identified
- The conversation elicited was made voluntarily and in good faith without any kind of inducement[67]

While being used, unmistakable police paraphernalia must be concealed or, when visible, disguised.

Some thought should be given to converting an enclosed, moderate-sized truck or van to suit the needs of lengthy, fixed surveillances. Disguises for an automobile include: extra sets of license plates (both in-state and out-of-state); window and bumper stickers; a set of props in the car's trunk such as: a shopping bag filled with groceries, a briefcase, and a few changes of outer clothing and headgear. The area of operation will suggest other props.

Night surveillance also requires that officers have appropriate equipment available. There are two types of night vision technology: infrared and image intensification.

Infrared equipment detects heat variations among the objects in front of it and produces an image that looks like a black-and-white negative. ... Image intensification uses a tube to gather existing light and amplify it thousands of times to create a fluorescent green image.[68]

In recent years the capability of night vision equipment has improved dramatically, largely as a result of research done for the military.

Blending In

A surveillant must blend with the neighborhood of the operation. (A few props already have been suggested.) The aim is to play a role the locals will accept without question or suspicion. For example, in a congested urban environment the investigator might assume the identity of a laborer or an office worker; in a rural area, that of a delivery worker or farmer. With ethnic groups, the problems become difficult: a white cannot be disguised as a black, the stereotypical Irishman as the stereotypical Italian, or a Slav as an Arab. In these situations another tack must be taken. Again, the aim is to be accepted in the neighborhood, not necessarily seem indigenous to it. Ubiquitous figures on the inner-city sidewalk, like the practical nurse, welfare worker, rent collector, and insurance adjuster, come to mind. Other practical matters also must be planned: providing relief for the surveillant's personal necessities and time off, and, where applicable, securing a supply of public transit tokens or passes.

If the subject enters a theater or other similar venue where there is an admission charge, the detective should *not* gain entry by showing his or her credentials. A common technique to identify a "tail" is to enter facilities that require payment or, in some cases, enter a building where a pass, ticket, or some other form of passage is required.

Discontinuing the Surveillance

Usually, a surveillance can be discontinued without repercussions, but should the subject directly or indirectly indicate that its existence is suspected, breaking off contact requires caution. It must be made certain that the investigator has not been placed under counter-surveillance by the subject or an associate; accordingly, the investigator should not return directly to the station house until sure that no such reverse surveillance is being used. In the event of a direct challenge, it is important to be prepared with a response that has been thought through, rehearsed, and is almost instinctive for the surveillant. An improvised response would not ring true; it would only confirm the subject's suspicions. Neither should the investigator immediately deny being a police officer, but rather react with some irritation: impatient comments such as "Why are you bothering me" or "I don't know what you're talking about." This approach might work and avoid the consequences of being "made." These suggestions are offered as practical responses in a given situation. A good surveillance operative or team will practice various approaches to avoid detection.

PROCEDURE FOR INTERCEPTION OF WIRE OR ORAL COMMUNICATIONS

Title III, Section 2518 of the Omnibus Crime Bill (as amended by the Electronic Communications Privacy Act of 1986) describes how to obtain an order from a judge authorizing the interception of a wire or oral communication. The detailed, comprehensive procedures resemble those traditionally employed to obtain a conventional search warrant. In federal cases, the application for an interception order must be approved by the attorney general (or a specific designee); in state cases, by the principal prosecuting officer of the state or its political subdivisions. The application must be in writing and sworn or affirmed to, then submitted to the appropriate federal or state judge for approval. The judge may issue an *ex parte* order authorizing the interception if it is determined, on the basis of the facts submitted by the applicant, that:

(a)   there is probable cause for belief that an individual is committing, has committed, or is about to commit a particular offense enumerated in section 2516 …;

(b)   there is probable cause for belief that particular communications concerning that offense will be obtained through such interception;

(c)   normal investigative procedures have been tried and have failed or reasonably appear to be unlikely to succeed if tried or to be too dangerous;

(d)   except as provided in subsection (11), there is probable cause for belief that the facilities from which, or the place where, the wire, oral, or electronic communications are to be intercepted are being used, or are about to be used, in connection with the commission of such offense, or are leased to, listed in the name of, or commonly used by such person.[69]

The order may not remain in effect longer than is necessary to achieve its objectives, and no longer than 30 days in any event. It must be executed promptly, minimizing any interference with communications otherwise not subject to interception, and must terminate upon attainment of the authorized objective. There is no limitation on the number of extensions that may be granted but, as in the original application, each must provide the requisite information and show probable cause. In executing the order the investigator must do all that is possible to avoid unnecessary intrusions upon innocuous communications, thereby respecting the right of privacy.

COMPUTER SURVEILLANCE

Increasingly, law enforcement is devoting attention to specific types of electronic bulletin boards, chat rooms, social networking sites, and other Internet sources to help identify criminals, especially pedophiles, child pornographers, and potentially violent groups. (See Chapter 11 for more information on this surveillance technique.)

CONCLUSION

In the "old" days some would argue that surveillance was as much an art as it was a science, but as noted in this and later chapters, science continues to be an increasingly important aspect of criminal investigation. "Old-fashioned" shoe leather is being enhanced by surveillance technology. Nevertheless, in the end a case may ultimately depend on the work of experienced surveillants who can work the streets. A good detective will work on these skills and learn how to combine and best use the various tools and techniques of surveillance.

NOTES

1   *United States v. Jones*, 565 U.S. 132 S.Ct. 945 (2012).

2   *Giancana v. Johnson*, 335 F.2d 366 (7th Cir. 1964).

3   *Giancana v. Johnson*, No. 63 C 1145 (N.D. Ill. 1963).

4   Ibid.

5   379 U.S. 1001 (1969).

6   See http://www.utcle.org/eLibrary/preview.php?asset_file_id = 21137

7   *Olmstead v. United States*, 277 U.S. 438 (1928).

8   Ibid., 465.

9   Ibid.

10 Omnibus Crime Control and Safe Streets Act of 1968 ("Title III") 18 U.S.C. §§ 2510–2520 (1970).

11 *Blanton v. State*, 886 So.2d. 850 (2003).

12 *Berger v. New York*, 388 U.S. 41, 45 (1967).

13 Ibid., 71.

14 *Goldman v. United States*, 316 U.S. 129 (1942).

15 *Silverman v. United States*, 365 U.S. 505 (1961).

16 *On Lee v. United States*, 343 U.S. 747 (1952).

17 *Katz v. United States*, 389 U.S. 347 (1967).

18 Ibid., 351.

19 Ibid., 356.

20 *Dalia v. United States*, 441 U.S. 238, 247 (1979).

21 Ibid., 241.

22 Ibid., 255.

23 Ibid.

24 Ibid., 257.

25 Ibid., 258.

26 *United States v. New York Telephone Co.*, 434 U.S. 159, 160 (1977).

27 *Smith v. State of Maryland*, 442 U.S. 735 (1979).

28 Ibid., 745.

29 *Hinkston v. State*, 340 Ark. 530 (2000).

30 See http://www.sconet.state.oh.us/rod/docs/pdf/0/2009/2009-Ohio-6426.pdf

[31]   *State v. Hendricks*, 43 N.C. App. 245, 253 (1979).

[32]   *United States v. Knotts*, 460 U.S. 276 (1983).

[33]   Ibid., 276.

[34]   *United States v. Karo*, 468 U.S. 705 (1984).

[35]   Ibid., 707.

[36]   Ibid., 713. Despite this holding, warrants for installation and monitoring of a GPS device will obviously be desirable, as it may be useful, or even critical, to monitor the device to determine that it is actually located in a place not open to visual surveillance. Monitoring without a warrant may violate the Fourth Amendment.

[37]   Ibid.

[38]   Ibid., 718.

[39]   Public Law No. 99–508, 18 U.S.C. § 2510, et seq.

[40]   *Marshall v. United States*, 422 F.2d 185, 188 (5th Cir. 1970); *United States v. Wright*, 449 F.2d 1355, 1357 (D.C. Cir. 1971).

[41]   *On Lee v. United States*, 343 U.S. 747, 754 (1952).

[42]   *Hester v. United States*, 265 U.S. 57, 59 (1924).

[43]   Ibid.

[44]   *Katz*, supra note 16, 351.

[45]   *Commonwealth v. Hernley*, 263 A.2d 904 (1970).

[46]   *Hernley et al. v. Pennsylvania*, 401 U.S. 914 (1971).

[47]   Amato, Bill, & Rachel Heintz. "*Ryburn v. Huff* Affirms Police Decisions in Warrantless Entries," Chief's Counsel, *The Police Chief*, 79 (May 2012): 12–13.

[48]   *United States v. Kim*, 415 F. Supp. 1252 (D. Hawaii 1976).

[49]   Ibid., 1257.

[50]   *People v. Arno*, 153 Cal. Rptr. 624, 625 (1979).

[51]   *State v. Kender*, 588 P.2d 447, 449 (1978).

[52]   *Kim*, supra note 46, 1254; *Commonwealth v. Williams*, 396 A.2d 1286, 1290 (1978).

[53]   *Arno*, supra note 48, 627.

[54]   *Kyllo v. United States*, 533 U.S. 27 (2001).

[55]   *United States v. Dunn*, 480 U.S. 294 (1987).

[56]   Ibid., 294–295, 303–305.

[57]   *California v. Ciraolo*, 476 U.S. 207 (1986).

[58]   Ibid., 208.

[59]   *Florida v. Riley*, 488 U.S. 445 (1989).

[60]   Ibid., 844–845.

[61]   Ibid., 852.

[62]   *Dow Chemical v. United States*, 476 U.S. 227 (1986).

[63]   Ibid., 228.

[64]   Lois Pilant, "Achieving State-of-the-Art Surveillance," *The Police Chief*, 60:6, 25–34 (June 1993), 5.

[65]   Ibid.

[66]   Michael Saul, & Sean Gardener. "Kelly Shifts Policy on Stop and Frisk," *Wall Street Journal* (May 18, 2012, Pp. A1,18).

[67]   Pilant, 30–31.

[68]   Pilant, 26.

[69]   Omnibus Crime Control and Safe Streets Act of 1968 as amended by the Electronic Communications Privacy Act of 1986, Title 18, § 2518 (3).

IMPORTANT CASES

Agnello v. United States (1925)
Berger v. New York (1967)
Blanton v. State (2003)
California v. Ciraolo (1986)
Commonwealth v. Hernley (1970)
Commonwealth v. Williams (1978)
Dalia v. United States (1979)
Dow Chemical v. United States (1986)
Florida v. Riley (1989)
Giancana v. Johnson (1963)
Giancana v. Johnson (1964)
Goldman v. United States (1942)
Hernley et al. v. Pennsylvania (1971)
Hester v. United States (1924)
Hinkston v. State (2000)
Katz v. United States (1967)
Kyllo v. United States (2001)
Marshall v. United States (1970)
Olmstead v. United States (1928)
On Lee v. United States (1952)
People v. Arno (1979)
Ryburn v. Huff (2012)
Silverman v. United States (1961)
Smith v. State of Maryland (1979)

State v. Hendricks (1979)
State v. Kender (1978)
United States v. Dunn (1987)
United States v. Jones (2012)
United States v. Karo (1984)
United States v. Kim (1976)
United States v. Knotts (1983)
United States v. New York Telephone Co. (1977)
United States v. Wright (1971)

DISCUSSION QUESTIONS

1. What are the four perspectives that traditionally define the reasons and methodology of surveillance?

2. What are the legal issues related to surveillance?

3. What is the current legal status of wiretapping in the United States?

4. What is a "mail cover"?

5. What is the current legal status relating to the use of visual and sound enhancement devices?

6. What is "loose surveillance"?

7. What is "close surveillance"?

8. Explain "stop and frisk" as a police technique.

9. What must be established to obtain a court order to intercept wire or oral communication?

SUPPLEMENTAL READINGS

del Carmen, R. V., & Walker, J. T. (2011). *Briefs of leading cases in law enforcement* (8th ed.). Boston: Elsevier/ Anderson Publishing.

Ingram, J. L. (2011). *Criminal evidence* (11th ed.). Boston: Elsevier/Anderson Publishing.

Kanovitz, J. R. (2012). *Constitutional law* (13th ed.). Boston: Elsevier/Anderson Publishing.

CHAPTER 9

EYEWITNESS IDENTIFICATION
Guidelines and Procedures

When a crime has been witnessed by a victim or another person, either might be able to identify the offender. This possibility must be exploited without delay. The first step is to arrange for both victim and eyewitness to scrutinize the mug shot files of the Rogues Gallery; then, if this effort is unsuccessful, to reconstruct an image of the offender with an artist's sketch, facial-features kit, or computer-generated sketch. The reconstruction should be distributed within the department and, to enlist the public's cooperation, in the vicinity of the crime. If an arrest is ultimately made, a lineup should be held to see whether victim or eyewitness can identify the suspect.

Clearly, the methods employed to identify an offender before an arrest differ markedly from those used after arrest. Just the same, the investigator must bear in mind not only the limitations of eyewitness evidence, but also the potential for misidentification. The following recommendations will help to minimize this potential.

PHOTO FILES

In all states the laws require the photographing, fingerprinting, and collection of a DNA sample of anyone arrested for a felony or some of the more serious misdemeanors, such as possession of burglars' tools. (When a conviction does not result, the accused may be able to have all or part of the records expunged.) Mug shots—a full-face and a profile photograph—are commonly made; a group photograph may be made as well, when more than one individual is apprehended for the same crime. A personal description is recorded: age, height, weight, place of birth, scars and tattoos, social security number, and fingerprints [classification and file (Bertillon) number]. In addition, nicknames and aliases as well as any peculiarities in *modus operandi* are noted. This information correlated with the mug shots provides the basis for what is sometimes called an offender's "Rogues Gallery" file.

A file administrator must develop a system that permits only those photographs of likely offenders to be shown on demand to the case investigator and eyewitness. This could be accomplished with an ongoing set of mug shots classified by type of crime, object attacked, and method employed. For example, the following scheme would be practical: ROBBERY—bank—gas station—armored truck—supermarket; and so on. Rape classifications might include: victim followed (from bus stop, subway station, supermarket); victim pulled into automobile from sidewalk; victim ambushed (in a parking lot, building elevator, when opening garage door); and so on.

Mug shots are generally categorized by the type of crime, which might include subsets, such as business, vehicle, "strongarm," and so on. However, the use of relational databases has made it much easier to maintain cross-referenced files. Geographical parameters as well as physical characteristics may be used for other subsets and searches. A computerized mug shot file, discussed in the next section, offers a broad range of methods to narrow the number of photos to which a witness may be exposed. Going through hundreds of photos will frequently tire a victim or witness, which may hamper the ability to recognize a suspect.

Regardless of the classification scheme devised, the choice of person to take charge of the photo file is vital to its success. Indeed this individual becomes a filtering resource who can recognize and pull appropriate material to show to the victim. The longer he or she remains at that post, the greater is his or her value for investigators. The file manager must deal with the difficult decision of what and when to cull—to remove photographs no longer likely to be useful and retain those which might still be of use. Leaner files are preferable in light of the issue of viewer saturation, with its attendant look-alike problems.

Computerized Mug Photographs

Electronic data processing aids the investigator significantly. There are a number of software programs available for the retrieval of photographs stored in a computer database.

The computer's discriminatory capability is a major advantage over manual selection in a mug shot file. The more specific the information provided by an eyewitness (age, race, sex, hair color, scar, tattoo, type of crime and weapon, gang emblem or jacket, etc.), the fewer the mug shots that need be printed, thereby keeping viewer saturation to a minimum.

Using a Photo File

When a witness agrees (and some will not) to view a photo file, several precautions must be taken to minimize the chance of a misidentification.

1. A reasonable number of randomly arranged photographs should be shown to the witness regardless of whether an identification is made immediately upon viewing but one or two of them. In *Simmons v. United States*, the Supreme Court approved displaying only six photographs.[1] Many departments, however, require more. From an investigative standpoint, they find a higher number preferable.

2. A detective or other police officer must not offer an opinion as to which person in the mug shot display may have committed the crime. If a witness asks, it should be explained that this is not allowed because it is the eyewitness's unbiased opinion that is crucial.

3. Only one witness at a time should be permitted to view the mug shot display. Furthermore, one witness may not view photographs when another is present. All must act separately and out of earshot of each other.

4. After viewing a set of mug shots, a witness must not suggest by word or gesture to another witness that he or she has or has not made an identification.

5. When a positive identification is made and probable cause to warrant an arrest is thereby established, the remaining witnesses should not be shown more mug shots; instead the witnesses should be held in reserve to scan a lineup for the suspect if one can be arranged.[2]

6. Whenever a positive identification results, a record should be made of all photographs shown, and the witness asked to initial and date any photographs found to identify an offender.

When and where the procedure occurred and who was present should also be recorded. As soon as practicable, the investigator is to record anything the witness said upon making the identification.

7. In general, the use of mug shot photographs to identify an offender is an advisable practice only when a live, corporeal identification—such as a lineup—is not feasible.

8. Photographs should be presented in "as neutral a form as possible"[3] and should not be referred to as "mugshot" photographs.[4]

Taking these precautions ensures that the procedure will be fair and not subject to serious attack in court. Furthermore, the witness will have faith in any identification he or she made and will testify with greater confidence at trial.

BOX 9.1 IDENTIFICATION EXERCISE

In Chapter 5, you observed a photograph of Mike Fain. Assume these photos are part of a lineup. Can you identify Mr. Fain without going back to observe the photo?

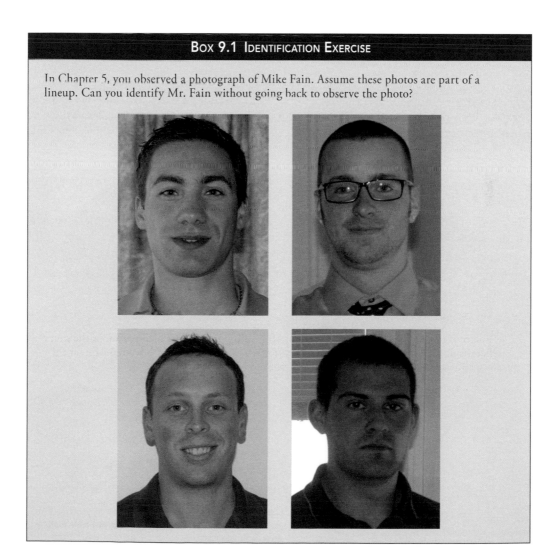

SKETCHES AND COMPOSITE IMAGES

If viewing photo files does not produce an identification of an offender, the next step is the use of a police artist or composite image kits. The likenesses produced can then be distributed to the force and other police departments (see Figures 9.1 and 9.2). In important cases the public can be involved through the media (newspapers, circulars, television). Anonymity can be granted to those who wish it by means of a hotline telephone number.

Using the Police Artist

Artists lend their talent for sketching facial images to the police. Such people are on the payroll of many departments, but civilian volunteers often serve equally well. Each develops a method of working with a witness. In one that has proved successful, the witness describes the offender and answers questions posed by the artist, who is then allowed to go to work free from interruption and, most important, without being observed by the witness. This prevents the witness from directing and shaping the artist's outlines. Consistent with Gestalt psychology, denying access to the image until its completion enhances viewer/witness perception of what changes are still needed. Typical comments evoked—"the eyebrows are bushier," "the eyes are closer together," "the lips are thinner," and so on—allow the artist to modify first attempts. This process is repeated until the witness is satisfied or the artist thinks the image cannot be improved.

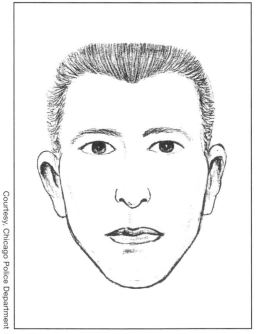

Courtesy, Chicago Police Department

Figure 9.1
Police artist drawing of a suspect based on the description by the only nurse (out of nine) to survive a mass killing.

Courtesy, Chicago Police Department

Figure 9.2
Photograph of Richard Speck from the files of a maritime union hiring hall in Chicago, obtained the day after the artist's drawing was made.

If there are two or more witnesses, the others do not participate in this process. But they can be asked—separately—to view the end product. If either finds it a good likeness, further modifications are unnecessary; if not, the process can be repeated—using the same artist or a different artist—with the second witness.

Using Composite Kits

Composite kits for creating facial images are commercially available. Identi-Kit is well-known in the United States; another, developed in Great Britain and available here, is Photo-Fit Kit. Complete with instruction manuals, both offer front face and profile selections for a wide variety of racial and ethnic origins. For example, Photo-Fit has a "Caucasian-Afro-Asian Front Face Kit" as well as a "Male Caucasian Profile Kit," and there are supplementary kits for Middle eastern features and those of North American Indians. The possible permutations and combinations offered in the "Female Caucasian Front Face Kit" and its accessories (age lines, eyeglasses, sunglasses, headgear) are claimed to be more than 2 billion. Many of the features in the "Male Caucasian Profile Kit" are interchangeable with those of the "female kit," thus extending the range of possibilities. As with the Rogues Gallery file, it is best to allocate a limited number of personnel to deal with witnesses who are choosing and assembling facial features to form a composite image of the offender. In addition to traditional transparency kits, software programs can be used to create composites. Such software lets users create endless combinations of faces. Some computerized composite systems include Identi-Kit, Faces 3.0, ComPHOTOfit, and Compusketch. Because each feature selected is readily identified by code number, prompt transmission of the information to distant police departments is feasible. See Figures 9.3–9.5.

Figure 9.3
Police photograph of suspect taken after apprehension.

Figure 9.4
Identi-Kit composite of same suspect, before apprehension.

Figure 9.5
Police artist's rendition of same suspect.

LINEUPS

When a suspect is apprehended and there is an eyewitness to the crime, the appropriate next step is an investigatory lineup. In fact, it is preferred over any other eyewitness identification procedure. In contrast to the photo display, the lineup (in Britain, the "identification parade") is corporeal: the suspect is placed within a group of people for the purpose of being viewed by eyewitnesses. It is utilized most often, but not exclusively, for the crimes of rape, robbery, and assault. The following recommendations apply (with exceptions where noted) to investigatory lineups as well as lineups held after adversarial judicial proceedings have been initiated.

A lineup should be conducted as soon as possible after the apprehension of a suspect. Three reasons are: (1) the shorter the interval between the lineup and the commission of the crime, the more reliable the eyewitness's memory; (2) an innocent person can be released quickly; and (3) if the suspect is released on bond before a lineup is held, this could delay or frustrate the process. Accordingly, a procedure ought to be adopted for speedily contacting all eyewitnesses, obtaining nonsuspect participants, and arranging for an attorney's presence if necessary.

Lineup Procedure

A properly operated lineup is important for two reasons. It bolsters the confidence of both eyewitness and investigator that the witness can, without help, recognize the offender in a group of apparently similar individuals, and helps to avoid subsequent legal challenges to its validity. Precautions need be taken to attain these ends.

Composition of the Lineup

The police must avoid any temptation to assist an eyewitness in making an identification. Though present at the procedure, they do not take part. The police must also exercise care in the selection of the participants and give consideration to such issues as: the number of participants in the lineup; the position the suspect selects; and the race, sex, physical characteristics, and type of dress worn by the participants.

Number and Position of Participants

Although some state courts have sanctioned a three-person lineup, the United States Supreme Court implicitly approved one comprising six people, including two suspects; that is, at least two nonsuspects for each suspect, a ratio of 2:1.[5] These numbers represent the minimum; they are acceptable only when additional nonsuspect participants cannot be located within a reasonable time. State courts generally require fewer participants for corporeal lineups than photographs for mug shot identification displays, based on the belief that a mug shot identification is less reliable.[6] Also, it is more difficult for police to find nonsuspect participants for a lineup than suitable photographs for a photo identification.

As to position in the lineup, a suspect should be permitted to choose a spot and, after each viewing, to change to any other spot. This forestalls any charge that a suspect's positioning by a detective led to an identification or was otherwise suggestive. Sometimes, such elemental fairness has led suspects identified in a lineup to confess more readily if interrogated soon thereafter.

Outward Appearance of Participants

The participants in a lineup must not be too dissimilar in appearance. To facilitate this effort, the following factors must be considered.

Race and Sex: The apparent race and sex of all participants should be as identical as is practical. If the suspect is black or female, a lineup composed only of white males would clearly be improper.

Physical Characteristics: Attention must be paid to matching or being reasonably close to the suspect in such particulars as:

Age, height, weight, build or body type, light versus dark complexion
Hair—color, style, length, mustache, beard, sideburns

Type of Dress: If the offender was described as wearing eyeglasses or sunglasses, or such distinctive clothing as a leather vest or purple shirt, all participants (if possible) must be wearing this garb or none should be. Because finding a purple shirt (much less several of different sizes) would be inconvenient, some departments provide overalls. It also would be improper to have several police officers in a lineup wearing uniform trousers with business jackets, while a suspect was outfitted in a suit; in other words, no suggestion is to be made concerning who in the group might be the offender. The Supreme Court, however, has approved a suspect's being required to put on some distinctive accessory or article of clothing that distinguished him or her and was remembered by the victim (e.g., adhesive strips on the sides of the perpetrator's face).[7] The face of each nonsuspect must also be shown taped with adhesive or Band-Aids. Finally, if a suspect's unusual appearance makes it impossible to assemble a group of not-too-dissimilar people, a lineup would have no purpose and should not be held. A photo display can serve in its stead.

Conduct of Lineups

Lineup participants must be cautioned to behave similarly and avoid conduct that would set them apart from the suspect. For instance, it would be improper to put a glum suspect in the midst of participants in good spirits. When a viewer/witness requests that one in the group utter specific words, assume a particular pose, or make a certain gesture, then each must be required to do so in turn. One viewer/witness should be permitted in the lineup room at a time. Only when the process is completed and each has stated independently whether an identification was made are they to be allowed to converse with one another.

Suppressing Suggestions

All investigators, other officials, and even eyewitnesses must be warned about a natural tendency to offer any comment, casual or pointed, within earshot of another viewer/witness. This prohibition applies to gestures or actions that could single out the suspect from the rest of the lineup participants. An impropriety may be regarded as impermissibly suggestive and could "give rise to a very substantial likelihood of irreparable misidentification."[8] Though the Court's words bear upon a "pretrial identification by photograph," they should be regarded as applicable to lineups.

Recording the Procedure

The lineup procedure must be recorded. This includes written notation of such items as time, place, names of participants and others who were present, in addition to any statement by a viewer/witness or potentially suggestive remark made by anyone in the room. A color photograph—and when possible, sound and video recordings—serve to document how the lineup was conducted. Taking these precautions renders moot the fairness issue treated by the Court:

> ... the defense can seldom reconstruct the manner and mode of line-up identification for judge and jury at trial. ... in short, the accused's inability effectively to reconstruct at trial any unfairness that occurred at the line-up may deprive him of his only opportunity meaningfully to attack the credibility of the witness' courtroom identification.[9]

In summary, a properly conducted, fully documented lineup can blunt unfavorable judgments and criticism. At trial, it will enhance the credibility of the witness's identification.

Uncooperative Suspects

The suspect who refuses to participate in or threatens to disrupt a lineup can create a problem. To secure cooperation, a first step would be to inform him or her that no constitutional right of refusal to be part of a lineup exists. It should also be made clear that such refusal can be brought out in a criminal trial and its exact language will be preserved for this reason. If the outcome is an investigative standstill (i.e., the suspect continues to refuse to appear in a lineup), this can be remedied with a pictorial identification—placing a photograph of the suspect among others of similar appearance.

RIGHT TO AN ATTORNEY

The law concerning the right to have an attorney present at each eyewitness identification varies with the procedure; for example, there are different requirements for an investigatory lineup and one held after judicial proceedings are initiated.

Facial Recognition

The identification of individuals using new forms of technology has increased the ability to improve upon facial and other forms of personal identification. Historically, facial recognition by witnesses has proven to be questionable in many cases, and as courts rely less on witness identification, the availability of new technology may prove to be more effective. Closed-circuit video cameras in businesses and the general community are already being used to capture images of speeding drivers and toll booth and red light traffic violators with a high degree of accuracy. The number and availability of these have increased.

Box 9.2 Facial Recognition Software

Facial recognition software has improved significantly over the past decade, offering a new tool in the area of crime investigation. However, it is also a form of technology open to abuse, according to the American Civil Liberties Union (ACLU), raising the possibility of such use as an illegal search. Alessandro Acquisti, a researcher at Carnegie Mellon University, found that about 33 percent of 93 student volunteers in a study could be identified from a snapshot when compared with facial recognition technology. The students' photos were uploaded into a cloud computer with 261,262 publicly available photos. Using a webcam and the research "suggests that the identity of about one-third of subjects walking by the campus building may be inferred in a few seconds combining social network data, cloud computing, and an inexpensive webcam," according to professor Acquisti. Researchers, who were studying the impact of facial recognition technology on the right of privacy, noted that by using the information on Facebook, they could predict about 27 percent of the first five digits of an individual's social security number.

Source: Julia Angwin, "Face-ID Tools Pose New Risk." *Wall Street Journal* (August 8, 2011).

The Supreme Court allowed a conviction to stand based on a pre-arrest display of photographs in which no counsel was present, and held it to have been a valid procedure.[10] Subsequently, it ruled on a post-arrest photographic identification:

> ... the Sixth Amendment does not grant the right to counsel at photographic displays conducted by the government for the purpose of allowing a witness to attempt an identification of the offender.[11]

Accordingly, a suspect does not have the right to have an attorney present when an identification procedure—photo display, composite image, or sketch—is employed, whether the attempt to effect an identification occurs before or after arrest.

Lineups

In 1967 the Supreme Court decided that a post-indictment lineup was a "critical stage" of the prosecution's case and that, therefore, a Sixth Amendment right exists for a suspect to have counsel present.[12] Five years later it refused (in *Kirby v. Illinois*) to extend the right to counsel in a pre-indictment case:

> The initiation of judicial proceedings is far from a mere formalism. It is the starting point of our whole system of adversary criminal justice. For it is only then that the government has committed itself to prosecute, and only then that the adverse positions of government and defendant have solidified. ... It is this point, therefore, that marks the commencement of the "criminal prosecutions" to which alone the explicit guarantees of the Sixth Amendment are applicable.[13]

It is important to note that each state is free to exceed the constitutional requirements of *Kirby* (and *United States v. Wade*) in its own jurisdiction. Several have chosen to do so. The presence of counsel at a pre-arraignment lineup, while not required by *Kirby*, helps to ensure that due process standards are met.

Advising the Suspect

If a suspect has a *Miranda* or other right to an attorney, he or she also must be informed of the right to have a lawyer present at the lineup, that a lawyer will be provided free of charge should he or she be unable to afford one, and that the lineup will be delayed for a reasonable time in order for a lawyer to appear.

Waiver of Right

A suspect may waive the right to have an attorney at the lineup. The waiver may be oral or written, with the burden resting on the state—the police—to prove it was made knowingly and intelligently. At least one witness, preferably more, is needed to verify the waiver.

Role of the Suspect's Attorney

The attorney should be allowed to consult with the suspect, make suggestions about the procedure, and observe the conduct of the lineup. At hand as an observer rather than an advisor, he or she must not be permitted to obstruct or control the process. However, any suggestion the attorney makes that is not adopted should be recorded in writing.

The attorney should be cautioned to remain silent during the lineup, and may be present when the witness informs the investigator whether or not he or she was able to make identification. Only after this decision is conveyed and the lineup is concluded, and only if agreeable to the witness, may the attorney then speak to the witness.

ONE-ON-ONE CONFRONTATIONS (SHOW-UPS)

When a situation arises in which a proper lineup cannot be arranged quickly, a one-on-one confrontation or show-up may be utilized. As an identification procedure, confrontation frequently means bringing a suspect (within a short time frame) back to the scene or presenting a suspect to each eyewitness separately. For further information, consult *People v. Manion*[14] and/or *Kennaugh v. Miller*.[15]

Because the procedure is inherently suggestive, some compelling circumstance must be operative. For example, if a wounded eyewitness, suspect, or victim is in danger of death, a one-on-one confrontation may be set up when:

1. The permission of the physician in charge is obtained.

2. The time between the crime and the confrontation is limited—to within 20 minutes, preferably. (See the case law of the appropriate state; some states allow up to two hours.)

During a confrontation no comments or suggestions—such as "We found your wallet when we searched him" or "She confessed but we need your identification, too"—are to be made to a witness. An absence of incriminating commentary establishes the aura of impartiality that ought to characterize the procedure. Although there is no law or court decision that gives a suspect the right to have an attorney present at a one-on-one confrontation, it is prudent to keep a record of the procedure (as with a lineup). Later, if the case goes to trial and the investigator must respond to questions posed by the defense, the date, time, place, and statements made by the viewer or suspect will be available for ready reference.

RELIABILITY OF EYEWITNESS IDENTIFICATIONS

Eyewitness testimony has been studied by a number of behavioral scientists who belittle such testimony and believe that juries tend to overestimate the credibility of eyewitness accounts.[16] This outlook, however, is not shared by average citizens. Based on their own experience, they feel they can trust what they see with their own eyes. Jurors often transfer this credibility to the testimony of an eyewitness.

What Can Affect Witness Reliability?

- Procedures during lineups
- Witness stress or pressure
- Racial bias
- Lighting during crime
- Time between act and identification

In the absence of forensic evidence, the two most compelling kinds of evidence presented to a jury are the signed confession and the identification of the defendant by an eyewitness. The Supreme Court has placed more severe limitations on obtaining and using a confession as evidence than it has on securing and using the evidence of an eyewitness. Significant eyewitness identification cases are listed in the references.[17]

Jury Instructions on Eyewitness Identification

In a case involving damaging eyewitness testimony, the defense may ask a trial judge to give jurors special instructions to assist them in evaluating it. An explanation of jury instructions may help. First, readers should be aware that a defense attorney has this additional opportunity to protect a client's interests. Second, it is important that investigators be familiar with the contents of a carefully drafted set of jury instructions; then, they can spot and remedy any weakness before their evidence reaches the court.

In the appendix to his journal article, Sanders proposes an elaborate set of such instructions for an eyewitness identification case. He recommends they be read to the jury before the eyewitness is heard, and further, that each juror be given a copy before retiring to consider the evidence. They are as follows:

[One of the most important questions] or [the only important question] in this case is the identification of the defendant as the person who committed the crime. The prosecution has the burden of proving beyond a reasonable doubt, not only that the crime was committed, but also that the defendant was the person who committed the crime. If, after considering the evidence you have heard from both sides, you are not convinced beyond a reasonable doubt that the defendant is the person who committed the crime, you must find him not guilty.

The identification testimony that you have heard was an expression of belief or impression by the witness. To find the defendant not guilty, you need not believe that the identification witness was insincere, but merely that he was mistaken in his belief or impression.

Many factors affect the accuracy of identification. In considering whether the prosecution has proved beyond a reasonable doubt that the defendant is the person who committed the crime, you should consider the following:

1.   Did the witness have an adequate opportunity to observe [see] the criminal actor?

     In answering this question, you should consider:

     a.   the length of time the witness observed the actor;
     b.   the distance between the witness and the actor;
     c.   the extent to which the actor's features were visible and undisguised;
     d.   the light or lack of light at the place and time of observation;
     e.   the presence or absence of distracting noises or activity during the observation;
     f.   any other circumstance affecting the witness's opportunity to observe the person committing the crime.

2.   Did the witness have the capacity to observe the person committing the crime?

     In answering this question, you should consider whether the witness's capacity was impaired by:

     a.   stress or fright at the time of observation;
     b.   personal motivations, biases or prejudices;
     c.   uncorrected visual defects;
     d.   fatigue and injury;
     e.   drugs or alcohol.

     [You should consider also whether the witness is of a different race than the criminal actor. Identification by a person of a different race may be less reliable than identification by a person of the same race.]

3.   Was the witness sufficiently attentive to the criminal actor at the time of the crime?

     In answering this question, you should consider whether the witness knew that a crime was taking place during the time he observed the actor. Even if the witness had adequate opportunity and capacity to observe the criminal actor, he may not have done so unless he was aware that a crime was being committed.

4.   Was the witness identification of the defendant completely the product of his own memory?

     In answering this question, you should consider:

     a.   the length of time that passed between the witness's original observation and his identification of the defendant;
     b.   the witness's capacity and state of mind at the time of the identification;
     c.   the witness's exposure to opinions, descriptions or identifications given by other witnesses, to photographs or newspaper accounts, or to any other information or influence that may have affected the independence of his identification;
     d.   any instances when the witness, or any eyewitness to the crime, failed to identify the defendant;
     e.   any instances when the witness, or any eyewitness to the crime, gave a description of the actor that is inconsistent with the defendant's appearance;
     f.   the circumstances under which the defendant was presented to the witness for identification. [You may take into account that an identification made by

picking the defendant from a group of similar individuals is generally more reliable than an identification made from the defendant being presented alone to the witness. You may also take into account that identifications made from seeing the person are generally more reliable than identifications made from a photograph.]

I again emphasize that the burden of proving that the defendant is the person who committed the crime is on the prosecution. If, after considering the evidence you have heard from the prosecution and from the defense, and after evaluating the eyewitness testimony in light of the considerations listed above, you have a reasonable doubt about whether the defendant is the person who committed the crime, you must find him not guilty.[18]

More recent research on eyewitness identification has prompted legislation in New Jersey and Connecticut that mandates more definitive instructions to juries. The court is charged with explaining to jurors the factors that may affect a witnesses' reliability. It is likely that other states will expand rules relative to eyewitness identification and testimony.

CONCLUSION

One of the more rapidly changing aspects of criminal investigation involves eyewitness testimony. Recent Supreme Court decisions are likely to be further refined by the Courts as more research comes to the fore. It is incumbent upon the investigator to keep abreast of court decisions and actions by state legislatures to address issues related to faulty eyewitness accounts. Here again, the investigator must make every effort to "test" an eyewitnesses description and account of an observation.[19]

NOTES

[1]   *Simmons v. United States*, 390 U.S. 377, 385 (1968).

[2]   Ibid., 386, note 4.

[3]   *State v. Taplin*, 230 N.J. Super. 99 (1988).

[4]   *State v. Cribb*, 281 N.J. Super. 156 (1995).

[5]   *State v. Henderson*, 479 S.W.2d 485 (Mo. 1972); *Coleman v. Alabama*, 399 U.S. 1, 5 (1970).

[6]   *Simmons*, supra note 1; *United States v. Ash*, 413 U.S. 300, 322 (1973).

[7]   *United States v. Wade*, 388 U.S. 218, 220 (1967).

[8]   *Simmons*, supra note 1, 377.

[9]   *Wade*, supra note 7, 230–232.

[10]   *Simmons*, supra note 1.

[11]   *Ash*, supra note 6, 321.

[12]   *Wade*, supra note 7, 237.

[13]   *Kirby v. Illinois*, 406 U.S. 682, 689 (1972).

14   *People v. Manion*, 67 Ill. 2d 564, 367 N.E.d 1313 (1977).

15   *Kennaugh v. Miller*, 29 F.3d 36 (2002).

16   Elizabeth Loftus. *Eyewitness Testimony*, txt. ed. (Cambridge, MA: Harvard University Press, 1980); Daniel Yarmey, *The Psychology of Eyewitness Testimony* (Riverside, NJ: The Free Press, 1979); Brian R. Clifford and Ray Bull, *The Psychology of Person Identification* (Boston: Routledge & Kegan Paul, 1978).

17   *Wade*, supra note 7; *Gilbert v. California*, 388 U.S. 263 (1967); *Stovall v. Denno*, 388 U.S. 293 (1967); *Foster v. California*, 394 U.S. 440 (1969); *Neil v. Biggers*, 409 U.S. 188 (1972); *Manson v. Brathwaite*, 432 U.S. 98 (1977). These issues are covered in Shelvin Singer and Marshall J. Hartman, *Constitutional Criminal Procedure Handbook* (New York: Wiley & Sons, 1986).

18   Robin Sanders, "Helping the Jury Evaluate Eyewitness Testimony: The Need for Additional Safe-guards," *American Journal of Criminal Law* 12 (1984), 222–224.19.

19   Spadanuta, Laura (2012) "Witness History: A New Jersey Ruling on the Use of Eyewitness Identification in Criminal Trials Will Change How Such Evidence is Presented to Juries." *Security Management* (January, pp. 16–17).

IMPORTANT CASES

Coleman v. Alabama (1970)
Kennaugh v. Miller (2002)
Kirby v. Illinois (1972)
People v. Manion (1977)
Simmons v. United States (1968)
State v. Henderson (1972)
State v. Cribb (1995)
State v. Taplin (1988)
United States v. Ash (1973)
United States v. Wade (1967)

DISCUSSION QUESTIONS

1.   In all states anyone arrested for a felony what documentary evidence is required?

2.   When a suspect is arrested when should a lineup be conducted?

3.   What is the recommended number of persons for a lineup, and how should it be composed?

4.   What is the reliability of eyewitness identifications?

5.   What are some of the factors that might influence an individual's identification?

SUPPLEMENTAL READINGS

Boylan, J. (2000). *Portraits of guilt*. New York: Pocket Books.

Brewer, N. (2006). Uses and abuses of eyewitness identification confidence. *Legal and Criminological Psychology*, *11*, 1.

Clifford, B. R., & Ray, B. (1978). *The psychology of person identification*. Boston: Routledge & Kegan Paul.

Cutler, B. L., & Penrod, S. D. (1995). *Mistaken identification—the eyewitness, psychology, and the law*. Cambridge, NY: Cambridge University Press.

del Carmen, R. V., & Jeffery, T. W. (2011). *Briefs of leading cases in law enforcement* (8th ed.). Boston: Elsevier/Anderson Publishing.

Ingram, J. L. (2011). *Criminal evidence* (11th ed.). Boston: Elsevier/Anderson Publishing.

Kanovitz, J. R. (2012). *Constitutional law* (13th ed.). Boston: Elsevier/Anderson Publishing.

Leinfelt, F. H. (2004). Descriptive eyewitness testimony: The influence of emotionality, racial identification, question style, and selective perception. *Criminal Justice Review*, *29*(2), 317–340.

Loftus, E. F., & Doyle, J. (2007). *Eyewitness testimony: Civil and criminal* (4th ed.). LexisNexis.

Loftus, E. F., & Ketchum, K. (1991). *Witness for the defense: The accused, the eyewitness and the expert who puts memory on trial*. New York: St. Martin's Press.

Moak, S. C., & Carlson, R. L. (2012). *Criminal justice procedure* (8th ed.). Boston: Elsevier/Anderson Publishing.

Parliament, L., & Yarmey, A. D. (2002). Deception in eyewitness identification. *Criminal Justice and Behavior*, *29*(6), 734–736.

CHAPTER 10

INTERROGATION OF SUSPECTS AND HOSTILE WITNESSES

Guidelines and Procedures

Probably no subject in the area of crime investigation has been so discussed or hotly debated in recent years as that relating to the subject of interrogation. Although the focus has largely been on the interrogation of suspected terrorists at the facility on the Guantanamo naval base, or at various other international sites, the issue has sparked legitimate concern as to what the difference is between interrogation and torture. Unfortunately, there is no uniform agreement, even at the highest levels of government.

Today, many investigators believe that the sole purpose of interrogation is to get a confession. This may be in part a lingering heritage of English common law: in earlier times, a lack of confession was often viewed as a serious deficiency in the Crown's case, enough to cause a judge or jury to acquit the accused. The weight given to confession as a means of solving a crime continues to the present day. Despite this, the investigator should realize that an interrogation can also be used to

Figure 10.1
In this 2005 file photo released by the U.S. military, ankle cuffs are shown locked to the chair and floor in an interrogation room at Guantanamo Bay Naval Base, Cuba. Allegations of abuse in Guantanamo have surfaced, including the use of controversial interrogation techniques such as "waterboarding."

gather information or statements that can contribute to building a case in the absence of a confession. However, a common defense in such cases is that remarks made by a suspect during an interrogation should not be included if the confession is thrown out by the courts.

The potential of the forensic sciences—especially criminalistics—as its partial replacement for establishing guilt is yet to be fully realized. In the United States, Supreme Court decisions have placed limits on the interrogative procedures that may be used to secure a confession; they reflect the importance it retains. In Great Britain, the Judges' Rules (formulated in 1912 and since modified) govern investigative behavior. The aim of judicial guidance in either country is to ensure that a confession is trustworthy and that it was made voluntarily—not under duress.

The *Miranda* warning precedent has had a major impact on interrogations, especially with regard to career criminals, who will frequently request a lawyer. Because an interrogation must cease at this point until a lawyer is present, the use of interrogation has become increasingly complex. Interrogation of nonsuspects and uncooperative witnesses is not covered under *Miranda*, and does frequently offer a valuable avenue during the course of an investigation.

THE PURPOSE OF INTERROGATION

The purpose of interrogation is to elicit information from a suspect who may suppress the facts, or from people whose answers might be influenced by close ties to a suspect. Though spouses, parents, accomplices, and friends will not often willingly divulge what could be damaging to a suspect's best interests, these sources may still provide potentially prejudicial information. Although obtaining information detrimental to the suspect's case is the primary goal of the interrogative process, other results may be achieved.

1. Establish the innocence of a suspect by clearing up facts that seem to point to guilt (although a frequent, important result, this is ignored in much of the literature in the field);

2. Obtain from the suspect or relatives and friends of the suspect:
    *   The names of accomplices;
    *   The facts and circumstances surrounding the crime;
    *   Follow-up leads provided unwittingly, or with ulterior motive, such as faking an alibi;
    *   The location of stolen goods;
    *   The location of physical evidence, such as documents, a weapon, or a burglar's tool.

3. Obtain from the suspect alone:
    *   An admission—an express or implied statement tending to support the suspect's involvement in the crime, but insufficient by itself to prove guilt;
    *   A confession—an oral or written statement acknowledging guilt.

WHY PEOPLE CONFESS

An understanding of why it is possible to obtain a confession may be found in the works of M.W. Horowitz,[1] and Ivan Pavlov (as interpreted by William Sargant).[2] The law enforcement community—academics as well as practitioners—has generally taken little notice of Horowitz's paper examining the psychology of confession. Pointing to a problem as ancient as history itself, Horowitz asks, "Why does it occur?":

> Why not always brazen it out when confronted by accusation? Why does a person convict himself through a confession, when at the very worst, no confession would leave him at least as well off (and possibly better off) from the point of view of the physical and social consequences of his act?[3]

Horowitz goes on to discuss how readily some college students suspected of cheating admitted their guilt when faced with strong evidence of collusion:

> ... no accusations of an explicit nature were made [to the students]. There were no stern or frowning faces. All involved persons were simply and directly confronted with the evidence, namely, the coincidence of answers on adjacent papers, and asked if there was some explanation of the coincidence. The question was asked simply, calmly, and directly.
>
>   When so confronted the involved persons confessed, much to the surprise of all. Clearly, cheating could not be proved in any accepted legal sense in these cases. Guilt was presumptive, only. Nevertheless, all did confess without being pressed. That pressure existed is nearly certain because of the nature of the situation. *But it was intrinsic in the psychology of the situation, and not induced* (emphasis added).[4]

This experiment demonstrates the powerful influence of evidence, particularly physical evidence, in building on the internal, self-generated, psychological pressure of a guilty person. Horowitz then notes that confession (even to offenses not committed) can be obtained through duress such as torture, brutality, and excessive or prolonged psychological pressure. But, he adds, this is unnecessary if the suspect is indeed guilty, and if certain other social psychological conditions prevail.

Horowitz: Basic Concepts

An understanding of Horowitz's five social-psychological concepts will help to explain why a person confesses. They are: (1) accusation, (2) available evidence, (3) friendly and hostile forces, (4) guilt feelings, and, finally, (5) confession as a way out.

Accusation: The person under interrogation must be mentally or visually aware of an accusation. The accusation may be explicit—made directly at the start of an interrogation, or it may be implicit in the interrogator's attitude and demeanor—communicated by nothing more than a raised eyebrow. As a result, the person perceives that he or she has been accused or, based on guilt feelings, projects such a perception. According to Horowitz, whether the accusation is explicit or implicit makes no essential difference in the suspect's social-psychological situation.

Some consequences flow from the perception of accusation. One is the feeling that one's psychological freedom and movement are curtailed; another is being placed on unsure ground where the familiar clues governing behavior in normal situations are missing. Being interviewed for a job can produce a similar feeling. In either situation, the accused is largely supported by available ego defense responses. There is

> ... no role if you will, that he can utilize in this situation. He must behave, then, in stereotyped and compulsive ways. He feels that he has been personally attacked, hemmed in, constricted. This perception of accusation to the guilty person must inevitably produce defense for an attacked ego. Indeed even innocent persons frequently feel guilty when falsely accused.[5]

Whether guilty or innocent, the individual is in a difficult position. Feeling cornered, freedom is the main concern, but the route appears blocked. The strength of the perception of accusation is subjective; it is "a function of the person rather than a function of the objective strength of the authority itself."[6]

Evidence is Available: The first response, especially of the guilty person, to the realization of being accused is to become worried and psychologically unsettled.

> [The accused's] ... perceptual structure is unstable. This is so because he does not know exactly how much is actually known to the accuser. Perhaps the accuser is bluffing, in which case one might brazen it out. Perhaps the accuser knows all, in which case one is better off to ask for sympathetic treatment or to argue for extenuating circumstances. Most usually, the truth lies between these extremes but the accused doesn't know exactly where.[7]

An accusation in and of itself implies that a certain amount of evidence is indeed available. When hard evidence is produced, any logical person will infer at some point in the interrogation that he or she "is caught with the goods." Their psychological position becoming precarious, freedom is even more threatened. It is not essential, however, that hard evidence be produced—believing that it is available may suffice. The accused may "read into what may be innocent things in reality, portents which need not be there."[8] Hence, failing a polygraph examination often leads to confession (though the failure is not admissible as evidence in court—except by stipulation). Hearing that an accomplice is "just starting to talk" or that crime scene evidence has been taken to the laboratory may reinforce natural anxiety and provoke a confession. Indeed, the considerable potential of physical evidence is not taken advantage of by many investigators, owing to a lack of training and education in understanding crime laboratory results. This point has been made before, and probably will be again; it is worth reemphasizing. Playing one co-offender against the other (using the revelations of each on the other) is an additional means of indicating that "evidence is available." Also useful is framing a question to imply that its answer is already known (e.g., "You bought the gun, not your partner—is that correct?")

Motive is not normally thought of as evidence, but if it has been determined—especially for crimes in which it is particularized rather than universal, as in homicide—this information can be put to good use during interrogation. The victim may be able to suggest a motive. Sometimes it can be surmised by the shrewd investigator from facts developed during the investigation or from similar cases. Because suspects believe that motive has evidentiary value, they often believe that it has furnished evidence by providing a reason for the crime.

Forces—Friendly and Hostile: It should be obvious from the foregoing that any factors contributing to psychological uneasiness will also be conducive to confession. Accordingly, any legally permitted action that either reduces the forces friendly to the accused, or increases the hostile forces, can enhance the likelihood of a confession:

> ... the suspect must perceive ... that the total hostile array of power exceeds the total array of friendly power that he can martial [sic]. ... In short, the person must believe he is alone, or nearly alone. He is cut off from succor. His situation is such that salvation lies only in him.[9]

This is why an interrogation is not conducted in the comfort of the suspect's living room, convivial drinks in hand, surrounded by supportive family members. On the contrary, the characteristically dreary police station house minimizes forces friendly to the suspect.

Guilt Feelings: Guilt feelings must be present in order for a confession to be forthcoming:

It should be … clear that if a person does not feel guilt he is not in his own mind guilty and will not confess to an act which others may regard as evil or wrong and he, in fact, considers correct.[10]

Confession, therefore, is rare when the "hit man" in a gangland killing is apprehended and questioned. The code of silence *(omerta)* among these criminals acknowledges that death is the rightful punishment for those who break it. The assignment to execute anyone is a clear indication of gangland trust; the execution carried off, a path to advancement. From this perspective, there is little if any reason for the gunman to feel guilt. The killer was "only carrying out orders" or "the punk had it coming." Hard empirical evidence, therefore, confirms that admissions of or confessions to gangland killings are rare, even when police know the killer's identity and interrogate him or her. Horowitz's statement on guilt feelings helps to explain this phenomenon.

Ordinarily, most people feel guilt as a consequence of wrongdoing, their sense of right conduct having been violated. When it moves beyond mere self reproach, the feeling becomes strong enough to cause the person's inner peace to crumble. Then other factors—an accusation, physical evidence, or both—have a cumulative effect by generating psychological stress. As stated at the onset, Pavlov also studied this process. Understanding his theory (explained below) can increase the chances of obtaining a confession. Although his study considers how stress was induced in dogs, it may apply to humans as well.

Confession: Confession should be presented as a way out. Under interrogation, people are aware of their vulnerability and weakness when accused by "an authority with a high ratio of power compared to the forces [they] can martial [sic]." Perceiving "that there is good evidence of [their] guilt," they feel guilty, are mindful of loneliness, inner ferment, and the need for relief.[11] At this point in the process, investigators should make them aware that confession is the path to deliverance and mental freedom. Meanwhile, it must be made easy for the person to confess. A crowd of onlookers—police chief, captain of detectives, district attorney, reporters—is not conducive to this end. This is why privacy and anonymity are the rule in religious and psychiatric practice. Confessing may well be "good for the soul," but a person about to do so must be made to feel comfortable. Any residual hesitancy must be removed with assurances that their emotions are at least understood, if not shared. Sentiments that could convey this might include: "Tell me about it, and you will feel better," "I've heard what you're going to tell me before," "You're not the first to do this, and you're probably not the last," or "Lots of people have had the same idea." Minimizing the ethical considerations and seriousness of their conduct makes it easier for a person to confess.

Ivan Pavlov's classical study of conditioned reflex established a relationship between induced stress and the nervous system and helps explain why individuals confess. Though humans have not been deliberately conditioned, a signal is nevertheless received when a suspect realizes that incriminating evidence (induced stress) exists. The process is similar to Horowitz's results: the stronger the evidence, the stronger the signal; the greater the threat to freedom, the greater the stress. For example, the questioning of relatives or associates may reveal some apparently innocuous details about a suspect's past. If, during a subsequent interrogation of the suspect, the investigator picks up on them, the suspect may suppose that his or her life is an open book. The guilty person might then jump to conclusions, infer that their participation in the crime is also known, and confess. Though an innocent person is unlikely to be similarly affected, a guilty person may well receive an increased

en.wikipedia.org

Figure 10.2
Ivan Pavlov is widely known for first describing the phenomenon of classical conditioning, the basic concepts of which can be applied to the interrogation and confession of suspects.

signal and feel greater stress when the authority making the accusation is a chief of detectives or a district attorney specifically called in to handle the interrogation.

Anxiety Waiting: Pavlov's observations seem applicable to human behavior. For example, it is a common experience for an individual to become tense while remaining in readiness, expecting something to happen—especially if the anticipated result is of some concern. Thus, a suspect awaiting an alibi check may become anxious because of the time it entails (particularly if the alibi proffered cannot bear checking); as may, to a lesser extent, a person who is forced to wait for an investigator to complete other business after being brought to the station house for questioning. Sometimes, it is productive to ask an individual who has denied involvement with a crime to "think it over" and "come back tomorrow." The effect on a guilty person will be prolonged tension. Except for the inconvenience, the innocent should be relatively unaffected.

Physical Condition: The Wickersham Commission revealed in 1931 that the "third degree," which it defined as "the extraction of confessions through police brutality," was a "widespread, almost universal practice."[12] Although it is not acceptable today, instances of the abuse of prisoners and suspects continue to be a problem in some departments. For those curious about just how far civilized methods of interrogation have come, the Wickersham Reports are recommended reading.[13]

Occasionally, however, an opportunity may present itself to obtain a confession from a suspect who is exhausted.

WHY SOME DO NOT CONFESS

By now the reader will understand that obtaining a confession is not a simple matter. After all, Horowitz's experiments involved a noncriminal, rather homogeneous group of people. Investigators know quite well that all guilty persons—particularly those facing severe sanctions—are not as ready to confess as one might assume, even when Horowitz's five basic conditions have been met. There are several reasons why even a guilty person will not acknowledge, much less confess to, involvement in a crime:

- Some suffer no pangs of conscience and have no need to relieve guilty feelings.

- Some are fearful of the consequences if they betray their accomplices.

- Some have learned (having been through the mill) that only by talking do they dig their own grave.

- Under *Miranda*, it would require an unusual set of circumstances for an attorney to fail to advise a client to remain silent.

INTERROGATION: GUIDELINES AND PROCEDURES

The practice of criminal interrogation in the United States has been significantly affected by decisions of the Supreme Court, most significantly by *Miranda v. Arizona* in 1966. This being so, it is essential to consider the guidelines laid down in *Miranda* before the procedure involved in conducting an interrogation can be treated.

Miranda Guidelines

The *Miranda* doctrine spells out the constitutional rights and procedural safeguards, including the waiver of those rights that must be conveyed to a person before any interrogation may be undertaken. Chief Justice Warren delivered and summed up the opinion of the Court as follows:

> Our holding will be spelled out with some specificity in the pages which follow but briefly stated it is this. The prosecution may not use statements, whether exculpatory or inculpatory, stemming from custodial interrogation of the defendant unless it demonstrates the use of procedural safeguards effective to secure the privilege against self-incrimination. By custodial interrogation, we mean questioning initiated by law enforcement officers after a person has been taken into custody or otherwise deprived of his freedom of action in any significant way.* As for the procedural safeguards to be employed, unless other fully effective means are devised to inform accused persons of their right of silence and to assure continuous opportunity to exercise it, the following measures are required. Prior to any questioning, the person must be warned that he has a right to remain silent, that any statement he does make may be used as evidence against him, and that he has a right to the presence of an attorney, either retained or appointed. The defendant may waive effectuation of these rights, provided the waiver is made voluntarily, knowingly and intelligently. If, however, he indicates in any manner and at any stage of the process that he wishes to consult with an attorney before speaking there can be no questioning. Likewise, if the individual is alone and indicates in any manner that he does not wish to be interrogated, the police may not question him. The mere fact that he may have answered some questions or volunteered some statements on his own does not deprive him of the right to refrain from answering any further inquiries until he has consulted with an attorney and thereafter consents to be questioned.[14]

The words of the Court also spell out what the police must do to comply with the *Miranda* ruling.[15]

THE RIGHT TO REMAIN SILENT
At the outset, if a person in custody is to be subjected to interrogation, he must first be informed in clear and unequivocal terms that he has the right to remain silent. For those unaware of the privilege, the warning is needed simply to make them aware of it—the threshold requirement for an intelligent decision as to its exercise.

ANYTHING SAID CAN BE USED AGAINST THE INDIVIDUAL
The warning of the right to remain silent must be accompanied by the explanation that anything said can and will be used against the individual in court. This warning is needed in order to make him aware not only of the privilege, but also of the consequence of forgoing it. It is only through an awareness of these consequences that there can be any assurance of real understanding and intelligent exercise of the privilege. Moreover, this warning may serve to make the individual more acutely aware that he is faced with a phase of the adversary system—that he is not in the presence of persons acting solely in his interest.

RIGHT TO COUNSEL
The circumstances surrounding in-custody interrogation can operate very quickly to overbear the will of one merely made aware of his privilege by his interrogators. Therefore the right

---

* This is what we meant in *Escobedo [v. Illinois]* when we spoke of an investigation that had focused on an accused.

to have counsel present at the interrogation is indispensable to the protection of the Fifth Amendment privilege under the system we delineate today.

Accordingly we hold that an individual held for interrogation must be clearly informed that he has the right to consult with a lawyer and to have the lawyer with him during interrogation under the system for protecting the privilege we delineate today. As with the warnings of the right to remain silent and that anything stated can be used in evidence against him, this warning is an absolute prerequisite to interrogation. No amount of circumstantial evidence that the person may have been aware of this right will suffice to stand in its stead. Only through such a warning is there ascertainable assurance that the accused was aware of this right.

If an individual indicates that he wishes the assistance of counsel before any interrogation occurs, the authorities cannot rationally ignore or deny his request on the basis that the individual does not have or cannot afford a retained attorney.

An individual need not make a pre-interrogation request for a lawyer. While such request affirmatively secures his right to have one, his failure to ask for a lawyer does not constitute a waiver. No effective waiver of the right to counsel during interrogation can be recognized unless specifically made after the warnings we here delineate have been given. The accused who does not know his rights and therefore does not make a request may be the person who most needs counsel.

COUNSEL FOR THE INDIGENT
In order fully to apprise a person interrogated of the extent of his rights under this system then, it is necessary to warn him not only that he has the right to consult with an attorney, but also that if he is indigent a lawyer will be appointed to represent him. Without this additional warning, the admonition of the right to consult with counsel would often be understood as meaning only that he can consult with a lawyer if he has one or has the funds to obtain one. The warning of a right to counsel would be hollow if not couched in terms that would convey to the indigent—the person most often subjected to interrogation—the knowledge that he too has a right to have counsel present. As with the warnings of the right to remain silent and of the general right to counsel, only by effective and express explanation to the indigent of this right can there be assurance that he was truly in a position to exercise it.

THE WISH TO REMAIN SILENT
Once warnings have been given, the subsequent procedure is clear. If the individual indicates in any manner, at any time prior to or during questioning, that he wishes to remain silent, the interrogation must cease. At this point he has shown that he intends to exercise his Fifth Amendment privilege; any statement taken after the person invokes his privilege cannot be other than the product of compulsion, subtle or otherwise. Without the right to cut off questioning, the setting of in-custody interrogation operates on the individual to overcome free choice in producing a statement after the privilege has been once invoked. If the individual states that he wants an attorney, the interrogation must cease until an attorney is present. At that time, the individual must have an opportunity to confer with the attorney and to have him present during any subsequent questioning. If the individual cannot obtain an attorney and he indicates that he wants one before speaking to police, they must respect his decision to remain silent.

WAIVING ONE'S RIGHTS
If the interrogation continues without the presence of an attorney and a statement is taken, a heavy burden rests on the government to demonstrate that the defendant knowingly

and intelligently waived his privilege against self-incrimination and his right to retained or appointed counsel.

An express statement that the individual is willing to make a statement and does not want an attorney followed closely by a statement could constitute a waiver. But a valid waiver will not be presumed simply from the silence of the accused after warnings are given or simply from the fact that a confession was in fact eventually obtained.

Moreover, where in-custody interrogation is involved, there is no room for the contention that the privilege is waived if the individual answers some questions or gives some information on his own prior to invoking his right to remain silent when interrogated.

ADMISSION OF STATEMENTS

The warnings required and the waiver necessary in accordance with our opinion today are, in the absence of a fully effective equivalent, prerequisites to the admissibility of any statement made by a defendant. No distinction can be drawn between statements which are direct confessions and statements which amount to "admissions" of part or all of an offense. The privilege against self-incrimination protects the individual from being compelled to incriminate himself in any manner; it does not distinguish degrees of incrimination. Similarly, for precisely the same reason, no distinction may be drawn between inculpatory statements and statements alleged to be merely "exculpatory." If a statement made were in fact truly exculpatory it would, of course, never be used by the prosecution. In fact, statements merely intended to be exculpatory by the defendant are often used to impeach his testimony at trial or to demonstrate untruths in the statements given under interrogation and thus to prove guilt by implication. These statements are incriminating in any meaningful sense of the word and may not be used without the full warnings and effective waiver required for any other statement.

In dealing with statements obtained through interrogation, we do not purport to find all confessions inadmissible. Confessions remain a proper element in law enforcement. Any statement given freely and voluntarily without any compelling influences is, of course, admissible in evidence. The fundamental import of the privilege while an individual is in custody is not whether he is allowed to talk to the police without the benefit of warnings and counsel, but whether he can be interrogated. There is no requirement that police stop a person who enters a police station and states that he wishes to confess to a crime, or a person who calls the police to offer a confession or any other statement he desires to make. Volunteered statements of any kind are not barred by the Fifth Amendment and their admissibility is not affected by our holding today.

Congressional Action

In 1968, two years after *Miranda*, Congress (as part of a crime control bill) passed a law that applied only to federal prosecutions. The intent was to get around *Miranda* and allow voluntary confessions to be admitted into evidence. In 1997, Attorney General Janet Reno directed federal prosecutors not to argue that *Miranda* warnings can be disregarded, and in a letter to Congress, she stated that the 1968 law was unconstitutional. In 1999, however (31 years after *Miranda*), the 4th Circuit U.S. Court of Appeals permitted the resurrection of the 1968 law that had never been invoked. In a 2–1 ruling, it reaffirmed the admissibility of voluntary confessions. In *United States v. Dickerson*,[16] the defendant had voluntarily confessed to a series of bank robberies, but it was only later that he was read the *Miranda* warnings. In *Dickerson v. United States*,[17] however, the court held that any law passed by Congress that seeks to overturn the *Miranda* decision is unconstitutional.

Implementing the *Miranda* Warnings

As a means of compliance with the *Miranda* decision many police departments have cards printed that spell out the constitutional rights of the individual (see Figure 10.3). One of these cards may be given to the person in custody, but the officer also must verbally inform the individual of each right. If necessary (owing to some difficulty in language, hearing, or intelligence), or if requested, the rights should be explained further to the individual.

The courts have ruled that any statements made outside the context of *Miranda* rules are allowed. In *United States v. Barnes*, the suspect was arrested and invoked his right to counsel before making several statements. The officer told Barnes that he was being booked for illegal possession of a firearm, and he replied that he "didn't think so." After the officer asked him what he meant by that statement, Barnes told him that it was not illegal for convicted felons to carry weapons. These statements are considered volunteered (and admissible in court) because they were spontaneous and not made during an interrogation.[18]

Waiving One's Rights

The concern, first expressed by the police after *Miranda*, that no one would agree to be interrogated is not supported by experience. Fewer individuals exercise their rights than do those who waive them.

1. You have the right to remain silent. This means you do not have to answer any questions.

2. If you answer any question, anything you say can be used against you in court.

3. You have the right to legal counsel. This means you may secure the services of a lawyer of your own choosing and seek his or her advice. You may also have him or her present with you while you are being questioned.

4. If you cannot afford to hire a lawyer, one will be appointed to represent you before any questioning takes place, if you so wish. This will be done without any expense to you.

5. If you decide to answer questions now without a lawyer present, you retain the right to stop answering at any time. At that time you still have the right to seek the advice of a lawyer before continuing to answer questions.

Figure 10.3
Miranda warning card.

It is incumbent on the investigator to prove that the person voluntarily and knowingly waived his or her *Miranda* rights and decided to answer questions posed by the investigator. The language of *Miranda* is significant on this point:

> Whatever the testimony of the authorities as to waiver of rights by an accused, the fact of lengthy interrogation or incommunicado incarceration before a statement is made is strong evidence that the accused did not validly waive his rights. In these circumstances the fact that the individual eventually made a statement is consistent with the conclusion that the compelling influence of the interrogation finally forced him to do so. It is inconsistent with any notion of a voluntary relinquishment of the privilege. Moreover, any evidence that the accused was threatened, tricked, or cajoled into a waiver will, of course, show that the defendant did not voluntarily waive his privilege. The requirement of warnings and waiver of rights is a fundamental with respect to the Fifth Amendment privilege and not simply a preliminary ritual to existing methods of interrogation.[19]

Fortunately the Court indicated in its decision that an "express statement that the individual is willing to make a statement and does not want an attorney, followed by a statement" may serve as proof for the waiver of the individual's rights.[20] In practice there are two ways to accomplish this. One is to ask the individual the following questions, each of which must be answered affirmatively:

1. Do you understand each of the rights which have been explained to you and which you have read?

2. Keeping these rights in mind, do you now wish to talk and answer questions regarding _____?

The second method is to obtain a signed, witnessed "waiver of rights" form as shown in Figure 10.4. These should be available in several languages.

Interrogation in Practice

To conduct an interrogation it is important to establish its purpose and be familiar with the underlying principles, as discussed earlier. In addition, the investigator must be prepared to evaluate the responses throughout the questioning. Finally, if the outcome is a confession, the results must be documented for possible later use in court. Because, on occasion, others besides a suspect are interrogated, the term *subject* will be used below to describe the person being interrogated.

Preparation

The success of an interrogation rests on several factors, among which preparation is one of the most important. Accordingly, a diligent investigator will:

1. Personally visit the crime scene in important cases, or refresh memory by reviewing the crime scene photographs.

2. Review the entire file so as to be thoroughly familiar with all the details of the case.

3. Be aware of how any physical evidence that was discovered is useful in reconstructing the crime or in connecting a suspect to the crime scene or victim.

I have had my rights explained to me and have read a statement of them. I understand what my rights are. I do not want an attorney at this time. I know and understand the consequences of what I am doing. I am willing to answer questions and to make a statement. No threats have been made to me. No coercion or pressure of any kind has been exerted against me. No promises have been made to me.

DATE: _____   _____
                                                      (Signature)

TIME: _____

LOCATION: _____

WITNESS: _____   DATE: _____

                                                             TIME: _____

WITNESS: _____   DATE: _____

                                                             TIME: _____

Figure 10.4
"Waiver of rights" form.

4. Learn as much as possible about the subject from his or her family and friends. If the subject's name appears in the records of the department, the facts and circumstances of each and every incident recorded in the files should be studied. Anyone in the department who knows or has had contact with the subject should be queried for any helpful insights they might be able to provide. In addition, anything that is of concern or interest to the subject should be learned. This would include such matters as: What job does he or she hold? Is he or she of a religious bent? Does he or she have hobbies and other interests—such as specific sports played or watched?

5. Ascertain which elements of the crime can be proved by the existing evidence and which still need to be proved. Any possible incriminating facts disclosed by the subject should be followed up, particularly when they relate to those elements still to be proved.

The aim at the outset of such preparation is to get the subject to talk (see Item 4 above) and keep talking. This permits the investigator to question the subject in a logical fashion with the purpose of arriving at the facts, particularly those not yet known (or proven) about the crime.

The Setting

The conduct of an interrogation is best served if the barriers to communication are minimized. The amount of privacy and time, the room arrangement, and the tone set by the investigator can significantly influence the conduct and progress of an interrogation. These and related matters are considered next.

Privacy

A subject in a criminal investigation usually does not wish to be queried in public. Also, a person is unlikely to confess unless it is made easy to do so. Thus, a private, one-on-one conversation in a setting free from interruption and distraction is especially suitable. The suspect or interviewee should not be permitted to carry a smart phone or other recording device into the room. In most cases the investigator should not bring a phone into the room or should turn the phone off. (Exceptions to this might occur if there is a prearranged plan to have the detective called, either as a ruse that is connected to the investigation or the detective may want to have someone, such as a family member, try to convince the subject to cooperate.) It is becoming more common for interrogations to be recorded, which is advisable, both audibly and in video. Recording may be covert or overt, depending on Department policy, and a decision as to whether or not the subject should be told of the recording will frequently depend on the situation and an assessment of the subject's feelings toward recording. (This subject is discussed further later in this chapter.)

The Room

The room in which an interrogation is conducted should contribute to its success rather than provide distractions that defeat it. Unfortunately, many police departments ignore the importance of having a proper room available for this purpose. A proper room has a decor that precludes distractions of sound or sight. Thus, a sparsely furnished, relatively soundproof, windowless room with bare walls and subdued light would help to keep the questioning focused and on track.

The arrangement of furniture can facilitate or hamper communication. For example, a judge's bench or that of a desk officer in a police station enhances the superior–subordinate relationship by its elevation, the separation it provides, and its ornateness and spaciousness—thus hampering communication. Even a plain table set between two persons is considered to be a barrier—physical and psychological—to communication. Accordingly, some practitioners believe the furniture in an interrogation room should consist of two chairs, and absolutely nothing else.[21] Others disagree, claiming it would be ridiculous to have a room with just two chairs in it.[22] The chairs should be plain, unpadded, and straight-backed with no arms, with the interrogator's chair four to five inches higher and easily moved. The subject's chair, placed with its back to the door, should be anchored to the floor or otherwise made difficult to move by employing rubber tips on the leg ends.[23] The purpose is to allow the interrogator to move closer and closer to the suspect as the latter's feelings of guilt develop to the point of wanting to confess. Propinquity creating a more intimate relationship, it is easier for the subject to confess.

Although the perception of privacy is paramount if a confession is to be obtained, the need to have others witness the interrogation can be met by installing a two-way mirror. The two-way mirror has become so commonplace in the media and film that a subject is likely to be constrained in talking. Closed circuit (CCTV) cameras have become more common, but it is advisable to have at least two cameras in opposite corners that are equipped with sensitive audio recording. Having others who are involved in the case observe and listen to the interrogation is a form of insurance that some clue is not missed or not followed up thoroughly by additional questioning. These and other suggestions made to the interrogator during a break (taken for personal and humane reasons) can be invaluable and contribute to an effective interrogation.

There are many methods of recording an interrogation. These will be treated later in this chapter under "Documenting the Interrogation."

Creating the Tone

It is important at the outset to create an atmosphere that will govern the interrogation. This is done with several objectives in mind: to make it easy for the subject to talk (and confess); to establish that you are in control of the questioning; to avoid distractions that allow the subject's mind to stray from the matter at hand; and to prevent interruptions that break the continuity of the narrative description or thought pertaining to the event under investigation.

The importance of the room setting in achieving some of these objectives has already been described. The manner in which the investigator carries and conducts himself or herself is another significant factor in creating the tone that will govern the interrogation. For example, consider the following aspects of an investigator's behavior and how they may influence the outcome of an interrogation.

Interrogation by Male and/or Females

In most interrogations it makes no difference whether the investigator is a male or female, although traditionally females have been used in sex crime cases where the subject is a female. This is also common in some types of cases involving juveniles, or where the suspect is a female. However, it would be wrong to conclude that women are necessarily more or less effective in handling interrogations and the ultimate decision on who should handle the interrogation involves a number of variables, including but not limited to experience, nature and type of case, suspect criteria and personal bias or perceptions.

It is true that some males express a bias or hostile attitude toward females, whereas females may be uncomfortable with males. But, there is very little research in this area, and this is an area where a supervisor should confer with the detectives on their backgrounds, experience, and opinions related to the subject. In many cases the detectives may work in tandem, taking turns to see who is more likely to establish a rapport with the subject. Ultimately, the goal is to obtain a confession or to develop further information to advance an investigation.

Multiple Interrogators

Most interrogations are conducted by an individual detective in a one-on-one session with the subject. Other sessions may be handled in tandem with the detectives taking turns, and in some cases two investigators may work together. In either of two latter approaches it is critical that the second investigator observe all of the questioning, being particularly aware of statements made by the subject. Failure to do this is likely to result in the subject learning various points of information from the queries by the initial investigator, and then using it in responding to other investigators.

In two-on-one sessions it is common to use the good guy–bad guy approach or a number of variations on the technique. Because most career criminals and a large number of citizens are well aware of this approach an interview strategy should be developed.

Dress and Appearance

A decently groomed, conservatively dressed investigator creates a business-like appearance and a first-impression respect that helps to set the tone of the inquiry. On the other hand, display of police equipment—gun, handcuff, badge and the like—is likely to be counterproductive because of its distractive potential. Similarly, flashy clothing and sloppy appearance are discouraged because of the credibility problem that they may create.

Diction

One's manner of speech and choice of words also have influence over the tone of a conversation. Although good diction is important in many situations, it may be a barrier to communication if the subject comes from a deprived economic class or a different culture. This not-uncommon situation calls for a knowledge of street language, current jargon, and even the argot of professional criminals if the investigator is to understand and be understood. Often it is advisable to soften the terms and words critical to establishing the elements of the crime. Thus the subject "went into" rather than "broke and entered" the apartment. They "took" the television set rather than "stole" it. They are asked "to tell the truth," not "to confess." Employing euphemisms to diminish any harshness that attends the description of the individual's action or crime makes it easier for that person to admit it.

Mannerisms

Any distinctive trait or habit of the investigator that may cause the subject's attention to become unfocused or his or her mind to wander is to be avoided. Blinking the eyes or waving the hands excessively, twitching of the mouth or limbs, doodling, pacing the floor—all are examples of mannerisms that can be counterproductive because they are a source of distraction during interrogation.

Attitude

It is important to establish at the start of the investigation that your job is to investigate the complaint. It is as much your job to prove that a subject was not involved as it is to prove that he or she was. This then is the subject's opportunity to tell his or her story. If a wrong accusation has been made by an accomplice, now is the time to "get the facts out on the table and clear the matter up." Open-mindedness, a willingness to be convinced, and a concern that an innocent person not be unjustly charged are attitudes that should be conveyed by word and deed. With experience, vicarious or personal, an investigator should be able to mention cases in which, though it looked bad in the beginning for a subject, the matter was ended when a little checking established that he or she was telling the truth.

Taking Command of the Situation

An investigator must at all times be in control of the interrogation. It can be lost if the investigator succumbs to his or her emotions (temper, frustration, etc.), has to grope for questions to ask, or allows the subject to take over the session by asking questions in place of answering them. Indeed, it is in just this manner that some subjects are able to ascertain whether the evidence against them is weak or strong. They may also try to defeat the purpose by giving unduly long answers or offering extraneous information. An investigator keeps control not by physical intimidation (which would be illegal) but rather by "selling" himself or herself to the subject, being on top of the investigation, and using clear thinking that keeps the questions and answers focused on the purpose of the interrogation. Utilizing those factors that are important in creating the tone of the interrogation also helps to establish the investigator as person who is in command of the situation.

Conducting the Interrogation

Preliminaries

Prior to beginning an interrogation, a few preliminary precautions must be observed. The first is concerned with the capacity of the subject to understand and respond rationally to questions. If a subject is intoxicated, under the influence of other drugs, or exhibiting any abnormal emotional reactions, this may be good reason for not commencing (or continuing) the interrogation. In these circumstances, the advice of a physician may be needed to determine when, and if, the process may begin (or continue) with assurance that the subject's responses will be rational and intelligent. Although it is not illegal to interrogate a suspect under the influence of alcohol or drugs, the investigator should recognize that this may be used by the defense to argue that the person was not in control of his or her faculties. For this reason, if an interrogation is conducted under these circumstances it is advisable to conduct a second session when the individual is sober.

Where possible a determination of the subject's "psychological" profile can be beneficial. In this regard much research has been conducted on emotional stress, proclivity to lie, disorientation, and sexual, racial or social bias.

The second precaution pertains only when the person to be interrogated is a suspect. Surprisingly, there are those who will respond affirmatively if asked whether they committed a particular crime. Captain Robert Borkenstein, a former commanding officer of the Indiana State Police Laboratory—before administering a lie detector test—asked a suspect who had been transported several hundred miles for the test if he was guilty. The response was a quick "yes." Further inquiry by Borkenstein as to why the suspect had not told the investigators who had been with him all day and questioned him earlier evoked a reply that is as surprising as it is instructive: "They didn't ask me." There are more than a few such persons who merely need to be presented with an opportunity to admit their guilt at the outset. Good practice requires that this opportunity be provided for them.

Beginning the Interrogation

After *Miranda* warnings have been given and the suspect has agreed to be questioned, the first few inquiries are directed toward establishing that the suspect can remember, is in touch with reality, and responds rationally. Questions such as the following can be used to accomplish this:

- What is your full name?
- Where are you now?
- What time is it?
- Where do you live?
- Do you have a job?
- What day is it?
- Where do you work?
- Do you know my name?
- Do you know my occupation?

If the answers to these questions indicate that the suspect knows what is going on, he or she should (generally) then be informed of the crime about which he or she is to be questioned, the location and time it happened, and the identity of the victim(s).

The Body of the Interrogation

If a *res gestae* statement implicating the suspect was uttered by the victim, witness, or even the suspect, it is appropriate (usually at the beginning) to make use of it during the interrogation. One may commence by allowing the suspect to offer, without interruption, a statement of his or her involvement or noninvolvement. Ample opportunity must be given to the suspect to advance any explanation he or she cares to express. The tack to be taken will vary depending on what has been said and how it squares with the information developed independently during the investigation. If there is a complete denial of having been in contact with the victim or of having been at the crime scene, it is important to establish whether the denial is valid. If a claim is made that there was some previous contact with the victim or the scene, it is important to ascertain when and under what circumstances. If the possibility of a prior contact is denied, the suspect is forestalled from later offering a credible explanation for any evidence—tangible or from an eyewitness—that places him or her at the scene or in contact with the victim. If in making the denial the suspect fails to mention any of the following, it is appropriate to inquire further as to:

- His or her whereabouts at the time of the crime;

- Who he or she was with at the time;

- What he or she was doing at that time;

- Whether there was anyone who had an opportunity to observe him or her at that time, and who they are.

These responses must be verified or determined to be inaccurate. If accurate and they exculpate the suspect, it is appropriate to reevaluate the individual's "suspect" status at this point. If inaccurate, however, the suspect should be asked to explain each discrepancy. For a guilty person this will be difficult to accomplish, and sooner or later it becomes apparent that there is "evidence available against him or her." (See Horowitz, Point 2.)

— Evaluation of Responses

Throughout the interrogation the manner of response as well as the answers must be evaluated. A talent for good analytical thinking, an ability to read body language (i.e., to recognize nonverbal cues), and the knowledge and experience needed to recognize signs of lying—these provide the means for detecting whether a subject is telling the truth, stretching it, or lying. The physiological symptoms of lying are known to many because almost everyone has had the experience of telling a lie. Even for a minor falsehood, some persons blush, develop sweaty palms, experience an increased heart rate, have trouble looking the other person in the eye, or display signs of uneasiness such as a twitching of the cheek or licking of the lips. A major lie exacerbates these symptoms and adds at least three others:

1. Just as experiencing an intense emotion can give one a "lump in the throat" so can a lie affect the larynx or "Adam's apple," causing it to move up and down excessively.

2. The carotid arteries in the neck stand out and can be noticed throbbing.

3. The mouth becomes dry, apparently by inhibiting the salivary glands. To relieve this condition the subject may try to wet the lips, work cheeks and tongue to produce saliva, or ask for a glass of water.

It hardly requires mention that these symptoms do not constitute legal evidence. It should also be pointed out that, perhaps with the exception of mouth dryness, these symptoms to a lesser degree can be caused by nervousness. Because most persons suspected of a crime and being interrogated about it are likely to be nervous, there is a question as to the degree of manifestation of the symptoms. With experience, an investigator often can detect the difference between the signs of "normal" nervousness and those caused by "guilty knowledge." (The value of video recording cannot be overstated because it is frequently possible to detect facial or body language movements that might have gone unnoticed.) Physical body movements, such as wringing hands, touching the face, or shaking a leg may also indicate nervousness, an effort to cover up a lie or misrepresentation. But it is worth noting again that such characteristics do not necessarily incriminate an individual, and it is the observation by an investigator over time that is more likely to lead to more accurate conclusions.

An invitation to take a lie detector (polygraph) test may be appropriate at the point when these symptoms appear or perhaps after the subject has been caught making contradictory statements that have been pointed out but remain unexplained.

The "Break"

Although not a part of Horowitz's analysis of why people confess, it is appropriate to discuss what in police circles is called the *break*. The symptoms of lying (already described) may be part of the break, i.e., the point in the interrogation at which the investigator recognizes that the person is about to confess. Such recognition is the result of experience but it manifests itself in several ways. Some early signs include the cessation of denial of involvement in, or commission of, the crime, and the repetition of phrases like "not that I remember." Such behavior might be followed by "What if" questions such as "What if a person didn't intend to _____?" or "What if this is the first time?" or "I have never been in trouble before; wouldn't that be taken into consideration?" Other signs consist of a display of uneasiness: shifting the body in the chair frequently; chain smoking when otherwise a light smoker; casting the eyes on the floor; and so on. It is at this point that the individual needs to be shown gently that confession is the way out (recall Horowitz, Point 5).

Documenting the Interrogation

Where a confession has been made, it is important to document that it was not obtained as a result of coercion or duress, that it was freely and voluntarily made, and that it is trustworthy.

Recording Statements and the Confession

Perhaps the most suitable means for demonstrating that an interrogation was conducted using civilized police practices and that the confession is trustworthy and voluntary is to record the session with a video-sound recorder (tape or digital). Technological advances in video and sound equipment have made this an important tool and financially feasible.

Increasingly more departments are turning to video recordings, and with the advent of digital recording the capability to utilize the results of an interrogation is increased. Even seasoned investigators frequently "read into" a statement, making it easy to misinterpret or even miss a vital clue. Further, a video recording provides a visual recording of body language and other "subsurface" actions. Review of the recording may make it possible to determine physical signs when a person is lying, such as avoiding eye contact, touching a part of his or her face, or hunching his or her shoulders. Even in cases in which a lawyer is present, who may advise the client not to respond to a certain question, there is likely to be a body language or other visual clue. This is usually most effective with direct questions, such as: "Did you kill John Smith?," "Do you own a firearm?," and so on.

Often overlooked or ignored are videos made in connection with vehicle stops, the crime scene or arrests. Many police vehicles are now equipped with visual recording devices for traffic stops. These may be valuable in preparing for the interrogation.

Where an interrogation takes place outside a police facility, usually following an apprehension, then the interrogation should be made with an audio recorder. Both video and audio must be treated in the same fashion as any other physical evidence, i.e., their identification and custody must be considered. In order to introduce such evidence in court there are additional requirements as to how the recording is made. These may be found in some state court decisions. The following guidelines cover the key points:

1. The recorder (tape or digital) must be capable of recording conversation; a video recorder must be able to record visually in addition to recording conversation.

2. The operator must be competent.

3. The recording must be authentic and correct.

4. No changes, additions, or deletions may be made in the recording.

5. The operator should state at the beginning of the recording the time it began running, and the recorder should be left on at all times during the interrogation. The time when the recording ends (or stops) must also be stated for the record. Compliance with this recommendation, however, is not always feasible. For example, some suspects state to detectives that they will not confess while the video camera (or tape recorder) is running.

6. If a recorder breaks during the session the recording should not be discarded. Where possible a new recording should be started, with a new time of beginning and ending.

Care must be taken during an interrogation not to coerce the suspect. Any number of individuals have been put on trial and found guilty by a jury but, then, years later had their convictions overturned when a court ruled they had been falsely accused and convicted. Just as false (often coerced) confessions play a major role in these cases, so does DNA evidence, but to impugn the confession and throw out the conviction. According to a 2010 assessment, there have been 280 post-conviction DNA exonerations in the United States, 213 of them occurring since 2000.[24]

One report examined the overturned convictions of 340 individuals (327 men and 13 women) over a 15-year period between 1989 and 2003. It found that 51 of these cases (15%) involved false confessions. There were several different types of cases overturned for such admissions. For example, in 1988 in Austin, Texas

> ... Christopher Ochoa falsely confessed to rape and murder in order to avoid the threat of the death penalty—and along the way falsely implicated his friend, Richard Danzinger; both were sentenced to life in prison, and both were exonerated by DNA in 2001, three years after the real criminal sent a letter to [then] Governor Bush confessing to their crimes."[25]

In another case a man convicted of rape and murder confessed to the crime and spent ten years in prison and was paroled before DNA evidence later indicated that another person had committed the crime. He said that he confessed because of persistent interrogation techniques. Professor Brandon Garrett at the University of Virginia Law School notes that between 1976 and 2010, forty people falsely confessed to crimes that they didn't commit and were later exonerated by DNA evidence. The reasons why a person confesses vary, but some experts note that those likely to confess when they are innocent is more common among the mentally impaired, young people, and individuals who are "easily led." [26]

There are many benefits for recording interviews and interrogations. The following benefits have been articulated by many in the criminal justice field:

•   Recording custodial interviews is a tremendous benefit to the criminal justice system. A permanent record is created of what was said and done, how suspects acted, and how officers treated suspects. Officers are no longer subjected to unwarranted allegations about abusive conduct; those who may be inclined to use improper tactics cannot do so because their actions and words are being recorded.

- Voluntary admissions and confessions are indisputable. Defense motions to suppress based on alleged coercion and abuse drop off dramatically, and the few that are filed are easily resolved by the recording.

- Without the need to make detailed notes, officers are better able to concentrate on suspects' demeanors and statements. They no longer have to attempt to recall details about the interviews days and weeks later when recollections have faded.

- In most instances, the ability to obtain confessions and admissions is not affected by recording. Most states permit police to record covertly. However, if a suspect realizes a recording is to be made and refuses to cooperate if recorded, the officers simply make a record of the suspect's refusal and proceed in the "old-fashioned" manner with handwritten notes.

- Later review of recordings affords officers the ability to retrieve leads and inconsistent statements overlooked during the interviews.

- Recordings are valuable for training new officers in proper interrogation techniques and for experienced officers to self-evaluate and improve their methods.

- Public confidence in police practices increases, because recordings demonstrate that officers conducting closed custodial interviews have nothing to hide from public review.[27]

Types of Cases Videotaped

Although 57,000 criminal cases involving videotaped suspects' statements were examined in a survey cited in 2005, an endnote cautions: "As a result, the findings of this national survey … must be taken as preliminary."[28] Even so, the results disclose that 83 percent of agencies videotaped statements in homicide cases. The practice is also utilized in many other crime cases, but usage decreases as perception of seriousness decreases; for example: rape (77%); aggravated battery or assault (71%); armed robbery (61%); drunk driving (59%); unarmed robbery (45%); burglary (44%); and other property crimes (34%).[29]

A Consensus Favoring Videotaping

Geller states that on the basis of this exploratory study, videotaping appears to be a distinctly useful tool. "It is seen as simultaneously furthering the criminal justice system's pursuit of disparate objectives. … a striking 97 percent of all departments that have ever videotaped suspects' statements continue to find such videotaping, on balance, to be useful. Likewise, agencies visited were asked, knowing what they know of videotaping now, if they would do it again. Every agency said yes."[30]

Reducing the Confession to Writing

If the interrogation and confession have not been recorded according to these guidelines, it is wise to obtain, if possible, a confession written in the suspect's hand. Although less desirable, it can also be dictated to a stenographer. If dictated it must be typed and signed, or if the suspect is unwilling to sign the document, acknowledged by the suspect as his or her statement before a witness.

Prior to *Miranda*, many recommendations were made by textbook writers that involved the investigator in structuring the confession statement. In the post-*Miranda* era, these older practices are considered to be undesirable because they may affect the credibility of the document. Jurors, for example, may find it difficult to believe that in a free and voluntary statement a person is likely to ensure that he or she has covered each and every element of the crime in his or her narration. Similarly, there is criticism of the use of the question-and-answer form of confession. Some believe there is too great a possibility of controlling the suspect's story and influencing the suspect's answers through suggestive questions.

Coaching a suspect to write a confession, in which the investigator supplies wording can also be troublesome at trial. Where defense counsel can secure prior written confessions obtained by a particular investigator it is possible to conduct computerized examples of word usage and placement that help to identify a writer.

Witnessing the Confession

After a confession acknowledging guilt, many persons experience a quieting effect and peace of mind. By the time a statement is put in writing, a witness to its signing can often be brought in without objection from the suspect. If possible, for reasons of credibility, it is best to have a disinterested citizen serve as witness; if not, a civilian member of the department should be used. As a last resort, another sworn member in addition to the investigator may serve as a witness to the signing.

It is important that the address of the witness and a typed (or printed) spelling of his or her name be obtained in addition to a signature. Sworn members of the force may use title, badge number, and assignment in lieu of a street address

Time and Personal Needs Register

The time an interrogation commenced and any recesses taken to attend to the personal needs of the suspect should be recorded. Personal needs include such things as food and drink, use of the toilet, telephoning, and smoking. If interrogation sessions are recorded, this information should automatically be made part of the recording. Some departments also use a "Time and Personal Needs Register" to refute an allegation of coercion or duress that might be raised subsequently. If food and drink are purchased for the suspect, it is advisable to obtain a receipt for the purchase and to ask the cashier to write on it the name of the purchaser and the person for whom it is being purchased, together with the restaurant and cashier's name, the date, and the time.

CONCLUSION

Just as an understanding of Horowitz and Pavlov can improve an investigator's ability to conduct an interrogation, so can it ensure that the process be humane. No investigator wishes to have an innocent party confess to a crime. A crude test might be to judge from experience just how much stress would fall short of eliciting a confession from the innocent person, yet cause many of the guilty to cave in under the pressure of conscience.

In any event, evidence beyond the confession should also be sought as a means of corroborating guilt. For example, shortly after a confession is obtained, it may be possible to have the suspect lead investigators to the fruits of the crime, or to physical evidence such as the weapon or tool used.

Sometimes the suspect will agree to reenact the crime, and in the process mention a fact to which only the guilty party would be privy. A confession may be therapeutic, provoking the need to "tell all" (including other crimes committed by the suspect). Two important reminders should be considered: one, that a written confession should be limited to the crime under investigation—any mention of others being prejudicial to the defendant; and two, though confirmation of confession is highly desirable, it has all too often been ignored in practice.

NOTES

[1]   M.W. Horowitz, "The Psychology of Confession," *Journal of Criminal Law, Criminology, and Police Science*, 47:2 (1956), 197–204.

[2]   William W. Sargant, *Battle for the Mind: A Physiology of Conversion and Brainwashing* (New York: Doubleday, 1957; Springfield, IL: Greenwood Press, 1975).

[3]   Horowitz, op. cit., 197.

[4]   Ibid., 198.

[5]   Ibid., 200.

[6]   Ibid., 201.

[7]   Ibid., 200.

[8]   Ibid., 202.

[9]   Ibid.

[10]   Ibid., 203.

[11]   Ibid.

[12]   President's Commission on Law Enforcement and Administration of Justice, *The Challenge of Crime in a Free Society* (Washington, DC: U.S. Government Printing Office, 1967), 93. [Commissioned by Lyndon Johnson.]

[13]   National Commission of Law Observance and Enforcement, *Report on Lawlessness in Law Enforcement*, No. 11 (Washington, DC: U.S. Government Printing Office, 1931). [One of 14 reports of the Wickersham Commission appointed by Herbert Hoover in 1929.]

[14]   *Miranda v. Arizona*, 384 U.S. 436 (1966) at 444.

[15]   Ibid., 467–478.

[16]   *United States v. Dickerson*, 166 F.3d 667 (4th Cir. 1999).

[17]   *Dickerson v. United States*, 530 U.S. 428 (2000).

[18]   *United States v. Barnes*, 195 F.3d 1927 (8th Cir, 1999).

[19]   *Miranda*, supra note 1, 476.

[20]   *Miranda*, supra note 1, 475.

[21]   Richard O. Arther and Rudolph R. Caputo, *Interrogation for Investigators* (New York: William C. Copp and Associates, 1959), 7.

22   Clifford H. Van Meter, *Principles of Police Interrogation* (Springfield, IL: Charles C Thomas, 1973), 56.

23   Arther and Caputo, op. cit., 8–9.

24   http://www.innocenceproject.org/Content/Facts_on_PostConviction_DNA_Exonerations.php

25   S.R. Gross, K. Jacoby, D.J. Matheson, N. Montgomery, and S. Patil, "Exonerations in the UnitedStates 1989 through 2003," *Journal of Criminal Law and Criminology*, 95:2 (2005), 546.

26   John Schwartz. "Confessing to Crime, but Innocent: Research Questions Police Interrogations." *New York Times*. September 14, 2010. p.A14.

27   Thomas P. Sullivan, "Electronic Recording of Custodial Interrogations: Everybody Wins," Journal of Criminal Law and Criminology, 95:3 (2005), 1129–1130.

28   William A. Geller. *Videotaping Interrogations and Confessions* (Washington, DC: U.S. Department of Justice, March 1993), note 1.

29   Ibid., 3.

30   Ibid., 10.

Important Cases

Dickerson v. United States (2000)
Escobedo v. Illinois (1964)
Miranda v. Arizona (1966)
United States v. Barnes (1999)
United States v. Dickerson (1999)

Discussion Questions

1. What is the role of an investigator in an interrogation?

2. Horowitz identifies five social-psychological concepts as to why a person confesses. What are they?

3. What are some of the reasons a person will not confess?

4. What does a *Miranda* warning establish?

5. What must the police advise a suspect to comply with *Miranda*?

6. Why is the "setting" of an interrogation important?

7. What are some preliminary questions that should be used to determine if the suspect is rational and in touch with reality?

8. When a suspect denies committing the crime, the investigator should pursue a line of questioning that focuses on information that can be verified. What are some of the types of questions?

9. What are the attributes of an effective interrogator?

10. What is the best method for recording an interrogation? Why is this advisable?

SUPPLEMENTAL READINGS

Fast, J. (2000). *Body language: The essential secrets of non-verbal communication*. New York: MJF Books.

Fisher, R. P., & Geiselman, R. E. (1992). *Memory-enhancing techniques for investigative interviewing: The cognitive interview*. Springfield, IL: Charles C Thomas.

Geracimos, A. (Jan. 12, 2006). CSI: Language analysis unit. *The Washington Times*, B1, B4.

Gudjonsson, G. H. (2003). *The psychology of interrogations and confessions: A handbook*. Hoboken, NJ: Wiley.

Hess, J. E. (2010). *Interviewing and interrogation for law enforcement* (2nd ed.). New Providence, NJ: LexisNexis Matthew Bender.

Hess, J. E. (2011). *Interviewing and interrogation for law enforcement* (2nd ed.). Boston: Elsevier/Anderson Publishing.

Inbau, F. E. (2004). *Criminal investigation and confessions* (4th ed.). Boston: Jones and Bartlett.

Lang, A. F., Jr., & Beattie, A. R. (2009). *War, torture and terrorism: Rethinking the rules of international security*. New York: Routledge.

Lykken, D. T. (1998). *Tremor in the blood: Uses and abuses of the lie detector*. New York: Plenum Trade.

Macdonald, J. M., & Michaud, D. L. (1992). *Criminal interrogation*, (rev. & enl. ed.). Denver: Apache Press.

Navarro, J., & Marvin, K. (2008). *What every body is saying: An ex FBI agent's guide to speed-reading people*. New York: HarperCollins.

O'Connor, T., & William, C. (Dec. 2005). Understanding the psychology of child molesters: A key to getting confessions. *The Police Chief*, *72*(12), 70–76.

Pease, A., & Pease, B. (2004). *The definitive book of body language*. New York: Bantam Dell.

Sargant, W. W. (1957). *Battle for the mind: A physiology of conversion and brainwashing*. New York: Doubleday. (Springfield, IL: Greenwood Press, 1975; Cambridge, MA: Malor Books, 1997).

Turvey, B. (2011). *Criminal profiling: An introduction to behavioral evidence analysis* (4th ed.). New York: Elsevier/Academic Press.

Welch, M. (2009). American 'Pain-Ology' in the war on terror: a critique of 'scientific' torture. *Theoretical Criminology*, *13*(4), 451–474.

Zulawski, D. E., & Douglas, E. (2002). Wicklander: *Practical aspects of interview and interrogation* (2nd ed.). Boca Raton, FL: CRC Press.

Part D

THE INFLUENCE AND IMPACT OF TECHNOLOGY

At this point, the many ways in which technology is impacting both new forms of criminality and the investigative function should be obvious. The following chapters provide a more vivid description of the social, criminological, legal, and investigative issues facing law enforcement, and particularly those charged with understanding the phenomenon and building criminal cases in what has certainly become a new and, at times, a very uncertain environment.

CHAPTER 11

THE INFLUENCE OF TECHNOLOGY
ON CRIME INVESTIGATION

INTRODUCTION

Most observers, when asked about technology in law enforcement and the investigation of crime think initially of forensic science. Pressed further, they might likely mention the automobile, the telephone, the two-way radio, and the computer. Perhaps some will identify education and training. Although most people tend to think of technology as being an invention tied to a machine, it is actually defined as the application of science to human endeavors; in this case, the investigation of crime. Thus, fingerprint analysis, blood typing, the microscope, and the scale are all technological applications, but systemic crime scene analysis, blood splatters, interviewing and interrogation techniques, and investigative speculation might also be called technology. Unfortunately, many of the advances, as well as failures, lack a scientific or research basis and were adopted on the basis of observation, experience, and perhaps untested theory.

Even fingerprinting is based on the belief that no two persons have the same fingerprint, a theory tested when three FBI analysts and an external consultant positively matched the fingerprint of an American to the Madrid bombing in March 2004, and were proven wrong. Apparently, this was the first time that two fingerprints were so closely matched that they were able to fool not just one but three experts. This should not be viewed as a criticism of the field but rather an observation that technology takes many forms and in some cases may be relied upon too heavily, but errors in judgment can have the effect of sending innocent people to jail, and perhaps to death. In this regard, care must be taken in adopting or adapting technology to the investigative function.

In contemporary society the advances in science and technology are generating a broad range of inventions. Crime in the United States has fluctuated significantly since records have been kept. Despite very sophisticated statistical techniques, there continue to be disagreements by criminologists on why crime increases or decreases. The evolution of crime control has run the gamut of preventive patrol to community policing, and the clearance rate of crimes solved by investigation has also fluctuated.

Although criticism, drawbacks, legal decisions, and the impact of change have influenced crime investigation, the focus has not changed: it is to solve crimes, protect the innocent, and bring the guilty to justice. Increasingly, greater emphasis is placed on technology because the so-called traditional aspects of detective work—pounding shoe leather and talking to people—have given way in large part to new and other ways of supplementing interviews and interrogation. Today, the investigator can turn to other forms of gathering information and conducting an investigation.

Indeed, interviewing and interrogation are critical aspects of the investigative model, but it is the availability of new tools that form the basis of this section.

In many ways, criminal investigation has been affected by changes in procedures and tactics based on legal precedents and the demands of societal change and expectations. These changes have had an impact on everything from interviewing and interrogation methods to the introduction of new tools designed to support the detective, not the least of which have been in communication, basic computer technology, and the evolution of a process focused, as more than one detective has remarked, "on shoe leather." "Hitting the bricks" has been the tried and true method of crime investigation for a hundred years. Today, though, there is an increasing emphasis on so-called "knowledge management," influenced by various forms of technology, and while knowing the street is still important, an understanding of technological capabilities occupies much more of an investigator's time.

It is probably safe to say that the next decade in the field of criminal investigation will change dramatically, resulting in the need for a new breed of detectives, focused in large measure on greater specialization, improved training and education, a more diverse work force, and greater dependence on technology—which can be defined as the application of science to human endeavors. The scientific method is defined by *Merriam-Webster's Collegiate Dictionary* as: "principles and procedures for the systematic pursuit of knowledge involving the recognition and formulation of a problem, the collection of data through observation and experiment, and the formulation and testing of hypotheses."[1]

At the same time, there will likely be changes in crime and criminal activity, including wholly new criminal enterprises that emerge as a result of globalization, technology, commerce, and the movement of people throughout the world.

Changing technology has had a profound impact on almost every facet of life throughout the world. Some argue that change is coming so fast it is hard to keep up. In many ways, we are forced to rely on technicians to install, repair, and otherwise serve as a backup in our homes and the workplace. We may know what the technology does, but understanding how it works is more likely to be problematic. Smart phones, multi-dimensional television and video systems, intrusion devices, and robotics of one sort or another are now commonplace in most American homes, and these are just a small fraction of the influence that technology plays in our everyday lives. Advances in forensic science, medical technology, vehicles and travel, economic transactions, computers, smart phones, massive amounts of new software, videography and body scanning are but some of the advances in technology that are common in most developed countries.

The impact on criminal investigation is much more advanced than most seasoned investigators might imagine, and for many younger investigators, much of this technology is an integral part of their lives. How technology is being used, and how it can be used in different ways, is becoming more important. Just as understanding changes in criminal law and procedure should be a part of an investigator's continuing education and training, the use of new technology must be included. With this should also come new approaches, as well as new ideas, for the utilization of technology.

Beyond advances in communications, crime scene examination, forensic science, and computerized records systems, more commonly referred to now as information technology, there are much more sophisticated approaches to crime analysis (geospatial and visualization); the use of surveillance equipment (night vision, drones, cameras); the application of sophisticated data manipulation using a concept known as "artificial intelligence" and data mining (in records, searches, and analysis); search technology (such as Google, Facebook, and Wikipedia); crime reconstruction (crime scene, forensic psychology and profiling); new types of weapons (lethal and nonlethal); new models of criminal behavior (fraud, Internet, drug trafficking); social media (Twitter, Facebook, blogs, etc.); and computing (applications or "apps," game theory, and terrorism).

Perhaps most important is an emphasis on the ability of law enforcement to identify new ways in which technology can enhance policing and criminal investigation. The business term is "thinking outside the box," which applies also to investigative function. Today's criminal population has learned to make use of technology in ever-increasing ways, whether it is in the more traditional crimes of murder, robbery, rape, and burglary or in relatively new forms of crime, such as Internet fraud, identity theft, pedophilia, human trafficking, illegal designer drugs, or terrorism (domestic and global). With this in mind, today's detective must continuously employ and develop new ways and new methods to combat the changing nature of criminal activity.

Today, computers come in all shapes and sizes, ranging from smart phones to so-called supercomputers. The vast majority of Americans now have computers in their homes, which may be desktops, laptops, iPads or other tablets, and, of course, smart phones. In addition, computers in vehicles can also include monitoring equipment, GPS devices, voice-activated telephones, televisions, toll cards (such as E-ZPass), and equipment that can notify a central location if there is an accident or an emergency requiring assistance. Much of this technology is available throughout the world and, in some places, such as Japan, the technology is even more sophisticated than it is in the United States. In most major cities, computers are now installed in police vehicles. In short, computers have become an integral part of society, and are used every day by millions of people for a variety of tasks.

However, the ultimate success of the computer is closely related to the hundreds of thousands of applications ("apps") that are available to the consumer. In this context an application may be defined as a particular program that enables an individual to perform a specific task, whether it is playing a game; looking up information; reading a book, newspaper, or magazine; planning a trip or checking on congestion on a highway; or communicating via Internet—an activity known as using social media. This includes text messaging, Twitter, blogs, and any other form of communicating in which an individual or an organization can pass or receive information. Social media has been a major source of information that contributed to the so-called "Arab Spring" movement that overthrew the governments of Egypt and Libya through organized protest movements. These advances in technology have had a profound positive effect on societies throughout the world. On the other hand, computer technology, or information technology, has also proven to be a major source of concern in law enforcement and national defense.

Illegal computer use and so-called cybercrime represent some of the major topics of concern at the national, state, and local levels, and one that has been increasing exponentially throughout the world. Cybercrime involves a broad range of criminal activity using computers and other forms of information technology. Closely related to cybercrime is cyber-terrorism, which involves activities designed to sabotage, obstruct, or support violent group movements. Rapid improvements in cellular technology represent another area of potential abuse and criminal activity because cellular technology today contains much more than traditional telephonic communication. Sarah Stephens, a vice president with Aon Risk Solutions in San Francisco, notes that today's mobile devices are equipped with high-resolution cameras, global positioning systems, and other applications that can put the user at risk. Mobile devices can also provide a means for criminals to hack into personal or corporate information. [2]

The investigation of cybercrime usually involves a high degree of specialized knowledge, and will frequently necessitate the assistance of experts. This chapter addresses some of the more common types of computer and cybercrime. Criminal activity using various forms of technology is virtually borderless, operating globally, and frequently confounding jurisdictional issues.

The investigator should be familiar with the resources available to assist in an investigation, and have at least a basic knowledge of the types of tactics employed by the criminal element. The

Federal Bureau of Investigation maintains cyber investigation units in each of its 56 field offices, with more than 1,000 advanced cyber-trained FBI agents, analysts, and forensic examiners. At the same time, most large city police departments now maintain cybercrime units, some of which are attached to a crime analysis section.

On a "higher" level, cybercrime usually involves criminal networks or groups. In 2011, the FBI was investigating more than 400 reported cases involving corporate account "takeovers" involving losses of as much as $85 million.

Rapid improvements in cellular technology represent another area of potential abuse and criminal activity because cellular technology today contains much more than traditional telephonic communication.

Rapid increases in information technology, including computers, smart phones, data storage, and digital imagery, have had a major impact on domestic and international communication, global business practices, and social interaction. The expansion of these types of crime, some of which have been in existence for decades, have resulted in more specialized aspects of criminal investigation. In addition to the more traditional role of the detective, the emergence of crime and intelligence analysts has increased dramatically, and today virtually all federal agencies and larger police departments employ analysts, many of whom work directly with field operatives.

On the national level, the Federal Bureau of Investigation, the Department of Homeland Security, and the Central Intelligence Agency employ analysts as part of the intelligence and investigative process. The concept of predictive policing is based on the premise that information collected in many forms provides the basis for using technology to develop intelligence that can be used in the field to combat crime or terrorism. The full impact of cybercrime has yet to be realized, largely because criminals introduce new schemes and methods to avoid detection on an ongoing basis.

At the outset it should be recognized that law enforcement continues to increase its use of computers, software, and information technology. Criminal investigation has been enhanced considerably through the use of commercial programs involving relational databases, geospatial imagery, temporal analysis (activities over time), artificial intelligence, and criminal profiling. The result has been the development of a new type of investigator, sometimes referred to as a *cyberdetective*. These specialists bring a new dimension to the field of crime investigation, and as with advances in forensic science, their contributions are becoming increasingly important. Unfortunately, in many ways it is safe to say that law enforcement continues to be behind the curve in knowledge of computer technology and cybercrime.

Cybercrime generally falls into three categories:

- Cases in which technology is integral to commission of a crime (electronic fraud, money laundering, child pornography).

- Cases in which the technology is used to commit a crime (identity theft, computer sabotage, theft of privileged information).

- Cases in which technology is used as an incidental aspect of a crime (data and image storage, Internet and cellular communication).[3]

The investigator should be familiar with the more common types of crime using information technology. The National Institute of Justice's *Electronic Crime Scene Investigation: A Guide for First Responders* is an important publication that should be of interest to all investigators.[4] Some of the material for this chapter was culled from this NIJ guide, as well as other publications.

BOX 11.1 COMMON TYPES OF CYBERCRIME

- Child pornography and exploitation
- Economic related fraud
- Electronic stalking and harassment (cyberstalking)
- Extortion
- Gambling
- Identity theft
- Illegal drug activity
- Intellectual property crimes
- Mail and wire fraud
- Money laundering
- Prostitution
- Software theft
- Telecommunications fraud
- Terrorism
- Transporting stolen property
- Data theft
- Electronic sabotage

It is virtually impossible to determine the monetary amounts of various types of IT crime, but costs and losses easily run into billions of dollars and may have already come close to reaching a trillion dollars. Such high-volume crimes as child pornography and identity theft, two types of crime that cross national and international borders, involve thousands of individuals, both as perpetrators and victims.

The U.S. National Consumers League (NCL) data in 2007 indicated that the total losses of Internet fraud amounted to $17,508,480, and the most frequent schemes were fake checks (29%), general merchandise (23%), auction (13%), Nigerian advance fee loans (11%), lotteries (7%), phishing (3%), advance fee loans (3%), friendship and sweetheart swindles, (1%), and Internet access services (1%).[5] A growing industry in counterfeit documents exists, including driver's licenses, personal identification cards, and other forged documents, which can be bought online through web sites, some of which originate in China and Panama.

Reported cybercrime numbers are quite low compared to reality, according to many experts, who note that many victims fail to report Internet fraud because of the embarrassment associated with being scammed. In addition, some large companies and corporations do not report cybercrime and cyber attacks because they may fear customer lack of confidence, or do not wish to draw attention to the vulnerability of their system.

Individuals involved in economic fraud are more likely to be older than those involved in "hacking" or software piracy; child pornographers cut across international dimensions that may involve persons from two or more countries; identity theft is usually either an individual or group-related

---

BOX 11.2 A TYPOLOGY OF INTERNET FRAUD

- Identity theft
- Credit card fraud
- Online auction fraud
- Short firm fraud
- Advance fee fraud
- Direct investment fraud
- Drug sale scams
- Prize/sweepstakes fraud
- Social engineering and internet fraud

Source: Tae J. Chung, "Policing Internet Fraud: A Study of the Tensions Between Private and Public Models of Policing Fraudulent Activity in Cyberspace with Particular Focus on South Korea and Special Reference to the United Kingdom and the United States." Unpublished dissertation, The University of Leeds School of Law, Leeds, UK (December 2008), 64.

---

criminal activity; and terrorist web sites may involve numerous persons. Enterprise and organized crime groups have taken to the use of various forms of technology to elude detection and foster communication.

Investigations following the September 11, 2001, terrorist attacks in the United States and the foiled attack in England in August 2006 revealed a global computer network used by terrorists to communicate, as well as the use of computers, especially the Internet, to gather information about targets and to do research on everything from bombs to building layouts and tracking air transport vulnerabilities.

Emerging databases and search engines on the Internet enable individuals to gather information on virtually any subject, including biographical data on millions of individuals. For instance, the Google search engine has integrated several public information databases into its basic search capabilities. Anyone can now enter a Vehicle Identification Number (VIN) into the search engine and get free a basic report on the history of the vehicle from CarFax.com and other similar enterprises.

As the amount of public information about individuals has increased, the availability of inexpensive, portable storage capacity has also increased. For instance, today it is possible to carry gigabytes of information on a storage device the size of a pack of chewing gum. These portable storage devices allow a person to carry as much as 16,000 pictures (at 500KB each) or more than 100,000 pages of text in their pocket, plugging it into a computer only when needed. The most popular of these devices are the so-called flash or USB drives, because they allow users to transport many gigabytes of data that can be plugged into any computer (Windows or Macintosh) without restrictions of computer ownership or permissions.

Handheld personal digital assistants (PDAs), electronic organizers, iPods and iPads, and memory cards may also be used to store information that may be of interest to investigators (see Figure 11.1).

Additionally, smart cards and other small devices may contain their own microprocessors that enable a card to hold and change information, such as fund balances (known as debit cards). Removable storage devices come in many different forms, ranging from the early floppy disks, to zip disks, CDs and DVDs, and tape drives, to name a few.

Photo taken by Evan-Amos. Screen copyrighted by Apple Inc.

Figure 11.1
First-generation iPad home screen.

A further complicating factor in cases involving various forms of electronic technology involves case preparation and the presentation of evidence for court. Because this is a relatively new area in which law breakers frequently know more about the technology than investigators or the courts, there is the increasing problem of not being able to present a case that can be understood by a jury. Everything from initial investigations to the collection, presentation, and admissibility of evidence is important.

Electronic evidence is, by its very nature, fragile. It can be altered, damaged, or destroyed by improper handling or improper examination. For this reason, special precautions should be taken to document, collect, preserve, and examine this type of evidence. Failure to do so may render it unusable or lead to an inaccurate conclusion.[6]

SYSTEMIC COMPONENTS

At the heart of virtually all information technology lies a computer system or central processing unit (CPU). Generally, these systems contain a data storage component and a "hard" drive that is programmed to run the system. The introduction of *cloud computing* represents another dimension that can hamper investigations. The computing power of today's technology is enormous, enabling the user to run a broad range of programs, commonly referred to as software, in conjunction with internal and external drives.

The computer contains a number of files that are connected to different types of software, such as word processing, spreadsheets, databases, e-mail, or web sites. Some of these programs, such as dictionaries and directories, may not be alterable, whereas user-created files are developed by the user and generally prove to be the most valuable from an investigative standpoint. One of the major exceptions involves downloaded images or documents that may be used in developing a *prima facie* case, such as for child pornography.

Some of the more important files that an investigator should be familiar with appear in the accompanying sidebar, "File Types of Interest."

Moreover, the development of high-quality peripheral devices, such as scanners and printers, has increased opportunities for the criminal element to perform further illicit activities, including counterfeiting, various types of fraud, child pornography, and identity theft.

File Types of Interest

- Address books
- Audio or video files
- Bookmarks
- Calendars
- Databases
- Documents, correspondence files
- E-mail files
- Favorite sites
- Images and graphics
- Indexes
- Spreadsheets
- Voicemail
- Social networking accounts

LEGAL ISSUES

In many ways investigation involving various forms of technology, especially computers and the Internet, are complicated by a myriad of legal issues, court decisions, and policy issues of organizations. Because case law in this area is relatively new, there are times when the investigator may be operating in uncharted territory, or may come up against newly designed software or innovative criminal activities. (For example, terrorists and organized criminals frequently communicate within interactive games making it difficult to intercept using conventional technology.) Further, because many of the laws and policies may be based on individual state laws, they may not be applicable from one state to another. For this reason, when in doubt, the investigator should consult with appropriate legal counsel.

On the federal level, there has been a steady stream of decisions by circuit courts that serve to give better clarification to the procedures that must be followed by investigators. Generally, a search warrant is required to conduct an investigation of the contents of a computer's hard drive, or to gather information from an Internet source (e-mail or Internet service providers—ISPs). A suspect may give permission for an investigator to conduct a search of his or her computer, but it is advisable to get this permission in writing. Courts have become more involved in Fourth Amendment issues related to the search and seizure of computers and data culled from ISPs.[7]

The search of a computer or other electronic device is generally developed from search warrants in other more traditional contexts, with Fourth Amendment guarantees that protect a person from unreasonable searches and seizures being an important consideration. The highest privacy interest is attached to private dwellings.[8]

In searches and seizures of computers and other forms of electronic storage, the investigator is generally required to establish probable cause to obtain a warrant. This includes reasonable grounds to believe that the data to be seized actually exists and will provide evidence of a crime, the location of what will be searched, and a reasonably detailed description of the information or data that will be retrieved.[9]

The primary issue in computer-related cases centers on an individual's right to privacy regarding information stored in a computer or other device. There are numerous locations from which information can be obtained. As it relates to digital forensics, the most important case law for investigators is the decision rendered in *Daubert v. Merrell Dow Pharmaceuticals, Inc.* (509 U.S. 579, 1003), that addresses the issue of the admissibility of expert witness evidence. The so-called "Daubert Test" of Rule 702 of the Federal Rules of Evidence requires that expert testimony must:

1.   Be grounded in knowledge.
2.   Have a valid scientific connection.
3.   Be supported in scientific journal publications.[10]

Sources of Information

- The home
- The workplace
- Personal computers and other portable devices
- Social networking sites (e.g., Twitter, Facebook, MySpace, LinkedIn)
- Internet service providers (ISPs)
- Chat rooms
- Web sites
- External storage devices

Home Computers

As indicated above, home computers and other personal and portable devices fall under the purview of the Fourth Amendment of the U.S. Constitution, which protects citizens from unreasonable searches and seizures. A search warrant requires permission to gain entry to the residence or portable devices in possession of a suspect. As noted, the warrant must include a statement as to what technological equipment (computers, storage devices, cameras, printers, etc.) is to be searched, what is to be sought, and why the warrant is requested. The investigator must show probable cause for the search, which may be based on a variety of circumstances, such as prior knowledge based on the experience of the investigator; the past criminal record of the suspect; or information provided by informants and victims. There is no reasonable expectation of privacy when the information was openly available, where the device has been stolen, where control of the device was given to another person, or where the individual owner loses control of the device.[11] In cases in which the home or computer may be shared by another person, the other person may give permission to search the computer, but not access to password-protected files.[12]

Workplace Computers

Workplace searches present a somewhat different issue, and it has been held that an employee does not necessarily have a right to the expectation of privacy.[13] However, in determining an individual's expectation of privacy, Stephen W. Cogar suggests that the following questions should be considered:

- Is the employee's office shared?

- Is the hard drive password-protected?

- Is the computer physically locked?

- Is the office locked, and if so, who has access?

- Can the files be accessed remotely through a network program?

- Is there an employee policy in place regarding computer usage that states that files can be searched or monitored?

- Is the policy enforced uniformly?

- Is there evidence that the employee was aware of the policy?

- Is software used to monitor computer use, and are employees aware of the practice?

- Do work stations contain a message when the computer is accessed that the computer can be monitored?[14]

In many instances, employees may contend that they were not aware of company policy, which may negate permission given by the employer to conduct a search. For this reason it is advisable to seek a search warrant whenever possible.

Internet Service Providers

When a suspect may be anonymous, using a screen name or other form of e-mail address, the best source of identification is likely to be an ISP, such as America OnLine (AOL); Comcast, Earthlink,

Windstream, and so on. Although the content of information may be protected under the Fourth Amendment, the Courts have held that the identity of the subscriber is not protected. However, a number of recent cases in which the government has sought to obtain information from Internet service providers, specifically in terrorism-related cases, have sparked debate, and it is likely that the issue will be addressed by the Supreme Court in the future.

While under certain circumstances a person may have an expectation of privacy in content information, a person does not have an interest in the account information given to the ISP in order to establish an e-mail account. This is considered non-content information.[15] This includes: name; billing address; and home, work, and fax telephone numbers. The Stored Wire and Electronic Communication and Transactional Records (SWECTRA) Act requires ISPs to disclose non-content information to the law enforcement community pursuant to legal authorization.[16] The Cyber Security Enhancement Act of 2003, which is part of the Homeland Security Act of 2002, "makes it easier for police agencies to obtain investigative information from Internet service providers (ISPs) and shields from lawsuits ISPs who hand over user information to law enforcement officers without a warrant."[17]

Cases involving terrorism investigations permit disclosure of more non-content information than is permissible in other types of criminal investigations. The USA PATRIOT Act "can force the disclosure of a subscriber's name; address; local and long distance telephone connection records, or records of session times and duration, length of service (including start date and types of service utilized; telephone or instrument number or other subscriber number or identity, including any temporary assigned network address; and means and source of payment for such service of a subscriber)."[18]

Chat Rooms and Social Networking

One of the most common forms of communication today is the use of social media that have changed in large measure the way Americans relate to each other. Twitter (a free "microblogging" social networking service that enables users to send and read messages known as "tweets," which allows posts of up to 140 characters); text messaging; social networking sites such as Facebook, MySpace, and LinkedIn; and Internet "chat rooms" have made it possible to exchange photos and other data on a variety of communications technology. These methods of communication have become commonplace in the United States and most other developed and developing countries. The emerging capabilities of new forms of communications technology provide a broad range of opportunities available to users, including access to geospatial technology, relational databases, visualization, sophisticated statistical and analytical tools, and access to thousands of web sites.

The many advantages notwithstanding, the potential for utilizing these technological advances for criminal purposes represents a challenge for law enforcement. Two of the more common investigative approaches include identifying pedophiles and child molesters, and investigations of child pornographic images on web sites and in the possession of individuals.

"Sting" operations by police departments, in which investigators communicate with suspected pedophiles who are trying to lure children into illicit relationships, have become commonplace in a number of state and local agencies.

> Child pornography and individuals who possess pictures or video (collectively "images") that are sexually exploitative of children represent one of the darkest sides of the Internet.

Investigating and prosecuting child pornography cases inevitably involves more than just the evidence that certain images were found on a computer used by the defendant...

Child pornography investigations often involve people who are quite knowledgeable about technology, computers, and the Internet. They trade images with other collectors within their own towns and around the world using, for example, Web sites, file sharing, e-mail, buddy lists, password protected files, or *encryption* (emphasis in original).[19]

With the growth of social networking sites on which many young people post revealing or sexually explicit photographs, the problem has become more complex, and some sites have agreed to remove individuals who have a criminal record involving children from access.

Web Sites

Today there are thousands of web sites, making it possible to gather information on almost any subject. Some of these are nothing more than propaganda sites, devoted to fostering ideological positions, racism, ethnic hate, and dissatisfaction with the government. Free speech rights protect these sites, and many of them draw a fine line between what is legal and what is illegal. The fact that an individual visits a web site is not a crime, and an investigator must take care in how such information is used. In cases involving pedophiles, the fact that they subscribed to or visited web sites may serve as circumstantial evidence when a sex crime is involved.

A number of federal agencies monitor the web sites of suspected violent groups, largely as a means of keeping track of potential criminal activity. However, it should be noted that care must be taken in attempting to develop cases based on information from a site. Web sites also serve as one of the largest libraries in the world, providing not only information about people, places, and things. Many web sites may also be targets for hackers trying to disrupt an organization.

INVESTIGATING HIGH-TECH AND IT CRIME

A thorough discussion of investigative methods involving high-tech crime is beyond the scope of this chapter, but it is important to have a basic understanding of the type of crimes that an investigator may come across. Because computers have become so common in everyday life, it is important to recognize that a vast amount of information can be obtained from what appears to be normal record keeping. This may include address and telephone records, bank account records, e-mail transactions between suspects, and other personal data.

The Computer Crime and Intellectual Property Section of the U.S. Department of Justice and the specialized computer investigation units of the Federal Bureau of Investigation are available to assist local law enforcement in technology-related investigations. The investigator facing a crime scene involving computers should protect the area and call for an evidence technician conversant with computer technology. However, there may be situations in which this is impossible. For example, if a computer virus has been introduced, or a self-destruct system implanted by an "intruder," it may be necessary to take preliminary action to preserve the equipment. (See Box 11.3 for available guides from the National Institute of Justice (NIJ) on Internet Digital Evidence.)

In other cases, the investigator may be seizing or protecting a computer that has been or is being used in the commission of a crime. In such cases, the suspect may have built programs into the

---

BOX 11.3 NIJ GUIDES ON DIGITAL EVIDENCE

Electronic Crime Scene Investigation: A Guide for First Responders:
http://www.ojp.usdoj.gov/nij/pubs-sum/187736.htm

Forensic Examination of Digital Evidence: A Guide for Law Enforcement:
http://www.ojp.usdoj.gov/nij/pubs-sum/199408.htm

Investigations Involving the Internet and Computer Networks:
http://www.ojp.usdoj.gov/nij/pubs-sum/210798.htm

---

computer designed to destroy the evidence necessary for proving that a crime has been committed using the equipment. Thus, the investigator must have some basic familiarization with the types of criminal activity he or she might encounter, how they are generally carried out, and the procedures necessary for the safeguarding of evidence and preliminary investigations. The investigator should also be familiar with those agencies or organizations that might also be able to assist in such investigations. A number of federal agencies, such as the FBI and the Secret Service, now have cybercrime experts located in every major field office.

Because cybercrime and other forms of high-technology crime may involve multiple jurisdictions, or involve a federal offense, it is important to communicate with appropriate agencies or organizations early in the process. For example, fraud involving interstate communication by electronic communication is likely to fall under the jurisdiction of the U.S. Postal Service. The use of a computer to transmit child pornography—much of which actually originates abroad—may involve multiple jurisdictions. The Immigration and Customs Enforcement (ICE) agency can be of assistance in crimes carried out in the United States as well as other countries.

It is extremely important that a detailed record be kept of all actions taken during the investigation. This may prove helpful when it is necessary to reconstruct events or design a particular strategy and may be very important when such cases reach the trial stage.

At the outset, the investigator must be extremely careful not to destroy evidence that may be on a computer, a disk, or other electronic storage mechanism. Sophisticated criminals using computers are likely to use passwords or other program methods that are designed to erase data if not properly accessed. It may be possible, though, for experts to recover data that appears to have been erased. Thus, unless an investigator is thoroughly familiar with this type of investigation, it is best to leave the equipment untouched until an expert can be called. One should not turn the computer off or on or ask the suspect to assist unless an expert is present.

Most experts agree that training and education of investigators must increasingly include a basic knowledge of computers and how they can be used in criminal activities. In many cases, the investigator will have to rely on the victim to explain how a crime was carried out, and what damages may be attributed to the offender. The investigator, frequently in cooperation with legal counsel, will be faced with determining what crime took place and the legal standards and jurisdiction that are involved.

Of the crimes that are predominantly carried out using various forms of technology, child pornography and exploitation, electronic and economic fraud, identity theft, and gambling are quite common. The following illustrations and case studies provide an overview of the more common methods employed.

Courtesy, Peter Massey, Department of Forensic Sciences, University of New Haven

Figure 11.2
This photo illustrates the type of crime scene that may be encountered in cybercrime investigations. Note clues, such as the eyeglasses and the business card in the ashtray. This type of investigation will usually necessitate a computer expert.

The Internet has become a notorious tool for pedophiles, child pornographers, and other child sex abusers. ICE, the Postal Inspection Service, and the FBI generally investigate international providers. Depending on how information comes to authorities, federal, state, and local law enforcement may handle local investigations of users. Users of child pornography may also be pedophiles who are active in recruiting children for photos or using chat rooms to entice children to meet them.

A growing number of states have expanded or initiated child exploitation units, which usually include a computer specialist who is familiar with the methods used by suspects who make contact with young people through chat rooms as a means of luring victims to a prearranged location. When a parent or other person makes a complaint, the investigator should be thoroughly familiar with local laws relating to solicitation of a minor. Generally, it must be proved that the suspect was aware that the individual was a minor and in most cases it will be necessary to prove that something more than a meeting was planned. For this reason, it is important to obtain prior communications. If a meeting is arranged, it must be proved that the suspect was actually going to make contact and that a positive identification of the suspect has been made.

Economic Crimes—Fraud, Embezzlement, and Identity Theft

There are a great many types of economic-related fraud, including business fraud and embezzlement, perhaps the largest of which was the Enron case in Texas, which involved a broad range of criminal activities. A major component of this scheme involved computer usage for money transfers and communication. The sale of products that are not delivered as well as misrepresentation by sellers has become a growing problem, and investigations may involve multiple jurisdictions and countries.

Keeping transactions within the computer allows the suspect to destroy information rapidly. However, in many cases, transactions may have been sent to one or more other computers or organizations with which the suspect is conducting business. Further, with the development of small storage devices that can hold enormous amounts of data, as well as cloud computing, it will be increasingly common for criminals to maintain suspect records separate from the computer.

One of the more common types of electronic fraud involves the use of stolen or forged credit cards. Despite efforts by companies to create "safer" credit cards using photos and fingerprints, this problem continues to grow, due in some measure to the ability to purchase products and services over the Internet. Identity theft is one of the fastest-growing crimes in the United States. Criminals use a variety of means to secure information. They then use this information to commit fraudulent purchases, acquire other forms of false identification, receive large cash advances, and establish fraudulent lines of credit in the forms of loans and other credit cards.

A number of schemes involving telecommunications fraud have arisen with the increase in the number of cell phones available throughout the world. Each type of telecommunications offering, from voice to wireless data, is vulnerable. For instance, through fraudulent access to networks, perpetrators can avoid paying for wireless service, steal and resell long-distance minutes, hijack a network device to send unsolicited commercial e-mail or pornographic spam to unsuspecting end users, or use stolen cell phones to make large numbers of calls.

Additionally, a number of organized crime groups, frequently with international connections, have developed sophisticated fraudulent credit card rings. Investigations of these types of activities must be handled quickly because perpetrators are likely to move frequently to avoid apprehension. Unfortunately, in many cases, the victim whose number or card has been stolen is not aware of the crime until he or she receives a statement.

On a higher level, fraudulent wire transfers, bank fraud, telecommunications fraud, and money laundering have also become commonplace. In many instances, the illegal activities are carried out across borders and will involve multiple jurisdictions. Electronic funds transfers have made it possible for individuals to move funds to offshore accounts, to gain entry illegally into funding institutions and make transfers, and to embezzle large amounts of money. Section 2314 of Title 18 of the U.S. Code makes it illegal to transport interstate computer data[20] and stolen computer hardware worth at least $5,000.[21]

Economic espionage has also become a major problem. Although relatively little attention is paid by law enforcement to the issue of economic espionage, patent or intellectual property infringement, or the stealing of trade secrets, this is an area in which the amount of criminal activity has been growing steadily. In many cases, the companies being victimized are unaware of the problem or do not have procedures for reporting or investigating such activities. Estimates of annual misappropriations and fraud (frequently committed by trusted employees) of U.S. companies amount to more than $250 billion. Although statutes differ by states, the elements of computer fraud make it unlawful for any person to:

- Use a computer or computer network,

- Without authority, and

- With the intent to: (a) obtain property or services by false pretenses; (b) embezzle or commit larceny; or (c) convert the property of another.[22]

Computer Hacking/Cracking and Sabotage

One of the more pervasive illegal uses of the computer is hacking, more correctly cracking, which generally involves entering a computer system illegally or without knowledge of the victim. The term *hacker* generally refers to individuals whose goal is to reduce ther lines of code without inhibiting the program to operate optimally. The term *cracker*, on the other hand, is used more often to describe a person who attempts to destroy, change, or steal programs or information. Often undertaken as what hackers refer to as an "intellectual challenge," the practice has become a major problem in both the public and private sectors. A growing number of individuals and "clubs" throughout the world have been involved in developing methods to break codes or find ways to enter a system, and they have frequently been successful in "crashing" web sites, altering information, and introducing viruses. In Internet slang, the term "white hat" refers to nonmalicious, ethical hackers, including those who

---

BOX 11.4 CASE STUDY: HACKERS

Russian hackers obtained American identities and software developed by Microsoft as part of their attack on Georgia during the five-day conflict in 2008 between the two countries. This was the first time cyber-attacks were known to have coincided with a military campaign. According to the report, the attacks, using social networking sites such as Twitter and Facebook, disabled 20 web sites, including those of the Georgian President, the defense minister, the National Bank of Georgia, and major news outlets.

Source: Siobhan Gorman, "Deciphering Cyber Attacks," *The Wall Street Journal* (August 18, 2009), 11.

---

perform penetration tests and vulnerability assessments. A "black hat" hacker is a hacker who violates computer security for malicious reasons or personal gain.

Table 11.1 defines some of the terms involved in economic-related criminal activity. "A number of states criminalize the dissemination of viruses, worms and other forms of malware [malicious

Table 11.1
Computer Terminology

Clipper chip	A computer chip for encryption as a means of protecting computerized information.
Encryption	A means of protecting communication and electronic commerce. Can be used by organized crime or terrorist groups to conceal illegal activities.
Logic Bomb	A virus that is dormant until a particular time (which can be days, months, or years) or when a particular command is entered in the computer.
Pinging or Spamming	A form of vandalism, or sabotaging, that involves bombarding an e-mail address with thousands of messages using automatic remailer tools.
Remailer	A program that makes it possible to send thousands of messages to an e-mail address.
Trapdoor	A means for bypassing the security controls of a computer mainframe system (usually installed by programmers to permit then to enter the system to check when things go wrong).
Trojan Horse	Software embedded in a popular and trusted computer software program (maybe unknown to the user) that is stealing secrets, modifying the database, or deleting specific items of information. It is not usually considered a virus because it does not replicate itself and does not spread.
Virus	A program designed to attach itself to a file, reproduce, and spread from one file to another, destroying data, displaying an irritating message, or otherwise disrupting computer operations.
Worm	Software that works its way through a single computer system or a network, changing and destroying data or codes.
Packet Sniffer	A program that examines all traffic on a section of network to find passwords, credit card numbers, and other information of value.

Table 11.1
(Continued)

SATAN	A security loophole analysis program designed for use by system administrators (and abused by electronic intruders) to detect insecure systems.
File Infector	Computer viruses that attach to program files and spread when the program is executed.
Boot Sector Virus	A computer virus that infects the sectors on a disk that contain the data a computer uses during the boot process. This type of virus does not require a program to spread, and may cause the destruction of all data on a drive.
Macro Virus	A computer virus that infects the automatic command execution capabilities (macros) of productivity software. Macro viruses are typically attached to documents and spreadsheets.
Cracking	The process of trying to overcome a security measure.
Black Hat	A term used to describe a hacker who has the intention of causing damage or stealing information.
Crackers	People who break into a computer system with intent to damage files or steal data, or who are driven to hack highly secure systems.
Denial of Service Attack	An attack that causes the targeted system to be unable to fulfill its intended function.
IP Spoofing	An attack whereby the attacker disguises himself or herself as another user by means of a false IP network address.
Letterbomb	An e-mail containing live data intended to cause damage to the recipient's computer.
Malware	A term for malicious software.
Phreaking	When a person hacks telephone systems, usually for the purpose of making free phone call.
Phracking	When a person combines phone phreaking with computer hacking.
Trap and Trace Device	A device used to record the telephone numbers dialed by a specific telephone.
War Dialer	Software designed to detect dial-in access to computer systems.
Computer Emergency Response Team (CERT)	An organization that collects and distributes information about security breaches.
Firewall	A device designed to enforce the boundary between two or more networks, limiting access.
Keystroke Monitoring	The process of recording every character typed by a computer user on a keyboard.
Pretty Good Privacy (PGP)	A freeware program designed to encrypt e-mail.
Warez	Slang for pirated software.
Zeus Malware	Program installed on a telephone by imbedding a link in a message text

software]. Many of these prohibitions target the dissemination of a 'computer contaminant.' 'Computer contaminant' is defined as encompassing viruses, worms and other harmful programs."[23]

Professional crackers are involved in garnering classified or sensitive information that they can sell to others. Zeus Malware is one example of a program installed on a telephone by imbedding a link in a text message

In recent years, governments have also been involved in using the computer to steal or pass information. Investigations of this nature require sophisticated knowledge of the computer and should not be attempted without consulting a technical advisor.

Closely related to hacking is computer sabotage, which may involve the actions of a disgruntled employee to destroy an employers' database or make an external attack on a computer database.

Illegal Drug Activity

Drug traffickers have taken to using the Internet for distribution of drugs, communicating between groups, and keeping records of transactions. Organized crime groups have developed sophisticated methods for the transfer of funds to other countries or offshore accounts, frequently by establishing electronic business "fronts" or by "purchasing" high-cost items with illegal cash and then "selling" the items abroad as a means of recovering the cash.

Terrorism

Although this subject is covered in more detail in Chapter 23, it is important to recognize that terrorist groups use the Internet as an increasingly important means of communication. They also use the Internet to gather information about individuals, possible targets, and ways of making explosives or other weapons.

CYBER-CRIME INVESTIGATION AND THE ELECTRONIC CRIME SCENE

There are a number of considerations that should be observed when dealing with a high-tech crime scene. The National Institute of Justice (NIJ) Guide stresses the importance of documentation in detail. The following steps are recommended:

- Observe and document the physical scene, such as the position of the mouse and the location of components relative to each other (e.g., a mouse on the left side of the computer may indicate a left-handed user).

- Document the condition and location of the computer system, including power status of the computer (on, off, or in sleep mode). Most computers have status lights that indicate the computer is on. Likewise, if fan noise is heard, the system is probably on. Furthermore, if the computer system is warm, that may also indicate that it is on or was recently turned off.

- Identify and document related electronic components that will not be collected.

- Photograph the entire scene to create a visual record as noted by the first responder. The complete room should be recorded with 360 degrees of coverage, when possible.

- Photograph the front of the computer as well as the monitor screen and other components. Also take written notes on what appears on the monitor screen. Active programs may require videotaping or more extensive documentation of monitor screen activity.[24]

The computer has come of age in law enforcement as departments and other agencies develop applications through which this technology can benefit the field. In many cases, the technology and the application software—the programs used to handle and manipulate the data—exist in various forms but require modification for law enforcement purposes. In other cases, software is available (frequently through hardware vendors) that has been designed specifically for police work. Included in this category are programs ranging from relatively simple data-storage programs to extremely complex systems for tasks such as imaging (for storing photographic images on the computer) and optical scanning (for storing fingerprints for later retrieval).

In the field of criminal investigation, the computer has not yet come close to the potential it offers as an investigative tool. Although one reason for this is a lack of sufficient funding, other considerations also limit computer utilization—for example, concern about the right to privacy, a lack of trained technicians, and an entrenched resistance by officers who have little understanding of the computer's capabilities.

As new generations of computer-literate personnel move into the law enforcement profession, there is likely to be a growing trend toward acceptance. Many federal agencies have begun to develop and adopt computer-based systems that go far beyond mere data storage and retrieval. A number of police departments—including those in Chicago, Los Angeles, and Houston—have invested millions of dollars in automated fingerprint identification systems (AFISs) and are seeing their value in the investigative function. Illustrative of this potential value is a case involving a forcible rape in which a latent fingerprint was lifted from the handbag of the victim. Fingerprint analysis provided no suspects. However, more than a year later, a suspect arrested in a burglary was surprised to learn that, despite the passage of time, his prints identified him as the rapist. (At the time of the rape, he had been too young to be fingerprinted, despite his long record as a juvenile offender.) This illustrates the capability of technology to solve what in all likelihood would have remained an unsolved case.

Computers are also being used for developing crime patterns; for artificial intelligence, and, with imaging, for storing online mug shots of suspects and photographs of stolen artwork or other valuable collections.

Perhaps the greatest innovation in programming software in the past decade has been the development of very sophisticated relational databases, and linking and geospatial programs for law enforcement purposes. A relational database makes it possible to combine a large number of individual databases into a system that makes it possible to link a broad range of disparate variables for search and profiling purposes. The Chicago Police Department's CLEAR program makes it possible to link millions of records from different sources (including other police departments) to provide a powerful tool for investigators. The program utilizes artificial intelligence, photographs, images, and geospatial techniques in addition to text-based records. Some of these include:

- Nickname database
- MO file
- Informants file
- Business locator index with emergency telephone numbers for business owners
- Case file indicating which cases are assigned to which investigator
- Skills index listing the names of those who can assist with specific needs, such as language skills, scuba divers, technicians, etc.

- Intelligence file offering a source for various bits of information that can be pieced together to form a clearer picture of suspects or crime patterns. (This file, which usually requires the expertise of an analyst or other individual familiar with the technology, represents one of the more significant changes appearing in the field of criminal investigation.)

- Stolen property files

- Building layouts and schematics

- Tattoo files

- Gang symbols and descriptors

- Motor vehicle records

- Victimization files

The FBI utilizes Rapid Start Teams, which are teams of experienced investigators and technical experts who can quickly load information from hundreds of leads and investigative tips into a database to assist in major case investigations. Established in 1995, the Rapid Start Team has assisted in numerous high-profile cases, including the Oklahoma City Bombing in 1995, the Atlanta Olympics Bombing in 1996, and the 9/11 attacks in 2001. Rapid Start Teams are also available for child abduction cases and other major cases.

On an individual basis, investigators can use PCs, laptops, PDAs, and other devices to maintain their own data sources, address and telephone files, case information, as well as for numerous other applications.

If a picture is worth a thousand words, imaging technology offers immense possibilities. One of the most obvious uses today is through computer-based identification kits, which make it possible to prepare a composite of a suspect relatively easily. However, the quality and color of newer monitors and systems make it possible to have a four-color, instant-access mug shot book readily available. Indeed, coupled with search technology, the investigators can feed in information on *modus operandi*, physical descriptors, type of victim, and so on, to call up groups and individuals in various categories for the victim to view on the scene.

Electronic surveillance takes many forms, and is being used more frequently in terrorism and organized crime investigations. Some of these, most of which require a court order, include:

- Telephone wiretap

- Electronic intercept of oral conversation

- Voice paging

- Digital display paging

- Cellular telephone intercepts

- Pen register

- Internet or computer communications intercept

Additionally, there are also a great number of sources on the Internet that are available to investigators to seek information.

THE FUTURE

Computer-related crime deserves more attention from a futures perspective, largely because of the rapidly changing nature of technology. One can only speculate as to the types of crime the world will face in the years to come. Of particular importance to the investigator is the ability to foresee ways in which new forms of technology will be embraced by criminal elements. Cybercrime is not an American innovation, and today borders are no obstacle to criminals who can use many forms of communication and transportation to carry out criminal activity. Some of this involves what are now traditional types of crime, such as fraud, child pornography, cyber-attacks on national security, and stalking. Others involve relatively new types of crime, such as data manipulation, asymmetric warfare, identification theft, and cyberbullying. A report by the Intelligence and National Security Alliance, a nonprofit group, points out that "the growing increase in sophisticated cyber-attacks has moved beyond acceptable losses for government and businesses that simply threaten finances or intellectual property." [25]

Figure 11.3
The Pentagon's U.S. Cyber Command logo. The logo contains an embedded 32-character string of secret code in its logo, causing a stir among bloggers and curious techies eager to decipher the veiled message.

Army General Keith Alexander, commander of the U.S. Cyber Command, and Director of the National Security Agency (NSA), at a conference on cyberwarfare in 2011, said that "massive losses of private and public data in recent years to computer criminals and spies represent the largest theft in history," adding that, "Threats posed by cyber-attacks on computer networks and the Internet are escalating from large-scale theft of data and strikes designed to disrupt computer operations to more lethal attacks that destroy entire systems and physical equipment." [26]

Gordon Snow, Assistant Director, Cyber Division, Federal Bureau of Investigation, in testimony before a Congressional committee warned in 2011 that cyber criminals represent a major threat to financial and business corporations. He noted that, "[T]he number and sophistication of malicious incidents has increased dramatically over the past five years and is expected to continue to grow."[27]

AP Photo/Department of Defense

Defense Concerns

The Pentagon's cyberstrategy announced last summer [2010] calls for treating the cyberdomain as equal to the air, land, sea and space domains and leveraging U.S. technology to improve cyberdefenses for government and the private sector.

On information theft, General Alexander said the problem is so pervasive that there are two categories for major companies: firms that are aware they have been hacked and the rest who remain unaware of the problem.

Information technology offers investigators one of the most important advances in law enforcement, and is a growing area of development. Most federal agencies and many police departments are now employing crime analysts—specialists schooled in this technology—who can serve as an important source of support to field investigators.

NOTES

[1]   *Merriam-Webster's Collegiate Dictionary*, 11th ed. Merriam-Webster, Inc. Springfield, MA. 2003

[2]   Greenwald, Judy. "Mobile devices may be small, but data risks are enormous." *Business Insurance*. July 31, 2011.

[3]   Susan W. Brenner. "Defining Cybercrime: A Review of State and Federal Law." In Ralph D. Clifford, ed. (2006). *Cybercrime: The Investigation, Prosecution and Defense of a Computer Related Crime*, 2nd ed. (Durham, NC: Carolina Academic Press).

[4]   U.S. Department of Justice, *Electronic Crime Scene Investigation: A Guide for First Responders* (Washington, DC: National Institute of Justice, July 2001). See http://www.ncjrs.gov/pdffiles1/nij/187736.pdf.

[5]   Tae J. Chung. "Policing Internet Fraud: A Study of the Tensions Between Private and Public Models of Policing Fraudulent Activity in Cyberspace with Particular Focus on South Korea and Special Reference to the United Kingdom and the United States." Unpublished dissertation, The University of Leeds School of Law, Leeds, UK (December 2008), 64.

[6]   Supra note 3, 4.

[7]   Stephen W. Cogar, "Obtaining Admissible Evidence from Computers and Internet Service Providers." *FBI Law Enforcement Bulletin* (Washington, DC: U.S. Department of Justice, 2003), 11.

[8]   *Welsh v. Wisconsin*, 466 U.S. 740, 748 (1984); Ivan Orton, "The Investigation and Prosecution of a Cybercrime." In Ralph D. Clifford, ed., *Cybercrime: The Investigation, Prosecution and Defense of a Computer Related Crime*, 2nd ed. (Durham, NC: Carolina Academic Press, 2006), 126,

[9]   Donald Resseguie, *Computer Searches and Seizure*, 48 Clev. St. L. Rev. 185 (2000).

[10]   Carrier, Brian (2003) "Open Source Digital Forensic Tools: The Legal Argument." www.digital-evidence. org/papers/opensrc_legal.pdf. ; *Daubert v. Merrell* (509 US 579, 1999)

[11]   Rolando V. del Carmen and Jeffery T. Walker, *Briefs of Leading Cases in Law Enforcement*, 8th ed. (Boston: Elsevier/Anderson Publishing, 2012), 61–70.

[12]   *Trulock v. Freeh*, 275 F.3d 391 (4th Cir. 2001).

[13]   *United States v. Simons*, 206 F.3d 392 (4th Cir. 2000).

[14]   Cogar, loc. cit.

[15]   *United States v. Hambrick*, 225 F.3d 656 (4th Cir. 2000).

[16]   Cogar, 14.

[17]   Frank Schmalleger, *Criminal Law Today: An Introduction to Capstone Cases*, 3rd ed. (Upper Saddle River, NJ: Pearson/Prentice Hall, 2006), 411.

[18]   Cogar, 15.

[19]   U.S. Department of Justice, Office of Justice Programs, "Digital Evidence in the Courtroom: A Guide for Law Enforcement and Prosecutors" (Washington, DC: National Institute of Justice, 2007), 53.

[20]   *United States v. Farraj*, 211 F. Supp. 2d 479 (S.D.N.Y. 2002).

[21]   Brenner, 54.

[22]   Schmalleger, 418.

[23]   Brenner, 84.

24   Supra note 4.

25   L. C. Baldor. ABC15.com, 09/12/2011, retrieved from http://www.abc15.com/dpp/news/science_tech/study-warns-us-must-develop-cyber-intelligence-wcpo1315837910497

26   Gertz, Bill. "Computer-based attacks emerge as threat of future, General says." *The Washington Times*, September 13, 2011.

27   Gordon M. Snow, "Statement before the House Financial Services Committee, Subcommittee on Financial Institutions and Consumer Credit." Federal Bureau of Investigation, Washington, D.C. (September 14, 2011).

IMPORTANT CASES

Daubert v. Merrell Dow Pharmaceuticals, Inc. (1993)
Trulock v. Freeh (2001)
United States v. Farraj (2002)
United States v. Hambrick (2000)
United States v. Simons (2000)

DISCUSSION QUESTIONS

1.   Why is changing technology important in criminal investigation, and how will these changes affect future investigators?

2.   Why is so-called cybercrime of increasing concern?

3.   What are the three categories that cybercrime usually falls into?

4.   What are some of the common types of cybercrime?

5.   Why are cybercrimes frequently difficult to prosecute?

6.   What types of computerized files can be of importance to an investigator?

7.   The *Daubert* test requires what criteria in order to qualify as an expert witness?

8.   Why is an understanding of chat rooms and social networking important?

9.   Why must an investigator be familiar with the various types and characteristics of computer-related crime?

10. In general, what are the legal elements of computer fraud?

SUPPLEMENTAL READINGS

Amoroso, E. G. (2011). *Cyber attacks: Protecting national infrastructure.* Boston: Elsevier.

Blitzer, H. L., Stein-Ferguson, K., & Huang, J. (2008). *Understanding forensic digital imaging.* Boston: Academic Press.

Casey, E. (Ed.). (2002). *Handbook of computer crime investigation: Forensic tools and technology.* San Diego: Academic Press.

Clifford, R. D. (Ed.). (2006). *Cybercrime: The investigation, prosecution and defense of a computer related crime* (2nd ed.). Durham, NC: Carolina Academic Press.

Johnson, T. A. (Ed.). (2006). Boca Raton, FL: CRC Taylor & Francis Press.

Kovacich, G. L., & Jones, A. (2006). *High technology crime investigator's handbook: Establishing and managing a high-technology crime prevention program* (2nd ed.). Boston: Butterworth-Heinemann/Elsevier.

Moore, R. (2011). *Cybercrime: Investigating high-technology computer crime* (2nd ed.). Boston: Elsevier/Anderson Publishing.

U.S. Department of Justice, *Electronic crime scene investigation: A guide for first responders* (2nd ed.). Washington, DC: National Institute of Justice.

CHAPTER 12

CRIME ANALYSIS AND COMING ATTRACTIONS IN THE INVESTIGATOR'S TOOLBOX

CRIME ANALYSIS

One of the more rapidly growing influences on crime investigation is in the field of crime analysis. This now goes far beyond the use of pin maps, which were followed by crime maps on acetate layers so that one could look at crime patterns at various times of day or days of the weeks. This gave way to computerized mapping in the 1970s and 1980s, and today is giving way to crime analysis and the use of highly sophisticated relational database programs that prove to be much more valuable to both police administrators and investigators. "Crime analysis is a field of study and practice in criminal justice that utilizes systematic research methods and data, supports the mission of police agencies, and provides information to a range of audiences."[1]

Computer Terminology

Artificial Intelligence – A program designed to simulate human intelligence.
Database – Data arranged for retrieval.
Digital Computing – Computing that performs operations based on a series of digits.
Algorithm – Mathematical rule to solve a problem.
Bit – Basic unit of computing represented by just two digits, 0 or 1.
Data Set – A collection of related computer records.
Flat File – A file of data that has no internal hierarchy.
Query – A specific request for data from one or more databases.

The Relational Database

A traditional database is generally viewed as a collection of information or data arranged to research complex relationships between variables, enabling the investigator to view and "test" theoretical concepts. There is an enormous range of databases usually associated with a particular organization or function, such as auto licenses and registration; medical records; personnel records, or arrest records. Many of

Geographic Database Locations

- Local (cities and towns)
- State
- Federal
- International
- Public sector
  - Available to the public, usually for a fee
- Private sector
  - Corporations and businesses
  - Credit Research Unions

these databases can be transferred in what is commonly referred to as a "flat" file, which will have any number of variables associated with the file's purpose. These files may contain millions of variables or categories.

Records and files may also be "housed" in a variety of settings. Geographically, these may be databases ranging from the local to the international level.

Essentially, a relational database enables the analyst to enter information on hundreds, if not thousands, of variables. Constructing a crime-related database is as much an art as it is a science. The way it is constructed, and the power or capability of the software program, will have an impact on the way data can be analyzed. Various models can be obtained by manipulation of the data to focus on different intelligence and operational goals. For example, a relational database construct can be used to:

- Identify suspects
- Identify acquaintances
- Compare geospatial attributes
- Analyze crime scenes and *modus operandi* (MO)
- Develop various types of "linking" models
- Analyze temporal aspects of specific criminal activity
- Analyze investigative effectiveness
- Create operational plans
- Analyze specific variables, such as names, nicknames, tattoos, telephone numbers, addresses, criminal records (convictions, probation, parole, gang and organizational affiliations, weapons)

A relational database makes it possible to draw from a much broader range of data sets in a variety of ways. The experienced crime analyst should be able to "construct" certain types of searches in a way that visualizes them in various ways, displayed as a link chart or other format

Crime Mapping

Crime mapping represents another technique of crime analysis. It is used widely in police departments to track trends and to visualize a broad range of topics that are of value to administrators, supervisors, and line personnel, such as crime patterns, traffic accidents, personnel deployment, and building maps, as well as so-called hot spots. "The literature on hot spots is as prevalent and as varied as the definition of hot spots. Generally, hot spots are viewed as small geographic areas that experience higher than average levels of crime for consistent periods of time."[2]

Crime mapping in the investigative process has a variety of uses. For example, a map depicting the locations of stolen vehicles and their drop-off points may lead to indications of how the vehicle

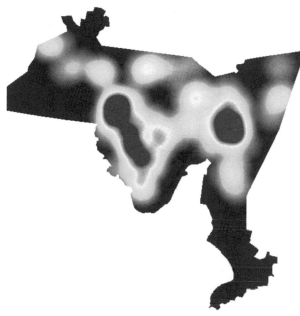

Figure 12.1
A heat map of robberies over a three-month period in an urban center.

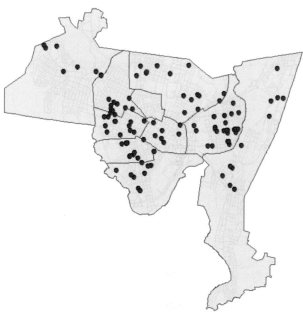

Figure 12.2
A "point" map of robberies over a three-month period in an urban center.

was being used, the proximity of the thief's residence, or the existence of a nearby "chop shop" when vehicles are stripped. Crime maps can also be used to analyze where certain types of crimes are more prevalent, or to identify locations where known criminals live.

Figures 12.1 and 12.2 illustrate a "heat map" of robberies over a specified period of time, which could be used to "isolate" particular areas where robbery teams are more active.

Database Usage

A successful database is dependent upon the number of variables, which may be defined as minutia, or the inclusion of details about the crime, the criminal, the location, and other variables identified within the database. Unfortunately, in the vast majority of criminal investigations, a wealth of information goes unreported. Even basic information may not be reported, for instance, serial number or detailed description of property; the actions and "tale" of a perpetrator; description of clothing worn, such as a baseball cap; or other accurate and specific details provided by victims, witnesses, or even suspects. If entered into a relational database, all of this data can be retrieved by a crime analyst in ways that would have been virtually impossible a decade ago.

Figures 12.3 and 12.4 indicate the type of search that can be conducted, moving progressively through each link chart to narrow down a list of suspects. In Figure 12.3, the analyst first searches for all

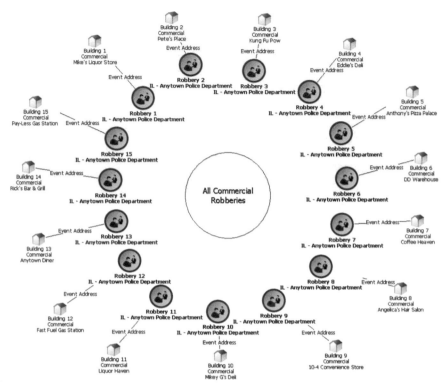

Figure 12.3
Link chart: Search for All Commercial Robberies.

commercial robberies. In Figure 12.4, the search is developed by adding commercial robberies with two or more perpetrators.

Figure 12.5 shows a link chart after the search has been narrowed to include a handgun and the addition of the nickname "Pancho" or "Poncho." Three robberies contain the variables described.

Perhaps it should be noted that this particular set of link charts is relatively simple and illustrative of the techniques that a crime analyst or investigator may use. It is important to recognize that the sequence in which the variables are added is important, and if a key variable is omitted, it is likely it will eliminate a possible suspect. Further, manipulation of the search may also provide the same or similar data, but it is important to work from the specific details (in this case, the specific variables were: commercial robbery, with a handgun, by two individuals). The nickname may or may not be a key factor, and it may have been worthwhile to work from a single individual with a handgun to explore the possibility that the perpetrator may have worked other robberies alone, or with a different partner. In essence, this represents the "art" of crime analysis.

What might have happened if all of the data was entered into the larger database? See Figure 12.6 for an idea. Obviously, this approach is virtually useless, and explains the importance of knowing how to conduct an investigation using link charts and crime mapping (visualization) in investigations.

The crime analyst working with the investigator should be able to manipulate, add, or delete variables, such as recently released parolees or subjects on probation for burglary. In essence, this

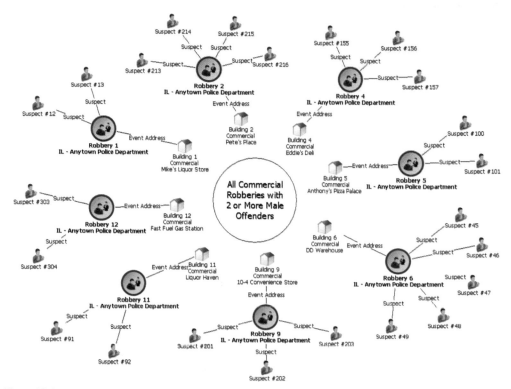

Figure 12.4
Link chart: Search for All Commercial Robberies with Two or More Perpetrators.

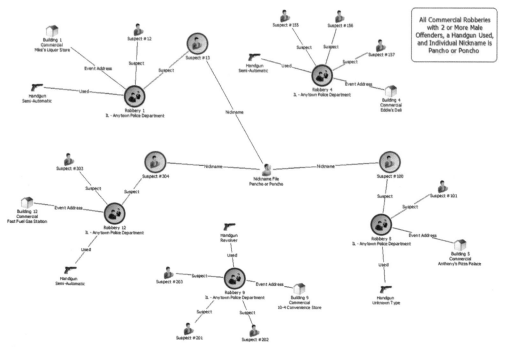

Figure 12.5
Link chart: Search for All Commercial Robberies with Pancho or Poncho.

Figure 12.6
Results of link chart without narrowing down information.

type of search is based almost exclusively on the types of information being collected and stored in the database. The analyst can also refine the search by reducing the time frame, restructuring the geographic area, or increasing the individuals arrested for other crimes. Where cooperation exists between jurisdictions, data from other towns may be integrated into the search. The more experience an analyst gains, the more likely he or she will be able to assist the investigator.

In the simulated robbery investigation above, the detective would prepare a list of variables that should include:

- Past commercial robberies

- Two or more perpetrators

- Physical descriptors – male white, male Hispanic

- Weapon (handgun – silver automatic)

- Prior arrests for robbery

- Tattoo – skull

- Nickname – Pancho or Poncho

An exception to this rule involves artificial intelligence, in which a program is designed to "look" at options, usually based on algorithms, to solve a problem. Put another way, it is a method whereby the computer is "asked" to analyze a large data set, or, in some cases, reports, records, or other written forms, and supply mathematical "judgments or conclusions" that would be virtually impossible to detect by hand. An example might be to query one or more databases to identify the frequency of an event and its relationship to other variables that may not appear obvious. This is frequently used in code-breaking, predicting possible events, and analyzing writing styles.

In many ways, crime analysis is not all that different from programs used by the government in counterterrorism and private organizations to analyze anything from spending habits to reading preferences and Internet usage. However, the vast majority of federal, state, and local law enforcement jurisdictions are woefully behind in the application of more sophisticated analyses and investigative strategies. The need for trained analysts is discussed in several other sections of this book, but this must also be accompanied by the availability of new information technology and up-to-date programs. All of these are costly and beyond the reach of many, if not most, police agencies.

Future advances will depend in large measure on a much greater emphasis on shared resources and cooperation. Philip Mudd, a former Deputy Director of the Counterterrorist Center at the Central Intelligence Agency (CIA), senior intelligence advisor at the FBI, and more recently a senior advisor at Oxford Global Analytica and senior research fellow at the New America Foundation's Counterterrorism Strategy Initiative, points out that the domestic threat to the United States is broad, including gangs, cyberthreats, and more than 10,000 murders every year. He notes that government intelligence must be useful and tactical, and requires cooperation and sharing with public and private organizations.[3]

Crime analysis represents an important contribution to the investigative function, and future criminal investigators will be expected to have a basic understanding of the ways in which this form of technology can be utilized. The following section addresses the application of principles applied to criminal investigation.

COMING ATTRACTIONS IN THE INVESTIGATOR'S TOOLBOX

At the outset it may be wise to address the naysayers and the skeptics who are likely to argue that some of the ideas and thoughts presented in this section are merely pie-in-the-sky or impossible propositions. For the authors, who bring more than 100 years of experience to the fore, it is not difficult to look back and point out the many changes in law enforcement that trampled the nonbelievers. The following represents a means of viewing the future from a broader perspective rather than accepting the *status quo*.

Surveillance

As noted in Chapter 8, and in other places throughout this text, surveillance is the observation of a subject under suspicion, or the act of watching. The tradition and strategy covered in most of the literature on criminal investigation focuses on the types and methods employed in following a suspect. In some cases, surveillance may involve following a person (relative, spouse, friend, or someone who is usually close to the subject) in the hope that they will lead to a suspect. Surveillance is also used

Figure 12.7
A police aerial surveillance drone.

in kidnapping, hostage-taking, and stalking cases, either to gather information or to protect a victim or witness.

In addition to eye contact, a surveillant may rely on binoculars, video cameras, or the use of GPS equipment. GPS equipment is becoming increasingly more common, but as noted earlier, it is also the subject of limits from the court decision in the *United States v. Jones* (2012).[4] One-on-one surveillance is difficult, and multiple teams are usually employed in major cases. This is also an area that requires a high degree of training and expertise.

Traditional surveillance is likely to be replaced or enhanced by several tools that may not be generally available to local police, but are being used extensively by the military, the Defense Intelligence (DIA), the Central Intelligence Agency (CIA), the National Security Agency (NSA), the FBI, the Drug Enforcement Administration (DEA), and other federal agencies.

Rapid advances in camera technology have made it possible to film from satellites, a tactic that was used in surveilling the hideout of Osama Bin Laden. Satellites do have the drawback of orbiting the earth, usually leaving a period when observation is cut off. Nevertheless, if one is looking to compare changes in a location over time, or the movement of vehicles or aircraft, satellites are a useful tool likely to become available for major crimes in the future. The use of planes is another tool available to some of the larger police departments and some state agencies, as well as the FBI and DEA, who maintain fleets.

The development and use of drones, which are unmanned aerial vehicles (UAVs), originated in the military. Drones continue to play a key role in identifying and killing terrorists, and are being used in the United States by the DEA on the Mexican border, as well as in other types of operations.

Drone technology has reached the point at which it is used in the private sector for a variety of operations, including police reconnaissance, border surveillance, inspecting oil equipment, aerial filming, checking crops, and surveilling wildlife. Their relatively low cost makes it likely that there will be increasing use by law enforcement in the future. Future technology is focusing on the development of so-called "robotic flies" that "look—and fly—like ladybugs, dragonflies and other insects."[5] Their application offers a number of possibilities, according to Chris Anderson, editor of *Wired* magazine, including the ability "to fly into a drug trafficker's house."

Aerial photography is being used on airplanes and drones in the United States to identify drug crops, to track the movement of illegal goods, and in counter-terrorism operations. The use of aircraft or similar equipment provides an eye-in-the-sky approach that can prove to be much less expensive than employing teams of surveillants on the ground over lengthy periods of time, or in multiple locations. How this type of equipment is used in the future will depend in large measure on "out-of-the-box" thinking within the field and research institutes.

Drones vs. Helicopters

The rapid technology in drones may replace helicopters, or provide a new tool for police departments that can't afford to maintain a helicopter fleet. Ben Miller, a drone pilot in Mesa County, Colorado, said: "There's nothing they do that manned aircraft couldn't. We just can't afford manned aircraft."

Source: Anderson, Chris. "Here Come the Drones." *Wired magazine.* July, 2012. p.103.

Of particular interest in surveillance operations is the concept of "marking" or "painting," a practice in which an individual, a vehicle, or other movable object can be marked or identified, enabling the camera to follow movements. The application can be used from aircraft and helicopters, but from a law enforcement viewpoint, it is probably more valuable from a fixed position in a tall building to monitor movements in a large area, such as a stadium, ballpark, or other large venue.

In loose surveillance operations, where visual contact may not be necessary, it may be possible to track an individual's movements by keeping track of actions that are recorded, such as passing through a toll booth using an electronic toll-collection system such as E-ZPass, making withdrawals from cash machines, or using credit cards in locations where there are likely to be cameras, such as department stores and supermarkets. In many cases, the devices also record other details beyond video footage, such as the date, time, and amounts of cash withdrawals; changes in clothing or physical description; or other actions.

In some cases, it may be possible to couple this type of surveillance data to track an individual's movements and actions over time. Most people are creatures of habit, and individuals generally develop patterns, such as the route they take to work, where they have breakfast or lunch, or how they spend their leisure time. In the so-called "Grey Lord" case some years ago in Chicago, investigators knew that certain judges who were under suspicion frequently had breakfast together in a particular diner and sat in the same location. Court-approved wiretaps were used to gather information that resulted in a number of convictions.

Telephone and smart phone examination may be used to track numbers called or received by date and time of day, and, in some cases, it may also be possible to determine the location at which a call is made or received. The same can also be said of the use of social media, particularly in the case of "tweets," texting, or Facebook posts.

As technology improves, the ability to keep track of individuals and their actions will become more common. However, as noted here and in other chapters, many of these techniques are being scrutinized by the courts in a number of cases at the state and federal level, and either currently require search warrants, or are likely to be the subject of future requirements. For this reason, it is imperative that the investigator be familiar with court decisions, and use of such techniques may require consultation with legal advisors or prosecutors.

Records

As noted earlier, in American society, records on an individual begin at birth, or even while still a fetus. For example, medical records and gene technology are rapidly making it possible to know a great amount of information before a person is born, such as prior drug use by the mother, blood type or DNA analyses, or certain types of diseases that may be a part of the child's genealogy. As medical and scientific research expands, an individual's lifespan may be charted in ways that can influence an investigation.

In fact, the amount of information compiled on an individual over time is enormous, often making it virtually impossible to decipher, particularly in cases where the investigator may not be sure what type of evidence is important to the investigation. It is not unusual, as an investigation proceeds, to have to go back over various aspects of data to pursue leads. In some cases, it may be necessary to construct a historical profile of a suspect that might include where he or she lived and worked, who his or her friends were, and what kinds of activities he or she was involved in, such as gambling or illegal drug use. Any number of cases have been made by determining who was a suspect's cell mate or friend in the past. An individual's habits or interests may change over time, and there are cases in which an individual is married to more than one person or living in more than one households at the same time, while neither family or partner was aware of the other one.

One might think that a thorough records search would uncover alternate lifestyles. There are many techniques that may serve to make this difficult, including changing one's name, getting a new driver's license, using someone else's social security number, moving to another state or country, or simply stealing someone else's identity—a tactic that proves relatively easy if the person whose identity is being stolen is deceased. Some kidnappers have been known to change a child's identity and raise the child as if he or she were their own.

BOX 12.1 HIDING IN PLAIN SIGHT

James "Whitey" Bulger.

James "Whitey" Bulger, also known by a number of aliases, managed to elude capture by the FBI for more than 16 years, from 1995 until 2012, when the former wanted fugitive and his girlfriend, Catherine Greig, were captured in a quiet neighborhood apartment building in Santa Monica, California, where they lived for at least 13 years.

Implicated in at least 19 murders, Bulger, who led the so-called Winter Hill Gang in Boston, has been described as an FBI informant and an Irish mob hit man. In the years before his capture, he apparently led a quiet life, avoiding contact with neighbors, growing a beard, and using the false identity of Charlie Gasko from Chicago.

Despite an intensive manhunt following his indictment in 1995, Bulger was able to carry on a relatively normal life. He was captured in 2011, when a neighbor recognized him on CNN and called the FBI. The neighbor collected more than $2 million in reward money.

In most cases, the investigator is confronted with numerous records in different locations and databases. Government records, such as those for driver's licenses, vehicle registration, arrest and court records, and other local records, are relatively easy to retrieve, but are usually maintained on a town, city, or state level. Without specific information, it is difficult to cull out suspects.

At the federal level, there are numerous databases, some of which are available to law enforcement, such as crime-related records, customs and immigration information, and postal information, but most personal records, such as social security information, are not open, and require a warrant for release. Here again, an investigator is not likely to be successful if "fishing" without specific identifiers.

Perhaps the most comprehensive databases are in the private sector, and these are growing both in size and methods of use on an extraordinary scale, due largely to information technology designed to explore personal attributes of an individual, such as indebtedness, buying and travel habits, employment, income, property ownership, and in some cases criminal activities and family relationships. It is likely that these databases will continue to grow exponentially, and already are encompassing international records.

At the local level, police records are, for the most part, woefully inadequate in most departments. Even reported crime and arrest records frequently leave much to be desired. State records may provide little more than the name, identification, and types of crime for which an individual has been arrested, or is on probation or parole. Data on *modus operandi* (MO), acquaintances, and areas of operation are less likely to be available, and if so, are more likely to be embedded in the actual arrest report.

The application of more sophisticated crime analysis, as noted earlier in this chapter, is beginning to change the way investigations are conducted. This tool should enhance the use of records and the way in which they are analyzed as police departments increase their information technology (IT) efforts. Nevertheless, it should be noted that the most promising aspect of using records in crime investigation will depend in large measure on the way in which the field understands and applies insight into how newly developed records systems can be used. In this regard, attention should be paid to new types of sources and ways to enhance their use.

For example, with nothing turning up at nearby pawnshops, one enterprising investigator, in a small town plagued by a rash of burglaries, created a list of persons who attended flea markets and sold secondhand goods. He ran the names of sellers through a state database of probation and parole offenders, matching names and narrowing the list down to locals in the region, and eventually refining the list enough to visit several flea markets. As a result, he located and arrested a suspect who later gave the names of other individuals who committed burglaries and sold merchandise that he knew to be stolen.

Photography and Imaging

Perhaps the most significant improvement in photography since invention of the Polaroid camera and film has been the application of digital technology. The applications in criminal investigation have been enormous in both single imaging and videography. Not only has clarity been improved, but the ability to transmit and store images electronically continues to show great promise. As noted earlier, it is possible to photograph distinct images and transfer them immediately from satellites, aircraft, and great distances.

This technology has not been lost on criminal elements, for it is also possible to alter images relatively easily, and is used in counterfeiting, fraud, child pornography, and document alterations.

Digital imagery in cameras, smart phones, laptops, and a host of other devices makes it possible to place this technology in the hands of the investigator and exchange or search images in relatively new ways. For example, so called "Real-Time" Crime centers are using digital imagery to use geo-spatial videos to view crime scenes from above (using Google maps), transfer images of suspects from security cameras, monitor changes in locations over time (temporally), and make it possible for an officer or detective to photograph a crime scene or suspect immediately through hand-held devices. (This does not take the place of a crime scene analyst, but can support this effort in several ways.)

Using digital imaging is relatively inexpensive compared to more traditional approaches using older techniques of processing and printing. One can take hundreds of photos, and select the most graphic, at little cost, making it possible to photograph even minute evidence specimens *in situ*. (In such cases, it is advisable to keep and store *all* photos on a microdisc or jump drive in the event a defense counsel challenges the veracity of the data.)

Digital imaging is now being used in a number of places, such as airports and sporting events, to film hundreds or even thousands of persons and immediately process them through a suspect database. Current technology also makes it possible to film and record license plates and run them through a database of stolen or suspicious vehicles.

The Total Recall Corporation is one of several companies that provide closed-circuit television (CCTV) equipment that can be used for a variety of surveillance activities, including digital wireless networks, thermal imaging, GPS tracking, and other equipment compatible with a variety of so-called "best of breed" products. The use of security cameras and other forms of imaging surveillance is rapidly gaining traction.

Body scanning or advanced imaging technology (AIT) is used largely by airports. In 2012, there were 630 image technology machines being used at 150 airports. Privacy concerns have caused the leading providers to develop newer approaches that eliminate naked images. Future research is moving toward the goal of unobtrusive scanning that will make it possible to "search" an individual as he or she passes through a portal. There are likely to be any number of investigative applications in this area as the technology improves. A number of companies are experimenting with other types of technology, such as improved "wands," shoe scanners, "backscatter" (X-rays), or millimeter-wave scanners.[6]

Imaging has also become more prevalent in the tracking of tattoos, which have become more common in society over the past several decades. Gang tattoos are commonly recorded in law enforcement records, and have proven to be of value by gang crime units. Tattoos are also frequently recorded in arrest reports. Digital imaging has advanced the ability to search for matching tattoos. One of the more interesting cases involved a tattoo on an individual whose image represented the recreation of a homicide (see Box 12.2).

BOX 12.2 TATTOO LEADS TO MURDER CONVICTION

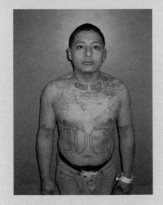

Permission granted by Captain Parker, Sheriff, Headquarter Bureau-Newsroom, LA Sheriff's Department.

The tattoo on a murder suspect in a four-year-old murder case in California led to conviction when LA County Sheriff's homicide investigator, Kevin Lloyd, while reviewing tattoos of gang members recognized the "art work" of 25-year-old Anthony Garcia on his chest, depicting the liquor store robbery/murder that had occurred in 2004, right down to the detail of Christmas lights and the direction the 23-year-old victim fell. A miniature helicopter on the suspect's chest, referring to his nickname, "Chopper,'" led to a 2008 investigation that ended in 2011 when Garcia was arrested. Garcia told undercover detectives about the shooting, and eventually confessed.

Source: Robert Faturechi, "Gang Tattoo Leads to Murder Conviction." *Los Angeles Times* (April 22, 2011).

Crime Reconstruction

Traditional methods of crime reconstruction will be enhanced by tools capable of producing multi-dimensional images, infrared and high-elevation imaging, and advanced computer-designed imaging. Location mapping utilizing techniques developed by Google to portray neighborhoods and geospatial imaging will enable the laboratory to prepare an almost live visual impression of a neighborhood, or the relationship of a building or other object, such as a vehicle, that could be used for court presentations, physical surveillance planning, or to determine the "atmosphere" of a street or neighborhood.

Digital imaging and the availability of relatively small high-resolution cameras, including even cell phones, will enable an officer or investigator to record a crime scene or the injuries to a victim almost immediately, as an initial endeavor prior to the arrival of a crime scene unit or ambulance. This will require better training of field operatives, and although it will not replace the need for an evidence technician, the practice can also be used to establish a "first look" that may prove valuable in later crime reconstruction.

These are just a few of the many changing tools available to law enforcement. There are many more being developed, including new methods for identifying documents and handwriting. The investigator must be aware of new changes and open-minded enough to see the possible applications to their work.

NOTES

[1]   Rachel Boba Santos. *Crime Analysis and Crime Mapping*. 3rd Edition. Los Angeles: Sage, p. xv.

[2]   Rebeccah Paynich and Bryan Hill, *Fundamentals of Crime Mapping*. Boston: Jones and Bartlett, 2010, p. 193.

[3]   "Think Tank Perspective: Interview with Philip Mudd." *Security Management*. June, 2012, pp. 26, 39.

[4]   *United States v. Jones* (2012).

[5]   Judy Dutton. "Drones of the Future" in "Here Come the Drones." *Wired*. July, 2012, p. 111.

[6]   Matthew Harwood. "Full-Body Scanning Report." *Security Management*. June, 2012, pp. 53–62.

DISCUSSION QUESTIONS

1. How has crime analysis become more effective as an investigative tool?

2. What is a relational database?

3. How can crime mapping be used to assist investigators?

4. What are some of the emerging or enhanced development areas that are of interest to investigators?

5. How and why can drones and unmanned aircraft be used in investigations?

6. How is digital imaging replacing more traditional methods of crime scene reconstruction, surveillance, and geospatial analysis?

SUPPLEMENTAL READING

Brunty, J. L., & Helenek, K. (2013). *Social media investigation for law enforcement.* Boston: Elsevier/Anderson Publishing.

Parker, R. N., & Asencio., E. K. (2008). *GIS and spatial analysis for the social sciences: Coding, mapping and modeling.* New York, NY: Routledge.

Section II

APPLYING THE PRINCIPLES TO CRIMINAL INVESTIGATION

Most working detectives hold that their work is unique, that few tasks even come close. To some degree this is true, but the authors of this text maintain that the criminal investigator's job is largely just another kind of inquiry—a reconstruction of the past. Because others with a similar concern for the past (ranging from historians to geologists) employ the scientific method in their endeavors, so too must the detective. Section II, therefore, provides coverage of managing criminal investigations, a general treatment of methods of inquiry, the use of induction and deduction in scientific reasoning, and the sources of information available for reconstructing past events. This section deals with the investigation of some of the more common penal law crimes (i.e., those against the person, those against property). Categorizing crimes in this way may well be useful for didactic reasons, but the distinction fades when subjected to more careful analysis: a burglar's aim is to steal property of value in order to then pawn or sell it, yet a person feels not only its loss but also a sense of having been violated; likewise, arson adversely affects individuals directly or through increased insurance rates, just as homicide seriously affects direct victims as well as their loved ones.

When perusing the chapters in this section, the reader will quickly note that motive is very important to the development of suspects. For some crimes, however, ascertaining motive can be difficult. For instance, murder is generally committed for a variety of reasons; therefore, in any treatment of criminal investigation, it is necessary to expand on the motivation a perpetrator might have had for committing the crime. Despite the fact that it can often be the key to the solution of crimes, motive is seldom treated in criminal investigation texts, except with regard to the informant looking for monetary or other compensation from the police.

There are two kinds of motive: general and specific. A general motive is one that applies to most—if not all—offenders; for example, the burglar or robber looking for profit with the least effort. A specific motive is one that relates the offender to the victim or object of the crime, which has been selected for a specific reason. An example might be the owner of a business who has lost customers to a competitor and "arranges" to burn down the rival's building.

With a specific motive established, a list of potential suspects can be compiled through the process of deduction. Using this as the generalization, the particulars (a list of individuals perceived to have such a motive) can be compiled. The list may then be shortened by determining who had the opportunity with respect to time and place, and who possessed the temperament to commit the crime or arrange for its commission. Although motive is not an element that must be proved in court, juries generally feel more comfortable about convicting a defendant who can be shown to have one. Consequently, establishing a particularized motive has both investigative and probative significance.

Without a particularized motive, the investigation of crimes having a universal motive (for example, rape and robbery) is rendered more difficult. A compensation, however, is the fact that these crimes often have an eyewitness. Except in cases of date rape, this is apt to be more useful in proving guilt than in identifying and apprehending the perpetrator.

This section emphasizes investigative activities that point to likely suspects, to the honing of any list developed, and to the search for additional evidence. Depending on what any new evidence supports or fails to support, the original hypothesis regarding the suspect(s) is either enhanced, downgraded, or rejected. Considerably more space is allotted to homicide than to other crimes because:

1.   It has a greater impact on a community than does any other felony; the public expects this crime to be handled competently and expeditiously.

2.   It is the ultimate challenge to an investigator, demanding the highest professional standards if the case is to be proved in court.

3.   Success in solving homicide requires familiarity with all possible investigative moves; each new development calls for an evaluation of the next step to be taken.

4.   The skills acquired in solving a homicide can serve well when applied to other crimes.

CHAPTER 13

MANAGING CRIMINAL INVESTIGATIONS

INTRODUCTION

Management of the criminal investigation function generally involves two components: the first being the direct investigation of criminal activity, and the second being the administrative management of an investigative unit. Direct investigation includes those cases handled by one or more investigators, usually with minimal supervision or oversight. In more complex investigations that involve numerous investigators and specialists, a supervisor may oversee and guide the investigation. Administrative management may fall under the direction of the Chief of Detectives, the head of a division, such as the Forensics unit, or divisional units in large police departments, and may include:

- Selection and training of investigators

- Reports and records

- Resource allocation

- Personnel supervision and management

- Crime analysis (which in some agencies is handled by another unit at the department level)

- Assessments of effectiveness

- Handling of citizen complaints and external inquiries

- Fostering research

Traditionally, the investigative division within a medium- or large-size police department, as well as within federal agencies, is organized with subunits or squads—such as homicide and serious assaults, sex crimes, robbery, burglary, automobile theft, missing persons, and general assignment units. In federal agencies, other specialized units are usually designated to handle certain types of crimes. In smaller departments, the divisions are usually identified as for crimes against property and crimes against persons.

One of the more troubling aspects of law enforcement administration is the friction that frequently exists between units (e.g., patrol versus detective) and a lack of cooperation between local and federal investigators, and between federal agencies. Since the events of September 11, 2001, a major reorganization at the federal level and efforts to increase cooperation at all levels has resulted in some successes, but much still needs to be done. Patrol officers continue to refer to detectives euphemistically as the "brains" or the "suits."

Friction and the lack of cooperation between different units and agencies is a major impediment to successful investigations. Failures by the patrol force or other first responders to protect a crime scene, handle witnesses, or file incomplete reports may well determine whether a case is solved.

Participation of investigative units in research on specific issues related to crime and its investigation has become more commonplace. Of particular interest is the desire to test long-held suppositions, practices, and methods. Much of this research has been on confessions, the use of DNA, and erroneous practices.[1]

HISTORICAL ANTECEDENTS

When drafting the Constitution, the Founding Fathers delegated law enforcement to the states. The primary reason was historic—rooted in the age-old abuses of police power by monarchs. Charles Dickens details in *A Tale of Two Cities* the abuses of a bad king: how Louis XVI's arbitrary, spiteful use of the *lettre de cachet* and many another corrupt practice contributed to the French Revolution. The language of the Declaration of Independence summarizes George III's own "long train of continued abuses" that ultimately led American colonists to revolution before winning the right to frame a written constitution.

Another reason the founders delegated law enforcement to the states, rather than nationalizing it, was pragmatic. Crime was local in nature; few colonists had the transportation, time, or opportunity to move from settlement to settlement. When adopting the Constitution, therefore, they drafted the Tenth Amendment to reserve law enforcement for the individual states. Each state in turn enacted penal laws and gave over the enforcement and prosecution of them to its counties and subdivisions. Over the years there has been an erosion of local control as the U.S. Congress has increased the jurisdiction of various crimes to federal law enforcement, largely as a result of growth in travel, communications, and public sentiment.

Much of the research on criminal investigation begins with the so-called RAND Reports on the criminal investigation process in the 1970s by Chaiken, Greenwood, and Petersilia, which focused on detective productivity, and where it was found that "less than half of all reported serious crimes receive 'any serious consideration by an investigator.'"[2]

CONVENTIONAL INVESTIGATIVE ARRANGEMENTS

It was not until the nineteenth century that police departments were formally organized in this country, appearing first in the major cities. Before long, the need for an investigative arm was recognized and, slowly, detective bureaus were established. Personnel selection was based partly on political considerations, or friendship—often that of the police chief. This practice has continued; even today in too many jurisdictions "clout" is a prerequisite to appointment as detective.

Bad practice, however, can evoke unintended consequences. This policy divided the force into separate camps—uniformed and detective. Excluded from what was perceived to be the most interesting aspect of "the job"—solving crime—the contribution of the uniformed officer was lost to what should have been a cooperative effort. In addition, the somewhat relaxed, sometimes nonexistent supervision that became the detective's lot caused a welling of animosity and envy. In New York City, it was not uncommon for a uniformed officer, assigned to safeguard a crime scene until detectives arrived, to comment: "Well, here come the brains." Over time, detective bureaus tended to become insulated from the department, building their own power bases among judges, prosecutors, and politicians. This state of affairs is described by a former head of the New York City Police, Patrick V. Murphy, in *Commissioner* in which Murphy relates how carefully he had to tread when attempting to effect change in the detective bureau.[3]

Detective bureaus have customarily been organized as follows: As specialists, detectives handle particular crimes (for example, homicide, automobile theft, burglary); as generalists, they handle any kind of case as reported. Specialization also can be based on a categorization of offenses into crimes against the person and crimes against property. Detectives may be assigned to central headquarters (likely in small departments), to local precincts or districts, or to the two in combination. Specialized squads are generally at central headquarters. Detectives handling run-of-the-mill cases usually work out of precincts or districts and call on specialists for cases judged to be important. If the victim is a prominent person or the crime promises to attract media attention, it is termed "heavy." Whether or not a detective "caught a heavy one," they still "caught all squeals" (New York jargon for cases reported during their tour of duty). Although this results in an uneven distribution of work, it is often tolerated in the belief that things average out in the long run. From a management view, however, it is an unsatisfactory division of labor.

Crime in the streets has been a major campaign issue in United States elections over the years. The election of Lyndon Johnson in 1967 resulted in a flood of federal money to improve law enforcement. Funds were used in various ways. Most promising from the perspective of this chapter was the emphasis on higher education for police officers and the beginning of professionalized law enforcement. Today, virtually all police agencies are headed by individuals with college degrees, and the percentage of all personnel with a college education has increased significantly. These professionals have learned the value of and the need for empirical research; they were taught to have an open mind when attempting to translate the results into practice. A significant outcome of federally funded research into improving the criminal investigative function is described in the next section.

MANAGING CRIMINAL INVESTIGATIONS (MCI)

In the literature of the field, a collection of empirically tested suggestions for improving the investigative process emerged in the 1970s and 1980s and was known as MCI or *Managing Criminal Investigations*.[4] The MCI model was based upon four measurable criteria:

1. Number of arrests
2. Number of cases cleared (one arrest may clear many crimes; several arrests may clear but a single crime)
3. Number of convictions
4. Number of cases accepted for prosecution

The first two considerations are fundamental to the control of criminal investigation by today's police administrators; they are the responsibility of the detective and police supervisors. The third involves the jury, judge, and especially the prosecutor. The fourth depends on the standards set by the prosecutor, the results of Appellate and Supreme Court decisions and the ability of the detective to meet them. To some degree, the performance of a detective can affect the outcome of all four.

The Elements of Managing Criminal Investigations (MCI)

Five elements are viewed as significant in the management of criminal investigations: (1) the initial investigation; (2) case screening; (3) management of the ongoing investigation, (4) police–prosecutor relations; and (5) continuous monitoring of the investigative process.

Five Elements of MCI

1. The initial investigation
2. Case screening
3. Management of the ongoing investigation
4. Police – prosecutor relations
5. Continuous monitoring of the investigative process

The Initial Investigation

There is a major difference between traditional investigation efforts and the management of the investigative function. Greater responsibility for the initial investigation has been delegated to the patrol officer responding to the radio call. The aim is to have the uniformed officer obtain all the information available at the crime scene, so that this task need not be repeated should a detective be assigned to continue it. There are, however, implications of this procedural change that are overlooked in the literature. For instance, the patrol force needs in-depth training in the recognition and preservation of physical evidence at the crime scene. If moved, trampled, or touched, the investigative and probative value of such evidence can be greatly diminished or even destroyed in certain situations. In many departments, the use of Crime Scene Units has been implemented to handle specific felony cases.

Case Screening

Case screening is used to determine whether a case should be followed-up on because it appears to be unsolvable or to recommend further investigation. Experience clearly demonstrates that every case is not solvable at the outset, but using data from cases that were successfully investigated, empirical research has identified "solvability" factors. The presence of these factors suggests that a solution is possible if the case is pursued further. Those factors deemed significant are:

- Is there a witness to the crime?
- Is a suspect named?
- Can a suspect be described?
- Can a suspect be located?
- Can a suspect vehicle be identified?

- Is stolen property traceable?

- Is physical evidence present?

- Is there a distinguishable *modus operandi* (MO)?

A negative answer to all or most of these questions constitutes grounds for closing a case. If these factors are present, their quality and number must be evaluated. For this purpose, in some departments a weighting system has been developed for some crimes.[5]

Should the sum of the weighted factors in a particular case equal or exceed a specified value, additional investigation is advised. In many departments, an experienced supervisor will review the initial recommendation. If the closing of a serious case is recommended, the case is reevaluated by another supervisor. The case screening process removes cases from the workload, thus making resources available for those holding greater promise of solution. This approach also creates more time for detectives to prepare for their court testimony in cases accepted for prosecution.

Where a decision is made not to pursue an investigation the complainant should be informed that the evidence does not justify further efforts at the time, and if further information or evidence becomes available the case may be reopened. In either event, the complainant should be instructed to report to the police any additional information that may subsequently be discovered from neighbors, later recollection, or other sources. Depending on the importance of the information, a case may be reopened, and given the increasing ability to use analytical technology to "link" crimes, the case may be pursued in the future.

Management of the Continuing Investigation

Under traditional arrangements, a detective "caught" cases by chance. This means that the individual on duty was responsible for all cases that came in and for deciding which to pursue and which to "set aside," or keep in a personal file, off the official record, as warranting no further effort. This practice has many shortcomings. One is that caseloads are uneven because they are dependent on the day of the week that the tour of duty happens to fall (weekends are the heaviest). Another shortcoming is the inefficient use of special talent. This becomes obvious when a good burglary investigator catches a sex crime, and a good sex crime investigator is assigned to a burglary. An added shortcoming is the lack of continuity resulting when a detective keeps an investigation "secret" and is unavailable for an unexpected development when he or she is off-duty. Another flaw is the fact that a detective determines the size and nature of the workload, has little accountability, and operates in an atmosphere of low visibility.

Management of the investigative function focuses on eliminating these shortcomings by establishing administrative controls and organizing investigative resources more effectively. The former may be accomplished through perceptive supervision, case review, and reporting; the latter by turning to the specialist/centralized model (while preserving its advantages and minimizing its disadvantages). The expansion of the role of the patrol officer and crime scene technician is pivotal, as is the expectation of better communication between officers and detectives.

However, recent research indicates that "detective work has remained essentially unchanged during the three decades since 'Rand's landmark study of detectives conducted during the 1970s.'"[6]

To organize resources more effectively in selected categories of cases, modern management places greater responsibility on the patrol force, especially in relatively minor cases that are not likely to be handled by an investigator. This approach develops a pool of talent that can be identified in the patrol force when career advancement opportunities arise.

Police–Prosecutor Relations

The traditional practice in the criminal justice system has been for each segment to act independently with little concern for other component parts. For instance, the police seldom talk to—much less exchange ideas and opinions with—corrections officials, judges, or prosecutors. Many uniformed officers and detectives hold the view that they have an adversarial relationship with the prosecutor's office. Effective management emphasizes mutual cooperation and understanding. Thus, the prosecutor evaluates and marshals police evidence before initiating criminal proceedings to determine if the office standards for charging, indicting, and convicting an offender have been met. If they have not, the prosecutor should explain what must be done to meet those standards.

With the goals of cooperation and understanding in mind, MCI outlines five essential steps:

1. Increased consultation between executives of the agencies;

2. Increased cooperation among supervisory personnel of the agencies;

3. The use of liaison officers to communicate to police personnel the investigatory techniques and evidence standards that the prosecutor requires to file a case;

4. Improved case preparation procedures, including the use of forms and checklists;

5. Developing a system of formal and informal feedback to the police on case dispositions (dismissal, continuance, or other outcome of court action).

Improved relations depend not only on a firm commitment by both police and prosecutors, but also on common sense, a willingness to learn through trial and error, and training.

Investigative Monitoring System

A case monitoring system is set up to give administrators continuous feedback on the investigative process and the quality of personnel performance. The monitoring might focus on the percentage of cases assigned for continuing investigation, and whether the interval between assignment and case closure has changed (a reduction being desirable). If sufficiently detailed, the system will identify problems and facilitate the development of remedies. With respect to personnel performance, monitoring can be put to use in building a profile of each detective's abilities, assessing productivity, and identifying any need for retraining.

Monitoring, whether of the investigatory process or its individual members, presents difficulties not readily perceived. A basic one evolves because the systematic assessment of quantitative data requires intellectual skills that differ from those acquired through traditional investigative experience.

Cold-Case Investigations

In recent years, greater emphasis has been placed on so-called cold-case investigations that involve reopening old cases, usually murder, missing persons, and sex crimes. In a number of police departments cold-case squads have been established and staffed with seasoned investigators. The New Haven Police Department in Connecticut, for example, hired a number of retired detectives as consultants to assist on cold-case investigations.

The cold-case methodology usually begins with a systematic review of all records, both official and from the public sector (newspapers, television news videos), and the establishment of a computerized database organized by subject areas, such as victim, witnesses, suspects, crime scene information and photos, physical evidence and forensics reports, and other background information. This analysis enables the preparation of sophisticated linking diagrams, time series analysis, and mapping or geospatial presentations.

From this point investigators generally move to interviews or to following up on leads that may not have been apparent during the initial investigation. Although there is always the likelihood that over time people may forget or remember facts in a different way, there is also the possibility that individuals feel less threatened over time, or may come forward with new information that was not initially reported.

Potential Benefits of MCI

The MCI model represented an important change in the investigation of crime. It has evolved over the years, largely as a result of improved technology and the introduction of more modern management techniques. Among the benefits of the program have been:

1. An increase in productivity through the better use of available resources or through tangible rewards for superior performance.

2. Reallocation of the resources made available through case screening to other endeavors, such as:
    a. Proactive investigations—aiming investigative efforts at those notorious criminals whose activities contribute disproportionately to the totality of crime in the community.
    b. Formation of Task Force Units to address specific, transitory crime problems.
    c. Better preparation of cases submitted to the prosecutor.

3. Rejection of favoritism as the basis for the selection of detectives. Utilizing the pool of talent recognized in the patrol force through monitoring, i.e., patrol officers adept in handling initial investigations. By selecting those who have demonstrated competence, it is likely that more cases will be handled and solved in a professional manner.

4. Better educated and trained investigators.

Human Resources

Historically investigators have been drawn from the patrol force in police departments, usually based on examinations or direct selection by administrators. Often their movement into investigation has been based on their arrest records as patrol officers and their educational background.

Although this model is not without merit, there has been an increasing emphasis on the need for specialists, particularly in the areas of crime analysis, sex crimes, fraud, crime scene investigation, and counter-terrorism. The trend, therefore, appears to be moving toward a focus on individuals with special skills. In response, many universities have implemented more specialized curricula within criminal justice programs and other departments. Some of these programs include majors or minors in fraud investigation, forensics, computer science, arson investigation, national and homeland security, and forensic accounting. Many investigative positions are now being held by civilians or police officers with these types of skills.

One of the fastest growing areas has been cybersecurity, which is also one of the fastest-growing fields at the federal level. At the state and local level, the number of crime analysts and positions in computer technology has also seen rapid growth.[7]

The lack of qualified personnel has prompted the federal government to support educational programs as a national strategy. The national Initiative for Cybersecurity Education (NICE) is charged with increasing and improving overall cybersecurity.[8] Increased emphasis on training present and future investigators is also a major priority, according to Dr. John DeCarlo, a former Chief of Police in Connecticut, and currently an Associate Professor at the University of New Haven.

As noted earlier in the text, the days of "pounding shoe leather" as the primary methodology for investigations has given way to technology and crime analysis. CompStat and Real-Time Crime Centers are but two relatively new approaches in the area of criminal investigation.

COMPSTAT AND REAL-TIME CRIME CENTERS

The introduction of CompStat in the early 1990s in the New York City Police Department, under the direction of then–Police Commissioner William J. Bratton, brought a quantitative approach to measuring effectiveness in policing, and more recently has come to include criminal investigation units.[9]

Essentially, CompStat "is a management process through which the NYPD identifies problems and measures the results of its problem solving activities."[10] Eventually, the CompStat model expanded to include a number of other programs, such as SATCOM (Strategic and Tactical Command), which combined and integrated various databases on career criminals. This model proved especially helpful to investigators in handling cases involving gangs and drug activity.

As CompStat has morphed into a range of programs in other police departments, the concept of utilizing statistical and geospatial models has had an impact on the management of the criminal investigation function. Today, with the introduction of a new generation of software, sophisticated databases, and linking and mapping programs, the investigation of crime has taken new forms.

Ultimately, though, the success of a criminal investigation depends largely on the ability of investigators, their expertise, and the ability to bring to the fore the personal and support tools necessary to effective case management. In this regard, the individual characteristics of an investigator's psychological makeup and training are critical. The concept of *predictive policing*, developed in the Los Angeles Police Department under former Chief William Bratton and Captain Sean Malinowski, has shown great promise as an investigative tool that complements the CompStat model. Predictive policing is a technological concept designed to assist investigators by using analytical, temporal, and geospatial data to identify suspects, trends, and patterns of crime. "Real-Time Crime" centers, such as those in Los Angeles and New York, are designed to provide on-the-spot information to field personnel. These centers draw upon a broad range of databases and records systems to assist patrol and investigative units. They may include, in addition to police and federal databases, motor vehicle driver and registration records; medical facility records; housing and real estate records; utility company records; and license application records.

Relatively routine investigations represent the vast majority of cases in the criminal justice process, and are no less important than complex investigations. In such cases, the investigator will determine the investigative strategy and course of action; request specialist assistance, such as crime scene and laboratory units; interview witnesses and suspects; make arrests; and present the case to a prosecutor. The vast majority of these cases, if handled properly, result in plea bargaining and a conviction.

Figure 13.1
Officers work in the New York City Police Department's Real-Time Crime Center at Police Headquarters. The program provides instant access to computerized records and live feeds from a growing number of surveillance cameras to keep an eye on high-crime neighborhoods.

Complex investigations, on the other hand, are more likely to involve numerous investigators, specialists directly (such as forensic accountants, laboratory personnel, or surveillance assistance), and other criminal justice personnel (such as prosecutors, computer technicians, or undercover personnel). These investigations may also involve other law enforcement agencies, multiple jurisdictions, and administrative oversight, and may operate over lengthy periods of time. Such cases are frequently brought before a grand jury prior to an arrest, and will also involve heightened media attention.

In preparing and carrying out an investigation, it is important to understand one's own strengths and weaknesses. The following section addresses some of the psychological aspects of crime investigation.

THE PSYCHOLOGY OF CRIME INVESTIGATION

The term *mind-set* is frequently used to explain the posture an investigator must take to avoid jumping to conclusions; formulating opinions based on prior experience or actions of witnesses or suspects; or just plain biases. At the outset it is important to recognize that it is virtually impossible in any situation to avoid speculating or formulating conclusions based on the information at hand. For example, most people, when they first meet someone, make conscious or subconscious decisions about the individual based on a number of variables, such as dress, speech, personality, body language, or the observations of others. How often do you conclude that you like or dislike someone at first, only to change your mind later as you get to know the person? Or, in sizing up something by observation, such as viewing a photograph or picture, how frequently do you find that another person has a different perception of what they see?

Perhaps the biggest problem an investigator faces is in understanding their personal psychological makeup. We all bring to any situation our own beliefs, experiences, morality, and ethical standards based upon a great many factors. These may include upbringing (relationships with family), education, training, motivation, and personal goals. Most people in the United States also bring the history of another culture, usually through grandparents or parents, which can also influence our beliefs. Americans also tend to be competitive by nature, with a strong desire to succeed. Much has been written about the psychology of police officers and why individuals choose this career over another.

The desire to become an investigator may be based on any number of reasons, such as: serving the community, prestige, money, or the satisfaction of "breaking" a case. There are both positive and negative motives, the most important factor being one's personal understanding of one's own motivation and personality. It is important to recognize one's own strengths and weaknesses, as well as one's personal likes, dislikes, and biases. Why is one investigator more successful than another? What does the phrase "top-notch investigator" really mean? How should an investigator be evaluated—on the basis of cases solved, arrests, indictments, convictions, or innocent persons freed? In most investigative units, success is measured by cases solved by arrest, but a great many other variables come into play, not the least of which are the difficulties associated with solving a case. Nevertheless, in most investigative units, supervisors and other members of the unit do have perceptions about who are the best investigators—frequently formed from a personal perspective, seeing others as more or less effective than themselves.

U.S. society glorifies "number one" in many aspects, especially when it can be quantified in some way—the number of wins in sports, the number of successful operations in medicine, the highest grade point average in education, and so on. This emphasis on competition can prove to be disastrous when it comes to the investigation of crime, particularly when the pressure is on an investigator to solve a case.

Social-Psychological Issues

An individual's personality is based on a great many factors that, according to some experts, begin shortly after conception. There are several stages in a person's life cycle that influence behavior. Very few youngsters grow up with the desire to be a criminal investigator (notwithstanding a child's early desire to be a police officer or a firefighter), but an early emphasis on the desire to learn about many things—usually through reading and observing—sets the stage for an inquisitive life. Research has shown that "experts-in-training keep their mind's box open all the time, so that they can inspect, criticize and augment its contents and thereby approach the standards set by leaders in their fields."[11]

The making of an expert investigator is no simple matter and, as the psychologist Herbert Simon has noted, "The 10 year rule states that it takes approximately a decade of heavy labor to master any field."[12] The skills associated with criminal investigation involve a great many attributes, tied in no small measure to one's physical and mental processes.

Cognition

Cognition is the process of acquiring knowledge by the use of reasoning, intuition, or perception. In some cases, we learn by doing or observing (experience), and in others through training, education, and reading (learning). The phrase, "it may not be as it seems," is particularly true in a criminal investigation. Our cognitive ability can be developed over time, but it is also important to recognize that our observations can be in error. Subconscious thought is usually based on prior experiences or visual "implants," as well as on what we consider statistical inferences. For instance, a conclusion that a spouse committed a murder may be based on the knowledge that in most cases involving the murder of a husband or wife, the crime was committed by the spouse.

Developing cognitive ability is important because it reduces the tendency to jump to conclusions, and helps one to recognize the necessity of weighing all of the facts in a case. What appears to be a suicide may be tested by observation: did a left-handed man shoot himself with the pistol in his right hand? Is the direction of a stab wound consistent with the suspect's height or whether the person is right- or left-handed?

Personality

Ego defense mechanisms, from a psychoanalytic perspective, are subconscious parts of an individual's personality, and they frequently play a role in behavior. The psychological and psychiatric literature refer to the concepts of the id (which forms instinctual behavior), the superego (defined as one's conscience, or perceptions of right and wrong), and the ego (which operates to protect the "self" from perceived threats or in reaction to stress). An understanding of defense mechanisms is important for an investigator because of the various pressures that frequently occur during an investigation. Examples may involve pressure to solve the case, a desire not to lose "face" in front of a suspect or interviewee, or perhaps the threat of force or retaliation by a suspect. It is not uncommon for a person being interviewed to say, "I'll have your job" when they feel threatened, or as a means of putting the investigator "on guard."

In most cases, these are idle threats, but they may influence the investigator's behavior and reasoning. This is especially true in cases in which an individual is short-tempered or perhaps subconsciously afraid of losing control of the interview. The investigator should recognize that just as he or she is "sizing" up a suspect, the suspect is also doing the same thing of the investigator. When a suspect is able to shift the line of questioning by guile, lying, or threatening behavior, it can influence the outcome of the interview. By the same token, a suspect may use a variety of other techniques, such as playing to the investigator's self-esteem ("I know you'll believe me because you are smart.") or character ("Look, we both come from the same background.") In some cases, the suspect may attempt to antagonize the investigator in order to make him or her use force or lose control. Such actions may later be used by the defense in arguing that a statement or confession was coerced.

Composure is a critical aspect of personality, and the seasoned investigator will recognize the so-called "hot buttons" that may distract him or her from concentrating on the critical elements of the case. This is why the investigator should be familiar with his or her own personality traits. To respond appropriately, a person only needs to review instances in which he or she was embarrassed, ridiculed, said something they didn't really mean, or lost control.

Observation

Seeing is believing. Or is it? Developing one's powers of observation frequently involves going beyond what we see at first glance, or being able to analyze a crime scene by identifying clues that are not visible to the casual observer. The position of a body, blood splatters, the presence of trace evidence (frequently not visible to the naked eye), the condition of the suspect, the "movement" that took place at a crime scene, and objects that are out of place may all be important, but they are of no value unless they are observed, and preferably recorded.

Like other physical characteristics, the power of observation can be improved with practice. Research indicates that we tend to be more observant of things that we like or dislike. We go through life viewing a great many things each day, but most of what we see goes unrecorded in our minds, lost in a myriad of inconsequential images.

Visual clues, such as body language, persons "out of place," the placement of vehicles or furniture, the contents of a wallet or a suspect's pockets, or the "arrangement" of a crime scene provide the investigator with information that may prove important later. Nevertheless, research indicates that most people's recollections of visual images are poor and frequently inaccurate.

CONCLUSION

The management of a criminal investigation, from the administrative and supervisory level to the investigator, as viewed in this chapter, is generally thought of as a routine matter, with the exception of major cases. In this case, "routine" is a much-maligned term because there is much that goes on that many investigators take for granted. Whether a case is solved or unsolved, a large number of decision points may come into play. A so-called simple burglary, or any felony, for that matter, begins with a reported or "discovered" crime and progresses through a series of actions usually based on what are termed "best practices." However, research on the investigative function has shown that many of the best practices of the past have given way to new techniques, new technology, and new procedures (many of them dictated by court decisions). In some departments, case loads have increased, or so-called "crime waves," such as an increase in homicides, have compelled administrators to reassign or restructure the investigative unit to address public and media pressure. This may be understandable, but it also emphasizes the importance of managing investigations and the investigative process, challenging the term "routine."

The following chapters address the methodology, legal implications, and evidentiary issues in a criminal investigation, and are followed by chapters on the more serious types of crime facing the investigator.

NOTES

1   Some examples include research in Texas on arson investigation; research by David Schroeder at the University of New Haven on DNA and crime investigation; and the National Academy of Sciences Report on Forensic Laboratories.

2   Chaiken, J.M., P.W. Greenwood, and J. Petersilia. *The Criminal Investigation Process: A Summary Report*. Rand Corporation, Santa Monica. (1976). Cited in: John J. Liederbach, Eric J. Fritsch, Charissa I. Womack. "Detective Workload and Opportunities for Increased Productivity in Criminal Investigations." *Police Practice and Research: An International Journal*. (Routledge: Taylor & Francis.) Volume 12, Number 1. February 2011, p. 50.

3   Murphy, Patrick V, *Commissioner*, New York, Simon and Schuster, 1977.

4   Peter W. Greenwood and Joan Petersilia, *The Criminal Investigation Process*, Vol. I, *Summary and Policy Implications*, Vol. III: *Observations and Analysis* (Santa Monica, CA: RAND, 1976); Ilene Greenberg and Robert Wasserman, *Managing Criminal Investigations* (Washington, DC: U.S. Government Printing Office, 1979); John E. Eck, *Solving Crimes: The Investigation of Burglary and Robbery* (Washington, DC: Police Executive Research Forum, 1983); Peter B. Bloch and Donald R. Weidman, *Managing Criminal Investigations* (Washington, DC: U.S. Government Printing Office, U.S. Department of Justice, 1975).

5   Eck, loc. cit.

6   John J. Liederbach, Eric J. Fritsch, Charissa I. Womack. "Detective Workload and Opportunities for Increased Productivity in Criminal Investigations." *Police Practice and Research: An International Journal*. (Routledge: Taylor & Francis.) Volume 12, Number 1. February 2011, p. 50.

7   According to one report, "The annual federal government information security market is expected to grow from $9.2 billion in 2011 to $14 billion in 2016…Spending by defense agencies is expected to grow from $4.4 billion in 2011 to $6.7 billion in 2016. Intelligence agency spending is expected to grow from $2.3 billion to $3.6 billion." Source: *Security Management*, June, 2012.

8   John Wagley. "Developing a Cybersecurity Staff." *Security Management.* June, 2012. Pp. 70–74.

9   Eli B. Silverman, *NYPD Battles Crime: Innovative Strategies in Policing* (Boston: Northeastern University Press, 1999), 97 99.

10   Vincent Henry, *The CompStat Paradigm: Management Accountability in Policing, Business and the Public Sector* (New York: Looseleaf Law, 2002), 5.

11   Philip F. Ross, "The Expert Mind: Studies of the Mental Processes of Chess Grandmasters Have Revealed Clues to How People Become Experts in Other Fields as Well." *Scientific American*, August 2006, 70.

12   Ibid., 69.

DISCUSSION QUESTIONS

1.   What are the two components of managing an investigations unit?
2.   According to the text, what is one of the most troublesome aspects of successful investigations?
3.   According to some researchers, what role should the patrol force play in criminal investigations?
4.   What is the role of the prosecutor in a criminal case?
5.   What is a case monitoring system?
6.   What is a "cold-case" investigation?
7.   What is CompStat?

SUPPLEMENTAL READINGS

Brown, M. F. (2001). *Criminal investigation: Law and practice* (2nd ed.). Boston: Elsevier/Butterworth-Heinemann.

Green, E., Lynch, R. G., & Lynch, S. R. (2013). *The police manager.* Boston: Elsevier/Anderson Publishing.

Jetmore, L. F. (2008). *Path of the hunter: Entering and excelling in the field of criminal investigation.* Flushing, NY: Looseleaf Law.

Kania, R. R. E. (2012). *Managing criminal justice organizations: An introduction to theory and practice* (2nd ed.). Boston: Elsevier/Anderson Publishing.

Thurman, Q. C., & Jamieson, J. D. (2004). *Police problem solving.* Newark, NJ: LexisNexis Matthew Bender.

CHAPTER 14

RECONSTRUCTING THE PAST
Methods, Evidence, Examples

METHODS OF INQUIRY

It brings insight to divide the principal methods of inquiry into two broad, distinct categories: those that reconstruct the past and those that discover or create new knowledge. The first is the method of the historian, archeologist, epidemiologist, journalist, and criminal investigator; the second, that of the scientist in general (as well as the creative artist). Although usefully stated as a dichotomy for the sake of a conceptual distinction, these methods finally fuse in the minds of the better thinkers and practitioners, for the reconstruction of the past often makes use of the scientific method, while science and art build on and digress from the past. Further reflection suggests that any thorough inquiry employs techniques common to both. This certainly applies to the best practice in criminal investigation. Disciplines as diverse as geology, physical geography, physical anthropology, forensic medicine, statistics, computer technology, and criminalistics can make a contribution. Indeed, the discrete methods they employ may be seen as a continuum, with the ideal drawing on history, science, and art in varying proportions depending on the subject under probe. Therefore, just as the model investigation must utilize both principal methods of inquiry, so must the model investigator. This is not to say that a unique investigative technique may not be developed to deal with a specific problem, and be helpful with others as well. For testing the authenticity of a confession, for example, the tools of psycholinguistics could be put to use. That they have not been put to use thus far indicates the wide range of resources yet to be tapped by criminal investigators.

More than 30 years ago, the sociologist W.B. Sanders[1] and the historian Robin Winks[2] saw the relationships between their fields and the field of criminal investigation. They see the parallels between the ivory-towered inquirer and society's more familiar figure, the detective: both study human behavior and both employ information-gathering practices such as interviews and observations. Sanders recognizes that the sociologist can learn from the detective, among other things, how to combine several methods of inquiry (or research) and sources of information (or data) into a single inquiry. Winks's selection of essays by writers and historians reveals how scholars penetrate rumors, forgeries, false accounts, and misleading clues to unravel old mysteries. Not only do the essays "point up the elements of evidence within them to emphasize leads and clues, straight tips, false rumors, and the mischief wrought by time," they demonstrate that the historian and detective are on common ground when confronting the techniques and pitfalls of dealing with evidence.[3]

> The historian must collect, interpret, and then explain his evidence by methods which are not greatly different from those techniques employed by the detective, or at least the detective of fiction. ... Perhaps the real detective trusts more to luck, or to gadgetry, or to informers than does

the fictional hero. … Much of the historian's work then, like that of the insurance investigator, the fingerprint man, or the coroner, may to the outsider seem to consist of deadening routine … yet the routine must be pursued or the clue may be missed, the apparently false trail must be followed in order to be certain it is false; the mute witnesses must be asked the reasons for their silence, for the piece of evidence that is missing from where one might reasonably expect to find it is, after all, a form of evidence itself. … We are all detectives, of course, in that at one time or another we all have had to engage in some genuine deductive routine. Each day we do so, if only in small ways. By the same token, we are all historians, in that we reconstruct past events from present evidence, and perhaps we build usable generalizations upon those reconstructions.[4]

Attention will now be turned to the scientific method; then to the means for reconstructing the past.

The Scientific Method

Evolving from the efforts of many workers over the course of several thousand years, the scientific method is a way of observing, thinking about, and solving problems objectively and systematically. As the prestigious nineteenth-century student of science Thomas Huxley emphasized, its use is not limited to scientists. A lesson Huxley learned early was "to make things clear," and his easy, plain-talking style in the opening paragraphs of this piece serves well as an introduction to the scientific method.

The method of scientific investigation is nothing but the expression of the necessary mode of working of the human mind. It is simply the mode by which all phenomena are reasoned about, rendered precise and exact. There is no more difference, but there is just the same kind of difference, between the mental operations of a man of science and those of an ordinary person, as there is between the operations and methods of a baker or of a butcher weighing out his goods in common scales, and the operations of a chemist in performing a difficult and complex analysis by means of his balance and finely graduated weights. It is not that the action of the scales in the one case, and the balance in the other, differ in the principles of their construction or manner of working; but the beam of one is set on an infinitely finer axis than the other, and of course turns by the addition of a much smaller weight. You will understand this better, perhaps, if I give you some familiar example. You have all heard it repeated, I dare say, that men of science work by means of induction and deduction, and that by the help of these operations, they, in a sort of sense, wring from nature certain other things, which are called natural laws, and causes, and that out of these, by some cunning skill of their own, they build up hypotheses and theories. And it is imagined by many, that the operations of the common mind can be by no means compared with these processes, and that they have to be acquired by a sort of special apprenticeship to the craft. To hear all these large words, you would think that the mind of a man of science must be constituted differently from that of his fellow men; but if you will not be frightened by terms, you will discover that you are quite wrong, and that all these terrible apparatus are being used by yourselves every day and every hour of your lives.[5]

Definitions

Before proceeding to an example of the scientific method in criminal investigation, several terms require definition (see Box 14.1). They are: induction, deduction, classification, synthesis, analysis, hypothesis, theory, *a priori*, and *a posteriori*.

BOX 14.1 SOME KEY DEFINITIONS

Inductive Reasoning – The process of reasoning beginning with specific information to form a general conclusion.

Deduction – The process of reasoning that begins with a generalization and moves to a particular or specific conclusion (fact).

Classification – The systematic arrangement of objects into categories that have one or more traits in common.

Synthesis – The combining of separate parts or elements that lead toward a conclusion.

Analysis – Examines all information available in an effort to separate the data into relevant parts for further study.

Hypothesis – Forms the basis for an examination of information to form an assertion or tentative guess.

Theory – A scheme of thought with assumptions chosen to fit empirical knowledge or observations.

A priori – Deductive or theoretical reasoning based on cause and effect, where a conclusion is based on self-evident principles.

A posteriori – Inductive reasoning based on empirical facts acquired through experience or experimentation to form general principles.

Induction is a process of reasoning based on a set of experiences or observations (particulars) from which a conclusion or generalization is drawn. It commences with the specific and goes to the general. As to the result secured, however, care must be exercised. This warning is implicit in Huxley's "sour apple" lesson. For another illustration, consider the man who notes that of the 10 species of bird he has observed, all are able to fly. When he induces from this observation that all birds fly, he will be incorrect. Though not always recognized as such, the penguin is a bird. At one time, its short paddles covered with hard, close-set feathers served as wings. Now, it moves swiftly and gracefully through water, having over the eons become adapted to this medium; the penguin does not fly. The ostrich is another example of the fallacious conclusion that all birds fly. Induction, therefore, can lead to probabilities, not certainties. When integrated over a lifetime, however, inductive experience is an important component of the so-called common sense that supposedly governs human behavior.

Deduction is a process of reasoning that commences with a generalization or a premise and by means of careful, systematic thinking moves to a particular fact or consequence. For example, if one begins with the statement that "All persons convicted of a serious crime are felons" (the major premise), then adds the fact that "Jack was convicted of a serious crime" (the minor premise), that "Jack is a felon" (the conclusion) may be deduced. This is a syllogism, a form of deductive reasoning that moves from the general to the specific. If the original premise is valid, the logical consequences must be valid. In logic (the science of correct reasoning), deduction leads to certainties and not to probabilities; in criminal investigation, the generalization cannot be so precisely formulated as to always be relied upon as valid. Only in fiction is a Sherlock Holmes able, after a quick glance at the mud on the butler's shoe, to state unequivocally that it originated from but one meadow. In the real world, the criminal investigator cannot mouth certitudes while an awed partner (like Dr. Watson) stands by and accepts them on faith. Because of the illogical, often perverse quality of human behavior, deduction does not necessarily lead to certainty.

Classification is the systematic arrangement of objects into categories (groups or classes) based on shared traits or characteristics. The objects in each category, having one or more traits in common, are chosen to suit the classifier's purposes. They may be natural (in accord with the observed order of things), logical, or even purely arbitrary. The science of classification is called *taxonomy*. Biology has developed a taxonomy to classify organisms; chemistry, to analyze compounds; law enforcement, to file fingerprints, bullets, DNA, a wide range of typefaces, and automobile paints.

Synthesis is the combining of separate parts or elements. For purposes of criminal investigation, those elements that, when combined, provide a coherent view of the crime and its solution, are: the evidence provided by witnesses, forensic examinations, and the facts disclosed by records.

Analysis starts with the whole (whether a material substance, thought, or impression), and then involves an effort to separate the whole into its constituent parts for individual study. Hence, on being assigned to investigate a crime, the investigator seeks relevant information from three separate sources—people, records, and the physical evidence found at the crime scene.

A *hypothesis* is a conjecture that provisionally accounts for a set of facts. It can be used as the basis for additional investigation and as a guide for further activity. Because it is an assertion or tentative guess subject to verification, the pursuit of more evidence is required of the detective (or scientist). Along the way, the hypothesis may have to be adjusted, causing the investigation (or inquiry) to change direction depending on whether the original conjecture is substantiated or disproved as new facts are uncovered. As corroborating data accumulate and are analyzed, the hypothesis moves toward the next phase of proof—a theory.

A *theory* is a somewhat verified hypothesis, a scheme of thought with assumptions chosen to fit empirical knowledge or observations. As a theory becomes more solidly based and evidence accumulates, it evolves into a methodical organization of knowledge applicable to any number of situations. It should predict or otherwise explain the nature of a specified set of phenomena. The ultimate theory presents a grand conceptual scheme that both predicts and explains, while keeping assumptions as few and as general as possible. In science, the ultimate is often achieved; in criminal investigation, a less decisive "somewhat verified hypothesis" is the best that can be expected at the present time.

A priori (Latin for "from the previous cause") is defined: from a known or assumed cause to a necessarily related effect; from a general law to a particular instance; valid independently of observation. In some instances, *a priori* conclusions are reached through reasoning from assumed principles, which are regarded as self-evident. Thus, it is deductive and theoretical rather than based on experiment or experience.

A posteriori is a term denoting reasoning from empirical facts or particulars (acquired through experience or experiment) to general principles; or, from effects to causes. It is inductive.

Problem Identification

The first step in reconstructing the past or unraveling the mysteries of the universe is to identify the problem. What is the question? Although the techniques and methods for problem-solving have been systematized as the scientific method, the state of affairs regarding problem identification—namely, recognizing what it is, precisely—is less than satisfactory. Indeed, operational research, which is concerned with correctly stating the problem to be studied, was conceived of in England by scientist J.D. Bernal when he solved a problem submitted by the military during World War II. Informed that his solution did not work, Bernal investigated further only to find that, although he had solved the problem given him, it was not what was actually troubling the military. Painstakingly, he was obliged to reformulate and restate the problem for them before the solution could be applied.

Texts dealing with public relations reveal that problem identification is a major concern. It begins with an interview of the client to ascertain what the problem is believed to be. Then, a search of the literature is made to learn more about the apparent issues. Finally, there is an attempt to restate the problem. This procedure is the basis on which an effective public relations program can be developed.[6] Although problem identification is seldom the concern of the criminal investigator, the problem statement pertains to two situations in the criminal justice system. One occurs when a crime is committed on the borderline of two jurisdictions; the other, when it is difficult to determine what crime was committed. If it is a question of jurisdiction, an investigator may either seek to obtain the case, or convince the investigator working the other jurisdiction to accept it. The choice can depend on several factors: Is the case likely to be publicized? Is it inherently interesting or important? Is there a chance to make a "good arrest"? As to determining what crime was committed, this is usually quite simple because the elements of major crimes (burglary, robbery, murder, manslaughter, assault, rape, and arson) are well-known to the experienced investigator. However, the increasing use of computers, the Internet and social media have added a new dimension to criminal investigation that may well be less defined. This is further complicated by the fact that most criminal activity using computers or the Internet involves more than one jurisdiction, frequently making the activity a federal crime— where the federal government may have jurisdiction, or in some cases involving transnational criminality jurisdiction may be questionable. The advice of legal counsel is advisable, however, when the determination is a complicated one: Is it a case of extortion or third-degree robbery? In crimes involving consent, such as fraud, was consent granted or withheld? Does the mere scorching of the paint on a house, without fire, satisfy an element of arson? Or does an Internet threat amount to extortion?

SCIENTIFIC REASONING APPLIED TO A CRIMINAL INVESTIGATION

The use of the scientific method in criminal investigation is illustrated by the following situation, based on an actual case. A detective, called to the scene where a young woman had been murdered in her apartment, found the table set for two. There were melted-down candles, wine, supper still warm on the serving cart, and a radio softly playing. Finding no evidence of forced entry or struggle, the detective hypothesized that the woman admitted the killer into her home, probably as her dinner guest. In subsequent questioning of the victim's family, friends, and business associates, one name, that of her former lover, continually surfaced; indeed, several people indicated that his earlier behavior during a quarrel had been forgiven, and that this was to have been a reconciliation dinner.

The hypothesis that the killer was an invited guest is somewhat verified by the facts obtained through interviews. Needing additional information, however, the investigator must consider the following possibilities: Can the friend be located at his place of business, home, or other usual haunts? Is flight indicated? If so, is any clothing or other item such as razor or prized trophy missing? Did the suspect cash a large check or withdraw money from his bank the day of or on the morning following the homicide? If affirmative answers are obtained and applied inductively, the weight of evidence in support of the hypothesis is even greater. The former lover may now be considered the prime suspect (the generalization). An inductive result, however, is not necessarily a certainty: flight may be evidence of guilt, but it is not proof. The suspect could have innocently gone on a vacation at what would, in retrospect, have been an inopportune time. Assuming that information from relatives and friends has failed to trace him, the homicide investigator must now discover his whereabouts.

The next logical step in the investigative process is deduction. The characterization of the lover as the prime suspect (the generalization) leads to the question: "Where would he be likely to flee?" (answers to which are the particulars). Possible locations are suggested by such considerations as: Where was the suspect born? Had he lived for a time in some other area? Does he have a favorite vacation spot? With additional facts or details elicited, investigative activities will seek answers (again, particulars) to other questions, such as: What else might he do to earn a living? Who might he write or telephone? Will he try to collect his last pay check either by mail or other means? Will he continue to pay union dues? Will he change his driver's license? A sufficient amount of acquired and utilized facts (particulars) should allow the investigator to come to a generalization through the process of inductive reasoning.

The generalization about the likely whereabouts or location of the subject permits the investigator to deduce the particulars (such as addresses) needed to apprehend the suspect. Again, reasonable premises (e.g., that suspects will turn up at their usual haunts) may prove to be invalid because of the illogical, often perverse aspects of human behavior.

In summary, the cyclical process of scientific reasoning—moving from induction to deduction, and vice-versa—is applicable to criminal investigation as a means of reconstructing past events. A noted philosopher of science, Hans Reichenbach, recognized the similarities in the thought process shared by scientist and detective:

> I should like to mention the inferences made by a detective in his search for the perpetrator of a crime. Some data are given such as a blood-stained handkerchief, a chisel, and the disappearance of a wealthy dowager, and several explanations offer themselves for what has happened.
>
> The detective tries to determine the most probable explanation. His considerations follow established rules of probability; using all the factual clues and all his knowledge of human psychology, he attempts to arrive at conclusions, which in turn are tested by new observations specifically planned for this purpose. Each test, based on new material, increases or decreases the probability of the explanation; but never can the explanation constructed be regarded as absolutely certain.[7]

RECONSTRUCTING THE PAST: SOURCES OF INFORMATION

The information needed to reconstruct the past is available through three sources: people, physical evidence, and records. Historians' efforts to shed light on the distant past are largely confined to researching records. Art and epic poems (physical evidence) and folk tales (people) are also researched. Criminal investigators, more concerned with the immediate past, often put all three sources to use. Table 14.1 summarizes and compares the sources of the historian and the criminal investigator.

People

As long as general, specific, or intimate knowledge concerning an individual endures, it can be acquired by those who know how. People are social beings, and information on them can usually be found in the possession of family and relatives, work or business associates, and others who share their

Table 14.1
History and Criminal Investigation as Methods of Study of Past Events: Sources of Information Common to Both; Available Ancillary Disciplines

SOURCE OF INFORMATION		ANCILLARY DISCIPLINES AVAILABLE TO ASSIST IN THE STUDY OF A PAST EVENT	
HISTORY	CRIMINAL INVESTIGATION	HISTORY	CRIMINAL INVESTIGATION
PHYSICAL EVIDENCE		**PHYSICAL EVIDENCE**	
1. Fossils 2. Bones 3. Human remains	1. Impressions (finger, tool, tire, shoe) 2. Narcotics 3. Paint 4. Bullets 5. Blood 6. Flora	1. Paleontology 2. Geology 3. Zoology 4. Physical anthropology 5. Archeology	1. Criminalistics 2. Chemistry 3. Biology 4. Physics 5. Immunology 6. Botany
RECORDS AND DOCUMENTS		**RECORDS AND DOCUMENTS**	
1. Memoirs 2. Letters 3. Official documents 4. Manuscripts 5. Books 6. Paintings, other artwork 7. Coins 8. Epic poems	1. Fraudulent checks 2. Threatening notes 3. Kidnap letters 4. Miscellaneous documents	1. Paleography 2. Art history 3. Linguistics 4. Numismatics 5. Information theory—storage and retrieval	1. Criminalistics 2. Questioned document expertise 3. Photography
PEOPLE		**PEOPLE**	
1. Folklore 2. Cultural survivals	1. Victim 2. Eyewitnesses 3. Suspects 4. Others related to victim, suspects, and crime scene	1. Cultural anthropology 2. Ethnology	Techniques rather than disciplines are available. 1. Questioning 2. Surveillance 3. Use of Informants

recreational interests. It can also be picked up accidentally through those who were witness to, or the victim of, a crime. The careful investigator identifies and exploits all potential sources. Some people will talk willingly; some will be reluctant to disclose what they know. Investigators must learn how to overcome resistance and retrieve facts that were overlooked, forgotten, or thought not important enough to mention. Meanwhile, they must guard against deliberate distortions or attempts to mislead, thwarting such maneuvers through skillful questioning. Talking with people and unobtrusively observing them and the places they frequent may be useful. Tips or decisive information furnished by informants can also be significant in moving an investigation toward a conclusion.

Physical Evidence

Any object of a material nature is potential physical evidence. The scientific specialties that undertake most examinations of physical evidence are forensic medicine and criminalistics. Their purpose being the acquisition of facts, the following questions arise: What is this material? If found at a crime scene, can it be linked to, or help exonerate, a suspect? Can it be used to reconstruct what happened (especially when witnesses give conflicting accounts)? In a homicide, what was the cause of death?

In the conduct of everyday affairs, people employ physical evidence in decision making, but few note this fact. For example, when looking for a house they will examine the condition of the paint, plaster, and plumbing; determine its location relative to transportation, schools, and churches; then inspect the surrounding neighborhood. The ultimate decision is based to a large extent on this kind of evidence; indeed, it is the way many day-to-day decisions are made.

Records

Records are a form of physical evidence. They receive separate treatment in this text, however, because they are widely scattered, voluminous, and have specialists devoting full time to their storage and retrieval. Modern society relies on both paper and electronically stored records by amassing the information collected day in and day out. Later this can prove useful in a criminal investigation. For example, telephone company records of toll calls can establish that two people who deny any relationship had indeed been in communication. Records need not be printed or handwritten. They may be stored in digital form or on film or tape. One famous historic example is the White House tapes that provided the "smoking gun" evidence in the Watergate cover-up of the Nixon Administration.[8] This case clearly demonstrates the power of physical evidence over verbal testimony.

Innovative Applications

History and archeology are academic disciplines that reconstruct the past through information from people, physical evidence, and records. Some unusual investigative efforts employing classical techniques have gained attention in the press as well as in scholarly literature. They demonstrate that the means for reconstructing the remote past are applicable to the immediate past. Hence, criminal investigation is not unique; it shares the approaches sanctioned by scholars in established disciplines. The following examples will illustrate.

Industrial Archeology

Uncovering traces of an ancient civilization in a temple or amphitheater sounds more romantic than finding what remains of an old factory. Yet the classical techniques of archeology are now being used

> ... to discover and record how American industry moved from colonial cottages to the vast mechanized and automated complex it is today. Although the industrial revolution began in the U.S. only about 200 years ago, there already are tremendous gaps in the knowledge of how it occurred.

Records and artifacts of entire industrial processes, including some in use as recently as the 1920s, either have been lost or, often, were never made. And the machines and buildings that would give clues to how an industry evolved are rapidly being destroyed or buried by parking lots, housing developments and new factories. If Patterson (New Jersey) is any indication, American cities are being buried several times faster than ancient Troy; the archaeologists in Patterson found foundations barely a century old at depths of eight to twelve feet. ... It took over 5000 years for fifty feet of debris to build up over ancient Troy.[9]

Lest such behavior be thought of as that of a few eccentric archaeologists, it is significant to note that more than one university has set up an Institute of Industrial Archeology.[10]

Garbageology

Another contemporary form of archeology is *garbageology*, the "science of rubbish" or the study of garbage.[11] Discarded material can be revealing when analyzing present-day consumer trends. So too are the different facets of a family's shopping habits, better disclosed through the study of its trash than through buying surveys. There is, however, the issue of an individual's right to privacy, even though refuse left on a sidewalk is abandoned property and its removal not theft. The journalist who took five plastic bags of trash left in front of a celebrity's home unwittingly gave fresh meaning to Shakespeare's lines: "Who steals my purse steals trash; 'tis something, 'tis nothing," for Iago knows only too well that the trash will indeed "filch ... [his] good name."[12] Whether from contemporary rubbish or the ruins of antiquity, reconstructing the past can reveal how people live(d).

Theological Detective Work

Candidates for sainthood in the Catholic Church undergo an investigation that has been described as "theological detective work."[13] To be declared a saint, a candidate must "... have to be responsible for two miracles, specifically medical miracles."[14] Scrutinizing such candidates involves performing archival searches; sifting through diaries, poems, and letters; and interviewing people. Because an important goal is to find a stain on the candidate's character, theological detective work is akin (in the reverse sense) to criminal investigation wherein the protection of the innocent has an equal claim. As a process of inquiry, beatification is always exhaustive and expensive. Like criminal investigation, it has its share of critics who claim there are better ways to spend time and resources.

This brief survey of a few novel examples of inquiry suggests that the study of criminal investigation is not one of narrow vocational interest; instead, it lies within the educational tradition that produces generalists rather than narrow specialists. Because industrial archeology, garbageology, and the process of canonization share the same purpose—that of reconstructing the past—the astute student will perceive that what is learned through the study of criminal investigation can be applied to a broad range of theoretical and practical problems.

Data Mining and Information Gathering

Data mining involves the use of computers or data secured from private companies to explore and retrieve information that can be analyzed to form conclusions about potential suspects or types of criminal activity. Information gathering involves the collection of information on individuals or groups who may be involved in, or familiar with others involved in, criminal activity. This borders on the problem of profiling when the focus is on a particular race or religious group, and has been the subject of criticism of police focusing on Muslims, or on young blacks or Hispanics in connection with gang activity.

Data mining also involves the use of relational databases, artificial intelligence, and algorithms to test theories and formulate probability estimates. In the business sector, for example, by determining what types of periodical subscriptions, online purchases, and credit purchases an individual makes, a profile can be determined about his or her personal, career, and purchasing interests; psychosocial preferences; and movement (travel). This information is frequently sold or shared between companies, and is a major factor in marketing.

In criminal investigation, profiles of pedophiles and online child pornography rings have been successful avenues of pursuit. Relational databases and linking programs also provide a means of examining large amounts of information to identify suspects and their contacts with others.

Caution must be taken in this area, given the concerns about law enforcement invading the private lives of citizens. The courts and Congress have been critical of some of the tactics involved in seeking to identify terrorists by using data mining or questionable information-gathering techniques.

FURTHER COMMENTARY ON THE INVESTIGATIVE PROCESS

Peripheral issues surface from time to time regarding the investigative process. They involve such questions as: Is luck important to the outcome of an investigation? Is a skeptical attitude of value to an investigator? Is there such a thing as an investigative mind-set? Some cases and examples are provided below to illuminate these issues.

Luck or Creativity

Rather than merely an exercise in objective, systematic thinking, criminal investigation is believed by experienced detectives and some scholars of the investigative procedure to involve an element of luck.[15] As careful analysis will suggest, it is not good fortune alone. It is "chance which can be on our side, if we but stir it up with our energies, stay receptive to its every random opportunity, and continually provoke it by individuality in our hobbies and our approach to life."[16] William Beveridge devotes an entire chapter to this matter, which he summarizes as follows:

> New knowledge very often has its origin in some quite unexpected observation or chance occurrence arising during an investigation. The importance of this factor in discovery should be fully appreciated and research workers ought deliberately to exploit it. ... Interpreting the clue and realizing its possible significance require knowledge without fixed ideas, imagination ... and a habit of contemplating all unexplained observations.[17]

See Box 14.2.

BOX 14.2 TWO CASE STUDIES SHOW THE UNKNOWN FACTOR OF CHANCE

Case One:

This case involved an aged widow, a recluse living in an apartment-hotel. Her meals delivered daily, the evening tray would be placed in her locked foyer by the night shift elevator operator. After he left she would retrieve the tray, and upon finishing, replace it in the foyer to be picked up several hours later. Occasionally, the night shift operator had an opportunity to talk with the woman, but then only briefly. When the evening tray had not been replaced even by breakfast time, and the morning tray had remained untouched, the day shift operator notified the building manager. Using a pass key, the manager found the woman apparently dead on the bedroom floor; on the kitchen table were the remains of the evening meal of the previous day. The medical examiner established that she had been strangled. It was a case of criminal homicide.

The day shift operator was questioned but could supply no useful information; other tenants had not seen or heard anything suspicious. Checking out the victim's background, friends who visited, and other possible leads occupied the investigators for the remainder of the day. They then focused their questions on the night shift operator who had delivered the last tray of food she had touched. Except for her failing to replace it, he observed nothing unusual, he said, adding that even this had not surprised him, because it was not the first time it had occurred. Asked to account for his own dinner hour, he reported that it had been meatloaf as usual at the corner cafeteria; after that, a smoke on the street outside the restaurant.

To the detectives assigned to the case it looked like a protracted investigation. As they returned to the station house close by and passed the cafeteria, one of the two suggested, "Let's check on the operator's story, and see if anybody remembers seeing him last night." The slight possibility that he had not had dinner there was dashed when the cashier, the owner's wife, stated unequivocally that she had seen him: "He always comes in when he works. He likes our food and prices." The detective probed further, inquiring about the meatloaf served the previous night. The cashier's reply was a surprise, "It's odd that you ask. Yesterday we had trouble with the ovens and the cook couldn't bake. It's the first time in more than a year that meatloaf was not our Thursday night special." Needless to say, the detectives did not continue on their way back to the station house; instead, they quickly returned to the hotel to conduct an intensive interrogation of the night shift operator.

Was it chance or was it thoroughness that prompted the check on the man's story? Had chance prompted the inquiry about the meatloaf? Had experience suggested the most trivial of statements be verified?

Case Two:

This case started innocuously enough when a U.S. Army .45 automatic pistol disappeared from a tavern in a small university town. The detective who responded to the report made proper notifications (within the department and to other law enforcement agencies) pertaining to gun theft, but did little else. A month later, however, an armed robbery occurred in a bank 20 miles away; the weapon the robber brandished, a U.S. Army .45 automatic. The disappearance of the pistol from the tavern still unsolved, and there being no clues except for the eyewitness descriptions of the bank robber, the federal agent assigned to the case decided to follow up on the uncleared gun theft.

The agent's diligence uncovered the information that a carpenter had been working in the back of the tavern during the time the gun disappeared. On the outside chance that the carpenter had seen or heard something, the agent made an appointment for an interview at his home. Arriving early and invited in by the carpenter's wife, he observed a photograph on the piano. Its smudged surface had caught his eye. "Is that a picture of your husband?" he inquired. Walking over to it, she answered, "Yes, it is. And you know, he did a dumb thing a few days ago. He ruined it trying to see

Beveridge drew on Pasteur's well-known aphorism, "In the field of observation, chance favors only the prepared mind," when he wrote:

> It is the interpretation of the chance observation which counts. The role of chance is merely to provide the opportunity and the scientist has to recognize it and grasp it.[18]

In any investigation, it is easier to perceive clues or hints when the mind is prepared through interest or experience. As already suggested, a creative, albeit critical, nature is also helpful for suspecting potential or actual criminality.

Investigative Mind-Set

Just as hindsight brings clear vision, so does *investigative mind-set* provide foresight, and possibly insight, to the creative investigator. The terms *mind-set* and a *set mind* are antithetical; one should not be mistaken for the other. A set mind is scarcely useful to the investigator, the cerebral faculty being neither developed nor strengthened by an inflexible outlook. Investigative mind-set on the other hand, is to some extent a gift at birth. It can, however, be developed through practice and experience. More than mere suspicion, it is doubt or misgivings based on experience that, in combination with a critical faculty, often perceives a connection between two apparently unrelated items or bits of data, and looks for what does not fit the situation. What exactly is wrong? Is there anything out of place? Unusual? If so, why? Two maxims speak to the practical value of a skeptical outlook: such old proverbs as the Latin "Believe nothing and be on your guard against everything," and the Persian "Doubt is the key to knowledge." The philosopher René Descartes developed a theory of knowledge based on doubting everything—including his own existence. He said, "I think, therefore I am," employing the aphorism to show how the doubt had been resolved to his satisfaction. Examples of investigative mind-set are found in the 9/11 World Trade Center case.

These details about intelligence gathering suggest that some attributes are shared by criminal investigators and intelligence agents, even though one is reacting to a crime already committed, while the other is trying to fathom future activities of a targeted person. These shared characteristics include:

- Investigative mind-set
- Interrogation methods
- Surveillance capabilities—including technical means
- Perseverance
- An ability to "think outside the box"

BOX 14.3 A CASE STUDY SHOWS THE VALUE OF INVESTIGATIVE MIND-SET

The 9/11 World Trade Center Attack

The terrorists who leveled the World Trade Center on September 11, 2001 were, in retrospect, able to enter, leave, and explore the country for potential opportunities that would allow them to accomplish their villainous goals. One prospect was to enroll as students in pilot flight training schools. They showed little interest in learning how to take off and land; rather, they wanted to learn how to pilot a commercial jet while airborne. Anyone with an investigative mind-set would regard this behavior as suspicious. Two FBI agents did so. One, on July 10, 2001, sent a communication to headquarters "outlining links between a group of suspected Middle Eastern terrorists and the Embry-Riddle Aeronautical University ... The agent (Kenneth Williams) ... suggested that the FBI should canvass U.S. flight schools for information on other Middle Eastern students. He speculated that bin Laden might be attempting to train operatives to infiltrate the aviation industry."[a] The other agent, Coleen Rowley, a Minneapolis field office lawyer, sent a

Apprehended terrorist Zacarías Moussaoui.

U.S. Department of Justice

13-page letter to the newly appointed Director of the FBI warning him about, among other things, how "instructors at the Pan Am flight school near Minneapolis–St. Paul had phoned the FBI the previous day reporting that a student, in bad English, had showed up asking for instruction on how to fly a 747."[b] When FBI agents arrived at the student's motel, they asked for his immigration papers. "[W]hen the documents showed evidence of a possible visa violation, agents from the Immigration and Naturalization Service arrested (Zacarias) Moussaoui on charges of overstaying his visa."[c] Despite evidence obtained from French intelligence that Moussaoui "was not only operational in the militant Islamist world but had some autonomy and authority as well,"[d] Rowley's request for permission to obtain a search warrant to study the contents of (Moussaoui's) laptop was denied by a superior at headquarters. "Only after September 11, 2001, did the FBI successfully obtain a warrant to search Moussaoui's belongings; among other things the search turned up crop dusting information ... and a notebook that contained an alias eventually traced to the roommate of hijacker Mohammed Atta."[e]

It is perhaps relevant to remark at this point on the relationship between criminal investigation, which is a reactive endeavor, and intelligence, which is a proactive endeavor.

"It was old-fashioned interrogation and eavesdropping that first led U.S. agents to the Qaeda [sic] plotters. In the summer of 1998, only a couple of weeks after bin Laden operatives truck-bombed two U.S. Embassies in Africa, the FBI got a break: one of the Nairobi bombers had been caught. ... (He) was supposed to have killed himself in the blast. Instead, he got out of the truck at the last moment and fled. He was arrested in a seedy Nairobi hotel, ... (and) questioned by the FBI, ... Among the information he gave agents was the telephone number of a Qaeda [sic] safe house in Yemen ... U.S. intelligence agents began listening in on the telephone line of the Yemen house, described in government documents as a Qaeda [sic] 'logistics center,' where ... the African bombings and later the Cole attack in Yemen—were planned. ... [I]ntercepted conversations on the Yemen phone tipped off agents to the January 2000 Kuala Lumpur summit [meeting].... After the meeting, Malaysian intelligence continued to watch the condo at the CIA's request, but after a while the agency lost interest. Had agents kept up the surveillance, they might have observed ... Zacarías Moussaoui."[f]

BOX 14.3 (CONTINUED)

Zacarias Moussaoui pleaded guilty to all charges against him (conspiracy to commit acts of terrorism transcending national boundaries, to commit aircraft piracy, to destroy aircraft, to use weapons of mass destruction, to murder U.S. employees, and to destroy property). He was sentenced to six consecutive life terms without the possibility of parole. In early 2010, a federal appeals court denied his appeal and affirmed the conviction and life sentence.

[a] Barton Gellman. "Dots That Didn't Connect," *The Washington Post National Weekly Edition*, (May 27–June 2, 2002), 10.

[b] R. Ratnesar and M. Weisskopf, "How the FBI Blew the Case," *Time*, (June 3, 2002), 28.

[c] Loc. cit., col. 2.

[d] Loc. cit., col. 3.

[e] Ibid., 31, col. 3; 32, col. 1.

[f] M. Isikoff and D. Kaidman, "Terrorists Who Got Away," *Newsweek*, (June 10, 2002), 24, 25.

The Development of Mind-Set

In day-to-day reading, a news story occasionally triggers the mind to question its details and reflects a developing investigative mind-set. If articles are clipped and files maintained as stories unfold, original suspicions may be confirmed or denied. As the reader's ability improves through practice, more validations and fewer misjudgments will occur.

Conscientious students will find that the study of old newspaper and magazine files in libraries and "surfing" the Internet helps stimulate those intuitive responses that characterize investigative mind-set. A great deal of time may be required to find suitable case examples, but with patience—a primary investigative attribute—there is intellectual gold to be mined.

What evidence and proof consist of in science, law, and criminal investigation are the subject of the next section. Table 14.2 summarizes this information.

EVIDENCE AND PROOF

A chance observation, such as a detective's noting the marred surface of a photograph (as in the case of the U.S. Army pistol theft), represents an investigative opportunity. It does not constitute evidence of probable cause. Sometimes chance may raise a mere suspicion, a sense that the nature or quality of what is observed presents "interesting possibilities" worthy of follow-up. To be of further value to the investigator, it must be supplemented by an apperceptive noting and recording of facts—seen and understood in the light of past experience. The chance observation and apperception coming together in this process inductively provide grounds for a hypothesis or a belief that leads to a tentative generalization. For example, a detective's attention was called to a vehicle parked across the street from a bank, the bank president having observed it there several times in the past month. Additional suspicion was aroused when it was again seen an hour or so before opening time on one day, and just before closing time the following day. A check of its license plate revealed that the car was not stolen; its registered owner was a local resident with no police record. Despite this, the detective, acting on a sense of "interesting possibilities" in the nature of what had been observed, briefed the radio car

Table 14.2
Evidence and Proof: In Science, Law, and Criminal Investigation[a]

CATEGORY	I	II[b]	III[b]
DEGREES OF PROOF	**INTUITIVE**	**SPECULATIVE**	**PROBABLE CAUSE**
EVIDENCE Kind	Guess; hunch; gut feeling.	Impression; surmise.	Facts that a reasonable, prudent person would accept as a basis for decisionmaking.
Quantity	Virtually none that can be identified and articulated to another person.	Not sufficient to be convincing.	*Prima facie*: presumptive but rebuttable.
Degree of uncertainty	Considerable.	Apparent.	Less than apparent but still quite possible.
USAGE IN Science	Discovery and hypothesis formulation.		Basis for theory development through testing of hypothesis.
Law (in the U.S.)	Exercise a peremptory challenge in jury selection. Defense may move to suppress this kind of evidence.		Satisfies requirement for an arrest or issuance of a warrant for search and seizure of evidence. Basis for going on to the next stage of a legal proceeding. If no defense is made, *prima facie* evidence for every element constitutes a *prima facie* case that is sufficient to support a conviction in criminal cases.
Criminal Investigation (in the U.S.)	Useful during the first stages of investigation. Basis for decisions on what to monitor, what to investigate, and what direction—at least initially—an investigation should take.		Obtain a search warrant or an arrest warrant.

Table 14.2
(Continued)

IV	V	VI[c]	VII[c]
PREPONDERANCE OF THE EVIDENCE	CLEAR AND CONVINCING	BEYOND A REASONABLE DOUBT	SCIENTIFIC CERTAINTY
Additional facts, increasingly supportive, obtained through eyewitness testimony, or the examination of documents and other physical things—fingerprints, toolmarks, bullets, recordings, and so on. A forensic scientist may be required to interpret and evaluate the significance of this evidence for legal use.[d]			Factual data and details arrived at by methods of analysis of known precision and accuracy.
Over 50 percent of the facts are in support.	Only slightly less than proof beyond a reasonable doubt.	Sufficient to preclude every reasonable hypothesis except that which it tends to support.	Overwhelming but still probabilistic.
Some is permitted.	A little may remain.	Almost none.	Essentially none.
Basis for theory development through continued testing of hypothesis.		Theory.	Scientific law that accounts for the known, observed facts.
Basis upon which most civil cases are decided. Suggests need to plea bargain in criminal cases and offers to settle in civil cases. Meets burden of proof such as under RICO. Revocation of probation, conditional discharge, and supervision.	A U.S. President may be impeached (accused).[e] A mentally ill person may be committed involuntarily. Supports a decision in a civil case involving moral turpitude and fraud.	Basis upon which a criminal case is decided ora U.S. President removed from office.	Seldom achieved.
Obtain an admission or confession by pointing out the evidence against the suspect as part of the questioning. Induce a suspect who is a potential informant to talk. Verifies investigation is proceeding in the proper direction. May suggest use of civil processes rather than criminal prosecution in a given case.		Satisfies the quantity of legal proof required to convict in a criminal case.	Seldom achieved.

[a]Although depicted as seven categories for didactic reasons, such a division may also (and should) be viewed as a continuum.

[b]Reasonable Suspicion. A category of proof that is less than probable cause but more than speculative, it was invoked by the managers for the House of Representatives in the impeachment and trial of President William Jefferson Clinton. This category of proof is not recognized in science.

[c]The U.S. Supreme Court has not looked favorably upon attempts to define "beyond a reasonable doubt" because it found the words themselves sufficiently descriptive. (Consult *Miles v. United States*, 103 U.S. 312 (1981)). "Beyond a shadow of a doubt" is a colloquial term that falls between Categories VI and VII. Proof "beyond a shadow of *any* doubt" falls into Category VII.

[d]Circumstantial evidence falls into Category III-VI. It is evidence not bearing directly on the fact in dispute, but on various attendant circumstances from which a judge or jury may logically infer the occurrence of the fact in dispute. It is indirect evidence by which a principal fact may be arrived at inductively. It is far more common than direct evidence, i.e., eyewitness testimony or a confession.

[e]This standard of proof was invoked in the political impeachment of President Richard Milhous Nixon.

patrol covering the car owner's residence about the bank's uneasiness. A week later the sector car patrol officer spotted an out-of-state vehicle parked in the driveway of the house. A check disclosed that the vehicle was registered to an individual with a bank burglary record, whose *modus operandi* was to burn around the dial of a safe with an acetylene torch.

By now, the detective's thinking had moved by degrees from the mere suspicion or "intriguing possibilities" stage to one that at the very least called for some follow-up measures. Official interest was still based on speculation however, with additional facts needed to prove that the bank was indeed to be "hit." Local welding equipment suppliers were alerted and provided with photographs of both individuals. As prearranged, when a customer resembling either one came in for a tank of acetylene, police were alerted and surveillance of the purchaser—now a suspect—was begun.

It is clear from the foregoing that evidence consists of a number of facts that point to a conclusion. In this case, if the bank is broken into, that fact would prove intent to commit burglary, but if the detective waits for the suspect to emerge, loot in hand, it would provide sufficient evidence to support and prove the charge of burglary. The number and kind of facts, together with the ambiguity or doubt associated with each fact, dictate the level of evidentiary value. When enough facts are available, proof becomes possible depending upon the purpose, criteria, and requirements of the discipline in which the proof is offered. As pointed out earlier, Beveridge suggests discoveries result when attention is paid to the slightest clue. A certain attitude of mind (capable of a quantum leap from limited evidence) is required for the discovery stage, whereas the unquestioned proof stage has distinctly different evidentiary requirements. In criminal investigation, similarly, there are two standards of proof: "probable cause" for a legal arrest and "beyond a reasonable doubt" for a conviction. In civil cases the standard is "a preponderance of the evidence"; the House Judiciary Committee in its impeachment deliberations proposed as the yardstick "clear and convincing" evidence.[19] Although each standard seems discrete, it should be viewed as a continuum of evidence and proof.

Evidence, then, is the means by which a fact is established. When the number of facts collected and confirmed is sufficient, depending on whether it is a civil or criminal matter, the point in question is proved. In civil law, a preponderance of the evidence is required; in criminal law, it must be "beyond a reasonable doubt" (see Table 14.2).

Conclusion: Investigation—Art or Science?

The concept of continuous succession—a continuum—is helpful in understanding other aspects of the investigative process; specifically, to examine two polar views: investigation as an art versus investigation as a science. But if art and science are part of a continuum, where does the separation point lie? Further reflection suggests it is determined by the subject under consideration: for the physical and biological sciences, it is far to one side; for culinary creativeness, it leans toward the arts (since any chef can read a cookbook and follow directions). For criminal investigation, the separation point is moving by degrees toward science. The field is becoming a focus of academic study and research, one in which the impact of forensic science is felt more and more. See Box 14.4

BOX 14.4 SUMMARY OF THE SCIENTIFIC METHOD AND ITS APPLICATION TO CRIMINAL INVESTIGATION

The Steps Involved may be Summarized as Follows:

SCIENTIFIC METHOD	CRIMINAL INVESTIGATION*
1. State the problem.**	1. What crime was committed?
2. Form the hypothesis.	2. In what jurisdiction?
3. Collect data by observing and experimenting.	3. Hypothesize as to possible suspects based on information known about the victim or gathered from witnesses, physical evidence at the crime scene, and motive (if determined).
4. Interpret the data as a test of the hypothesis.	4. Seek out pertinent records. Continue effort to locate and interview additional witnesses. If possible, obtain from each potential suspect's person (home or automobile) exemplars for comparison with physical evidence discovered at the crime scene. Interview witnesses again, if necessary, based on information acquired after initial interviews.
5. If the data support the hypothesis so far, continue to collect additional data (as a logical consequence of the hypothesis).	5. Review and evaluate the evidence so far available relative to making a case—for and against—each suspect. Focus the investigation on the most likely suspect.
	After *Miranda* warnings, interrogate the suspect.
6. Draw conclusions (which, if the data are sufficiently supportive, may lead to a theory).	6. Seek additional evidence (possibly through follow-up measures) that supports (or disproves) the hypothesis that the suspect was the offender.
	7. If evidence amounting to probable cause has been developed, arrest suspect. Continue seeking evidence to support or refute the guilt of the defendant.

*Criminal investigation generally commences as an inductive process with deductive reasoning integral to it.

**Problem recognition precedes this stage and is, perhaps, the driving force leading to an investigation of the problem. As part of the process, the issue must be clearly formulated by "stating the problem."

NOTES

[1]   W.B. Sanders, ed., *The Sociologist as Detective* (New York: Praeger, 1974).

[2]   Robin W. Winks, ed., *The Historian as Detective* (New York: Harper & Row, 1969).

[3]   Ibid., XXIV.

[4]   Ibid., XIII, XVII, 4.

[5]   Thomas H. Huxley, *Collected Essays, Vol. II: Darwiniana* (London: Macmillan, 1970), 363–365.

[6]   E.L. Bernays, *The Engineering of Consent* (Norman, OK: University of Oklahoma Press, 1956), 9 ff.

[7]   Hans Reichenbach, *The Rise of Scientific Philosophy* (Berkeley: University of California Press, 1951), 9 ff., 232.

[8]   "The Republicans' Moment of Truth," *Time*, (29 July 1974), 10.

[9]   J.E. Bishop. "Industrial Evolution," *The Wall Street Journal*, (June 26, 1975), 40.

[10]   R.A. Buchanan, *Industrial Archeology in Britain* (London: Penguin Books, 1972).

[11]   J. Beck. "Study of Garbage Threatens Privacy," *Chicago Tribune*, (July 18, 1975).

[12]   "Trashy Journalism," *Time*, (July 21, 1975), 40.

[13]   L.R. Gallese. "The Good Fight: American Saint's Cause Took Century of Work, Millions in Donations!" *The Wall Street Journal*, (June 25, 1975), 1, 19.

[14]   Ibid.

[15]   Charles E. O'Hara and Gregory L. O'Hara, *Fundamentals of Criminal Investigation*, rev. 5th ed. (Springfield, IL: Charles C Thomas, 1973), 22.

[16]   J.H. Austin. "The Roots of Serendipity," *Saturday Review World*, (Nov. 2, 1974), 64.

[17]   William I. Beveridge, *The Art of Scientific Investigation*, Modern Library rev. ed. (New York: Random House, 1957), 55.

[18]   Ibid., 46.

[19]   U.S. Congress, House Committee on the Judiciary, Hearings on H. Res. 803, 93rd Cong., 2nd sess. "Summary of Information," 19 (July 1974), 5. "Debate on Articles of Impeachment," 24, 27, 29, 30 (July 1974).

IMPORTANT CASE

Miles v. United States (1981)

DISCUSSION QUESTIONS

1.   What is the scientific method?

2.   What is inductive reasoning?

3.   What is deductive reasoning?

4.   What is the difference between classification and synthesis?

5.   What is the difference between a hypothesis and a theory?

6.   What is data mining?

SUPPLEMENTAL READINGS

Barzun, J., & Henry, F. G. (2004). *The modern researcher* (6th ed.). Belmont, CA: Thomson/Wadsworth.

Copi, I. M., & Cohen, C. (2010). *An introduction to logic* (14th ed.). Upper Saddle River, NJ: Pearson/Prentice Hall.

Davidson, J. W., & Mark, H. L. (2009). *After the fact: The art of historical detection* (6th ed.). Boston: McGraw-Hill.

Fisher, D. (1995). *Hard evidence: How detectives inside the fbi's sci-crime lab have helped solve america's toughest cases.* New York: Simon & Schuster.

Kukura, T. V. (Feb. 1991). Trash inspections and the fourth amendment. *FBI Law Enforcement Bulletin, 60*(2), 27–32.

Lang, A. F., Jr. & Beattie, A. R. (Eds.). (2009). *War, torture and terrorism: Rethinking the rules of international security.* New York: Routledge.

Woodward, K. L. (1996). *Making saints: How the catholic church determines who becomes a saint, who doesn't, and why.* New York: Simon & Schuster.

Winks, R. W. (Ed.). (1978). *The historian as detective: Essays on evidence.* New York: HarperCollins.

CHAPTER 15

CRIME AND CONSTITUTIONAL LAW
The Foundations of Criminal Investigation

Any serious study looking into the understanding and control of crime gains insight from a wide variety of disciplines. A list might include history, criminal justice, political science, sociology, computer science, psychiatry, and even biology. Because the concern of this text must be narrow, it is limited to how crimes are solved—using legal means. With this in mind it would be advantageous at the outset to define some elementary terms in the field of criminal investigation: crime, criminal law, case law, and the Model Penal Code.

Likewise, understanding the relationship of the Constitution to the American legal system serves to provide the investigator with the knowledge to better comprehend the foundations and framework of criminal law, criminal investigation, and criminal procedural law.

CRIME

The search for the meaning of this word begins with *The American Heritage Dictionary*. It defines "crime" as:

> An act committed or omitted in violation of law forbidding or commanding it, and for which punishment is imposed upon conviction.[1]

The dictionary does not specify what is forbidden or commanded, spell out what is required to prove guilt and obtain a conviction, or provide any guidelines for the conduct of the investigation and the presentation of evidence at trial. These details must be sought in the criminal law of each jurisdiction.

The legislature defines crime by enacting penal statutes that govern behavior for which punishment can be meted out. Behavior can be viewed as (1) inherently bad (*malum in se*, e.g., the deliberate killing of another human being), or (2) against public policy (*malum prohibitum*, e.g., committing arson in order to defraud). Public perception of crime varies over time and across cultures.

Public perception has also changed regarding the way wealth is acquired. Many families that are today's pillars of society acquired their "old money" through now-outlawed *malum prohibitum* business practices, whereas some "new money" involves behavior that may yet be outlawed (e.g., "white-collar crime" in general, which presently is a sociological rather than a legal term).

CRIMINAL LAW

American definitions of crimes are rooted in English common law, which in turn is based on custom and usage in England. Despite their common origin, state criminal laws can vary not only on punishment but, surprisingly, on the definition of the constituent elements of each crime. Moreover, every state's penal code has separate sections dealing respectively with substantive and procedural criminal law.

Substantive criminal law describes the forbidden acts and the punishment to be inflicted when the law is broken. *Procedural* criminal law deals with how the state may go about arresting and convicting a suspected offender.

Substantive Criminal Law

Crimes are divided into two classes: *felonies* are crimes of a more serious nature; *misdemeanors* are less serious, perhaps even trivial. A more significant distinction is made on the basis of punishment provided by statute: felonies are punishable by death or imprisonment for one year or more in a state prison; misdemeanors by imprisonment for less than one year or by a fine, or both. A further distinction is inherent in the sanctions imposed: a convicted felon is prohibited from holding public office or engaging in a licensed occupation; a misdemeanant is not similarly disadvantaged.

The Elements of a Crime

The penal laws enacted by a state legislature to cover wrongful behavior spell out what constitutes a crime. The phrase *elements of the crime* describes the specific acts that, taken together, compose the crime. For example, loosely stated, the elements of burglary are: (a) breaking, (b) entering, and (c) with intent to commit a crime; the elements of robbery are: (a) the taking of property, (b) from another person, and (c) by force or the fear of force. If each and every element of a crime is not proved, a defendant cannot be convicted for that crime.

Corpus Delicti

The *corpus delicti* or body of a crime has two components: one, that each element of the crime is satisfied; two, that someone is responsible for inflicting the injury or loss that was sustained. When the state has proved the *corpus delicti* beyond a reasonable doubt, the prosecutor has met the burden of proof required for a jury (or judge) to convict.

Procedural Criminal Law

Procedural criminal law flows from the constitutions of the United States and the respective states. In its decisions, the Supreme Court interprets the United States Constitution or exercises its supervisory power over the federal system of criminal justice. Of greatest importance to procedural criminal law is the Bill of Rights—especially the Fourth through the Ninth Amendments, in which the actions permitted or forbidden by the government in criminal matters are spelled out. By specifying the course of action required or prohibited in each phase of the legal process, the Bill of Rights protects the accused from unjust treatment by the state. Precisely because a violation will render illegally obtained evidence inadmissible at a subsequent trial, procedural limitations placed on investigative behavior are raised throughout this text.

CASE LAW

The language of the penal law is necessarily general, leaving it up to the trial judge to decide whether a particular set of details surrounding an alleged crime fits or does not fit its requirements. The cumulative wisdom of such judicial decisions is referred to as case law; it interprets the meaning of the law. In the language of the statute on burglary, for instance, "break" is an element of the crime. But suppose an offender is able to reach through an open window to unlock a door. Does that constitute a break? Is it a break if the door was ajar and the offender merely had to walk in? The case law of each state supplies the answer for that state. Should a novel issue be raised when relevant case law does not exist, the decisions of other jurisdictions are then searched to learn how the point in question was settled. Sources for the annotated statutes (state law codes) that embody the case law of each state are treated at the end of the chapter.

THE MODEL PENAL CODE

In an effort to make criminal laws more uniform, a Model Penal Code was proposed by the American Law Institute (ALI) in 1962 and updated in 1981. The ALI is a nationwide body with membership drawn from the bench, the bar, and law schools. The code was intended to bring a unified approach to criminal law through an examination of its philosophical foundations, the elements that defined specific crimes, and the provisions for sentencing and correction. Its main thrust and purpose was an attempt to be organized and more civilized in using the power of the state against the individual. Professor Herbert Wechsler, a principal architect of the Model Penal Code, stated:

> ... penal law governs the strongest force that we permit official agencies to bring to bear on individuals. Its promise as an instrument of safety is matched only by its power to destroy. If penal law is weak or ineffective, basic human interests are in jeopardy. If it is harsh or arbitrary in its impact, it works a gross injustice on those caught within its toils. The law that carries such responsibilities should surely be as rational and just as law can be.[2]

The ALI Model Penal Code has not yet been widely accepted, though some aspects have found their way into the criminal law of some states. Even if it were to be universally adopted, it is important to realize that the development of case law would continue, while the differences now found between states would most likely be diminished.

SOURCES OF STATE LAW

The best place to research cases concerning a particular type of crime in a certain state, dependency, or territory is a law school library where current law codes for all of the United States and its possessions are to be found. The codes (annotated statutes) are shelved and indexed alphabetically by state; usually there is commentary following each section of the code, and relevant cases may be cited therein. Additional research involves Shepard's Citations, available from LexisNexis, which publishes a comprehensive "How to Use" booklet in conjunction with its volumes. Shepard's will direct the investigator to the appropriate sources where case texts and analyses are located. Online services by LexisNexis and Westlaw can be searched, as can various web sites on the Internet. Other possible sources might be a large public library or a superior court center. State and local prosecutors will also generally have a law library that may be accessible.

THEORIES ON CRIME[3]

American criminology perspectives have their roots in Western influences and have been used to help explain criminality since the inception of the criminal justice system. The main perspective applied to crime is the Classical school of thought, and many of the concepts developed in the eighteenth century are still used today. It is important to use theoretical perspectives not only to explain why individuals participate in criminal behavior but also in order to better formulate investigative theories.

Psychological approaches to criminal behavior are characterized by concern with mental defect and abnormal mental processes in individual personalities. Sigmund Freud's psychoanalytic theory focuses on three tenets of the personality: the id (pleasure principle), ego (reality principle), and superego (conscience). This approach sees crime as occurring when an imbalance is present among these three principles, which is usually during the early stages of life.[4] According to attachment theory, developed in the 1950s, individuals who do not form healthy relationships as children are more likely to participate in criminal behavior. B.F. Skinner developed behavior theory, which is based on rewards and punishments for specific behaviors: positive rewards, negative rewards, positive punishments, and negative punishments.

Social structure theories concentrate on the economic structure of society and help explain criminal behavior committed by the disadvantaged classes. The lower-class structure is characterized by underemployment, poverty, aggression, and an imbalance with the other social structures. Social disorganization theory stems from the ecological Chicago School and focuses on lack of consensus and opportunity among class structures.

Criminology of place, also referred to as environmental criminology, concentrates on architecture and geography in explaining criminality. The main idea developed from this theory is the "broken windows" thesis, which states that run-down and deteriorated buildings produce a delinquent attitude among residents.[5] It helps explain the psychological consequences of residing in low-income and crime-prone areas.

en.wikipedia.org

Figure 15.1
French sociologist Emile Durkheim popularized the term "anomie," which describes a lack of social norms.

Strain theory attributes criminality to struggles of the lower class to meet socially defined goals through legitimate means. Emile Durkheim popularized the term *anomie* (without norms) in his 1897 publication *Suicide*, which described anomic societies as rapidly changing with the presence of alternate (often illegitimate) methods to achieve socially acceptable goals (see Figure 15.1).[6] Robert Merton modified this concept into strain theory to explain criminal behavior as the result of individuals seeking societal goals through illegal means.

General Strain Theory (GST) was introduced in 1992 by Robert Agnew. It provides a micro-level perspective to the strain approach. Agnew describes strain as an individual reaction to negative social relationships that can cause "negative affective states" that can lead to antisocial behavior.[7] For example, when a teenager's parents get divorced, he or she is likely to feel anger and frustration and may respond to this by participating in delinquent behavior.

Culture conflict theory combines social disorganization and strain theories to help explain differences among socially different groups. Walter Miller developed a set of focal concerns that characterize the lower-class subculture, including: trouble, toughness, smartness, excitement, fate, and autonomy.[8] Richard Cloward and Lloyd Ohlin applied social disorganization and strain theories to gang subculture to help explain differential opportunity theory. The gang acts as a means to attain legitimate economic and social status even though illegitimate and illegal means are utilized. Three types of gangs are described: criminal, conflict, and retreatist.[9] Gresham Sykes and David Matza developed a taxonomy of ways that individuals in certain subcultures justify their criminal behavior. These techniques of neutralization contain five methods: denial of responsibility, denial of victim, denial of injury, condemnation of condemners, and an appeal to higher loyalties.[10] Many offenders possess working moral standards and must justify their criminal behavior by using the above methods.

Social process theories focus on the relationships between individuals and society and emphasize learned behavior as the main motivation to commit crime. Social learning theory states that all behavior, including criminal, is learned through social interaction and communication.[11]

The differential reinforcement perspective was developed by Ronald Akers and Robert Burgess in 1966 as an extension of Sutherland's differential association theory. The theory states that learned criminal behavior is affected by direct conditioning (differential reinforcement), which occurs when behavior is rewarded or punished.[12] Individuals may learn from the outcomes by either direct contact, imitation, or observing the process. Albert Bandura's modeling theory of aggression explains the development of aggressive behavior by an individual's observations of others.[13] This theory is significant because it allows learning behavior and reinforcement to occur through several modes, including media programs.

Social control theories focus on reasons why the vast majority of the population chooses not to commit crimes. Containment theory seeks to explain conformity to norms and rules by the concepts of inner and external containment. Inner containment, also referred to as self-concept, involves an individual's ability to follow the group's accepted roles. External containment includes group goals and expected norms.[14]

Labeling theory helps explain the struggle between individual perception and outsider perception. First developed by Frank Tannenbaum in the late 1930s, the dramatization of evil is explained as the process by which an offender is labeled as inherently bad or negative by outsiders who, consequently, make the individual believe the label. The individual then modifies his or her personality and behavior to fit the outsider's image.[15] Primary deviance concerns the initial act or behavior that causes the initial labeling; secondary deviance explains the self-fulfilling prophecy that occurs when the labeled person begins to act in accordance with the labeler's image. Howard Becker further expanded this theory, noting that labels are determined by the dominant ruling social power, called moral entrepreneurs.[16] He maintains that deviance is a subjective concept and changes depending on the labeler's perspective.

Life-course theories focus on the difference between career criminals and temporary or adolescent offenders. Robert Sampson and John Laub developed the life-course approach in the late twentieth century and state that criminal activity is likely to occur when social bonds are broken or weak.[17] Positive relationships in life make up social capital, and an inverse relationship between social bonds and criminality exists.[18]

Michael Gottfredson and Travis Hirschi developed an integrated theory of crime in their work, *A General Theory of Crime*. This theory focuses on concepts from the Classical school and the idea of self-control.[19] It recognizes that criminals are able to belong to socially acceptable and conventional groups and activities while still participating in criminal behavior and that most individuals commit deviant acts at some point in their lives.

The conflict perspective (critical criminology) focuses on the struggle between the group that makes laws and norms and the groups that must abide by them. Radical criminology, also called Marxist criminology, focuses on the capitalist system of society and the lack of consensus between those in power and those affected by the powerful. Feminist criminology also concentrates on the struggles between classes like Marxist and left-realist criminology, but it focuses on gender inequality. Freda Adler and Rita Simon helped form this theory in the 1970s and concentrated on the differences between male and female criminality. They predicted that female crime rates will increase as females become a more equal part of society.[20]

American criminology encompasses a wide array of perspectives that encourage a well-rounded and diverse approach to explaining criminality. It is important to realize that some criminology perspectives best explain certain criminals and behavior and that the approaches should be viewed as a whole rather than individually.

CONTROL OVER INVESTIGATIONS THROUGH CONSTITUTIONAL LAW

The quest for justice was one of the primary incentives for the colonists to come to America. Both Pennsylvania and Georgia were established in part as idealistic experiments in government: the former by Quakers seeking freedom of religion; the latter by James Oglethorpe and his settlers (some of whom, as debtors, were imprisoned in England). Other unfortunates also fled Europe for the new world and the opportunity to improve the condition of their lives.

Although subjects of the Crown, the settlers did not typically think or act as their compatriots in England. Indeed, their Dutch, Swedish, German, Scottish, and English ancestries partly accounted for this, as did the new manners and ideas that evolved from their struggle to tame a wilderness. The culture of the native American Indians also exerted an influence for change. During the next century and a half, therefore, British rule increasingly led to dissatisfaction. It culminated in "The Unanimous Declaration of the Thirteen United States of America in Congress."[21] It is revealing to note the importance the settlers attached to their colonies as sovereign states. Nowhere in the document, now known as the Declaration of Independence, does the word "nation" appear.

The government that would conduct the greater part of the war against the mother country was set up in 1777 under the Articles of Confederation. A short time after the Revolution it was clear that the Articles of Confederation needed to be revised. To deal with the numerous problems that were manifest, the nation would need effective government. Finally, in 1787 a constitutional convention met in Independence Hall in Philadelphia, and from those historic deliberations, two particularly important governing principles emerged. The first concerned the distribution of power between the central government and the sovereign states. The powers finally given up by the 13 original states were carefully defined. One they would retain was control over the criminal law.

The adoption of the new Constitution was delayed by the insistence of the original 13 states that a Bill of Rights (the first 10 amendments) be made an integral part of the document. These amendments placed limits only on the powers of the federal government. It took 77 years and the passage of the Fourteenth Amendment to give the Court a constitutional basis to intervene in a state criminal matter. It was not until the Warren Court (1953–1969) that any extensive set of overruling decisions cloaked criminal defendants in state courts with the mantle of protection afforded by the Bill of Rights.

The Preamble to the Constitution states:

We the People of the United States, in Order to form a more perfect Union, establish Justice, insure domestic Tranquility, provide for the common defence, promote the general Welfare, and secure the Blessings of Liberty to ourselves and our Posterity, do ordain and establish this Constitution for the United States of America.

As the Preamble asserts, the first reason for forming "a more perfect Union" is to establish justice. The basic human drives are for food, shelter, and procreation. Once these needs are provided for, the next instinct to be found universally across cultures is the quest for justice. Philosophers, writers, and political scientists endlessly speculate on the meaning of justice. Hence, those engaged in law enforcement, and especially in criminal investigation, are entrusted with an awesome task. If they carry it out improperly or insensitively, they not only dishonor themselves and their agencies, but also the aspirations of humankind.

Criminal Justice In the Articles and Amendments

With the exception of treason, no crime is defined in the Constitution; indeed, only a few matters affecting criminal justice can be found throughout its seven Articles:

Article I (Re: The Legislative Branch)
… in Cases of Impeachment … the Party convicted shall nevertheless be liable and subject to Indictment, Trial, Judgment and Punishment, according to Law. (Section 3, par. 7).
… the Writ of Habeas Corpus shall not be suspended. … (Section 9, par. 2).
… no Bill of Attainder or ex post facto Law shall be passed. (Section 9, par. 3).

Article II (Re: The Executive Branch)
… the President … shall have Power to grant Reprieves and Pardons for Offenses against the United States. … (Section 2, par. 1). … he … shall appoint … Judges of the Supreme Court. … (Section 2, par. 2).

Article III (Re: The Judicial Branch)
The judicial Power of the United States, shall be vested in one supreme Court. … (Section 1, par. 1).
… the supreme Court shall have appellate Jurisdiction, both as to Law and Fact, with such Exceptions, and under such Regulations as the Congress shall make. (Section 2, par. 2). The Trial of all Crimes … shall be by Jury … (Section 2, par. 3). Treason against the United States, shall consist only in levying War against them, or in adhering to their Enemies, giving them Aid and Comfort. No Person shall be convicted of Treason unless on the Testimony of two Witnesses to the same overt Act, or on Confession in open Court. (Section 3).

Article IV (Re: The States and its Citizens)
> A Person charged in any State with Treason, Felony, or other Crime, who shall flee from Justice, and be found in another State, shall on Demand of the executive Authority of the State from which he fled, be delivered up, to be removed to the State having Jurisdiction of the Crime. (Section 2, par. 2).

Article VI (Re: The Supreme Law)
> This Constitution ... shall be the supreme Law of the Land; and the Judges in every State shall be bound thereby, any Thing in the Constitution or Laws of any State to the Contrary notwithstanding. (par. 2).

The Bill of Rights

The first 10 amendments were adopted in 1791. Several of them affect the administration of criminal justice. Past Supreme Court decisions having the greatest influence on investigative practice are based on the Fourth, Fifth, Sixth, and Eighth Amendments.

Fourth Amendment
> The right of the people to be secure in their persons, houses, papers, and effects, against unreasonable searches and seizures, shall not be violated, and no Warrants shall issue, but upon probable cause, supported by Oath or affirmation, and particularly describing the place to be searched, and the persons or things to be seized.

Fifth Amendment
> No person shall be held to answer for a capital, or otherwise infamous crime, unless on a presentment or indictment of a Grand Jury, except in cases arising in the land or naval forces, or in the Militia, when in actual service in time of War or public danger; nor shall any person be subject for the same offence to be twice put in jeopardy of life or limb; nor shall be compelled in any criminal case to be a witness against himself, nor be deprived of life, liberty, or property, without due process of law; nor shall private property be taken for public use, without just compensation.

Sixth Amendment
> In all criminal prosecutions, the accused shall enjoy the right to a speedy and public trial, by an impartial jury of the State and district wherein the crime shall have been committed, which district shall have been previously ascertained by law, and to be informed of the nature and cause of the accusation; to be confronted with the witnesses against him; to have compulsory process for obtaining Witnesses in his favor, and to have the Assistance of Counsel for his defence.

Eighth Amendment
> Excessive bail shall not be required, nor excessive fines imposed, nor cruel and unusual punishments inflicted.

Although judicial and correctional practice is affected, the Eighth Amendment has little influence over criminal investigative behavior.

Ninth Amendment
> The enumeration in the Constitution, of certain rights, shall not be construed to deny or disparage others retained by the people.

The Ninth Amendment was intended to cover any right not expressly mentioned in the first eight amendments. One text attempting to explain the Constitution writes of the Ninth: "In practice it has been of no importance."[22] Another text, well aware that "Courts virtually ignored the Ninth Amendment for 175 years after its adoption," believes its mere presence was sufficient to keep the federal government from attempting to restrict any fundamental right of a citizen, even though that right was not expressly stated in the Constitution.[23]

Tenth Amendment
> The powers not delegated to the United States by the Constitution, nor prohibited by it to the States, are reserved to the States respectively, or to the people.

The Tenth Amendment reserves for the states the area of criminal justice. Federal law enforcement agencies derive their enforcement and investigative powers from four constitutional clauses in Article 1, Section 8:

> The Congress shall have Power To lay and collect Taxes, Duties, Imposts, and Excises ... (Clause 1);
> To regulate Commerce ... among the several States ... (Clause 3);
> To provide for the Punishment of counterfeiting the Securities and current Coin of the United States (Clause 6);
> To establish Post Offices and post Roads (Clause 7).

Thus, it is through Clause 3 that the FBI derives its authority to prosecute kidnapping, auto theft, Mann Act infractions (interstate prostitution), and so on. Many Treasury Department agencies are authorized through Clause 1 on taxing (which is used to regulate the sales of firearms and narcotics) or Clause 6 on counterfeiting (the Secret Service was one of the first federal policing agencies; its presidential protection duties were later acquired for reasons of convenience), whereas the postal inspector's authority has remained narrow.

Fourteenth Amendment
> Section 1. All persons born or naturalized in the United States, and subject to the jurisdiction thereof, are citizens of the United States and of the State wherein they reside. No State shall make or enforce any law which shall abridge the privileges or immunities of citizens of the United States; nor shall any State deprive any person of life, liberty, or property, without due process of law; nor deny to any person within its jurisdiction the equal protection of the laws.

THE SUPREME COURT AND CRIMINAL JUSTICE

Our federal court system rests on a very simple statement in Article 3, Section 1, of the Constitution:

> The judicial Power of the United States, shall be vested in one supreme Court, and in such inferior Courts as the Congress may from time to time ordain and establish ...

In Section 2, Clause 2, of this Article the appellate jurisdiction of the Supreme Court is described:

> ... In all the other Cases before mentioned, the supreme Court shall have appellate Jurisdiction, both as to Law and Fact, with such Exceptions, and under such Regulations as the Congress shall make.

Thus, Congress is given the power to define what the appellate jurisdiction of the court will be. The legislative branch may increase or decrease this function of the Court as it sees fit; however, it has been reluctant to do so. If the issue is one of interpretation: whether a law or procedure—either state or federal—is in accord with the Constitution, then the power of the Court is beyond the reach of the Congress. The historic decision in *Marbury v. Madison* settled this matter by ruling that the Judiciary Act of 1789 was unconstitutional in giving the Court the power to issue a writ of *mandamus*.[24]

The Judiciary Act of 1789 provided necessary congressional authorization for the Court to re-examine, reverse, or affirm the final judgments of the highest courts of the states.

> ... The Supreme Court shall also have appellate jurisdiction from the ... courts of the several states, in the cases herein after provided for ...[25]

The constitutionality of this act was first challenged in 1816 by a private citizen (*Martin v. Hunter's Lessee*)[26], then again in 1821 by a sovereign state (*Cohens v. Virginia*).[27] The Court affirmed its appellate review power in both cases. In addition, the Eleventh Amendment (relating to limitations on the "judicial power of the United States") was expressly held not to preclude the exercise of the Court's appellate review power even in a criminal prosecution in which the state itself is a party.[28]

From time to time, especially before the Civil War, several proposals have been introduced to abolish or limit the Court's power to review state court cases.[29] Thus far, such attempts to curb its review power have been doomed.

Incorporating the Bill of Rights Through the Fourteenth Amendment

The myriad problems of the twentieth century—resulting from the closing of the frontier, the onset of industrialization, the emergence of the United States as a world power, a burgeoning population, and urban growth—have exerted their influence for change in the distribution of power between the states and the federal government. Many people argued that such change should be effected by fresh interpretations of the Constitution. In the New Deal era of the late 1930s, the Court began to adopt this idea.

Other influences also caused a re-examination of state law enforcement practice. The reports in 1931 of the National Commission on Law Observance and Enforcement (the Wickersham Commission), the rise of totalitarianism in Europe and elsewhere, and the appointment of judges whose philosophical outlook reflected New Deal liberalism all helped focus the Court's attention on individual liberties. Criminal cases that might previously have been rejected were selected for scrutiny and commentary. As a result, the highest courts of the states were on the road to being stripped of the authority to act as the final arbiters of law enforcement activities. This has profoundly affected the investigative process.

Of course, not all Supreme Court justices adopted this view at once; rather, as succeeding presidents from Franklin Roosevelt on made appointments to the Court, it was taken up in varying degrees by each justice as his or her judicial philosophy was constructed. Throughout its history, the Court has overruled itself less than 200 times; it took 143 years to overrule 133 cases. In the 16 years of the Warren Court, however, an additional 44 cases were overruled, principally in the area of criminal law.

At the risk of oversimplification, and disregarding the nuances involved, the following explanation of the broad points of view that separate the Court into two schools (where law enforcement is concerned) should help to understand the trend. One is a legalistic or traditionalist philosophy; the other, a justice-oriented philosophy. The legalistic school favors a close adherence to and a relatively strict interpretation of the Constitution. Rather than extending supervisory power over law enforcement practice to include state agencies, it confines it to federal agencies and procedure. The term "judicial restraint" describes this outlook; "original intent" and "strict construction" also indicate that the Constitution is to be interpreted narrowly or literally. As vacancies occur on the bench, presidents with strict constructionist views of the Court's role in interpreting the Constitution nominate justices who share their views.

Since the early 1940s, however, the justice-oriented school acquired support among Court members, and state criminal law enforcement practice began to be affected. The so-called judicial activist school believes that justice is the yardstick to be applied in a case, as opposed to merely using the law. In reaching decisions, this school considers the findings and fruits of scholarship in other disciplines (like sociology or psychology) when interpreting the Constitution. The more we apply civilized standards in weighing investigative behavior, the less is the likelihood that any action that shocks the conscience of the community will be tolerated. In their view, the rights of the individual are paramount, and the whole power of the state cannot be pitted against the individual without assistance of counsel.

By the last quarter of the twentieth century, through a process of selective incorporation, almost all the safeguards of the Bill of Rights had been extended to cover state law enforcement practice. To understand how this occurred, the language of the Fourteenth Amendment must be reexamined:

> All persons born or naturalized in the United States, and subject to the jurisdiction thereof, are citizens of the United States and of the State wherein they reside. No State shall make or enforce any law which shall abridge the privileges or immunities of citizens of the United States; nor shall any State deprive any person of life, liberty, or property, without due process of law; nor deny to any person within its jurisdiction the equal protection of the laws.

Through the *due process* and *equal protection* clauses of this amendment, the Court has elected to incorporate the provisions of the Bill of Rights and apply them to the states in a piecemeal fashion. Of the first eight amendments, only the Second, Third, Seventh, and the grand jury clause of the Fifth remain unincorporated. A case also can be made for the bail clause of the Eighth Amendment. In the decision extending the Sixth Amendment right to a jury trial, Justice White spoke for the Court:

> ... many of the rights guaranteed by the first eight Amendments to the Constitution have been held to be protected against state action by the Due Process Clause of the Fourteenth Amendment. That clause now protects the right to compensation for property taken by the State; the rights of speech, press, and religion covered by the First Amendment; the Fourth Amendment rights to be free from unreasonable searches and seizures and to have excluded from criminal trials any evidence illegally seized; the right guaranteed by the Fifth Amendment to be free of compelled self-incrimination; and the Sixth Amendment right to counsel, to a speedy and public trial, to confrontation of opposing witnesses, and to compulsory process for obtaining witnesses.[30]

The Supreme Court's 2012 ruling over Arizona immigration laws made it clear that immigration is a federal issue and that a State cannot go beyond federal rules. However, the Court also held that state law enforcement officials, in an arrest or stop, could question an individual's immigration status "if they have reason to suspect that the individual might be in the country illegally." In the view of many legal scholars, this decision is likely to result in new cases affecting immigration law.[31]

MILESTONE DECISIONS AFFECTING INVESTIGATIVE PRACTICE

Law is but one of many institutions devised by society to control social behavior. Not static, it slowly evolves with the culture of the civilization it serves. In some areas of the world, law exerts little influence on the process of criminal investigation, but in the United States its effect is far-reaching. For countries of Anglo-Saxon heritage, the primary sources are threefold: common law and doctrinal writings, the legislature, and case law through judicial interpretations. The Supreme Court exerts its greatest influence in the area of case law.

The Constitution grants original jurisdiction to the highest tribunal in a very limited number of special cases that are seldom tried before the Court. Instead, the Supreme Court decides cases that originate in lower federal courts or the highest appellate courts of the states. It is asked to decide criminal law issues of two kinds: those unwittingly created by police behavior and those involving apparently new interpretations of law or custom as urged by defendants through their attorneys. *Rochin v. California* concerned a police-created issue. In this case, overzealous enforcement exceeded the bounds of civilized practice.[32] In *Gideon v. Wainwright*, defense counsel argued for a more liberal interpretation of the "right to counsel" clause.[33] Against the latter, police have little influence, but against the former they can exercise considerable control. Such control should be automatic when police investigative behavior is governed not only by the letter of the law, but also by its spirit. For better or worse (depending on one's viewpoint), criminal investigative practice has been altered by the Court. The next section traces the evolution of the Court's decisions with regard to the meaning of probable cause, the legal concept limiting the power of arrest and the seizure of evidence by law enforcement officers.

PROBABLE CAUSE: ITS EVOLUTION AND SIGNIFICANCE

Statutory authority for police officers to make felony arrests without warrant is generally restricted to crimes committed in their presence, or to cases in which they have reasonable grounds for believing a person has committed (or is committing) a felony. Similarly, the "reasonable" standard applies when seeking a search warrant; there, the applicant must be a reasonably cautious person who believes that *seizable property* will be found; namely, contraband, the fruits of crime, the instruments of crime (e.g., a weapon), or other relevant evidence. Where it is to be discovered—on a particular person, or in his or her home, garage, automobile, or other particular place—must also be specified. It is in the Fourth Amendment that the term *probable cause* appears. The constitutional requirement of "reasonableness" is rooted here. In *Ker v. California*,[34] through the *due process clause* of the Fourteenth Amendment, state law enforcement agencies have had the federal interpretation of Fourth Amendment probable cause imposed on them. Crucial to law enforcement officers, this constitutional imperative governs arrests or searches with or without warrants. For this reason, a more extensive examination of probable cause (including its historical meaning) is necessary for a full understanding of this judicial view.

One of the earliest comments on the meaning of probable cause is found in *Locke v. United States* (1813).[35] Chief Justice John Marshall spoke for the court in this decision:

> The term "probable cause" according to its usual acceptation, means less than evidence which would justify condemnation; and, in all cases of seizure, has a fixed and well known meaning. It imports a seizure made under circumstances which warrant suspicion.[36]

Sixty-five years later, the concept of probable cause was modified in *Stacey v. Emery* (1878):

... if the facts and circumstance before the officer are such as to warrant a man of prudence and caution in believing that the offense has been committed, it is sufficient.[37]

Thus, probable cause shifted from the bare suspicion test of Marshall to the idea of the prudent, cautious person. In *Carroll v. United States*,[38] and subsequently in *Brinegar v. United States*,[39] the term "reasonable" is added to the judicial discussion. In *Carroll*, the Court stated:

Probable cause exists where "the facts and circumstances within their [the arresting officers'] knowledge, and of which they had reasonably trustworthy information, [are] sufficient in themselves to warrant a man of reasonable caution in the belief that" an offense has been or is being committed.[40]

Brinegar throws further light on the question:

In dealing with probable cause, however, as the very name implies, we deal with probabilities. These are not technical; they are the factual and practical considerations of everyday life on which reasonable and prudent men, not legal technicians, act.[41]

The language of the Court seems clear. Nevertheless, the real problem of determining exactly what constitutes probable cause becomes apparent from the specific facts in a particular case.

It is plausible to argue that (owing to experience) the police recognize criminal behavior that the reasonable and prudent person (owing to unfamiliarity) would be unaware of and might, therefore, ignore. Hence, the law places police in the stultifying position of having information based on experience, observation, and interpretation, without the ability to employ it in decision making. Is this not comparable to forbidding the physician to act on clinical observations of a patient because the "reasonable and prudent" person is unable to recognize them? To many people, this position seems indefensible, but with regard to probable cause, it is the legal view governing the conduct of police officers.

In *Rios v. United States* (see Box 15.1) the fact that the officers had insight based on their police training and experience is not considered to be proved by the fact that contraband evidence was indeed in the defendant's possession. Against this logical, defensible argument sits the dictum of *Johnson v. United States* (1948)—that an arrest is not justified by what the subsequent search discloses.[42] Some respond that this is not an exercise in logic, that because individual liberty is at stake, society cannot afford the luxury of placating police officers.

The police argument may be cogent to many in the law enforcement profession; it is rooted, however, in a *crime suppression model* of criminal justice, whereas the Court's reasoning is rooted in a *due process model*. In a democracy the latter model finds greater acceptance from lawyers (and presumably the people); the former model is more popular with the police.

The Court does not address the issue of a difference in perception resulting from the vocational training and experience of a police officer. Rather, even though reasonable persons might draw the same inference from the evidence, a neutral, "disinterested" magistrate must be called upon to make the judgment. The frustration of police (among other things, it takes time to obtain a warrant) and the increased crime suffered by society are among the costs against which the promise to "secure the blessings of liberty" must be weighed. One who is a citizen first and a police officer second is likely to support the Court's view. But the beliefs of one who is a police officer first and then a citizen would be shaped by the crime suppression model. It might profit those so persuaded to examine how confident they are that some of their law enforcement colleagues would not unwittingly, and in their minds for the best of reasons, whittle away their fundamental

---

BOX 15.1 CASE STUDY: *RIOS V. UNITED STATES*

In a 1960 case, *Rios v. United States*, the Court stated:

> As in most cases involving a claimed unconstitutional search and seizure, resolution of the question requires a particular evaluation of the conduct of the officers involved. ... At about ten o'clock on the night of February 18, 1957, two Los Angeles police officers, dressed in plain clothes and riding in an unmarked car, observed a taxicab standing in a parking lot next to an apartment house at the corner of First and Flower Streets in Los Angeles. The neighborhood has a reputation for "narcotics activity." The officers saw the petitioner look up and down the street, walk across the lot, and get into the cab. Neither officer had ever before seen the petitioner, and neither of them had any idea of his identity. Except for the reputation of the neighborhood, neither officer had received information of any kind to suggest that someone might be engaged in criminal activity at that time and place. They were in possession of no arrest or search warrants.

> The taxicab drove away, and the officers followed it in their car for a distance of about two miles through the city. At the intersection of First and State Streets, the cab stopped for a traffic light. The two officers alighted from their car and approached on foot to opposite sides of the cab. One of the officers identified himself as a policeman. In the next minute there occurred a rapid succession of events. The cab door was opened; the petitioner dropped a recognizable package of narcotics to the floor of the vehicle; one of the officers grabbed the petitioner as he alighted from the cab; the other officer retrieved the package; and the first officer drew his revolver.

Further along in the opinion the Court comments:

> ... upon no possible view of the circumstances revealed in the testimony of the Los Angeles officers could it be said that there existed probable cause for an arrest at the time the officers decided to alight from their car and approach the taxi in which the petitioner was riding.

Source: *Rios v. United States*, 364 U.S. 253, 255, 261 (1960).

liberties. Present-day Americans have achieved with relatively little struggle what others paid for with great suffering. We need reminding that it is a price many people are still paying throughout the world.

CONTROL OVER INVESTIGATIVE PRACTICE

Not all Supreme Court decisions affecting law enforcement regulate or limit police conduct. Throughout the text (in Chapters 7 and 8 on informants and surveillance, for example), cases are cited that essentially support investigative practice.

As a result of the 9/11 attacks and reorganization of the government a great many court decisions have impacted law enforcement. Martin Alperen's text, *Foundations of Homeland Security: Law and Policy*, brings into focus many of the legal and legislative changes that have occurred since 9/11, in many cases outlining the problems associated with the government mandate to implement widespread organizational change designed to cope not only with terrorism but also national security, emergency management, and natural disasters. The author provides a comprehensive overview of the development of homeland security law that impacts federal, state, local, and tribal jurisdictions, as well as the private sector.[43]

The landmark cases that in some way restrict or regulate investigative practice are described in Table 15.1. This furnishes a bird's eye view of the issues while providing enough information to permit further pursuit of the matter by anyone interested.

Table 15.1
Milestone Decisions Affecting Investigative Practice under the 4th, 5th, and 6th Amendments of the United States Constitution

FOURTH AMENDMENT	ASPECT OF LAW ENFORCEMENT AFFECTED	SIGNIFICANT CASES*
Clause 1. "The right of the people to be secure in their persons, houses, papers, and effects, against unreasonable searches and seizures shall not be violated; …" (Concept involved: personal security and right to property.)	A. Search and seizure (Inadmissibility of evidence seized in an illegal fashion.)	**Federal Cases** *Weeks v. United States* 232 U.S. 383 (1914) *Wong Sun v. United States*, 371 U.S. 471 (1963) **State Cases**** *Mapp v. Ohio* 367 U.S. 643 (1961)
Clause 2. "… and no warrant shall issue, but upon probable cause …" (Concept involved: arrest powers.)	B. Arrest (The meaning of probable cause—right to stop and question; right to take a person into custody; standard for obtaining a search warrant.)	**Federal Cases** *Brinegar v. United States* 338 U.S. 183 (1948) *Rios v. United States* 364 U.S. 253 (1960) *United States v. Ventresca* 380 U.S. 102 (1965) *Terry v. Ohio* 392 U.S. 1 (1968) *Spinelli v. United States* 393 U.S. 410 (1969) *United States v. Santana* 427 U.S. 38 (1975) **State Cases**** *Aguilar v. Texas* 378 U.S. 108 (1954) *Coolidge v. New Hampshire* 403 U.S. 443 (1971)

FIFTH AMENDMENT	ASPECT OF LAW ENFORCEMENT AFFECTED	SIGNIFICANT CASES*
Clause 3. "; nor (shall any person) be compelled In any criminal case, to be a witness against himself;" (Concept involved: compulsory self-incrimination.)	A. Confessions (Incompetent under the self-incrimination clause if not free and voluntary, no threats or violence used, no promises made, direct or indirect, or any other improper influence exerted or mild pressure employed.) B. Compulsory testimony (Evidence obtained through a legal grant of immunity on the state level cannot then be used against the person on the federal level, or vice-versa.)	**Federal Cases** *United States v. The Saline Bank of Virginia* 1 Pet 100 (1828) *Bram v. United States* 168 U.S. 532 (1897) *Hardy v. United States* 186 U.S. 224(1902) *Ballman v. Fagin* 200 U.S. 186 (1906) *Wan v. United States* 266 U.S. 1 (1924) *Smith v. United States* 348 U.S. 147 (1954)

Table 15.1
(Continued)

FIFTH AMENDMENT	ASPECT OF LAW ENFORCEMENT AFFECTED	SIGNIFICANT CASES*
		State Cases** *Brown v. Mississippi* 279 U.S. 278(1936) *Haynes v. Washington* 373 U.S. 503(1963) *Malloy v. Hogan* 378 U.S. 1 (1964) *Murphy v. The Waterfront Commission of New York Harbor,* 378 U.S. 52 (1964) *Miranda v. Arizona* 384 U.S. 346(1966) *Colorado v. Colorado* 479 U.S. 157 (1986)
Clause 3. "; nor (shall any person) be deprived of life, liberty, or property without due process of law. (Concept involved: due process)	C. Interrogation during detention (Confessions.) D. Admissibility of evidence	**Federal Cases** *McNabb v. United States* 18 U.S. 332 (1943) *Upshaw v. United States* 335 U.S. 410 (1948) *Mallory v. United States* 354 U.S. 449 (1957) *Dickerson v. United States* 530 U.S. 428 (2000) **State Cases*** *Brown v. Mississippi* 297 U.S. 278 (1936) *Rochin v. California* 342 U.S. 165 (1952) *Miranda v. Arizona* 384 U.S. 436 (1966) *Edwards v. Arizona* 451 U.S. 477 (1981) *New York v. Querles* 467 U.S. 649 (1984) *Kaupp v. Texas* 538 U.S. 626 (2003) *Missouri v. Seibert* 542 U.S. 600 (2004)

Table 15.1
(Continued)

SIXTH AMENDMENT	ASPECT OF LAW ENFORCEMENT AFFECTED	SIGNIFICANT CASES*
Clause 2. "... to be confronted with the witnesses against him;" (Concepts involved: Access to evidence, Right of cross-examination. Fundamental fairness implicit in the concept of ordered liberty.)	A. The investigator's and prosecutor's ability to persuade the individual to appear as a witness in court.	**State Cases**** *Pointer v. Texas* 380 U.S. 400(1965)
Clause 3. "... and to have the assistance of counsel for his defense." (Concept involved: right to counsel, essentials of a fair trial.)	A. Adversary system of justice emphasized. B. Pretrial disclosure of investigative reports to defense counsel. (This affects the report writing efforts of investigators.)	**Federal Cases** *Jencks v. United States* 353 U.S. 657 (1957) *Massiah v. United States* 377 U.S. 201 (1964) *United States v. Dionisio* 410 U.S. 1 (1973) *United States v. Henry* 477 U.S. 264 (1980) **State Cases**** *Brady v. Maryland* 373 U.S. 83(1963) *Gideon v. Wainwright* 372 U.S. 335 (1963) *Escobedo v. Illinois* 378 U.S. 478 (1964) *Miranda v. Arizona* 384 U.S. 436 (1966)

*The terms "federal" and "state" indicate where the case originated. In a sense they are all federal cases, as the definitive decision was made by the U.S. Supreme Court.

**As a result of these decisions, federal practice and rules of criminal procedure are applied to state and local law enforcement through the "due process" clause of the 14th Amendment.

CONCLUSION

The Rule of Law is an indisputable aspect of the American criminal justice system and one of the most important precepts of democracy. Throughout history the American criminal justice system has adapted to change, sometimes grudgingly, and there is not always consensus among the police or the public. Nevertheless, it is not the police who make the laws, nor should the police take it upon themselves to ignore legal precepts, as has been done in the past and will likely be done by some in the future. Unfortunately, hardly a week goes by without some revelation of police abuse of authority, or a violation of the law that leads to an arrest and conviction of a police officer who felt that he or she was "above the law." It should not need to be mentioned to a future or present investigator that it is not worth going to jail or losing one's job by breaking the law to achieve an illegal end. But history shows that this is still a common problem.

NOTES

1   The American Heritage Dictionary of the English Language, 2nd College Edition, s.v. "crime."

2   H. Wechsler "The Challenge of a Model Penal Code," *Harvard Law Review*, 65 (1952), 1097–1098.

3   The authors are indebted to Ginny Wilson, who prepared the following section on crime theories.

4   Sigmund Freud *Beyond the Pleasure Principle* London: Inter-Psychoanalytic Press, 1922).

5   James Q. Wilson and George Kelling. "Broken Windows: The Police and Neighborhood Safety." *Atlantic Monthly*, (March 1982), 1–11.

6   Emile Durkheim, *Suicide: A Study in Sociology* (New York: Free Press, 1987).

7   Robert Agnew "Foundation for a General Strain Theory of Crime and Delinquency," *Criminology*, 30:1 (2002), 235–263.

8   Walter Miller "Lower Class Structure as a Generating Milieu of Gang Delinquency," *Journal of Social Issues*, 14:3 (1958), 9–30. 322.

9   Richard A. Cloward and Lloyd E. Ohlin, *Delinquency and Opportunity: A Theory of Delinquent Gangs* (Glencoe, IL: Free Press, 1960).

10 Gresham Sykes and David Matza, "Techniques of Neutralization: A Theory of Delinquency," *American Sociological Review*, 22 (December 1957), 664–670.

11 See, for example, Edwin H. Sutherland, & Donald R. Cressey. (1978). *Criminology* New York: Lippincott.

12 Robert Burgess and Ronald L. Akers, "A Differential Association-Reinforcement Theory of Criminal Behavior," Social Problems, 14 (1966), 363–383.

13 Albert Bandura, "The Social Learning Perspective: Mechanisms of Aggression," in Hans Toch, ed. *Psychology of Crime and Criminal Justice* (Prospect Heights, IL: Waveland, 1979).

14 Walter C. Reckless, *The Crime Problem*, 4th ed. (New York: Appleton-Century-Crofts, 1967).

15 Frank Tannenbaum, *Crime and the Community* (New York: Atheneum Press, 1938); see also, Edwin M. Lemert, *Social Pathology: A Systematic Approach to the Theory of Sociopathic Behavior* (New York: McGraw-Hill, 1951).

16 Howard Becker, *Outsiders: Studies in the Sociology of Deviance* (New York: Free Press, 1963).

17 Robert J. Sampson and John H. Laub, "Crime and the Life Course," in *Criminological Theory*, edited by Francis T. Cullen and Robert Agnew (Los Angeles: Roxbury), 2006, 187–198.

18 Robert J. Sampson and John H. Laub, *Crime in the Making: Pathways and Turning Points through Life* (Cambridge, MA: Harvard University Press, 1993).

19 Michael R. Gottfredson and Travis Hirschi, *A General Theory of Crime* (Palo Alto, CA: Stanford University Press, 1990).

[20] Freda Adler. *Sisters in Crime* (Prospect Heights, IL: Waveland, 1975, reprinted 1985); Rita James Simon, *Women and Crime* (Lexington, MA: D.C. Health, 1975).

[21] Daniel T. Borstin. "America: Our By-product Nation," *Time*, (23 June 1975), 70.

[22] Bruce Findlay and Esther Findlay, *Your Rugged Constitution* (Stanford, CA: Stanford University Press, 1950), 213.

[23] Paul Brest, *Processes of Constitutional Decision Making* (Boston: Little, Brown, 1975), 708.

[24] *Marbury v. Madison*, 5 U.S. (1 Cranch) 137 (1803).

[25] U.S. Judiciary Act 1789. Sec. 25. 1 Stat. 85.

[26] *Martin v. Hunter's Lessee*, 14 U.S. (1 Wheat.) 304 (1816).

[27] *Cohens v. Virginia*, 19 U.S. (6 Wheat.) 264 (1821).

[28] Ibid.

[29] M.S. Culp, "A Survey of the Proposals to Limit or Deny the Power of Judicial Review by the Supreme Court of the United States," *Indiana Law Journal* 4, 386 (1928).

[30] *Duncan v. Louisiana*, 391 U.S. 145 (1968).

[31] Liptak, Adam. "Court Splits Immigration Law Verdicts; Upholds Hotly Debated Centerpiece, 8–0." *The New York Times.* June 26, 2012. Pp. A1, A13.

[32] *Rochin v. California*, 342 U.S. 165 (1952).

[33] *Gideon v. Wainwright*, 372 U.S. 335 (1963).

[34] *Ker v. California*, 374 U.S. 23, 33 (1963).

[35] *Locke v. United States*, 11 U.S. (7 Cranch) 339 (1813).

[36] Ibid., 348.

[37] *Stacey v. Emery*, 97 U.S. 642, 645 (1878).

[38] *Carroll v. United States*, 267 U.S. 132 (1925).

[39] *Brinegar v. United States*, 338 U.S. 160 (1948).

[40] *Carroll*, supra note 38, 162.

[41] *Brinegar*, supra note 39, 175.

[42] *Johnson v. United States*, 333 U.S. 10, 16 (1948).

[43] Alperen, Martin. (2011). *Foundations of Homeland Security: Law and Policy.*John Wiley & Sons, New Jersey.

IMPORTANT CASES

Aguilar v. Texas (1954)
Ballman v. Fagin (1906)
Brady v. Maryland (1963)

Bram v. United States (1897)

Brinegar v. United States (1948)

Brown v. Mississippi (1936)

Carroll v. United States (1925)

Cohens v. Virginia (1821)

Colorado v. Colorado (1986)

Coolidge v. New Hampshire (1971)

Dickerson v. United States (2000)

Edwards v. Arizona (1981)

Escobedo v. Illinois (1964)

Gideon v. Wainwright (1963)

Hardy v. United States (1902)

Haynes v. Washington (1963)

Jencks v. United States (1957)

Johnson v. United States (1948)

Kaupp v. Texas (2003)

Ker v. California (1963)

Locke v. United States (1813)

Malloy v. Hogan (1964)

Mapp v. Ohio (1961)

Marbury v. Madison (1803)

Martin v. Hunter's Lessee (1816)

Massiah v. United States (1964)

McNabb v. United States (1943)

Miranda v. Arizona (1966)

Mallory v. United States (1957)

Missouri v. Seibert (2004)

Murphy v. The Waterfront Commission of New York Harbor (1964)

New York v. Querles (1984)

Pointer v. Texas (1965)

Rios v. United States (1960)

Rochin v. California (1952)

Smith v. United States (1954)

Spinelli v. United States (1969)

Stacey v. Emery (1878)

Terry v. Ohio (1968)

United States v. Dionisio (1973)

United States v. Henry (1980)

United States v. Santana (1975)

United States v. The Saline Bank of Virginia (1828)

United States v. Ventresca (1965)

Upshaw v. United States (1948)

Wan v. United States (1924)

Weeks v. United States (1914)

Wong Sun v. United States (1963)

DISCUSSION QUESTIONS

1. Why should an investigator be familiar with the U.S. Constitution and the American legal system?

2. From what legal system is the American legal system relating to crime drawn?

3. What is the difference between substantive criminal law and procedural criminal law?

4. Explain what is meant by the "elements" of a crime.

5. What is *corpus delicti*?

6. What is meant by the term "case law"?

7. What is strain theory?

8. What is culture conflict theory?

9. What crimes appear in the Constitution?

10. What amendments to the Constitution, based on past Supreme Court decisions, have the greatest influence on criminal investigation?

SUPPLEMENTAL READINGS

Brown, S. E., Esbensen, F. A., & Geis, G. (2013). *Criminology: Explaining crime and its context* (8th ed.). Boston: Elsevier/Anderson Publishing.

del Carmen, R. V. (2009). *Criminal procedure: Law and practice* (8th ed.). Belmont, CA: Thomson Wadsworth.

del Carmen, R. V., & Walker, J. T. (2012). *Briefs of leading cases in law enforcement* (8th ed.). Boston: Elsevier/Anderson Publishing.

Felkenes, G. T. (1988). *Constitutional law for criminal justice* (2nd ed.). Englewood Cliffs, NJ: Prentice Hall.

Garner, B. A. (Ed.). (2009). *Black's law dictionary* (9th ed.). St. Paul, MN: West.

Hall, K. L., & James, W. E, Jr. (2008). *The oxford guide to united states court decisions* (2nd ed.). New York: Oxford University Press.

Hogue, A. R. (1985). *Origins of the common law*. Indianapolis: Liberty Press.

Jones, M., & Johnson, P. (2012). *History of criminal justice* (5th ed.). Boston: Elsevier/Anderson Publishing.

Kanovitz, J. R. (2013). *Constitutional law* (13th ed.). Boston: Elsevier/Anderson Publishing.

Moak, S., & Carlson, R. L. (2013). *Criminal justice procedure* (8th ed.). Boston: Elsevier/Anderson Publishing.

National Commission on Law Enforcement (1931), *Report on lawlessness in law enforcement.* Washington, DC: U.S. Government Printing Office. [This is Report No. 11 of the Wickersham Commission appointed by President Herbert Hoover in 1929.].

Pollock, J. M. (2013). *Criminal law* (10th ed.). Boston: Elsevier/Anderson Publishing.

Schwartz, B. (1993). *A history of the supreme court.* New York: Oxford University Press.

Segal, J. A., & Harold, J. (1993). *Spaeth: The supreme court and the attitudinal model.* New York: Cambridge University Press.

Singer, S., & Marshall J. H. (1986). *Constitutional criminal procedure handbook.* New York: Wiley Law. Out of print.

Travis, L. F., III (2012). *Introduction to criminal justice* (7th ed.). Boston: Elsevier/Anderson Publishing.

Williams, F. P., III, & McShane, M. D. (1998). *Criminology theory: Selected classic readings.* Cincinnati: Anderson Publishing.

CHAPTER 16

EVIDENCE AND EFFECTIVE TESTIMONY

INTRODUCTION

A criminal investigation may be culminated in one of the following ways:

- The case is unfounded.

- The case is "cleared" by arrest for another crime or the suspect is deceased.
  - —While there is no precise definition of a "cleared case," generally the term refers to a case in which the suspects are charged or the case is closed administratively.

- The suspect pleads guilty to the crime(s) or to a lesser offense.
  - —The majority of cases brought before the courts in the United States result in a "plea bargain" in which the prosecution and the defense agree to accept a guilty plea for a lesser crime, or for an agreed-upon sentencing recommendation.

- An "indictment" or "information" is filed
  - —Felony cases in most jurisdictions require action by a grand jury, which is a "one-sided hearing" by the prosecutor before a jury that determines whether a *prima facie* case exists, or, in other words, that there is a probability that the defendant committed the crime. The grand jury will hand down an "indictment" if they conclude that a felony has been committed, or an "information" if it is concluded that the crime was a misdemeanor.

- The case is referred for trial.

This chapter addresses the process of a criminal trial with regard to the presentation of evidence and testimony of the investigator. A courtroom trial must establish the guilt of a defendant, proved beyond a reasonable doubt, during which legally obtained evidence (that is, evidence that is admissible in court) is presented to a jury (or judge, if trial by jury is waived). After hearing all the evidence, the jury or judge evaluates it, determines the facts, and based upon those facts makes a judgment of "guilty" or "not guilty." When a jury cannot reach a decision, which in most cases requires agreement by all voting members of the jury, the judge will nullify the trial in what is known as a "hung jury." The prosecutor has the option of retrying the case with another jury.

Initially and throughout this process the investigator is largely responsible for (1) establishing that a crime was committed, and (2) developing evidence to prove beyond a reasonable doubt that a particular individual is guilty of that crime. For future reference, one should carefully note the date and time when each bit of evidence became known or was developed by the investigator.

At the trial stage, it is the prosecutor's responsibility to present the evidence in court. Here, a few cautionary words about teamwork are in order: if a prosecutor and investigator do not work together, the presentation in court will be adversely affected—and so will the case against the defendant. Criminal prosecutions have been lost not only because a state's attorney had not prepared (through pretrial conferences) civilian witnesses to testify, but also because the police had not induced them to be available and in court at the proper time.

WHAT IS EVIDENCE?

Evidence is anything a judge permits to be offered in court to prove the truth or falsity of the question(s) at issue. It is classified as: testimonial, real, or demonstrative. Testimonial evidence is given orally by a witness. Real evidence is any tangible object or exhibit offered as proof. Demonstrative evidence can be a chart, drawing, model, illustration, or experiment. Some evidence may be classified as all three; for example, the results of forensic examinations presented in court can be testimonial, real, and/or demonstrative.

Evidence can also be classified as either direct or circumstantial. Direct evidence is evidence that, in itself, proves or refutes the fact at issue; for instance, a confession. Most often, direct evidence is testimonial—based on what a witness saw or heard—but it sometimes involves the other senses. Circumstantial evidence is indirect proof from which the fact at issue may be inferred. Most forensic testimonial evidence is circumstantial.

Direct, circumstantial, testimonial, real, and demonstrative evidence are not mutually exclusive. Testimonial evidence can be either direct or circumstantial; real evidence is also demonstrative evidence; and both real and demonstrative evidence are tangible evidence in contrast to verbal or testimonial evidence. The following scenario may clarify this:

> A bank robbery was interrupted by an off-duty police officer just entering a bank. Shots were exchanged and the officer was killed, the fleeing robber pausing long enough to pick up the fallen officer's revolver. Based on a reliable informant's tip, a search warrant was obtained and the suspect's garage searched. Evidence being found, the suspect was arrested. Later, the friend to whom he gave the gun for safekeeping voluntarily turned it over to the police.

At trial subsequently, a detective described the finding of "bait" money (handed over to the robber by the teller) buried in the dirt floor of the robber's garage. The marked money itself is real evidence. Discovering its hiding place to be the defendant's garage is an example of circumstantial evidence. The detective's witness-stand account of the discovery is testimonial evidence. The friend's witness-stand statements concerning her receipt of the police officer's revolver are examples of two kinds of evidence: testimonial and real. The photographs and a sketch showing the location of the buried loot before and after its retrieval are examples of demonstrative evidence.

A popular misconception about circumstantial evidence is that it ought not be believed; another, that it is a weak kind of evidence at best. The court, however, can insist on proper safeguards to ensure that a conviction resting solely on circumstantial evidence is sound—logical, convincing, and related to the contested issue. Circumstantial evidence can be, and often is, a most persuasive type of proof.

Historical Background of the Rules of Evidence

A means for settling both civil and criminal disputes is—after food, shelter, and procreation—high on the list of human needs. Just as various rules have evolved to secure justice, so have procedures to implement them. Historically, 16 systems have been recognized as constituting a well-defined, organized, continuous body of legal ideas and methods.[1] Two systems remain dominant in modern times: the Romanesque and the Anglican.[2] The Romanesque was developed in the 1200s. Known as an inquisitorial system of criminal justice, it is still operative in Continental Europe and Latin America. In this judge-directed and judge-dominated system, guilt or innocence is decided by a judge. There are few rules controlling the amount or type of evidence that must be considered. Underlying the need for few and less strict rules is the belief that a judge is better able to evaluate evidence than a jury of laypersons.

The Anglican legal system, or common law system, was inherited from England and is operative in the United States. Comprising an elaborate set of rules to govern the evidence that may be heard by a judge and a lay jury, it is an adversarial system in which the defendant in a criminal case is presumed innocent until proved guilty. This must be done to the satisfaction of a jury, and not solely that of a judge, as in the inquisitorial system.

Developments in the United States

During the past two centuries, a system of rules for the presentation of evidence has been established in the United States. In some instances the rules are the result of centuries of deep thought and experience. In other instances the rules have been established in a haphazard manner without much thought. Although the United States inherited the English system, rules concerning the admissibility of evidence have taken separate developmental paths and are not the same in the two countries.... Due to legislation and court decisions, some of which interpret constitutional provisions, the rules for obtaining and weighing evidence are now more restrictive in the United States than in England. ...

In an effort to obtain more uniformity in court procedures, the United States Supreme Court in 1972 adopted the Rules of Evidence for United States Courts and Magistrates. ... However, in accordance with federal laws, the proposed rules were required to be transmitted to Congress for approval. The House Judiciary Committee wrestled with the provisions for nearly a year, and finally approved a modified version in early 1974 by a vote of 377 to 130. Before approving the Supreme Court draft of the rules of evidence, the House Judiciary Committee changed provisions concerning privileged communications. ...[3]

Congress allowed the Federal Rules of Evidence to become federal law in 1975, after enacting the modifications to the rules proposed by the Supreme Court. The Rules are not carved in stone. It should be expected that, from time to time, they will be added to and revised.

The Rules of Evidence

For practical purposes the rules of evidence are rules of exclusion. Emphasis is placed throughout this text, therefore, on legal investigative behavior. This means: securing a search warrant to obtain evidence, arresting only on probable cause, administering *Miranda* warnings before interrogating a suspect, and respecting the right to counsel and the need for due process. An investigator sensitive to these concerns is unlikely to have evidence that was obtained in the course of the investigation excluded at trial.

Relevancy, materiality, and competency are other grounds on which an attorney relies to exclude evidence.

Relevancy is concerned with whether there is a connection between the evidence and the issue to be proved. Relevant evidence tends to prove or disprove a fact.

Materiality is concerned with whether the evidence is sufficiently important to influence the outcome of the issue being contested. Does it throw enough new light on the issue to warrant taking the time for its presentation and consideration?

Competency is concerned with the quality and kind of evidence being offered (or the person offering it). Competent evidence is that which is admissible under the rules of evidence for the purpose of proving a relevant fact.

As a general rule, evidence will not be excluded if neither prosecution nor defense makes an objection to its admission. Though not likely, a judge may also make a motion to exclude evidence.

Relevant Evidence

Relevant evidence—its admission and exclusion—is succinctly described in the Federal Rules of Evidence, Rules 401, 402, and 403.

Rule 401.   *Definition of "Relevant Evidence"*
"Relevant evidence" means evidence having any tendency to make the existence of any fact that is of consequence to the determination of the action more probable or less probable than it would be without the evidence.[4]

Rule 402.   *Relevant Evidence Generally Admissible; Irrelevant Evidence Inadmissible*
All relevant evidence is admissible, except as otherwise provided by the Constitution of the United States, by Act of Congress, by these rules, or by other rules prescribed by the Supreme Court pursuant to statutory authority. Evidence which is not relevant is not admissible.[5]

Rule 403.   *Exclusion of Relevant Evidence on Grounds of Prejudice, Confusion, or Waste of Time*
Although relevant, evidence may be excluded if its probative value is substantially outweighed by the danger of unfair prejudice, confusion of the issues, or misleading the jury, or by considerations of undue delay, waste of time, or needless presentation of cumulative evidence.[6]

In summary, it would appear that logic and common sense are to be utilized when deciding whether a piece of evidence is relevant. Relevancy by itself is not sufficient, however; the evidence must also be material and competent.

Material Evidence

Lawyers and judges often treat the terms *relevant* and *material*—and particularly their opposites—*irrelevant* and *immaterial*—as interchangeable.[7] They are not, of course. In distinguishing between the two, one court wrote:

As used with respect to evidence, "material" has a wholly different meaning from "relevant." To be relevant means to relate to the issue. To be material means to have probative weight, that is, reasonably likely to influence the tribunal in making the determination required to be made.[8]

Another view with regard to the same issue is that all material evidence is necessarily relevant, but all relevant evidence is not necessarily material. Evidence is not material if its effect on the outcome is likely to be trivial. Furthermore, evidence, though material, may be inadmissible because it is not competent.

Competent Evidence

The third prong in the test for admissibility (the most important from an investigative viewpoint) is *competency*. Competency involves either the nature of the evidence itself or the person through whom it is offered in court. It is interesting and informative to note that even after having consulted several law dictionaries, an intelligible definition of competent evidence remains elusive. In one dictionary, it is "to be legally qualified or legally fit";[9] in another, "the quality of evidence offered which makes it proper to be received";[10] in still another, "evidence relevant to the issues being litigated."[11]

Such definitions being of limited value, the concept involved is best understood by turning to examples of incompetent evidence. There, the most common grounds for exclusion are invoked when the evidence was obtained in violation of the United States Constitution, state and federal statutes, or rules established by courts. Increasingly, evidence obtained in violation of state constitutional provisions, as interpreted by state courts of last resort, is being held incompetent.

Constitutional Grounds

Evidence that has been obtained in violation of the Constitution ... is inadmissible not because it is irrelevant or immaterial but because it is incompetent *as determined by the courts* (emphasis added).[12]

Statutory Incompetence

... [S]ome evidence is not admissible because a state or federal statute prohibits the admission of the evidence. For example, § 2515 of the Omnibus Crime Control and Safe Streets Act of 1968, as amended, provides that evidence obtained by wiretapping or eavesdropping, when conducted in violation of the statute, is inadmissible in any court or other official proceeding. ... Evidence produced in contravention of ... similar statutes will be excluded from court use not because it is irrelevant or immaterial, but because the statutes specifically provide that the evidence is not admissible or usable in court.[13]

Similarly, evidence based on a privileged communication is not admissible by statute; any such proposed testimony is ruled out as incompetent. A privileged communication is any statement made by one person to another with whom a special relationship of trust and confidentiality exists. The most common examples include husband/wife, clergy/church member, attorney/client, and physician/patient; some jurisdictions also include accountant/client and reporter/source. A few examples of evidence deemed incompetent by court rules are:

- The evidence is unreliable (hearsay evidence)

- The evidence is so prejudicial (e.g., gruesome homicide scene photographs) that it could inflame the jury and its detrimental effect outweigh by far its probative value

- The evidence might lead to undue sympathy or hostility on the part of the jury

- The evidence would be disruptive of trial procedure (e.g., a surprise alibi raised at the last moment while at trial)

- The evidence would waste the court's time (e.g., repetitive, cumulative evidence being unnecessary)

WHAT IS EFFECTIVE TESTIMONY?

The investigative effort reaches its final, decisive stage when the results are presented at trial to court and jury. Unless accomplished effectively, the outcome could be a disappointment: a defendant might be found guilty of a lesser count in the indictment or even found not guilty. An investigator may well ask, "What, exactly does 'accomplished effectively' mean?" Testimony that is both understandable and believable would partially fill the bill. These two qualities, together with preparation regarding substantive matters and deportment, sum up "accomplished effectively."

Understandable Testimony

It is important that investigators be able to articulate the investigative activities leading to the indictment of the defendant. The method employed (for almost all court testimony) follows a question-and-answer (Q & A) format. The investigator responds to questions from both prosecutor and defense counsel. In so doing, the investigator must speak plainly and avoid police jargon that may not be comprehensible to a lay jury. Some jurors will recognize police shorthand, but few will know what "a DD 13 is." Hence, "I forwarded a DD 13 to see if the DOA owned the car" is not informative—thus, an ineffective statement. On the other hand, "I asked the records bureau for the name of the registered owner of the vehicle bearing license plate ABC-123" is informative enough to be effective. Answers should be couched in simple, everyday language and should be responsive to the questions. The ability to do this rests in part on a mastery of the details of the investigation. Hazy answers reflect a lack of command over every detail; this can be avoided by a careful pretrial review of crime scene notes, sketches, photographs, and case reports.

Anyone called to testify for the first time is naturally apprehensive; some people, including investigators, never quite conquer this feeling. Hence, witnesses mumble and give inaudible answers even though it is axiomatic that what a juror does not understand is evidence lost. Another critical consequence of a timid presentation is that the witness's credibility is diminished. In summary, understandable and believable testimony are inseparable: what cannot be understood will not be believed.

Believable Testimony

A criminal trial has two sides. The prosecution has the burden of proof beyond a reasonable doubt, and the defense must convince the court of the state's failure to do so. The defense need prove nothing; in most cases it will deny the charge and enter testimony in support of its contention of innocence. The jury's task is to decide which facts among all those presented are to be believed.

What then makes one witness more believable than another? And how can investigators enhance their credibility? Obviously, the witness with firsthand knowledge of the details of the case, who does not have to refer to notes, and whose facts square with common sense, creates a favorable impression. The good impression is heightened further if no prejudice, direct or indirect, is expressed against the defendant. A deputy sheriff's witness-stand response to a defense question in a murder trial surely diminished his credibility the moment he declared, "I'm here to see him burn!"

Even the *appearance* of overzealousness is to be avoided. For instance, an investigator unwilling to agree to anything that might assist the defendant is likely to reply to the defense question "Isn't it possible the gun went off accidentally?" with a flat-out denial: "No, that was not possible." Ruling out *all* possibilities is something a jury would find hard to swallow. A proper response might be, "Yes, that is a possibility;" or to add "Yes, but I do not believe the facts support the likelihood of that having happened" (assuming that the facts reasonably support the added contention).

It is also appropriate when testifying to display a concern for the plight of both victim and accused, as well as an obvious sincerity when presenting the facts that led to the indictment. In summary, an investigator should avoid leaving the overall impression with a jury that he or she is an automaton reeling off names, dates, and jaded answers. Rather, the investigator should be perceived as a human being very much aware of the gravity of the situation.

Behavior and Appearance

From the moment an investigator is called to the witness stand and walks into the courtroom, he or she is under scrutiny by the jury. The witness's carriage when proceeding to the stand—and demeanor while on it—can enhance or diminish the impact of the testimony. Just as conduct is important, so too is general appearance. The investigator/witness should be groomed as for a job interview.

Figure 16.1
On the witness stand, New York State Police Investigator Drew McDonald describes part of a crime scene. The defendant, Christopher Porco, was accused of killing his father with an ax and injuring his mother in their home.

CROSS-EXAMINATION

The Purpose

Immediately following the investigator's direct testimony, defense counsel will begin the cross-examination; its purposes are:

1.   To satisfy the obligation to a client to test any evidence being offered, if there is doubt about it.

2.   To develop facts favorable to the defense.

3.   To discredit the witness.

4.   To destroy the character of the witness, his or her story, or both.

Facts Favorable to the Defense

It is possible to develop facts that are advantageous to the defense (1) by eliciting a response from the investigator that suggests or acknowledges illegal behavior, or (2) by showing that there were others who had a motive, were considered suspects, and have not been ruled out. Defense counsel may try to establish that prevailing conditions (e.g., weather, light, etc.) contributed to a misjudgment of the victim's behavior and provoked the reaction from the defendant.

A competent attorney will seize upon any opportunity warranted by the testimony to build the case for the defense. In a narcotics arrest, for example, no mention was made on direct examination of a fingerprint having been found on any of the glassine envelopes containing the heroin. On cross-examination, the investigator might be asked casually whether any fingerprints were found on the evidence. If, as is most likely, the answer is "no," counsel may appear to ignore the response and go on to other matters. If such an issue raised by the Q & A is ignored by the prosecutor on redirect examination, defense counsel may argue in closing that the absence of the client's fingerprint on the envelopes proves that the defendant did not handle them. Most jurors, believing that fingerprints are invariably left when touching an object, may be persuaded. Had an expert in the development of fingerprints been summoned to testify, however, the record could have been set straight—fingerprints are not necessarily found on narcotics glassine envelopes. Similar issues surround the presence, or lack thereof, of DNA evidence. In some cases, such as rape, it is expected that a DNA examination of the victim would be conducted. It is the prosecutor's job to be alert to such possibilities, but an investigator who senses potential problems should bring them up with the prosecutor as soon as possible after leaving the witness stand.

Discrediting the Witness

Approaches taken to discredit a witness:

* Bringing out any latent evidence of bias or prejudice
* Testing the memory of the witness, the aim being to elicit statements inconsistent with or contradictory to the direct testimony
* Revealing, through adroit questioning, the direct testimony to be unreasonable and, therefore, of questionable credibility
* Showing that the direct testimony was inaccurate, mistaken, or the result of an oversight

Destroying the Witness's Testimony

One ultimate result of the adversary system, which pits defense against prosecution, is the demolition of a case through cross-examination. This need not happen if the investigator is alert, prepared, and truthful. If a witness is untruthful (especially if it involves a crucial piece of evidence) and this is admitted to on the witness stand, the witness's testimony is destroyed in the eyes of a jury.

Strategy and Tactics

A *leading question* is one that in its very asking supplies an answer. Often, it merely requires a "yes" or "no." This is permitted on cross-examination but not on direct examination. As a strategy, leading questions allow the defense to testify (albeit indirectly). Even attorneys with fearful reputations as cross-examiners will treat a witness "with kid gloves" when leading questions help the defense. Off the stand, one investigator remarked on completing his testimony, "Well, that wasn't too bad. How come he's considered so tough?" Having elicited admissions somewhat inconsistent with direct testimony, defense counsel had let the investigator off lightly. The questioning would have been much more severe (or, as some cops would put it, the "wraps would have been taken off") had his admissions not been favorable to the defense or had there been a chance to destroy rather than merely discredit him.

Some tactics intended to fulfill the ends of cross-examination include: bewildering a witness with rapid-fire questions, harassing or humiliating the witness through verbal browbeating, or intimidating or embarrassing the witness by physically approaching him or her in a confrontational way or by invading his or her personal space. Judges are supposed to protect witnesses against unfair cross-examination, but many are lenient and allow great latitude in this regard. Under these conditions, the proper response is to answer respectfully while maintaining an unruffled demeanor and exhibiting no signs of resentment. Though it may be hard to accept at the time, nothing personal is meant: counsel is merely doing a job. The investigator must bear in mind that lawyers, convinced that cross-examination is the acid test, take advantage of latitude granted by the judge. If the witness remains in command of the facts and behaves in a civil manner, there is little to fear from cross-examination.

Miscellaneous Comments

Early in an investigator's career it would be profitable to attend a few criminal trials, especially to observe a criminal lawyer renowned for cross-examination prowess. Though it might be less instructive, observing a run-of-the-mill cross-examination would be less intimidating and perhaps comforting.

Objections as to Form and Substance

Investigators are often astonished and feel quite let down when on the witness stand they are prevented from testifying about what they believe a jury ought to hear. Because unfamiliarity with the rules of evidence can be responsible for this, an understanding of some rules may assuage this disappointment. An objection to a question is based either on the way it was phrased or on its substance. Attorneys use "objection as to form" when a question is unclear or confusing, improperly phrased, or argumentative.

If sustained, the judge may then suggest that the question be rephrased. A question to which there is no definite answer is considered misleading and thus inadmissible "as to form." Leading questions and questions having two parts are objectionable for the same reason. Objections "as to substance" are based on the relevancy, materiality, or competency of the question; such qualities were discussed earlier in the chapter.

Alleged Prior Statements

During cross-examination, some attorneys will pick up a document and read from it. What was read then is attributed to the witness who will be asked whether he or she made the statement. Rather than offer a denial or express agreement, the witness should ask for an opportunity to read the document. Sometimes the statement will indeed be that of the witness but taken out of context. Seeing it in its entirety may enable the witness to set the record straight.

Use of Notes

It has been pointed out that it is best for an investigator to prepare for trial by being thoroughly conversant with the facts. Usually this is feasible; the exception is a complicated investigation extending over several months. In that event, it may be necessary to refer to notes and reports while testifying. Before doing so, the judge's permission is required. A witness is not permitted to read from them directly, but a review of them is allowed before answering. Scrambling through notes to locate the information is not the way to impress a jury. Credibility is enhanced when properly kept notes allow the witness to find the information promptly. The attorney may ask to see the notes, and the judge almost certainly will grant the request. Unbusinesslike, disorderly notes can be used to discredit an investigator. In addition, the fact that some are not available because they were destroyed (or not brought to court) may also create an unfavorable impression with the jury—especially if it believes the normal procedure would be to preserve them and bring them to court.

Use of Audio or Video Recordings

As noted earlier in the book, the use of audio or video recordings during interviews and interrogations is commonplace today. Copies of the recording must be made available to the defense, and the investigator should be familiar with the contents of the recording prior to taking the stand. In addition to viewing or listening to the recording, a transcript should be made and studied. Because such recordings are frequently lengthy, the defense may try to "trip up" the investigator with such questions as "Did you say ..." or "Did you ask the defendant if ...?" Prior to answering such questions, the investigator should ask to review the recording if there is any doubt in his or her mind.

"Yes or No" Answers

If it suits the purposes of an attorney, a "yes or no" answer may be demanded of the investigator on the stand. Rather than be intimidated and accede to the demand, it is appropriate for the witness to appeal to the judge on the grounds that the answer requires qualification or explanation and that a straight "yes" or "no" would be misleading. Unless this is perceived as evasive, the judge usually will not hold the witness to a "yes" or "no." In appealing to the judge, the investigator also sends a message to the prosecutor to bring the matter up again on redirect examination.

Timing the Response

An investigator on the witness stand may be surprised and uncertain as to why counsel raised an objection to a particular question. Therefore, it is advisable that a question not be answered too quickly; first, to be certain that it is understood and to allow sufficient time to formulate a reply; second, to permit the prosecutor to state an objection and have the judge rule on it.

CONCLUSION

A familiarity with the rules of evidence coupled with the realization that defense counsel is merely living up to the legal duty he or she owes to the client can make a cross-examination less of an ordeal. The investigator who is thoroughly prepared and understands what constitutes effective testimony should find that the initial apprehension (felt by most investigators early in their career) will diminish and finally disappear when more experience is gained in testifying.

NOTES

[1]   John H. Wigmore, *A Panorama of the World's Legal Systems* (St. Paul, MN: West, 1928).

[2]   John H. Wigmore. *Wigmore on Evidence*, 4th ed., 13 vols. (Boston: Little, Brown, 1970–89).

[3]   Jefferson L. Ingram, *Criminal Evidence*, 11th ed. (Boston: Elsevier/Anderson Publishing, 2011), 12–13.

[4]   Fed. R. Evid., 401.

[5]   Fed. R. Evid., 401.

[6]   Fed. R. Evid., 403.

[7]   Ingram, op. cit., 170.

[8]   *Weinstock v. United States*, 231 F.2d 699 (D.C. Cir. 1956).

[9]   Michael M. D'Auria, Gary D. Helfand, and Herbert F. Ryan, *Legal Terms and Concepts in Criminal Justice* (Wayne, NJ: Avery, 1983), 25.

[10]   *The Law Dictionary*, 7th ed. (Cincinnati: Anderson, 1997), 92.

[11]   Steven H. Gifis, *Law Dictionary* (Woodbury, NY: Barron's Educational Series, 1975), 38.

[12]   Ingram, op. cit., 236–237.

[13]   Ibid., 237

IMPORTANT CASE

Weinstock v. United States (1956)

DISCUSSION QUESTIONS

1. What are the ways in which a criminal case may be culminated?

2. What is the difference between direct and circumstantial evidence?

3. What is meant by "understandable testimony"?

4. What are the two sides of a criminal trial, and what are the roles of the prosecution and the defense?

5. What is a "leading question"?

6. Is an investigator permitted to refer to notes?

SUPPLEMENTAL READINGS

Brown, P. M. (2007). *The art of questioning: Thirty maxims of cross-examination.* Clark, NJ: Law Book Exchange.

Hanley, J., Schmidt, W. W., & Robbins, R. K. (2006). *Introduction to criminal evidence and court procedure* (4th ed.). Berkeley, CA: McCutchan.

Imwinkelried, E. J. (2009). *The new Wigmore: A treatise on evidence: Evidentiary privileges.* Austin, TX: Wolters Kluwer Law & Business.

Ingram, J. L. (2012). *Criminal evidence* (11th ed.). Boston: Elsevier/Anderson Publishing.

Saltzburg, S. A. (2006). Trial tactics. *Criminal Justice, 20*(4), 47–49.

CHAPTER 17

HOMICIDE

INTRODUCTION

One of the most feared crimes is murder—it can completely immobilize a community hit by a series of localized killings. Media publicity and the growth of social media have served to "popularize" crime, and a murder will undoubtedly have an impact on a community. Where the murder is committed by an unknown person, especially coupled with another crime such as robbery or home invasion, the result is likely to be fear and uncertainty. The removal of such offenders following a competently conducted investigation is not only a gratifying result for the investigators and officials who direct it, but for the general public as well.

Murder is a word that resonates in one way or another with virtually every level and facet of society. It is associated with fear, fascination, and curiosity—largely because most people cannot imagine, much less comprehend, why and how a person can take the life of another. For instance, the 9/11 attacks on the World Trade Center and the Pentagon brought the nation to a standstill. The psychological impact was immeasurable, and the economic loss in the billions of dollars.

Murder represents one of the major challenges for the investigator, bringing to the fore virtually all aspects of a criminal investigation. Even when the perpetrator is known, the investigator must take care in handling the case and preparing the case for court. One cannot anticipate a guilty plea or know what approach the defense counsel will take—such as invoking self-defense, accident, or one of many other defenses. When a suspect has not been identified, even one mistake can result in a failure to solve the case or can serve to open a line of defense. Due to its impact on the community, and because the investigator skilled in handling homicide cases should then be capable of managing other felony investigations, the reader will find that this crime receives more comprehensive treatment than the other crimes covered in this text.

DEFINITIONS

Homicide is the killing of one human being by another. All homicides are not criminal: they may also be justifiable or excusable. (Self-inflicted death is treated by the police as homicide until it can be established as suicide.)

Justifiable homicide involves the intentional but lawful killing of another. The state commits justifiable homicide in carrying out a death sentence handed down by a judge after conviction. Justifiable homicide is also committed when a police officer kills a bank robber who shoots at the officer while attempting to escape; or when an individual, believing his or her life is being threatened with a weapon, kills in defense of self or family. In the last example, should the weapon used to threaten—a gun, perhaps—subsequently prove to be an imitation, it would, even so, remain a case of justifiable homicide.

Excusable homicide involves one person killing another by accident without gross negligence and without intent to injure; for example, the hunter who honestly mistakes another person for game. The following scenario is another example: around 2 A.M. a police officer pursues a suspected burglar fleeing down a dead-end alley. He orders the suspect to halt, put up his hands, and not move; instead, the suspect turns around. The officer, observing a shiny object in the suspect's hand and believing it to be a weapon, fires and kills the suspect. The questions that will inevitably be raised are:

- What are the circumstances of the case?
- What were the physical characteristics such as lighting, visibility, suspect, action?
- Did the suspect whirl and crouch, or turn slowly?
- Did the suspect say anything?
- Was there a shiny object? Was it a gun or other weapon?

When the circumstances are determined, the issue of whether a case is excusable homicide can be settled.

Suicide is the taking of one's own life. Although not deemed a crime, suicide is considered a grave public wrong in many jurisdictions throughout the world.

Criminal homicide is the unlawful taking of a human life. There are two kinds of criminal homicide: murder and manslaughter.

Murder is the unlawful killing of another human being with malice aforethought (premeditation). Killing a person during the commission of a felony also constitutes murder—even when the killing is unintentional. Most murder convictions are for felony murder rather than for premeditated murder.

Manslaughter is the unlawful killing of another without intent—expressed or implied—to effect death.

Further classifications of unlawful homicide—such as first-degree (in police/prosecutor jargon: "murder one") versus second-degree murder; voluntary manslaughter (heat of passion) versus involuntary manslaughter (reckless or vehicular); and so on—are to be found in the penal laws of the states. The annotated statutes of the state in which the crime was committed must be consulted to determine which category of homicide fits a particular case. The term *homicide* will be employed throughout this chapter without further reference to the subcategory into which it legally falls.

Corpus Delicti

The *corpus delicti* is the collection of basic facts establishing that a crime has been committed and that some person is responsible. Regardless of the classification of an unlawful homicide, the investigator must marshal evidence for each element of the *corpus delicti* in order for the prosecutor to obtain an indictment or for the judge to hand the case over to a jury. The elements for unlawful homicide are:

1. The death was not the result of suicide, natural causes, or accident, thus establishing that it was a homicide. (This is the province of the forensic pathologist.)

2. Some person was responsible for the unlawful death. (Establishing the identity of the person is the province of the investigator, evidence technicians, and criminalists.)

The circumstances surrounding the death will determine whether the charge will be murder or manslaughter.

Demographics

Of all crime statistics, those on homicide are probably the most reliable. This is because two agencies of government—the police and the medical examiner (or coroner)—have jurisdiction, file separate reports, and compile data. The *Uniform Crime Reports* (UCR) disclose the number of murders and non-negligent manslaughters in the United States for each calendar year. Although the numbers increase or decrease from one year to another, three peaks (based on homicides per 100,000 population) have been noted for the twentieth century. The first occurred in 1933 when there were 9.7 homicides per 100,000; then the number fell to a low in the late 1950s and early 1960s.[1] The second peak, in 1980, hit 10.2 per 100,000. After a period of decline, the homicide rate peaked again in 1991 at 9.8 per 100,000.[2] The homicide rate has slowly decreased to its 2008 rate of 5.4 per 100,000[3] and further decreased to a rate of 4.8 per 100,000 in 2010.[4] Some perspective may be gained on UCR data if they are juxtaposed against statistics for another country or another time. For example, present-day Canada's low annual homicide rate remains at 1.62 per 100,000.[5]

In 2010, the most recent year for which data were available, of the 12,996 murder victims for whom gender was known, 77.4 percent were male. Of the offenders for whom gender was known, 90.3 percent were males. Concerning murder victims for whom race was known, 50.4 percent were black, 47 percent were white, and 2.6 percent were of other races. Of the offenders for whom race was known, 53.1 percent were black, 44.6 percent were white, and 2.3 percent were from other races. Single victim/single offender situations accounted for 48.4 percent of all murders reported. Of the homicides for which the type of weapon was specified, 67.5 percent involved the use of firearms. This percentage decreased from 71.9 percent in 2008. Concerning the known circumstances surrounding murders, 41.8 percent of victims were murdered during arguments (including romantic triangles). Felony circumstances (rape, robbery, burglary, etc.) accounted for 23.1 percent of murders. Figure 17.1 shows murder by victim–offender relationship, and a breakdown of the "Family" category is provided. In the "Other Known" category seen in the pie chart, "acquaintance" was the relationship description for the bulk of offenses (2,723), followed by "friend" (396), "girlfriend" (492), "boyfriend" (131), "neighbor" (92), "employer" (13), and "employee" (8).[6]

It is commendable that among serious felonies, homicide has a high clearance rate, and that it is declining in absolute numbers. However, in the case of stranger-to-stranger killing cases, ascertaining the particularized motive (if any) and working from motive to murderer is very difficult. Because many robbery and narcotics cases also have a generalized motive (and some develop into homicides), particularized motive is of little help as an investigative aid. An important development with regard to homicide was the appearance in 1997 of *Homicide Studies*, an interdisciplinary international journal. Its goal is to bridge the gap between academician and practitioner as well as between different disciplines, and ultimately to assist in the formation of more effective public policies and programs. Such interdisciplinary research can help us understand the causes of homicide so that we may learn how to reduce and perhaps even prevent it.

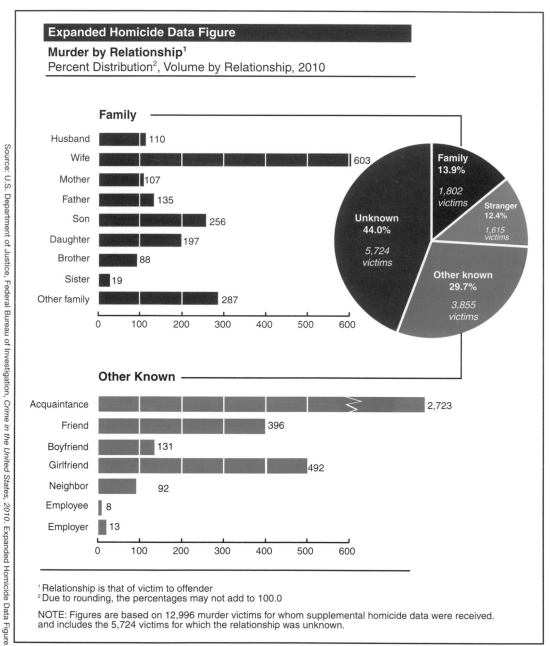

Figure 17.1

Murder by Victim-to-Offender Relationship.

OVERVIEW OF INVESTIGATIVE ACTIVITIES

A broad survey of homicide investigation is presented in this section. Outlining what needs to be done in apparently logical order creates an impression that there is a step-by-step procedure to be followed, but adhering to a prescribed course of action is often not feasible. Rather, the investigator must be prepared to seize upon any development that seems important and see that it is followed through and fully exploited, while remaining watchful for other developments to emerge. One should record the date and time any tactical maneuver is taken in response to new information, as preparation for a "when" question from defense counsel during a trial or other hearing. There are risks involved in such jumping around—other aspects of the investigation may be eclipsed, ignored, or overlooked. Hence, a comprehensive checklist will not only preclude this unfortunate result, it will serve as a reminder of the fundamentals that are part and parcel of a thorough investigation. Later, when preparing to testify in court, the investigator will find the list invaluable.

Recording the crime scene (with sketches and photographs), interviewing, and examining records were covered earlier in the text. Other procedures, such as ascertaining motive and assessing its value, are dealt with for the first time and treated here at some length.

Assuming the crime was committed in the investigator's jurisdiction, the following procedure is in accordance with normal practice:

INVESTIGATIVE ACTIVITIES IN A HOMICIDE
1.   Record crime scene (photographs, sketches, notes).
2.   Recognize, collect, and preserve all physical evidence:

To facilitate reconstruction of the crime.

To link a suspect to the victim, crime scene, or both.

To identify a substance (poison, narcotic, blood, semen), or an object (bludgeon, gun) in order to locate its source and trace its owner.

3.   Identify the victim.
4.   Establish the cause, manner, and time of death.
5.   Ascertain the motive for the crime:

From the way the crime was committed—using evidence at the scene, and trauma inflicted on the victim for psychological profiling.

From those who had knowledge of the victim's activities (social, familial, business). From documents written by or sent to the victim—diaries, letters, or documents relating to financial or business dealings of the victim.

6.   Seek additional information.

Interview people to check on the background and activities of the victim; obtain leads from those who knew the deceased; seek a possible informant; consider surveillance in some cases.

Examine records to ascertain business interests of the victim; trace source of murder weapon through manufacturer's records or firearms registration records.

Review intradepartmental electronic communications on a daily basis. Scan the police information network for possibly related criminal activity in other jurisdictions. Check on previous arrests to compare *modus operandi*.

Review social media where possible to gather information on possible suspects, collect information between individuals on "tweets" or Facebook that may relate to the crime. Obtain exemplars from any suspect (or from his or her home, garage, vehicle, etc.) for comparison with similar physical evidence discovered at the crime scene. [Note that research by the Institute for the Study of Violent Groups (ISVG) at the University of New Haven found that gang members frequently communicated with each other on social media to "brag" about their crime.]

7. Question suspects (after administering *Miranda* warnings).

Allow suspects to make any statement they wish, including those that are exculpatory. Check any statement in regard to suspect's knowledge of what happened in order to compare it against facts revealed through reconstructing the event, using available autopsy and physical evidence. The forensic pathologist can be very helpful in reconstructing the event; this should be attempted early in the investigation, preferably within the first 48 hours in a conference involving all investigators and technical personnel. Obtain an admission or a confession. During questioning, make use of forensic laboratory reports and other evidence of guilt that link the suspect to the crime.

PARTITIONING RESPONSIBILITIES

The investigation of a homicide can involve several persons—a crime scene evidence technician, criminalist, forensic pathologist, and detective or investigator. The responsibility for investigative activities in most cases can be partitioned as shown in Table 17.1.

MOTIVE

Importance

Motive is an important factor in pointing to possible suspects in a homicide. Often there is a personal relationship between victim and perpetrator that, if subjected to stress, may impel one of them to kill the other. If the underlying cause can be found, deductive reasoning may lead the investigator back to the one who logically might have been so motivated. Further investigative efforts are then required either to develop additional evidence of guilt or to eliminate the suspect entirely. Because it will provide some focus to the investigative process, it is useful to understand the most common motives for homicide.

The following classification treats ostensible motives as they appear to detectives initially, or as they are alleged by offenders after apprehension. Usually, deeper psychological motivations are not considered; in the absence of a psychiatric study of the killer, they are generally unknown. But psychological profiling can be of help in solving some cases.

Table 17.1
Dividing Up Investigative Responsibilities

INDIVIDUAL	ACTIVITY–RESPONSIBILITY
Evidence Technician	• recording crime scene (1) • recognizing, collecting, and preserving physical evidence (2)
Criminalist	• recognizing, collecting, and preserving physical evidence (2) *Sometimes responsible for::* • recording crime scene (1)
Forensic Pathologist	• identifying the victim (3) • estimating the time of death (4) • establishing the cause and manner of death (4) *Sometimes contributes to:* • recognizing, collecting, and preserving physical evidence (2) • ascertaining the motive for the crime (5)
Forensic Anthropologist	• recognizing, collecting, and preserving physical evidence (2) • Identifying the victim (3)
Detective (Investigator)	• recording crime scene (1) • recognizing, collecting, and preserving physical evidence (2) • ascertaining the motive for the crime (5) • seeking additional information (6) • questioning suspects (7) *Develops authentic information for:* • identifying the victim (3)

The numbers in the table correspond with those used in "Investigative Activities in a Homicide" in the preceding section.

Categorizing Motives

The following list covers most of the apparent reasons that impel one person to kill another. Sometimes it can be a combination of motives:

- Financial gain

- Sexual gratification

- Apparently sex-connected homicides

- Emotional factors

- Self-protection

- Removal of an inconvenience or impediment

- Apparently motiveless crimes

- "Thrill" killing

Financial Gain

Killers prompted by the expectation of financial gain include: the beneficiary of a will or insurance policy of a spouse or relative, the surviving spouse in a community property state, the merchant who stands to profit from the death of a business associate, the so-called "lonely hearts" killer, and the poisoner (see section on multiple killings).

When financial gain is the precipitating factor, deductive reasoning from motive to possible suspect(s) is often fruitful. There are exceptions, however. In robbery cases when the victim resists and is killed, the motive is seldom particularized; then, the answer is to solve the felony utilizing techniques appropriate to that felony. This would pertain to a burglary/homicide. The motive of a "lonely hearts" killer or poisoner is also financial gain, but in these cases a paper record of financial transactions connecting killer and victim is more likely to remain. Such transactions might include signing the home ownership deed over to the killer, opening a new checking or savings account in the name of the victim and killer, or even using a credit card.

Sexual Gratification

The classic example of sex as a motive for homicide is lust. Wanting a new or younger mate has led to the murder of a spouse, particularly in community property states where husband and wife own equal shares in their accumulated wealth (and the survivor need not settle for half the estate—as would ordinarily be the case with divorce). Both motives of sex and financial gain offer clues as to who might profit from the victim's death.

Apparently Sex-Connected Homicides

The psychological motivations for crimes of this kind are quite different. The killing of homosexuals and of young boys and girls (particularly girls) by older men appears to be of sexual origin. However, this is unlikely to aid in the identification of a suspect unless the slayer's *modus operandi* is on record.

Sadism—obtaining sexual satisfaction by inflicting pain on others—generally is not carried out to the point of death, yet there are some who do cross the threshold into homicide when not satiated by cruelty alone. Biting and mutilating may precede or follow the actual killing. There often is no prior connection between offender and victim, so motive is not helpful in leading back to the killer. On the other hand, a psychological profile may be constructed using inductive reasoning. It would begin with the recognition and interpretation of the evidence at the crime scene, including the trauma inflicted on the victim. According to the type of offender described, the profile would suggest the most beneficial interrogative approach. Additional data generated (according to FBI literature) might include: the murderer's sex, race, age bracket, employment history, socioeconomic status, sexual adjustment, past record of offenses and, in some cases, a prediction as to whether the individual will strike again. Psychological assessment and the details needed for constructing a profile are given more extensive treatment in Chapter 4.

Some murders are committed simultaneously with or immediately after the sex act, as a concomitant of sexual gratification. In other cases, gratification is achieved through the act of killing rather than through the act of sex; the assertion of power over the victim is the primary motivation—any sexual gratification is secondary. If these cases are initially perceived as ostensible sex homicides, the result may be a misdirected investigative effort. The inaccurately assessed crime scene can allow serial murders to escape detection for long periods of time. (See the discussion of ViCAP later in this chapter.)

Along with a study of the crime scene and the victim's body, interviews can provide important information by questioning those who might have been present when the victim and perpetrator were likely to have met (in a tavern or a school yard, for instance). A description of the offender and possibly of an automobile may be obtained from such eyewitnesses.

In some homicides thought to be sex-connected, peers or bar companions may know a good deal about the suspect: where he or she lives; if he or she is a recent arrival, where he or she comes from, occupation, and so on. Informants, surveillance, and canvassing are often employed in solving these cases. In child homicides, canvassing the neighborhood in the vicinity of a school yard or playground may produce a partial identification of a suspect or an automobile. Surveillance would then be worthwhile, with surveillants positioned to observe a subsequent effort to lure another victim.

Emotional Factors

Strong emotions—anger, jealousy, revenge, envy, hatred—can provoke a person to commit manslaughter or premeditated murder. A typical case of manslaughter is the lover or spouse caught *in flagrante delicto* and killed in the heat of passion. On the other hand, if the aggrieved partner plans and carries out the killing, it is premeditated murder.

Broken nuptial engagements, domestic quarrels, and altercations in general can escalate and lead to homicide when they exceed the bounds of dispute. As a rule, homicides motivated by strong emotion are readily solved, many being manslaughter cases with witnesses present. But even premeditated murder permits potential suspects to be identified deductively once motive is established.

Killings that involve the working out of emotional fantasies are called fantasy murders; they are sex-related as a rule, but not always sex-dominated. Some serial killings fall into this category.

Self-Protection

Self-protection as a reason for homicide should be recognized as a feasibility in specific situations. One example would be the criminal (caught in the act of committing a crime) whose escape is interrupted or hampered by the victim. Another would be a murder committed as a result of the realization of the eventual danger that would be posed by an eyewitness should the offender become a suspect. Another example, perhaps more frequent in occurrence, is that of an offender known to the victim (often a child or teenager) who kills to silence the victim. In such situations, self-protection is the motive for the removal of the eyewitness as a potential informant.

Interrupted Crimes

Home burglaries in particular are sometimes interrupted by the unforeseen return of the resident; if the burglar's escape is hampered, a homicide can ensue. An important early step in this kind of investigation would be to trace the movements of the victim just prior to the time of death. Murder during a robbery may occur because the victim resists or another person enters the scene.

In one case, the victim told a friend she had to go back home for papers needed for an appointment with the family lawyer. When she failed to keep the appointment, a concerned relative went to her apartment and found her murdered. No signs of a forced entry could be detected, but a partial palm print was developed on a bedroom lamp that had been moved from its usual place. A few months later, a young hardware store employee and lock specialist was apprehended for the burglary of a nearby sporting goods store; again, there were no signs of forced entry. A review of unforced entry cases in the area, coupled with the hardware store record of the employee's lock work, disclosed that in both cases he had changed the locks shortly before the burglaries (and homicide) occurred. Palm print evidence established that the hardware store employee handled the woman's bedroom lamp, located far from the hall door on which the lock work was done. When questioned about the woman's death, the intruder admitted that her unanticipated early return had surprised him, and that a struggle ensued which ultimately led to her death.

Eliminating an Eyewitness

The killing of an eyewitness (as a secondary homicide) may immediately follow a primary homicide. When homicide-suicide has been ruled out, the case is viewed as a dual criminal homicide. The chance that one of the victims was an eyewitness to the first (primary) homicide should also be considered. Checking on the background of each victim often determines who was most likely the intended victim and who the potential eyewitness (or secondary victim). Investigative efforts then can be concentrated on solving the initial (primary) homicide.

Slaying a Potential Informant

When the motive for a secondary homicide is the silencing of a potential informant, it will have investigative value only if some connection existed between killer and secondary victim that made the victim privy to the activities of the killer. Because the secondary victim could have incriminated only a limited number of individuals, the investigator must discover who they might be, and who among them had the opportunity (as to time and place) to commit the secondary homicide. Furthermore, if the suspect in the secondary homicide and the motive for the primary homicide are congruent, the hypothesis asserting the suspect's guilt is reinforced. Additional investigative effort will be necessary, but the result will be doubly satisfying if the case is made.

Removal of an Inconvenience or Impediment

A blackmailer, an unwanted child, a feeble parent blocking the takeover of a family business—each is an example of an obstacle to be removed. Once an investigator perceives that the very existence of the deceased was a major inconvenience or impediment to another person, the prospects of solving the homicide are enhanced. Records and people are important sources of information in such cases; they can support the hypothesis that the removal of an obstacle was the motive. Depending on how the crime was committed, physical evidence may link the victim or crime scene to the killer; for instance, a weapon could be traced to the offender's household.

Apparently Motiveless Crimes

There are two distinct kinds of homicide that appear motiveless or senseless: those of stranger killing stranger and those in which a person other than the intended victim is killed.

Stranger Killing Stranger

Although far less frequent than killings involving friends or acquaintances, this kind of homicide is on the increase in the United States. The adolescent male acting on a dare or the gang member asserting manliness (machismo) shoots to kill the first stranger he encounters. Encountering the stranger isn't always necessary; such shootings come from high-rise buildings as well as from passing cars. Nor is it necessary to be male; adolescent girl gangs are proliferating. Alcohol and other drugs often play a role in these senseless crimes. The solution of such crimes is frequently based on information obtained through a neighborhood canvass, from informants motivated by a substantial community reward, from pawn shop records, and from people who saw or heard the discharge of a firearm and reported it.

"Thrill" Killing

The murder of vagrants, the homeless, or other individuals based on their race or ethnic background may be carried out by perpetrators who describe their action as being "for the fun of it."

Mistaken Identity

Infrequently, a homicide will appear to be without motive, and—after a thorough check on the victim's background—quite senseless. Though the time or site may suggest the killing was intentional, no reason can be found. For example, a businessman was shot upon emerging from his apartment house at about 6:30 A.M., apparently by two men who just before that were observed loitering outside the building. The deceased's business and social background furnishing no possible motive, the case remained unsolved. Several months later, in the vicinity of the first homicide, another man was shot at the same time of day as he emerged from a building bearing the same house number but on a different street. When apprehended and questioned, the perpetrators confessed that they were hired killers. The first slaying had been a case of mistaken identity; the second was committed to rectify the mistake: this time they got both house and street number correct.

The very absence of motive is, in itself, significant. Here, it enabled investigative activities to concentrate on a neighborhood canvass and to find in both cases that the various bits of evidence matched: descriptions of victims and loiterers; occurrences at same time of day and same day of the week; two targets in the same neighborhood, in similar kinds of buildings with identical numerical addresses; and so on.

In another homicide, that of a Kansas farm family (see the Clutter case in the section on multiple deaths), the possibility of a mistake was considered. Investigators were about to fan out over several states and check everybody who had ever worked for the family. Before this exhaustive plan could be implemented, an informant changed the course of the investigation and led to a solution. The informant, a prison inmate who once worked for the Clutters, had shared everything he had learned about Mr. Clutter's way of doing business (where he kept his files, his cash flow, etc.) with his former cellmate. The news of the massacre overcame the prison-culture tenet to tell authorities nothing; he offered information to investigators implicating his former cellmate as one of the killers.

Homicides like those of the businessmen previously mentioned occur when a criminal tracks down the wrong person. Another example concerns an Ohio man who thought he was shooting his ex-wife and the man with whom she had fled to Florida. Instead, he had broken into the home of a family whose car in the driveway had a "vanity" license bearing the initials of the man he was pursuing. Upon arriving in Florida, the woman—knowing she had made a narrow escape and still fearing for her life—reported to local police the threats her husband had made. When they investigated the break-in and murder, the police recalled her report. The detectives making inquiries at the mobile home park brought along the photograph she had provided of the husband; employees readily identified him as the man who had been looking for a couple newly arrived from the north. As this case demonstrates, people are an important source of information. To prove guilt in court, however, it is necessary to collect all available physical evidence—here, the key piece of evidence was a firearm found in the trunk of the killer's vehicle. It is important to note that even when the motive seems apparent, it is still a hypothesis to be proved or discredited. Clinging tenaciously to what is ultimately the wrong motive can be hazardous; not only is precious investigative time lost, but it gives an offender the opportunity to eliminate any trail leading to him or her.

Determining Motive

In addition to understanding the motivations for homicide, it is necessary to be acquainted with how motive may be ascertained. Three major sources of information—crime scene, people, and records—serve this purpose.

Crime Scene

In addition to physical evidence, there are other kinds of evidence from which to surmise motive. As pointed out elsewhere in the text, the experienced homicide detective may be able to form a "crime picture" of the offender based on familiarity with similar crimes. This approach has been refined and to some extent codified. For some homicides, therefore, a psychological profile of the offender may help to ascertain motive (see Chapter 4).

People

The most productive source for determining motive is people—family, friends, business associates, and others who had more than a passing acquaintance with the deceased. As indicated previously, several reasons can prompt one person to kill another: some involve premeditation; some, a heat-of-the-moment impulse. With regard to the latter, a certain number are for trivial reasons; for others, however, the reason can be enormous, deep-seated, and compelling. A thorough background check on the deceased may provide insight into a likely motive for the homicide. From this determination, a list of people harboring such a motive can be compiled, and then narrowed, by considering who had the opportunity, means, and temperament to commit the crime. If victim and potential suspect come from a culture in which face-saving or male dominance is the norm, and the victim is female, then interpersonal relationships must be examined. What might merely be a lack of courtesy may be, in another culture, perceived as an insult to be repaid; such a confrontation often escalates—with lethal results.

Records

Records are also of help in suggesting motive. Financial gain may be indicated if a large insurance policy was issued or a will changing beneficiaries was signed just prior to the homicide. Records might reveal a history of "sharp" business practices or debt default, of family quarrels or disturbances requiring police response, or of filing for separation or divorce—any of these can leave a paper trail to the person motivated by anger, hatred, or the need to retaliate.

THE CRIME SCENE AS THE FOCUS OF THE INVESTIGATION

In homicide cases particularly, the crime scene can be a rich source of physical evidence—if care is taken to recognize it. To reconstruct how the crime was committed, or determine what actually happened, physical evidence must be recognized before it can be recorded, collected, and preserved. Moreover, there may be but one chance to accomplish this. In fact, legal requirements can limit the crime scene search to a single opportunity, should the property owner refuse to allow a second search. Other reasons for a thorough initial search include the possibility that the scene may be damaged by weather conditions (rain, snow, temperature), building construction in (or the tearing down of) the premises housing the crime scene, or other factors.

Another consideration arises when a dead body is in plain view. Because decency and dignity obligate investigators to shield it from public gaze, a cover must be carefully selected. This may create a problem; for example, investigators in the Nicole Brown Simpson/Ronald Goldman double-murder case used an old blanket from the home of the suspect's former wife (one of the murder victims). Because the accused had been a frequent visitor there, defense counsel maintained that fibers and hairs found at the scene could have dislodged from the blanket only to fall on the victims' bodies. Had a vinyl shower curtain or a new (painter's) drop cloth been selected, any potential for adding evidence to the crime scene would have been mitigated.

At the outset of the homicide investigation, the crime scene is the center point around which important questions revolve:

* Is this an unlawful homicide?

* Is this a homicide disguised as a suicide?

* Who is the deceased?

* What was the motive for the killing?

* Is there physical evidence present that may link the killer to the crime scene or the victim or could be useful in reconstructing the crime?

* What happened and/or how was the crime committed?

A somewhat different and complementary perspective was promulgated in late 1997 by a National Medicolegal Review Panel consisting of 144 highly experienced professionals from across the country.[7] Almost 60 percent of the reviewer network had medical backgrounds, in contrast to 31 percent who had law enforcement backgrounds. The title of its research report, *National Guidelines for Death Investigation*, suggests the difference between death and homicide investigation.

The purpose of the report was to identify and delineate the "set of investigative tasks that should and could be performed at every death scene."[8] To this end, coroners (especially in rural areas) and medical examiners can be assured that they now have the "means for substantially enhancing performance in fulfilling their far-ranging responsibilities."[9] Furthermore, adherence to the guidelines "may also serve to prevent innocent people from being accused of criminal activity when, in fact, a crime was not committed or the person suspected was not involved."[10]

The benefits of conforming to these guidelines stand in sharp contrast to the situation that existed before they became available:

> … With no "official training" required for elected coroners, it is difficult for the elected coroner to know what should be done in investigations. Most elected coroners have begun their jobs with little or no knowledge as to how and what they need to do. Having a set of national guidelines for medicolegal death investigation would ensure that at least the elected coroner would have a "cookbook" to follow and would have some idea of what is expected of him/her in every case.[11]

The guidelines cover in considerable detail the following: investigative tools and equipment, arriving at the scene, documenting and evaluating the scene, documenting and evaluating the body, establishing and recording descendent profile information, and completing the scene investigation.

Is This an Unlawful Homicide?

One element of murder or manslaughter that must be proved in court is whether the death was a result of an action or an omission that is neither excusable nor justifiable. This task being the responsibility of the medical examiner's or coroner's office, the forensic pathologist provides expert testimony on the cause and manner of death. This matter is given more extensive treatment in the next section, "The Body as the Focus of the Investigation."

To the investigator coming upon a crime scene it is important to point out that appearances are not always what they seem; cause of death is not necessarily obvious from viewing the body. In one case, an observant police officer saw a man leave an apartment house with a newspaper-wrapped package under his arm, return to the building, and re-emerge 10 minutes later with another package from which some apparently human toes protruded. On accompanying the man back to his apartment, the officer was confronted with the sight of a dismembered female body, a blood-splattered kitchen and bathroom, and what would appear to be an open-and-shut case of criminal homicide.

But not necessarily. The chain of events started the night before when the man in question met the woman at a bar, and after some heavy drinking took her to his apartment, then passed out. Waking in the morning to find a dead woman in his bed, he assumed he had killed her before blacking out. His attempted cover-up—dismembering and disposing of the body—had been exposed by the observant officer. The autopsy determined the death was from natural causes.

Is This Homicide Simulated as Suicide?

Simulating (or staging) a crime to cover up another crime is fairly rare, but it is not unheard of: to cloak homicide, arson and automobile accidents are the most common expedients; to conceal larceny—especially when an inventory is imminent—burglary may be used. Such crimes are detected because the simulation is often "overstaged" by an offender who is too anxious that investigators not miss the point.

Books that graphically detail how to terminate one's life open up the possibility of such information being misapplied (e.g., simulating a suicide to cover up a murder). Geberth, the author of a well-known work on homicide investigation, claims that "there are a significant number of such suicides occurring throughout the country."[12] He discusses three case histories of cases that were classified as suicides due to the similarities between the case and the information in the book *Final Exit*. Each was on file as a suicide because of the similarities between the death and the preparatory steps taken in the suicide: a plastic bag over the victim's head, a copy of the book *Final Exit* found beside the body, a note or letter(s) encompassing the recommendations prescribed in the book.[13]

The investigator must bear in mind how relatively easy it would be to gather such props in order to make a criminal homicide appear to be a suicide. To determine whether an apparent suicide falls into that category, Geberth provides a checklist.[14] Following is a checklist modified for the purpose of this text: an asterisk is placed next to those steps that, if followed, should help to differentiate a criminal homicide from a *Final Exit*-type suicide:

INVESTIGATIVE CHECKLIST

1. Is *Final Exit* or a similar book or web site on a computer at the scene?

2. Is there any underlining, written entry, or other markings related to what is observed at the scene, i.e., did the highlighted part(s) of the book serve as a model for the act of self-deliverance?

3. Is there other evidence for an act of self-deliverance, i.e., a suicide note (or other letters), perhaps accompanied by a Living Will and/or a Durable Power of Attorney for Health Care?

*4. Care must be exercised when touching or handling the suicide note (or other document) until it has been examined for fingerprints. To assess any latent prints that may be developed, the finger and palm prints of the deceased and all persons who were present at the scene or who are considered to be close to the deceased, must be obtained for comparison purposes.

*5. If there is a plastic bag over the head of the deceased (or if one is present at the scene) it must be examined for fingerprints. Any latent print that is developed must be compared with the known prints, as suggested above. A print present on the plastic bag (other than that of the deceased) must be evaluated against any explanation offered for its presence, taking into consideration the account given before the print was developed.

*6. Is the substance of the suicide note (or letter) expressed at the literacy level of the deceased? Or does the "last letter or note" duplicate almost exactly what is suggested in *Final Exit* or a similar work? An illiterate (or semiliterate) person may copy the words out of the book, but it should give rise to some suspicion if a literate person did so.

*7. If the note or letter is handwritten, its authenticity must be established. Is the handwriting (or hand printing) that of the deceased? If typed, was the instrument—typewriter or computer— available to the deceased? Was the deceased able to type or use a computer?

*8. All medicine containers must be gathered—including those that are empty. If a label bears the name of any of the drugs mentioned in *Final Exit* (or a similar book or web site) as useful for self-deliverance, any remaining contents should be analyzed. From the label (which shows the quantity dispensed) and a drug dosage table (one can be found in *Final Exit*), determine if a lethal dose was available to the deceased. If an autopsy and a toxicological analysis were carried out, check the results against the content of the containers.

Any information at variance with what might be expected should be followed up until any discordant or jarring results are clarified or a criminal homicide is settled upon.

Who is the Deceased?

Victim identification is of singular importance in homicide cases; otherwise, the crime will rarely be solved. The experience of numerous investigators bears witness to this assertion, for only after an identification has been made can a motive for the killing be established and then utilized to generate potential suspects. Correctly identifying the victim, therefore, is crucial. In addition to its investigative value, the identification is part of the *corpus delicti*; thus, it has probative value as well.

In many homicide cases identification is easy. It is speedily accomplished by relatives, friends, neighbors, and business associates who have known the victim for some time and can be relied upon to perform this function. On the other hand, if the victim was known casually or for a short time—as, for instance, the new roomer by a landlady—an identification based on such limited acquaintance is considered a "presumptive ID" and not deemed reliable.

Confirming an identification by independent means is therefore advisable. Identification by two unrelated persons who knew the victim well or by one person and a document (such as a driver's license) in the victim's possession with matching description or photograph is adequate for a positive ID. Jewelry, although not in itself sufficient for an identification in a criminal homicide, can make a contribution if it is engraved or of unusual design.

Fingerprints should be checked—especially if the body is not readily identified. (Of course, this is fruitless if the victim has not been previously fingerprinted.) Advances in single-digit technology may make it possible to link the victim to another crime. Missing persons records should be reviewed. The victim's clothing should be examined; if a laundry dry cleaning mark is found (either visually or by ultraviolet light) and a laundry file is maintained, it must be checked. A photograph of the victim (and laundry mark, if not identified) can be distributed in the community, and a public appeal made through newspapers and television. The roles of medical and dental evidence are discussed later in the text.

Figure 17.2
Can you determine from this photo whether this is a suicide or a homicide? Note the position of the rifle. The answer can be found later in the chapter.

What Was the Motive?

To be of investigative value, it is vital that any psychological evidence suggestive of the killer's motive be recognized at the crime scene and interpreted. An informed effort to estimate what kind of a person could have committed the crime is called *psychological profiling* (see Chapter 4). Apt to be useful in homicides involving sex, sadistic torture, disembowelment, or genital mutilation, a psychological profile may enable investigators to choose among those likely suspects whose aberrant behavior has been noted in the community and who appear capable of committing such a crime. Follow-up is obviously necessary to prove or disprove clues provided by this means.

The lack of apparent motive in a homicide raises the possibility of a mistake. A neighborhood canvass should be undertaken in search of a living individual whose description and behavior are consistent with those of the deceased; then a background check made on that individual. If a motive is found to explain why his or her sudden demise would be desirable, there is some chance that the motiveless crime was a case of mistaken identity.

Is There Associative Evidence Present?

Evidence that can link the perpetrator to the crime scene or victim is of two kinds: (1) evidence brought to and left (often unintentionally) at the scene; and (2) evidence taken deliberately or accidentally from the scene. Examples of the first kind are: fingerprints; spent bullets and cartridge cases; and blood, hair, and fibers from the person or clothing of the perpetrator. Examples of the second kind include: easily carried loot such as small appliances; rug and clothing fibers; broken glass particles imbedded in clothing or in the rubber heel of a shoe; smeared fresh paint or blood spattered on clothing; and so on. A mutual transfer of evidence is also feasible—clothing fibers, blood, or hair—from victim to killer during a struggle, and vice versa.

The sources of associative evidence suggest what might be looked for at the crime scene; they are:

- Traces of the person
    Finger and palm prints
    Blood, semen, saliva, hair
    Bare footprints
    Other skin patterns such as ear prints and lip impressions
    Teeth marks

- Traces of wearing apparel
    Shoe prints
    Weave pattern and stitching of clothing and gloves
    Clothing accessories

- Impressions left by
    Weapons—firearms, cutting or stabbing devices
    Tools—jimmies, metal cutters, hammers, metal punches
    Shovels—used to bury a body or weapon (Some types of soil, such as clay, retain striation marks left by the digging edge of a shovel.)

The discovery, preservation, and investigative value of physical evidence are treated extensively in Chapters 2 and 3.

Reconstructing What Happened

There are scientific means available to reconstruct the crime; that is, to determine how it was committed and what happened. The purpose is to allow any account of the event advanced by a suspect or witness to be compared with the reconstructed facts. Therefore, before anything is moved it is vital that the initial appearance of the crime scene be faithfully recorded through notes, sketches, and particularly photographs—including video pictures.

The use of computer-aided design (CAD) systems has become more common and useful in reconstructing crime scenes. This approach frequently offers a visual model that can be manipulated to test various theories, such as the path of the bullets fired, movement of individuals, and proximity to other objects. For example, if a suspect contends that the shooting was an accident that occurred while he was sitting down cleaning a shotgun, the height and location of pellets on the wall may serve to discredit the story.

The kinds of clue materials most frequently involved in the reconstruction of a crime are firearms and blood evidence. Other determinations might include: estimating the time needed to perform an act, pinpointing the exact time of a telephone call, making a theoretical analysis of a certain phenomenon, or conducting experiments. For example, how does a particular coffee table topple when struck during a struggle? Does it land on its side or turn upside down? A theoretical calculation of its center of gravity by a physicist, coupled with controlled experimentation by a qualified scientist, will provide a more reliable answer than an investigator's rudimentary tests at the scene.

Unexplained, significant differences between the facts disclosed through scientific reconstruction of evidence, and facts alleged by a suspect or witness, can be put to good use in subsequent interrogations (see Chapter 2 on crime reconstruction and Chapter 10 on confessions). Owing to its serendipitous nature, physical evidence may, when least expected, bring to light what actually happened. For example, though human hair seldom serves this purpose, when the need arose to determine which of two inebriated individuals was the driver of a car that killed two people in an unwitnessed accident (with each accusing the other), examination of the hair imbedded in the damaged windshield on the passenger side provided an indisputable answer.

The major contribution of the forensic pathologist to homicide investigation rests on the autopsy. Should a pathologist respond directly and promptly to the crime scene, he or she may also assist by offering an opinion as to the kind of weapon used in the killing. This information will facilitate a search for the weapon in the surrounding area and along possible escape routes.

THE BODY AS THE FOCUS OF THE INVESTIGATION

When examined by properly trained forensic scientists the victim's body can provide evidence of investigative and probative value. The testimony of the forensic pathologist figures significantly in this endeavor; it is required to prove one of the elements of homicide—that death was the result

The photo in Figure 17.2 is of a suicide. The rifle was held to the man's stomach, and he leaned over to fire into his midsection.

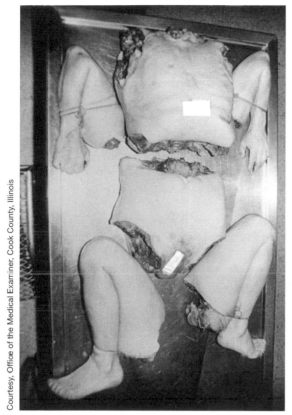

Courtesy, Office of the Medical Examiner, Cook County, Illinois

Figure 17.3
Unidentified dismembered body. Neither fingerprints (criminal or civil) nor medical records could be found; homicide remains unsolved.

of a criminal act. In addition to shedding light on the cause and manner of death, he or she may be able to testify about some of the circumstances surrounding the event, thus permitting a reconstruction of the crime—how and when it was committed. An experienced forensic pathologist can provide facts useful in constructing a profile of the killer, for instance, a description of the blows—their number and location—and the way they were inflicted. Other forensic scientists (e.g., odontologists, radiologists) may be able to identify the victim through the study of evidence obtained from the body—by X-rays of the teeth, for example.

Who is the Deceased?

In general, the most common means of identifying the victim are successful in permitting investigators to move on to other pressing matters. But sometimes body and facial features are unrecognizable (or missing if the body was dismembered, see Figure 17.3), and clothing or jewelry is not present. In these circumstances, the forensic pathologist and forensic odontologist may be able to identify the body through a comparison of skeletal and dental X-rays, or through unique features such as a surgically repaired organ, spinal cord defect, scar, birthmark, or tattoo (see Figure 17.4). An exemplar, a medical and dental record, or photograph of the feature taken before death is required for such a comparison to be successful.

Establishing the Cause and Manner of Death—The Autopsy

A death may be from natural causes, accident, suicide, or criminal act. When the first three are ruled out, it falls under the criminal law. The forensic pathologist, using medical autopsy, determines the cause and manner of death, and also evaluates the circumstances of the death. In gunshot cases, for

Courtesy, Denis Kelly

Figure 17.4
Body tattoos can be important in the identification of the deceased.

instance, cause and manner are determined in part by the circumstances surrounding the discovery of the body. Answers to the following questions, therefore, can reveal whether a death was suicidal, accidental, or criminal.

- Are there signs of a struggle?
- Could the injuries have been self-inflicted? The location of the entrance wound, the powder pattern, and the trajectory of the bullet in the body are important to this determination.
- What was the location of the weapon (or other object) that inflicted the injury or injuries?
- Is there a suicide note? Is it in the deceased's handwriting or printing?

In addition to its probative value, in the event that death was the result of a criminal act, the autopsy reveals detailed information. This affords the investigator, assisted by the pathologist, an opportunity to reconstruct the crime (should that be necessary).

Autopsy did not become a widely accepted, integral part of homicide investigation until the nineteenth century. Before that and continuing to this day, its principal purpose is the study of disease, particularly terminal disease. A medicolegal autopsy is a postmortem, scientific and systematic, internal and external examination of a corpse by a physician, the forensic pathologist. Involving as it does the practice of medicine, confidentiality must be maintained, albeit the patient is deceased.

The External Examination

The external examination of the corpse is a significant part of a total medicolegal autopsy. The pathologist will also want to see the clothing of the deceased, and the weapon (see Figure 17.5). Yielding details (such as scars or tattoos) that facilitate an identification, the external examination also provides what is necessary to reconstruct inductively the circumstances of the death—what happened, how and when it happened, and whether the body was moved after death.

Courtesy, Office of the Medical Examiner, Cook County, Illinois

Figure 17.5
Clothing fibers on bullet retrieved from body. One should not wash the bullet and destroy evidence. Fibers are important in garment identification.

The Internal Examination

The internal examination of the cadaver involves making incisions (generally of the scalp, chest, and abdomen) to remove organs, tissues, and fluids. Following a gross visual inspection, samples are taken for further study under the microscope and for chemical analysis by a toxicologist. The test results and the external examination allow for the formation of an expert opinion on the cause and manner of death. Sometimes, however, the cause of death cannot be determined.

Reconstructing the Crime

Answers to the following questions arising from autopsy evidence and its interpretation will help the investigator to reconstruct a homicide: Was the body moved after death? What occurred, and how did it occur? How much time would it take to inflict the injuries?

After committing a crime, a killer may move the victim's body to create the appearance of accidental death. To accomplish this, other aspects of the crime scene will have to be staged. In one case, asphyxiating the victim with a pillow in a drunken rage before blacking out created a problem for the murderer on regaining consciousness in the morning. Taking some time to think, he decided to carry the body to a full bathtub, place an electric hair dryer in the water, and turn on the current. The fact that the body had been moved was immediately apparent to the investigator, and the simulated electrocution was rendered a failure (see postmortem lividity below).

If there are two victims, the perpetrator may arrange the bodies to make it appear that they killed each other or that it was a murder-suicide. Another reason for moving a victim's body is to limit the scope of the investigation; a sudden disappearance can look like a missing person case instead of a homicide. Serial killers sometimes bury their victims in remote, unfrequented places to avoid detection. Another compelling reason for moving a body from the site of a homicide is the perpetrator's realization of the close connection between himself or herself and the crime scene.

Investigators have some means for determining whether a body has been moved from the site of the killing. One involves the circumstances surrounding the discovery and the place of the discovery; another, the phenomenon known as postmortem lividity.

Circumstances and Where Found

The appropriateness of the deceased's clothing, considered in conjunction with the place of discovery of the body, may suggest that the crime was committed elsewhere. For instance, a dead woman found in a garbage receptacle clothed in a nightdress was likely killed somewhere else. The chances of solving such cases are improved if the site of the murder can be determined. If the site is under private control or ownership, and there is a known connection between the controller and the victim, questioning that individual is in order. If the site is theoretically open to the public but seldom used, the investigator should determine who knew the victim and who had access to that locale and would feel safe from detection while committing the crime.

Postmortem Lividity

Livor mortis *(postmortem lividity)*[15] is a reddish, purplish-blue discoloration of the skin due to settling of blood, by gravity, in the vessels of the dependent areas of the body. In dependent areas pressed against a hard surface, the vessels are mechanically compressed by the pressure and blood cannot settle in them. This gives these areas a pale coloration. Lividity can be evident within 30 minutes of death and, because of clotting (which may take up to three to four hours), it will remain where it started, even if the body is subsequently moved. If signs of lividity can be seen on the top and side surfaces of the body, the inference can be drawn that it was moved after death.

Forensic Entomology

Entomology is the branch of zoology dealing with insects. The kind of insect(s) found on a body may prove it was moved, there being "city flies" and "country flies." In one case, such proof was provided when a cadaver discovered in a rural area was found to be infested with "city flies." The environment—indoor versus outdoor—influences the kind of insect species to be found on decomposing bodies.

> Some species of insects were restricted to remains discovered indoors; others were associated with remains in outdoor situations. Knowledge of the species associated with different habitats may serve to provide information concerning the history of the remains.[16]

When the entomologist fails to find insects on a body, this may indicate that the body was indeed moved, and that the suspect's denial is false. Entomologists study where a body is discovered as an ecological problem, then interpret their findings in terms of locality (i.e., is the body's insect population consistent with that of the environment of its discovery?). If it is not, then one can surmise that the body was moved from somewhere else. When a body has been moved, locating the site of the homicide can be critically important. Investigators may have a candidate site in mind:

> In an investigation of this sort the entomological examination will have to be conducted on that area, rather than on the body itself. This is because the presence of the body may affect the species composition of the soil beneath it, and these changes will remain detectable after the body has been moved. In indoor situations, the presence of certain corpse-associated insects will reveal the fact that a body had been placed there at some earlier time. There are even cases in which it was shown that murder victims were transported from place to place in a particular car.[17]

Similarly, investigative interest sometimes centers on who or what frequented a certain area. Tiny insects and organisms collected on clothing or in vehicles can indicate that a person or vehicle was in a certain locality.[18] Other information entomologists may be able to provide include answers to:

1. How did the death occur?
   When the body is in an advanced state of decay, it may be possible to offer an opinion.

2. Was the body mutilated after death?
   Insect secretions or bites sometimes seem to have a pattern, appearing to have been inflicted by a handmade tool. If a similar pattern were observed in another homicide shortly thereafter, investigators might infer that a disturbed person was involved. Clearly, this would be an unproductive effort if the mutilation pattern is that of insects.

3. Was this animal, especially a species protected by law, killed illegally?
   A conflict regarding time of death—(1) as "told" to an entomologist by studying the insect population and (2) the story told by a suspect as to where or when the carcass was discovered—can have significance for an investigator.[19]

Entomological information is most effectively utilized in the interrogative stage of an investigation, by invoking Horowitz's "Evidence is Available" principle looking toward a confession.

What Time or Times are Involved?

It is often important to know the time of death. Some reasons include:

- To question the individual who appears (from initial interviews) to be the last one to have seen or talked with the victim

- To look for flaws in a witness's account when it is in conflict with the forensic pathologist's estimated time of death

- To protect the innocent—often, one person immediately seems the likely suspect, and the sequence of events relative to the homicide can have inculpatory or exculpatory consequences

Last Person to See the Victim Alive

The last person to see the victim alive (besides the killer), not realizing that he or she possesses information of value, may have useful clues that remain undiscovered unless sought by the investigator. Hence, it is important to allow witnesses to recall the last contact with the victim in their own way, after which the investigator can follow up with questions that ensure disclosure of all potential information:

- What was the state of mind of the victim?

- Were there any signs of agitation or nervousness?

- Was there anything unusual in the behavior of the victim?

- Was anything said that, upon reflection, now seems important?

- If the witness is being re-interviewed after the investigation is under way, were facts developed independently that now suggest additional questions?

Checking a Witness's Story

It is important to check a witness's story. For instance, the establishment of time of death in the following case caused an individual to become a suspect. The victim had told a business associate of an after-dinner appointment—naming the individual to be met, but not the place or purpose of the meeting. As the last person to see the victim alive, this individual was questioned. He claimed, however, that the appointment was never kept, that he had waited more than an hour before leaving for another engagement, and that his first inkling of the crime came from the morning news.

If the pathologist's estimated time of death was substantially the same as the appointment time, the man who was to be met should be considered a potential suspect. Developing a motive involving this suspect would support the hypothesis that he was the killer, and indicate the need for a thorough follow-up to generate evidence that confirms (or refutes) the hypothesis.

Time of Death

Time of death is more accurately determined in manslaughter cases (witnesses often being present) than in murder cases. In the absence of a witness, the forensic pathologist estimates time of death, basing it on as many factors as possible. *Rigor mortis*, body temperature, and other factors are used for this purpose.

Rigor Mortis

Rigor mortis,[20] the stiffening of the body after death, is the result of chemical changes within muscle tissue. Evident at first in the small muscles of the hands and jaws (in two to four hours), it becomes more obvious in the larger muscles (in four to six hours), and is fully developed in 12 hours, where it remains until postmortem decomposition begins. Decomposition is affected by extremes of heat and cold; it occurs very slowly in cold weather, more rapidly in hot weather. Clearly, the extent of rigor mortis can be useful in establishing the approximate time of death.

Body Temperature

The live body is able to maintain a constant temperature of about 98 degrees Fahrenheit regardless of weather and type of clothing. After death, its temperature falls to that of the surrounding medium. The rate of fall can be affected by a number of factors; for instance, how the deceased was dressed or covered or the surface on which it is lying may influence heat loss. However, when a clothed adult body is in a room with normal heat, the formula below allows for an estimate of the interval between time of death and time of recording of rectal temperature. It assumes an average drop in temperature to be 1.5 degrees Fahrenheit per hour, that the ambient temperature was about 70 degrees Fahrenheit, and that the deceased had a normal body temperature of 98.6 degrees Fahrenheit at death.[21]

$$\frac{98.6 - T}{1.5} = N$$

Where: T = body rectal temperature in degrees Fahrenheit
N = number of hours elapsed since death

Several factors can affect the cooling rate; thus, the results have greater validity in the first 12 hours than after a longer interval. If no thermometer is available, feeling the body can yield a more subjective estimate: if the armpits are warm to the touch, death most likely occurred within the last few hours; if the body overall is cool and clammy, the elapsed time since death is approximately 18 to 24 hours.

Other Factors

In addition to bodily changes (postmortem lividity, rigor mortis, heat loss), other factors that can also help in estimating time of death include stomach content, insect growth, and external factors.

Stomach Content: As part of the autopsy, the stomach and small intestines are examined for undigested food. This procedure was developed by twentieth-century pathologists as one of the factors that might suggest time of death. Unlike other postmortem markers, digestion comes to a complete end at death. It provides two important pieces of information—what the deceased ate for the last meal and how long ago it was eaten. When "what" is coupled with "where"—the victim's home or a restaurant he or she frequented—the information obtained can affect the outcome of the investigation. In theory, at least, a medical examiner who knows the approximate time and quantity of the victim's last meal should be able to extrapolate time of death based on the rate that food might be expected to pass out of the stomach into the intestine.[22]

Insect Growth: There are other scientists besides the pathologist whose expertise can be useful in estimating time of death: the forensic entomologist (of which there are few) studies insects from egg laying and larvae growth to fully developed adulthood. Entomologists regard the human cadaver as an ecosystem in which certain insects appear and depart on a predictable schedule; they know, for example, that the eggs of houseflies hatch into maggots in 24 hours. Specific knowledge about the time required for each growth stage permits the specialist to estimate time of death for a body on which insect specimens were observed, recorded (by color photography if possible), and collected. If practicable, the entomologist should visit the crime scene to collect specimens, and do so at the autopsy as well. For such evidence to be reliable, the life cycles of the specific insects obtained from the cadaver must be replicated. Insect evidence in the form of eggs and larvae can sometimes be difficult or impossible to identify, but DNA now permits formerly difficult specimens to be identified.[23]

External Factors: Clues from the victim's residence and personal habits can be of assistance in estimating time of death. Gathering this information is the function of the investigator who then shares it with the pathologist.

Victim's Residence

Neighbors are often able to state when the victim was last seen alive. Additional information can be gleaned from such observations as: any food on the table, dishes in the sink, newspapers or mail not picked up, blinds or shades drawn or open, electric lights on or off, or a watch or clock stopped by its having been damaged (possibly from a struggle).

Personal Habits

If the deceased habitually performed certain daily tasks (e.g., walking the dog, leaving the house to buy cigarettes, going to work, picking up the mail, telephoning friends and family—or receiving calls from them), failure to do so establishes boundaries for estimating time of death.

Time Sequence

In some homicides the time available to the killer to carry out the crime can become an important issue; in others, there may be evidence that the killer delayed in leaving the scene. In either event the investigator should appreciate the implications of the time factor.

Accuracy

Forensic pathologists cannot pinpoint time of death; rather, based on when the victim was last seen alive and when the victim was found dead, they can state the interval of time during which death could have occurred. When the time span is great, the forensic pathologist may be able to narrow these limits—by utilizing insect growth, for example.

Was There Sufficient Time?

The sequence of events surrounding a homicide can be of great importance in fulfilling the obligation to protect the innocent. The investigator should ascertain whether the interval of time was sufficient for the suspect to inflict the injuries. An example will clarify this:

A young man returned home early one evening to find that his mother had been viciously assaulted and left for dead. Instead of dialing 911, he called the friend with whom he had spent the evening and was advised by his friend's father to call the family doctor. As the doctor was out of town, his wife suggested that the young man call an ambulance. Not long thereafter, the friend, an ambulance, and police arrived.

Now a potential suspect, the young man was asked by the police to strip. Investigators found no evidence of involvement in the struggle that had obviously taken place: no blood was on his body or clothing; a minor injury to a knuckle was accounted for (the suspect claiming it resulted when repairing his car); and no physical evidence was found to tie him to the homicide. Just the same, the fact that he was slow to summon assistance was viewed as peculiar, as was his failure to weep or display any other emotion. Along with the fact that he was the first to discover the crime, these particulars made the young man a prime suspect.

Initially, little investigative effort was put into establishing the time of each event surrounding the homicide; subsequently, important differences developed. Had there been sufficient time to commit the crime? This issue was resolved when the friend's father recalled in an interview that the telephone call from the young man had coincided with the fire engine sirens from the firehouse across the street. From this fact and the time the suspect was last seen, the pathologist could answer in the negative: there had not been sufficient time for the brutal murder—including as it did the breaking of several large bones and mutilation of the body.

Delayed Departure—Its Significance

Homicides have been made to appear incidental to an interrupted burglary. This deception is more likely in a manslaughter case, but it can materialize when a premeditated murder plan goes awry. The perpetrator, knowing that he or she will be suspected will sometimes take jewelry and valuables as a way to avoid this possibility.

In one case, a watch was removed from the victim's wrist. She had suffered a brutal beating and blood had seeped through the watchband and dried, leaving an outline of its design on her wrist. It, however, would be a rare burglar-turned-killer who would linger long enough for this to happen; the natural impulse is to escape. Thus, evidence that an offender delayed leaving the scene of a homicide should be a red flag to the investigator, suggesting a connection between victim and killer—a killer who felt secure from interruption while devising and executing a plan to throw investigators off the track.

Time Line

Defense investigators, particularly in cases involving several witnesses, now utilize the time line flowing from witnesses' stories. The purpose is to pick up inconsistencies or impossibilities regarding when the event occurred. For example, if a wife claims to have been with her husband four days ago, and forensic entomological evidence establishes that the victim was not alive four days ago, a case may be opened or its investigation intensified.

When answers to the quaternary issues (opportunity, means, motive, and audacity) are forthcoming, the investigation is off to a good start. Establishing a time line is helpful with regard to opportunity.

What Occurred?—How Did it Occur?

What occurred in a homicide may be determined from the kind of injury inflicted on the victim. Trauma results when violent or disruptive action causes physical injury or when a toxic substance is introduced into the body. A bullet, a bludgeon, and a sharp weapon produce visibly different injuries. To understand an autopsy report, the terms must be defined:[24]

Abrasion	A superficial, scraped surface area of tissue produced by friction. The result of a blunt force (see Figure 17.6).
Contusion	A hemorrhage beneath the skin; a bruise. If blood vessels are ruptured and considerable bleeding occurs, it is a hematoma.
Fracture	A break or crack of a bone or cartilage. A fracture with the skin broken—an open wound, perhaps with the bone exposed, is a compound (or open) fracture. A simple (or closed) fracture is one in which there is no break in the skin.
Incision	A relatively clean cut that results when a sharp instrument or force is applied to a small, limited area of tissue.
Laceration	A tearing of tissue, generally with ragged edges, caused by stretching the tissue beyond its ability to rebound. The result of a blunt force.
Wound	The result of a blunt or a sharp force. A wound is an injury—especially one in which the skin is pierced, cut, torn, or otherwise broken; however, a wound need not necessarily have open skin. A hematoma (a localized collection of blood, usually clotted, in tissue) is a wound.
Trauma	The result of any force—blunt, sharp, or penetrating. A hit-and-run automobile accident can result in lacerations, fractures, and on occasion, abrasion. A knife or ice pick produces incisions; even a dull axe leaves an incision but its opposite end will produce a laceration. All of these incidents result in trauma.

If the pathologist is able to state with some certainty what kind of weapon was used, the investigator can search for it along the paths the perpetrator may have taken in fleeing the crime scene. When a suspect is developed, his or her home, garage, and automobile can be searched for the weapon. The search and seizure laws must always be kept in mind; otherwise, the evidence may not be admissible. This could materially damage a case since a weapon can serve to link an offender to the crime.

Gunshot wounds are of particular interest; from them it may be possible to determine how and what occurred. They are an important source of information, which the forensic scientist interprets for the homicide detective.

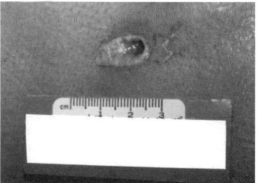

Figure 17.6
Gunshot wound of entry (at oblique angle) showing abrasion on the lateral side of the entrance.

Office of the Medical Examiner, Cook County, Illinois

Gunshot Wounds

A gunshot wound is the result of the discharge from the barrel of a gun—flame, hot gases, smoke, partially burned and unburned powder particles, and the projectile itself (bullet, wad, or shot).[25] The nature of the wound inflicted is a function of the distance between victim and muzzle at the time of discharge (assuming no object—such as a cigarette lighter in a shirt pocket—was struck by the bullet in flight between weapon and wound), and of the characteristics of the weapon itself (see Figures 17.7–17.9). Both entry and exit wounds can be observed on a body. Distinguishing between

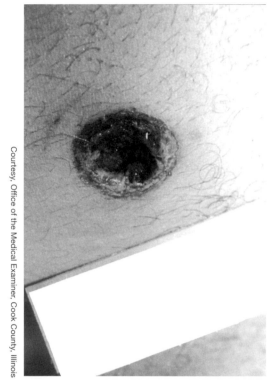

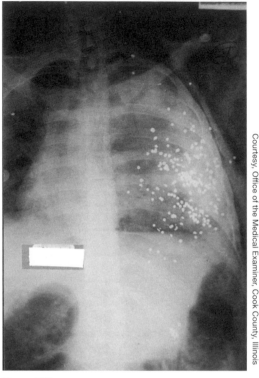

Figure 17.7
Shotgun contact wound.

Figure 17.8
X-ray of body shows pellets dispersed after striking bone.

them may allow the crime to be reconstructed, as may any blood spatter pattern produced—especially when the victim is shot at close range.

Entrance Wounds—Firing Distance

There are three kinds of entrance wounds: contact, near discharge, and distant discharge. A contact wound results when a small weapon is fired while in contact with the skin (a closed wound) or up to a distance of two or three inches from the body (see Figure 17.10), or a large caliber weapon (or rifle) is fired up to a distance of six inches from the body. A near discharge wound is the result of firing at a distance of six to 24 inches for handguns, and six to 36 inches for rifles. In reconstructing the possibility of suicide, the near discharge distance cannot exceed the deceased's arm length (unless there is some mechanical contrivance rigged to allow firing the weapon from a distance). A distant discharge wound results when a weapon is fired from a distance greater than 24 to 36 inches, respectively, for handguns and rifles (see Figure 17.11).

Characteristics of Entrance and Exit Wounds

Entrance wounds (assuming the bullet is not tumbling or misshapen at the time of entrance) are round or oval in appearance (see Figures 17.12A–D); their edges form an "abrasion collar" with the skin surface inverted—depressed and crater-like. Contact wounds inflicted over thick bone structure

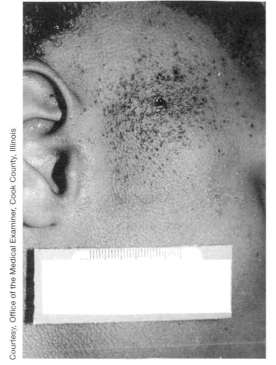

Figure 17.9
An example of stippling (tattooing). Firing distance approximately six inches.

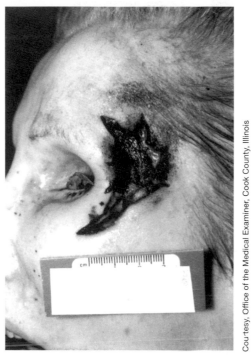

Figure 17.10
Close contact wound of the head with splitting of the skin. This is a suicide. Splitting of skin is due to gaseous discharge from weapon.

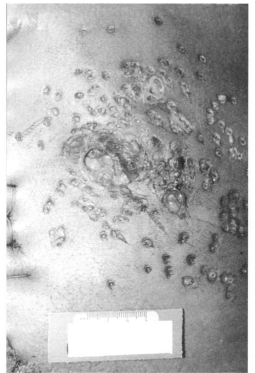

Figure 17.11
Shotgun entrance wound showing satellite wounds from pellets. Firing distance approximately six to eight yards.

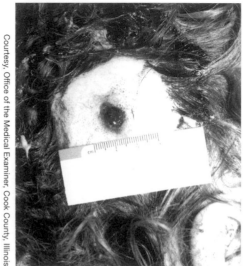

Figure 17.12A
Bullet entrance wound of head.

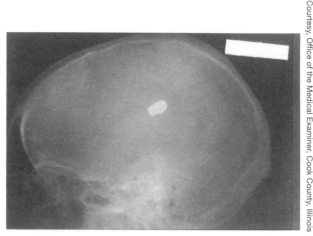

Figure 17.12B
X-ray of head showing lodged bullet.

Figure 17.12C
Copper-jacketed bullet removed from head.

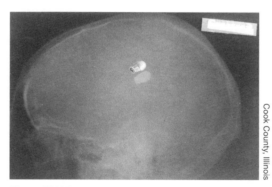

Figure 17.12D
Comparison of bullet with X-ray of lodged bullet.

have an irregular, stellate (star) shape; their edges are everted—pushed outward. The tearing of the tissue surrounding a contact wound results from the gases that, having entered the wound, seek to reverse direction and escape (see Figure 17.10). The laceration is irregular in appearance; it may be oval-shaped with no abrasion around the edges, but it can and usually will have an abrasion.

An exit wound results when a bullet, emerging from the body, splits the skin. This skin will exhibit greater tearing if the bullet emerges when it is no longer spinning on its axis—wobbling in its passage through the body. This can happen after striking a bone; if the emerging bullet carried bone splinters with it (and possibly some large pieces of bone), the wound may be mistaken for a laceration caused by a blunt force.

Once in the body, bullets have been known to behave erratically. There are several reported instances of a bullet entering a limb and following a blood vein back to the heart to be deposited in an upper chamber; or lodging between the skin and the skull, sometimes traveling between the two

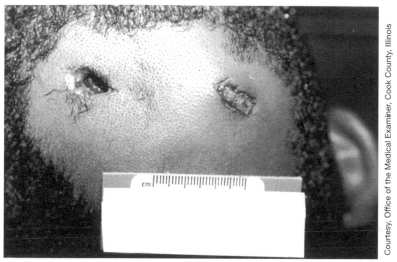

Figure 17.13
Bullet lodged underneath the skin above ear. Exit wound next to it at left. This illustrates the eccentric behavior sometimes observed of bullets as they pass through the body.

(see Figure 17.13). In at least one instance a bullet entered the victim's temple, traveled between the skin and skull around the head, and exited at the other temple.

Number of Wounds

When the number of entrance and exit wounds is the same, it is evident that all bullets that entered the body exited as well. Should the entrance number be greater than the exit number, one bullet (or more) remains in the body to be retrieved as potential evidence. Whether a particular wound is an entrance or an exit wound is best determined by the pathologist. If the distinction is of significance in reconstructing the crime and expert testimony is required, a forensic pathologist must make this determination.

Cutting and Stabbing Wounds

Although a wound may appear to the casual observer or untrained police officer to be the result of cutting or stabbing, in fact it is often difficult to determine cause (see Figures 17.14–17.16). For instance, a penetrating stab wound can be mistaken for a bullet wound; a gunshot wound may resemble cleavage by a knife or axe; a laceration on the scalp (from falling on a smooth hard surface such as a table or floor) can resemble a dull knife wound. These determinations often require the expert opinion of the forensic pathologist.

Accidental deaths from cutting or stabbing are relatively rare, but examples might include: being impaled on a picket fence, sliding from a hayloft onto a pitchfork, or tripping onto the teeth of a rake. The circumstances surrounding the death as well as the practices and habits of the deceased will help the medical examiner/coroner decide. Deaths from cutting or stabbing are generally suicidal or homicidal.

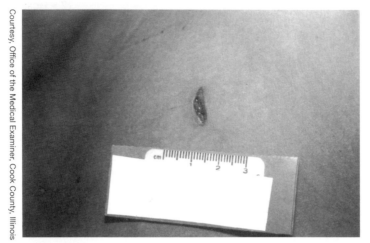

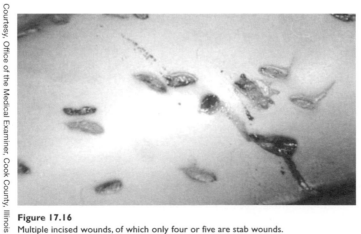

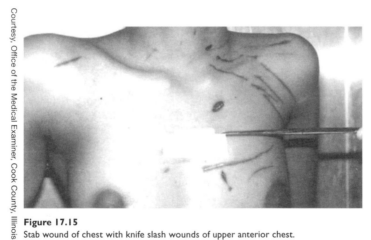

Figure 17.14
Stab wound.

Figure 17.15
Stab wound of chest with knife slash wounds of upper anterior chest.

Figure 17.16
Multiple incised wounds, of which only four or five are stab wounds.

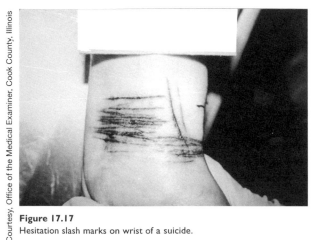

Figure 17.17
Hesitation slash marks on wrist of a suicide.

Suicidal Wounds

In feudal times, stabbing oneself or falling on one's sword was a more common way to commit suicide. Today, suicides by stabbing or cutting are more likely to involve a knife or razor, a broken bottle, glass, or other sharp-edged instrument. Seldom the result of one deft incision, usually a number of short superficial cuts are inflicted before the wounds are fatal (see Figure 17.17). These slight, often shallow cuts, known as *hesitation marks*, typify suicide and suicide attempts. (Even when a gun is used, there may be evidence that hesitation shots were fired.)

The parts of the body usually assaulted in such attempted suicides are the wrists, the throat, and sometimes the ankles. If the attempt is successful, the victim is usually found where the act took place. In some unsuccessful suicides by cutting or stabbing, the individual may decide to seek help, leaving the scene of the initial assault and a trail of blood behind.

Homicidal Wounds

Stabbing (not cutting) is often the cause of a homicidal wound—even when the weapon is a knife (see Figures 17.18A–D). Because victims will instinctively try to defend themselves, the forearm may bear slash marks, or if a knife grasped in self-protection is pulled away by the attacker, the palm and fingers will be cut deeply. These are known as defense wounds (see Figure 17.19). The upper parts of the body—most often the chest but also the side and back of the neck—suffer wounds that result in death. An autopsy can track the internal path of a stab wound. An upward thrust is normally (but not necessarily) indicative of homicide. It is easier to stab oneself with a downward or horizontal thrust; such a track usually points to suicide. Criminal homicide, however, cannot be ruled out; in such a case, blood will often be found scattered throughout the area of conflict—evidence of the victim's attempts to ward off the attacker and escape. The absence of a cutting weapon at the scene suggests homicide, but the experienced investigator knows that such evidence is often taken from the scene by the first person to discover the body.

Blunt Force Wounds

Wounds that are the product of neither a penetrating nor a cutting instrument are termed *blunt force wounds*. Various weapons are able to produce such wounds: a hammer, a stout branch, a two-by-four, an iron pipe, a brick or large stone, or an automobile. Blunt force wounds can be caused merely by falling from a height and striking the head, or landing feet-first on a hard surface. The injuries vary from lacerations, bruises or contusions, bone fractures, internal bleeding, and severe crushing wounds, most often to the head, neck, chest, and abdomen. The wound may not necessarily be the same

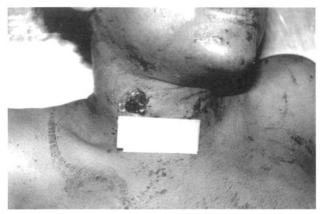

Figure 17.18A
Perforating stab wound of the neck, showing entrance and exit.

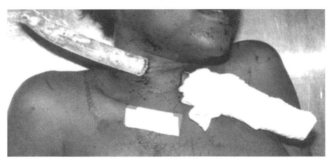

Figure 17.18B
Same through-and-through stab wound, with knife in place.

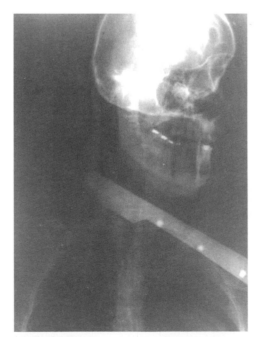

Figure 17.18C
X-ray from front.

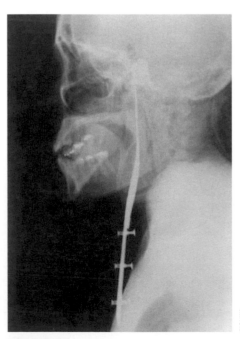

Figure 17.18D
X-ray from side.

All photos in Figure 17.18 Courtesy, Office of the Medical Examiner, Cook County, Illinois

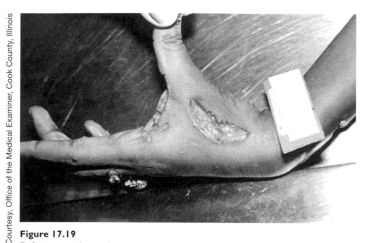

Figure 17.19
Defense incised wound.

Courtesy, Office of the Medical Examiner, Cook County, Illinois

size and shape as the crushing weapon. Despite this, a forensic pathologist often can suggest the kind(s) of weapon(s) used, thereby allowing the homicide investigator to conduct a search for the weapon. If found, it might bear traces of the victim's skin, blood, hair, clothing fibers—evidence that can have probative value.

Blunt impact weapons may also produce blood spatter which, if properly interpreted, can help to reconstruct the crime and determine what happened (see Chapter 2). Should this interpretation not agree with the suspect's explanation, the investigator can take full advantage of the difference by informing the suspect that contradictory evidence is available (one of Horowitz's principles of interrogation; see Chapter 10).

Asphyxiation

The medical term *asphyxiation* describes death caused by interference with the supply of oxygen to the lungs. Although the cause may be accidental (e.g., from food lodged in the windpipe, or drowning), of greatest interest to the homicide investigator are deaths from smothering, strangulation, hanging, poisoning, and drowning. Some drownings that appear accidental may be attempts to cover up criminal homicide; hanging and poisoning deaths, on the other hand, often are mistaken for criminal homicide when in reality they are suicides or accidents.

Smothering

Deaths from smothering are frequently encountered in infanticide, in which it is sufficient to place a hand over the infant's mouth and nose. Adults can also be killed deliberately by smothering. The assailant in these cases is usually more powerful than the victim and uses a pillow, cloth, or plastic pressed tightly over the face. It is not uncommon to use greater-than-necessary force; thus, scratches and bruises from the struggle will remain on the body. Their interpretation, together with autopsy findings, are best left to the forensic pathologist.

In most of these cases, the offender has a close relationship with the victim. A consideration of who had motive, opportunity, and the nerve to follow through should lead to some possible suspects. Because in these cases the offender is not a hardened criminal, any evidence provided by the pathologist and family members that is raised during the interrogation is (again in accordance with the principles of Horowitz) likely to result in an admission or confession.

Strangulation

A person may be strangled manually or with a ligature such as a clothesline, electric lamp wire, belt, necktie, nylon stocking, scarf, and so on. The external signs of manual strangulation on a corpse are different from those left by a ligature. In both types of strangulation, however, the internal signs are hemorrhage and damage to the interior structure (bones and cartilage) of the neck, throat, and larynx. They are disclosed through an autopsy.

Manual: Suicide by manual self-strangulation is virtually an impossibility; accidental throttling is also relatively rare. When the death is sudden and the injury slight and apparently unintentional, accidental strangulation is indicated. If, however, the signs of injury are obvious and severe, it is unlikely that the death was accidental. When death clearly resulted from manual strangulation, there is a strong presumption of felonious homicide. It may be surprising to learn that the hands are not commonly used to strangle; for one reason, it is difficult to throttle a healthy adult—a male especially—unless the attack is by stealth, or the victim is stunned by a blow or under the influence of alcohol or other drugs.

Following rape or attempted rape an assailant may try to eliminate the victim/eyewitness by choking. During a quarrel, one person may seize another by the throat to stifle an outcry for help. If this causes death, the attacker's intent would be a decisive factor as to whether it is murder or manslaughter. Witnesses should be queried about any spontaneous utterances made before or during the altercation, particularly by the assailant. If the intent was to silence the victim's call for help, murder is an appropriate charge.

Reconstructing some manual strangulations may reveal how they happened. The reconstructions are based on the probability that the force required to asphyxiate will leave an external pattern of finger marks (including fingernail marks) on the victim's neck. If the assault is from behind, the assailant generally uses both hands; if a frontal assault, one hand. The physical evidence may or may not square with the offender's account; if it does not, the discrepancy can be put to good use for interrogative purposes.

Ligature: Some strangulation deaths are caused by a broken wire, machine belt, or other ligature wrapping itself around the victim's neck. The nature of the circumstances together with eyewitness accounts of the incident should attest to its being accidental and not a crime. The intentional use of a ligature as a means of homicide is rare (except for lynchings and official executions), but when one is committed, a horizontal groove or furrow cut by the ligature is often visible on the throat, and normally is about the width of the ligature, and is located (on a male) at a level with or below the Adam's apple (see Figure 17.20). Signs of bruising and blood congestion just above and below the furrow indicate the victim was alive when it was applied. Because attempts are made to cover up a homicide by simulating suicidal hanging, these contusions have investigative and probative significance.

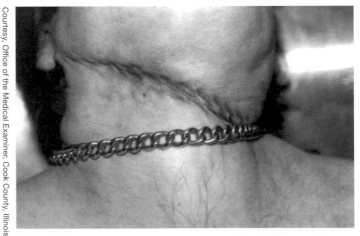

Figure 17.20
Strangulation by hanging—chain ligature showing patterned abrasion.

Courtesy, Office of the Medical Examiner, Cook County, Illinois

The pathologist will also examine the inside of the eyelids and the facial skin for another sign of strangulation: pinhead-sized red dots that are minute hemorrhages called *petechiae*. It is also not uncommon to find that the victim has bitten the tongue.

If a ligature is knotted, photographs (including one-to-one size) should be taken before it is removed, and a cut made as far as possible from the knot, with the cut ends carefully and securely tied together and labeled as such. Although rather unusual as evidence, the use of an unconventional knot can suggest a vocation (or hobby), and examining the victim's recent experience with anyone in that occupation may provide investigative insight.

Hanging: Although a form of strangulation, some hangings require separate treatment. The majority are intentional and thus suicidal (see Figure 17.21), but occasionally there are attempts to cover up criminal homi

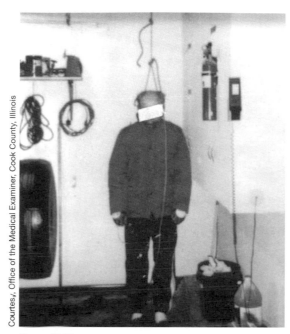

Figure 17.21
Suicidal hanging—note feet are on the floor.

cide by making it appear that the victim committed suicide by hanging. If the autopsy is competent, this ruse should fail. Autoerotic deaths, a form of hanging, are indeed accidental. Being unfamiliar with eroticized death, the relatives and friends of the victim—and even a few detectives—will almost invariably insist that the hanging was a case of murder.

Autoerotic deaths occur when an individual engages in a solitary, sex-related activity whereby he or she is asphyxiated accidentally. There is some physiological support for the belief that oxygen deprivation to the brain intensifies sexual arousal. When there is too much oxygen deprivation, however, the person loses control of the autoerotic exercise and dies of asphyxiation by being suffocated or hanged. The body may be found with the head covered by a plastic bag or with a ligature around the neck. If male, the decedent is often nude, or sometimes dressed in women's clothing (see Figure 17.22), his limbs shackled in a form of bondage with a mirror positioned for self-observation; if female, erotic paraphernalia such as an electric vibrator or dildo may be

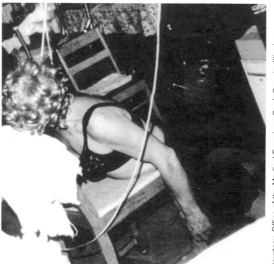

Figure 17.22
An example of autoerotic death by strangulation.

present. There is no evidence of suicidal intent such as a note. In a famous example, in 2009, character actor David Carradine was found hanging from a rope in a hotel room in Bangkok, Thailand. Two autopsies were conducted and it was concluded that the death was not caused by suicide. Police speculate that this was an accidental death caused by autoerotic asphyxiation.

Of the two modes of death—suffocation and hanging—hanging is a more common effect of autoeroticism. A bit of cloth or other material is often found wrapped around the ligature; its purpose, to prevent marking of the neck which would require some explaining to inquisitive relatives or friends, should the exercise turn out as expected—providing enhanced sexual arousal with no fatality. If this was a frequent practice, parallel rope marks (and possibly rope fibers) on an overhead pipe or top edge of a door (used as support) are likely to be present. They should be looked for after any suspected autoerotic fatality.

If most of the accompanying clues described are not present and the young victim is thought to be normal and well-adjusted, a ruling of accidental death rather than murder will almost certainly be incomprehensible to relatives. Treating the grieving family sympathetically will help to alleviate their anguish, and eventually lead to an acceptance of the autoerotic death finding.

Poisoning

Carbon monoxide is a colorless, odorless gas that is produced when any carbon fuel is incompletely burned. It is the primary cause of death due to inhalation injury. Familiar sources are coal and gas appliances such as stoves, refrigerators, hot water heaters, furnaces, and automobiles. The exhaust pipe fumes of an automobile are all too often seen as a convenient way to commit suicide.[26]

Defective home gas appliances are responsible for accidental deaths by carbon monoxide asphyxiation. Very small concentrations—one part per 1,000 parts of air—breathed for about an hour cause headache, nausea, dizziness, and confusion. Carbon monoxide accumulates in the blood, so that even smaller concentrations—one part per 10,000—have similar effects if breathed overnight. Awakened by headache and realizing something is amiss, the sufferer often will try to open a window or leave the room, but disorientation makes this impossible. Frequently, the victim stumbles and hits a radiator, table corner, or other hard object, opening a head wound that bleeds profusely. The floundering will make the room look like a battle occurred. In many cases, the victim will die before reaching fresh air and the accidental death will have signs of a felonious homicide.

Young children, owing to their high metabolic activity, succumb more readily to carbon monoxide poisoning than do adults; however, it is possible for all the people sleeping at one residence to die from carbon monoxide leaking into a home with its windows sealed shut.

Carbon monoxide turns blood to cherry red and produces a patchy, pinkish color in the lividity of the corpse. Armed with this knowledge, together with what can be learned from relatives and neighbors about the circumstances surrounding the death(s), the investigator can focus on the source of the gas and see that it is no longer a danger. The autopsy and toxicological analysis will confirm cause of death to be carbon monoxide, and with its source identified (generally a defective gas-burning appliance), establish a case of accidental death rather than criminal homicide.

Drowning

Drowning causes approximately 3,000 deaths in the United States each year (including both accidental and intended deaths). Most deaths from drowning are accidental; a few are suicidal. A large number of drowning deaths involve young children. Adults who drown in bathtubs are usually found to have contributing factors such as natural disease or toxicological abnormalities. Criminal homicide by drowning is largely limited to infants and small children, but adults can be overpowered and drowned. Usually, however, this requires accomplices. Attempts have been made to cover up a criminal homicide by placing the corpse in a bathtub filled with water to simulate a drowning. This ploy is called for when the connection between victim and killer is obvious and the latter will almost immediately be suspected. The manifestations of a true drowning (or other type of asphyxiation) and those of putting a dead body into water are sufficiently distinct to be differentiated by autopsy. The medical examiner/coroner, of course, determines whether the death is accidental, suicidal, or criminal.[27]

Burns

The very young and the very old are at greatest risk from burn accidents. In all fire deaths, the forensic pathologists should attempt to determine:[28]

- The positive identity of the deceased, especially if the body is charred beyond visual recognition
- Whether the deceased was alive prior to ignition of the fire, or whether the fire was set and the body burned in an attempt to conceal a homicide
- The cause and manner of death
- Whether contributing factors are present, such as alcohol/drug intoxication

Suicide by burning is quite rare in this culture; rarer still is burning a victim with the intent to kill. Accidental death resulting from burns is more common, particularly among the young and the elderly. A burned corpse may be of interest to the homicide detective because attempts have been made to cover up criminal homicides by making them appear to have been the result of smoking in bed. Hence, the question of accident versus cover-up needs to be considered whenever human remains are discovered at the scene of a fire. The medical examiner/coroner can be helpful in furnishing answers to the following concerns:

- Are the remains those of a human being?
- How is the body to be identified?
- Was the deceased alive or dead when the fire started?
- Who was the deceased? Sex? Age? Height?

Are the Remains of Human Origin?

A partially consumed body poses no problem as to its human origin. On those rare occasions when all flesh has been destroyed, the skull, skeletal bones, and especially the teeth, are likely to remain. The latter are most indestructible by fire; they generally can be recognized as human (see Figures 17.23 and 17.24). The issue of the origin of a bone or bones is raised occasionally when skeletonized remains are discovered outdoors in a sparsely settled area. They may be a mix of human and animal bones, or bones of animal origin only. Should there be any question, a forensic pathologist is consulted. In some cases, the pathologist may wish to seek the opinion of a forensic anthropologist before arriving at a definitive answer.

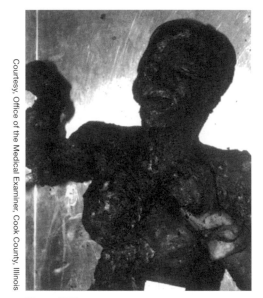

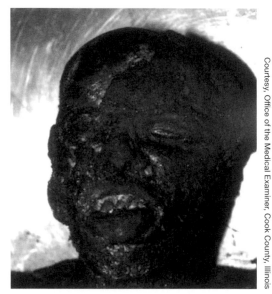

Figure 17.23
Charred remains from a house fire/arson. Note pugilistic attitude of arms, a characteristic of death by fire.

Figure 17.24
Face no longer recognizable, identification was made by comparing teeth with antemortem X-rays.

The Victim—Alive or Dead when the Fire Started?

In attempting to cover up a homicide by having it appear that the victim died as a result of a fire, the killer often makes a serious error based on ignorance. Though it is not common knowledge, two relatively simple procedures can determine if a person was dead or alive before the fire. The first is by autopsy of the air passageway to the lungs and the lungs themselves, inspecting for the smoke deposits that will be present only if the victim was breathing when the fire was started. The second method is a toxicological analysis of the blood for carbon monoxide. Because red blood cells combine preferentially with carbon monoxide (rather than oxygen), the gas will be found in the blood of a victim who was alive at the time of the fire. The absence of smoke deposits and carbon monoxide signifies that the individual was already dead, killed by another means.

Antemortem and Postmortem Injuries

In reconstructing a crime, it is sometimes important to know whether an injury was sustained before or after death. Cover-ups have been attempted by claiming an injury occurred after death, when it was actually inflicted before (and was the cause of the) death. The perpetrator's obvious intention is to corroborate the account he or she gave to investigators. Differentiating between an antemortem and a postmortem injury can be difficult when the injury occurred within minutes of—or very close to—the time of death; a longer time span makes it easier for the pathologist to estimate when an injury was inflicted. This pertains whether it was before or after the death. It is a matter for the expert to decide.

PEOPLE: THOSE WHO KNEW THE VICTIM

The most obvious persons to be interviewed are family members, close associates, co-workers, and social acquaintances of the victim. Some seek out the investigator to impart what they know and believe to be of value; others, either not realizing that they have relevant information or feeling reticent about any contact with police, do not come forward. Still others, not being especially close to the victim, may refrain from becoming involved in a homicide investigation; if reassured, they might cooperate. The competent investigator will cultivate and explore all of these potential sources (see Securing Cooperation in Chapter 6).

Information that may be elicited by interviewing a victim's associates includes:

1. The suggestion of a motive for the crime.

2. The naming of a suspect or suspects and providing the reasons for such charges or beliefs. (At this point immediate follow-up may be required if the suspect is likely to flee the area.)

3. Describing the usual activities and habits of the deceased permits his or her movements to be traced at the time of, and just before, the death. The last person to see the victim alive may provide valuable insights: Was the deceased's state of mind apparently normal? Did he or she seem depressed, anxious, or agitated? Does the last person to talk with the victim recall any pertinent remarks or expressions of concern?

Canvassing

Canvassing as a tactic in the search for witnesses is generally confined to the immediate crime scene area. In homicide investigation, the various places and locations visited by the deceased on the fatal day should also be revisited with the purpose of identifying anyone who was in contact with the victim. Follow-up will depend on all the facts generated through the canvass and other investigative efforts. To enlarge upon any hints or bits of information that might have been gleaned, it would be appropriate to place an individual under surveillance, or seek the help of an informant.

Informants

There are a number of homicides in which perpetrators appear to have successfully avoided detection, but after the initial fear of apprehension passes, they will relax their guard and talk, finding gratification in bragging about their exploits. At this point informants can provide what was overheard (often in a neighborhood bar). Various factors motivate informants. They may be out for a monetary reward, currying future favors, or trying to make a deal with the police—either seeking leniency in connection with a matter currently under investigation or being prosecuted, or looking for revenge on one of the perpetrators.

Follow-up measures include surveillance of the suspect (by wiretaps where permitted); review of the physical evidence discovered at the crime scene; and ultimately, interrogation.

Questioning Suspects

A suspect may be interviewed or interrogated, depending on the evidence. If, for instance, a person has been named as a possible suspect but no supporting reasons are cited, or a charge is based on mere suspicion, the proper procedure is an interview; its purpose, to learn what the individual knows about the crime and where he or she was at the time of death. The information must then be checked out. This might involve cross-checking with other people or require a reconstruction of the event, utilizing the physical evidence at the scene. When (and if) sufficient evidence is gathered and the investigation has shifted from a general inquiry to one focusing on a particular suspect, the interrogation process begins and *Miranda* warnings are in order.

The purpose at this juncture of the interrogation is to determine what the suspect is willing to disclose about the crime, and what connection (if any) exists between the suspect and the crime scene. Whether exculpatory or incriminating, a statement must still be checked against the alleged facts. This is true for all facts developed during the investigation—including those divulged by a reconstruction. Ultimately, if the case against the suspect continues to build, with support increasing for the hypothesis of guilt, the purpose of the interrogation shifts toward obtaining an admission or confession.

THE VALUE OF RECORDS IN HOMICIDE INVESTIGATION

Records can be an important source of information: providing insight into the motive for the crime, allowing the fatal weapon to be traced to its source or ownership, and documenting previous activities of the victim or suspect (which relate the motive to the killing). Special efforts must be expended to discover the existence of records, particularly those not maintained for law enforcement purposes.

Insight into Motive

Who Benefits?

A person who stands to gain from a criminal homicide as the beneficiary of an insurance policy, a will, or other inheritance may become a suspect. Individuals may also become suspects if it is learned that their former friendly relations with the deceased had soured to the extent that police were called to restore peace, or the deceased filed a civil suit. A person may also become a suspect if he or she was very recently made a beneficiary and had the means, nerve, and opportunity to commit the crime.

Written Materials

If diaries, letters, or even blogs exist, they may reveal or hint at a motive for the crime (and even name the perpetrator), or disclose a hostile business or personal relationship. Unlike records that are routinely maintained and accessible to law enforcement, diaries or letters must be hunted down. They may be withheld by family members because of their intimate nature, or because their potential value to the investigator is not fully appreciated. Careful interviewing of close friends of the deceased is required if such evidence is to be located and made available.

Computer Records

A search of the victim's or suspect's computer may produce a diary or other information that will assist in the investigation. Telephone numbers, e-mails, social networking activity, and other electronic records can be extremely valuable. In several cases involving shootings by juveniles, computerized records proved valuable in helping to establish motive and methods in an attack.

Tracing Ownership

An item of physical evidence—whether discarded when fleeing from the crime scene or brought to and left there by the perpetrator—represents an opportunity to trace its ownership. For example, the Mannlicher-Carcano rifle used to assassinate President John F. Kennedy and found in the Dallas book depository was soon traced to Lee Harvey Oswald through business records and Oswald's post office box in that city. On the other hand, 54,000 records had to be checked for the owner of a pair of eyeglasses, a crucial piece of physical evidence in the famous "Leopold and Loeb" case in 1924 (in which two college students—Nathan Leopold Jr. and Richard Loeb—killed a teenage boy in their quest to commit the "perfect crime"). When it was determined that the glasses found near the body were not the victim's, the optical firm that sold them was traced through a faint, diamond-shaped mark on the lenses. The unique hinges on the eyeglass frames were a new item of manufacture dispensed to but three customers. Only the third customer—Leopold—failed to produce his pair upon request, and this brought him into the network of suspects.

In another homicide case, it took hours of library research just to identify an item of physical evidence, whose purpose was not obvious or known to anyone who examined it. It was a fabricated piece of metal, found in a lover's lane frequented by college students. Library reference books listing trade associations that might be of assistance were consulted. Photographs of the evidence were then mailed to a number of possible manufacturers. The piece of metal was finally identified as a part for a stove, itself a new item dropped from production because it did not sell. The stove's former manufacturer was located in a state more than 1,000 miles from the college town where the evidence was found. A check of college registration records turned up the name of one student from the distant state. The human blood on his car's front seat fabric was the break needed in the case. Records were also crucial in tracing the ownership of the contents of the bundle discarded by Martin Luther King Jr.'s killer (see Chapter 5). VIN (Vehicle Identification Number) records helped trace the van used to transport the explosives set off in the New York World Trade Center bombing in 1993. The individuals who rented the van were on record with the rental agency.

Previously Recorded Activities

In addition to files maintained routinely to aid in criminal investigation, other police and judicial records should be probed. For example, there could be telephone calls to police complaining of a disturbance of the peace—a family quarrel or a noisy party. (Some even may be recalled by a member of the uniformed force before they are retrieved from the tapes.) There will also be court records when a person is put under bond not to interfere with the victim or when a divorce petition involving the victim is on file. Such records can suggest who to interview, and may also disclose:

- Unpaid bills
- Status of loans (including any mortgages)
- Credit problems
- Bank accounts (any significant movement of funds)

- Employment (job changes and reasons for them)

- Recent business transactions (Were they legal? Who was involved?)

- Safety deposit boxes (Were they recently purchased, used, or closed?)

- IRS records (Was more money reported than accounted for, indicating illegal activity?)

- Insurance policies (Who were the beneficiaries? Was policy of recent origin? Is there a double indemnity clause?)

- Wills (Who were the heirs? Is the estate in a healthy financial condition? Who is the executor? When was the will made?)

- Other records, if obtainable, should include:
  Medical records
  Psychiatric records
  Military records

Follow-Up Action

Through police computer information networks, current knowledge of investigative activities within a department (or in other departments) can be exchanged. The extent of the sharing varies among departments within a state. Computerized systems often employ acronyms: LEADS stands for Law Enforcement Automated Data System; PIMS for Police Information Management System; and NCIC for the National Crime Information Center (operated by the Federal Bureau of Investigation).

The utility of crime information systems is enhanced when the reporting of major crimes or arrests is accurate, and when it is done promptly and routinely. Thus, in a homicide investigation, useful information may be obtained through daily perusal of the computer printouts. For example, computer reports describing bank robbery/homicide perpetrators may help investigators recognize a potential suspect based on the *modus operandi* of a robbery. Pooling the information developed might help to clear more than one crime.

Other useful law enforcement files for follow-up having been treated elsewhere in the text, only a few need be mentioned in passing: arrest records, "moniker" (nickname) and fingerprint files, firearms evidence files, and so on.

COVER-UP ATTEMPTS

Sometimes, a killer makes an effort to disguise a crime. Several means are employed to make the death appear accidental or explainable, to misdirect the efforts of investigators (diverting them to someone else or persons unknown), or to conceal the perpetrator's own involvement.

Accidental Means

A relatively common means used to cover up a homicide is to make the death appear accidental—the result, for example, of driving into a ditch or cleaning a gun. Not so common but worth noting are arson and poisoning.

Vehicles

Inspecting a motor vehicle that has caused a death can determine if it has been tampered with; for example, a brake line nut loosened to allow fluid to leak with each application of the brake, or an accelerator made to stick in the feed position. Another kind of cover-up is the use of an automobile to run over the victim's bicycle or motorcycle to make it appear that the damage was caused by striking a telephone pole, curb, or other fixed object. To detect the deception in such cases, the services of a forensic scientist (physicist, engineer, or pathologist) and a mechanic are needed. They will ask: Is the damage to the vehicle or trauma to the victim consistent with that known to be sustained when striking or being struck by such an object? If not resolved satisfactorily, the issues raised by these questions can be significant in any subsequent interrogation.

Firearms

In supposedly accidental gun deaths, the deceased's occupation, hobbies, and interest in weapons should be checked out. They can be consequential when interpreting the tests to be discussed here. The crime laboratory can sometimes determine muzzle-to-victim distance through examination of gunpowder residue on fabric, a garment, or the body itself; then, based on a comparison with test firings of the suspect weapon at known distances, the information can be used to reconstruct the crime. The suspect's account of what happened should be checked against the laboratory finding, and any discrepancy utilized later in interrogation.

The detection of significant levels of barium and antimony (primer residue) on the back and thumb web of the firing hand, when there is little or no residue on the nonfiring hand of the victim, is considered evidence that the deceased discharged a firearm. Primer residue is easily removed from the skin—intentionally, unintentionally, or by natural absorption. Since there is no barium and antimony in most .22 rimfire cartridges, a lack of these substances on the victim's firing hand does not warrant a conclusion that he or she did not discharge the weapon.

Fire

Setting fire to a mattress to make it appear that the victim was careless about smoking in bed has been used as an attempt to mask criminal homicide. This matter is given further treatment in the arson chapter; here, it will suffice to note that forensic pathology plays a key role in proving a victim was dead before the fire. The use of apparent homicide to cover up insurance fraud is another twist; insurance investigators are confronting a flood of cases in which intense fire consumes the victims and makes identification difficult or impossible. Often the insured is found to be a recent arrival—sometimes from a third-world country in which scant fingerprint, medical, or dental records exist. It is comparatively easy under these circumstances to substitute the body of a countryman or vagrant to serve as the victim of an "accidental" fire.

One case involved a newcomer in a community who, early on, let neighbors know that his hobby was tinkering with cars. Then, to set the stage for accidental death from a gasoline fire, he said he needed to borrow pliers to fix a leaking carburetor. The stratagem worked; the burned body was assumed to be that of the newcomer. However, when investigators juxtaposed the facts with the probabilities in the case—a recently issued life insurance policy carrying an exorbitant death benefit and the likelihood of a tinkerer having to borrow a simple tool—the facts became clues which, by induction, led investigators to uncover the sham.

Poisons

Some poisoners, when caught, will claim that they put the poison in a medicine capsule with the intention of committing suicide, only to find that the victim took it accidentally. Rather than report the death immediately (the normal response to an accidental death), they will hide the body and claim the person is missing; then, if it is discovered, allege they acted out of fear of not being believed. In such cases, they take shelter under a second cover-up to account for the first. (See Cover-Up Attempts.)

Explainable Means

Two common cover-ups are employed to make a crime explainable: (1) simulating a felony (motor vehicle homicide, burglary, robbery, or kidnapping) to account for death; and (2) claiming self-defense. Another ruse (developed further in the section on missing persons) is to provide inquisitive neighbors with a plausible reason for the absence of a spouse or live-in companion.

Simulated Felony

Most people have neither the knowledge nor the ability to stage the scene of a crime with a fair degree of verisimilitude. The experienced investigator is often able to recognize a poorly conceived and executed scenario. When a suspect is questioned, any nervousness (from having committed the crime) or anxiety (because an explanation might be implausible) hints at a cover-up. Reconstructing the event and checking the results against the suspect's account can pay dividends if a cover-up has been attempted.

One case example concerns the motor vehicle homicide of an elderly woman much beloved in her neighborhood. There was a severe thunderstorm on the night of the murder, the prolonged downpour washing away any broken headlight glass or other debris (such as damaged grillwork) that could link a vehicle to an accident scene. At about 11:00 the same night, just after a change of shift, a factory employee came to the police station to report that his car was stolen while he was at work. Remarking that he had heard of the death, he wondered aloud if the thief might have hit the woman after stealing his car. The detective, noting the remark as curious, asked why he thought so; the man offered no reason for the notion, only expressed his need for the car and the hope that he would soon have it back.

The abandoned vehicle was discovered later that night by patrol car officers. The damage to its windshield and two side windows seeming excessive for a break-in and theft, the detective's first step was to call the mobile crime laboratory. Evidence technicians quickly determined that the break-in had been simulated, the windows having been broken from the inside and the windshield as well as front side windows cracked. Their experience indicated that the simulation of theft had been carried too far: the extensive damage making visibility nil, it would have been difficult if not impossible to drive the car. The laboratory noted a broken headlight lens, but because of the storm no accident scene glass was available to link the vehicle to the scene of the homicide. Evidence technicians also noted that hood damage was consistent with striking a person.

The police decided not to notify the car's owner of its recovery and the crime laboratory's examination, but to leave it in place. Inductive reasoning had led the detective to conclude: (1) that the car had not been stolen, and (2) that it might have been involved in the homicide. When the man reported finding his car the next morning, the conclusion was given support, for stolen vehicles are rarely recovered by their owners.

As part of the case follow-up, the detective also learned that a ladder placed against the perimeter wall of the plant where the car owner worked (which was fenced in, with access allowed only to those with proper identification through the front gate) permitted workers to have a drink at the local tavern while the time clock punch card would indicate they were on the job. Utilizing the facts in the interrogation—simulated theft, atypical recovery of the car, and the freedom to leave the plant and return—the investigator required little time to elicit a confession from the factory worker.

Self-Defense

The following case illustrates the use of a claim of self-defense to cover up a killing. In his statement to the police, a husband claimed he had called his estranged wife on the morning of the shooting to ask that she come to pick up her mail and sign an insurance check. He said he expected her in the late afternoon after work; instead, she showed up at midday. He also claimed that, after she had signed the check, he reached for it and the pen only to look into a pointed gun and to implore her, "No, no, don't shoot, Jenny!" He stated that he then turned sideways to reach for a gun hidden under a cushion; his wife fired once and missed, the bullet lodging in the couch; and only then did he pull the trigger of his gun, killing her.

Ballistics tests determined that the bullet retrieved from the couch had been fired by his weapon. The autopsy disclosed that the victim had been shot twice: once in the side of her body, and once in the back of the head. The number of shots did not comport with his claim of self-defense; neither did the location of the head wound. These facts, in addition to the strained marital relation, led the jury to convict him of second-degree murder.

Diversionary Means

Several diversionary means can be used to deceive an investigator, including the following tactics.

First Person to Report the Crime

Some people believe that if they discover or are the first to report a crime they will not be suspected—that the mere fact they came forward will be construed as showing honesty and integrity. Such credence is misplaced; many a criminal has come to regret this naïve assumption. Therefore, recognizing a potential diversionary tactic for what it may be, experienced investigators customarily consider and check out the person who discovers the body or first reports the crime.

Contrived Alibi

Another diversionary tactic is to contrive an alibi. For example, a man murdered his wife and children at about 7:00 P.M.; at about 8:30 P.M., just after calling his brother-in-law ostensibly to discuss a matter of mutual interest, he left on a business trip. Arriving some 150 miles away, he put in a long-distance call to his home through the motel operator. Receiving no response, he surmised, presumably for the benefit of the motel operator, that his wife and children must be sound asleep. He asked to be awakened at 7:30 A.M. so he could place another call to his family. Again, his call was unanswered. Expressing concern to the operator, he asked that a call be placed to neighbors to look in on his family. It was shortly thereafter that he claimed to have first learned of the tragedy.

In her contacts with the guest, the motel operator received the impression of a person who was not being straightforward and whose nervousness and anxiety were excessive. A background check on the family, the forensic pathologist's estimate of time of death, and the operator's suspicions led to an interrogation and later to an indictment.

Ruse

This case example of a cover-up by misdirection involves an attempt to have it appear that two women had engaged in a "cutting match"; this term and the following scenario were suggested by the man in whose apartment the double homicide took place. A background check on him and the victims disclosed that he and one woman had lived together for years, while the other woman was his new lover. The bodies were side by side; a carving knife was found next to each victim. Blood spatter patterns and the distribution of two types of blood in the patterns led investigators to reconstruct an event quite different from that suggested by the male who rented the apartment—the first person to report the crime. Investigators later learned from his confession that somehow the women had met, discovered his "double dealing," and confronted him. The ensuing quarrel led to the murders and the attempted cover-up.

Other red herrings can be put out to mislead an investigation. One is to report a person missing in order to cover up a homicide. This is discussed in the section on missing persons. Another is to fake kidnapping—including leaving a ransom note, a jimmied door, or a broken window.

Partial Cover-ups

Some killers attempt a partial cover-up instead of taking the stronger measures already described. Realizing that the police are looking for them, or at least soon will be, they go into hiding or take flight. Some conceal or destroy incriminating evidence such as a weapon, stained clothing, letters, or records; some think an adequate expedient is to remove bloodstains. Partial cover-up measures are more likely when the homicide is not premeditated.

Flight, the assumption of a false name, or the concealment or destruction of evidence are interpreted in the investigative phase as consciousness of guilt. Having raised the possibility that a particular individual is the offender, the investigator should seek additional evidence to support the hypothesis. If the circumstances surrounding the flight, the destruction of evidence, and so on are carefully explained to a jury, they can have probative value at trial.

MISSING PERSONS

Missing person cases are treated in this chapter because of the fear commonly expressed by relatives that the vanished family member has been the victim of a homicide. From the police viewpoint there are two kinds of missing persons cases, each having different consequences with regard to law enforcement follow-up. One kind is voluntary: the missing person has created circumstances suggesting an abduction, suicide, or accidental death. The other is involuntary: the missing person was abducted and is being held captive or is in fact dead, the victim of a criminal homicide. The murderer accounts for the disappearance by telling inquisitive neighbors that the victim is caring for a sick relative or friend living some distance away. The murderer may even attempt to mislead the police in this way, should pressure from family or friends precipitate official inquiries. Almost immediately after the police leave, the killer takes off for parts unknown.

Apparently Involuntary Disappearances

Most families believe that the disappearance of a relative, especially a child, is not voluntary. Some adolescents in a rebellious stage run away from home; such disappearances, of course, are voluntary. Just as the reasons for a child, adolescent, or adult to suddenly vanish will vary, so do the appropriate investigative efforts.

Children

Conventional police wisdom on missing children cases dictates that some disappearances are not cause for official concern; thus, a "24-hour rule" often governs the response. However, the rule is not invoked when there are signs of foul play or when a very young child abruptly vanishes. These circumstances call for an immediate, intensive search. Although police quickly recognize the potential for harm to the very young, as social science research suggests, the basic assumption that runaways are not at risk is ill-founded. Moreover, abuse and neglect can be involved even when a child has been abducted by a parent.

A linkage is believed to exist between the violence of a criminal and a childhood marred by physical, psychological, or sexual abuse. It has led to the development of a comprehensive multistate network for the exchange of information on missing or abducted children. Known in Illinois as the I-Search Program (Illinois State Enforcement Agencies to Recover Children), it defines a missing child as one whose whereabouts is unknown. Several states having joined the program, a jurisdictional issue should no longer permit cases to slip through the cracks of the criminal justice system—to remain uninvestigated and unsolved.

LEADS (Law Enforcement Automated Data System), a further refinement, improves the means for locating missing children and preventing their abduction. LEADS is connected to the FBI's National Crime Information Center (NCIC); hence, descriptive physical data and dental records can be entered into NCIC, making it possible to determine if the missing child was found dead elsewhere. Should a child be found subsequently, either dead or alive, a comparison can be made with data in the National Unidentified Person's File.

Another effort is the National Center for Missing and Exploited Children (NCMEC), which was federally funded in 1985. Since 1984, NCMEC has assisted law enforcement with more than 174,000 child cases, resulting in the recovery of more than 160,000 children. Most cases of missing children are runaways, followed by abductions by family members, and a small percentage abducted by strangers. In the last quarter of 2011, the NCMEC's Call Center received an average of 535 calls per day. Since its inception in 1984, the Call Center has responded to more than 2.5 million calls.[29]

In October 2002, a significant report was released from the National Incidence Studies of Missing, Abducted, Runaway, and Thrownaway Children (NISMART) that chronicled the 797,500 cases of missing children in 1999. A total of 203,900 of these cases involved family abductions, and 98 percent of the children involved were located. There were 58,200 cases of missing children who were abducted by non-family members, with about 99 percent of those located. Sixty-one percent of missing child cases in 1999 were reported to law enforcement officials, and 48 percent can be attributed to runaway/thrown-away cases.[30]

Recognizing that "missing children investigation is a somewhat neglected and underdeveloped area," the National Center for Missing and Exploited Children has addressed this problem by publishing a manual[31] and classifying each case according to definitions provided by the Office of Juvenile Justice and Delinquency Prevention (OJJDP):

> *Family Abduction*: When a family member (1) takes a child in violation of a custody agreement or decree; or (2) in violation of a custody agreement or decree fails to return a child at the end of a legal or agreed-upon visit, with the child being away at least overnight.
>
> *Non-Family Abduction*: The coerced and unauthorized taking of a child into a building, a vehicle, or a distance of more than 20 feet; the detention of a child for a period of more than an hour; or the luring of a child for the purposes of committing another crime. Stereotypical kidnappings are non-family abductions in which (1) the child is gone overnight; (2) is killed; (3) is transported a distance of 50 miles or more; (4) is ransomed; or (5) in which the perpetrator evidences an intent to keep the child permanently. The perpetrator needs to be a stranger.
>
> *Runaways*: Children who have left home without permission and stayed away overnight, or children who are already away and refuse to return home—depending on their age and amount of time away.
>
> *Thrownaways*: Children who (1) have been directly told to leave the household; (2) have been away from home and a caretaker refused to allow the child back; (3) have run away but the caretaker has made no effort to recover the child or does not care whether the child returns; or (4) have been abandoned or deserted.
>
> *Lost, Injured or Otherwise Missing*: Children, missing for various periods of time (from a few minutes to overnight), depending on the child's age, disability, and whether the absence is due to an injury.[32]

Various checklists and other resources for law enforcement can be found on the NCMEC web site.[33]

A special problem with young children missing for several years is the change in their appearance as they mature. Medical illustrators have developed aging profiles that make it possible to project what a child or individual will look like in future years with some degree of accuracy. This process has been put to effective use in creating a color representation of a child's face as he or she grows older.

Commercial enterprises (dairy, telephone, direct media companies) have attempted to help develop information about missing children. By distributing computer-updated photographs of the maturing child coupled with a toll-free telephone number, they seek to involve the general public. Other official efforts include legislation to require county and school district clerks to notify police of requests for an abducted child's birth certificate or school records.

Another innovation is the AMBER (America's Missing: Broadcast Emergency Response) Alert program, which was created in 1996 as a legacy to nine-year-old Amber Hagerman, who was kidnapped and brutally murdered while riding her bicycle in Arlington, Texas. Residents contacted radio stations in the area and suggested they broadcast special alerts over the airwaves so that they could help prevent such incidents in the future. In response, the Dallas/Fort Worth Association of Radio Managers teamed up with local law enforcement agencies in northern Texas and developed this innovative early warning system to help find abducted children. CodeAmber.org went live on August 23, 2002. On April 30, 2003, President George W. Bush signed the Prosecutorial Remedies and Other Tools to End the Exploitation of Children Today (PROTECT) Act of 2003 into law. This Act codified the national coordination of state and local AMBER Alert programs, including the development of guidance for issuance and dissemination of AMBER Alerts and the appointment of a national AMBER Alert Coordinator. As of December 2008, 432 abducted children were recovered as a result of the AMBER Alert Program.[34]

In child homicide cases, death can either be caused by another child or an adult. If the latter, the slaying is often sex-related; this motivated serial murderer John Wayne Gacy to kill more than 30 prepubescent and adolescent males in the Chicago area. Leads may be provided by law enforcement records on recently released sex offenders; these files have information on *modus operandi*, location, and so on. Leads may also come from a canvass of the victim's playmates, individuals who were able to observe the child's movements and activities, or those who frequent his or her environment (school, playground, after-school haunts). Because the perpetrator may have to entice at least a few children before succeeding in tempting one, a partial description of the individual or vehicle, as well as the MO, may be learned. If a suspect is developed, surveillance is in order.

Death at the hands of another child is difficult for most people to comprehend. At one extreme, it happens almost accidentally as the outcome of child/adolescent exploration; at the other extreme, it may be the result of the pleasure derived from the excitement and thrill of killing. Within the psyche of a child killer in the latter cases there often are pain, rage, and a sense of ineffectiveness. Killing seems a way out; circumstances becoming unbearable, a child may strike out against the one perceived responsible, even if it is another child.

Family and playmates usually provide the key to solving homicides committed by children. They may not volunteer a name or a motive, but interviewing them separately about various aspects of family life might produce insights. Confronting one interviewee with the statements of another during requestioning is often a fruitful exercise. Given the relative unsophistication of the child-turned-killer, obtaining an admission or confession is fairly simple.

Adults

The investigator should be mindful that the unexplained disappearance of an adult is a frightening experience for family and friends; in general they fear foul play. It is important to note, however, that an adult may lawfully leave home, job, and normal haunts without notice, provided the family does not become a community burden.

There are people, usually middle-aged, who disappear to take up a new life, as often as not with a younger mate. To soften the impact and account for the departure, they contrive an explanation. Some will leave evidence of apparent suicide—for example, arranging for their car to be found parked on a bridge over a large river running to the ocean, with an article of their clothing on the railing. Some will simulate an accident. In one such case, a father took his small son to the ocean for a day at the beach. When other bathers noticed the child playing alone and unminded at the water's edge, they notified the police. Later that day, when husband and child had not returned, the wife reported them missing. It was assumed the husband had drowned; this was the contrived explanation.

An experienced investigator will sense that something is wrong. The situation has the earmarks of a simulated missing person's case, employing a relatively common stratagem, e.g., a disappearance near a large body of water (an ocean, gulf, or sea). This lends plausibility; the perpetrator is relying on the fact that not all bodies are recovered under such circumstances.

Another fairly common deception is making it appear that the missing person has been the victim of a felony. A robbery and abduction might be simulated; sometimes the "missing" person's empty wallet will be left in a conspicuous place. Again, the experienced detective will be distrustful. An examination of the personal and business affairs of the missing person may produce support for the suspicion that the disappearance was contrived.

Obviously, missing persons cases are not always criminal homicides, but persons reported missing may indeed be homicides. Generally in a true homicide case, the disappearance is sudden and mysterious and the victim often is a female. The age factor should be significant to the investigator. When a young woman in her twenties at a social gathering leaves to go to the lavatory or refreshment stand and vanishes, leaving no trace, the likelihood of a serial murderer like Ted Bundy must be considered. If the victim is older and lives alone—single or widowed—a "lonely hearts" killer is more likely. The investigation of these kinds of cases is treated later in this chapter.

Adolescents

Police usually treat the missing adolescent as a runaway who is sure to turn up sooner or later, but this is not always so. In the John Wayne Gacy case in Illinois, for instance, a missing teenage boy's family insisted he was not a runaway and that the circumstances surrounding the disappearance called for more than routine police action. Finally, because the case fell within the jurisdiction of a relatively small police department, it was investigated vigorously. Gacy became an immediate suspect when it was noted that different parents reporting disappearances under similar circumstances had previously provided his name to other police departments; this had not been shared among the several jurisdictions involved. After his arrest, however, remedial steps were taken; now, such information enters the law enforcement computer network. It should no longer be lost between the cracks of the criminal justice system.

Misleading Reports

In the event of a misleading report, there is generally a connection between the individual making the fictitious report and the "missing" person; hence, the need for a cover-up. The possibility of homicide must be considered if there is an unusual delay in making the report. More than a day would be unusual unless a satisfactory explanation is offered. By interviewing family and friends, conducting a neighborhood canvass, and making a thorough background check, the investigator will often discover a motive and strengthen the suspicion that the report is a diversionary effort.

MULTIPLE DEATHS

Serial murders are frequently the subject of television and newspaper reports; this fuels public awareness and curiosity. The term, however, has become a common refrain, with the result that the incidence of serial murder is greatly exaggerated. Media speculation also makes this crime seem a modern phenomenon, which it is not. The reader who recalls Jack the Ripper in England or Bluebeard (real name: Giles de Rais) in fifteenth-century France knows that multiple homicides by a single killer have been around for years. All the reporting, however, does have its "up" side; on-the-spot coverage enables law enforcement agencies to recognize similarities in homicides committed over time and in wide-ranging areas (see the discussion of ViCAP later in this chapter).

All multiple killings are not the work of serial murderers. A Charles Whitman who indiscriminately shoots from the University of Texas tower is not a serial murderer, but a mass murderer. Other useful distinctions can be made among those responsible for multiple deaths. As a consequence, the investigation and solution of a case will differ depending on the classification into which the particular case falls. For example, most mass murderers either commit suicide, are killed by the police while committing the crime, or are taken into custody following negotiations at the scene.

Before police agencies can coordinate their efforts, serial killings must first be recognized as the work of one individual. "Lonely hearts" cases and crime-spree killings differ from serial murders, though less careful analysis may put them into one category. The following section treats multiple homicides according to whether they were all part of one episode or were a series of events spread over a period of days, months, or even years. It discusses the differences and nuances involved, while keeping the focus on the investigative measures employed to solve each kind of case.

Several Mortalities—All Part of One Event

Double homicide is the most common kind of multiple death. Less frequent, and often involving more than a few victims, is family slaughter by one of its own members; or the murder of all persons in a household by an intruder bent on robbery, burglary, or rape. The least frequent kind of multiple death, random mass murder, usually accounts for the greatest number of fatalities per event.

Double Homicide

The most common kind of double homicide is criminal homicide followed by suicide. For example, chronic ill health or financial worry can cause a married pair to decide to end their lives together. The forensic pathologist can provide considerable help in establishing which death was a homicide and which a suicide. (There may be insurance, as well as legal, implications to these findings, e.g., determining which last will and testament governs.) A background check of family and friends will often provide a reason. Sometimes a note is left behind; not infrequently, there is a pact between the victims. It would be worthwhile to find out if any prerequisite steps were taken, like purchasing a weapon, medicine, or poison. Such evidence, when coupled with the medical examiner's findings, can obviate further investigative effort by indicating that the perpetrator took his or her own life.

Another somewhat common double homicide is the shooting of a retail store clerk and a customer during a robbery. Here, the disposition rests on solving the robbery. From time to time, an individual is murdered merely for happening to be with the target, being an unwitting witness who must be eliminated. In such cases, the luckless bystander is peripheral to the solution of the case.

If the killings are the work of mobsters, statistics suggest that even when the motive is ascertained, solution and conviction are unlikely. If not of gangland origin, motive provides an important lead requiring exploration and follow-up on people, physical evidence, and records.

Family Residence Murders

The scene of some multiple deaths is the victims' home. There are three kinds of perpetrators: a family member; an ex-family member—husband, or former lover or friend; or a stranger (who invades the residence to commit a felony). When perpetrated by a family member, the case is usually amenable to solution, but solution is considerably more difficult when an unknown factor such as a home invader is responsible. Home invasions in which multiple individuals are murdered are frequently related to illegal drugs or vendettas. Evidence of torture may also be related to efforts by the perpetrators to gain information.

Intrafamily Killings

In family killings, an adolescent son rather than a daughter or parent is more likely to be the guilty party. The fact that there are no signs of forced entry suggests the crime was committed by someone with access to the premises. Intruders, however, can gain entry simply by ringing the doorbell and then pointing a weapon at whomever responds. Hence, a lack of evidence of forced entry does not necessarily rule out an intruder.

Initial investigative steps include a background check of all family members and a neighborhood canvass. A psychological profile should also be considered. Disclosure of any odd behavior or significant change in lifestyle, such as unanticipated flight or other uncharacteristic act of a family member, obviously warrants investigation. All are signals suggesting involvement; they call for a check on the whereabouts claimed by the individual at the time the crime was committed.

It might be productive to inquire whether anyone would profit from the death of the victim(s), or whether there are hints or suspicion of interest in the occult or demonology (satanism). The weapon used offers another investigative opportunity: Who had a familiarity with it? Owned it? Had access to it? Knew where it was kept?

Home and Workplace Invasions

In most cases, homes are invaded for the purpose of carrying out a felony—robbery, rape, and so on. The workplace or public building is generally invaded for a different reason: often there is a perception of injustice or a need to vent anger. For instance, the first of several notable violent incidents involving workers took place in an Edmund, Oklahoma, post office in 1986, when a disgruntled discharged employee indiscriminately shot 14 former coworkers. Since then the number of workplace violence cases has increased substantially. Three cases of home invasion are discussed below.

Home Burglary-Turned-Homicide: This case began as a burglary, then became a double homicide when a sleeping teenager awakened. The struggle that ensued aroused her brother and resulted in the deaths of both young people. Nothing of value was stolen from the premises.

Consideration was given to the fact that after midnight the intruder had climbed through an open bedroom window overlooking the backyard. Investigators speculated that the perpetrator cased the neighborhood for ground-floor windows left ajar. To apprehend the suspect, an innovative fixed surveillance was felt to be justified.

The strategy and tactics of the surveillance employed were as follows: Four unmarked cars were assigned to the area and ordered to respond promptly to every prowler call after midnight. Instead of proceeding to the immediate vicinity, they were to park one block away—one each to the north, east, south, and west—and wait two hours while observing any movement on the street. Following a call months later, detectives watched an individual walking rapidly for several blocks and moving between houses located in the middle of the block as if looking for an opportunity to commit burglary.

When the walker was intercepted, it was learned he did not reside in the area; rather, he lived four miles away. He was dressed all in black and wore tennis shoes though the temperature was below freezing. The pawn tickets in his wallet inducing them to believe he was a burglar, investigators asked to search his home. He granted permission readily—probably to keep official focus off murder and on burglary, and to establish himself as cooperative. Should there ever be questions about the double homicide committed nine months earlier, his denials, he believed, would be accepted at face value.

A search of the suspect's flat produced numerous television sets and other small electrical appliances; this confirmed the suspicion that a burglar had been caught. The suspect's cooperation was unflagging; he tried to identify the source of each stolen item shown him. When a certain flashlight with its reflector cavity stuffed with orange-colored paper (recovered at the scene of the double homicide) was presented, he exclaimed "Where did you get that? I couldn't remember where I put it." The memory lapse and admission of ownership were unfortunate for him; the intruder had dropped the flashlight at the scene of the double homicide.

The suspect confessed and agreed to reenact the crime. At the scene, his spontaneous comments about the placement of furniture (which had since been moved) bore witness to his presence there on the night of the killings. Also useful in corroborating his confession was the physical evidence—hair, blood, and the twig of a cherry tree.

In some break-ins, robbery or rape is intended rather than burglary. Either crime may motivate artisans or delivery/repair personnel, who in the course of their work spot people who are well off or particularly vulnerable. At some later time, perhaps bolstered by alcohol, they make their move. Occasionally, traces of the intruder's occupation are left behind: by a fuel delivery man, an odor of oil; by an upholsterer, an upholstery cord (used to tie up the victim while searching for a safe); and so on. Usually, though, such evidence will not be present. Nevertheless, a fruitful avenue of inquiry may be opened up by checking on recent (within the last six months or so) repairs or deliveries for which a stranger had to come into the home.

The Clutter Case: This home invasion started as a robbery and ended as a quadruple homicide. A well-publicized case, it is recounted in Truman Capote's nonfiction novel *In Cold Blood*. Seemingly without motive, using a 12-gauge shotgun and a knife, the killers slaughtered the Clutters and their teenage son and daughter; the only family survivors were two elder daughters living away from home. There were no signs of struggle; the victims, gagged with adhesive tape and tied hand and foot with cord, were found in different locations through the house. Based on these facts, investigators speculated that at least two persons had invaded the farmhouse that night.

Robbery was discounted as a motive because two rings remained on the woman's fingers; however, a pair of binoculars and a gray Zenith portable radio were missing. No shotgun shell cases were found (it was learned after their apprehension that the intruders had been careful to remove them). The physical evidence unknowingly left behind, a potential link to the suspects, was a bloody "Cat's Paw" half-sole impression found on a cardboard box in the basement. Also, when the enlarged crime scene photographs were printed, investigators saw the imprint of another shoe not visible to the naked eye, one with a diamond-shaped pattern on its sole.

People who knew the family were questioned and records were checked. Meanwhile, other information was developed; for example, Mr. Clutter had taken out a large, double indemnity insurance policy just eight hours before his death—its beneficiaries, the surviving daughters.

The father had raised objections because of religious differences to his (now deceased) daughter's steady boyfriend. (An interrogation and subsequent lie detector test eliminated the youth as a suspect.) Other promising leads had to be ruled out. A farmer who tied rope with knots identical to those that bound the victims was in another state on the fatal night. A piece of information that seemed incriminating and important—a month before the crime, an alcoholic father and son who had had a confrontation with Mr. Clutter over a minor business deal were heard to say, "Every time I think of that bastard, my hands start to twitch. I just want to choke him!"—was also rendered useless by good alibis.

It was feasible, thought investigators, that they had a case of mistaken identity. Had the intended victim been another rancher, spared because a hired killer took a wrong turn on unfamiliar roads? Just as this line of inquiry proved fruitless, so too were all efforts to locate the stolen binoculars and radio in pawn shops throughout several states. (As it would later turn out, a need for cash forced the killers—who, meanwhile, had fled to Mexico City—to sell both items to a police officer there, thus placing the stolen property out of reach.)

Meanwhile the former cellmate of one of the killers remained in the penitentiary, the man who—having once worked for Mr. Clutter—had talked so freely about the thousands of dollars expended each week to operate the ranch. Knowing he bore some responsibility for the reports of the massacre being broadcast over the prison radio, this prisoner's need to tell somebody was overwhelming, yet prison culture made it quite clear that inmates did not inform on each other. However, he opened up to a fellow prisoner with a religious bent who persuaded him to talk. The warden arranged to have him "called out" of his cell.

Conscience or civic duty aside, the cynic might speculate on the roles played by the reward and the possibility of parole. Needless to say, the authorities were interested in what the informer knew. Having worked for Mr. Clutter, he had told his former cellmate (now the killer) about the $10,000 turned over at the ranch each week. This led to extensive questioning by the cellmate: Where was the ranch? How did one get there? How was the house laid out? Was there a safe and where was it kept? Ultimately a plan unfolded; there was talk of robbing and then killing Mr. Clutter to leave no witnesses. The informant told authorities of having heard about another prisoner who shared in the plan. When "sprung," both were to "score big."

Primed with this information, along with descriptions and photographs of the two suspects, investigators decided not to go public. This strategy, they believed, would facilitate locating the killers by allowing them the delusion that they were free. It proved a wise course. On their return from Mexico, the suspects threw caution to the wind, electing to "hang paper" (i.e., pass bad checks). Needing cash, they purchased merchandise for pawn. It worked until a television salesperson had the foresight to jot down the license number and make of their car on the back of a check. These facts found their way into investigators' hands long after the suspects had left the area for Las Vegas. On arrival, their intention was to pick up a general delivery parcel, pass more checks, and leave in 24 hours. By this time, however, a description of their car and license had been shared by police departments over many states. As it pulled away from the post office, the wanted vehicle was spotted by police officers in a patrol car. The parcel they had collected contained two pairs of boots: one sole bore the "Cat's Paw" trademark; the other, a diamond-shaped pattern.

The four detectives sent by the Kansas Bureau of Investigation to question the suspects deferred any mention of the Clutter murders. Interrogating them separately, they employed the strategy of "anxiety waiting" (see Chapter 10). When the evidence and the lies each had told were massed against them, confessions were elicited.

As the old maxim has it, "chance favors the prepared mind." In the Clutter case, it might well be argued that luck struck twice: first, when the killer's cellmate decided to become an informer; second, when they were apprehended after—and not before—picking up the boots. The first argument suggests that the case would have gone unsolved had the cellmate not come forward; however, to move the stalled investigation, a canvass of all those who had worked for Mr. Clutter was being considered. Since most of these people were scattered through Kansas (and elsewhere), this would have been a formidable task—no wonder British police call the canvass "intensive inquiry"—but carried through it would have led to the cellmate who probably would have told his story to investigators.

As to the second argument. It was, admittedly, sheer chance that the package containing the physical evidence linking the killers to the crime scene did not languish in the dead-letter office. This result would have come to pass had the suspects been picked up as they arrived at the post office to claim it—rather than afterward.

Mass Murders

There are two kinds of mass murder—those resulting from a crime spree spread over a period of time, and those in which all deaths occur in one (generally random) shooting event. The latter kind is by far the easier to handle.

Random Shootings—All Victims Die in One Event

Many of the perpetrators of these massacres are misfits unable to cope in society. Often "loners" with few emotional ties and some bottled-up anger, they seek relief by killing total strangers (in most instances), generally by gunfire. Largely a twentieth-century phenomenon, this kind of mass murderer may be trying to exert control over a world that seems out of control. (See Table 17.2.)

In general, cases of one random shooting event are easily solved: the offender is killed by the police in the act of mowing down his (or her) victims, commits suicide, or is taken into custody (after negotiations). There is also an abundance of supplementary information available—e.g., eyewitness accounts, physical evidence (firearms), records (weapon sales, mental health)—which allows evidence to be developed with little difficulty (see Figure 17.25).

Multiple Killings—Separate Events Spread Over Time

In addition to crime-spree mass murderers (see Table 17.3), three other types of killers are responsible for multiple deaths—serial murderers, "lonely hearts" killers, and poisoners. Motive is usually an important factor in the solution of murder, but it contributes little to the solution of mass murders and serial killings. Motive plays a more significant role in solving homicides committed by "lonely hearts" killers and poisoners.

Crime-Spree Mass Murders

Although crime-spree mass murder cases occur infrequently, they are generally solved:

1. when they are recognized as the product of a crime spree—often motivated by robbery and rape—that results in the deaths of victims who are generally unknown to the killer;

Table 17.2
Selected Cases of Random Killings—All Victims Die in One Event

DATE	NAME	NUMBER OF VICTIMS	LOCATION	OUTCOME
Sept. 6, 1949	UNRUH, Howard	13 killed, 4 wounded	On the street in Camden, NJ	Committed to a mental hospital.
July 15, 1966	SPECK, Richard F.	8 killed	Student nurse dormitory of Chicago community hospital	Sentenced to electric chair.
Aug. 1, 1966	WHITMAN, Charles J.	16 killed, 33 wounded	Fired rifle from observation tower on the campus of the University of Texas at Austin, TX	Slain by the police.
Sept. 25, 1982	BANKS, George	13 killed, 1 wounded	In two homes, Wilkes-Barre, PA	Convicted of murder.
Feb. 19, 1983	NG, Benjamin Kin MAK, Kwain Fai (Willie) NG, Wai Chiu (Tony)	13 killed	Wah Mee Social (Gambling) Club, Seattle, WA	B.K. Ng and K.F. Mak convicted for murder. W.C. Ng disappeared.
April 15, 1984	THOMAS, Christopher	10 killed	"Palm Sunday Massacre," Brooklyn, NY	Convicted for manslaughter.
July 18, 1984	HUBERTY, James Oliver	21 killed, 15 wounded	McDonald's Restaurant In San Ysidro, CA	Killed by the police (SWAT Team).
Aug. 20, 1986	SHERRILL, Patrick H.	15 killed, 6 wounded	U.S. Post Office at Edmund, OK	Suicide at end of rampage.
Jan. 17, 1989	PURDY, Patrick Edward	5 killed, 30 Injured	Schoolyard in Stockton, CA	Suicide at end of rampage.
March 13, 1996	HAMILTON, Thomas	17 killed, 14 wounded	Dunblane Primary School, Dunblane, Scotland	Suicide at end of rampage.
April 20, 1999	HARRIS, Eric KLEBOLD, Dylan	13 killed	Columbine High School, Littleton, CO	Suicide at end of rampage.
Dec. 26, 2000	McDERMOTT, Michael	7 killed	Edgewater Technology, Wakefield, MA	Convicted of seven counts of first-degree murder; seven consecutive life sentences without possibility of parole.
March 21, 2005	WEISE, Jeffrey	9 killed, 15 wounded	In home and at Red Lake High School, Red Lake, MN	Suicide at end of rampage.
April 16, 2007	CHO, Seung-Hui	32 killed, 25 wounded	Virginia Polytechnic Institute and State University (Virginia Tech), Blacksburg, VA	Suicide at end of rampage.
Nov. 5, 2009	HASAN, Nidal Malik	13 killed, 30 wounded	Fort Hood Military Base outside Killeen, TX	Charged with 13 counts premeditated murder and 32 counts of attempted murder.
July 20, 2012	HOLMES, James	12 killed, 58 wounded	Century 16 Cinema, Aurora, CO, during showing of *The Dark Knight Rises*	Charged with 24 counts first-degree murder and more than 100 other violent offenses.
Dec. 14, 2012	LANZA, Adam	26 killed (20 children)	Sandy Hook Elementary School in Newtown, CT	Suicide at end of rampage.

AP Photo/The Roanoke Times, Alan Kim

Figure 17.25
In this April 16, 2007, photo, injured occupants are carried out of Norris Hall at Virginia Tech. In the largest mass murder in modern U.S. history, Seung-Hui Cho shot and killed 32 people and wounded many others in two separate attacks, approximately two hours apart, before committing suicide.

2. when the public, becoming involved through media coverage, reports sightings of the wanted criminal. This may ultimately lead to apprehension—if police surveillance and other follow-up activities have not succeeded. Many reports will be erroneous; just the same, each must be followed up quickly—such killers depend on mobility to avoid capture. Should flight take them back to where they formerly lived (as is often the case), the likelihood of their being recognized and reported is increased.

Serial Murders

The serial murderer is usually a male who is prompted by a sexual or aggressive drive to exert power through killing. Because each serial murderer has the same motivation, the value of motive in solving such homicides is nullified. An added hindrance is the general lack of any previous connection between victim and killer.

An exception is found in the case of serial killer Judias Buenoano.[35] Over a 12-year period, she murdered her son, his father, her second husband, and a (common law) husband in order to collect their insurance. Subsequent attempts to kill her latest boyfriend—first by poisoning and then blowing up his car—were unsuccessful. The discovery that she had insured him for $500,000 without his knowledge led to an investigation and a reexamination of the above-mentioned deaths. Three separate trials for each victim resulted in three convictions—one carrying the death sentence.

In general, the serial killer is intelligent. When brains and a good appearance are combined with a beguiling (albeit superficial) charm, winning a victim's confidence is not difficult. What differentiates serial killers from other murderers, however, is that they know right from wrong; what they lack is a conscience impelling them to do right. These criminals genuinely relish their victim's terror; for them, murder is the ultimate thrill, and this distinguishes them from the "average" killer. Not

Table 17.3
Selected Cases of Crime-Spree Killings—Victims Die in Several Events Spread Over Time

DATE	NAME	ASSOCIATED CRIMES	NUMBER OF VICTIMS	LOCATION	OUTCOME
1958 (9 days)	STARKWEATHER, Charles FUGATE, Caril Ann		11 killed	Nebraska; Wyoming	Convicted of murder. Starkweather—executed in 1959; Fugate—life sentence, but released in 1976.
1971–72 (8 months)	McCRARY, Sherman McCRARY, Carolyn McCRARY, Danny TAYLOR, R. Carl TAYLOR, Ginger	Robbery Kidnapping	22 killed (at least 10 are connected by ballistics tests)	Texas; Wyoming; Florida; Kansas; Missouri; Oklahoma; Nevada; Utah; Colorado; Oregon; California	S. McCrary and R. Carl Taylor convicted of murder.
1982	COLEMAN, Alton BROWN, Debra		7 killed	Wisconsin; Illinois; Indiana; Ohio	Convicted of murder. Coleman executed in 2002 by lethal injection. Brown's Ohio death sentence commuted to life imprisonment; Indiana death sentence still stands.
1987	SIMMONS, Ronald G.	Incest Spouse abuse	14 family, 2 others killed, 4 wounded	Dover, Arkansas; Russellville, Arkansas	Convicted of murder. Executed in 1990 by lethal injection.
1997–1999	RESÉNDIZ, Ángel	Robbery Rape	10 killed	Florida; Illinois; Kentucky; Texas	Found guilty of capital murder and sentenced to death. Executed in 2006 by lethal injection.
2002 (20 days)	MUHAMMED, John Allen MALVO, Lee Boyd "The DC Snipers"		10 killed, 3 wounded	Maryland, Virginia, Washington, DC	Muhammed—Virginia: Convicted of murder and sentenced to death; Maryland: Convicted of 6 counts of murder. Sentenced to 6 consecutive life terms without parole. Malvo—Virginia: Convicted of murder. Maryland: Pleaded guilty to 6 counts of murder. Sentenced to 6 consecutive life sentences without parole. Muhammed executed in November 2009.
2010	SPEIGHT, Christopher Bryan		8 killed	Appomattox, VA, 3 locations	Surrendered to police.

driven by conventional motives, therefore, they select their victims at random: perhaps some physical or mental attribute galvanizes them into action, or they are attracted by the seductive prospect of a corpse with its promise of erotic pleasure. Necrophilia can be defined as:

1. A morbid liking for being with dead bodies.

2. A morbid desire to have sexual contact with a dead body, usually of men to perform a sexual act with a dead woman.[36]

Serial killers, therefore, present the investigator with an additional burden in both quality and degree: their mobility, the absence of any prior association with the victim, and their use of remote burial sites all represent some of the difficult obstacles to be overcome. Indeed, the difficulty in solving serial murders may account for the drop in the homicide clearance rate from about 82 percent before World War II to 61.2 percent in 2007.[37]

When a serial murderer continues to operate in the same locale, disposing of the bodies becomes a problem. Serial murderers Wayne Williams and John Wayne Gacy dumped some victims from a bridge into a river. When a river or stream casts up murder victims, it is possible with technical help to estimate from which bridge they were thrown so that it can be placed under fixed surveillance. Although expensive in terms of personnel, surveillance has the potential for solving such homicides. It can become a tedious assignment, requiring close supervision of the surveillants to assure alertness and compliance with its special demands.

In a study of more than 200 serial murder cases Dirk C. Gibson noted that "most serial murderers communicate about their murders during or after the murders." In his analysis of the communications of 10 serial killers he concludes that:

1. A significant number of serial killers engaged in communication with law enforcement, the media, and/or victims' families.

2. This communication was deliberate, intentional, and purposive.

3. In several cases the purpose of this communication seemed to be to deliberately leave clues.

4. There were several modes of communication. These included notes left at the crime scene, messages left on the bodies, wall writing, phone calls, letters, notes found on killers, e-mails, crime plans, crime records, and diaries.

5. Despite the diversity of serial killer communication, there were certain common content themes. These included:
    a. Taunts and insults aimed at law enforcement. These were typical serial murder messages. Serial killers enjoy ridiculing their pursuers, and they frequently did so. The Unabomber, the BTK Strangler, the Zodiac, and Jack the Ripper all took pleasure in harassing and taunting law enforcement.
    b. Reinjury to victim's loved ones. This was commonplace, as the killer called or wrote family members or friends to share details about the torture they inflicted on the victim prior to an equally painful and terrifying death. The Zodiac, the BTK Strangler, and the Unabomber especially seemed to enjoy causing emotional pain.
    c. Threats of future murders. These were quite common, as killers bragged and boasted about their planned murders. Jack the Ripper, the Zodiac, the DC Sniper[s], and the BTK Strangler all threatened to commit further murders.
    d. Clues to the killer's identity. Kaczynski [the Unabomber] was caught when someone, his brother, recognized his communication.

e.   Issuance of demands. Although not quite as common as the previous theses, serial killers did sometimes try to extort things from someone. The DC Sniper[s] tried to cash in on the sniper killings by requesting $10 million to stop. The Zodiac and the Unabomber successfully demanded free, unedited media placement of their communications.

f.   Explanations. Some killers, such as the Mad Butcher, have explained the cessation of their crimes. Others, including the Black Dahlia Avenger, have tried to justify their killings through explanations. John Robinson [serial killer convicted in 2008 of killing several women] tried to convince people that his victims were still alive.

6.   Diversity characterized the communication style of every serial killer studied. They made telephone calls, left notes or other writing at crime scenes, mailed letters, and/or kept diaries and records of their serial escapades.[38]

See Table 17.4 for information on some notorious serial murders.

The Violent Criminal Apprehension Program (ViCAP)

The Tenth Amendment to the United States Constitution retains for the states the enforcement of criminal laws. The fact that law enforcement is a local responsibility in the United States undoubtedly contributes to the ability of serial murderers to commit so many homicides and remain at large. Whenever the criminal moves to a new locale, the prospect of apprehension is reduced; the greater this distance, the smaller the likelihood that the work of a transient killer will be detected. Not to be overlooked is the lack of cooperation between different police departments. Although not common, "bad blood" does exist between departments—perhaps the result of a previous experience in which one agency felt its public image was damaged by the other.

This led to the development at the national level of the Violent Criminal Apprehension Program (ViCAP). Located at the Federal Bureau of Investigation Academy in Quantico, Virginia, it became operational in June 1985. To be effective, the program must receive reports on homicides within the jurisdictions of local and state police departments. As might be expected, the ViCAP Crime Report Form had to be modified based on practical experience with its use. The primary purpose of the form was to recognize and match cases having an apparently common perpetrator; initially, however, it asked for too many details.

Not every homicide is suitable for consideration by the ViCAP program. Criteria for submission and acceptance are:

Homicides: solved, unsolved, attempted (particularly if an abduction is involved); appear to be random, motiveless, or sexually oriented; suspected or known to be part of a series.

Missing Persons: if the circumstances indicate a strong possibility of foul play and the victim remains missing.

Unidentified Dead Bodies: if the manner of death is known or suspected to result from criminal homicide.

Submission criteria and suggestions regarding how a police agency recognizes when it may have a serial-killer problem are essentially the same. The decline in the homicide clearance rate (from 93 percent in 1961 to 64.8 percent in 2010) may in part be attributed to serial killers for two reasons: (1) "their habit of extensive interstate travel"; and (2) the fact that they are generally not known to their victims.[39]

Table 17.4
Some Notorious Serial Murders

DATE	NAME	LOCATION/NUMBER OF VICTIMS	KIND OF VICTIM	MANNER OF KILLING	TRADEMARK	OUTCOME
The 1940s Arrested March 1949.	FERNANDEZ, Raymond BECK, Martha "The Lonely Hearts Killers"	New York, Michigan, Minnesota and various other states. At least 5 killed. Many attempts; number of successes unknown.	Widows and spinsters who seem to be well-off.	Strangulation. Dismemberment.	Found likely victims through correspondence in reply to a column in a "lonely hearts" magazine.	Both convicted of murder. Executed by electrocution in 1951.
1962–1964	DE SALVO, Albert Henry "The Boston Strangler"	In and around Boston, MA. 13 killed.	Mostly older women, but some young; all single.	Strangulation. Stabbing. Beating.	Tied an item of clothing—a stocking or bra—around the neck of the victim.	Pleaded guilty to sexual assault charges. Sentenced to life imprisonment. Stabbed and killed in prison in 1973.
1963; 1970–1971	KEMPER, Edmund	California, (San Francisco Bay area and Santa Cruz). 8 killed.	Family (grandparents, mother). Young women hitchhikers.	Strangulation. Shooting. Knifing.	Dismemberment of victims' bodies. Necrophilia.	Convicted of first-degree murder. Sentenced to life imprisonment.
1970–1971	CORONA, Juan	Yuba City (Sutter County), California. 25 killed.	Migrant farm workers.	Stabbing. Slashing of face, neck, and scalp.	Chop wounds inflicted by machete (or thin metal cleaver). Victim buried in a shallow grave.	Convicted of murder (1973). On appeal ordered retried (January 1978). Convicted of murder again in 1982. (Trial lasted 7 months and cost an estimated $7 million.) Sentenced to 25 consecutive terms of life imprisonment.
1971–summer of 1973	HENLEY, Elmer Wayne CORLL, Dean BROOKS, David	Houston, TX, and vicinity. Yorktown, Lake Sam Rayburn, and High Island, TX. 27 killed.	Boys between age 13 and 18.	Strangulation. Shooting. Blows with a blunt weapon. Kicking.	Rape. Torture. Castration of some victims.	Henley—Convicted of murder (1974). Sentenced to 6 consecutive 99 year terms in prison. Corll—Shot and killed by Henley in 1973. Brooks—Convicted of murder (1975). Sentenced to life imprisonment.
1971–1973	BUENOANO, Judias "The Black Widow"	Florida, Colorado. 5 victims—4 killed; 1 survived.	Relatives or boyfriends.	Arsenic poisoning, drowning.	Insured victim for large sums.	Sentenced to death in electric chair. Electrocuted in Florida in 1998.

Table 17.4
(Continued)

DATE	NAME	LOCATION/NUMBER OF VICTIMS	KIND OF VICTIM	MANNER OF KILLING	TRADEMARK	OUTCOME
1974–1978	BUNDY, Theodore (Ted) "The Love Bite Killer"	Washington, Utah, Colorado, Florida. 36+ killed.	Young women with blond or light brown hair parted in the middle.	Crushing skull with a club. Strangulation with nylon stocking or pantyhose. Stabbing.	Ingratiated self through smooth talk—using the name Ted. Faked injury (arm in a sling or leg in cast) and asked for help. Entered victim's bedroom in early morning or after midnight. Young women disappear suddenly; body not found until much later (if at all) in isolated area. Butchered some.	Convicted of 3 counts of murder. Sentenced to death. Executed by electrocution in 1989.
1975–1978	GACY, John Wayne (Jack)	Illinois (Chicago and its suburbs). 33 killed.	Adolescent boys.	Choking. Strangulation by rope.	Tricked victims into being handcuffed. Buried bodies in crawl space beneath his home. Also dumped victims into Des Plaines River.	Convicted of 33 counts of murder. Executed by lethal injection in 1994.
1975–1983	LUCAS, Henry Lee "The Hands of Death"	A drifter, he confessed to killing 188–336 persons in 26 states—mostly Florida and Texas. Later repudiated many of his claims.	Men, women, and children, often picked up as hitchhikers.	Bludgeoning. Stomping. Shooting. Hanging.		Convicted of murder. Sentenced to death. Commuted to life imprisonment in 1998. Died in prison from natural causes in 2001.
1976–1977	BERKOWITZ, David "Son of Sam"	NYC boroughs: Queens, Bronx, and Brooklyn. 5 killed, 7 injured.	Mostly young women, but some young men.	.44 caliber revolver.	Victims generally shot late at night in supposedly safe neighborhoods, often while seated in a parked car.	Pleaded guilty to 7 counts of murder. Sentenced to 6 consecutive life sentences.

Dates	Name	Location / Victims	Method	Disposal	Sentence
1977–1979	BIANCHI, Kenneth BUONO, Angelo "The Hillside Stranglers"	Los Angeles, CA; Washington state. 12 killed.	Strangulation—manually or by ligature.	Females, often prostitutes, who were unknown to them; age range: 17 to 30.	Discarded bodies on a hillside (or a roadside) for all to view their handiwork.	Bianchi—Pleaded guilty to 7 counts of murder. Sentenced to life imprisonment without parole. Buono—Convicted of 9 counts of murder. Sentenced to 9 consecutive life sentences. Died in prison in 2002.
1978–1981	SUTCLIFFE, Peter "The Yorkshire Ripper"	England. 13 killed, 7 other attempts.	Used a hammer to bludgeon and a screwdriver to stab and mutilate victims.	Prostitutes.	Striation marks on the bodies of victims left by the screwdriver.	Found guilty of murder. Sentenced to life imprisonment, ordered to serve at least 30 years.
1979–1981	WILLIAMS, Wayne	Atlanta, GA. 28 killed.	Asphyxiation—usually by strangulation. Blows to the head.	Black males—teenagers and young adults.	Attracted victim by offer of a role in a movie or money for a homosexual act. Dumped victims into a river from the bridge above.	Convicted of 2 counts of murder. Sentenced to 2 consecutive life sentences.
1982–1984	EYLER, Larry	Indiana, Illinois, Kentucky, Wisconsin. 23 killed.	Stabbing with knife or ice pick. Sometimes severed head of victim or dismembered body, throwing parts into dumpster.	Young men and boys, ages 14 to 28. Many street people with connections to homosexual community. Many picked up as hitchhikers.	Discarded bodies in out-of-the-way areas. Victim was partially dressed with pants pulled down to ankles.	Sentenced to death for murder (1984). Died of AIDS in 1994 before execution.
1984–1987	HARVEY, Donald (dubbed "The Kiss of Death" by coworkers)	Ohio, Kentucky. 21 killed in Cincinnati; 9 others killed elsewhere.	Poisoning of a drink or dessert with cyanide, rat poison, or petroleum distillate.	The elderly and the critically ill.	Used his position as a nurse's aide or orderly in a hospital to administer the deadly concoction.	Cincinnati—Convicted on 28 counts of aggravated murder, 7 counts of attempted murder, 1 count of felony assault. Sentenced to 7 consecutive life sentences and 3 terms of 7–25 years imprisonment. Kentucky—Convicted of 9 counts of murder. Sentenced to 8 life terms plus 20 years imprisonment.

Table 17.4
(Continued)

DATE	NAME	LOCATION/NUMBER OF VICTIMS	KIND OF VICTIM	MANNER OF KILLING	TRADEMARK	OUTCOME
1978–1991	DAHMER, Jeffrey	Milwaukee, WI.	Young men and boys (mostly African-American or Hispanic)	Drugged victims, strangled or dismembered them, cannibalized some.	Lured victims to his apartment for a drink or to take pictures.	Convicted of 15 counts of murder. Sentenced to 15 consecutive life sentences. Bludgeoned to death by a fellow prisoner in 1994.
July 15, 1982–1998	RIDGWAY, Gary "The Green River Killer"	Northern Oregon and the Seattle-Tacoma areas of Washington state. 48 killed.	Young women, mostly prostitutes.	Strangulation.	Dumped bodies in river, in ravines in the mountains, along logging trails, and in urban sites such as the back of a Little League field. Concealed bodies to prevent their being found quickly. When and where contact has been made, the victim is unknown.	Pleaded guilty to 48 counts of first-degree murder. Sentenced to multiple life sentences without parole.
1989–1991	WUORNOS, Aileen	Florida (highways of northern and central Florida). 6 killed.	Middle-aged white males.	Handgun.	Found victims by hitchhiking as prostitute throughout Florida's highways. She would later state that she killed them out of self-defense after they raped (or attempted to rape) and beat her. She also robbed them.	Convicted of first-degree murder. Sentenced to death. Pleaded guilty to 4 additional murders. Sentenced to 4 death sentences. Executed by lethal injection in 2002.

1974–1991	RADER, Dennis "BTK Killer"	In and around Wichita, KS. 10 killed.	Mostly women, but one family and their two children.	Bind, Torture, Kill.	Bound and tortured his victims until they would eventually die; would become sexually aroused as he watched them struggle and die. Began contacting the media and police until his eventual capture.	Pleaded guilty to the murders and sentenced to 10 consecutive life sentences without parole.
1984–2000	ROBINSON, John	Kansas, Missouri. 6 killed.	Females interested in BDSM (Bondage, Domination, Sadomasochism).	Bludgeoning.	Met women online interested in BDSM, using the online pseudonym "Slavemaster." Killed the women after sex. Disposed of many of them in chemical barrels.	Kansas—Convicted of 3 counts of murder. Sentenced to 2 death sentences and life imprisonment. Missouri—Pleaded guilty to 3 murders. Sentenced to life without parole.
1995–1996	GILBERT, Kristen "Angel of Death"	Veteran Affairs Medical Center in Northhampton, MA. Four killed (suspected of 40+ murders).	White males middle aged to elderly.	Would inject patients at the hospital where she was a nurse with epinephrine (a heart stimulant).	Killed her victims because she enjoyed the thrill of creating medical emergencies.	Convicted for the murders and sentenced to 4 consecutive life sentences without the chance of parole.
1981–2006	SANCHEZ, Altemio "Bike Path Rapist"	Many crimes took place near bike paths around Buffalo, NY. Killed 3. Raped at least 14.	Women.	Strangulation.	Convicted on DNA evidence. Anthony Capozzi was wrongfully convicted of two of Sanchez's murders.	Sentenced to 75 years in prison with no possibility of parole.
1997–2000	RESENDIZ Angel	Known to have killed at least 12 people, usually along railroad lines.	Random victims. Men and women	Robbery, murder	Traveled illegally on railroads, committing crimes in a number of states.	Executed in 2007 by lethal injection.

When a case is solved by a local authority before submission to ViCAP and the offender is known or has been arrested, a Crime Report Form should still be forwarded; cases in ViCAP's files may then be compared against the facts supplied. The aim is to find a match between the known offender and unsolved cases. When separate homicides are linked, the detectives in the different jurisdictions are informed of each other's interest; to coordinate efforts, their respective contact information is exchanged.

It should be noted that ViCAP can only be as good as the data supplied. As a national law enforcement resource, it can increase the likelihood that violent criminals—especially serial murderers—are recognized early, identified, and ultimately apprehended.

The Role of Routine Police Work in Solving a Serial Murder

Several notorious serial murderers have been apprehended as a result of routine police work: preventive patrol (Bundy); responding to a domestic disturbance involving a bizarre fire-setting attempt, and following through on a ticket for illegal parking (Son of Sam); checking for required tax stamps or stolen plates on a vehicle (Yorkshire Ripper); and following up on the last known contact of a missing teenager who disappeared after a job interview (Gacy). (See Table 17.5.) Most of these cases were the subject of intensive investigation; before being solved, they required sizeable resources: forensics, personnel, and computers. The case of the Yorkshire Ripper is an example. Absorbing more than five years of official effort, it cost about $8 million. Police received three letters and a tape cassette signed "Jack the Ripper"; the letters promised more murders and taunted them for incompetence. Considerable effort was spent analyzing material subsequently found to be a hoax.

Cases receiving inordinate media coverage cause an equally inordinate quantity of misleading and vexatious information to pour in to the police. Most, if not all, tips are shams. Just the same, on the outside chance that a real tip may have been provided, everything must be investigated. This means that precious resources will be squandered. In New York, for instance, the Son-of-Sam investigation required 200 detectives to be assigned exclusively to the case, the expenditure of $5 million, and about a year of investigative effort before David Berkowitz was identified and apprehended. A letter Berkowitz wrote to reporter Jimmy Breslin (published in the *Sunday Daily News*) brought on a flood of telephone calls to the police "hotline." Local precinct switchboards also were jammed by callers, all naming their suspect. For several days, more than 300 separate investigations per day were needed to follow up on ultimately useless information.

The ViCAP program offers the prospect of reducing the need for such extensive investigations by:

- Recognizing serial murders earlier than heretofore possible
- Pooling the clues from each case and—once a series of unrelated homicides is perceived to be the work of a serial murderer—compiling and narrowing the list of possible suspects by induction
- Clearing up other unsolved murders when an arrest is made

"Lonely Hearts" Killings

The term "lonely hearts" killers describes murderers who prey on lonesome people. They examine the personal columns of newspapers, magazines, and Internet chat rooms with great care, select prospective victims, and then correspond with them (or with those who reply to their own notices in personal columns). Starting off as pen pals, they follow up with telephone calls, and eventually

Table 17.5
Circumstances Leading to the Solution of Some Serial Murder Cases

CASE	ROUTINE POLICE WORK	BEHAVIOR OF SUSPECT
BERKOWITZ, David "Son of Sam"	Following up on tickets issued for illegal parking in Brooklyn, Berkowitz's car was the only one not belonging in the neighborhood, i.e., It was registered in another county. Following up some days later in the Bronx, an army duffel bag with a machine gun protruding from it is observed in his car parked on the street outside his apartment.	Berkowitz is suspected by neighbors of shooting two dogs for no apparent reason. A fire is set in another neighbor's doorway and Berkowitz is suspected.
BUNDY, Ted	Checking on restaurant after closing time, patrol officer observes unknown vehicle prowling the area. Officer makes a U-turn and follows suspicious car, which then attempts to speed away. When stopped, driver produces a stolen credit card for identification.	Assaults officer and attempts to escape.
GACY, John Wayne	Adolescent momentarily left his pharmacy job near closing time to talk about summer work with a contractor outside in the parking lot. Not returning, his disappearance is reported to the police. Gacy is observed in the pharmacy that day at 6 P.M. and 8 P.M. Gacy is verified to be a contractor	Gacy, realizing he is under surveillance, slows down, speeds up, and after pulling into a restaurant parking lot, invites investigators to have a cup of coffee with him.
LUCAS, Henry Lee	Arrested on a weapons charge. (Inspection of a driver's license and a vehicle—with owner's consent—of what is in plain view can result in the discovery of an item or material that suggests further investigation may be necessary. Obtaining the voluntary consent of the individual to accompany the officer to the station house legitimizes questioning, even though insufficient evidence for probable cause exists.)	When stopped by police when driving, Lucas walks back to the officer's car, regardless of whether he had anything to hide at the moment, in order to keep police away from his car.
SUTCLIFFE, Peter "The Yorkshire Ripper"	Officer observes known prostitute entering automobile. Discovers in license check that plates are not registered to vehicle. Driver is brought to police station for further investigation. Suspect's need to use the toilet shortly after relieving himself is noted and viewed as suspicious. Toilet is searched and possible murder weapon found. Follow-up search in the vicinity of site of apprehension leads to discovery of additional incriminating evidence.	At site of arrest, and shortly thereafter at station house, suspect asks for permission to relieve himself.
WILLIAMS, Wayne B.	Several missing children's bodies found floating in stream. Suspect's auto license noted through surveillance of a bridge from which victims were thought to have been thrown.	Suspect is observed with each of several victims shortly before they disappear.

arrange a meeting. By means of charm, a reassuring voice and manner—whatever it takes—they finally are able to learn whether the prospective victim has bank accounts or other assets. If they deem the potential reward worth the effort, attention is then lavished on the victim-to-be, with marriage or promise of marriage the ultimate bait. At this stage, they may take out an insurance policy on the life of the intended victim. "Lonely hearts" killers are most often males who work alone, but sometimes they work in pairs, perhaps with a female posing as a sister.

A famous case is that of Raymond Fernandez and Martha Beck; together they killed female spinsters, often burying the bodies in the victims' own basements. Indeed, disposing of and accounting for the disappearance of the slain individual are two major problems facing the "lonely hearts" killer. Explaining to friends and neighbors that he and his new wife (the victim) intend to visit distant relatives or perhaps resettle enables the killer to take off. He can transport the body in a large trunk without arousing suspicion, and bury it before departing. Although friends and neighbors might regard this as strange behavior, not until some time has passed—when no letters, calls, or holiday cards have been received—do they suspect foul play and report it to police.

By this time, the killer's trail is faint and difficult to track. Sometimes, though, a victim refuses to turn over control of her assets, and her signature must be forged after she is murdered. Such documents can link the killer to the crimes of forgery and homicide. There is little doubt that some "lonely hearts" killers have gotten away with murder. Yet others have been tripped up by those who became skeptical and reported their suspicions to police. In such circumstances, the VICAP program will allow more such offenders to be recognized and apprehended.

Poisonings

This section deals with mass poisoners and with those who, like most murderers, intend to kill just once. Homicide by poisoning is relatively rare today. Those who employ it to seize their victims' assets are somewhat akin to "lonely hearts" killers. They often befriend their prey and become live-in companions; in this way, they ensure a supply of victims. Another method is to run a boarding house for the elderly living on private pensions or Social Security. Should boarders need help with everyday problems—shopping, errands, picking up parcels, and so on—they are easily persuaded to have their checks cashed as well. This practice becomes routine, and it need not cease after the poison victim dies. When finally disposed of, the victim is replaced by a new paying guest. Poisoners must use care when selecting their victims—those without relatives or friends can disappear with no questions asked.

In the past, multiple homicide by poisoning was not uncommon.[40] In 54 A.D., Nero became emperor of the Roman Empire after his mother (Agrippina the Younger) poisoned, among others, her husband and uncle—the emperor Claudius. By the Middle Ages, poisoning had flowered into an art form. Those who practiced the poisoner's art were Catherine de Medici, and Cesare and Lucrezia Borgia (though modern writers say of Cesare's half-sister that "she was a lady much maligned").[41] In 1709 Mme. Toffana furnished the white arsenic (to make "Acqua Toffana"); it killed more than 600 people. Food tasters became a royal prerequisite, and during the reign of Henry VII, poisoners were boiled to death in England. In those days, conviction rested solely on circumstantial evidence, such as the onset of symptoms or any malicious intent attributed to the suspect. Not until 1781 did Joseph J. Plenck observe what is considered obvious today, i.e., the only certain sign of poisoning is the identification of the poison itself in the organs of the body; however, "… it remained for the rise of scientific methods in modern times to make the practice more risky for poisoners."[42] To put this in perspective, it should be noted that in 1831 James Marsh developed the definitive test for arsenic—historically, one of the most widely used poisons. This is an example of the early interaction of science with criminal investigation in furnishing credible evidence that can be offered as proof in court.

A poison is a substance that, when taken in small doses, causes an individual to sicken or die. It generally works by affecting a major organ—liver, kidney, brain, lungs—or the autonomic nervous system. Symptoms can be mistaken for those of a natural illness: acute bacterial food poisoning (so-called ptomaine poisoning) and acute arsenical poisoning resemble each other. Hence, if a toxicological examination is not conducted when a sudden onset of symptoms and death follow the ingestion of food or drink, a criminal homicide may not be recognized and a poisoner could go free. (See Table 17.6 for effects of some poisons after and before death.)

If several people had the same food or drink, and only one became ill but did not die, a bungled poisoning is a possibility. Owing to inexperience, many poisoners believe that too much poison will be detected. They hold back, causing sickness but not death, then must increase the doses until the desired result is achieved. Some poisons act cumulatively: each dose precipitates acute symptoms until

Table 17.6
Effects of Some Poisons After and Before Death

MANIFESTATION AFTER DEATH	POSSIBLE POISON
Pupil of eye—contracted	Opiates
Pupil of eye—dilated	Atropine (Belladonna), scopolamine
Skin is cherry red in color	Carbon monoxide, cyanide
Skin of face and neck is quite dark (compared to normal complexion of the victim)	Aniline, hypnotics, nitrobenzene, strychnine
Burns—mouth, lips, nose	Strong acid—nitric, hydrochloric, sulphuric; also oxalic and carbolic acids Strong bases—sodium or potassium hydroxide, i.e., lye or caustic potash
Odor of peach pits	Cyanide
Odor of garlic	Oxalic acid, phosphorous
Odor of disinfectant	Carbolic acid (or other phenol)
MANIFESTATION BEFORE DEATH	**POSSIBLE POISON**
Diarrhea (severe and unexplained)	Metallic compounds of arsenic, mercury, copper, antimony, lead, sodium fluoride
Vomiting and/or abdominal pain	Metallic compounds, food poisoning, sodium fluoride
Convulsion	Strychnine, nicotine, sodium fluoride
Sudden, quick death after ingestion	Cyanide
Abdominal pain	Metallic compounds, food poisoning

a lethal level is reached. Thus, if a person were to have repeated symptoms (a week, a month, or even several months later) with no prior record of such symptoms and is otherwise in good health, the death should be regarded as suspicious. At the very least, a toxicological analysis of the body organs and fluids should be performed.

The symptoms manifested before death are of utmost importance, as are the appearance and odor of the body after death. All can offer clues to the kind of poison that might have been used.

Investigating a Suspected Poisoning

Not every suspected poisoning case is necessarily a criminal homicide. There is no felony involved in at least three situations in which a poison causes a death:

1.   accidentally taking an overdose (particularly a narcotic);

2.   accidentally taking the wrong medicine;

3.   deliberately taking poison.

When poisoning is suspected, it is crucial that the source and kind of substance be determined. The following investigative steps should be taken:

1.   Interview the family, the physician (if any), and any others who have had recent contact with the deceased.

2.   Examine the premises where the death occurred and collect all potential evidence relating to the possible substance used. Who brought it in the house? Why?

3.   Transmit the evidence to the laboratory for examination by a toxicologist.

4.   Check records of the pharmacy that filled the prescription and other possible commercial sources of the poison.

Among the facts to be ascertained by initial interviews are:

1.   The date and time of death. When was the victim found and by whom?

2.   The time the victim's last meal was eaten. What was eaten?

3.   The date and time the deceased was last seen alive. Was the deceased in his or her usual state of health? Was he or she behaving normally? If not, when did the change in appearance or conduct occur?

4.   A complete description of the victim's physical symptoms and behavior prior to death. Was any odor detected? (This information can help in distinguishing between acute and chronic poisoning situations.)

Significance of Acute and Chronic Symptoms: The symptoms of acute versus chronic poisoning are:

Acute	Chronic
The person is in apparent good health, when the symptoms (including death) appear shortly after drinking, eating, or taking medicine; or several persons are afflicted at the same time after eating or drinking the same food or beverage.	The individual appears to suffer from a persistent malaise or chronic ill health, and the cause is difficult to diagnose or otherwise understand. When the person leaves his or her usual food/beverage setting (most often by leaving home for a vacation or other trip), the condition improves but recurs upon returning home.

Mass poisoners normally use substances that produce acute symptoms; for example, several victims (unconnected to each other) living scattered throughout an area will exhibit similar symptoms, then sicken and die in a short time. Running a thorough background check will usually reveal what, if anything, they shared in common. For instance, in the Chicago area in 1982, it was found that just before a quick death from cyanide poisoning, each victim had taken newly purchased over-the-counter medicine (Tylenol).

Mass poisoners are usually motivated by revenge, hate, discontent, and even extortion (by threatening to poison a company's product). They often see themselves as having been unfairly treated—in life generally or in the business world particularly. If the motive can be learned, the investigation has taken a significant turn. Sometimes the poisoner will volunteer crucial information through a letter to the media or a note planted at the scene, or a public appeal will induce the poisoner to share the reasons for the discontent. The appeal may be coupled with an offer (perhaps from a well-known newspaper columnist) to address the concerns of the offender. Written communications obtained in this way are valuable physical evidence; handwriting and typewriting specimens as well as finger or palm prints (if any) may tie a suspect to the crime.

Chronic symptoms of poisoning are more likely when the criminal is inexperienced and unfamiliar with the amount of poison required. Insufficient dosages are often administered since the victim must fail to detect the poison when eating or drinking.

A variation in type is the poisoner with the so-called "Florence Nightingale complex." Here, each of several individuals is administered poison on separate occasions. As each victim becomes sick, the poisoner, having previously let on to neighbors that he or she is a nurse, is called in to restore the person to health; and does so. It is only when a death occurs (rather than a restoration of health through the ministrations of the nurse) that the police are likely to become involved. "Nurse" poisoners who "help" their victims are like arsonists who see themselves as heroic when they "save" people from fires they themselves set. The investigator who learns from friends and neighbors of the deceased about similar sudden illnesses and restorations to health—by a neighbor/nurse—should be alert to the possibility of poisoning and to the fact that this individual needs to be checked out.

Physical Evidence at the Scene of Death: In cases of accidental suicide—an overdose or prescription medicine taken by mistake—the suspected substance is generally located with little difficulty (often on a night table or chair). The substance, together with any illicit drugs, hypodermic syringes, and needles that may be found, must be marked, preserved, and transmitted to the proper laboratory for analysis. The hypodermic needle requires special handling: the tip must be inserted carefully and securely into a stopper.

Medicine Cabinet: The entire contents of the medicine cabinet should be collected for examination and analysis.

Food: In addition to any uneaten food present at the scene, condiments, sugar, flour, baking powder, and so on, should be collected for analysis later; also any food in garbage containers.

Beverages: Milk, fruit juices, beer, wine, liquor, or any unsealed container of liquid that might have been consumed should be collected and refrigerated for possible analysis. An alcoholic beverage is often employed to administer a poison; it helps to mask the taste of the toxic substance. Any cup, glass, or other vessel the victim might have used should be seized.

Other Sources: Possible sources of poison within a household are rat and roach powders, ant traps, and garden insecticides. They should be looked for and collected.

Body Excretions: Diarrhea and vomiting are symptoms of poisoning. Accordingly, vomit and fecal matter must be collected separately in containers, and then sealed to preserve any volatile poison present.

Transmission of Evidence: For identification and security against tampering, it is important that physical evidence be handled to meet the requirements of both the lawyer and the toxicologist. Its transmission to the laboratory is part of the chain of custody. The forensic pathologist should submit the appropriate organs obtained by autopsy to the toxicological laboratory for analysis.

Checking Records: If a prescription medicine appears to be the source of the poison—either by overdose or mistaken ingestion—the records of the dispensing pharmacy should be checked and the physician who wrote the prescription interviewed. When the medicine has been identified by the toxicologist, the results must be compared with what was ordered and dispensed. Any serious disparity—for example, poison substituted for medicine—must be investigated.

Records are sometimes kept on toxic compounds, supplying the date, to whom furnished, and the amount obtained. A follow-up inquiry can determine if the individual who bought the material (or any suspect) performed work requiring the use of the toxic material.

When a possible known source of the poison is established, a sample should be obtained to determine the trace (chemical) elements present as impurities and contaminants. A similar analysis should be made of the suspected poison discovered at the scene or in the home of the suspected poisoner. Depending upon the qualitative and quantitative results, especially if both specimens have the same combinations of unusual trace elements, it may be possible to identify the known source of the fatal poison. If access to the source is limited, the investigator's task is much simpler.

DYING DECLARATIONS

A *dying declaration*[43] (also known as an *antemortem statement*) is hearsay evidence. Though generally not admissible in court, it is allowed into evidence in homicide cases in certain jurisdictions. When allowed (as an exception to the rules of evidence), the dying declaration has proved persuasive even though it is neither supported by the oath of the victim nor subjected to cross-examination. The underlying reasoning behind its credibility is the belief that human beings about to "meet their Maker" are strongly motivated to tell the truth. When close to death, supposedly, people do not lie.

An investigator's testimony on a dying declaration is subject to cross-examination. If the following recommendations are adhered to, few if any problems should be encountered when introducing the dying declaration on the witness stand.

The value of a dying declaration is illustrated by the successful prosecution of a homicide on New York's waterfront, which was accomplished largely because a dying declaration was used to convict three defendants of the murder of a dock boss. Because homicides on the waterfront are not often solved, and successful prosecution is even more infrequent, this case was well-known as the first in many years to lead to a conviction.

To be admissible as evidence, a dying declaration must meet several conditions:

1. The victim must believe he or she is about to die.
2. The victim must have no hope of recovery.
3. The victim's declaration must:
   Identify the person responsible for his or her condition.
   State the circumstances and manner by which the mortal injuries were inflicted.

4. The victim must be rational and competent.

5. The victim must die from the injuries received.

The last two conditions are met through the testimony of the investigator and forensic pathologist. The first three are met by asking the victim to reply to the following questions:

- What is your name?

- Where do you live?

- Do you now believe that you are about to die?

- Do you have any hope of recovery?

- Are you willing to make a true statement as to how and why you were injured?

The dying declaration may be oral, but it should be recorded on a tape or digital recorder, if possible. It also may be written, either by the victim or the investigator, and signed by the victim. It is useful, though not required, to have the declaration witnessed by a member of the public. A video is ideal, but unworkable in many cases; very often a dying declaration is made in an ambulance bearing the victim to a hospital.

Concluding Commentary

This chapter illustrates how the three sources of information—people, physical evidence, and records—are employed to solve homicides. It includes crimes with no apparent motive in which the killer seems to have escaped undetected (cases that confront the detective with a true mystery), and other kinds of homicides more easily handled by the trained, perceptive investigator. As the most serious of all crimes, it is fortunate that there are significantly fewer homicides than other major offenses. Several reasons account for the high rate of solution:

1. The resources that departments are willing to invest are greater than those allocated for other crimes. Large departments can assign personnel from other units to check out all leads as they develop in the course of an investigation. Smaller departments arrange to pool investigative talent, drawing from nearby communities.

2. For most homicides a particularized motive exists that prompted its commission. When ascertained, a list of suspects can be developed and honed by considering who among them had the opportunity, the means, the ability, and the necessary backbone to commit the crime. Investigative efforts can then concentrate on proving or disproving a suspect's involvement.

3. Physical evidence inadvertently left at the crime scene (e.g., a fingerprint, fired bullet, etc.) or taken from it (blood of the victim, fibers, etc.) may be available to link a suspect to the scene or the victim.

4. More than in most crimes, considerable physical evidence may be at hand to permit a reconstruction. The details revealed thereby can be checked against those provided by a suspect and possibly used in an interrogation aimed at obtaining a confession.

5. Investigative effort seeking to identify the perpetrator also may produce the evidence needed to prove that the defendant was the killer. The forensic pathologist provides the evidence—that the death was not natural or accidental, but criminal.

NOTES

[1] *Historical Statistics of the United States, Colonial Times to 1970, Bicentennial Ed.*, Part I (Washington, DC: U.S. Bureau of the Census, 1975), 414.

[2] U.S. Department of Justice, Federal Bureau of Investigation, *Uniform Crime Reports* 1975–2005 (Washington, DC: U.S. Government Printing Office).

[3] U.S. Department of Justice, Federal Bureau of Investigation, *Crime in the United States 2008*. See http://www.fbi.gov/ucr/cius2008/offenses/violent_crime/murder_homicide.html

[4] http://www.fbi.gov/about-us/cjis/ucr/crime-in-the-u.s/2010/crime-in-the-u.s.-2010/tables/10tbl01.xls

[5] http://www.statcan.gc.ca/pub/85-002-x/2011001/article/11561-eng.htm

[6] http://www.fbi.gov/about-us/cjis/ucr/crime-in-the-u.s/2010/crime-in-the-u.s.-2010/offenses-known-to-law-enforcement/expanded/expandhomicidemain

[7] Steven C. Clark, *National Guidelines for Death Investigation* (Washington, DC: U.S. Department of Justice, Office of Justice Programs, 1997).

[8] Ibid., 1.

[9] Ibid., xx.

[10] Loc. cit.

[11] Ibid., xxii.

[12] Vernon J. Geberth, *Practical Homicide Investigation: Tactics, Procedures, and Forensic Techniques*, 3rd ed. (Boca Raton, FL: CRC Press, 1996), 379–388.

[13] Ibid.

[14] Ibid.

[15] Dominic J. Di Maio and Vincent J.M. Di Maio, *Forensic Pathology* (New York: Elsevier, 1989), 21–25.

[16] M. Lee Goff, "Comparison of Insect Species Associated with Decomposing Remains Recovered Inside Dwellings and Outdoors on the Island of Oahu, Hawaii," *Journal of Forensic Sciences*, 36:3, (1991), 748–753.

[17] Y.Z. Erzinclioglu. "Forensic Entomology and Criminal Investigations," *Police Journal*, 41:1, 5–8 (Jan. 1991), 7.

[18] Ibid., 8.

[19] Ibid., 6–8.

[20] Vincent J. Di Maio, & Suzanna E. Dana, *Handbook of Forensic Pathology* (Austin, TX: Landes Bioscience, 1998), 21–22.

[21] Ibid.

[22] Ibid.

[23] Ibid.

[24] Di Maio and Di Maio. op. cit., 87–107, 171–206.

[25] Vincent J.M. Di Maio, *Gunshot Wounds: Practical Aspects of Firearms, Ballistics, and Forensic Techniques* (New York: Elsevier, 1985), 67–77, 103–121.

26   Di Maio, & Dana. op. cit., 169–171.

27   Ibid., 187–191.

28   Ibid., 161–173.

29   See the National Center for Missing and Exploited Children web site at http://www.missingkids.com/missingkids/servlet/PageServlet?LanguageCountry=en_US&PageId=2810

30   National Incidence Studies of Missing, Abducted, Runaway, and Thrownaway Children, NISMART-2 (Washington, DC: Office of Juvenile Justice and Delinquency Prevention, 2002).

31   Stephen E. Steidel, ed., *Missing and Abducted Children: A Law Enforcement Guide to Case Investigation and Program Management*, 2nd ed. (Alexandria, VA: National Center for Missing and Exploited Children, 2000).

32   David Finkelhor, Gerald Hotaling, and Andrea Sedlak, *Missing, Abducted, Runaway, and Thrownaway Children in America, Executive Summary* (Washington, DC: U.S. Department of Justice, Office of Juvenile Justice and Delinquency Prevention, 1990).

33   See the National Center for Missing and Exploited Children web site at http://www.missingkids.com

34   See the Amber Alert web site at http://www.amberalert.gov/

35   Chris Anderson and Sharon McGeheen, *Bodies of Evidence: The True Story of Judias B. Buenoano: Florida's Serial Murderess* (New York: Lyle Stuart, 1991).

36   *Mosby's Medical, Nursing, and Allied Health Dictionary*, 5th ed. (St. Louis, MO: Mosby, 1998).

37   http://www.fbi.gov/about-us/cjis/ucr/crime-in-the-u.s/2010/crime-in-the-u.s.-2010/clearances

38   Dirk C. Gibson. *Clues from Killers: Serial Murder and Crime Scene Messages* (New York: Barnes and Noble, 2007), 3, 210–211.

39   Terrence J. Green and Jane E. Whitmore. "ViCAP's Role in Multiagency Serial Murder Investigations," *The Police Chief*, 60:6, 38–45 (June 1993), 42.

40   Louis J. Casarett and John Doull, *Toxicology: The Basic Science of Poisons* (New York: Macmillan, 1975), 4–9.

41   Baron Corvo [Frederick Rolfe]. *A History of the Borgias* (Westport, CT: Greenwood Press, 1975), 204.

42   Casarett and Doull, op. cit., 6.

43   Ronald L. Carlson, *Criminal Justice Procedure*, 7th ed. (Newark, NJ: LexisNexis Matthew Bender, 2005), 179–180.

DISCUSSION QUESTIONS

1.   According to the text, why does murder represent a major challenge for the investigator?

2.   What is the definition of homicide?

3.   What is the difference between justifiable and excusable homicide?

4.   What are the most common motives for committing a murder?

5.   What is the purpose of reconstructing the crime?

6.   In order to establish that a homicide has been committed, what must be proven?

7. What is *rigor mortis*, or *postmortem lividity*?

8. What are some of the sources of associative evidence that may appear at a crime scene?

9. Before a thorough crime scene search is begun, what is the first action that should be taken at a crime scene?

10. What is the purpose of an autopsy?

11. What is entomology?

12. What is the purpose of examining the stomach and small intestine content of the deceased?

13. What are some of the types of physical injuries that a victim might sustain?

14. What are the three kinds of entrance wounds in a shooting?

15. What is asphyxiation?

16. What is the difference between mass murder and serial murder?

17. What is the ViCAP Program?

18. What is a dying declaration?

19. What are the three primary sources of information employed to solve homicides?

SUPPLEMENTAL READINGS

Benecke, M. (2005). *Murderous methods: Using forensic science to solve lethal cases.* New York: Columbia University Press.

Bevel, T., & Gardner, R. M. (2008). *Bloodstain pattern analysis: With an introduction to crime scene reconstruction* (3rd ed.). Boca Raton, FL: CRC Press.

Di Maio, V. J. M., & Di Maio, J. D. (2001). *Forensic pathology* (2nd ed.). Boca Raton, FL: CRC Press.

Dupras, T. L., & Schultz, J. J. (2011). *Forensic recovery of human remains: Archaeological approaches* (2nd ed.). Boca Raton, FL: CRC/Taylor & Francis.

Fisher, B. A. J. (2004). *Techniques of crime scene investigation* (7th ed.). Boca Raton, FL: CRC Press.

Fish, J. T., Miller, L. S., & Braswell, M. C. (2011). *Crime scene investigation* (2nd ed.). Boston: Elsevier/Anderson Publishing.

Geberth, V. J. (2006). *Practical homicide investigation: Tactics, procedures, and forensic techniques* (4th ed.). Boca Raton, FL: CRC/Taylor & Francis.

Geberth, V. J. (2006). *Practical homicide investigation: Tactics, procedures, and forensic techniques* (4th ed.). Boca Raton, FL: CRC/Taylor & Francis.

Geberth, V. J. (2010). *Sex-Related homicide and death investigation: Practical and clinical perspectives* (2nd ed.). Boca Raton, FL: CRC/Taylor & Francis.

Humphry, D. (2002). *Final exit: The practicalities of self-deliverance and assisted suicide for the dying* (3rd ed.). New York: Delta Trade Paperback.

Lee, H. C. (1998). *Dr. Henry C. Lee on crime scene investigation and reconstruction: Criminal law expert in residence '98.* Boston: MCLE.

Ressler, R. K., Burgess, A. W., & Douglas, J. E. (1988). *Sexual homicide: Patterns and motives.* Lexington, MA: Lexington Books.

Saferstein, R. (2009). *Forensic science: From the crime scene to the crime lab.* Upper Saddle River, NJ: Pearson/Prentice Hall.

Spitz, W. U. (2006). *Spitz and Fischer's MedicoLegal investigation of death: Guidelines for the application of pathology to criminal investigation* (4th ed.). Springfield, IL: Charles C Thomas.

CHAPTER 18

ROBBERY

INTRODUCTION

Robbery has strong psychological and social implications within the community. Robbery affects millions of Americans every year. Not only do victims suffer, but relatives and friends also must cope with the trauma of a loved one's victimization. Robbery involves either violence or the threat of violence, and the theft of property. It confronts the victim with a high probability of physical injury, emotional trauma, and frequently a feeling of helplessness.

Today, we know much more about robbery than we did 10 years ago. However, much of this information relates to sociological and demographic variables, and is less than helpful in aiding in its investigation. Robbery investigations employ all the elements involved in criminal investigation: people (victims and witnesses), method (*modus operandi*), physical evidence, crime analysis, and records. It is a confrontational crime, thereby placing the victim in a position to be an eyewitness—even if the suspect is disguised.

Robberies have considerable impact on the community. They engender fear and reduce the quality of life in a neighborhood, and political pressure is often brought to bear on the police department to solve them. For these reasons, supervisors will, if possible, assign their most trusted and capable investigators to robbery cases.

In 2010, most robberies occurred on streets and highways (43.2%), with robberies of commercial establishments accounting for an additional 22.9 percent. Residential robberies accounted for 17.3 percent of the total. The remainder were miscellaneous types.[1]

Firearms were used in 41.4 percent of robberies in 2010. Strong-arm robberies accounted for 42.0 percent of the total.[2]

The rate of robbery victimization in 2010 was 1.9 per 1,000 persons, and blacks and Hispanics were victimized more than twice as often as whites (3.6 per thousand for blacks and 2.7 per thousand for Hispanics). The rate of robbery victimization has also decreased from 2007, when it was 2.4 per 1,000 persons.[3]

Statistics also indicate that offenders using guns have a higher probability of carrying out the robbery than do those using other weapons. These statistics provide a background for the investigator and a frame of reference as the investigation proceeds.[4]

Almost 70 percent of robberies are committed by a stranger—about one-half of these by more than one offender. Most armed robberies and assaults occur on the street after dark. Most victims do not perceive that they are about to be robbed. The actual event usually takes place in a relatively short period of time.[5] In such cases, the victim may tend to perceive things that did not occur, and care should be taken to walk the victim through a reconstruction of events. This may prove helpful in developing an MO and in searching through files for similar cases.

The investigator should be aware that victimization studies indicate that about one-half of all robberies are never reported to the police. This fact can be important because the investigator may want to use the media and other community resources to ask victims who have not reported the crime to come forward in order to develop information about suspects and their description.

Definitions

Generally, robbery involves the taking of property from a person by the use of force or the fear of force. The Model Penal Code offers the following definition:

A person is guilty of robbery if, in the course of committing a theft, he or she:

(a)   inflicts serious bodily harm upon another; or

(b)   threatens another with or purposely puts him in fear of serious bodily injury; or

(c)   commits or threatens to commit any felony of the first or second degree.

An act shall be deemed "in the course of committing a theft" if it occurs in an attempt to commit theft or in flight after the attempt or commission.[6]

Robbery is generally defined for statistical purposes as:

The unlawful taking or attempted taking of property that is in the immediate possession of another, by force or threat of force.

Because theft or attempted theft is an important element of robbery, the investigator should be familiar with the definitions of theft and related offenses. Although the definitions from the Model Penal Code provide general information, the investigator must be thoroughly familiar with the definitions of the jurisdiction in which he or she works.

PEOPLE

Victims and Witnesses

Robbery victims come from all walks of life. Robbers run the gamut from unsophisticated juveniles to experienced career criminals. Males are victimized almost two times as often as females (2.4 per 1,000 males versus 1.4 per 1,000 females); and persons between the ages of 12 and 24 have a higher probability of victimization than those who are older (0.7 per 1,000 between 12 and 14; 2.7 per 1,000 between 15 and 17; 5.9 per 1,000 between 18 and 20; 3.7 per 1,000 between 21 and 24; and 2.5 per 1,000 between 25 and 34).[7]

Types of robberies include street robberies, residential robberies (usually termed "home invasions"), robberies in schools, bank and armored car robberies, and other commercial robberies. The most common commercial robberies involve convenience stores, gas stations, liquor stores, drug stores, cab drivers, and other businesses or activities that frequently operate during evening hours and involve cash transactions. (See Figure 18.1 for one year's breakdown of robberies by type of target.) Significant increases in so-called "carjacking" offenses have made this a high-priority crime in many jurisdictions.

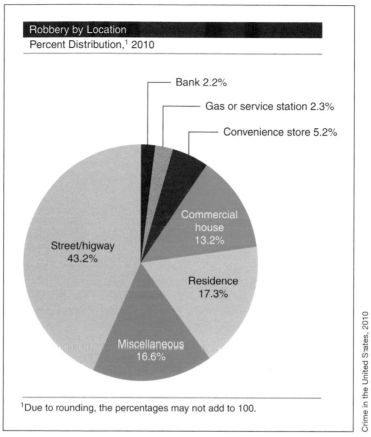

Robbery by Location
Percent Distribution,[1] 2010

- Bank 2.2%
- Gas or service station 2.3%
- Convenience store 5.2%
- Commercial house 13.2%
- Residence 17.3%
- Miscellaneous 16.6%
- Street/higway 43.2%

[1]Due to rounding, the percentages may not add to 100.

Crime in the United States, 2010

Figure 18.1
Robbery by Location.

Not surprisingly, the probability of victimization is related in large measure to where individuals live, their occupation, and their "availability" as targets. Most victims do not make good witnesses because the incident occurs quickly, a high degree of stress is involved, it is often dark—at least in street robberies, and the suspects often wear masks. Facial identification is frequently difficult for this reason. However, a good investigator working carefully can elicit information that may be buried in the victim's subconscious. Police artists, identification kits, and computer imaging systems can be used to help create a drawing of the suspect.

The investigator should be aware that facial identification, while important, is not the only source of information. Clothing, physical marks (e.g., a scar) or characteristics (e.g., a limp), type of weapon, and words (i.e., "tale") used by the perpetrator to convey that robbery is intended can be invaluable. The robber's tale is extremely important in establishing an MO.

When investigating robberies committed by juveniles, one should be aware that perpetrators may continue to wear the clothing worn during the robbery and/or use the same weapon again. Determining where and when the robbery took place also can be important in developing a profile and for crime pattern analysis.

Keeping in mind that the victim is likely to be traumatized by the event, the investigator should take care in conducting the interview. Initially, interviews should be conducted individually when there is more than one victim. The victim should first be asked to describe in his or her own words what actually took place. The investigator should attempt to obtain answers for the questions: who, what, when, where, how, and why. During this stage careful notes of the specifics should be taken. After the victim has explained what happened, the investigator should begin to work carefully through specific items of information. Some departments provide a checklist that is useful in obtaining specific information. The investigator should recognize that victims are prone to inadvertently giving inaccurate information; for example, height and weight are difficult to estimate accurately and are often reported incorrectly.

Robberies fall into categories based on the kind of force or threat employed:

Armed robbery involves the use of a weapon such as a firearm, knife, or other dangerous weapon. Other terms for this include: *holdup, stickup, heist,* and *hijacking.*

Strong-arm robbery involves the use of physical force to commit the robbery. Other expressions for this include: *mugging* and *muscle job.*

There may be more than one victim, and there may be more than one suspect. In more spectacular robberies involving some degree of planning—such as a bank or armored car robbery—there usually will be witnesses, and every effort must be made to locate them.

Bank robberies, although not one of the most common forms of robbery, represent a serious problem because they are reported in the media and therefore lead to public concern. In a study of bank robberies, Deborah Lamm Weisel notes:

The likelihood of catching a bank robber on or near the scene is higher than other crimes. This is because most bank robberies are reported very quickly, most occur during daylight hours, many have multiple witnesses, and some produce photographic images that can be used to canvass the surrounding area for suspects. Consequently, many robbers are caught the same day. In fact, the clearance rate for bank robbery is among the highest of all crimes—nearly 60 percent.[8]

There were 5,628 bank robberies in 2010, according to FBI statistics, amounting to more than $42 million in losses, of which $8.19 million was recovered. The average amount of loss nationwide in a robbery was about $7,600.[9] See Table 18.1.

Table 18.1
Bank Robbery Statute Violations by Regions, Geographic Divisions, States, and Territories (January 1, 2010 – December 31, 2010)

REGIONAL SUMMARY	BANK ROBBERIES	BANK BURGLARIES	BANK LARCENIES	BANK EXTORTIONS
Northeast	985	3	0	2
North Central	1,050	20	4	1
South	1,790	36	4	4
West	1,691	12	1	6
Territories	30	3	0	0
Totals	5,546	74	8	13

Source: Bank Crime Statistics (BCS). Federal Insured Financial Institutions. January 1, 2010 – December 31, 2010. Federal Bureau of Investigation.

Bank Robberies

Bank robberies are most commonly committed by:

- A single individual
- Without displaying a weapon
- Individuals who are older than in other robberies
- Perpetrators during the daytime

In a study of 163 bank robbery cases in the Northeast by Angelica Zdonek, most bank robberies occurred on Friday (19.3%), followed by Thursday (18.6%), and then Tuesday (18%). This data is similar to what the FBI found in 2010, where Friday (19.7%) had the most occurrences, then Tuesday (18.3%), and Monday (17.7%) and Thursday (17.7%). Moreover, most bank robberies occurred during the third week of a month (27%), while the smallest number of robberies occurred on the last week of a month (10%). Between April and August, most occurred in May (23%) and the least number in April (17%). In 135 of the 163 cases, 83 percent were committed by a single individual. In 23 of the cases, two perpetrators were involved (14%); in three cases, three persons were involved (2%); and in two cases, four persons (1%) were involved. In 26 cases, a weapon was displayed, a handgun in 22 cases, and a knife in four cases. In the vast majority of cases, a note was handed to a teller. In the 62 cases in which a perpetrator was arrested, four were between the ages of 18 and 19; 26 were between the ages of 20 and 30; 16 were between the ages of 31 and 40; nine between the ages of 41 and 50; and seven older than 50 years of age. In one case the perpetrator was 75 years old. In 88 cases where data was available, 37 of the perpetrators were observed fleeing in a vehicle; 50 fled on foot; and one fled on a bicycle.[10]

The use of weapons in a bank robbery has generally declined over the years because most robberies are committed alone by a single individual, most of whom do not have a prior record. There are important differences between amateur and professional bank robbers (see Table 18.2).

As Weisel notes, professional robbers are more likely to use firearms, escape in vehicles, and travel further to select targets.

The detective handling a robbery investigation must isolate the victim and witnesses and then interview them separately. He or she also must quickly identify and protect the crime scene. This aspect of the investigation is frequently overlooked or handled poorly, largely because the crime scene may actually be in more than one place (e.g., within a building where the robbery took place and outside where a getaway vehicle was parked). There is also a tendency to want to interview witnesses too quickly, which may result in a loss of information or varied accounts based on misconceptions.

In many instances the initial phase of the investigation is handled by the patrol force, and there is a desire to broadcast a physical description of the robbers and vehicle as soon as possible, and even to remove the victim from the scene to accompany patrol officers in a search for the suspect. Such actions, though understandable, can complicate the investigation. In some cases it is almost impossible to preserve the crime scene because so many curious bystanders have entered the area. If not kept separated, witnesses also may influence each other in providing descriptive and other information.

Table 18.2
Distinguishing Professional and Amateur Bank Robbers

	PROFESSIONAL	AMATEUR
Offenders	• Multiple offenders with division of labor • Shows evidence of planning • May be older • Prior bank robbery convictions • Travels further to rob banks	• Solitary offender • Alcohol or other drug use likely • No prior bank crime • Lives near bank target
Violence	• Aggressive takeover, with loud verbal demands • Visible weapons, especially guns • Intimidation, physical or verbal threats	• Note passed to teller or simple verbal demand • Waits in line • No weapon
Defeat Security	• Uses a disguise • Disables or obscures surveillance cameras • Demands that dye packs be left out, alarms not be activated, or police not be called	
Robbery Success	• Hits multiple teller windows • Larger amounts stolen • Lower percentage of money recovered • More successful robberies • Fewer cases directly cleared • Longer time from offense to case clearance	• Single teller window victimized • Lower amounts stolen • Higher percentage of money recovered • More failed robberies • Shorter time from offense to case clearance, including more same-day arrests • Direct case clearance more likely
Robbery Timing	• Targets banks when few customers are present, such as at opening time • Targets banks early in the week	• Targets banks when numerous customers are present, such as around midday • Targets banks near closing or on Friday
Target Selection	• Previous robbery • Busy road near intersection • Multidirectional traffic • Corner locations, multiple vehicle exits	• Previous robbery • Heavy pedestrian traffic or adjacent to dense multifamily residences • Parcels without barriers • Parcels with egress obscured
Getaway	• Via car	• On foot or bicycle

Source: Deborah Lamm Weisel, *Bank Robbery*. Washington, DC: U.S. Department of Justice, Office of Community Oriented Policing Services, 2007.

Consulting videotapes from closed-circuit television monitoring systems in businesses, apartment buildings, elevators, and other locations is important. Cameras may also be located in parking lots or other areas away from the crime scene (see Figure 18.2).

Robbery investigations depend on the ability to reconstruct the event, to develop physical descriptions and, perhaps most important, to establish the *modus operandi*. Because individuals are creatures of habit, they are likely to say or do similar things in different acts. The ability of the investigator to identify these "calling cards" can go a long way toward solution of the crime.

The investigator who bases a case solely on eyewitness testimony is endangering the case and the possibility of a conviction. The investigator should carefully develop an interview plan, both in terms of the sequence of individuals involved and the sequence of questions asked. All too often investigators "feed" information to individuals being interviewed.

Figure 18.2
In this image taken from surveillance video, a man points a handgun at the head of an employee while robbing a medical marijuana dispensary in Los Angeles.

Victims and witnesses generally fall into categories based on physical and emotional/psychological factors. These categories help determine the interview plan, the validity of the information, and the direction in which the investigation will head.

In addition to interviewing victims and witnesses, the investigator should remember that important information may also be gleaned from officers who arrived on the scene, as well as secondary witnesses who, though they may have arrived after the event took place, may have seen or heard something that was overlooked in the preliminary investigation.

Individuals—including the officers who handled the preliminary investigation—should not be permitted to hear or take part in the initial interviews of others. At a later time it may prove worthwhile to conduct group interviews, but this should be done only after everyone has been interviewed alone and after the investigator has compared notes with any partners or assistants.

Ideally the victim should be interviewed first and witnesses interviewed in descending order on the basis of those who appear most reliable. A classic mistake often made during interviews is grouping individuals in the same location as they await the interview, or permitting those who have been interviewed to mingle with those who have not.

Physical and Emotional Factors

Physical Factors:
Age
Sex
Race
Stature
Eyesight or other physical infirmities
Injury

Emotional/Psychological Factors:
Degree of distress
Whether or not a prior victim
Ego
Attitude toward police
Attitude toward race

Victim and witness perceptions may vary considerably. Short individuals, for example, will likely perceive the suspect as being taller than will witnesses who are tall. Elderly witnesses may have varying perceptions of age. Young witnesses may be able to provide more information on specific types of details, such as automobile descriptions, types of clothing, and mannerisms. When a victim has been robbed before, he or she may be able to provide details resulting from that unique frame of reference.

Sometimes victims (particularly males) experience ego problems because they did not act as they felt they should. Care should be taken to assure the individual that a lack of action or resistance was a wise course.

In addition to information provided by victims and witnesses, the investigator should identify and gather any physical evidence. All too often there is an assumption that the rapidity of the event precludes the possibility of physical evidence being present, but such a possibility should never be ruled out.

The Robbery Suspect

In 2010, persons under the age of 25 accounted for 64.2 percent of all robbery arrests. This is a major increase from 2005, when persons under the age of 25 accounted for 53 percent of all robbery arrests. Younger suspects tend to operate within a geographical radius of two miles from their residence. While males are overrepresented in robbery arrest statistics, making up 87 percent of all offenders, the racial breakdown has changed significantly over the past decade. Whites now represent 43.3 percent of all robbery offenders, with blacks and other races representing 55 percent and 1.7 percent, respectively. For the most part, these offenders are also likely to commit street crimes and commit multiple offenses in a relatively short period of time, frequently under the influence of alcohol or other drugs. In 2010, more than a quarter of all robberies were cleared. According to the 2010 Uniform Crime Reports, juveniles comprised only 14 percent of robbery clearances.[11]

Street and Commercial Robberies

Most robberies involve more than one offender operating against a single victim. About one-third of robberies involve three or more offenders. The number of offenders in an offending group is usually age-related. Young robbers tend to act in groups, and are more prone to commit street robberies, whereas older robbers are more likely to commit commercial robberies and frequently operate alone or with a partner. Robberies at automated teller machines usually involve a lone offender who accosts the victim who has just made a withdrawal, and according to Michael Scott, "There is some evidence that offenders who commit street robbery (including ATM robbery) are different from those who commit commercial robbery."[12] Although juvenile suspects may have prior arrest records, they may be difficult to retrieve because they were handled in a juvenile court and are unobtainable. Nevertheless, the frequency of events is in the investigator's favor. Information should be sought from youth investigators, informants, beat officers, neighborhood residents, and others who have access to possible suspects. A review of past arrests of robbery suspects who utilize a similar MO may prove useful.

Professional robbers are more likely to be older and to have a prior arrest record. Frequently they have been convicted of a crime. Older offenders are more likely to plan the act, but the plan is sometimes no more than "casing" the location. Well-planned and well-executed robberies will usually be obvious to the investigator and will involve large sums of money or merchandise. The professional robber is also much more likely to operate over a wide geographic area, in some cases across jurisdictional boundaries and even state lines. He or she is also more likely to use firearms, automobiles, masks or disguises, and lookouts. In some instances, professionals use hand-held radios for communication and to monitor police radio frequencies.

The professional robber represents a different challenge from the so-called opportunist robber who selects victims by chance. Because this type of robbery is executed less frequently and over a wider geographic area, it is much more difficult to establish a pattern or useful MO. In these cases the investigator must resort to the use of records, physical evidence, and robbery analysis techniques to be successful.

Residence and Home Invasion Robberies

Residential and home invasion robberies are generally of two types, the first being the robbery at a home where the perpetrators believe that the victim or victims are wealthy and likely to have cash and valuables present. These types of robberies appear to be on the increase, and many also result in physical injury to the victims. They are more likely to occur in wealthier neighborhoods, and the robberies are committed "blindly" without knowledge of the occupants. In the second type of home invasion, frequently committed by street gangs or drug dealers, where the primary motive is not robbery, the motive may be to recover illegal drugs, demand payment on a loan, or threaten or kill an occupant. The number of home invasion cases appears to be increasing. In 2010, 17.3 percent of all robberies involved a residence.[13]

CONDUCTING THE INVESTIGATION

Physical Evidence

General crime scene protection and search measures should be observed at the robbery scene and in other key locations, such as a vehicle recovered after use in the crime. Some specific types of physical evidence should be considered at robbery scenes:

1. Footprints may be present.

2. Fingerprints may be left in proximate locations. For example, the suspect in a store robbery may have handled merchandise prior to carrying out the robbery; in a bar there may be fingerprints on the glass or bottle used; in a handbag snatching in which the item is recovered there may be fingerprints on the handbag or its contents, or footprints where it was recovered. There may also be fiber traces on recovered material.

3. Saliva may be present on discarded facial masks.

4. Body secretions, fiber evidence, or other trace materials may be present on the victim's clothing if there was a scuffle or the use of force.

5. When a suspect has been identified or apprehended, trace material may be present on the suspect's clothing that will link him or her to the victim or the scene.

6. Physical evidence may be available where a weapon is recovered. Blood samples, skin or tissue residue, or even toolmarks should not be overlooked. In one robbery-homicide case the perpetrator struck the victim with a serrated hammer. The blow was struck with such force that an impression that matched the weapon was left on the skull.

7. Fingerprints or trace evidence can be left on the articles recovered. A watch taken during a robbery, which was later pawned and recovered by police, produced a partial print that helped convict the suspect. In a rape/robbery, a suspect was identified more than a year later when a fingerprint recovered from the victim's handbag was run through the computerized fingerprint system known as AFIS (Automatic Fingerprint Identification System) when the suspect was arrested for another crime.

Records and Other Sources of Information

A robbery suspect will probably have a prior arrest record. The manner in which records are used may determine the success or failure of the investigation. By a process of elimination it may be possible to narrow the range of suspects considerably. In departments that use a computerized record system it may be possible to initiate "blind" searches. Some of the variables that can reduce a list of suspects include:

- Sex
- Race
- Age (although this can be deceiving)
- Color of hair
- Specific descriptors (such as a tattoo)
- Clothing (particularly hats or jackets)
- Type of weapon
- Geographic location
- Type of vehicle used
- Number of subjects involved
- Tale told or words used by suspect
- Videos from prior robberies

This partial list of variables provides an indication of the ways in which a potential list of suspects can be developed and then reduced.

Most robbery suspects will commit more than one crime. If, over time, it is possible to link crimes to one person, a more accurate profile can be developed and used to plan a strategy for apprehension. In addition to police department records, consideration should be given to other records, including:

1. Court records
2. Prison records (particularly recent releases)
3. Other law enforcement agency records (including federal, state, and local)
4. Other agencies (unemployment offices, schools, housing offices, drug rehabilitation programs, etc.)
5. Credit card companies (particularly when cards were taken in the robbery)
6. Motor vehicle bureau records

Numerous other sources of information may be pursued. These include:

1. Other investigators

2. Information from patrol officers

3. Informants

4. Individuals arrested in other cases

5. Stores where particular types of weapons may be purchased

6. Closed-circuit television recordings recovered at the scene

FOLLOW-UP ACTIVITIES

Successful robbery investigations depend heavily on the ability of the investigator to recognize significant variables that can be used to research past crimes as a measure of identifying and locating suspects. When all leads have been exhausted with reference to the immediate investigation, the solution will frequently lie in past crimes.

Recognizing patterns, geographical locations, the types of victims, and the number and characteristics of associates should be a high priority in the follow-up sequence of the investigation. By putting this information together it is frequently possible to add to the information about suspects. Having accomplished this, the investigator should begin to review arrest records of individuals who fit the composite *modus operandi* and physical characteristics.

Where this fails, the investigator should relay information to other jurisdictions, requesting their cooperation in crimes of a similar nature, or those in which potential suspects may have been arrested.

CONCLUSION

Research concerning robbery indicates that most street robberies are not well-planned, and the choice of victim is based on both circumstances, usually associated with time of day and location, and the perceived vulnerability of the victim. More sophisticated or professional robberies, on the other hand, generally display varying degrees of preparation. All of these factors should be a part of the robbery investigator's store of knowledge. The literature in this area is rich with information that can be of assistance. The National Criminal Justice Reference Service in Washington, DC, can provide a comprehensive annotated bibliography that should not be overlooked.[14]

NOTES

[1] U.S. Department of Justice, Federal Bureau of Investigation, *Crime in the United States 2010*. See http://www.fbi.gov/about-us/cjis/ucr/crime-in-the-u.s/2010/crime-in-the-u.s.-2010/violent-crime/robberymain

[2] Ibid.

[3]   Truman, J.L. (2011), "Criminal Victimization, 2010"; *National Crime Victimization Survey*, U.S. Department of Justice. Retrieved from http://bjs.ojp.usdoj.gov/content/pub/pdf/cv10.pdf

[4]   Bureau of Justice Statistics (BJS). See http://www.ojp.usdoj.gov/bjs

[5]   U.S. Department of Justice, Bureau of Justice Statistics, *2005 National Crime Victimization Survey* (Washington, DC: U.S. Government Printing Office, 2006).

[6]   American Law Institute Model Penal Code, 1895. As adopted at the 1952 annual meeting of the American Law Institute at Washington, DC, 24 May 1962, 145.

[7]   Truman, J.L. (2011), "Criminal Victimization, 2010"; *National Crime Victimization Survey*, U.S. Department of Justice. Retrieved from http://bjs.ojp.usdoj.gov/content/pub/pdf/cv10.pdf

[8]   Weisel, Deborah Lamm, *Bank Robbery* (Washington, DC: US Department of Justice, 2007), 3.

[9]   Johnson, Patrick. (2011), "FBI data for 2010 show number of bank robberies declining nationwide and in Massachusetts." *The Republican* (April 5, 2011).

[10]   Zdonek, Angela (2011) [Unpublished research paper. University of New Haven.]

[11]   U.S. Department of Justice, Federal Bureau of Investigation, *Crime in the United States 2010*. See http://www.fbi.gov/about-us/cjis/ucr/crime-in-the-u.s/2010/crime-in-the-u.s.-2010/clearances

[12]   Michael Scott, *Robbery at Automated Teller Machines*. U.S. Department of Justice, Office of Community Oriented Policing. Washington, DC. 2001, p. 3.

[13]   U.S. Department of Justice, Federal Bureau of Investigation (2010), *Uniform Crime Reports: 2010*. (Washington, DC: U.S. Government Printing Office).

[14]   The National Criminal Justice Reference Service (Washington, DC) can be reached at 800/851-3420 or http://www.ncjrs.gov

DISCUSSION QUESTIONS

1.   Where are most robberies committed?

2.   Generally, what are the elements of robbery?

3.   In addition to facial identification, what are other sources of information?

4.   What are the characteristics of a bank robbery?

5.   Do victims and witnesses in a robbery frequently offer different perceptions?

6.   Persons under the age of 25 account for what percentage of robbery arrests?

7.   What are the characteristics of professional robbers?

8.   What are two types of residence and home invasion robberies?

9.   What are some of the types of physical evidence that should be considered in robbery investigations?

10.   What are some of the variables that can be used to search records?

SUPPLEMENTAL READINGS

Banton, M. (1985). *Investigating robbery*. Brookfield, VT: Gower.

Glensor, R. W., & Peak, K. L. (2004). *Crimes against tourists*. Washington, DC: U.S. Department of Justice.

Klaus, P. (Mar. 1999). Carjacking in the United States, 1992–96. *Bureau of Justice Statistics Special Report*.

Klaus, P. (July 2004). Carjacking, 1993–2002. *Bureau of Justice Statistics Crime Data Brief*.

Matthews, R. (2002). *Armed robbery*. Portland, OR: Willan Publishing.

U.S. Department of Justice (2005). *Crimes against persons age 65 or older, 1993–2002*. Washington, DC: Office of Justice Programs.

Wagner, W. E. (1999). *Burglary/robbery investigation*. Indianapolis: Public Safety Training Council.

Wright, R. T., & Decker, S. H. (1997). *Armed robbers in action: Stickups and street culture*. Boston: Northeastern University Press.

CHAPTER 19

SEX CRIMES

INTRODUCTION

The investigation of rape and other sex crimes represents a significant challenge for the criminal investigator. The manner in which the investigation is conducted can have an impact not only on a successful conclusion in court, but also on the psychological and social well-being of the victim. Sex crimes, more so than many other forms of criminal activity, are likely to leave an emotional scar that can last a lifetime.

The focus of this chapter is on the crime of rape. However, it is important to recognize that virtually all sex-related offenses demand special attention. To begin with, interviewing victims, witnesses, and even offenders requires a high level of compassion and skill. One of the fastest growing types of crimes today is the general category of Internet-related sex crimes.

In 2012, the definition of rape was revised for the Uniform Crime Report (UCR) by the U.S. Department of Justice to include cases involving any gender (male or female) of the victim or perpetrator. It also includes those cases in which the victim was unable to give consent because he or she was temporarily or permanently incapacitated by a mental or physical condition, which includes being under the influence of alcohol or other drugs, or age (see Box 19.1).

The success of the investigation will also frequently depend on the collection of physical evidence. The nature of proof in sex offenses, unlike most other crimes, traditionally has required some corroboration other than the victim's testimony. Sex crimes also arouse the concern of the community, and there is likely to be political and public pressure on the police to solve the case. If not handled properly, this pressure can contribute to a faulty and hasty investigation. Rape is also the felony that is least reported to the police. In 2010, rape victims accounted for 0.7 per 1,000 households, with a probability of victimization being higher in metropolitan areas. This number increased 48.5 percent from 2009, with a rate of 0.5 per 1,000 households, but decreased from 2007 where the rate was 0.8 per 1,000 households.[1]

Research indicates that in 2010, 7 percent of rape or sexual assaults were committed by an offender with a firearm, which increased from 2007 when 1 percent of rape or sexual assaults were committed by an offender with a firearm, and it is estimated that about 50 percent of rape or sexual assaults were reported to the police. In 76 percent of the cases, the perpetrator was known to the victim, compared to 2007, where in 64 percent of the cases, the perpetrator was known to the victim.[2]

Understanding the definition and elements of the various kinds of sex crimes is important, for in many cases the offender maintains that the victim consented to the act.

Definitions

Sex crimes cover a multitude of offenses ranging from indecent exposure to forcible rape. The issue of mutual consent is frequently a key defense contention. However, it should be noted at the outset

---

Box 19.1 UCR REVISION OF RAPE

The revised definition of rape includes any gender of victim or perpetrator, and includes instances in which the victim is incapable of giving consent because of temporary or permanent mental or physical incapacity, including due to the influence of drugs or alcohol or because of age. With this redefinition, it is expected that the national crime statistics will better reflect the true incidence of reported rape in the United States.

When speaking about the change, David Cuthbertson, FBI Assistant Director, CJIS Division, said, "This change will give law enforcement the ability to report more complete rape offense data, as the new definition reflects the vast majority of state rape statutes." The goal of the updated definition is to more accurately demonstrate the totality of the response and investigative work done by law enforcement across the country.

The IACP has long advocated for this change. In early 2011, the IACP met with Vice President Biden's Office to discuss modernizing the UCR definition of forcible rape. In collaboration with law enforcement partners, the IACP drafted language to capture the reality of this crime.

Source: International Association of Chiefs of Police statement, 2012.

---

that the concept of mutual consent is not well defined in the law, and what may be perceived as consent may not in fact be the case. A prostitute can be raped. An individual under the influence of liquor or other drugs may not be in a position to psychologically (and legally) consent. Minor children cannot generally give consent. The incidence of "acquaintance rape," often known as "date rape," has in recent years gained attention and generated new case law.

Within the rubric of mutual consent lie a number of acts that may involve full consent between the parties, but that nevertheless are illegal within a particular jurisdiction. Examples of these include prostitution, adultery, homosexual acts, and other sex acts, such as anal intercourse. These crimes are rarely handled by investigative units and are not discussed in this chapter.

The most serious sex-connected crime from the perception of the public is forcible rape or sodomy, coupled with murder. It is important to recognize, though, that all rapes and serious sexual assaults must have a high priority in the investigative universe. They are frequently difficult to prove in a court of law, and offenders have gone free because of a lazy or sloppy investigation.

Corpus Delicti

The legal definition of rape generally involves the following elements:

A. Sexual penetration, however slight, of the victim's vulva or penetration of the anal cavity (sodomy);

B. By a person or persons without the victim's consent;

C. Or with a minor child.

Sex crimes include other forms of aberrant behavior with which the investigator should be familiar. These include:

1. Sexual assault

2. Child abuse and molestation, also known as pedophilia

3. Some forms of pornography

4. Indecent exposure

5. Incest

6. Stalking

STALKING

Not much research has been done on stalking, which generally involves conduct that is directed at a specific person or persons, that seriously alarms, annoys, intimidates, or harasses the person(s), and that serves no legitimate purpose. Stalking may involve telephone calls, notes or letters, e-mails, text messages, spying, confrontations, and following or observing a person or persons. It may be instituted for a variety of reasons.[3] Eighteen- to 24-year-olds are more often the victims of stalking, and stalking on college campuses is higher than for the average population. Six million women and men are victims of stalking each year. Two-thirds of female victims have been stalked by a current or former intimate partner. Most stalking involves unwanted telephone calls or text messages. Stalking victims who are raped identify a former intimate partner or a friend, roommate, or neighbor.[4]

Figure 19.1
A cocktail sits atop a "date rape drug detection coaster." Manufacturers claim that the coasters test for "date rape drugs" in drinks via test spots that turn dark blue if a splash of alcohol contains one of the common drugs used to incapacitate victims. Some law enforcement experts claim the coasters are ineffective and could lead to more assaults by creating a false sense of security.

A more common problem for local law enforcement is the use of the computer to stalk or harass individuals. In most cases, the sender is most likely to be anonymous. The prior section on legal aspects outlines the procedures involved in gaining access to the identity of an individual who is using the computer or telephone for illegal purposes.

A year-long study in 2006 of stalking victims found that about 25 percent of stalking suspects used e-mail (83%) or instant messaging (35%), and about 75 percent of the victims knew the stalker in some capacity. Overall, more than three million people over the age of 18 were stalking victims. Stalking was defined as "a course of conduct that would cause a reasonable person to feel fear." More than one in four stalking victims reported that some form of cyberstalking was used:

> Electronic monitoring was used to stalk 1 in 13 victims. Video or digital cameras were equally likely as listening devices or bugs to be used to electronically monitor victims (46% and 42%). Global positioning systems (GPS) technology comprised about a tenth of the electronic monitoring of stalking victims.[5]

Of the 3.4 million victims surveyed, 278,580 sustained injuries in attacks, including 38,590 (13.9%) victims who were raped or sexually assaulted, 52,080 who were seriously injured, and 276,440 who suffered minor or other injuries. A weapon was used in 138,630 attacks. The majority of offenders (64%) were between the ages of 18 and 29, and the majority of the victims were between the ages of 21 and 39 (71%).[6]

Two types of stalkers have been identified by New York homicide detective Vernon Geberth: the *psychopathic personality stalker*, and the *psychotic personality stalker*[7] (see Table 19.1).

Table 19.1
Types of Stalkers

The Psychopathic Personality Stalker	Usually a male from a dysfunctional family, who is likely to use violence as a form of control over a former girlfriend or wife, and who frequently displays homicidal behavior. This is the most common form of stalker.
The Psychotic Personality Stalker	A male or female who becomes obsessed with a particular person, such as an unobtainable love subject.
Celebrity Stalker	Follows someone who is famous, usually an entertainment or sports figure.
Lust Stalker	Usually involves desire for sexual (rape) gratification, or psychological gain or power over a stranger.
"Hit Man" Stalker	A professional killer who stalks his or her victims.
Love-Scorned Stalker	Involves prior personal relationship between the stalker and the victim.
Domestic Stalker	Involves anger against a spouse.
Political Stalker	Focuses on a political figure, usually not personally known to the attacker.

Adapted from V. Geberth, "Stalkers," *Law and Order* (October 1992), and R. Holmes, "Stalking in America: Types and Methods of Criminal Stalkers." *Journal of Contemporary Criminal Justice* (December 1993).

Understanding the reasons for stalking behavior is a critical part of the investigation. In the case of love-scorned and domestic stalkers, the suspect is usually known. He or she often may be known in the case of celebrity stalkers. In cases involving lust, contract murder, and political stalkers, the suspect is usually not identified. In the absence of letters, phone calls, or other warnings, the victim may tell the investigator that he or she "feels" they are being watched.

When telephone calls are being made, a pen register may be placed on the phone with the cooperation of the telephone company. This identifies the phone from which a call is being made. In the case of mail, leads may be developed by looking at postmarks to determine where the letter was posted.

The U.S. Secret Service maintains an extensive file on potential political stalkers or assassins, and the FBI maintains a sexual offender file that may be of assistance in cases involving lust stalkers.

In a study of more than 120 stalkers, Holmes found that, with the exception of love-scorned stalkers, most had the intent to commit murder. In the case of love-scorned stalkers, while they do not usually intend to murder the victim, they do have a propensity for violence, and many of these cases have resulted in a murder.[8]

Stalkers are also likely to commit identity theft or alter a victim's financial or other records, such as closing or opening accounts, removing money, or charging items on a credit card. A Bureau of Justice Study of 204,230 stalking victims found that more than half had financial accounts opened or closed by the stalker.[9]

Information from these sources provides both evidentiary evidence of stalking as well as the elements of other crimes. In such cases the investigator should take care to document transactions, interview bank officials who may have viewed the offender, and follow up other leads that may not be obvious at first. Charging the offender with other crimes, such as fraud, larceny, or forgery may have a greater impact on convincing him or her to confess in hopes of a lesser plea.

Identity Theft by Stalkers

In 2008, stalking offenders committed identity theft against 204,230 victims. Offenses that occurred:

Opened/closed accounts: 110,850 cases (54.3%)

Took money from accounts: 105,130 cases (51.5%)

Charged items to credit card: 60,790 cases (29.8%)

Source: "Stalking Victimization in the United States." *Bureau of Justice Statistics: Special Report.* U.S. Justice Department. January, Washington, DC, 2009.

CHILD EXPLOITATION

The Internet has become a notorious tool for pedophiles, child pornographers, and other child sex abusers. ICE, the Postal Inspection Service, and the FBI generally investigate international providers. Depending on how information comes to authorities, either federal, state, or local law enforcement may handle local investigations of users. Users of child pornography may also be pedophiles who are active in recruiting children for photos or using chat rooms to entice children to meet them.

A growing number of states have expanded or initiated child exploitation units, which usually include a computer specialist who is familiar with the methods used by suspects who make contact with young people through chat rooms as a means of luring victims to a prearranged location. When a parent or other person makes a complaint, the investigator should be thoroughly familiar with local laws relating to solicitation of a minor. Generally, it must be proved that the suspect was aware that the individual was a minor and in most cases it will be necessary to prove that something more than a meeting was planned. For this reason, it is important to obtain prior communications. If a meeting is arranged, it must be proved that the suspect was actually going to make contact and that a positive identification of the suspect has been made.

The Cook County Sheriff's Department in Illinois and the Texas Attorney General's criminal investigation unit have been successful in drawing out numerous pedophiles who believed they were communicating with a minor. One key to success has been the ability to establish and build cases that have not been viewed as entrapment. Generally, by studying the ways in which young people communicate on the Internet, law enforcement agents have been successful in getting the suspect to communicate freely. When arrested, the suspect is frequently found to have other incriminating material in his or her residence.

The U.S. Postal Inspection Service has stopped about 500 child molesters and been involved in the conviction of more than 250 persons for child sexual exploitation since 1997. Their research indicates a high correlation between child molesters and people involved in selling, purchasing, and trading child pornography. The Postal Inspection Service is an excellent source for assistance in cases involving the Internet or mail.[10]

In 2003, the Supreme Court held that sex offenders' photos and other information, such as an address, may be posted on the Internet as a means of providing citizens with information about potential threats.[11] At least 35 states provide this information. Such databases may also prove to be a good tool for investigators to develop suspects. However, care should be taken in jumping to conclusions, as well as making decisions to conduct interviews.

PEOPLE

Two aspects of sex crime investigation must receive priority handling. The first is seeing that the victim receives proper medical attention and a physical examination that can establish rape or sexual assault. The second is protection of the crime scene and, if a suspect is apprehended immediately or shortly thereafter, the collection and protection of his clothing—particularly undergarments. In addition, efforts should be made to locate witnesses who, although they may not have seen the crime, can place the suspect with or in proximity to the victim.

The attitude and demeanor of the investigator is crucial during these initial stages. A progressive law enforcement agency will have developed relationships with hospital emergency rooms and victim support groups that can be of great assistance. The medical practitioner conducting a rape examination is expected to follow a set of standard procedures that are a part of the case during its investigative and trial stages.

In rape cases there may be more than one crime scene requiring protection. For example, the victim may have been abducted and taken by car to another location and held there, or assaulted in one location and then taken to yet another location where she was released.

Because there might not be any other witnesses, it is necessary to establish an evidentiary link between the perpetrator and the victim that will serve to corroborate the victim's allegation. Even in cases in which the suspect admits that he was with the victim, but denies that a rape took place or says that the victim consented, it may be possible through physical evidence to attack the suspect's statements. For example, the presence of semen in the vagina may be used to refute an allegation that intercourse did not take place; and trace or fingerprint evidence may be used to show that the suspect was at a location where he denied being, such as the bedroom.

After the victim has received medical attention, a follow-up interview should be conducted. In many jurisdictions this interview is conducted by a female investigator if one is available. Under ideal circumstances it is prudent to have a psychologist familiar with sex crimes advise the investigator as questioning proceeds (this is not usually done in the presence of the victim). The psychologist should not take part in the interview, although in some cases it may be advisable to permit a representative from a victim support group to be present. This will depend on the emotional state of the victim and her desire to have an outsider present.

In practice, the first officer on the scene will likely conduct a preliminary interview. These interviews are critical; patrol officers should be trained in handling them. (A second officer or investigator should immediately be assigned to canvass the area or neighborhood for potential witnesses.) In addition, the time, manner, and nature of the interview may be affected if considerable time passes before medical authorities permit the victim to be interviewed by the investigator. For example, if there is serious physical or emotional trauma, the doctor may not permit an immediate interview. In such a case, the investigator must depend on the information from the initial interview. In addition, because there may be a tendency to "block" or subconsciously forget information due to trauma, the initial interview may be used later to help refresh the victim's memory.

The use of debilitating drugs such as rohypnol ("roofies") and gamma hydroxybutyrate (GHB) complicates an investigation because victims may not remember but only suspect that an assault has occurred. In these cases, the immediate gathering of physical evidence is especially pivotal to the investigation. For example, trace evidence of drugs can sometimes be obtained at the crime scene or information on manufacturing such drugs found on an offender's computer.

Victims and Witnesses

The preliminary interview should address the physical description of the offender, where the act occurred, and the circumstances surrounding it. The interview should be conducted in private, preferably with an impartial observer such as a nurse or female officer. Generally, the officer with the most experience should conduct the interview. However, circumstances may dictate otherwise—for example, if the victim is more comfortable with a female officer with less experience.

At this stage, the victim is frequently highly traumatized and may be hysterical. It is not necessary to focus on physical details of the act. If the victim alleges a rape, the officer should assume that one has occurred and operate on this assumption. It is usually advisable to let the victim tell her story uninterrupted and to take good notes. If time permits, the next stage of the interview should attempt to build on the victim's statements, taking care not to challenge or question statements. The officer should studiously avoid accusatory statements such as "Why were you in the bar?," "Why were you out late at night?," "Why did you go with him?," or "Why were you wearing that clothing?"

The interview should take into account such factors as age, psychological state, willingness to cooperate, and special circumstances. This involves an ability to "size up the situation." The officer should avoid leading questions and should respond to statements by nodding or asking, "Then what happened?" Confusion, disorientation, or fear may create inconsistencies in statements. Inconsistencies do not mean that the victim is lying. She may be avoiding certain items of information because she is psychologically traumatized, severely embarrassed, or worried about the reactions of a spouse, boyfriend, or some family member.

The goal of the preliminary interview should be to establish

1. a physical description of the offender or offenders;

2. the location or locations where the crime took place;

3. the identification of possible witnesses (Remember that even the fact that a witness can place the victim with an offender could be important. The fact that they "saw nothing" should not be a reason to dismiss them, or to refrain from obtaining their addresses and phone numbers.);

4. specific actions of the offender that are volunteered by the victim;

5. circumstances leading up to the attack;

6. information on any weapon or vehicle that may have been used;

7. specific information on the actual location of the assault (bedroom, back of a vehicle, etc.).

During the preliminary interview the officer must take care to be supportive and understanding. This is as important for female officers as it is for males. It is not unusual, subconsciously, to provide the victim with visual cues that indicate skepticism, disbelief, disapproval, or even hostility.

Unless there are very unusual circumstances, the interview should never be conducted in the presence of the husband, boyfriend, or other family member. In some cases the victim may insist on having a close friend in attendance. Again, this generally should be avoided unless a determination has been made that this will aid in the interview process.

The officer should refrain from telling individuals that the victim does not want them present; instead he or she should politely tell them that their presence is not advisable at this point and assure them that they will have an opportunity to speak to the victim as soon as possible. In some cases the victim may be afraid to face a husband, boyfriend, or parents who may be accusatory. An effort must be made by the investigator to be present, if at all possible, when the victim first meets with persons close to her after the assault. A victim-assistance counselor or psychologist can be of great assistance at this stage.

FOLLOW-UP INTERVIEWS

Follow-up interviews will usually be conducted by the investigator, and in some cases by the prosecutor. If the victim has recovered sufficiently to talk, this stage involves the development of specific information that will form the basis for a legal case. A trained rape counselor (many of whom have been victims of rape) with experience in handling and counseling rape victims can be of assistance in reassuring the victim. The use of counselors should be countenanced by department policy. Ground rules should be established for their utilization. The task of a counselor is not to conduct the interview; it is rather to lend support.

Ideally, the interview setting should be comfortable for the victim. Generally, the police station is to be avoided. The interview should be conducted with only the necessary people present—the investigator, the victim assistance counselor or psychologist, and perhaps the prosecutor. In some cases a stenographer may be needed. Doctors, nurses, police supervisors, and, of course, reporters are excluded; the fewer people, the better.

The investigator should ask the victim to tell her story from the beginning, apologize for having her repeat it, and explain that some questions may be asked again—not because the investigator does not believe her but because it will help later in conducting the investigation, arresting the perpetrator, and, most importantly, gaining a conviction. The investigator should explain that the more information the police have, the greater the likelihood that the case may not have to come to trial. The defendant is likely to plead guilty in cases in which the prosecutor has a lot of information.

The victim should be allowed to tell the story in her own words with minimal interruptions while the investigator makes notes of the areas in which more information is needed. The investigator should establish the basic points of information: who, what, when, where, how, and why. The elements of the crime must be established. Taking care not to "lead" the witness, the investigator should move from the general to the specific. If the victim appears uncomfortable providing the details of the commission of the crime, she should be allowed to come back to them later.

Many victims will have difficulty explaining certain sex acts. Questioning will be governed in large measure on the experience and comfort of the victim in providing graphic details. While taking care not to appear like a voyeur, the investigator should exhibit a sense of comfort in discussing the case.

In establishing the acts of the perpetrator, language familiar to the victim should be used. Terms such as *coitus, fellatio*, and *cunnilingus* may be alien to the victim. The investigator must not assume that the victim understands what has been said to her just because she nods agreement or says yes. She should explain what happened in her own words. If there are multiple acts, they should be identified and categorized in chronological order.

Because consent is a common defense against rape, care must be taken to determine the mind-set of the victim when the crime was committed. The actions of the perpetrator and the victim, including statements made and physical actions taken at that time, must be ascertained. The psychological state of the victim may have prompted her to acquiesce out of fear even though on the surface it may not appear that a threat was present. The victim's actions and words may be crucial to a conviction and must be carefully recorded.

Definitions

- **Coitus** – Physical union of male and female genitalia accompanied by rhythmic movements; sexual intercourse.
- **Cunnilingus** – Oral stimulation of the vulva or clitoris.
- **Fellatio** – Oral stimulation of the penis.
- **Rape** – Unlawful sexual activity, usually carried out forcibly or under threat of injury against the will usually of a female or with a person who is beneath a certain age or incapable of valid consent.
- **Sexual assault** – Illegal sexual contact that usually involves force upon a person without consent or is inflicted upon a person who is incapable of giving consent (as because of age or mental incapacity) or who places the assailant (as a family friend) in a position of trust or authority.
- **Statutory rape** – Sexual intercourse with a person who is below the age of consent as defined by law.

Source: *Merriam-Webster's Medical Dictionary*, 2006, pp. 168, 200, 304, 767, 829, 863.

Some victims may be reluctant to use profanity and may hesitate to repeat the words an offender used. Even some novice investigators have been known to omit profanity from reports even though it was used in a verbatim account of the crime.

The so-called "experience" or moral character of the victim may also be used against the victim during a trial, and the investigator should establish in detail what in the victim's mind constituted a lack of consent, and how or why the victim may have acquiesced. The fact that a suspect is unarmed and said to the victim, "I want to fuck you," and she acquiesced does not preclude rape if the victim felt she was being coerced. The fact that she had sexual intercourse with other men is immaterial.

In many cases there is a victim–suspect relationship, but this does not preclude forcible rape. In one case, the victim, who had been drinking, had sexual intercourse with one individual willingly, after which his friend entered the room and held her down and copulated with her, despite her protests and physical attempts to stop him. This is rape.

In recent years "date rape" has come to be a serious problem, one frequently ignored by authorities in the past. Greater recognition and sensitivity to this issue in society has prompted concern and action by law enforcement. In such cases the investigator must take special care in the interview phase to obtain information that establishes the sequence of events. The exact statements of the victim, witnesses, and the suspect may be crucial for prosecution. For this reason, it is important to try to record interviews.

The actions of the suspect after the act should also be determined if possible. Remarks initiated by the offender may constitute part of his MO. For example, phrases such as "I'll bet that's as good as you've had it" or "You liked it, didn't you?" reflect an inner need that is likely to be repeated with subsequent victims. Because the exact words used vary from rapist to rapist, phrases can characterize an MO and help to tie two or more rapes to one perpetrator. The victim may be able to provide other information that makes it possible to collect physical evidence linking the suspect to the scene. The suspect in one case went into the bathroom and discarded his and the victim's underwear in the toilet. The underwear was later recovered and used against him. In another case a suspect left a dress shirt in the garbage pail at the scene. He was linked to it through the laundry marks on the collar.

In developing a physical description of the offender, the investigator should make every effort to have the victim identify distinguishing marks or characteristics such as scars or tattoos—particularly those that are normally not visible. The investigator should ask if the offender was circumcised, and should be sure that the victim understands what circumcision is and what it looks like. If she does not know or is unsure, this should be noted, because the defense may try to lead the victim into a trap on this issue.

Interviews with the victim should be kept to a minimum; repeated interviews can cause trauma. On the other hand, the investigator must feel confident that all the necessary information has been collected. This may mean holding two or more sessions.

Interviews of witnesses in rape cases fall into two categories: (1) those who can testify that the offender was with the victim, and (2) those who may be able to testify to specific acts. Hostile witnesses may claim that the victim gave her consent; others may be ashamed at what they saw and might not want to cooperate.

With hostile witnesses efforts should be made to gather as much detail as possible. What they perceive as acquiescence may not be. In addition, if they are lying to help a friend, it may be possible to develop conflicting statements or descriptions of the actions. Such witnesses should be handled carefully; the investigator must not lead them in their responses.

Interviewing Children

Interviewing children requires great sensitivity and, unless there is an immediate necessity, these interviews should be conducted with the assistance of trained professionals.

Where there is an indication of rape or sexual abuse of a child, the offender is frequently known to the child. The investigator must keep in mind that the child may have been victimized by a parent. It is important to maintain eye contact, and to observe physical movements and the relationship between parent and child.

The preliminary interview may involve parents who have discovered that a crime has taken place. Often the suspect is known. In most cases in which such an allegation is made, the reporting officer need not conduct an interview immediately. It is better to wait for an investigator trained in such matters.

When a case of forcible rape or sexual abuse has just occurred, it may be necessary to conduct a preliminary interview. The child should be allowed to explain what happened in his or her own words. The investigator should try to secure an identification or physical description of the offender. Trained investigators, children's advocates, or counselors who are familiar with this type of investigation should be summoned immediately. The crime scene must be protected and the victim's garments obtained after taking the victim for medical attention. Several strategies commonly used to minimize the trauma of child victims include the use of anatomical dolls, drawings, and videotaped interviews.[12]

CONDUCTING THE INVESTIGATION

The investigation of sex-related offenses requires sensitivity. The investigator must be aware that the lives of victims, as well as alleged suspects, can be ruined through carelessness. The crime scene and the collection of physical evidence represent an important part of the initial phase of the investigation.

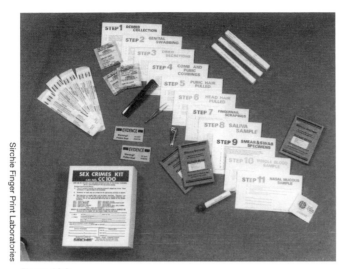

Sirchie Finger Print Laboratories

Figure 19.2
Sex crimes evidence collection kit.

Physical Evidence

In general, the collection of physical evidence in rape and sexual abuse cases should follow the recommendations outlined in Chapter 2. A sex crimes investigation kit should also be available to the investigator. These kits are designed to help in the collection and preservation of evidence, especially by medical personnel (see Figure 19.2).

The investigator should recognize that sex crimes may occur in multiple locations. Care should be taken to identify multiple crime scenes quickly, and immediate steps should be taken to protect them.

The goal of the crime scene search is to locate evidence that will:

1. link the victim and the offender to the crime scene;
2. establish that sexual relations took place;
3. establish that coercion, fear, or force was used; and
4. establish the offender's role or activity.

Establishing a link between the victim, offender, and crime scene may be necessary in cases in which the offender denies being present or claims that the victim was not present. This link has great investigative and probative significance. Rapid advances in DNA technology make establishing a link to the victim easier, especially when the suspect claims he was not present. In addition to fingerprint evidence, the investigator should look for evidence that may establish a DNA link. Cigarette butts, saliva, or blood, for example, can be especially important if the perpetrator used a condom.

In order to establish rape it is necessary to prove that penetration, however slight, took place. This is usually accomplished through a medical examination, which may show that intercourse took place. However, laboratory analyses may be hampered if the victim has taken a shower or douche. Analysis also can be impeded if the victim had intercourse with another individual just prior to the rape, or was attacked by more than one person. In the case mentioned earlier in which a victim had sexual intercourse with her boyfriend willingly, but awoke later to find that one of his "friends" had entered her room after he left and forced her to have sexual relations, the offender maintained that he had not had sexual intercourse, but instead merely had sat on the bed, propositioned the woman, and been refused. A crime scene search produced the victim's undergarments, which contained traces of semen. When examined to determine its blood group, the blood group found matched that of the accused, but differed from that of the victim and the boyfriend. When confronted with this evidence, the man confessed. Because it is more specific, modern DNA technology (testing for Y chromosomes) is even more helpful than blood grouping in resolving such an issue.

The use of force can be established through the recovery of weapons or material used to tie the victim down, or by showing the marks left through the use of force in restraining the victim. In one case involving a homicide, the rope fibers on a tree established that one of the victims had been tied to the tree.

Establishing the offender's actions or role can be accomplished in several ways, ranging from an analysis of the scene (such as moved furniture) to trace evidence and bloodstain patterns in different locations. In the case mentioned above, the offender denied being present at the scene. However, drops of his blood from a cut received in a struggle with one of the victims left a trail that not only established his presence, but also showed his movements and direction. It was established that he had not only been at the scene, but had moved to his vehicle and then returned to the scene.

Dale M. Moreau provides a list of some of the types of physical evidence that the investigator should be aware of and the means of collection and preservation that should be used with them (see Table 19.2).[13]

Table 19.2
Types of Physical Evidence and Their Collection Methods

Clothing	All clothing worn by the victim should be obtained and packaged in a sealed, secure condition. Each item must be packaged separately to avoid transfer of evidence from one item to another. Sections of Kraft-type paper or sturdy paper bags can be used for packaging purposes.
Head Hair	
Combing/Brushing	The head hair region of the victim should be combed or brushed for evidence. This requires an uncontaminated comb or brush used for the head area only. The comb or brush and adhering materials are then packaged and sealed.
Known Head Hairs	An appropriate amount of hair (one to two dozen hairs from each region sampled) to represent color, length, and area variation must be obtained. Hairs should be pulled whenever possible. Known hairs should be acquired after the head hair combing or brushing procedure is completed. These hairs are then separately packaged and sealed.
Pubic Hair	
Combing/Brushing	The pubic region of the victim should be combed or brushed for evidence. This requires an uncontaminated comb or brush for the pubic area only. The comb or brush and adhering materials are then packaged separately and sealed.
Known Pubic Hairs	An appropriate amount of pubic hair (one to two dozen hairs) to represent color, length, and area variation should be obtained. Hairs should be pulled whenever possible. Known pubic hairs should be acquired after the pubic hair combing or brushing procedure is completed. These hairs are packaged separately and sealed.
Combing/Brushing of Body Hair Regions Other Than Head and Pubic Area	In the event an individual is observed to have excessive body hair, a separate, uncontaminated comb or brush and appropriate packaging material can be used to collect any trace evidence that may be present.
Vaginal Swabbings	The vaginal cavity should be swabbed to detect the presence of spermatozoa or seminal fluid. An unstained control sample of the gathering medium must be retained and packaged separately.

Table 19.2
(Continued)

Oral Swabbings	The oral cavity should be swabbed to detect the presence of spermatozoa or seminal fluid. An unstained control sample of the gathering medium is retained and packaged separately.
Anal Swabbings	The anal region should be swabbed to detect the presence of spermatozoa or seminal fluid. An unstained control sample of the gathering medium is retained and packaged separately.
Microscope Slides of Smears Made from Vaginal, Oral, and Anal Swabbings	Any such slides prepared for the examination of spermatozoa should be retained along with the swabs used to prepare the smears.
Penile Swabbings	The penis should be swabbed to detect the presence of blood or other evidence. An unused control sample of the gathering medium is retained and packaged separately from the swab used to obtain the penile sample.
Vaginal Aspirate	In addition to vaginal swabbing, the vaginal vault should be irrigated with saline solution. Spermatozoa not obtained through the swabbing procedure may be recovered in this manner. The aspirate solution is placed in a separate tube or small vial. A control sample of the irrigation fluid is also retained and packaged separately.
Oral Rinse	The mouth of the person examined can be rinsed in order to remove spermatozoa not collected via the swabbing procedure. The rinse is expectorated into a tube or vial. A control sample of the rinse is retained and packaged separately.
Nasal Mucus Sample	This type of sample is acquired by having the individual being examined blow his or her nose on cloth. The mucus may contain spermatozoa that were deposited in the mouth or the facial area. An unstained portion of the cloth is needed as a control sample.
Fingernail Scrapings	Using appropriate materials (such as a flat wooden toothpick), the areas underneath the fingernails should be scraped for significant debris such as hairs, fibers, blood, or tissue. The gathering implement is retained. It is suggested that each hand be scraped individually and the resulting debris packaged separately.
Miscellaneous	
Debris Collection	Evidence substances not included in the previous discussion can often be observed during the examination of a person. Several individually packaged swabs or sections of cotton cloth should be available to collect such items as blood or semen found on the skin. Additionally, several separate containers should be included to collect debris taken from the clothing or body of the individual.
Known Blood	Blood should be drawn (by medical personnel) into a sterile test tube for blood grouping purposes. A minimum of 5 milliliters is recommended—preferably without the inclusion of a chemical anticoagulant or preservative.
Known Saliva	Saliva should be sampled from the person to assist in the determination of secretor status. An unstained control sample of the gathering medium is retained and packaged separately.
"Catch" Paper/Cloth	A section of paper or cloth should be provided on which the person (victim and suspect) can stand while undressing. Additionally, a separate piece of paper or cloth can be used to cover the examining table to collect any evidence that is dislodged during the examination. Such paper or cloth is carefully folded, marked, and sealed in a suitable container.

Physical evidence plays an important role in the prosecution of sexual assault cases. It helps establish the credibility of the victim and may be used to negate or support an offender's contentions. How the physical evidence is used will depend on the various elements of the case as it is being prepared. For example, fingernail scrapings from the victim may be used to tie the offender to the victim. Scrapings from the suspect may be used to place the suspect in a particular location as well as link him to the victim. Blood can be grouped and examined for its DNA pattern.

Some important considerations play a role in the use of physical evidence in both investigation and prosecution (see Table 19.3).

Table 19.3
Important Considerations for Physical Evidence

Blood	Modern blood-testing techniques make it possible for the laboratory to provide much more information than in the past. DNA analysis determines the genetic code that is unique to that individual; only identical twins will have the same genetic codes (see Chapter 2). Using this technique it may be possible to "individualize" the sample. Care must be taken in the collection of blood samples; efforts should be made to ensure that there is no mixing of body fluids.
Semen	Microscopic examination of semen may help determine if the sexual activity was recent. (Recent sexual activity will be indicated by live, mobile spermatozoa.) In most cases the crime laboratory deals with dead sperm because of the passage of time prior to examination. For this reason, if possible, a microscopic examination of a sample should be conducted as soon as possible. This is usually done in the hospital by a physician or trained medical microscopist. Semen can also provide evidence of blood type. More recent research indicates that it may be possible to identify an individual's genetic code by examining semen. Collecting semen samples from the victim will generally be handled at the hospital where rape "kits" should be available for use by a physician or nurse (see Figure 19.2). The investigator or crime scene technician should collect the clothing of the victim and the suspect whenever possible. Each item should be handled as a separate piece of evidence;under no circumstances should the garments be put in the same container. Care should also be taken with garments containing dried semen samples so that it does not flake off. They should not be folded as the semen sample may then crumble and be lost. In searching for semen samples it is common to use ultraviolet light because semen fluoresces. This is not a conclusive indication of semen, but it marks the area that should be handled carefully and protected.
Saliva	Saliva samples may be used to identify blood group and can also be used to identify genetic codes. Saliva is found less frequently than blood and semen; the properties of saliva make it look like water. Nevertheless, it may be possible to obtain a saliva sample from cigarettes, food, chewing gum, or bed sheets. It also may be present in bite marks on the victim. In collection, care should be taken not to touch the saliva directly as secretions on the fingers can contaminate it.
Hair	Hair can be taken from the head, chest, legs, or pubic area. Facial hair is less likely to be present unless the individual has a beard or mustache. An individual's DNA can be determined from a hair if the root is present.
Fibers	Fibers obtained from the suspect's clothing or from other material, such as rope or cord used to tie the victim, may be useful evidentiary material. Here again, it is important to note that each collection should be handled separately and clearly identified as to location.
Markings	Tool or weapon markings may be used to link the weapon or tool to the scene or victim, particularly if it is recovered in the possession of the suspect. For example, a screwdriver or other tool used in a forced entry may leave distinctive marks on the door or window. When a knife or other instrument is used as a weapon, it may be possible for a victim to identify, especially if it has any unusual characteristics.

When collecting or identifying physical evidence at the scene, particular care should be taken to note clearly where each piece of evidence is located. Do not rely on memory: use sketches, photographs, and notes.

Records and Other Sources of Information

The use of records and information in sex crimes cases follows the general pattern described earlier (see Chapter 5). However, a number of additional sources of information should be pursued.

The initial inquiry should be addressed either to the records department or crime analysis unit. A sex offender may have a prior arrest record, although not necessarily for rape. If another crime accompanied the rape, such as burglary or robbery, it is possible that the perpetrator committed the sex offense as a "crime of opportunity."

A computerized record system may be able to assist the investigator in identifying possible suspects based on physical description, prior arrests, or MO. The crime analysis unit may help by recognizing similar cases that can be compared to the present one. This effort should include queries to surrounding jurisdictions and, if the information obtained provides additional details, it is wise to follow up by querying other jurisdictions as well.

Unlike most other crimes, the sex offense may have a "specific" motive known only to the perpetrator. Do not assume that it was solely for sexual gratification. Rape is rarely associated with sexual gratification, and is more likely associated with a need for power.

The nature of the attack may also provide valuable clues. The type of weapon, geographical location, time of day, and the suspect's actions can all link him to other crimes or to past activities. In addition to law enforcement records, the investigator may want to explore other sources.

Profiling Offenders

In recent years emphasis has been placed on the development of rape offender profiles. Much of this research was pioneered by the Federal Bureau of Investigation's Behavioral Science Unit, part of the National Center for the Analysis of Violent Crime located in Quantico, Virginia. The methodology employed by the FBI in profiling violent offenders through the ViCAP program involves information collected from police departments, interviews with convicted offenders, and research results published by social scientists.

The FBI will assist local agencies on request. These requests usually should be made through the profile coordinator at the local FBI office. Police departments are asked to complete the ViCAP forms on offenders, which are then computerized at Quantico. The rape offender profile is based on the theory that an individual displays unique characteristics in personality, crime scene behavior, and method of operation.

The investigator should be aware that many of the commonly held assumptions about rape and rapists are inaccurate. Many rapists are married; they are not necessarily oversexed, they are not necessarily women-haters. Most are employed—but some are not, and their intelligence levels vary significantly. On the other hand, there are likely to be clues in the crime itself that can assist the investigator and that are believed to be subject to profiling.

The majority of rape offenders are not psychotic, but virtually all of them have deeply rooted psychological problems. According to A. Nicholas Groth, a psychologist who specializes in the study of sexual assault:

> Some men who ordinarily would never commit a sexual assault commit rape under very extraordinary circumstances, such as in wartime, but the likelihood of such a person's being a repetitive offender is very low. There are other men, however, who find it very difficult to meet the ordinary or unusual demands of life, and the stresses that we all learn to tolerate are unendurable and overwhelming to these individuals. The extent to which they find most life demands frustrating, coupled with their inability to tolerate frustration and their reliance on sex as the way of overcoming their distress, make the likelihood of their being a repetitive offender very high. Furthermore, they constitute an immediate and ongoing threat to the safety of the community.[14]

The investigator may find that a profile of the offender will assist in reducing or narrowing the range of potential suspects through identification of social and demographic characteristics.

In a study of 170 men who were convicted of sexually assaulting adults and 178 who were convicted of sexually assaulting children, Groth identified the following patterns for various types of rape:[15]

1. *Gang Rape.* In 9 percent of the cases in the study, the sexual offense involved more than one assailant. Most of these cases (90%) involved one victim; 77 percent involved offenders between the ages of 17 and 27.

2. *Elderly Rape.* In 18 percent of the cases, the suspect sexually assaulted a woman who was significantly older; in 12 percent, women over the age of 50 were attacked. Offenders were most likely to be young, white, single males, ranging in age from 12 to 38; 43 percent were in their twenties. All of the offenders showed life adjustment difficulties beginning with adolescence.

3. *Child Rape.* The individual who rapes children is likely to come from a disadvantaged background. He is usually relatively young and is rarely beyond age 40. Rape of children appears to be more class-related, the act is frequently devoid of a sexual or emotional involvement, and the suspect attacks different victims.

In their pioneering work on sexual homicide, Robert K. Ressler, Ann W. Burgess, and John E. Douglas developed a model for the criminal profile generating process (see Figure 19.3).[16]

Profiling aids a reasoned, systematic process for the investigation of rape and reduces the possibility of investigative error. In sex-related homicides there is a good possibility that the offender will strike again or that he has committed other crimes. Although the techniques for investigating a sex-related homicide are similar to those in any homicide investigation, this type of crime has unique characteristics that should be considered. The motivation of the offender may or may not have been homicide, but in most cases the perpetrator set out to commit a sexual assault. An exception to this is a sex-related homicide during a burglary or robbery in which the offender rapes and kills merely because a victim is present.

Of particular importance is the length of time the perpetrator remains at the scene. The longer he is there, the higher the probability of leaving trace evidence and other information that may assist in developing background information. Moreover, because the offender is likely to commit more than one attack, it is possible to bring together information from other crimes to develop a composite database.

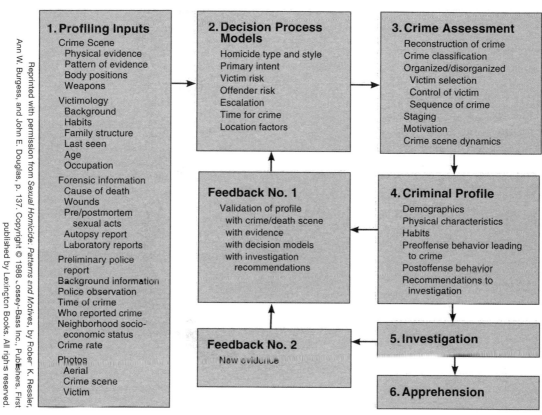

Figure 19.3
Criminal profile generating process.

Hazelwood and Warren, in a study of 41 serial rapists, found that:[17]

76 percent had been sexually abused as children

71 percent had been married at least once

54 percent had generally stable employment

52 percent scored above average on intelligence tests

51 percent had served in the armed forces

36 percent collected pornography

The mobility of American society makes it possible for an offender to commit crimes in many different states. Thus, every attempt should be made to share information with other jurisdictions.

FOLLOW-UP ACTIVITIES

The investigation of sexual assault requires an objective, reasoned approach. A sympathetic understanding of the trauma of the victim should be combined with an unemotional attitude toward the suspect. The investigator should not judge or let personal emotions interfere with the investigation. His or her primary task is to identify the perpetrator and build a case for prosecution. However, the emotional factors involved in such investigations create a greater probability of making mistakes.

When a suspect has been identified, the investigator should carefully check out the alibi and any other items of information that might serve to support the suspect's statements.

The use of police sketches, Identi-Kit images, or computerized graphics can be of particular use if the victim or witnesses can provide detailed descriptive information. However, the investigator should recognize that eyewitness identification frequently is flawed. For this reason, identification through sketches, photographs, or even lineups should be considered with caution. All too often there is a tendency to couple an eyewitness identification with a prior record as a basis for prosecution. Such evidence, though valuable, should be combined with a thorough investigation that endeavors to tie the suspect to the crime scene, to link him or her to the victim, and to counter any defense contentions of mistaken identity.

In many cases the offender will say that the victim actually induced the crime. Such claims may be difficult to prove in court; it is the investigator's responsibility, however, to explore all contentions, keeping in mind that the victim's background or reputation does not have any bearing on whether she was assaulted. Although interviews are an important part of this phase of the investigation, there are other ways in which an individual's statements can be verified or disproved. Contradictory statements, errors of fact, and descriptive comments should be explored during interrogation. For this reason it is important to keep good notes and to record statements if possible.

As the case progresses and more information becomes available, the investigator should maintain a set of computerized cross-referenced files for ease of access and comparison. Further, because there may be information available from other cases or from prior records, information management is particularly important.

In cases in which a suspect has a prior record, it is frequently useful to review court records or case and investigative reports for information. Information on *modus operandi*, accomplices, weapons, locations, and statements may all prove important.

It is important that photographic evidence be reviewed carefully. The investigator should scrupulously review crime scene sketches, laboratory reports, and witness statements. The review of evidence is particularly important in preparing the case for prosecution.

CONCLUSION

Sex crimes by their very nature arouse repugnant feelings and they can be difficult crimes to investigate for many of the reasons noted above. In many police departments sex crime investigations are handled by women for what may seem like obvious reasons. But, it should be noted that male detectives should not be excluded from such investigations because each case is unique. The most important factor is the ability to communicate with the victim or witnesses, and in most cases the offender will be a male who may feel inhibited talking to a female. Understanding the elements of the crime, and particularly the interviewing and interrogation techniques that are peculiar to this type of investigation, calls for experienced detectives, whether they are male or female.

Notes

[1]   http://bjs.ojp.usdoj.gov/content/pub/pdf/cv10.pdf; http://www.bjs.gov/content/pub/pdf/cvus05.pdf

[2]   Bureau of Justice Statistics, Office of Justice Programs. See http://bjs.ojp.usdoj.gov/content/pub/pdf/cv10.pdf

[3]   Ronald M. Holmes, "Stalking in America: Types and Methods of Criminal Stalkers." *Journal of Contemporary Criminal Justice*, 9:4 (1993), 317–327.

[4]   Robin Hattersly Gray. "Stopping Stalkers." *Campus Safety Magazine*. January February, 2012. Pp. 14–17. See also National Center for Victims Crime: Stalking Resource Center. Center for Disease Control and Prevention. U.S. Bureau of Justice Statistics 2009.

[5]   Katrina Baum, Shannon Catalano, Michael Rand, & Kristina Rose, *Stalking Victimization in theUnited States* (Washington, DC: U.S. Department of Justice, Bureau of Justice Statistics, 2009), 1–3.

[6]   Ibid.

[7]   Vernon Geberth. "Stalkers." *Law and Order*, 40 (Oct. 1992), 138–143.

[8]   Holmes, supra note 3.

[9]   Katrina Baum, Shannon Catalano and Michael Rand, "Stalking Victimization in the United States." Bureau of Justice Statistics: Special Report. U.S. Justice Department. January, Washington, DC 2009.

[10] See the web site of the U.S. Postal Inspection Service at http://www.usps.com/postalinspectors/

[11] Rolando V. del Carmen, Susan E. Ritter, and Betsy A. Witt, *Briefs of Leading Cases in Corrections*, 5th ed. (Newark, NJ: LexisNexis Matthew Bender, 2008), 340–341.

[12] Brian K. Payne and Randy R. Gainey, *Family Violence and Criminal Justice: A Life-Course Approach*, 3rd ed. (New Providence, NJ: LexisNexis Matthew Bender), 2009.

[13] Robert R. Hazelwood and Ann Wolkert Burgess, eds., *Practical Aspects of Rape Investigation: A Multidisciplinary Approach*, 2nd ed. (Boca Raton, FL: CRC Press, 1955).

[14] A. Nicholas Groth, with Jean Birnbaum, *Men Who Rape: The Psychology of the Offender* (New York: Plenum Press, 1979), 7.

[15] Ibid., 110–192.

[16] Robert K. Ressler, Ann W. Burgess, and John E. Douglas, *Sexual Homicide: Patterns and Motives* (Lexington, MA: Lexington Books, 1988), 137.

[17] Robert R. Hazelwood and Janet Warren, "The Serial Rapist: His Characteristics and Victims," *FBI Law Enforcement Bulletin*, 58:1 (Jan. 1989), 10–17.

Discussion Questions

1.   What were the major revisions made in Uniform Crime Reporting 2012 with reference to rape?

2.   What elements involve the legal definition of rape?

3.   What other types of sex crimes should the investigator be familiar with?

4.   What is the relationship of the Internet to sex crimes?

5.   What is a common characteristic of crime scenes in rape cases?

6.   What must the investigating officer be aware of during a preliminary interview of a victim?

7.   Why is consent, or lack of consent, of the victim important in rape investigations?

8.   Why can a rape offender profile be valuable in an investigation?

SUPPLEMENTAL READINGS

Carney, T. P. (2004). *Practical investigation of sex crimes: A strategic and operational approach* (3rd ed.). Boca Raton, FL: CRC Press.

Douglas, J., & Olshaker, M. (1999). *The anatomy of motive: The FBI's legendary mindhunter explores the key to understanding and catching violent criminals.* New York: Scribner.

Hazelwood, R. R., & Wolbert Burgess, A. (2009). *Practical aspects of rape investigation: A multidisciplinary approach* (4th ed.). Boca Raton, FL: CRC Press.

Holmes, S. T., & Holmes, R. M. (2009). *Sex crimes: Patterns and behavior* (3rd ed.). Los Angeles: Sage.

LeBeau, M. A., & Mozayani, A. (2001). *Drug-Facilitated sexual assault: A forensic handbook.* San Diego, Boston: Elsevier/Academic Press.

Savino, J., & Turvey, B. (2011). *Rape investigation handbook.* Boston: Elsevier/Academic Press.

CHAPTER 20

BURGLARY

INTRODUCTION

Burglary is a difficult crime to investigate. Success depends in large measure on the actions of the initial officer on the scene, and the efforts of crime scene technicians, the crime lab and fingerprint analysts. The dogged determination of the investigator in using interviewing skills, crime pattern analysis, and available records to identify a suspect is critical to successful investigations. Burglary is a crime that affects all strata of society. Losses range from relatively small amounts to millions of dollars; burglary suspects can have widely varying degrees of skill and expertise. In 2010, there were more than two million burglaries, costing victims an estimated $4.6 billion in lost property; overall, the average dollar loss per burglary offense was $2,119. Burglary accounted for 23.8 percent of the estimated number of property crimes committed in 2008.[1]

All too frequently, and particularly in the inner city, burglaries are given short shrift by the police, who may be deluged with large numbers of violent crimes against the person. Although burglary is viewed as a property crime in the Uniform Crime Reports, it has a direct impact on the victims who frequently feel violated by the offense. In many cases, although the burglary may not appear serious in terms of its dollar value, it may deprive a family of its most valued possessions.

Burglary affects a large segment of society. It is estimated that more than 70 percent of all households will be burglarized at least once over a 20-year period, and almost one-half of all urban residences will be victimized two or more times. According to the Bureau of Justice Statistics, the probability of being a household burglary victim is higher in the central city, in homes headed by younger people, in residences where six or more people live, and in homes in which the head of household is black.[2]

More than 60.5 percent of all burglaries involved forcible entry, and more than 33 percent were unlawful entries (without force); the remaining 6.4 percent were forcible entry attempts. Burglary occurs more often in the summer months. About 74 percent of burglaries were of residential properties. Most daytime burglaries involved residential facilities, whereas nonresidential burglaries occurred slightly more at night.[3]

The National Crime Victimization Survey has indicated that many rapes, robberies, and aggravated and simple assaults in the home occurred during an illegal entry.[4]

Although difficult to investigate, burglary usually offers a relatively large number of clues. The expanding capabilities of single-digit fingerprint systems, such as AFIS, and breakthroughs in DNA analysis offer significant tools in burglary investigations. Research indicates that the preliminary analysis of a burglary case can provide "solvability factors" that make it possible to focus on those cases with the highest probability of being solved.[5] Burglary investigation can bring a high degree of satisfaction to the person who is truly interested in the elements of solving a mystery.

Definitions

The Model Penal Code of the American Law Institute defines *burglary* as follows:

> A person is guilty of burglary if he enters a building or occupied structure, or separately secured or occupied portion thereof, with purpose to commit a crime therein, unless the premises are at the time open to the public or the actor is licensed or privileged to enter. It is an affirmative defense to prosecution for burglary that the building or structure was abandoned.[6]

The Uniform Crime Reports define burglary as the unlawful entry of a structure to commit a felony or theft. The use of force is not required to classify an offense as burglary.[7]

Although burglary is generally considered a property crime, it is important for the investigator to recognize that a theft need not be committed to establish a burglary charge.

PEOPLE

Victims

Burglaries take many forms and affect victims in different ways. The homeowner who loses a personal heirloom or other personal property—which may have little monetary value—may be more devastated than the businessperson who loses millions of dollars worth of insured goods.

Understanding the type of burglary, the characteristics of the offense, and the demographic characteristics of the victim can provide insight into the suspect and his or her background. For example, burglaries of middle-class or poor residences are more likely to be committed by juveniles, and the probability increases in cases in which entry is through a broken window, and again when the search appears to have been haphazard and the property taken is varied rather than specific. Burglaries in hotels are more likely to be committed by an older, more experienced professional. In a residential burglary, the method of entry and exit, as well as the type of search, will provide information about the suspect. (More experienced burglars will frequently unlock all the doors and even windows in a residence in order to exit quickly in case the owner returns.) The more professional burglar searches methodically (e.g., emptying drawers on the bed one at a time, then pulling the contents off after sifting through each one; see Figure 20.1); uses a specific type of tool for entry; takes only valuable property; and concentrates on wealthier victims. As one burglar put it, "You'll do time for a big job as well as a small job, so why increase the risks with a lot of small scores?"

Most commercial or business burglaries require a greater degree of expertise and frequently more planning than a residential burglary. Nevertheless, many burglars operate with very little planning or "casing" of the target and the victim. In burglaries involving large amounts of merchandise or very valuable property there is likely to be an inside informant working with the burglar. This is especially true in businesses that have a high employee turnover; it is important to ask the victim about employment records.

In addition to providing information about property stolen, the victim should be asked to review the past few weeks and recall any unusual events or the presence of individuals who seemed out of the ordinary. Other questions that might produce information of interest include:

- Is there anything unique about the timing of the burglary (e.g., valuables were there only on certain days, such as payroll money)?

- Have there been prior attempts or successful burglaries?

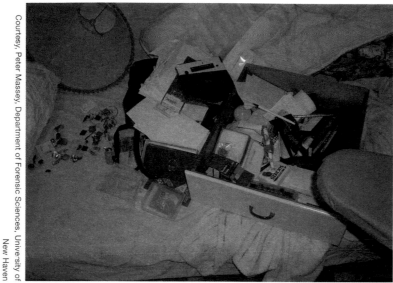

Courtesy, Peter Massey, Department of Forensic Sciences, University of New Haven

Figure 20.1
A burglary crime scene. Note how the perpetrator went through the drawer seeking valuables. The jewelry lies to the left of the drawer, which usually indicates a more sophisticated burglar who turns out drawers on a bed, then shakes each drawer off to search additional drawers.

- Who knew about the property and its location?
- Is the property unique, including items such as art objects?
- Have there been similar burglaries?
- Did any publicity appear in local newspapers (e.g., notification of a wedding indicating that people won't be at home)?

The Public

Although conventional wisdom holds that there are few witnesses to burglaries, in reality there are likely to be many more than one might suspect. In most cases the police make a cursory or half-hearted attempt to locate witnesses. A careful canvass of the immediate area should be made as soon as possible with a view to identifying or developing descriptions of potential suspects. If some time has passed since the burglary occurred, it may be worthwhile to interview persons who might have been on the scene at or near the time of the burglary. For example, in residential burglaries, besides neighbors, the canvass might also include the mail carrier, delivery persons, utility meter readers, and telephone company workers, among others. Residents should be asked if they observed any other individuals or suspicious vehicles in the vicinity.

One should also keep in mind that persons who are "out of place," such as juveniles during school hours, or "strange" vehicles and unusual activity at the burglary site may not be thought important by witnesses at first. Careful questioning can uncover this information.

In addition to witnesses at the scene, there will also be witnesses at the point where the property is disposed. Although these witnesses are not likely to be cooperative, pointing out that linking the stolen goods to the burglary could result in a charge of receiving stolen property will frequently elicit their cooperation. Of course, without adequate property identification this avenue is less hopeful.

Informants or petty criminals on the fringe of illegal activity in a neighborhood also can be a source of information. Most good burglary detectives have a good informant network, and are tied in with other sources of information, such as beat patrol officers, bartenders, truant officers, playground attendants, and other individuals who pick up information on illegal activities. Cultivating such sources is an important component of the investigator's work.

The Burglary Suspect

Professional burglaries represent different challenges. When large amounts of merchandise or warehouse goods are taken, identification of the truck or other vehicle used is important. Here again, witnesses may have seen the truck at or near the scene. The vehicle may even have received a traffic citation. Witnesses should be asked about vehicles that were out of place, such as a van where tractor trailers usually park, or whether there was an inordinate number of people on the truck (usually, a truck only has a driver and loader on it).

A sympathetic and unhurried approach to questioning the victim is important, not only because it helps alleviate much of the stress associated with victimization, but also because details provided about what has been stolen, the *modus operandi* of the burglar, or other aspects of the case may become critical as the investigation proceeds. Stolen items overlooked in the initial report may provide the link that helps solve the case. Items with serial numbers or individual marks, custom-made jewelry, original artwork, documents such as checkbooks or stock certificates, and even keys or personal tools taken by the burglar may be recovered later. In most cases the burglar will dispose of stolen items through a fence or even directly on the street, but some items may be kept for personal use.

In addition to stealing property, the offender may do things at the scene of the crime that can help identify or link him or her to the scene of the crime at a later date. One burglar thought it clever to leave disparaging notes on the walls of his victims' homes. When he was eventually apprehended, he was surprised to learn that handwriting analysis helped add several years to his sentence because the prosecution was able to charge him with multiple crimes. Other burglars may take food from the refrigerator, use the victim's facilities (perhaps to make phone calls), or display other forms of aberrational behavior that help establish a *modus operandi*.

Harry O'Reilly, a former New York City burglary detective who is something of a legend for his ability to solve cases, identified some of the more common techniques used by burglars to gain entry:[8]

> *Prying*: The use of a jimmy, screwdriver, tire iron, pry bar, or knife to force a door, window, or lock. The perpetrator may leave tool impressions on the point of entry (see Figure 20.2).
>
> *Picking*: Using a knife or professional locksmith's picks to open the cylinder of a lock.
>
> *Pulling*: Using an auto body repair tool called a dent puller or "slap hammer" to pull the lock's cylinder out.
>
> *Smash and crash*: Simply breaking a window to gain entry, and in the case of a store, reaching in and grabbing articles on display.

Cutting glass: Using a glass cutter to make a hole in order to reach in and open a lock or unfasten the latch. A small suction cup may be used, such as a toy dart, to keep the glass from falling inside and making noise. After the cut is made around the suction cup, the burglar simply pulls the glass out.

Slipping lock or "loiding": Originally celluloid strips were used, hence the term loiding, but they are frequently replaced now by credit cards and pocket knives (the knife may be filed down to make it narrower) or other thin objects, such as nail files, that are less identifiable as a burglar's tools. The card is slipped between the lock and the door jamb where there is no "dead bolt" or other latch.

Brute force: Kicking, breaking, or forcing a door with the body or an instrument. Where a door has been kicked in, the perpetrator may leave shoe or sneaker impressions.

Removing door panel: Kicking in or breaking the door panel, or unscrewing the panel on an aluminum door.

Entry through windows: Entry through windows is usually accomplished by breaking a hole through a pane and removing the broken glass so that the latch can be reached. In order to minimize the

Figure 20.2
Burglar's tools: on the left, a pry bar or jimmy; on the right, a lock and chain cutter.

noise from falling glass, the burglar may press a rag against the window; sometimes adhesive tape may be used. In some cases, the burglar may remove the entire window pane by removing the putty holding the glass in place. Entry may also be gained by forcing in a tool to push back a window latch. In such cases, tool marks should be looked for and samples of wood and paint should be taken for comparison if a tool is later found. A prybar, screwdriver, or other tool is also sometimes used in forcing a window.

Entry through doors: A burglar usually opens a door by using a prybar and jamb around the lock until either the bolt can be pushed back or the bolt is actually freed from the striker plate. This may be done by mere pressure from the body or by inserting a jack horizontally across the door frame. The lock might also be made accessible through a hole that is drilled, sawed, or broken in a door panel. Far too many doors are fitted with glass that is simply broken so that the lock may be reached. Entry can also be gained by cutting the hinge pins off by means of a bolt cutter. More commonly, however, the pins are simply knocked out with hammer and chisel or screwdriver.

Entry through basement windows and skylights: These windows are forced in the same manner as ordinary windows, but the investigator should pay special attention to the possibility that the burglar's clothes may have become torn and cloth fragments or fibers may have been left behind.

Entry through walls: Walls are either broken by tools or by explosives. A brick wall is easily broken by a hammer and chisel or a sledge hammer. In blasting, a hole is usually chiseled between two bricks and the charge is inserted. Small hydraulic jacks may be used to force holes into a wall.

Entry through floors: This method of entry is often preferred in the case of warehouses or other buildings that have a crawl space underneath. The burglar usually drills or saws a hole in the floorboards large enough to crawl through. Entry through walls and floors is also made when the criminal suspects or knows that the premises are protected by burglary alarms on doors and windows.

Safe cracking: A very specialized form of burglary that may involve burning, blasting, punching (see Figure 20.3), chopping (through the bottom) ripping, cutting, or peeling a safe.

"Second-story" job: Gaining entry to warehouses, factories, and other businesses through upper floor windows or roof.

Chicago Police Department

Figure 20.3
Broken safe, opened by punching through its dial.

This is only a partial list of burglary techniques, but it is important to recognize that it contributes in large measure to efforts to determine *modus operandi*. In addition to technique, a burglary typology can serve as a frame of reference for the investigator. Figure 20.4 is a matrix that may be useful in this effort if completed at the start of the investigation and compared with similar forms on file for previous burglary cases. If some common thread, such as an MO, is recognized, clues from the crimes can be pooled in an attempt to develop a suspect.

In burglaries of businesses, particularly where entry may have been gained through an adjoining wall or over a roof, it is likely that the perpetrator cased the location on a prior occasion. Employees should be asked about persons who either acted strangely, or asked questions about the building, or lingered for a long time.

In questioning burglary witnesses it is difficult to develop good physical descriptions unless the burglar had a distinguishing facial feature, such as a mustache. Because most witnesses will probably not be able to identify the suspects, this effort may serve mainly to develop general descriptions or other items of information. In such cases, the smallest details put together over several burglaries may help to develop a composite that leads to identification of the suspect.

CONDUCTING THE INVESTIGATION

Repetition is a predominant characteristic of burglary. Burglaries are generally committed over and over again until eventually the suspect is caught. Unfortunately, in most cases, very little information from one burglary to another is exchanged by investigators, which makes it difficult to clear cases. One of the best sources of information on prior cases is the patrol force. Officers collect a great deal of information, but even over a relatively small geographical area there may be five or more officers working during a seven-day period. When one considers the number of officers in a city or county, it becomes clear that much information is lost for lack of collation or analysis. Few burglary reports are designed to collect the unique elements of information that make it possible for the investigator to link prior cases. Fortunately, there has been significant progress over the past decade in this area. A number of forms now collect information that can help solve the crime rather than simply report it. However, the value of a report is

	RESIDENCE Apartment / house	BUSINESS Office / factory	OTHER Tractor trailer / warehouse, etc./ recreation vehicle, boat, etc./ hotel. etc.
1. Occupied Not occupied			

2. Day (Dawn to dusk)
   Evening
   (Dusk to midnight)			

3. Night (Midnight to dawn)			
4. Actual time			

5. Entry through:
   Door
   Window
   Roof
   Wall			

6. Means
   (See list of techniques
   in text.)			

7. Victim type
   Poor
   Middle class
   Wealthy
   Shop owner
   Business/corporation			

8. Search method
   Haphazard
   Specific area
   Methodical overall			

9. Characteristics in
   addition to theft:
   Property damage
   Murder / assault / rape
   Eat food
   Graffiti
   Other MO aspects			

10. Number of offenders
   Single
   Two
   More than two			

Figure 20.4
Burglary typology and method matrix.

only as good as the information collected. Patrol officers should be trained and supervised properly, and proper credit should be given to them when they provide information that helps solve a case.

Because the majority of burglaries are residential, and because research suggests that many of these are committed by juveniles, a good deal of information may be found on the street. In addition to the patrol force, juvenile courts, youth squads, and other youth service agencies may be of assistance.

Investigation of large professional burglaries, which may involve multiple jurisdictions, requires communication with other agencies. Major case squads will frequently be established, and information on their activities and sources of contact should be available. In some jurisdictions, such units meet periodically to discuss ongoing or unusual cases.

Professional associations and business groups, particularly those affiliated with the insurance industry, also can be valuable to the burglary investigator. In addition to providing information on specific groups, such associations can provide the investigator with other helpful information—such as burglary techniques being used, types of property most frequently attacked, and kinds of merchandise in greatest demand.

Research on burglary and burglars provides some information that will help the burglary investigator better understand the dynamics and career patterns of the crime. Generally, burglary offenders begin their careers at a young age, acting with other juveniles in break-ins or burglaries. In 2010, 22.7 percent of burglary arrests were of juveniles, with 6.2 percent under the age of 15. These percentages decreased in comparison to 2007, when 27 percent of burglary arrests were of juveniles, with 8.1 percent under the age of 15. White juveniles accounted for 61.7 percent of arrests, and black juveniles about 36.5 percent. In 2007, white juveniles accounted for 67 percents of arrests, and black juveniles about 31 percent. About 13 percent of all burglaries were cleared by arrest or exceptional means.[9]

Some offenders turn to more violent forms of crime, but career burglary patterns usually emerge, and some individuals develop specialties in certain types of acts, such as safe or art burglaries.[10]

Wright and Decker interviewed 105 burglars, finding that more than 50 percent had committed 50 or more burglaries during their criminal careers.[11] Table 20.1 illustrates how a burglary career develops over time.

Juvenile burglars commonly operate with an accomplice, and are even more likely to work in groups of three or more. More sophisticated burglars may operate in pairs, but research on them is inconclusive. The professional burglar will frequently operate with a lookout, and may use cell phones or walkie-talkies to communicate.

Most burglaries are not well planned. The choice of target is likely to be based on whether the perpetrator views it as an easy mark. An easy mark would be a place such as an unlighted residence, or one with high hedges, old windows, or easily opened doors. A small percentage of thrill-seeking perpetrators, commonly called "cat burglars," enter homes when residents are present, usually at night, and try to accomplish the crime without arousing the occupants.

In recent years there has been an increase in home invasions, in which a residence is entered while an individual or a family is present. These are usually carried out by groups or gangs, who may often commit crimes such as robbery, assault, rape, or murder. The viciousness of these crimes often defies imagination, and makes home invasions a high investigative priority. For the most part, though, burglars are looking for quick cash or goods they can fence. Tracking stolen property offers another avenue of investigation.

Patterns in the rates of household burglary and property theft have been similar to that of overall property crime. Households in the two lowest income categories—less than $7,500 per year and $7,500 to

Table 20.1
The Burglar's Career Path

BURGLAR	JUVENILE OFFENDER	LATE TEENS/ EARLY 20s	MID-20s/ EARLY 30s	CAREER BURGLAR
Activity Range	Usually close to home.	Wider pattern; use of vehicle for transportation.	Operates over a broad area; crosses jurisdictions.	May operate anywhere.
Burglary	Not planned well.	Better planned, but usually target of opportunity.	Selects targets; some planning.	Well-planned and researched; or uses a set MO.
Type	Residential.	Residential, or easy business target.	Business, some residential.	Corporations, larger businesses; specific wealthy targets.
Property Stolen	Anything in the open or easily taken.	Money, jewels.	Specific types of property or valuables, e.g., computers.	Very specific valuable targets.

$14,999 per year—were victims of burglary and theft at higher or marginally higher rates than households in all other income categories. For household burglary, the rate for households with six or more persons was higher than that for households in most other income categories. According to victimization surveys, 50 percent of burglaries and 31 percent of household thefts were reported to the police.[12]

Many burglars are drug addicts who can frequently be identified by the types of property they take. They usually fall into the second or third category of burglars listed in Table 20.1, but exhibit less sophistication in their activities. These burglars commonly steal television sets and other easily disposable items.

Some burglars turn to robbery (the taking of property from a person by force) as they get older. Relatively few become professional burglars, but those who do develop a high level of expertise in planning and carrying out their crimes.

Physical Evidence

For purposes of identifying perpetrators and making a case that will hold up in court, a wealth of physical evidence is usually available. Unfortunately, for a variety of reasons, crime scene searches are conducted in only a few cases, usually only where there has been a large loss, or where another serious crime such as assault, rape, or homicide is involved.

Research indicates that most crime scenes contain much more physical evidence than is discovered. Fingerprints are the most common form of evidence sought in a crime scene search, and other items of trace evidence and materials are often overlooked. Trace evidence can establish a link between the perpetrator and the crime scene. Blood, saliva, footprints, hair, and fibers may be present. The suspect may also leave behind items such as cigarettes, matchbooks, tools, clothing, or handwriting.

Successful crime scene processing begins with the initial officer on the scene. Even though a decision may be made not to call in an evidence technician, a crime scene search can and should be conducted. (See Chapter 3 for a method of conducting a crime scene search.)

Bear in mind that what may seem trivial at first may later prove to be a key piece of evidence. In one case, a matchbook containing no more than a woman's name in it enabled an investigator to clear up a string of burglaries. The matchbook had come from a local bar. The investigator located the woman, who said she had written her name on it for a guy she met there. This information, coupled with a sole print on a kitchen floor from an athletic shoe, tied the suspect to the scene. He also had a habit of eating food at the residences, which linked him to other crimes. The chipped screwdriver with which he forced doors provided further evidence when investigators went back to the scenes. Confronted with the evidence, the suspect admitted to more than 100 residential burglaries. The case was solved by an investigator who followed up a lead that some might have disregarded.

The search for physical evidence at a burglary scene will frequently require the assistance of the victim, who can be very helpful in identifying what has been moved or what does not belong. Often overlooked are toolmarks, personal items such as discarded cigarettes and matchbooks, and footprints outside the house (e.g., below windows). As indicated earlier, burglars often eat and drink whatever is available in the kitchen of the burgled home, thereby leaving traces of their DNA on a cup, bottle, or utensil used to consume the food or drink. It is through attention to the collection and examination of details that the British police have significantly increased the number of solved burglary cases.

As noted, one of the more promising advances in scientific criminal investigation has been the Automated Fingerprint Identification System (AFIS), which makes it possible to search criminal records for a single latent print.[13] This system is of particular value to burglary investigations, in which latent prints generally represent the most common form of physical evidence available. The utilization of evidence technicians at burglary crime scenes increases the probability of collecting latent prints.

AFIS technology is based on the ability to electronically scan and identify fingerprint characteristics and store them in digital form in a computer. Using ridge endings and bifurcations it is possible to create a digitized representation of the print, which can be stored in the computer (see Figure 20.5).

Although frequently overlooked, latent fingerprints represent a potential source of information that should not be ignored. Unlike for most other crimes, the suspect is usually in the house for some period of time and, because he or she is looking for things, objects are touched. In addition to the more common locations processed by crime scene technicians, other areas should be examined, including:

- beer and soda cans in the garbage
- items in the refrigerator that may have been touched, moved, or bitten—leaving a print or a bite mark
- toilet seat and the nearby wall
- the bottoms of dresser drawers that may have been removed for searching
- window locks that may have been opened from the inside as a means of escape in the event that the owner returned
- documents that may have been handled

On a rolled inked print, usually obtained from a prior arrest, it is possible to find 90 or more points on each finger, making the print distinguishable from all other single-digit prints. When a

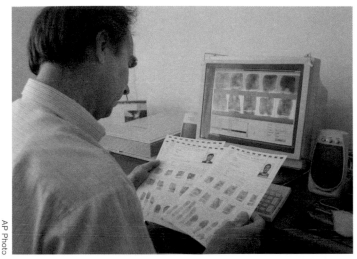

Figure 20.5
A specialist of the AFIS (Automatic Fingerprinting Identification System) compares fingerprints. Because latent prints are often the most common form of physical evidence
available for a burglary, AFIS is of particular value to burglary investigations.

latent (partial) print is recovered at the crime scene, it can be run through the system for a match.
Even a poorly developed partial print may provide enough information to conduct a successful search.
It takes just minutes to accomplish a 10-print search in a file of about 5,000 records, although it may
take longer to search for a match to a partial, single print. The ability of the investigator to provide
the names or record numbers of potential suspects can help reduce the search time.

Records and Other Sources of Information

The uniqueness of burglary investigation rests in large measure on the use of records and information about the stolen property. In even the smallest burglary there is likely to be something taken
that has a number or mark that individualizes it for identification purposes. In the age of computers
and other forms of technology, it is much easier to track items, to communicate and cooperate with
other agencies, and to work closely with companies and businesses that may be able to assist. This
chapter focuses on sources and information unique to the crime of burglary. Obviously, police records
will contain information on possible suspects, reports leading to the recognition of crime patterns
and MO, and property data. The key here is in knowing how to use department records and crime
analysis to search for variables that focus on the unique aspects of the case. (See the section on Crime
Analysis in Chapter 12.)

External information from manufacturers, businesses, and trade associations may also provide
valuable assistance. For example, most manufacturers include identification numbers and other
information on merchandise, such as where it was sold and additional details that may facilitate
identification. Sometimes the investigator will have a load of stolen merchandise but will not have a
victim. Tracing its sales point may indicate where, and possibly to whom, it was sold.

BOX 20.1 SOURCES TO AID THE INVESTIGATOR

- The National Crime Information Center (NCIC), a national database that is particularly useful in tracing weapons and items with serial numbers.
- The National Auto Theft Bureau (NATB), which provides information not only on stolen vehicles, but also on property taken from trucks.
- Credit card companies, which can provide information on the use of stolen credit cards, thus providing clues to a suspect's movements, sometimes helping to produce eyewitness descriptions by sales clerks (when the burglar has used the card).
- Chambers of commerce, which may assist in the investigation of certain types of crimes against businesses.

Today, using scanners and bar codes, it is also possible to more clearly identify merchandise. It is now possible for police departments to scan reports into a computer, making it much easier to retrieve information about specific items of property. Further, more sophisticated databases allow investigators to search for information.

FOLLOW-UP ACTIVITIES

The investigation of burglary involves several stages:

1.   Investigating the crime scene and collecting and preserving any available physical evidence.

2.   Interviewing potential witnesses.

3.   Interviewing known fences.

4.   Using informants.

5.   Examining records.

6.   Tracing property.

7.   Identifying suspects.

The successful conclusion of a case will frequently depend on the investigator's ability to handle a large amount of seemingly unrelated pieces of information in an analytical way.

In many cases burglars are known to the police. Most have prior arrests, and a large percentage of them are drug users. Most are young males. Generally, burglars must commit a relatively large number of crimes in order to meet their needs. They usually operate within a specific geographic area, but there are some signs that this is changing. Many burglars steal cars to carry out the crime. Distinguishing marks—such as method of entry, type of property taken, or method of search—are often left behind. All of these factors lend themselves to crime analysis. Computers, if used properly, are an important investigative tool. Even in large cities, where burglaries are relatively common, the investigator or crime analyst can frequently "sort out" burglaries committed by one or more individuals.

A "fence" is an individual who purchases stolen property, and knowledge of such individuals is worth developing. In many instances a fence will keep the property in his or her residence. In some cases it may be possible to gather information from an informant who can identify local fences, and who can identify the types of property in a suspect residence, that can then be used to secure a search warrant.

The computer also can be used in tracing property. The initial and follow-up reports must be as specific as possible in the identification of property. Brand names, specific marks, and serial numbers are important. Burglary investigations can generate a vast amount of information. Information overload can be avoided by using a relational database.

The availability of computers to investigators makes it possible to maintain comprehensive lists of stolen property that can be checked quickly where a suspect is in possession of merchandise. This is very useful where smaller items, such as laptop computers, cell phones, and other devices are found in a suspect's possession.

Under ideal conditions, some form of case screening will help. With a case-screening approach, individual investigators are assigned cases with common characteristics; some will work on residential, others on business cases—some on juvenile cases, others on professional jobs. Another effective but seldom used approach is the daily or weekly case review in which investigators meet to describe their cases and to identify common characteristics of burglaries and burglary suspects. With the exception of most juvenile burglars, many burglars are highly mobile and will move from one jurisdiction to another, making communication and information sharing with other jurisdictions important. In one major city, a string of burglaries was solved when an investigator attended a regional training seminar where he spoke to a colleague about a peculiar cat burglar who always drank a glass of milk at the scene and then washed the glass. The colleague named the suspect immediately. The burglar had moved from one jurisdiction to another after he was released from prison. Unfortunately, most cases are not solved that easily. Both luck and the prepared mind factor into it, and investigators help make their own breaks.

Having mastered the information concerning burglary types and career patterns, the investigator has taken a long stride toward developing expertise. Putting the aforementioned information together with an investigative plan is the initial step.

A short description prepared for the case report should emphasize the differences (variables) in burglaries. It should begin with the type of burglary and proceed to include the finer details. An example of this might be:

Residential burglary of middle-income, single-family house. Entry through broken rear window between 9:00 A.M. and 3:00 P.M.

Property taken:

1.   One 13″ portable television (Zenith)

2.   Approximately $20 in currency

3.   Unknown amount in coins from jar in bedroom

Search haphazard, left large television and other electronic goods. Suspect wrote "Thanks" on bedroom mirror with lipstick.

The follow-up investigation reveals:

•   Blood found on broken glass. No crime scene search conducted, but glass marked and maintained as evidence. Investigator lifted single fingerprint from mirror in bedroom. Sent to fingerprint section.

- Interviews with neighbors. A neighbor, Mary Smith (address) states that a male, white, 14–16 years old, knocked on her door at approximately 1300 hours and asked if "Joey" lived there. Suspect description: M/W/14–16 years/5' 4"/110 lbs./wearing black leather jacket.

The investigator can now ask the courts for a records check, and also check parole and probation records. Although it is unlikely that the television set will turn up as fenced property, the investigator can add this to his or her list of items when checking pawn shops, informants, or other outlets for stolen goods.

There are enough individual items in the report to assist in the continuing investigation. By keeping the case "alive," it is possible that a break will come. "Filing" it will mean less likelihood that it will be remembered. If a suspect is turned in—either through records, informants, or other information—there is physical evidence that may be brought into play. Although this is a relatively simple case, it is not an uncommon one.

For a more sophisticated burglary, a similar, although more detailed, investigative plan may be developed. The plan need not be written out for each case, but it should be considered, used as a guide, and referred to especially when a case stalls. Time management is a critical factor in the investigation because most investigators may be working on dozens of cases at one time. For this reason keeping records of stolen property is important.

"Solvability factors" have been adopted by a number of police departments as a means of screening cases to identify those with the highest probability of solution. Solvability factors focus on unique aspects of a burglary that are likely to be of assistance in providing leads.

A burglary checklist developed by Harry O'Reilly and Mark Ronaldes, a criminal investigator with the Granby (Connecticut) Police Department, is in use in many departments (see Box 20.2). The form is useful for both the patrol officer and investigator.

Some Solvability Factors

- Type of building
- Unique type of entry
- Type of search
- Distinctive property stolen
- Eyewitnesses
- Writing or markings left
- Crime scene characteristics
- Physical evidence

CONCLUSION

Burglaries test the innovative skills of an investigator who can make sense of a large amount of information related to the type of case, the MO of known burglars, and the ability to trace stolen goods. In most cases, burglaries are mysteries that can be solved by diligent investigation. Unfortunately, in too many cases, investigators are unwilling or unable to take the time necessary to complete a thorough investigation. But there is great satisfaction in telling a victim that their case has been solved.

BOX 20.2 BURGLARY CHECKLIST

1. Determine location of building—street and house number, street name, nearest proximity of homes, escape routes, etc. (residential—industrial—commercial).

2. Determine description of building—size, color, type, height, shrubbery, multi-family, one-story/two-story, wood frame, brick, etc.

3. Determine date and time (hour) of entry.

4. Determine date and time location was last known to be secure—estimate time of break.

5. Determine who reported burglary and how it was discovered.

6. Determine where the occupants were at the time of burglary—when did they leave?, were all doors and windows secure?, were keys available?

7. Determine upon arriving at scene the state and condition of the location—lights on, curtains drawn, windows open, doors ajar, furniture moved, etc.

8. Determine if location had recent visitors—strangers, servicemen, peddlers, tradesmen, lights/telephone/gas, etc.

9. Check other burglars in same section for similar *modus operandi*.

10. Determine point and manner of entering—measure distances and heights; diagram crime scene.

11. Determine manner (means) of entry—pass key, jimmy, saw, drill, pry bar, hammer, axe, wrench, etc. Compare tools with marks found on building, doors, windows, etc.

12. Photograph crime scene—exterior/interior, tool marks, evidentiary objects, place of entry/exit, injuries if any, etc.

13. Determine stolen property—compile list of stolen property, detailed description and marks of means of identification, approximate values, serial numbers, etc.

14. Determine if identifiable laboratory clues exist—fingerprints, footprints, tire marks, blood, fibers, etc. Photograph/diagram evidence prior to removing or lifting.

15. Determine names of any persons showing interest in stolen items. Were such persons familiar with location of stolen items?

16. Determine if burglar did anything other than steal—help self to food, ransack house, confine them to one specific area, etc.

17. For boarding house or apartment burglars, check all occupants and past occupants within reasonable time back, particularly any who took keys or had access to dwelling.

18. Conduct canvass to determine possible suspect information.

19. Contact pawnshops and secondhand dealers for stolen property. In addition, notify surrounding departments of property stolen and *modus operandi* of criminal.

Source: *Practical Burglary Investigation*, by Harry T. O'Reilly. Courtesy, Office of Security Programs, University of Illinois at Chicago, 1990

NOTES

[1]   U.S. Department of Justice, Federal Bureau of Investigation, *Crime in the United States 2010*. See http://www. fbi.gov/about-us/cjis/ucr/crime-in-the-u.s/2010/crime-in-the-u.s.-2010/property-crime/burglarymain

[2]   Ibid 1, *Uniform Crime Reports 1975-2005* (Washington, DC: U.S. Government Printing Office, 2006).

[3]   U.S. Department of Justice, Federal Bureau of Investigation, *Crime in the United States 2010*, op. cit.

[4]   U.S. Department of Justice, Bureau of Justice Statistics, *Report to the Nation on Crime and Justice*, 2nd ed. (Washington, DC: U.S. Government Printing Office, 1988).

[5]   John Eck, *Managing Case Assignments: Burglary Investigation Decision Model Replication* (Washington, DC: Police Executive Research Forum, 1979).

[6]   American Law Institute, A Model Penal Code. As adopted at the 1962 Annual Meeting of the American Law Institute at Washington, DC, 24 May 1962, 142.

[7]   U.S. Department of Justice, Federal Bureau of Investigation, *Uniform Crime Reports*. See http://www.fbi.gov/about-us/cjis/ucr/ucr

[8]   Harry O'Reilly, *Practical Burglary Investigation* (Chicago: Office of Security Programs, University of Illinois at Chicago, 1991).

[9]   U.S. Department of Justice, Federal Bureau of Investigation, *Crime in the United States 2010*, op. cit. See http://www.fbi.gov/about-us/cjis/ucr/crime-in-the-u.s/2010/crime-in-the-u.s.-2010/violent-crime/robberymain

[10]   Barry Fisher, *Techniques of Crime Scene Investigation*, 6th ed. (Boca Raton, FL: CRC Press, 2000).

[11]   Richard T. Wright and Scott H. Decker, *Burglars on the Job: Streetlife and Residential Break-ins* (Boston: Northeastern University Press, 1994).

[12]   U.S. Department of Justice, Bureau of Justice Statistics Bulletin, *National Crime Victimization Survey, 2007*. See http://bjs.ojp.usdoj.gov/content/pub/pdf/cv07.pdf

[13]   U.S. Department of Justice, Federal Bureau of Investigation, "Automated Fingerprint Identification Systems: Technology of Policy Issues," pamphlet (Washington, DC: U.S. Government Printing Office).

DISCUSSION QUESTIONS

1. What percentage of burglaries are residential?

2. What is the UCR definition of burglary?

3. What are some of the characteristics of different types of burglaries?

4. What are some of the techniques used by burglars to gain entry? Explain each.

5. Are most burglaries well planned?

6. Does the crime scene offer much evidence in burglaries?

7. Beyond latent prints what are some of the other aspects of a burglary investigation that should be considered?

8.   What is a "fence"?

9.   What are some solvability factors in a burglary investigation?

SUPPLEMENTAL READINGS

Jetmore, L. F. (2008). *Path of the hunter: Entering and excelling in the field of criminal investigation.* Flushing, NY: Looseleaf Law.

Wright, R. T., & Decker, S. H. (1994). *Burglars on the job: Streetlife and residential break-ins.* Boston: Northeastern University Press.

CHAPTER 21

ARSON AND EXPLOSIVES

INTRODUCTION

This chapter addresses two areas that require a high degree of specialization: arson and explosives investigations. The National Association of Fire Investigators (NAFI) and the Bureau of Alcohol, Tobacco, Firearms, and Explosives (ATF) both provide extensive training in bomb and arson investigation. Arson is one of the fastest growing crimes in the United States. It remains very costly in both economic and human terms.

Motives for arson vary from an intent to murder the occupants to doing it just "for kicks," the thrill often being accompanied by sexual excitement. Arson may alternatively be prompted by more personal aggression, such as a wish to mete out punishment or revenge, or to express racial or social hatred. Some commit arson to bolster their self-esteem. A burning building gives an impressive display of the arsonist's power, and moreover may give him or her an opportunity to indulge in heroics in fighting the blaze. Professional firefighters have been known to succumb to the temptation of arson. Some arsonists wish to draw attention to some disadvantage they suffer, such as unemployment. There are also some hardheaded motives. A fire is seen as an effective way to destroy evidence of some other crime such as theft or even murder.[1]

Bombings have become the weapon of choice in any number of criminal acts, including domestic terrorist group attacks, revenge attacks, and random attacks by deranged individuals. Most bombings in the United States are done with self-made bombs, referred to by the military as IEDs (improvised explosive devices). However, there is concern that terrorists may resort to more sophisticated ordnance and/or propelled munitions devices.

According to federal statistics issued in 2010, arsons involving structures (residential, storage, public, etc.) accounted for 45.5 percent of the total number of arson offenses; arsons involving mobile property accounted for 26 percent; and other types of property (such as crops, timber, fences, etc.) accounted for 28.5 percent of reported arsons. Arsons of industrial/manufacturing structures resulted in the highest average dollar losses (an average of $133,717 per offense), which is down from 2008 with an average of $212,388 per offense.[2]

In many areas of the country, authority for arson investigation is in the hands of state and local fire marshals, and in some, the police have concurrent jurisdiction. A fire has to be investigated, in certain cases extensively, *before* there is proof that a crime was committed—that the fire was of incendiary origin. Some unusual aspects of the crime of arson contribute to the difficulty of obtaining evidence to convict. They are:

1. The fire may consume all traces of its incendiary origin, especially if detecting and extinguishing it were delayed.

2.   Rather than remaining undisturbed until recorded properly and the physical evidence collected, the crime scene may be hosed down with powerful streams of water, or its contents moved outdoors.

3.   The perpetrator can use a timing device to delay the start of the fire, thus allowing an interim for an alibi.

4.   Falling debris or the collapse of a building may cover or destroy evidence of the fire's having been set.

5.   Freezing weather makes searching for evidence more difficult; if everything becomes caked with ice, search and recovery are further delayed. Extremely hot weather can evaporate volatile accelerants.

Arson is unquestionably one of the most difficult crimes to investigate, and is a topic that has come under particular scrutiny by the judiciary and the media. A 2009 report on the forensics of arson by a seasoned arson investigator indicated that one man may have died as a result of a conviction on the basis of what has been referred to as the mythology of fire forensic examinations.

The National Fire Protection Association (NFPA) establishes "guidelines and recommendations for the safe and systematic investigation or analysis of fire and explosion incidents" *(NFPA 921*, § 1.2.1). The NFPA guidelines are endorsed by National and International Associations of Fire Investigators, and their publication *NFPA 921* forms the basis for certification examinations for fire investigators.[3]

Definitions

The elements of the crime of arson differ more from state to state than do the elements of any other crime. Such words borrowed from the common law as "willful," "malicious," and "intentional" appear in combination or separately in the various statutory definitions of arson. More recently, some states

Department of Fire Science, University of New Haven

Figure 21.1
Professor Bruce Varga illustrates the importance of identifying and analyzing fire patterns to a group of undergraduate students.

have included "the use of explosives to injure property"; and, rather than having to rely on a charge of "attempted arson," they added "the preparation of a building for burning" to the arson statute per se. The degree of arson is keyed to the endangerment to life; as deadly as any gun, arson is a weapon against people as well as property. The fire started at night is considered more life-threatening than one set when most people are awake or unlikely to be present. Therefore, the question is asked: When the fire was started, was a person in the structure, or was it reasonable to expect anyone to be?

Corpus Delicti

The *corpus delicti* of arson has three elements:

1. That a fire or burning occurred in a structure or property (including vehicles, in many states) protected by law. To meet this requirement, the case law of a particular jurisdiction must be consulted to determine whether charring or merely scorching is sufficient to meet this requirement; or whether there must be an actual physical change in the material.

2. That the fire or burning was intentional: neither accidental nor attributable to negligence or natural causes, but the result of a criminal act.

3. That someone set the fire, caused it to be set, or otherwise furthered the act.

WHY IS ARSON SUSPECTED?

In strictly legal terms a fire is considered to be of accidental origin unless proved otherwise. However, all fire scenes should be treated as crime scenes until it is determined by competent authority that the fire was accidental. As firefighters know well, it is not unusual to be unable to make out a case for arson, even when experience strongly suggests the fire was not accidental. Their reaction (as described by one fire chief) is akin to that of the police when an officer is killed in the line of duty; in the performance of the firefighter's duties, arson has the potential to kill. Hence, when the police have the primary responsibility to investigate a fire, they should exploit the firefighters' eagerness to put their suspicions to the test; when the arson issue is raised, the first step toward proving the *corpus delicti* is taken.

As Rossotti notes, "by far the most common crime involving fire is the illegal burning of buildings. Owners burn their own property in order to make fraudulent insurance claims; but more often the criminal burns the property of someone else."[4]

People are usually responsible for questioning the source of the fire. Not only the victim, but customers, tenants, and business rivals may express the belief that the fire in question was most timely or convenient. This should open up reservations as to its origin. Physical evidence also can strongly suggest arson; for instance, when two distinctly separate fires are encountered at the same time in the same premises. Records are least likely to be of immediate service, but later in the investigation they may be invaluable in establishing a motive; for example, a large insurance policy taken out shortly before the fire occurred; or, over time, the same owner having several fires in different locations.

Rather than prejudge any fire or explosion, the investigator should question all information until it is verified. To minimize the loss of evidence, every fire scene should be treated as a potential crime scene; any conclusion as to its incendiary or accidental cause must be based on the totality of the evidence gathered. The investigator must then sort it, form a "working hypothesis" and, testing new information against that hypothesis, modify it as needed. If the data collected continues to support the hypothesis, the end product should fit the facts—that is, answer all challenges.

PEOPLE AS A SOURCE OF INFORMATION

Besides the firefighters who extinguish the blaze, other people can add to the pool of information collected through interviewing. They are: the person who discovered the fire; the owner or manager, and the tenants of the burned structure; company employees; business associates and business competitors; insurance and financial personnel; and TV camera technicians.

Who Discovered the Fire?

The person who discovered the fire can report on which part of the building was ablaze when he or she first noticed it. This helps to determine the point of origin. Additional information from residents and bystanders might include observations on how quickly it spread, whether the color and volume of smoke were unusual, and descriptions of people or vehicles seen in the area shortly before the fire.

Firefighters

Firefighters are able to pinpoint the origin of structural fires (in contrast to forest or grass fires) almost 50 percent of the time. Based on past experience, they are often the first to suspect arson and quick to recognize the unusual. Giving voice to their suspicions, they will note: flame height; how rapidly the fire expanded; smoke density, and any odd color of the smoke; odor redolent of organic accelerants; fire doors that are open but should be shut; and boxed merchandise blocking passageways and doors.[5] They will recall having responded previously to alarms from the same location, and whether a fire benefited the owner. A failed fire alarm or sprinkler system certainly will give firefighters pause (later, the investigator should have such equipment checked to see whether it was tampered with).

Owner or Manager of the Structure

The owner or manager of the destroyed property may be questioned twice: first, soon after the fire and before arson is suspected; then, when evidence obtained from people, the scene, and records supports a case for arson. The second round of questioning may be an interrogation.

During the first session of questioning, information should be sought concerning the interviewee's knowledge of the fire, e.g., how and why it started. It is important for the investigator to establish the expected fuel load (what was purported to be in the building—including any recent additions to or removal of stock or furniture) for later comparison with the amount of physical remains. The whereabouts of the interviewee at the time the fire started should be ascertained, as well as how he or she learned of the blaze. Questions concerning insurance coverage are also in order and the responses should be placed in the record. Suspicion should be aroused if the individual can produce a fire insurance policy on the spot when no other policies are immediately on hand; or if he or she can account quite readily for his or her whereabouts at the start of the fire and cite eyewitnesses, yet remain hazy concerning the hours just prior to the fire. When a case can be made for arson, especially arson-for-profit, a second round of interviewing is in order. At this point the investigator must be fully prepared to conduct an interrogation.

Employees

Employees of a commercial enterprise possess potentially useful information, which will be divulged if they are interviewed properly. They may tell what they know of any recent changes in business practice or (by repeating office gossip) offer a perspective on the firm's financial health that differs markedly from management's. Although such information does not constitute evidence in and of itself, it can give direction to a line of inquiry that otherwise might not be pursued by the investigator. For example, the owner's reputation as a gambler or womanizer suggests a need for ready cash. If accounts receivable records were destroyed in the fire, the clerical staff should be asked if a change in their overnight storage had been made. Employees (and tenants) should be questioned about the contents of the building: How was it distributed? Where was the stock? Where were the furnishings? They should be asked about any recent changes: Was new stock added or substituted for old stock that was moved or removed? Employees may report having observed fire hazards that management ignored. Any recent laxity requires a follow-up to find any connection between the hazard and the spread of the fire or its initial site.

Insurance and Financial Personnel

When insurance fraud is believed to have motivated the arson, the following people must be interviewed: the insurance agent who sold the fire policy to the owner, the claims adjuster, the insurance company's arson investigator, and the owner's creditors and bankers. In almost all cases, the insurance company will be conducting a parallel investigation to protect its interests in potential civil litigation. Frequently, the company's investigator, whether in-house or independent, has much more latitude than the public-sector criminal investigator, as insurance contracts generally require a building owner to allow company investigators on the site as often as they reasonably demand access. A criminal investigator, however, must either have a search warrant or permission from the owner, who thereby waives Fourth Amendment rights. Within the terms of the contract, the insured can be required to submit to examinations under oath, and may not refuse to answer any questions without jeopardizing his or her right to collect on a claim. Hence, cooperation (without collusion) is feasible between the public and private sectors. Public-sector employees have access to criminal and other records not available to the private-sector investigator. On the other hand, if an insured has invoked his or her Fifth Amendment rights with the criminal investigator, the company can be notified of this fact, and an exploration conducted under the auspices of the civil investigation. By disclosing any financial situation that could have prompted the arson, such inquiries can be useful in any subsequent interrogation.

Business Competitors

Business competitors can provide information on the economic health of the industry in general and the arson target in particular. If financial problems are manifest, this can be cited during interrogation to reinforce a supposition about the motive for setting the fire.

Other Possible Witnesses

Spectators at the scene, neighbors and tenants of commercial buildings, news media staff, and those found through neighborhood canvassing are other potential sources of information not to be overlooked.

For residence fires that occur during normal sleeping hours, occupants will generally be found out on the street. Any spectator not dressed appropriately for that time—that is, wrapped in bedclothes, street clothes thrown over nightdress, and so on—should be asked for identification. If one is a stranger to the neighborhood, how they came to be there should be ascertained. Suspicious behavior to be looked for among spectators at the scene includes: anyone making light of the situation, laughing, moving about constantly, or talking to other spectators (the investigator should find out just what was said), as well as the so-called "eager beaver" who provides unsought information or "helps" the firefighters with more enthusiasm than the situation warrants.

Neighbors or tenants in the same building or one nearby should be questioned because they may have observed unusual activity immediately before the fire was reported. Unusual activity would include, for instance, a vehicle speeding from the scene just prior to the fire. In cases of insurance fraud, it would be the removal of such valuable merchandise as high-quality men's suits, and their replacement with suits of low quality. If the shift was made during regular business hours, it would probably be noticed by other tenants (especially if the elevator was inconveniently tied up); if one was made after hours, it would be even more suspicious (at least in retrospect). In residential fires the removal of guns and electronic appliances, especially TVs, is common. Irreplaceable possessions like the family Bible, photographs, trophies, or certificates also are frequently removed prior to the setting of a fire.

News media reporters and photographers covering the fire may photograph the crowd gathered to watch. Photographs and films taken of bystanders at recent fires should be scrutinized to determine if the same individual appears at several fires, or whether a suspect generated subsequently was a spectator. Videos made by both professionals and amateurs have proved invaluable in documenting the course of large fires and the actions taken during their suppression.

Depending on the time and location of the fire, the investigator must consider the potential eyewitnesses who, during the course of each day, pass by the place routinely. If the target is on a bus route, there should be bus drivers, passengers, and people waiting for transportation. There also maybe service deliverers (U.S. Postal Service, United Parcel Service, trash pickup, laundry, food, etc.); pedestrians on errands or walking their dogs; and motorists driving by or sitting in parked automobiles. Considerable time and effort would be needed to ferret out witnesses from among so many people. Yet it may be worth it, as they can fall into the category of fortuitous witnesses (that is, people who fail to report the valuable information they possess—what they saw or heard—simply because they do not realize its worth).

CONDUCTING THE INVESTIGATION

The scientific method forms the basis for NFPA guidelines for conducting a fire examination, which include five components as a methodological approach:

1. The assignment is received and the investigator is notified of his or her responsibilities.

2. The investigator plans the investigation and assembles tools, equipment, and personnel.

3.   The scene is examined and data is collected.

4.   Physical evidence is collected, documented, tested, and evaluated.

5.   The scientific method is used to analyze the information obtained.[6]

The motives for committing arson are numerous, but can be summarized as follows: profit, spite, revenge, vandalism, and pyromania. Generally, motive is quite personal (that is, secret and having a particular purpose). When tentatively identified, it may send the investigator to search records, or require a surveillance, neighborhood canvass, and/or additional interviewing of those who might confirm or dispute the motive attributed to the suspect. This topic will be considered again, following the discussion on how the investigator obtains information from people and physical evidence.

The investigation of arson initially focuses on whether the ignition was intentional. This can frequently be determined by the presence of cans or bottles of gasoline or other flammable mixtures left at the scene or in close proximity. The location where the fire originated may also provide evidence by analysis of the way in which the fire progressed. This may be determined by the extent of charring that can indicate the length of burning, or in the case of windows where a very high temperature, indicating a longer burning period, may result in the melting of glass. "A faster build-up to a high temperature would leave cleaner windows with many cracks, whereas an even faster build-up would produce a few very large cracks."[7]

PHYSICAL EVIDENCE

The purpose of examining the scene and attempting to recognize and collect physical evidence in a case of suspected arson is threefold: first, to determine where the fire started (only when the origin is known can possible causes be searched for and eliminated); second, to establish whether the fire was intentionally set, thereby proving an element of the crime; and third, if the fire is determined to have been set, to connect the arsonist to the crime scene. However, the task of locating and recognizing physical evidence is a different one for arson than it is for most other crimes: some physical evidence may be destroyed by flames and heat, or washed away by pressure hoses. Despite this, telltale signs of where the fire started may remain, but the investigator must be capable of reading them. To do so, the following very elementary knowledge of the chemistry and physics of fire is needed.

COMBUSTION

Three components are required for fire: burnable material (a fuel), oxygen, and a heat source (which raises the temperature of the fuel to its kindling point). The relationship is expressed in the equation:

$$FUEL + OXYGEN + HEAT\ SOURCE = COMBUSTION$$

The first two components coexist all the time with no threat of fire. Only when the third—a heat source—is present can fire occur. The temperature of the heat source must be greater than the ignition (or kindling) temperature of the fuel; also, the heat source must be able to raise the fuel to its ignition point by direct contact, or by transferring the heat through radiation, conduction, or convection. Because each component can play a role in proving or disproving that the fire was set intentionally, it is important to understand the function of each.[8]

Fuels

All fuels have an ignition temperature, meaning that when raised to that point, they start to burn. The temperature of the heat source must be higher than the fuel's ignition temperature. Most fuels are organic (i.e., they are carbon compounds), as are the many products used in constructing and furnishing buildings, such as wood, paint, and fabrics used in rugs, draperies, upholstery, and bedding.[9]

When burning, carbon combines with oxygen to form carbon monoxide and carbon dioxide, releasing heat in the process:

$$\text{ORGANIC (CARBON) COMPOUNDS} + \text{OXYGEN} =$$
$$\text{CARBON MONOXIDE} + \text{CARBON DIOXIDE} + \text{HEAT}$$

Oxidation is the term used by chemists to describe the reaction of a chemical compound with oxygen. A compound such as linseed oil (a drying oil found in paints) combines at room temperature with oxygen and releases considerable heat as part of the oxidation process. Should linseed oil be left on rags that are piled up or dropped in a heap, thereby preventing the air currents from carrying away the heat, fire can break out. What may appear initially to be a suspicious fire will actually have been caused by spontaneous combustion, a result of the careless disposal of paint-waste rags. Most petroleum products—oils, greases, kerosene, and gasoline—are not drying oils and thus do not pose a spontaneous combustion risk.

When arson is employed to cover up a homicide, investigative use can be made of the fact that carbon monoxide is one of the by-products of combustion. Its absence in the blood of a dead person who apparently fell asleep while smoking in bed may unmask a cover-up attempt—a supposedly accidental death may be revealed to be a criminal homicide. A living person breathing carbon monoxide retains it in the blood because hemoglobin forms a stronger chemical bond—about 200 times stronger—with the deadly gas than it does with oxygen. A dead person's blood is no longer circulating; accordingly, carbon monoxide is not taken up by the body even though it is exposed to it.

Soot is another by-product of combustion. Its presence or absence in the respiratory passages of an alleged victim of a fire indicates whether he or she was alive or dead at the time of the fire. Soot will be detected only in those who were breathing at that time. The absence of soot in the windpipe and lungs of the deceased could indicate that a death first believed accidental—from falling asleep while smoking in bed—may actually have been homicide.

Oxygen

The earth's atmosphere, approximately 21 percent oxygen, remains constant through the cyclical processes of combustion (best described for living matter as oxidation) and photosynthesis. The carbon dioxide produced by combustion is used by green plants and trees for the photosynthesis of organic compounds and the simultaneous release of oxygen into the atmosphere, thereby maintaining the earth's oxygen supply at the 21 percent level. Fire requires at least 16 percent oxygen content to continue; concentrations between 16 and 21 percent promote heavy smoke production.

Investigative interest is aroused when a fire extinguishes itself through a shortage of oxygen (a level below 16 percent), and by the carbon dioxide and carbon monoxide produced. This situation arises only under certain conditions; for instance, when a fire is ignited in a building so tightly sealed and unventilated that it does not allow the oxygen to be replaced as it is consumed by the burning fuel. By extinguishing itself before it has consumed the structure, the fire may leave evidence of combustible material placed to spread the fire (see Trailers below).

Heat Sources

It is the temperature and size of the heat source that matters, fires usually being small at the beginning. If circumstances are favorable—a flammable gas or vapor, or a finely divided, solid material such as kapok is present—a mere spark can be the ignition source. A spark was all it took to set fire to the ocean liner *Normandie*, being refitted as a troop carrier during World War II. Naturally, sabotage was suspected. An immediate investigation, however, revealed that an acetylene torch had been used in disregard of such a known fire hazard—the proximity of highly flammable kapok. The ship was quickly engulfed in flames and the volume of water ultimately needed to quench the flames sank the liner at her berth in New York harbor. Because the welder could testify about how and exactly where it began, the initial site of the fire was readily determined. In the meantime, a thorough background check on the welder ruled out sabotage.[10]

Accidental Heat Sources

In cases of suspected arson, the initial site of the fire may be determined from the physical evidence and traces remaining after it is extinguished. Whether its origins were accidental or natural, some evidence of the cause will usually be found at its source. The most common accidental causes include:

Heating/Cooking Systems: Sparks from a fireplace (see Figure 21.2), dirty chimney, overturned space heater, exploding or leaking kerosene oil stove, or overheated greasy frying pan. Radiant heat from boilers, stoves, furnaces, faulty chimneys, or overheated equipment—motors, gear boxes with dry bearings. Vents and exhaust systems that allow flames or hot gases to escape and come in contact with combustibles.

Bruce Varga, Department of Fire Science, University of New Haven

Figure 21.2
Fireplace ash door opened directly into unprotected combustible crawl space.

Bruce Varga, Department of Fire Science, University of New Haven

Figure 21.3
External fire damage on a residence due to careless disposal of smoking materials.

Heating systems are the most common cause of fires, especially in the southern states where they tend to be portable (electric or liquid fueled). Cooking accidents are the most common cause of injuries resulting from fires.

Electrical System (Equipment and Appliances): Deterioration because of: worn insulation; misuse (overloaded circuits); improper installation (loose connections—especially with aluminum wire); defects (shorted circuits through a faulty switch, causing sparking or arcing); overheating caused by a loose connection; and any of the above coupled with neglect (grease collected in stove vents and hood filters).

Smoking: Careless use or disposal of cigarettes, cigars, or pipes, especially in bed and in living areas, is the cause of many fires, and the most common cause of death by fire. Ignition can be delayed up to 12 hours when smoking materials are improperly discarded (see Figure 21.3).

Matches: Fumes or vapors, virtually impossible to ignite with a glowing cigarette, are ignited easily with a spark from a match or a flame. Matches and lighters—with their exposed flames— probably are responsible for more fires than are the glowing embers of tobacco, if fires started by children playing with matches are counted. Though accidental fires do not result every time a child plays with matches, they can be a consequence of such activity. The investigator should look into the child's past behavior, which is not likely to have escaped the family's notice. Asking the family if precautions were taken to keep matches safe and asking the child whether he or she was able to obtain them would also be appropriate.

Natural Heat Sources

Occasionally, nature is responsible for starting a blaze. Some natural causes are: spontaneous combustion, which can make flammable material smolder and then burst into flame; lightning (especially in remote areas), which can start fires in structures (such as silos or barns) but more frequently causes forest fires; and—although a rare cause—sunlight, which can be concentrated on combustible material by the lens effect of a water-filled glass container or a concave mirror. Witnesses can help to establish whether conditions were right for such an occurrence: Was it a hot, sunny day? Was lightning seen in the area? How long had the fuel been there—hours, days, weeks?

Investigative Significance

Making a fire appear to have been the result of an accidental or natural cause may look like an easy cover-up to an arsonist. Investigative efforts must make certain that the cause was not so simulated. Cover-up attempts are usually associated with insurance fraud or with fires meant to conceal other crimes such as homicide or theft. Motive, especially pecuniary, can be an important factor in deciding to press on with the inquiry rather than accept the ostensible cause. The absence of (1) a natural cause, or (2) an accidental cause leads to an assumption of arson. If both are eliminated after a thorough investigation by a qualified expert, one element for a charge of arson—the fact that the fire was set willfully or maliciously—is sustainable.

Additional factors to be considered include: the nature of the fuel present; its physical form; whether the suspected source could provide enough energy to ignite a fire; and whether normal ventilation was tampered with, which otherwise would have cooled off the fuel faster than it could be heated.

Accelerants

A number of commercially available volatile liquids are used to start fires and help them spread more rapidly. Known as *accelerants* in the field of arson detection, some examples are: gasoline (or gasoline blended with diesel fuel, a precaution sometimes taken by arsonists); kerosene, lighter fluids; paint thinners (turpentine, mineral spirits, acetone); and toluene. All carry a high potential for danger, the greatest attaching to the most common accelerant by far—gasoline.

If gasoline and other extremely volatile fuels are ignited at concentrations between 1.5 and 6 percent, gasoline vapors may produce an explosion that shatters windows, pushes out walls (see Figure 21.4), and scorches the skin and clothing of the arsonist, who may be burned acutely on the back while making a hasty exit. By notifying hospitals, emergency clinics, and doctors of the need to report all cases of extensive burns, particularly back burns, the arson investigator may locate a likely suspect—certainly if the patient with severe back burns claims they resulted from having lighted a gas oven. In reality, an exploding gas oven would cause more frontal burns and less severe back burns. If the suspect is a hired professional, paid to torch the structure for the benefit of the owner or someone with a grudge against the owner, follow-up is obviously necessary. A possible ploy, which often succeeds with a novice or a youth, would be to inquire into the amount contracted for, feign surprise, and then let on that the going rate is higher. Feeling cheated, the inexperienced arsonist may blurt out the name of the individual who did the hiring.

John DeHaan

Figure 21.4
Low pressure, low velocity explosion damage, with exterior sooting and scorching, from a gasoline vapor explosion.

Point of Origin

In the investigation of any structural fire, it is critical first to determine its point of origin. There are two reasons for this. The primary one is to establish cause, because arson becomes probable should both accidental and natural causes be ruled out. The second reason is germane to the kind of debris remaining at the site: if an accelerant was used, some residue can be retrieved for laboratory analysis; if a fire-setting mechanism was employed, its parts can be collected as evidence.

Figure 21.5
Drawing of light bulb exposed to heat from oncoming fire. Gas pressure in bulb causes blow-out, which points toward the fire.

Locating the Initial Site

Three sources of information can help to determine where a structural fire originated.[11] The first source is provided by the fire patterns visible on partially consumed combustible material. In this age of high technology it may be surprising to learn that the prosaic shovel is a must if fire patterns are to be made visible, for a huge quantity of debris is the inevitable consequence of fighting a fire. Indeed, it is not uncommon for arson experts called to the scene to find a foot of rubble covering much of the site. The distorted shapes and other effects of intense heat on such objects as light bulbs or furniture springs are the second source of information (see Figure 21.5). The third source, one that may lead to the point of origin, was noted earlier in the chapter: the observations of the person(s) who first noticed the fire.

Fire Patterns

The intensity and duration of a fire can, with some confidence, be inferred from the fire patterns that can be observed on combustible material not completely consumed. When wood is the fuel, a blister or alligator-like pattern is usually present. Even on a noncombustible surface, such as a cement block wall, a pattern may be visible. Fire usually burns upward (by convection), then outward (by radiation and conduction). By examining where things are burned and where they are not, the investigator establishes the pattern of the burning. Surfaces exposed to oncoming flames are always burned more than surfaces not exposed—protected, on the lee side. Beveling takes place; this and the "V" pattern resulting from the flow of the fire (see below) are used to reconstruct its path.[12]

Pour Patterns: The kind of fire pattern that results from pouring an accelerant onto the floor of a room is particularly important. A pour pattern is clear, demonstrable evidence of the use of an accelerant (see Figures 21.6–21.8).

Alligatoring: Anyone who has observed the partially burned residue of a campfire is familiar with how the blisters on the logs resemble the skin of an alligator. The size of the alligatoring or checking is not useful to the investigator, for it is dependent on the type of wood and its cut rather than

Bruce Varga, Department of Fire Science, University of New Haven

Figure 21.6
Clearing fire debris and washing floor reveals ignitable liquid pour patterns.

Courtesy, Ron Mullen, Loss Investigation Services

Figure 21.7
A pour pattern on a floor is a good place to take samples.

on exposure to the fire. The single exception is the flat, baked appearance caused by low-intensity heating over a long time (see Crazing below).

   "V" Pattern: Fire, if unobstructed, will shoot upward and fan out, often registering as a "V" or a cone pattern left after the fire is put out (see Figure 21.9). When the "V" is distinct, the bottom of the cone sometimes points to where the fire started, or to where the fuel was burning. An ignition or

Brooksville Fire Department, Brooksville, Florida

Figure 21.8
A pour/drip pattern visible on carpet. Fire spread from room to room.

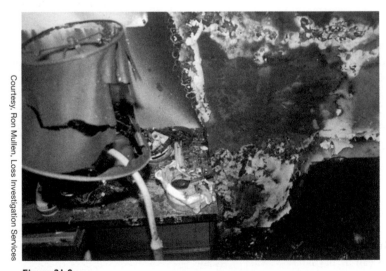

Courtesy, Ron Mullen, Loss Investigation Services

Figure 21.9
Fire pattern extends upward in a "V" from trash can, the initial ignition site.

fuel source may be found at the base of a "V" pattern. The action of interior structural fires, however, is not always this simple. Obstructions can prevent a fire from spreading; strong drafts from stairwells and elevator shafts can distort the "V"; and broken or open windows and doors can create drafts that dramatically alter the way the fire spreads and, therefore, the configuration of its fire pattern.

Charring: The charring of wood inevitably is observed in structural fires and can be an indicator of fire travel and point of origin (see Figure 21.10). Many arson investigators believe that the deeper the charring, the longer the fire burned at that spot. Because the longest burning time must be at the point of origin, observing the depth of char at various places can help them to trace the fire back to that point. This may be true sometimes, but too many complicating factors interfere with accuracy. One area, for instance, may be drenched by the fire hoses (and cooled) and an adjacent one completely missed. An accelerant itself may burn more intensely than the materials on which it was splashed, leaving a darker, recognizable char pattern of its own. Even when thrown on a vertical surface (such as a door), the resulting fire pattern indicates where the fluid was applied. Heavy charring in a corner of a room, which would otherwise be difficult to fathom, may have resulted because the accelerant flowed there across an uneven floor.

From an investigative viewpoint, the most useful facts relative to charring may be summed up as follows:

Figure 21.10
Charring as an indicator of fire travel and point of origin. It is clear from the charring that the fire traveled from left to right.

1. The depth of char is proportional to the intensity of the fire (if short in duration) and to the length of burning if the fire burns slowly for a long time.

2. Those places where intensity was greatest—directly over a fire, or where ventilation or drafts "fan" it—will have deeper charring.

3. The relative depth of char around a room may help locate sources of fuel or ventilation.

HEAT DISTORTION

Direct flames or atmospheric heat build-up can distort objects, thereby impressing telltale signs on materials (especially plastic) that partially melt, fuse, or crack when exposed to intense heat. Even without flames and charring, the direction of fire travel may be established through the deformation of some objects by heat.

Light Bulbs: The glass housing of a light bulb can be partially melted, and the distorted form that results will point in the direction of the oncoming fire (see Figure 21.11).

Spalling: Although noncombustible, cement can show exposure to intense heat through spalling. The signs that indicate spalling are surface discoloration, chipping, crumbling, or a flaky, chalklike appearance. Most often it results from exposure to radiant heat from a large,

Figure 21.11
Light bulbs melt first on side facing oncoming fire. Gas pressure in bulb causes blow-out to point toward heat source (fire).

Courtesy, Ron Mullen, Loss Investigation Services

Figure 21.12
Spalling on a concrete wall. Concrete spalling may indicate the use of a liquid accelerant. Look for patterns of discoloration around the spalling, and have a laboratory analyze samples of concrete or absorbent powder that has been allowed to stand on the concrete for about an hour.

established fire. Brown-black stains on the cement around the spalled area suggest the use of an accelerant, although experiments reveal it is very difficult to produce spalling with a liquid accelerant. A pattern or trail of spalling can be read like a fire pattern on any surface (see Figure 21.12).[13]

Crazing: A pattern or network of fine, irregular lines in glass and wood are termed craze lines. In glass and ceramic material they may be the result of rapid, intense heat, possibly because of the use of an accelerant. Craze lines on wood, found on the baked, flat surface of a board, are the result of relatively low heat over a long period of time.

Significance of Finding Point of Origin

When all relevant information sources (people, fire patterns, heat distortion) on the fire have been exploited, the fire's point of origin may be found at or close to the low point of the burned-out area. Multiple low points, signifying possible multiple origins, are highly suspicious. They signal an intentionally set fire. Questionable sites include: a closet, bathroom, attic, crawl space, the area beneath stairs—because accidental fires in such locations are rare. An unusual burn is another suspicious sign: the fire burning down instead of up, or fire developing as a result of a flashover when normally there would not be enough fuel on hand for this to occur. *Flashover* is a phenomenon that occurs when, in the growth of a fire, all the fuel in a room is ignited and flames flash over the entire area. Whenever arson is suspected, the point of origin, once located, must be examined for all possible sources of ignition and for any remaining traces of accelerant.

Ignition Sources

Once an area of origin has been established, the investigator can then turn to a search for ignition sources. Flame from a match or a cigarette lighter is the most common source for an incendiary fire, but except through exclusion, the use of either will not be apparent in a case of arson. In other words, only when no other possible source of heat can be found at the point of origin—no electric or gas outlet in the area; no spark, friction, or chemical source of heat; no child having access to the area or to matches; and no stored rags that could have undergone spontaneous combustion—is such a source indicated. The presence of an electrical outlet or appliance near or at the point of origin requires checking out, as does the possibility that overheating, or an arc (or spark) may have caused the fire. If such causes are to be eliminated, an expert is needed to perform these tasks.

Although less common as an ignition source, it is important to ascertain whether any mechanical (frictional), chemical, or natural source was present at the point of origin to account for the fuel's having reached ignition temperature. When all are eliminated, an inference that the fire was deliberately set is warranted.

Plants (Sets)

Arson investigators employ the term *plant*, or *arson set*, to describe a device that ignites the first fuel, or assists the initial flame to build in intensity. A timing mechanism may be included as part of the device. In addition, a trailer may be used to spread the fire to other parts of the structure.

Timing Devices: Arsonists employ timing devices to delay the start of a fire and allow them to establish an alibi. By this means, witnesses can be produced to attest to their presence in another place at the time of the blaze. The simpler the timing device, the more difficult it is to prove one was used, and the less likely it is to malfunction. The more complicated and clever the device, the fewer the people with the ability or the means to design, test, and build it.

Matches, Candles, Cigarettes, and Other Timing Devices: A simple but effective ignition and timing device involves the use of matches with a burning candle wrapped in excelsior or other readily flammable material. Generally, a candle three-quarters of an inch in diameter burns at about one inch per hour, making possible a few hours' delay. Blasting safety fuses and cannon/pyrotechnic fuses make shorter delays feasible (up to 10 minutes), by burning at a predictable rate of 24 to 60 inches per minute. Another means of causing ignition in a short time is the use of a matchbook and a burning cigarette. Candles may be used in combination with other fuels for delayed ignition. Another device, the road accident flare, is also easily obtained. A mattress or some readily combustible material may be placed near or wrapped around any ignition/timing device.

Phosphorus, a chemical element that ignites upon exposure to air, has been employed to start a delayed fire. When dissolved in a solvent that evaporates slowly, combustion is postponed until it is exposed to the air after the solvent has evaporated. Alternatively, phosphorus may be coated with paraffin, sewn inside the shoulder pad of a garment, then sent to a dry cleaner where the cleaning fluid dissolves the paraffin, exposing the phosphorus to the air. Dry cleaning shops involved in labor disputes or fighting a competitor have been burned out by this technique.

A lighted cigarette dropped accidentally or placed deliberately between upholstered chair cushions may smolder and incubate for three-quarters of an hour to four hours before bursting into flame (and may never go to open flame). A fire started within an upholstered chair will heavily char the chair's insides as well as the floor. The chair's coil springs will usually collapse, then be hardened by rapid cooling from the water doused on them. A fire started from the outside and engulfing the same chair would do more exterior than interior damage; the springs and floor underneath may remain virtually undamaged. Light bulbs or hot appliances wrapped in cloth rags or cotton batting will cause smoldering after several minutes, and later, flaming combustion. Figure 21.13 shows a cigarette that was intended to be used as an ignition device.

Bruce Varga, Department of Fire Science, University of New Haven

Figure 21.13
Homemade quarter stick of dynamite with cigarette as failed delayed ignition device.

Other more esoteric devices have been constructed. To time the start of a fire, the electric, telephone, or gas utility system can be altered. Electronic timers, alarm clocks, and other mechanical devices are also used, and can be set off by remote control—by telephone or radio signal. As a general rule, some physical trace of a timing device (if one was employed) is likely to be found in the debris remaining at the point of origin—provided that the point of origin is located and thoroughly examined.

Trailers: *Trailers* (or *streamers*) are used to extend the fire from the plant (or set) to other parts of the structure. Sometimes they lead from the starter plant to one or more secondary plants from which other trailers emanate. A wide variety of materials can be utilized for this purpose: newspapers, waxed paper, toilet paper, rags twisted into rope and doused with accelerant, gunpowder, certain motion picture film, and such flammable liquids as a mix of kerosene and gasoline, or a mix of gasoline and fireplace ashes.

In using trailers, the amateur arsonist might not make allowances for the replacement of oxygen in a relatively air-tight building that has no source of ventilation to restore the oxygen consumed by the fire. This causes the carbon dioxide and carbon monoxide (generated by combustion of the fuel and simultaneous reduction of the oxygen) to snuff out the fire. Left behind is visible evidence of the streamers and plants, photographs of which should convince a jury that arson was intended (see Figure 21.14).

Accelerants

Gasoline (the most common accelerant), turpentine, and kerosene are readily identified by their distinctive odors. When searching the crime scene for an accelerant, a shovelful of debris—ashes,

John DeHaan

Figure 21.14
Trailer across counter and into open cabinets failed to ignite contents.

wood flooring, carpeting, or upholstery, for instance—must be lifted, then sniffed. The sense of smell, however, is easily fatigued or dulled; it is not always reliable. Several attempts (perhaps by more than one person) may be necessary before an odor is detected; when it is, the debris must be collected and preserved for transmission to the laboratory.

The distinctive odors of many accelerants come from the impurities remaining after petroleum, pine tree wood, or other natural products are distilled. With care and some expense, they can be removed. This process yields a relatively odorless, flammable liquid that, when objections are raised about the fumes of ordinary oil house paints, serves as an acceptable paint thinner. Such products can also be used by the arsonist to mask the use of an accelerant. In such a case, some method other than lifting and sniffing must be found to discover the presence of an accelerant.

Detection Methods—For Use at the Crime Scene: Accelerants can sometimes be detected at the scene of a suspected arson by visual inspection, by odor, or by means of instrumental devices.

In addition to a pour pattern, other visual evidence of the use of an accelerant can be found when heat intensity is sufficient to melt, twist, or oxidize metals used in the construction of a building or piece of furniture (see Figures 21.15 and 21.16).

As noted above, detecting by scent is another method that can be employed in detecting arson at a crime scene.[14] The human olfactory nerve can be sensitive. A few people are capable of recognizing one part of gasoline in 10 million parts of air; the majority require a concentration of about 10 parts per million. Trained dogs have been successful in detecting gasoline at fire scenes; their sensitivity also is on the order of one part per million. Chemical dyes and instrumental means also can establish the presence of a flammable hydrocarbon in the debris at a crime scene. The "rainbow" effect to be observed on pools of water, caused by contamination from the oily residue found in many commercially available volatile fluids, suggests the presence of an accelerant, but may also be the result of naturally occurring decomposition (pyrolysis) products.

Figure 21.15
Melted aluminum in a low area (such as door sill in photograph above) is a good indicator of intense heat—as from a flammable liquid. A wooden door charred on the bottom edge is a strong indicator that an accelerant burned on the floor underneath the door.

Figure 21.16
Fire penetration from above resulting in distinct burn on supporting floor joist.

Another technique is the dye color test. If sprinkled over a suspected area, dyes soluble only in organic solvents can change to red or another color (depending on the dye). They are easy to use and low in cost. But just as dyes are the least sensitive detection method, they are the least specific: they may turn color even when no accelerant is present. Their low cost does make detection of odorless accelerants feasible. Thus, samples should be collected for the crime laboratory in which sophisticated equipment is available for analysis.

Finally, there are many instruments available for the detection of accelerants. Costing from a few thousand to hundreds of thousands of dollars, they vary widely in price as well as sensitivity, specificity, and portability. Underlying their operation is a broad range of scientific principles—from flame ionization and gas chromatography to infrared spectrophotometry and catalytic combustion/resistance analysis (see Chapter 2). Known as a *sniffer* in the jargon of arson investigators, the catalytic combustion device is the most common means employed to detect flammable vapors. Specificity to hydrocarbon accelerants being impossible with field devices, some false positive results will occur; therefore, any positive reading must be confirmed by collecting and submitting samples for further laboratory analysis.

Collection and Transmission: The volatility of accelerants requires that crime scene debris suspected of harboring flammable material be sealed tightly in new, quart- to gallon-sized paint cans or glass jars. A pure ignitable liquid sample should never be placed in a metal can.[15]

Polyethylene or polystyrene containers are unsuitable for collecting accelerants; they are deteriorated by or are permeable to petroleum products. The cans or jars should be filled until they are 80 to 90 percent full. They should not be exposed to the heat of the sun or left in a closed automobile or trunk during hot weather. To prevent the escape of flammable vapor, expeditious delivery to the laboratory is crucial. There, the evidence can be sampled (using head space or charcoal trap concentration) and then analyzed by gas chromatography. A fresh cellulose sponge, gauze, or cotton batting can be used to soak up small quantities of liquid, and then stored in a small, tightly covered glass jar or can. Flour, diatomaceous earth, or calcium carbonate can be spread on a wet concrete surface to absorb traces of gasoline or other petroleum distillate. The absorbent should then be sealed in a can to await analysis.

MOTIVE

After a fire has come under suspicion (based on information obtained from people and crime scene evidence), a knowledge of the wide differences both in motive and *modus operandi* of arsonists facilitates the search for the individual responsible. Property owners looking to collect insurance want everything completely burned down. They often take measures to ensure the fire's spread to all parts of the premises, and do so with little fear of being in the building since they are in control of it. Hence, a disabled alarm or sprinkler suggests the arsonist is an owner or holds another financial interest. Those looking for thrills rarely go to such lengths; it is sufficient that they see the flames and hear the fire engines. The kind of person whose name would crop up on a list of individuals seeking to collect insurance is unlikely to resemble the thrill-seeker in age and business background. Likewise, an attempt to make the cause of a fire seem accidental is not expected when the motivation is vandalism, spite, revenge, or hatred; rather, it suggests insurance fraud. Because the nature of a fire can provide clues to motive, the following discussion is designed to enhance the investigator's understanding and skill in dealing with this crime.

Financial Gain

Arson can result when a business or person gains financially, for example, by eliminating competition, through insurance fraud, or through welfare fraud (following the destruction of home and possessions). Often the greatest benefit accrues from swindling an insurance company.

Insurance Fraud: Liquidating a large inventory of unsold or obsolete merchandise—"selling" it to the insurance company by means of a set fire—is most likely when the goods are seasonal or produced by an industry that has suffered a severe downturn. Other scenarios include the need for: extensive renovation to meet new safety standards; costly retooling, or replacing of an outmoded plant, in order to remain competitive; or capital that is tied up (e.g., in a long-vacant building, whose sale would mean taking a great loss). In cases in which insurance fraud is suspected, the careful inspection of business, personal, and especially financial records is an obvious first step. If a thorough inventory of the firm's assets was kept, it will often become apparent why arson was seen as a solution.

Elimination of Competition: A strategically timed fire can undoubtedly benefit a surviving firm when its competitor is forced out of business by arson. For example, many companies rely on holiday buying to ensure adequate annual profits. If, as the season is launched, its inventory is received and then destroyed by a set fire, the business may be hard put to survive. Arson is intimidating at any time, but especially so for a struggling new business. When arson is suspected or proved, the victim more likely than not is able to suggest who might benefit. Because fire setters are often hired professionals, a list of the calls—local and particularly long-distance—charged to a suspect's business and residence telephones can be very useful to the investigator. If the records of several months prior to and following the fire are studied, a particular number may be noted that appears abruptly, then vanishes. Next, a background check on the recipient may turn up an individual with an arrest record or reputation as a fire setter. Because professionals usually demand ready money, cash is the most likely form of payment; therefore, an investigator's failure to examine bank statements for cash withdrawals and checks written is inexcusable. Surveillance may be called for; if the suspect is subsequently caught red-handed, a confession should be obtained for the first fire.

Moving and Resettlement Allowance: People who do not live below the poverty line cannot know the hardships endured by those who live on the edge. For the middle class a home fire is regarded as a calamity, the emotional impact of which is partially offset by insurance coverage. For the poor a fire may be seen as a way out. Possessions good for the junk heap can be replaced and the rundown house left behind. With the homeless given priority for public housing, and charitable organizations helping families to resettle, arson is sometimes seen as a viable option. It is resorted to from time to time, therefore, and should not be ruled out. When there is evidence to prove that the fire was set, and the family agrees to be interrogated, a confession is extremely likely.

Intimidation

Arson has been used to:

1.   instill fear regarding the safety of one's person or family;

2.   threaten economic loss; or

3.   effect a desired change in government or business policy.

Fear for Safety: The threat of arson has caused individuals to fear for their safety. It may be used either to prevent or force them to do something. Witnesses may be threatened with the torching of their home or business should they come forth with testimony in an upcoming criminal trial. Sometimes, owing to racial hostility, a home is burned when a new family moving into the neighborhood is not welcomed by the dominant group. In the event of witness intimidation, the motive is clear after a threat has been made. Before the fire is set, surveillance of the targeted property, the suspect, and associates is an effective strategy. Although there might seem to be too many suspects in a racially tense neighborhood, if the property and those who seem capable of disregarding the civil rights of others can be kept under surveillance, the offender(s) could be caught in the act.

Threatened Economic Loss: Arson has been used to intimidate management in labor disputes, especially when the settlement of a strike seems unlikely. Mobsters have sometimes extorted money from business concerns by torching a company vehicle as a signal that more serious repercussions will take place should compliance not be forthcoming.

Change of Policy: Arson has been used to press for a change in governmental policy. During the Vietnam War, government and quasi-military installations were set afire or bombed. It also has been used to induce action for the alleviation of other problems: for example, banks believed to be "redlining" a community (not approving mortgage loans for housing in the area) have received arson threats. In these cases, informants can be helpful by indicating promising suspects to be placed under surveillance.

Emotional Reasons

Jealousy, spite, revenge, and hatred are strong enough to cause some individuals to resort to arson to relieve the malaise produced by these emotions. In such arson cases, the victim usually is aware of the aggrieved individual and can provide the investigator with the name of the likely perpetrator.

Jealousy: Jealousy can cause a jilted sexual partner to resort to arson, by setting the property of a former lover or new lover afire. It is not uncommon for an unrequited lover to throw a Molotov cocktail against the front door of the person who has rejected him or her. Although similar to jealousy, envy is less useful in suggesting a possible suspect.

Spite: Domestic quarrels and feuds between neighbors are often marked by arson. Some property of value to the other party to the conflict is burned. In rural areas, a barn may be targeted; in cities, a vehicle.

Revenge: A relationship between employer and employee also can become so embittered as to cause the firm's business or equipment to be set afire. Family feuds and gang warfare provide excuses for revenge fires as well.

Hatred: Hatred is another strong emotion that sometimes is relieved through arson. The target may be the commercial property, automobile, or residence of the intended victim. Those so motivated have probably let others know of their feelings, or the victim may be aware of the animosity and furnish the names of possible suspects. The list can be pared down if necessary by considering who had the opportunity and who might be foolhardy enough to commit arson.

Dislike of an assigned task (a mild form of hatred) has caused arson to be employed as a diversionary tactic. The disruption, it is hoped, will eliminate the need to fulfill an obligation. For example, to force the postponement of a test, a student may start a diversionary fire in a dormitory or classroom. Such fires usually are set with material readily available—pages torn from a phone book, curtains, draperies, upholstered cushions, a waste basket. If a series of small fires (sometimes the first one or two will not be reported) is extinguished before they do extensive damage, an analysis of the time, day of the week, and the period separating them may be profitable. In one case, a chemistry class held a monthly examination, always on a Thursday; over a three-month period, several fires were set late at night on the Wednesday preceding the test. After the pattern was recognized, a course list of students who were faring poorly was obtained. Questioning each one separately led to a confession.

Concealment of Another Crime

Sometimes arson serves to conceal a homicide, account for an inventory shortage, destroy incriminating records, or distract police from another felony being committed simultaneously in the area. When the investigator realizes that arson was put to such use, heed should be given to whomever may have had a motive to commit the other offense.

Homicide: Attempts have been made to conceal a criminal homicide by having it appear that a person fell asleep while smoking and then died. Such attempts are doomed if a proper autopsy is conducted. The carbon monoxide level, soot inhalation, and fire patterns on the body must be consistent with the hypothesized reconstruction. The possibility of suicide by fire must not be overlooked; fires and even explosions have been set in structures and vehicles as a means of self-destruction.

Larceny: Sound business practice requires that an inventory count be taken regularly to ferret out theft. An employee who is periodically stealing from a firm can attempt to conceal a shortage through an apparent destruction by fire. When a fire occurs shortly before inventory time, the possibility that arson was a cover-up for larceny must be considered. When the resale value of a residence has dropped, owing perhaps to market conditions, a home owner may decide to "sell it" to the insurance company through arson. To maximize the reimbursement, expensive items are replaced by cheaper ones. An arson investigator must check to verify that the remaining contents (and ashes) are what would be expected from the inventory provided by the insured.

Fraud, Forgery, or Embezzlement: These crimes generally involve documents, some of which are needed to prove the *corpus delicti*. If such documents are unavailable because they were destroyed in a fire, crucial evidence will be missing and the prosecution made more difficult.

Other Crimes: A substantial fire requires the presence of the police to redirect traffic and see to it that spectators do not interfere with firefighters and are kept at a safe distance. With police so preoccupied, the criminal or an accomplice, having set the fire, is at liberty to commit another crime—a burglary or robbery, for instance—elsewhere in the jurisdiction.

Pyromania

Pyromania is defined as an irresistible impulse or compulsion to start a fire or set something on fire. Even though excitement or sensual gratification makes the motive clear, this kind of arson may be considered motiveless from an investigative viewpoint. In any event, because all pyromaniacs have the same inner drive, the term pyromania is too general to be useful in identifying an offender.

Modus operandi, however, can be a telltale sign; the investigator armed with this information can take the necessary steps to apprehend the pyromaniac. The arsonist motivated by profit wants to do maximum damage by penetrating deep inside the structure to set the fire. The pyromaniac, a creature of impulse who seldom forms any plans, must make do with material on hand: old newspapers, garbage chute refuse, the mattress from a baby carriage standing in a hallway, trash underneath a staircase, and so on. In other words, the fire is set wherever the fuel is found. When, for instance, many such fires occur in urban areas in the late evening hours when neighborhood bars are emptying, a pattern may be recognized: Are the fires set on the same day of the week? About the same time of night? Is there a linkage between them and payday? What local bars are within walking distance of the fire? Is the same kind of structure being attacked—apartment building, factory, garage, barn? Are they along the same route; if so, how does this relate to the locations of the local bars? If a fire-setting pattern becomes clear, the use of surveillance—fixed (of possible targets) and moving (of possible suspects)—is an obvious strategy, albeit an expensive one, in terms of work hours.

Recognition as a Hero

Some arsonists will set a fire in order to "discover" it and then "save" the inhabitants or contents. These so-called heroes tend to fall into certain, not necessarily exclusive, classes: volunteer firefighters, babysitters, volunteer librarians, night watch personnel. True heroes certainly exist—people who risk their own lives to save others, but when an individual manages to make a second heroic rescue not too long after the first, it is feasible that he or she is an arsonist. Questioning the suspect, then homing in on the details of the "discovery/rescue" during requestioning, will expose discrepancies and ultimately produce an admission or confession.

Vandalism

Run down or vacant buildings in deteriorating neighborhoods can become the target of adolescent gangs looking to vent anger or simply to relieve monotony. A set fire is good for a certain amount of excitement. Sometimes gang members "graduate" to setting fires for landlords of rent-controlled properties; having driven the tenants out, the owners realize increased revenues by subdividing the large flats. Motives varying widely in these situations, it would facilitate the investigation if a suspect gang member can be turned into an informant.

Churches and schools are vandalized and even torched from time to time. Often the individuals responsible are (or were) closely associated with the institution or congregation. But just as often, they are mischievous or malicious juveniles. Some are people who, feeling they have been unfairly treated, vandalize to redress a slight or recover self-esteem. The investigator must follow all leads, even those that seem trivial. When religious property is the target, bigotry and hatred are usually the underlying motives, and a hate crime may have taken place. Identifying the culprits can be difficult at best, unless an informant can be developed or an extensive surveillance conducted to catch them red-handed. A reward offered by church members may be helpful.

RECORDS

Some motives that drive a person to commit arson—intimidation, policy differences, emotions—may have been the consequence of an earlier provocation or quarrel requiring that the police be called.

Depending on the circumstances, the altercation could be a matter of a formal police record or merely a note in the memo pad of the uniformed officer who responded. In either event, the investigator must be diligent in following through to determine if any recorded evidence exists to support a motive for arson. Other law enforcement records to be checked out include those on recently released prisoners who were convicted of arson, with special attention paid to their *modus operandi* and the kinds of targets involved.

Fire Records

As part and parcel of an arson suppression program, many fire departments have recognized the value of the computer to store and retrieve data on suspicious or deliberately set fires. A complete Fire Incident Report should include the following information:

- Location of the incident

- Time and day of the week that the incident occurred

- Name of the occupant(s) of the premises

- Name and address of the owner of the premises

- Area of fire origin

- Source of heat-causing ignition

- Type of material ignited

- Damage: whether it is restricted, or extends beyond confines of the structure

- Estimated damage in dollars

When such data are collected and stored routinely at the state level, it will be more difficult for "fire-prone" owners and those convicted of arson-for-profit to avoid detection of their previous behavior by keeping on the move. The investigator should know that the insurance industry in this country maintains a Property Insurance Loss Register that records the prior fire loss history of individuals. Although most of the data in the Fire Incident Report is obtained easily, an owner's name and address may not be (see section on "Straw Owners"). Many states have instituted immunity laws to promote sharing of insurance company records with criminal investigators. Such legislation would allow an interchange without penalizing the insurers for releasing client information.

Straw Owners

In arson cases, especially arson-for-profit, uncovering hidden ownership or financial interest in the burned property can be a formidable task. It is complicated by the incidence of *straw ownership*, whereby the individual or business entity on record (i.e., the *straw owner* or *straw*) is a front for the real owner. If not set up for illegal purposes, straw ownership is lawful; however, the arrangement often seems questionable—bordering on "sharp" or shady business practice. By seeking answers to the following questions, the real owner may be discovered:

- Who owns the building in which the straw lives?

- For whom does the straw work?

- What attorney, management company, notary public, contractor, or tax advisor does the straw hire? Are any of these people also hired by the straw's boss (at work) or landlord (at home)?

- Who collects the rents for the burned building? (It is often the real owner in the guise of the collector who does so instead of the straw, who may be unknown to the tenants.)

Of those persons developed by the above line of inquiry, is there anyone whose financial affairs appear to be bordering on insolvency? Beacon signals to look for are:

- Bills that are not paid soon enough to qualify for the discount offered for prompt payment.

- Accounts receivable that are pledged to secure a loan or are sold at a high discount (20 to 40 percent) prior to their collection in the ordinary course of business.

- Taxes on (or collected by) the business that are not being paid as required by law (liens for unpaid taxes usually being a matter of public record).

If the business affairs of the suspect (who appears to be connected to the straw) seem in a state of potential insolvency, this obviously requires a follow-up. One approach would be to identify an employee who may feel insecure because of the downturn in the firm's financial strength, or who may otherwise be sufficiently disgruntled to be turned into an informant.

Follow-Up Activities

The investigation of arson—especially arson-for-profit—is a demanding task. The technical assistance of auditors, accountants, tax lawyers, real estate agents, and credit and financial managers will often be needed to get past the roadblocks set up to hide ownership of the property and the identity of the individual responsible. In such cases, circumstantial evidence may provide the basis upon which prosecution is possible. It can result from an admission that two separate fires in the premises occurred simultaneously; or from a finding that the door was locked, the occupant was present or in possession of the only key, and therefore had exclusive opportunity to start the fire. Opportunity may be established through canvassing: the suspect might have been seen in the area about the time the fire was first noticed.

Arson cases are also solved by direct evidence: the investigator observes the arsonist preparing to commit, or actually committing, the crime. To accomplish this, surveillance is obviously necessary. Undercover efforts can be effective. Posing as a jobless vagrant, for instance, allows the investigator to be ignored while observing the suspect entering or leaving a likely target just before the fire breaks out.

Bombing Investigations

When a threatened or actual bombing is reported, an after-the-fact investigation is begun in reaction to the incident. More often than not, however, the perpetrators are not arrested. A proactive approach has proved more productive in arresting and convicting those responsible for terrorist bombings.

Explosives

Several types of explosives are used by terrorists. In the United States, the most common explosive has been a pipe bomb using black powder. The materials necessary to make a pipe bomb are readily available in most countries and can be purchased in drug stores, hardware stores, and construction supply stores. In the 1993 World Trade Center explosion, a ureanitrate bomb was used. In Oklahoma City in 1995, the bomb consisted of a mixture of ammonium nitrate and fuel oil (called Anfo). Although homemade bombs have been used frequently, the availability of other types of explosives—particularly dynamite, TNT, and hand grenades—makes their use in the future more likely (see Table 21.1).

Detonation of an explosive device results in three primary effects: fragmentation, blast pressure, and fire. Fragmentation bombs produce shrapnel and are designed to be used against people. Homemade fragmentation bombs include such items as nails, steel ball bearings, or other materials

Table 21.1
Types of Explosive Devices

SEMTEX	A yellowish plastic explosive, about one-third more powerful than a similar amount of TNT. It has a texture like clay putty or clay, and can be molded. It is easy to transport because it will not explode without a detonator. C-4—Similar to SEMTEX, C4 is a plastic explosive that can be manufactured in solid or powder form. It is made in the United States and used by the U.S. Army and many allies, as well as by mining companies. It explodes at 26,400 feet per second.
HMEs (Home Made Explosives)	These usually involve the use of fertilizer. See Ammonium Nitrate.
IEDs (Improvised Explosive Devices)	Explosive devices formulated with the use of a variety of types of explosives and detonators, including military munitions and other common bomb-making materials.
Triavetone Triperoxide (TATP)	A liquid-based explosive created by mixing the two chemicals, which when combined create TATP, forming a white crystalline powder. The powder must dry before it can be used, and it is somewhat difficult to detonate. Could be ignited with a match or lighter in the case of a suicide bomber, as well as a detonator under optimum conditions.
Peroxide-Based Explosive	An improvised device that is relatively easy to detonate and easy to obtain on the open market. This type of explosive was used in the 2006 London train bombings.
Pipe Bomb	A device built with a length of pipe stuffed with explosive (usually black powder) and shrapnel, such as nails or BBs, sealed at both ends, and fitted with a detonator (see Figure 21.17).
Plutonium-229	Radioactive material that, when of weapons-grade quality, can be used in the making of nuclear bombs.
TNT (Trinitrotoluene)	Approximately twice as powerful as common dynamite, TNT has a lower explosive velocity than plastic explosives. It is made of nitric and sulfuric acid, and toluene. It is readily available in the United States and is usually produced in half-pound and one-pound sticks.
Ammonium Nitrate	Common fertilizer, when mixed with diesel fuel, has an explosive velocity of 3,600 feet per second. The bomb is "triggered" by a detonator, which is used to introduce an electrical charge, which causes the explosive to ignite. Detonation may be achieved in a number of ways, including using a timing mechanism, electronically, or by a fuse—all of which complete an electric (usually battery-operated) circuit in some way.

that spread out over the blast area. The blast from any explosive is capable of killing; the greater the amount of explosive used, the greater the damage. In addition, the very placement of the bomb can be designed to create a fragmentation explosion. A car bomb, for example, will create shrapnel from the metal parts as the vehicle is torn apart.

Some explosives can be traced through markers that are placed in the material by the manufacturer, making it possible to trace the source of the explosive. Unfortunately, this identification is limited largely to dynamite or TNT, and the large quantity used for industrial purposes may hamper tracing.

As mentioned earlier, *improvised explosive devices* (*IEDs*) is a common term for "homemade" bombs and became popular in the lexicon of bombs in the war in Iraq. Although the types of bombs used by insurgents in Iraq frequently use military ordnance, most have similar properties to the types of bombs listed below.

Car bombs are used to kill the occupants of a vehicle, to kill individuals in close proximity to the vehicle, or so-called "suicide" bombs in which a driver runs a vehicle into a facility or crowd of people, or parks the vehicle near a target.

Fragmentation bombs, as noted earlier, are designed to kill or maim people. In addition to homemade bombs, hand grenades, mines, and other antipersonnel devices are becoming more common.

Letter bombs consist of a relatively small amount of explosive, but enough to kill or maim. The explosive is placed in an envelope or package and is wired to detonate when it is opened. Letter bombs have resulted in several fatalities, including that of a federal judge in Alabama in 1989.

Aircraft bombs are usually designed to explode when a plane is in the air, ideally over water. Various means (air pressure, timing, etc.) are used to detonate the explosives.

Suicide bombers have yet to be a major problem in the United States, but experts believe that it is only a matter of time before this type of attack will be more common in this country.

As mentioned earlier, it is not uncommon for terrorists to plant a second explosive device designed to kill police or military officials who respond to the scene. Great care must be taken in responding to and protecting the scene. An investigator should never try to process a bomb scene until trained bomb-disposal technicians have cleared the area. Eric Rudolph used secondary explosive devices in attacks in Atlanta in 1997. Rudolph, a former Army Ranger, was responsible for several attacks in the southern part of the United States, including the 1996 Atlanta Olympics site, a lesbian nightclub, and several abortion facilities. He was able to elude police for more than seven years after the Atlanta bombings, and was captured in May 2003 by an alert police officer who caught him rummaging in garbage for food in rural North Carolina.

In addition to bombs, the availability of various forms of military hardware poses an increasing threat. An RPG (rocket-propelled grenade) or shoulder-mounted missile, such as the Stinger, can bring down a plane or can be fired

Cmdr. Joseph Grubisic, Bomb Squad, Chicago Police Department

Figure 21.17
A typical pipe bomb, a type of explosive commonly used by terrorists.

into a building from a distance. Because these devices are usually fired from discardable tubes, fingerprints and other trace evidence may be available.

The use of mobile and relatively simple mortars or missiles used by Hezbollah against Israel are designed to create fear and disrupt communities. Similar-type mortars or missiles have been used by groups in the United States.

CONCLUSION

Arson and explosives investigation are specialized types of investigations that will usually necessitate the assistance of a fire marshal or a federal investigator from the Bureau of Alcohol, Tobacco, Firearms and Explosives (ATF).

NOTES

[1]   Rossotti, Hazel, *Fire: Servant, Scourge and Enigma*, Dover Publications, Inc. New York, (1993), p. 83.

[2]   U.S. Department of Justice, Federal Bureau of Investigation, *Crime in the United States 2010*. See http://www.fbi.gov/about-us/cjis/ucr/crime-in-the-u.s/2010/crime-in-the-u.s.-2010/violent-crime/

[3]   National Fire Protection Association, *NFPA 921: Guide for Fire & Explosion Investigations* (Quincy, MA: NFPA, 2008).

[4]   Rossotti, p. 83.

[5]   J. D. De Haan, *Kirk's Fire Investigation*, 3rd ed. (Englewood Cliffs, NJ: Prentice Hall, Brady Books, 1990), 106.

[6]   Supra note 2.

[7]   Rossotti. p. 213.

[8]   De Haan. *Kirk's Fire Investigation*, op. cit., 6–33.

[9]   De Haan. *Kirk's Fire Investigation*, op. cit., 34–66.

[10]   De Haan. *Kirk's Fire Investigation*, op. cit., 67–92.

[11]   J. D. De Haan, "Determining the Point of Origin—Diagnostic Signs and Laboratory Analysis," *Fire and Arson Investigator*, 36:4 (1986), 37–40.

[12]   De Haan. *Kirk's Fire Investigation*, op. cit., 109–119.

[13]   D. V. Canfield, "Causes of Spalling of Concrete at Elevated Temperatures," *Fire and Arson Investigator*, 34:4 (1984).

[14]   De Haan. *Kirk's Fire Investigation*, op. cit., 135.

[15]   National Fire Protection Association, *User's Manual for NFPA 921: Guide for Fire and Explosion Investigations*, 2nd ed. (Sudbury, MA: Jones and Bartlett, 2005), 921.

DISCUSSION QUESTIONS

1. Arson and bombing investigations are usually handled by what types of investigators?

2. Why are arson investigations often difficult to investigate?

3. What are common elements in the definition of arson?

4. According to Rossotti, what is the most common reason for committing arson?

5. Why might photos of persons observing the fire be important in an investigation?

6. What are the usual motives for arson?

7. What types of commercially available accelerants can be used to start fires, and what is the most common one used in arson?

8. Why is point of origin of the fire important to the investigator?

9. Why is a pour pattern important?

10. What are some of the items that may be used to delay the start of a fire?

11. What is pyromania?

12. What should a complete fire incident report contain?

13. What is an IED or an HME?

14. What is ammonium nitrate?

15. What is meant by a secondary device?

SUPPLEMENTAL READINGS

Babrauskas, V. (2003). *Ignition handbook*. Issaquah, WA: Fire Science Publishers.

DeHaan, J. D. (2007). *Kirk's fire investigation* (6th ed.). Upper Saddle River, NJ: Pearson/Prentice Hall.

Gaynor, J. (2000). *Juvenile firesetter intervention handbook*. Washington DC: Federal Emergency Management Agency, and U.S. Fire Administration. Full text available at: http://www.usfa.fema.gov/usfapubs/

Icove, D. J., & DeHaan, J. D. (2012). *Forensic fire scene reconstruction* (3rd ed.). Upper Saddle River, NJ: Pearson/Prentice Hall.

Motavalli, J. (Mar. 21, 2005). Detectives in hot pursuit of evidence in the ashes. *The New York Times*, D9.

National Fire Protection Association (2011). *NFPA 921: Guide for fire & explosion investigations*. Quincy, MA: NFPA.

Noon, R. (1995). *Engineering analysis of fires and explosions*. Boca Raton, FL: CRC Press.

Stadolnik, R. F. (2000). *Drawn to the flame: Assessment and treatment of juvenile firesetting behavior*. Sarasota, FL: Professional Resource Exchange.

Section III

SPECIAL TOPICS

Section III presents a "potpourri" from which instructors may choose topics according to their interests or those of their students. A few chapters from earlier editions have been relocated here. In addition, the reader will find new information on global crime, reflecting the growing importance of international investigations and threats posed by criminal activity by foreign nationals in the United States and abroad.

Topics covered in this section also include increasing threats and emerging crime, terrorism and urban disorder, and enterprise crime. The reader should be aware that there is some redundancy in this section with several earlier chapters, where a topic may not have been covered in as much detail as it is in this section.

CHAPTER 22

INCREASING THREATS AND EMERGING CRIME

INTRODUCTION

In a rapidly changing societal environment characterized by increases in communication, technology, travel, social mobility, economic changes, and growth in immigration, both legal and illegal, police departments are finding themselves involved in new or changing forms of crime that will have an impact on the investigative function. In many ways, these types of crimes will also involve new investigative approaches, a greater reliance on technology, and cooperative relationships with other law enforcement agencies and the private-security sector.

Of particular importance in many of these types of crime is a thorough knowledge of the law, particularly where new legislation has been enacted, and the recognition that many of these types of crimes focus on specific population groups, such as the aged, ethnic minorities, and new immigrants. Problems include language translation, cultural traditions, fear of retaliation by offenders, and an apprehensive attitude toward cooperating with the police because of their experiences in countries from which they came. Immigrants from other countries have frequently developed their own communities in larger cities, a situation not unlike that of the great migration to the United States at the beginning of the twentieth century. This sometimes presents special problems for law enforcement.

An aging population in America has also resulted in the growth of retirement homes and communities for older citizens. Criminals and less-than-legal business organizations have been quick to take advantage of the elderly and migrant populations. The investigator should be aware of the unique issues that come into play in handling these types of cases.

IDENTITY THEFT

One of the fastest growing crimes in America is *identity theft*. The advent of the Internet and a proliferation of web sites have contributed to this phenomenon. Identity theft takes many forms, the most common of which is related to various types of fraud, theft, and misrepresentation. Criminal activity may range from single or multiple uses of credit cards to elaborate schemes resulting in losses amounting to hundreds of thousands of dollars. See Box 22.1.

Investigations related to theft and fraud will usually necessitate working with credit card and cell phone companies, the Postal Investigation Service, other federal organizations, and state agencies. Two of the more common methods of identity theft, known as "phishing" and "spoofing," involve

---

Box 22.1 Identity Theft: From US Code Title 18; Section 1028

(a) Whoever, in a circumstance described in subsection (c) of this section—

(1) knowingly and without lawful authority produces an identification document, authentication feature, or a false identification document;

(2) knowingly transfers an identification document, authentication feature, or a false identification document knowing that such document or feature was stolen or produced without lawful authority;

(3) knowingly possesses with intent to use unlawfully or transfer unlawfully five or more identification documents (other than those issued lawfully for the use of the possessor), authentication features, or false identification documents;

(4) knowingly possesses an identification document (other than one issued lawfully for the use of the possessor), authentication feature, or a false identification document, with the intent such document or feature be used to defraud the United States;

(5) knowingly produces, transfers, or possesses a document-making implement or authentication feature with the intent such document-making implement or authentication feature will be used in the production of a false identification document or another document-making implement or authentication feature which will be so used;

(6) knowingly possesses an identification document or authentication feature that is or appears to be an identification document or authentication feature of the United States or a sponsoring entity of an event designated as a special event of national significance which is stolen or produced without lawful authority knowing that such document or feature was stolen or produced without such authority;

(7) knowingly transfers, possesses, or uses, without lawful authority, a means of identification of another person with the intent to commit, or to aid or abet, or in connection with, any unlawful activity that constitutes a violation of Federal law, or that constitutes a felony under any applicable State or local law; or

(8) knowingly traffics in false or actual authentication features for use in false identification documents, document-making implements, or means of identification; shall be punished as provided in subsection (b) of this section.

---

efforts to have a credit card, computer, or cell phone customer give up information by claiming to be representatives of the company (see Box 22.2).

In some cases, there are likely to be multiple victims. In all cases, the investigator should make every effort to recover as much documentation, such as credit card and bank statements, as possible. If a computer has been involved, precautions should be taken to secure the computer for examination by a forensics laboratory. The U.S. Code (Section 1028, Title 18) makes it a federal crime to produce, steal, or use a false identification document; transfer or possess a false identification document that is used to defraud the government, or used to commit a crime that is a violation of federal law, or constitutes a felony under an applicable state or local law; or traffic in false identification documents. The term *identification document* includes any means of identification, name or number, used to identify a specific person. This includes such information as name, social security number, date of birth, driver's license, passport, tax ID number, or unique electronic or other form of identifying information.[1] See Figure 22.1.

BOX 22.2 PHISHING AND SPOOFING

Phishing is a computer scam in which a victim is contacted by e-mail, or in some cases by telephone, and is asked for his or her social security number or other sensitive information that can then be used to secure credit cards, open charge accounts, or otherwise use the information to defraud the victim.

Spoofing involves efforts by criminals to obtain caller ID numbers for the victim's cell phone, which can then be used to obtain information about the victim's identity. In 1996 the Federal Trade Commission (FCC) filed the first case against a mortgage company that allegedly used the information for telemarketing. There has been a proliferation of companies that sell so-called "SpoofCards" as telephone cards, which can be used by the perpetrators to pose as banks or other organizations. Although the sale of SpoofCards is legal in most states, these cards can provide criminals with sensitive information.

One example involves calls made from what appears to be a court and the victim is told that he or she has missed a jury duty appearance and must pay a fine. The person is then asked for a credit card number or bank account from which funds can be drawn. Another example involves use of the altered ID number to send malicious phone calls as a means of harassing the victim. In March 2005, police in New Jersey received a call from a woman saying she was being raped. When the police arrived, they found that the call had been "spoofed" by someone who entered her number as the one from which the call was sent.

Source: Becky Yerek, "Thieves Hot Tool: Caller ID." *Chicago Tribune* (July 16, 2006), I.

Figure 22.1
An FBI official speaks at a news conference announcing the arrests of dozens of people in an identity theft ring. U.S. and Egyptian authorities arrested dozens of people involved in an identity theft ring that victimized thousands.

When a suspect has been identified, it may be necessary to secure a search warrant that identifies property or other materials that may have been purchased by the perpetrator. For example, in many of these types of cases the perpetrator will secure materials, such as a television set or other electronics, that can later be identified as having been purchased using the victim's identity documentation.

Online Sting

In June 2012, an FBI "sting" operation resulted in the arrest of 24 suspects in what was described as the largest undercover operation focusing on international trading in stolen credit card numbers. "Operation Card Shop," using a fake website, provided a glimpse into the way criminals operate on the Internet. The fake website was described as a "marketplace for illegal activities," attracting thousand s of perpetrators who had stolen identity information from an estimated 400,000 victims.

Source: Reed Albergotti, "Arrests Total 24 in Online Sting." *Wall Street Journal* (June 27, 2012). P.C2

Because the elderly are frequently prone to being victimized by this type of crime, care should be taken in interviewing to document the victim's statements and record the details involved in the methods used by the perpetrator. For example, if a credit card was stolen from the victim, efforts should be made to determine where the theft took place and obtain a description of the suspect if available. Keep in mind that an elderly victim may be prone to forgetting, misreading, or interpreting a statement or action, or unclear as to how the crime was committed. Further, if the case goes to court, the defense attorney may attack witness or victim statements and how they were recorded. A common defense question is likely to begin with: "Are you absolutely positive that the victim…" For this reason it is imperative that a careful and accurate record be kept. In some cases, it may be worth recording the victim's statements.

INTERNET FRAUD

A growing number of what may be described as "lower-level" crimes are being reported. These involve use of the computer to change records, to make monetary transfers, or to victimize companies. Many of these types of crime are committed by employees or former employees. In some cases, a company itself may be involved in fraudulent activity. The Enron accounting fraud scandal in 2001, involving millions of dollars, is perhaps the largest example of company fraud. In such fraud cases, the investigator should secure the services of a forensic accountant and computer forensic specialists. According to a 2009 report, Americans lost more than $559.7 million in the year prior as a result of Internet fraud, compared to $336 million in 2006. Moreover, 61 percent of computers in the United States were infected with spyware.[2]

Internet fraud involves a large number of schemes. One of the more common types of "phishing" involves an Internet letter from a Nigerian official or some other international figure who promises a reward for helping them move funds out of their country. Other scams include offers to update a computer or requests for account information. If the victim responds, his or her computer may then be "monitored" by the offender.[3]

Another type of Internet fraud involves the sale of goods by computer, whereby the victim sends a check or makes a monetary transfer and the merchandise is never delivered. These cases are frequently difficult to investigate because the seller may be located in another jurisdiction. In order to make a case, the investigator must show that the criminal activity involves more than one case, which will also involve multiple victims.

Sections 1341 and 1343 of Title 18 of the U.S. Code can frequently be used to prosecute Internet or wire fraud when the crime takes place across state lines or via the U.S. mail or an interstate commercial carrier, such as UPS or Federal Express. The elements of mail and wire fraud include: (1) the intent to defraud, and (2) either the mail or a wire transmission was used to carry out the fraudulent activity. For example, the suspect may use the Internet to sell a fraudulent product or service and then use the mail to receive payment.[4]

The U.S. Postal Inspection Service warns of a growing number of foreign lottery-type scams. It is a federal violation to mail lottery tickets, advertisements, or payments to a foreign lottery. A common practice is to inform a victim by telephone or e-mail that they have won money. Given the increased use of the Internet there is no doubt that these types of crimes will continue to grow.

EXPLOITATION OF WOMEN AND CHILDREN

The exploitation of women and children for criminal purposes and the growth of child pornography have become serious issues for law enforcement. Child pornography has been fueled largely by the Internet, and its investigation will usually require cooperation with federal authorities because the criminal activity usually involves multiple jurisdictions and, in some cases, other countries. Mere possession of child pornography is a crime in many jurisdictions, but it should be recognized that most pedophiles who collect such materials are in communication with others who share photos, as well as individuals and groups who sell such materials. The International Police Organization (INTERPOL) serves as a "clearinghouse" for information on the exploitation of women and children (see Box 22.3).

Box 22.3 Interpol

INTERPOL aims to end the abuse and exploitation of human beings for financial gain. Women from developing countries and young children all over the world are especially vulnerable to trafficking, smuggling, or sexual exploitation.

Trafficking in women for sexual exploitation is a multi-billion-dollar business that involves citizens of most countries and helps sustain organized crime. A violation of human rights, it destroys the lives of its victims.

People smuggling implies the procurement, for financial or material gain, of illegal entry into a state of which that person is neither a citizen nor a permanent resident. Criminal networks that smuggle and traffic in human beings for financial gain increasingly control the flow of migrants across borders.

Human trafficking, such as for sexual exploitation, is distinct from people smuggling in that it involves the exploitation of the migrant, often for purposes of forced labor and/or prostitution.

Child sexual exploitation on the Internet ranges from posed photos to visual recordings of brutal sexual crimes. One of INTERPOL's main tools for helping police fight this type of crime is the INTERPOL Child Abuse Image Database (ICAID). Created in 2001, it contains hundreds of thousands of images of child sexual abuse submitted by member countries, thereby facilitating the sharing of images and information to assist law enforcement agencies with the identification of new victims.

Source: http://www.INTERPOL.org

The Child Pornography Protection Act (CPPA) was codified in 2001 as 18 U.S. Code (2251-2260) in response to the proliferation of images on the Internet. The prosecution of violations has been further complicated by the use of "virtual" child pornography, which does not necessarily depict a real or identifiable child. The use of "morphing" enables the user to create pornographic images by cutting and pasting to develop images that are almost impossible to discern as being fabricated. Under Sections 2251, 2252 (al-5), and 2256(8), the visual description of child pornography (minors engaged in sexually explicit conduct), as well as interstate transport, selling, or possession, by any means, including mail or computer, is illegal.[5] However, the Supreme Court, in *Ashcroft v. Free Speech Coalition* (2002),[6] found that the definition of "any visual depiction," be it computer-generated or a picture of a minor engaging in sexually explicit conduct, was too broad. In *United States v. LaFortune* (2008),[7] the Court said that a non-expert trier of fact could determine whether images were of real or virtual children without benefit of expert testimony. In *United States v. Irving* (2004),[8] the court declined to hold that the prosecution was required to present expert testimony proving that the children in the unlawful video images were in fact real, rather than virtual, children. The U.S. Postal Inspection Service and the Immigration and Customs (ICE) service have units that focus on this type of crime.

HUMAN TRAFFICKING AND THE EXPLOITATION OF ILLEGAL ALIENS

Human trafficking is a global problem. According to Barbara Moynihan and Mario T. Gaboury, "Today, the monetary value of human beings is increasing. Due to an explosion in population, it is easy and cheap to find slave labor... Trafficking victims are hostages, taken against their will, forced to engage in unwanted, dangerous and frightening activities. Labor trafficking can involve many hours of work, little or no time off, exposure to physical harm or disease, and no hope for rescue."[9]

In 2000, the Trafficking Victims Protection Act (TVPA) came into law and highlighted a growing new phenomenon involving the exploitation of women and children and the victimization of illegal immigrants. In 2005, the Act required a reporting system, resulting in a 2011 Bureau of Justice Statistics Special Report, *Characteristics of Suspected Human Trafficking Incidents, 2008–2010.* The data from 38 federally funded human trafficking task forces identified 2,515 cases/incidents involving forced prostitution, child sex trafficking, and other sex trafficking. Among the 389 incidents confirmed to be human trafficking by high-data-quality task forces, there were 488 suspects and 527 victims. Most of the cases (87%) involved a state or local law enforcement agency. Most (73%) of the victims were U.S. citizens, and the majority of sex trafficking victims (83%) were U.S. citizens. Child sex trafficking accounted for 55 percent of the cases. Among the 415 suspects for whom information on race and origin was reported, blacks represented the largest category (54%), followed by Hispanics (29%). Whites and Asians accounted for 6 and 7 percent of human trafficking suspects, respectively. Hispanics constituted the largest category of labor trafficking suspects (48%), while blacks accounted for the largest percentage of sex trafficking suspects (62%).[10]

Statistics dispel the myth that most victims involved in human trafficking are illegal immigrants, although it should be noted that a large number of unreported cases may be attributed to the fear of undocumented aliens to report being victimized.

Home Invasions

The number of home invasions in the United States, particularly as they relate to illegal drug activity, has also increased. Many of these cases involve the murder of the occupants, usually for revenge or for stealing drugs from their supplier. These cases are frequently associated with gang activity. Evidence of the torture of one or more of the victims is a strong indication of such activity.

Home invasion is the crime of entering a private and occupied dwelling, with the intent of committing a crime, often while threatening the resident of the dwelling. It is a legally defined offense in the United States, and applies even if entry is not forced. It can also apply if someone is invited into a home and remains on the premises after being asked to leave by the resident. Home invasion differs from burglary, which is usually defined as unlawful entry into any occupied or unoccupied building, with intent to commit one of a list of specified offences. Home invasion covers an intent to commit any crime.

As discussed in Chapter 18, some home invasions involve robbery. The victims are frequently elderly persons or homeowners who are thought to be wealthy. These victims are likely to be targeted by individuals who have been to the home previously, perhaps as delivery or repair personnel. The investigator should query the victims about prior visits or circumstances in which an outsider may have been privy to information suggesting the presence of valuables in their home.

One of the most infamous home invasion investigations in recent years took place following the murder of Jennifer Hawke-Petit and daughters Hayley and Michaela at their home in Cheshire, Connecticut, in 2007. During the invasion, Hawke-Petit died of asphyxiation due to strangulation while her two daughters were left bound in their beds, dying of smoke inhalation after the suspects doused the house with gasoline and set it on fire before fleeing. The victims were also raped and tortured during the invasion. William Petit Jr. survived the attack despite being bound and severely beaten while trying to help his family. Two paroled criminals were charged with capital felony and murder, aggravated sexual assault, arson, robbery, and kidnapping. They were convicted in 2012. In 2008, partly as a result of this incident, Connecticut passed a law ordering a 30-year mandatory sentence for home invasion, but numerous Connecticut residents have been campaigning for the passage of a "three strikes" law that would impose life sentences for repeat violent offenders.[11]

Investigations of home invasions should focus on what was taken. If items other than cash were taken, descriptions of property should be recorded in detail. Pawn shops and known "fences" should be examined in an effort to identify possible suspects. In most cases, home invasion crimes are committed by more than one individual, and the perpetrators are likely to be involved in multiple crimes.

Con Games

P.T. Barnum supposedly said "a sucker is born every minute," and judging by the number of victims of con artists, the statement holds true. Con or "scam" artists have developed an array of schemes designed to swindle naïve and unsuspecting citizens of millions of dollars each year. These types of criminals usually work in pairs and are highly mobile. By the time a victim realizes that he or she has been swindled, the perpetrators are usually far away.

For this reason, an important aspect of the investigation requires good communication between departments and a computerized database that makes it possible to link the cases. A records search should be made to identify individuals who have been arrested in the past for crimes of a similar nature.

THEFT OF PAINTINGS AND CULTURAL OBJECTS

The theft of and illegal transport of valuable art work and cultural objects has also increased in recent years, and usually involves a specialized form of investigation. The FBI and a number of the larger police departments now have units devoted to this type of criminal activity (see Box 22.4). Some departments in the United States and abroad also have web sites displaying stolen art work. "Over the last 50 years, the U.S. Department of Justice (DOJ) has ranked art crime behind only drugs and arms in terms of highest-grossing criminal trades. There are hundreds of thousands of art crimes reported per year, but, despite this fact, the general public only hears about the handful of big-name museum heists that make international headlines."[12]

The Los Angeles Police Department's "Art Theft Detail" is responsible for the investigation of all thefts and burglaries in which fine art is the primary object of attack. The detail also investigates fakes, frauds, and forgeries involving art. This unit has citywide jurisdiction and assists in protecting the artistic, cultural, and historical heritage of a city of 3.8 million people covering more than 450 square miles. It is the only full-time law enforcement unit in the United States devoted to the investigation of art crimes. The two detectives assigned to the Art Theft Detail target suspects who prey upon artists, art dealers, and collectors. The unit maintains close contact with the art community and provides stolen art information to galleries, art dealers, auction houses, museums, art associations, publications, and other law enforcement agencies—both nationally and internationally.[13]

Box 22.4 FBI ART CRIME TEAM

Founded in 2004, the FBI's Art Crime Team features several dedicated agents supported by special trial attorneys for prosecutions. The team also maintains the National Stolen Art File (NSAF), a computerized index of reported stolen art for use by law enforcement agencies around the world. The Art Crime Team has recovered more than 2,600 items valued at approximately $142 million. Such statistics must be understood in context, however. The cited values for art are based on the estimated open market value—that which art with legitimate pedigree may sell for at auction. Estimates of the black market value of stolen art based on the amount that undercover agents were asked to pay during sting operations is 7 to 10 percent of its perceived open market value.

Source: U.S. Department of Justice, Federal Bureau of Investigation, Art Crime Team, *http://www.fbi.gov/about-us/ investigate/vc_majorthefts/arttheft/art-crime-team* (accessed July 12, 2011). In Noah Charney, Paul Denton, John Kleberg. "Protecting Cultural Heritage from Art Theft: International Challenge, Local Opportunity. *FBI Law Enforcement Bulletin*. March, 2012.

Art Theft

Over the last 50 years, the U.S. Department of Justice (DOJ) has ranked art crime behind only drugs and arms in terms of highest-grossing criminal trades. There are hundreds of thousands of art crimes reported per year, but, despite this fact, the general public only hears about the handful of big-name museum heists that make international headlines.

Source: Noah Charney, Paul Denton, John Kleberg. "Protecting Cultural Heritage from Art Theft: International Challenge, Local Opportunity." *FBI Law Enforcement Bulletin*. March, 2012.

Noah Charney, the director of the Association for Research into Crimes against Art (ARCA), an international nonprofit research group based in Italy, is an internationally recognized "art investigator." He has written a number of books on art crime. In his most recent work, *The Thefts of the Mona Lisa*, he explores the problems of investigating a crime that involves numerous countries over more than a hundred years.[14]

Forgery and crimes of deception remain within the realm of individual con men and women and skillful artists. While no criminal profile exists for art thieves, who tend to be mercenary criminals with no experience or knowledge of the art world, forgers fit a specific profile, and their MO can be mapped in a way that if studied by the art trade might prevent future crimes.[15]

Figure 22.2
Badge of the Carabinieri Art Squad.

The MOs of art thieves and forgers are varied, and not really understood by the general public, who generally view this type of crime as being rare and glamorized, largely by the media and popular films. "The reasons for this are complex and fascinating. They require an understanding not only of organized crime but of the exclusive and often underhanded machinations of the international art community."[16] The art theft squad of the Talian Carabinieri is considered to be one of the best, largely because Italy is the center of global art-related criminal activity (see Figure 22.2).

Copies and "Knockoffs"

Although counterfeit product and patent and copyright violations generally represent a specialized type of investigation, the growth of this criminal activity involves losses estimated in billions of dollars. This type of criminal activity ranges from media (films and records) to copies of so-called "knockoffs" of high-cost products, such as watches (Rolex, Cartier, Tag Heuer), handbags (Gucci, Coach, Prada), designer clothing, and sports paraphernalia (see Figure 22.3). A growing problem is the introduction of counterfeit prescription drugs.

Of particular concern regarding these types of crimes is the involvement of organized criminal activity on a global scale, as well as evidence that the proceeds of some of these crimes are used to support terrorist groups.

Because most citizens do not view the sale of such merchandise as a major issue, it has not traditionally been an area of great concern to law enforcement. However, given the large amounts of money such activities generate, investigations involving major dealers are becoming more commonplace. The primary focus of such investigations will be on major traffickers, especially when organized crime groups are involved.

Body Parts

Rapid advances in medicine and the ability to replace body parts has resulted in what some feel is an "opportunity" for organized criminals to engage in the illegal securing and sale of body parts. In

Figure 22.3
U.S. Immigration and Customs Enforcement and Tampa Police Department officers box up hundreds of counterfeit NFL jerseys seized during a raid on a flea market booth just before 2009's Super Bowl XLIII.

other countries, such as India and China, the sale of kidneys by the poor has become increasingly common. Because it is possible to live with one kidney, the practice is not illegal in these countries. In the United States, however, the sale of kidneys is illegal (although one can volunteer to give up a kidney). As science makes it easier to transplant everything from ears to the cornea of an eye, the demand throughout the world is increasing.

Most reports of the taking and sale of body parts from the living are nothing more than urban legend, but there have been reported cases of the sale of body parts taken illegally or questionably from deceased persons. In the United States, most of the illegal trafficking in body parts centers on the illegal removal of organs that are sold by funeral parlors or removed during autopsies and sold without knowledge of the relatives of the deceased. A special report by *USA Today* reporter Stephanie Armour noted that body parts can be sold for thousands of dollars. Although some body parts are used for transplants, many of the parts are sold to research facilities or other buyers. In most cases, the buyers are not aware that the parts were stolen. Some examples of cadaver body parts are corneas for correcting or averting blindness; heart valves for repairing cardiac defects or damage; and bone, cartilage, and tendon for grafting, Approximate prices for fresh or frozen body parts can be seen in Table 22.1.[17]

Table 22.1
Approximate Prices for Fresh or Frozen Body Parts

BODY PART	PRICE COMMANDED
Brain	$500–600
Elbow	$350–850
Forearm	$350–850
Head	$550–900
Hand	$350–850
Knee	$450–650
Leg	$700–1,000
Shoulder	$375–650
Temporal Bones	$370–550
Torso	$1,200–3,000
Wrist	$350–850

Source: Adapted from *USA Today*, "Brokering Body Parts." Available from http://www.usatoday.com/graphics/body_parts/flash.htm

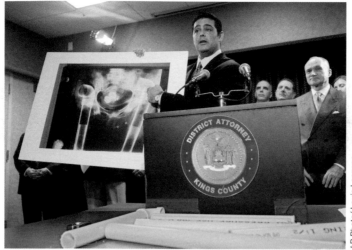

Figure 22.4
An assistant district attorney shows a photograph of an X-ray showing the pelvic area of a deceased person with PVC plumbing pipe inserted where bones belong. Michael Mastromarino was convicted in 2008 of enterprise corruption, body stealing, and reckless endangerment.

In 2006, for example, the Brooklyn district attorney charged Michael Mastromarino and his accomplices with stealing more than a thousand corpses—including that of Alistair Cooke, the well-respected host of *Masterpiece Theatre*—and dismembering and distributing them without screening the parts for disease. From an investigative standpoint in the United States, this type of criminal activity is rare, but something with which investigators should be familiar. See Figure 22.4.

SCHOOL AND WORKPLACE VIOLENCE

Violence and criminal activities in schools have become an increasingly important community issue. They represent difficult investigative issues partly because in many cases there was a complaint made prior to the incident by citizens or coworkers. Failure to follow up on complaints or other forms of information is likely to bring criticism upon law enforcement agencies. School bullying has become an increasingly public concern, and includes the use of the Internet to harass or intimidate a victim. Several cases have resulted in the victims committing suicide.

The number of violent attacks in the workplace, or on the perpetrator's associates or supervisors has emerged as an important investigative issue, largely because of the media publicity surrounding such an event. Hostility toward businesses or government agencies has also been a topic of concern. Of particular concern has been the number of school violence reports that have resulted in deaths of students and teachers. The Virginia Polytechnic Institute and State University attack in 2007 resulted in the murder of 33 students. One of the most tragic events occurred on April 20, 1999, in a high school in Columbine, Colorado, when two students, in a carefully planned attack, killed one teacher and 12 students. The shooters, Eric Harris and Dylan Klebold, were reportedly bullied constantly by their classmates, and this behavior was allegedly one of the reasons they carried out the attack. In the aftermath of the shootings, there was a widespread debate about gun control laws and firearm availability, particularly to minors.

Since Columbine there have been more than 80 school-related shootings. Of particular interest in the Columbine case are the many mistakes made by authorities prior to the event, the erroneous information provided by the media and through a web of rumors circulated throughout the town, and eventually throughout the country. Dave Cullen, an author and reporter, spent nine years unraveling the case. His account of the mistakes made by investigators, the law enforcement community and other authorities, including the media, in his book *Columbine*, provides a primer on follow-up investigations.[18]

One government report found 10 key similarities among 37 incidents that happened between 1974 and 2000.[19] These findings may have major implications for approaches to deter school violence and shootings:

1. Incidents of targeted violence at school rarely are sudden, impulsive acts.

2. Prior to most incidents, other people knew about the attacker's idea and/or plan to attack.

3. Most attackers did not threaten their targets directly prior to advancing the attack.

4. There is no accurate or useful profile of students who engaged in targeted school violence.

5. Most attackers engaged in some behavior prior to the incident that caused others concern or indicated a need for help.

6. Most attackers had difficulty coping with significant losses or personal failures. Moreover, many had considered or attempted suicide.

7. Many attackers felt bullied, persecuted, or injured by others prior to the attack.

8. Most attackers had access to and had used weapons prior to the attack.

9. In many cases, other students were involved in some capacity.

10. Despite prompt law enforcement responses, most shooting incidents were stopped by means other than law enforcement intervention.

Workplace violence drew national attention in the 1990s, following a series of shootings in postal facilities. These attacks are characterized by physical assaults, and in the more extreme cases, shootings. According to the Department of Labor, in 2010 there were 506 homicides in the workplace, which represents a decline of more than 50 percent from 1994, when 1,080 homicides were reported.[20]

The National Institute for the Prevention of Workplace Violence, Inc. maintains statistics on workplace violence and estimates the economic cost of workplace violence nationwide at around $121 billion a year. Nonfatal workplace assaults result in more than 876,000 lost workdays and $16 million in lost wages.[21]

Depending on the nature and severity of the incident, subsequent costs might be incurred due to lost productivity and/or materials (e.g., plant closings), debriefing/counseling, contract/sales losses, cleaning and refurbishing of impacted areas, increase in insurance costs, lawsuits, and settlements, PR measures to combat negative publicity, increased retention and recruiting issues, and organizational change initiatives. In addition, there is a profound impact on the business operations from decreased productivity, delayed shipments, lost sales, management distraction, increased absenteeism, worker compensation, and medical claims, etc.[22]

In conducting an investigation of a complaint, an effort should be made to develop background information on alleged suspects, such as previous arrests, a history of violent behavior, and the possession of firearms. In cases involving students, interviews with teachers and staff can provide important information on demeanor, propensity for violence, and prior incidents involving threatening behavior.

Special care must be taken in interviews with parents, who are likely to be hostile or defensive. When an individual appears to be prone to violence, a referral to counseling may be warranted. However, because a crime has not been committed yet, the investigator should avoid making accusations.

Following an event, standard investigative procedures should be followed relative to the crime scene, interviews, suspect statements, and recovery of weapons. A common defense is likely to be self-defense, and this should be a focus of the investigation in determining the facts and motive in the case.

Satanism, Cults, and Ritual Crime

Although groups involved in satanism, cult behavior, or ritualistic activities have a long history throughout the world, one of the more common aspects of these cases has been criticism of law enforcement, either for not conducting investigations or for handling confrontations poorly. For this reason the investigator should be familiar with the practices and methods of such groups because incidents are frequently preceded by complaints from citizens that go overlooked or ignored.

In cases in which such groups are known to be active in a community, information about their aims, leadership, and organization may be collected for background purposes. However, because many of these groups claim to be religious or social in nature, there is a fine line as to the types of information that can be collected. The investigator should be familiar with local rules and procedures relative to the collection of intelligence information.

Kenneth Lanning, FBI Supervisory Special Agent, Behavioral Science Unit at Quantico, studied the rising concern with cults and satanism by attending numerous seminars and conferences taught by law enforcement officials, usually police officers, and by looking for hard evidence of the alleged criminal activity engaged in by satanists or cult members.

Lanning concluded:

> Law enforcement officers need to know something about satanism and the occult in order to properly evaluate their possible connections to criminal activity. The focus, however, must be on the objective investigation of violations of criminal statutes. ... As a general rule of thumb, the law enforcement perspective can best be maintained by investigators repeatedly asking themselves what they would do if the acts in question were part of Protestant, Catholic, or Jewish activity.[23]

Larry Kahaner, in a book on cults that kill, asserts that satanic cult crimes are rarely solved. Based on interviews with the police and others, he details activity such as animal sacrifices and mutilations (see Figure 22.5), corpses drained of blood, satanic symbols carved on chests (see Figure 22.6), and even human sacrifices involving children.[24]

As long as estimates of satanic practices are belittled by some and overstated by others, the careful

Figure 22.5
Sacrificial sheep (head is to the right) found near ceremonial scene.

Courtesy, Robert J. Simandl

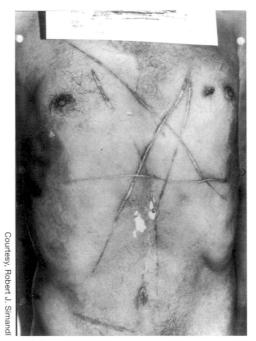

Courtesy, Robert J. Simandl

Figure 22.6
Pentagram carved on chest of an unidentified, homeless person who was kidnapped and sacrificed.

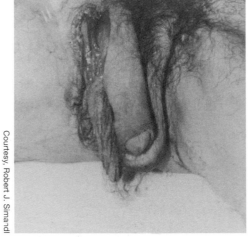

Courtesy, Robert J. Simandl

Figure 22.7
Genital mutilation. Right testicle removed in ceremonial act as part of a sacrifice or sadistic murder. Satanists believe the right testicle is a source of power. Such knowledge has significance in that such mutilation indicates motive and intent.

analysis of Jeffrey S. Victor, a prominent critic of the satanic legend helps to strike some balance:

> There are people involved in criminal activities who justify their crimes with some kind of make-shift ideology of Devil worship. There are a few psychopathic murderers who call themselves Satanists. There are also some people who sexually abuse children, using rituals and, perhaps, references to the Devil to manipulate the children. There are many teenagers involved in the various forms of juvenile delinquency who are also involved in "pseudo-Satanic" practices, which they may use to justify their crimes. However, these disparate forms of deviant behavior are not part of the same package.[25]

Satanic cults attract individuals searching for money, power, control, and/or political influence. In sum, they perceive themselves as petitioners who importune supernatural forces through ritual and who can, thereby, fashion events and individuals to their own liking.

At one time or another in the historical past, satanic rituals have involved the sacrifice of animals or babies (this included the drinking of their blood, which supposedly contains the life force), the eating of human flesh, and the mutilation of bodies for parts (for example, the heart, a finger of the left hand, or, as in Figure 22.7, a *right* testicle). A pentagram may be painted on the satanist's body, or carved on a victim's body; the bodies may be ornamented with the number 666, or a drawing of the Baphomet (a goat's head located inside an inverted pentagram within the smaller of two concentric circles—see symbols in Table 22.2 later in the chapter). Satanic cults employ utmost secrecy; their rituals might include child molestation, and child abuse involving incest or pornography. Such practices may be recorded in their private journal, often called *The Book of Shadows*.

Lanning compiled a list of "law enforcement problems" most often linked to satanic or occult activity: vandalism, desecration of churches and cemeteries, thefts from churches and cemeteries, teenage gangs, animal mutilations, teenage suicide, child abuse, kidnapping, and murder and human sacrifices.[26]

When the police receive a complaint concerning behavior that appears to meet the statutory elements of a penal law crime, the responsibility to conduct an investigation is clear. When a child becomes involved in a ceremony, rite, or similar observance, some states delineate which specific acts constitute the crime of *ritual abuse of a child*.

The "freedom of religion" clause of the First Amendment can pose a problem in the investigation of any group that claims it as a shield. The amendment, however, defends freedom of belief, not freedom of behavior. Because its protection is not absolute, the conjuring of a spiritual connection does not necessarily legitimize every venture carried out "in the name of the Lord." If the penal law did not apply to one and all—president and clergy, rich and poor—rather than the rule of law, the result would be a reign of terror. Accordingly, the investigation of cultic activity must be based on the alleged crime; then, facts to support or disprove the complaint can be gathered from people, records, and physical evidence.

People: Individuals immediately affected by cult activities (such as members' parents, spouses, relatives, and friends) are the most likely sources of information. Although any insights they provide on their loved one may well be conjectural, they are often specific about their concerns. The aberrant behavior they observe may precipitate their lodging a complaint with the police.

Cult survivors—people who voluntarily withdraw from a cult—are another potential source of information. They will know about a cult's leader, its membership, and any criminal activities. Nevertheless, such informants should be regarded with a healthy skepticism, for sometimes they are purposefully misleading the investigator.

Corrective measures, therefore, take a multifaceted approach, including:

- Maintenance of special records on satanic-type crimes
- Cooperative intelligence-gathering apparatus
- County or state task forces to coordinate investigations of satanic-related crime
- State and federal computer utilization for satanic-related crime
- Standardized report forms for satanic-related crime
- Development of reliable sources of information and possible informants
- Allocation of adequate departmental resources
- In-depth training for specialized investigators[27]

Investigative follow-up (if warranted by the evidence supporting the accusation) might include placing cult members under surveillance or infiltrating the cult. When human sacrifice is alleged, technical surveillance may be called for; before it can be installed, an exact location must be determined. Surveillance and undercover work, because they are expensive, are justified only for more serious breaches of the law.

Pawnbrokers and "fences" can provide information if a cult engages in burglary or larceny to obtain funds. Animal control officers, child abuse investigators, school officials, and parole and probation officers can be helpful should a suspect (or cult activity) come within the scope of their duties.

Physical Evidence: Potential sources of physical evidence (in which any illegal practice is suspected) are the site(s) of the ritual(s); another would be the cult disciple's inner sanctum. Locating a ritual site can be difficult, secrecy being a paramount concern to those involved. Should the cult believe it has been discovered, the site will probably be eradicated and moved. Game wardens, park rangers, and foresters are often responsible for exposing clandestine sites. Cemetery groundkeepers may report as vandalism what are actually attempts to steal human body parts. Such attempts may involve the larceny of decorative urns or bronze tablets and plates on mausoleums and caskets. Teenagers held for shoplifting or other minor crimes (especially when a first brush with the law) may divulge the location of rites carried out

BOX 22.5 THE WEST MEMPHIS THREE

The "West Memphis Three" is the name given to three teenagers who were tried and convicted of the mutilation and murders of three children in the Robin Hood Hills area of West Memphis, Arkansas, in 1993. The three adolescents were accused of killing the boys as part of a satanic ritual. Damien Echols was sentenced to death. Jessie Misskelley, Jr. was sentenced to life in prison, plus 40 years (he received two 20-year sentences in addition to the life sentence). Jason Baldwin was sentenced to life imprisonment.

The case has received considerable attention. Supporters believe the arrests and convictions were a miscarriage of justice and that the defendants were wrongfully convicted during a period of intense media scrutiny.

Two films, *Paradise Lost: The Child Murders at Robin Hood Hills* and *Paradise Lost 2: Revelations*, have documented this case, as have the books *Blood of Innocents*, by Guy Reel, and *Devil's Knot*, by Mara Leveritt. The documentary films and Leveritt's book were strongly critical of the verdict, and argue that the suspects were wrongly convicted.

In 2011, following the presentation of newly produced DNA evidence, the West Memphis Three reached a deal with prosecutors and entered *Alford* pleas, which allowed them to assert their innocence while acknowledging that prosecutors have enough evidence to convict them. The judge accepted the pleas and sentenced them to time served. They were released with 10-year suspended sentences, having served more than 17 years in prison.

Courtesy, Robert J. Simandl

Figure 22.8
Ceremonial site used by teenaged experimenters. The circle measured 9 feet in diameter.

by friends or acquaintances. This could lead to evidence of criminality.

Discovery of occult paraphernalia or literature in a person's possession does not necessarily reflect criminal behavior. See Box 22.5 for a well-known case involving allegations of a murder resulting from satanic ritual. The detective who is informed on this subject can help to allay parents' fears. If parents believe criminal activity is involved, they may be willing to assist the investigation in the hope of deterring more destructive behavior by the offender, not to mention earning lenient treatment should a conviction result.

It takes the initiated to recognize cult symbols or warning signs displayed at entrance path(s). The scene of ritual ceremony may be bounded by a circle nine feet in diameter to protect against outside evil and keep in the power of Satan (see Figure 22.8). It may comprise an altar (marble slab, stone, or wooden bench), ritual books, black candles (whole or melted), chalice or goblet, bell or drums, incense, sword or knives, and a cauldron (to hold blood, bones, even flesh). A cat-o-nine tail, a small velvet pillow, a right-handed glove, an

Table 22.2
Occult Symbols

Trail Markers		Directional trail markers come in many forms; some apply only to one group. A pentagram also has been used on a roadway, trail, or even a building to provide a bearing that leads to the site of the occult activity. The small circle in the marker sketched to the left indicates the starting place, while the path flows and ebbs as the terrain leading to the site changes.
Recognition Sign "Horned Hand"		The "horned hand" is a sign of recognition employed by those involved in occult matters.
Pentagram		Perhaps the oldest (and one of the most important) positive occult symbols. The spirit is represented at the top point. The other four points signify fire, water, earth, and air. Is also viewed as the consummate man—head at the top, feet at the bottom, and arms akimbo.
Inverted Pentagram		To Satanists, the inverted pentagram negates the positive nature of the pentagram. It is viewed as the degradation of the spirit into matter. It is also seen as the repudiation of the Holy Trinity. This is sometimes called the "Baphomet," which generally is depicted in a more elaborate fashion—a goat head within circles.
Triangle		This symbol is usually drawn or inscribed, on the ground as part of a ritual to indicate where Satan or another demon is expected to appear as a result of conjuring. It may vary in size in contrast to that of a circle.
Circle		This symbol may be painted or inscribed to serve as a means of protection from outside evil and to keep the power or force within its boundaries. In occult ritual practice, a diameter of exactly nine feet is prescribed.
The Mark of the Beast	666 FFF	There are several symbols for Satan based on the variations of 666—the "mark of the beast." Note that "F" is the sixth letter in the alphabet. (Revelations 13: 16–18)
Black Mass Indicators		These symbols indicate a black mass.
Blood Ritual Symbol		This symbol is indicative of animal and human sacrifices.
Sex Ritual Symbol		This symbol may be painted on or carved in stone to show the area being used for sexual rituals.
Baphomet		A goat head inside an inverted pentagram, contained within two concentric circles, is the usual sign of the Baphomet. (See the symbol above for the inverted pentagram.)

animal mask, small cages (either holding an animal or empty), finger bones, an inverted cross, or even a skull or a coffin may be present. A fire pit dug in the earth is not uncommon for an outdoor scene.

A path leading to the scene of an occult ritual may be marked with warning signs and path markers; other symbols indicate what kind of ceremony is intended. Table 22.2 provides some common examples. It is important to acquire familiarity with them, and learn how to interpret their significance.

The search of a suspected satanic ritual crime scene can expose the investigator to certain hazards that must be anticipated. Because secrecy and freedom from exposure are a major concern, satanists take strong protective measures. Some devices (and ritual paraphernalia) found at ritual scenes, which are employed to discourage intruders, are shown in Figure 22.9.

If an investigator is asked to examine a site suspected of destructive cult practices or criminal activity, he or she must adhere to the standards for a traditional crime scene search. The purpose is to find any evidence of lawbreaking. Requests can come from park rangers, game wardens, parents, relatives, or friends of someone thought to be involved with or to be the victim of a destructive cult.

Courtesy, Robert J. Simandl

A. *Block of wood—its sharp, protruding nails were covered with leaves.*
B. *Chain used to restrain animals awaiting sacrifice.*
C. *White candle used in ceremony.*
D. *Piano wire to be strung between trees at ankle and chest height.*
E. *Filet knife attached to tree branch, used to skin animals.*
F. *Sharp pointed stake—its tip dipped into a poisonous substance.*
G. *Flares to start fire and destroy ceremonial scene.*
H. *Chicken bones.*
I. *Ammunition.*

Figure 22.9
Devices and ritual paraphernalia found at ceremonial scenes.

For an outdoor scene, the ashes remaining in a fire pit must be sifted down to a level about three feet below the surface. Bones and teeth may be uncovered; and, if discovered (photographed), stakes used to spread-eagle captives may corroborate an allegation of torture. For an indoor scene, it is important to search the refrigerator for vials or bottles that appear to contain blood, and for the attendant syringes and hypodermic needles. Tucked away out of sight may be occult literature, student composition books, handmade drawings, poems, and essays. Such evidence can be obtained more easily from teenage "dabblers," whereas cults run by adults are usually too well organized and sophisticated to leave evidence so readily available.

Occult members mark off special days for celebrations that are centered around pagan holidays and festivals. Occult holidays are of investigative interest because they may provide motive (i.e., what crime was committed, and why). Although it need not be proved, it may be possible to infer intent from motive, and intent is often an element of a crime. For example, a cemetery may be vandalized or desecrated, the latter charge carrying a greater penalty; thus, the charge of random overturning of tombstones might be raised from vandalism to desecration. If the crime was carried out on the eve or day of an occult holiday, this fact would suggest motive, and consequently, intent. Breaking off an angel's wings on a cemetery statue (rather than merely toppling it) is another example of intent to desecrate.

Records: In addition to information that may be recorded in any written material found, there are other potential record sources: purchase receipts for handguns, assault rifles, chemicals; records of long-distance telephone calls; credit card statements; and the like.

PERSPECTIVES ON INTERNATIONAL CRIMINALITY

Throughout this text the terms "global" and "international" appear frequently, representing in no small way the implications of new and emerging aspects of the world order. Most Americans are familiar with issues related to illegal immigration, international fraud, so-called "knockoffs," counterfeiting of American currency and other documents, and, of course, global terrorism. The impact of global crime on the United States, on Americans, particularly those in the service of the country, and to some degree the United States' allies in other nations should not be underestimated.

Today, there are more U.S. law enforcement and private security officials working abroad than at any time in history. Additionally, hundreds of thousands of Americans have returned from military service in far-off lands, bringing with them broader perceptions of the world and other cultures, most with greater appreciation of the United States, but relatively few who embarked on careers in crime or other forms of violence. A great many are pursuing careers in criminal justice or national security.

The criminal investigator should be aware that global crime on the current scale knows no bounds. American corporations operating internationally are finding that fraud, theft, kidnapping, and violence are not limited to U.S. citizens and employees. The same is true of foreign companies operating within our borders. The Internet and electronic communication contribute to the problems of criminal investigation, as do international travel, the influx of illegal aliens, and relatively open borders. Many of the types of criminality across borders are addressed in earlier chapters, but for the most part, the field of criminal investigation has fallen behind in efforts to combat global crime.

Typology of Global Crime

Although it is difficult to identify any single type of global criminality, it is safe to conclude that cybercrime, fraud, drug trafficking, and illegal immigration represent major threats. The threat of terrorism, although relatively small, is a major concern and an area where a large number of personnel and budgets are focused, both within the United States and abroad.

The investigation of global crime falls largely within the province of federal law enforcement, although many of the cases originate or are discovered at the local level. Drug trafficking can involve numerous jurisdictions, as do the activities of organized crime networks and cases involving illegal aliens or the exploitation of legal aliens who may be in the country as students or on special visas. The investigator should be familiar with the various passports, visas, and types of visas. Although new technology has made it more difficult to copy documents, such as passports, there is a global market in counterfeit entry documents, driver's licenses, and social security cards. See Box 22.6 for a case study of an investigation of enterprise crime.

In many cases, there are symbiotic relationships between groups that have resulted in a global network of organized criminal activity. Cooperation in various forms of criminal trafficking, money laundering, and illegal enterprises involving technology (e.g., cybercrime) are the most common forms of these relationships. In adapting to a new world order, many criminal groups in Southeast Asia and the Middle East have reinvented themselves, both to evade international law enforcement efforts and to take advantage of new "markets" throughout the world.

At the heart of these criminal activities is the world market in illegal drugs, ranging from poppy production for heroin to new demands for psychotropic substances, such as methamphetamines and other forms of "designer" drugs like methylamphetamine (commonly known as ecstasy), gamma hydroxy butyrate (GHB), rohypnol, ketamine (Special K), methcathanone (Cat), and mescaline.

With the opening of China to the West in the 1980s and the fall of the Soviet Union in 1991, growing markets in illegal immigration and the exploitation of women and children have also become lucrative sources of income for organized crime. The technological advances of the past decade have fostered child pornography, money laundering, and Internet scams. Organized crime groups have become an integral part of this burgeoning international phenomenon.

BOX 22.6 CASE STUDY: OPERATION SWIPER

A New York investigation in 2011 resulted in the indictments of 111 suspects in a case that involved a global crime "network of counterfeiters, hackers, fences and thieves who made off with an estimated $13 million in fraudulent purchases." Known as Operation Swiper, the case involved enterprise crime networks in Europe, Asia, Africa, and the Middle East. Victims included citizens whose credit card information was obtained by restaurant employees using "skimming machines," and also working with international hackers and bank employees who aided in stealing personal information. Suspects used the card and other personal information to purchase high-end goods, electronic equipment, and designer clothes that were then fenced for cash. Police broke up the plans of other suspects to rob a bank, some of whom were planning to steal a cargo shipment at New York's Kennedy airport.

Source: Bob Harris and Al Baker, "111 Charged in Elaborate Identity-Theft Scheme." *New York Times* (October 7, 2011).

It is widely assumed that organized crime cannot exist to any substantial degree in the absence of corruption, and many countries find themselves facing growing levels of government, judicial and police involvement in corrupt activities that support criminal enterprises.[28]

The United Nations Office on Drugs and Crime (UNODC) and the International Police Organization (INTERPOL) are two of the major global organizations focusing on international crime. In the private sector, a number of organizations, including the American Society of Industrial Security (ASIS), are involved in cooperative relationships and intelligence collection with U.S. agencies. In addition, many countries have expanded the practice of assigning law enforcement officials to other countries to work closely with their counterparts in the host country, focusing on the investigation of transnational organized criminal groups. The United States is the largest participant in assigning federal agents to other countries. The Drug Enforcement Administration (DEA), U.S. Customs Service, Federal Bureau of Investigation (FBI), Immigration and Naturalization Service (INS), Secret Service (responsible for counterfeiting), and the U.S. Postal Inspection Service are but some of the American agencies with representatives abroad.

The disparity between developed and developing countries has grown larger over the past two or three decades. Organized criminal groups will frequently use poorer countries as a base of operations because police and government structures are either unable to cope with sophisticated, and often violent, groups or they take advantage of widespread corruption to protect their activities. Corruption of police and government officials has become endemic. Corruption takes many forms and may involve different levels of government as well as the private sector.

One should recognize that despite the opportunities for criminality, there are a great many benefits associated with globalization. As an economic and military power, the United States can be the victim of those who take advantage of an open and democratic society. However, it is worthwhile to mention that, although a number of countries and their citizens are involved in criminality, the vast majority of foreigners living in or working with American citizens are law-abiding, and often envious of the opportunities the United States has to offer. In most cases, individual criminals, groups, and corporations involved in criminal activities are working with American citizens. The United States, unlike perhaps no other country in the world, finds its strengths in diversity, whether it be ethnicity, race, or religion. The country was built on this framework. Its history is replete with the myths, the reality, and the records of criminal activity in many forms. It is incumbent on the professional investigator to approach his or her tasks in an objective and non-prejudicial manner. Indeed, within the field, great emphasis has been placed on hiring investigators with foreign language skills and knowledge of other countries' cultures, legal systems, and the perceptions that foreigners may have of law enforcement.

NOTES

[1]   Susan W. Brenner, "Defining Cybercrime: A Review of State and Federal Law." In Ralph D. Clifford, ed., *Cybercrime: The Investigation, Prosecution and Defense of a Computer-Related Crime*, 2nd ed. (Durham, NC: Carolina Academic Press, 2006), 45–48.

[2]   Internet Crime Complaint Center, *2009 Internet Crime Report*. See http://www.ic3.gov/media/annual report/2009_IC3Report.pdf

[3]   Robert Moritz. "Protect Yourself from Cyber Crooks." *Parade*, (June 25, 2006), 14.

4   *Ashcroft v. Free Speech Coalition* recognized as unconstitutional by *U.S. v. McCoy* (2009).

5   Brenner, op. cit.

6   *Ashcroft v. Free Speech Coalition*, 424 U.S. 234 (2002).

7   *United States v. LaFortune*, 520 F.2d 50 (1st Cir. 2008).

8   *United States v. Irving*, 452 F.3d 110 (2nd Cir. 2004).

9   Barbara Moynihan and Mario T. Gaboury, "Hidden in Plain Sight: Modern Day Slavery and the Rise of Human Trafficking. (p. 333). In Rita M. Hammer, Barbara Moynihan and Elaine M. Pagliaro, *Forensic Nursing: A Handbook for Practice*, 2nd ed. (Boston: Jones and Bartlett Learning, 2013), xiii.

10   Duren Banks and Tracey Kyckelhahn, *Characteristics of Suspected Human Trafficking Incidents, 2008–2010* (Washington, DC: U.S. Department of Justice, Office of Justice Programs, 2011). See http://bjs.ojp.usdoj.gov/content/pub/pdf/cshti0810.pdf.

11   Michael Benson, *Murder in Connecticut: The Shocking Crime That Destroyed a Family and United a Community* (Guilford, CT: Lyons Press, 2008).

13   See the web site of the Los Angeles Police Department at http://www.lapdonline.org

12   Noah Charney, Paul Denton, John Kleberg. "Protecting Cultural Heritage from Art Theft: International Challenge, Local Opportunity." *FBI Law Enforcement Bulletin*. March, 2012.

14   Noah Charney. *The Thefts of the Mona Lisa: On Stealing the World's Most Famous Painting* (Amelia, Italy: ARCA Publication, 2011).

15   Noah Charney, Paul Denton, John Kleberg, "Protecting Cultural Heritage From Art Theft: International Challenge, Local Opportunity. *FBI Law Enforcement Bulletin*. March, 2012.

16   Ibid.

17   Stephanie Armour. "The Body Parts Business: Illegal Trade in Bodies Shakes Loved Ones." *USA Today*, (Apr. 27, 2006), 1.

18   Dave Cullen, *Columbine* (New York: Twelve, 2009).

19   U.S. Secret Service and U.S. Department of Education, *The Final Report and Findings of the Safe School Initiative: Implications for the Prevention of School Attacks in the United States* (Washington, DC: U.S. Government Printing Office, 2002).

20   Bureau of Labor Statistics, "National Census of Fatal Occupational Injuries in 2011" (September 20, 2012). See http://www.bls.gov/news.release/pdf/cfoi.pdf

21   The National Institute for the Prevention of Workplace Violence, Inc., *2011 Workplace Violence Prevention Fact Sheet*, http://content.yudu.com/Library/A1tx1d/2011AWorkplaceViolen/resources/index.htm?referrerUrl = http%3A%2F%2Fwww.workplaceviolence911.com%2Fnode%2F975%2Fdone%3Fsid%3D4571

22   The National Institute for the Prevention of Workplace Violence, Inc., *2011 Workplace Violence Prevention Fact Sheet*. See http://content.yudu.com/Library/A1tx1d/2011AWorkplaceViolen/resources/index.htm?rcfrrerUrl=http%3A%2F%2Fwww.workplaceviolence911.com%2Fnode%2F975%2Fdone%3Fsid%3D4571:

23   Kenneth L. Lanning. "Satanic, Occult, Ritualistic Crime: A Law Enforcement Perspective," Quantico, VA. Behavioral Science Instruction and Research Unit, FBI Academy. Undated. (Also see: *The Police Chief*, Oct. 1989, 62–83.)

[24] Larry Kahaner, *Cults That Kill*. (New York: Warner Books, 1988), vii.

[25] Jeffrey S. Victor, *Satanic Panic: The Creation of a Contemporary Legend (Chicago*: Open Court, 1993), 216–217.

[26] Lanning, op. cit.

[27] Jerry Johnston, *The Edge of Evil: The Rise of Satanism in North America* (Dallas: Word, 1989), 238.

[28] Richard Ward & Daniel Mabrey, "Transnational Organized Crime in Asia and the Middle East." In *Handbook of Transnational Crime & Justice* (2nd edition) Philip Reichel & Jay Albanese (Eds.), Sage Publications, Forthcoming 2013.

IMPORTANT CASES

Ashcroft v. Free Speech Coalition (2002)
United States v. Irving (2004)
United States v. LaFortune (2008)
United States v. McCoy (2009)

DISCUSSION QUESTIONS

1. What are some of the types of identity theft?
2. What do the elements of mail and wire fraud involve?
3. Is possession of child pornography a crime?
4. Are human trafficking victims solely illegal aliens?
5. What are some corrective measures recommended in the investigation of possible satanic-related crimes?
6. What are some of the types of global crime?
7. What are some of the public and private organizations that focus on global crime?

SUPPLEMENTAL READINGS

Albrecht, C., Albrecht, C., & Albrecht, S. (2011). *Fraud examination* (4th ed.). Mason, OH: Cengage Learning/South-Western.

Australian Institute of Criminology (2005). *International police operations against online child pornography.* Canberra, Australia.

Casey, E. (2011). *Digital evidence and computer crime: Forensic science, computers, and the Internet.* Boston: Elsevier/Syngress.

Foy, D., Levy, J., & Burgess, R. (2004). *The scam handbook: The secrets of the con artist.* London: Barnes and Noble.

Hall, N. (2005). *Hate crime.* Portland, OR: Willan.

Johnson, K. O. (2004). *Financial crimes against the elderly.* Washington, DC: U.S. Department of Justice.

Kelly, R., Maghan, J., & Serio, J. (2005). *Illicit trafficking.* Santa Barbara, CA: ABC-CLIO.

Krone, T. (2005). *Queensland police stings in online chat rooms.* Canberra: Australian Institute of Criminology.

Manning, G. A. (2010). *Financial investigation and forensic accounting* (3rd ed.). Boca Raton, FL: CRC Press.

The New York Times. The organ grinder. See http://nymag.com/news/features/22326/index1.html#ixzz0cRJsvgUj

Ratliff, E. (Oct. 10, 2005). The zombie hunters. *The New Yorker,* 44–49.

Surowiecki, J. (Oct. 17, 2005). Cash for canvas. *The New Yorker,* 62.

Turvey, B. E., & Petherick, W. (2009). *Forensic victimology: Examining violent crime victims in investigative and legal contexts.* New York: Elsevier.

U.S. Department of Justice (1992), *Investigator's guide to allegations of "ritual" child abuse.* Quantico, VA: National Center for the Analysis of Violent Crime.

CHAPTER 23

TERRORISM AND URBAN DISORDER

INTRODUCTION

The events of September 11, 2001, with attacks on the World Trade Center and the Pentagon, marked a major change in the efforts of the American government to cope with the threat of terrorism (see Figure 23.1). This included the establishment of the Department of Homeland Security and a major reorganization of the government, designed to bring most federal law enforcement and intelligence functions under one "roof." (See Box 23.1 for the mission statement and organization of the Department of Homeland Security.) Although the Federal Bureau of Investigation continues to be the lead domestic agency responsible for terrorism investigations, a greater role has been placed on other federal, state, and local government agencies, the latter being focused largely on identifying threats. A number of training programs related to counterterrorism continue to provide training to local law enforcement. The State and Local Anti-Terrorism Training (SLATT) program, sponsored by the Bureau of Justice Assistance (BJA), provides training at no cost to state and local police agencies.

The USA PATRIOT Act (Uniting and Strengthening America by Providing Appropriate Tools Required to Intercept and Obstruct Terrorism) gives law enforcement expanded legal authority in the areas of gathering intelligence, surveillance, and the collection of information. The investigator should be familiar with the legal powers and limitations associated with terrorism investigations.

Although great emphasis has been placed on internationally initiated threats, many related directly or indirectly to al-Qaeda, it is important to recognize that a number of "homegrown" groups with a focus on violence continue to be of great concern. The FBI continues to express concern about the animal rights extremists and so called earth "eco" extremists. These include attacks on research facilities that use animals, and the destruction of property viewed by those who view facilities as a threat to the environment. Additionally, anarchists and anti-abortion militants as well as right-wing militant groups pose an ongoing threat.

Of particular concern to authorities has been the increase in suicide bombings in other countries. Vesna Markovic, Director of Collection for the Institute for the Study of Violent Groups, states that between 1990 and 2000 there were 134 suicide bombings carried out in 14 different countries worldwide, more than 50 percent occurring in Sri Lanka and nearly 20 percent in Israel, but between 2001 and 2011 there were 3,047 observed suicide bombings occurring in 40 countries, more than 46 percent in Iraq, nearly 25 percent in Afghanistan, and just over 12 percent in Pakistan.[1]

Many experts agree that this phenomenon will eventually occur in the United States. Research indicates that suicide or martyr bombers "may be of good economic and educational background

Bureau of Alcohol, Tobacco, Firearms, and Explosives

Figure 23.1
The attacks on the World Trade Center and the Pentagon on September 11, 2001, marked a turning point in efforts to combat terrorism.

and not typically from impoverished origins. They are thought to be indoctrinated from youth to have unyielding patriotic and/or religious views with no tolerance for others."[2]

Given the increasing concern associated with urban violence, this chapter includes a section on the role of law enforcement in responding to the growth of urban gangs, many of which operate across state borders and have international connections. The role of the criminal investigator in both counterterrorism and gang investigations frequently requires similar investigative techniques involving intelligence, surveillance, and case construction.

Generally, terrorism falls into one or a combination of typologies. The more commonly accepted forms of terrorism include:

Violent political movements—separatist movements or efforts to destabilize governments. In many cases such efforts may also be linked to religious or economic factors.

Single-issue or special-interest groups—movements that focus on a specific issue, such as anti-abortion, ecology, animal rights, or personal vendettas, usually against government agencies.

Racial, ethnic, or religious threats—attacks focusing on religious, racial, or ethnic minorities, and consisting of groups or individuals who use terrorist tactics to vent their hatred.

Global economic movements—use violence against international economic institutions, such as the World Bank, as a means of protesting the disparity between rich and poor nations.

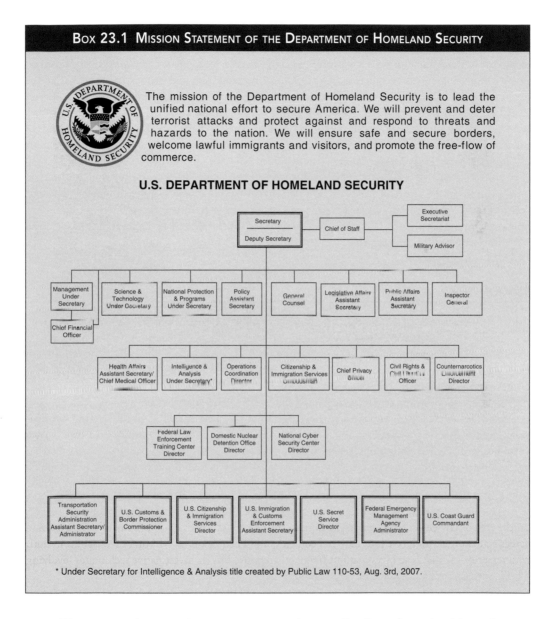

Box 23.1 MISSION STATEMENT OF THE DEPARTMENT OF HOMELAND SECURITY

The mission of the Department of Homeland Security is to lead the unified national effort to secure America. We will prevent and deter terrorist attacks and protect against and respond to threats and hazards to the nation. We will ensure safe and secure borders, welcome lawful immigrants and visitors, and promote the free-flow of commerce.

U.S. DEPARTMENT OF HOMELAND SECURITY

* Under Secretary for Intelligence & Analysis title created by Public Law 110-53, Aug. 3rd, 2007.

Hate groups and anti-immigration movements—a longstanding form of terrorist violence that involves generally well-organized and supported entities that frequently have a political base, which advocate violence by so-called "lone wolves" and cells operating independently using a tactic known as "leaderless resistance."

There may be considerable overlap between these types of individuals or groups, but from an investigative standpoint it is important at times to be able to distinguish between the baseline motives of the principal actors involved in perpetrating violence. It is also important to recognize that in virtually all of these typologies there are likely to be large numbers of individuals who may be sympathetic to a cause, but who do not provide anything more than vocal or financial support, or participate only in peaceful demonstrations. In a free society, freedom of speech and the right to protest are protected unless a law is broken. Undoubtedly, this may present some obstacles to an investigation, but this is an inherent right that must be protected, and history has shown that one of the most significant reasons for individuals to embrace a movement is the abuse of police power.

Two aspects of terrorism should be of interest to the investigator. First is the recognition that terrorist activity has the capability to kill or injure large numbers of people. The threat of weapons of mass destruction makes this type of investigation a major concern. Second is the fact that the most effective investigations of terrorism are actually aimed at preventing the act from occurring (that is, they are proactive). In most criminal cases, however, investigators are responding after a crime has been committed (i.e., reactive), and it is rare that investigations are mounted without some advance warning, usually in the form of intelligence analysis, a tip from an informant or from an undercover operative. Given the potential for widespread violence, the need for a proactive approach has become a high priority for law enforcement.

OVERVIEW

Prior to the September 11th attacks, the American public was lulled into the belief that terrorism was largely a problem that existed overseas. There was, of course, recognition by federal agencies and the intelligence community that the terrorist threat was greater than what was being reported in the media. The FBI, which had national responsibility for investigating domestic terrorism, focused efforts largely on internal groups and individuals who were believed to have ties to external terrorist organizations. Following the attacks on the World Trade Center and the Pentagon, the Bureau and other agencies, such as the Central Intelligence Agency (CIA), were criticized for not sharing information, and for a lack of cooperation in monitoring threats. The 2002 Joint Inquiry into Intelligence Community Activities Before and After the Terrorist Attacks of September 11, 2001, concluded that the lack of cooperation between agencies resulted in so-called "stovepiping" of information, in which intelligence data was not shared.

Although there have been significant improvements in intelligence sharing, both in the United States and other countries there continue to be some problems, particularly between local law enforcement and some federal agencies. Today, one of the major problems is the vast amount of information being collected and the ability to digest and determine both the meaning and the intelligence value of the data.

Over the years, the tactics, technology, and weapons used by terrorist groups have also changed. Although explosives continue to be the most frequently used weapons in the terrorist's arsenal, greater levels of sophistication (such as the use of aircraft in the 9/11 attack), the use of new timing and detonation devices, and the availability of more powerful explosives have increased the danger. Most experts believe that suicide bombings (see Figure 23.2), weapons of mass destruction (WMD), and the danger of Internet attacks (cyber-terrorism) on public- and private-sector computer systems will be an increasing concern. An emerging array of technology and sophisticated weaponry is readily available to a committed terrorist organization.

It is important to recognize that terrorism, like any other social phenomenon, has changed over the years. Much of the earlier research on terrorism and terrorists is outdated. For example, in the past, terrorist groups were quick to take credit for an act and seek media attention. Groups today are less likely to take credit for fear of being identified by investigators. Terrorists of the past in the

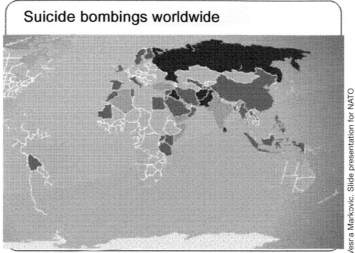

Figure 23.2
Blue indicates 1–5 suicide bombings; green 6–24 bombings, and red 25 or more bombings.

Suicide Bombings 1981–2010

Carried out (n = 2,892)

- 1980s (n = 41)
- 1990s (n = 99)
- 2000s (n = 2,753)

Gender

- Male (n = 2,745)
- Female (n = 151)

Source: Vesna Markovic. Slide presentation for NATO Conference. University of New Haven. (2012)

United States were likely to be college-educated, upper-middle-class youths. Such profiles are almost useless today, for involvement in terrorism covers a broad spectrum of society. In the past, there was likely to be a formal organized structure utilizing "cells" directed by a central authority. Today, most terrorist attacks in the United States are carried out by a small group, or even one or two individuals, whose ties to a formal organization are likely to be weak and whose acts are "individualized" and not part of a larger plan, except insofar as their views are consistent with those of a larger (usually law-abiding) organization.

As the nature and tactics of terrorism have changed over the years, so have the investigative approaches. The bombings of the World Trade Center in New York City in 1993 and the Alfred P. Murrah Federal Building in Oklahoma City in 1995 should have served as warnings to the American people that large-scale destruction and loss of life through terrorist activities represented a clear threat for the future. Prior to these and the 9/11 attacks, terrorism in the United States was largely attributed to fringe or splinter groups with a specific aim. Animal rights groups, anti-abortion attacks, militia movements, and hate crime violence perpetrated by so-called Skinheads or right-wing extremists were a primary focus of investigators in America. Violence perpetrated against Americans and American interests abroad represented an international focus, but such attacks were generally not of concern in terms of domestic investigations. Today, the United States faces new threats presented by international terrorists operating alone or in cells, sometimes supported by rogue governments, such as Iran and Syria, or by wealthy private individuals from countries friendly to the United States, such as Saudi Arabia.

Despite the demise of Osama bin Laden in the U.S. Navy Seal's attack on his compound in Pakistan in 2011, the al Qaeda organization, particularly the off-shoot group in Yemen, has continued to represent a threat. (For an account of this raid, see: http://today.msnbc.msn.com/id/47944034/ ns/world_news/) A number of foiled attacks in the United States by immigrants as well as American citizens are evidence of improved cooperation and intelligence.

Defining Terrorism

Although there are a number of definitions of terrorism, each includes in some way the phrase: "the use of force or the threat of force to achieve a political end." In recent years this has been modified in some sectors to read "… to achieve a political or criminal end." So-called narcoterrorism (the influence of illegal drugs to support some terrorist groups, or the use of terrorist tactics by drug groups to influence a population or government), gray-area phenomena, and various forms of extortion are frequently embraced in this broader definition, but the definition does not include more common criminal activity. There are many definitions of terrorism that, from an investigative standpoint, are virtually meaningless because they are vague and do not provide a clear *corpus delicti* for the crime. For purposes of this text, *terrorism* can be defined as the use of force or the fear of force to achieve a political or criminal end. Another definition, offered by the Vice President's Task Force on Combating Terrorism, provides some further clarification:

> [Terrorism] is the unlawful use or threat of violence against persons or property to further political or social objectives. It is generally intended to intimidate or coerce a government, individuals or groups to modify their behavior or policies.[3]

This definition currently provides a framework that encompasses relatively new legislation that includes more traditional types of crime under the USA PATRIOT Act and other legal entities in the homeland security framework. Local law enforcement's investigative activities may be more likely to focus on the more traditional crimes involved.

Ultimately, media exposure and world events have contributed to greater public awareness of terrorism as a public policy issue, and the investigation of terrorist activity has increasingly become a concern to law enforcement. Responsibility for crime scene protection and preliminary investigations rests largely with local law enforcement because they are the first to respond. As noted, successful investigations depend on a high degree of cooperation between local, state, and federal officials, as well as cooperation between geographic jurisdictions and, in many cases, other countries.

The most common types of crime in this area include:

- Conspiracy
- Murder (assassination)
- Kidnapping
- Hijacking (skyjacking)
- Bombing/Arson
- Robbery

- Extortion

- Manufacturing or possessing radiological, chemical, biological, or nuclear weapons or the materials necessary to make them

- Raising funds for terrorist groups as designated by the Secretary of State

- Cyber-attacks on computer and other technological systems

What makes terrorist crimes different is that they are frequently carried out by groups or individuals within a group. The motive for them is not usually monetary gain (except as a means to support the movement), they are frequently well-planned, and the acts themselves are designed to achieve some political aim.

Narcoterrorism is an exception to the general rule that monetary gain is not a motivation. Although narcoterrorism is more closely associated with criminal cartels in Mexico and Central and South America, there is an increasing use of violence related to illegal drugs in the United States. The difference between drug-related violence and narcoterrorism lies in the fact that the latter involves the use of terror to achieve a political aim. Of particular concern to American law enforcement are the activities of criminal gangs in Mexico, which also operate across the border and in some cities in the United States. In the United States, gangs and other groups involved in drug trafficking use violence to intimidate communities or eliminate witnesses. Mexican transnational gangs are numerous and some, such as the Los Zetas, are extremely violent. Figures 23.3 and 23.4 illustrate the relationships between the Mexican Los Zetas and the Sinaloa Cartel and their relationships to street gangs in the United States.

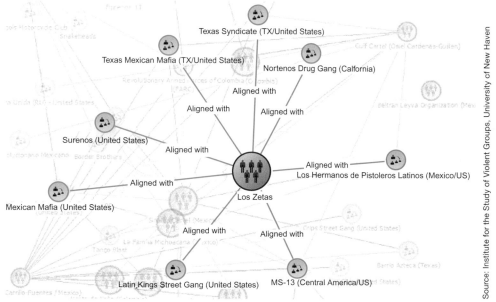

Figure 23.3
Los Zetas relationships to U.S. street gangs.

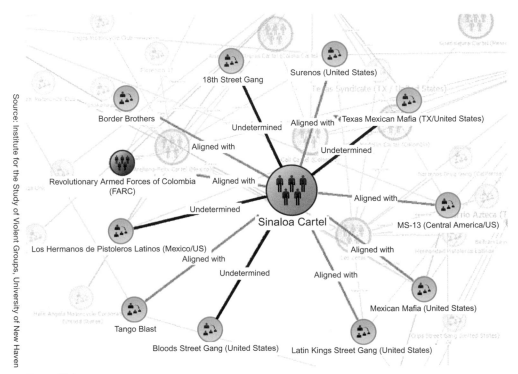

Source: Institute for the Study of Violent Groups, University of New Haven

Figure 23.4
Sinaloa Cartel and their relationship to other criminal organizations.

LEGAL ASPECTS

Intelligence Reform and Terrorism Prevention Act of 2004

The Intelligence Reform and Terrorism Prevention Act of 2004 was passed by both the House of Representatives and the Senate in December 2004. Prior to signing the Intelligence Reform and Terrorism Prevention Act, President George W. Bush described it as "the most dramatic reform of our nation's intelligence capabilities since President Harry S. Truman signed the National Security Act of 1947." Bush said the main purpose of the Act was "to ensure that the people in government responsible for defending America have the best possible information to make the best possible decisions."

The USA PATRIOT Act, formally the Uniting and Strengthening America by Providing Appropriate Tools Required to Intercept and Obstruct Terrorism Act of 2001 (H.R. 3162), was signed into law on October 26, 2001, in response to the terrorist attacks of September 11, 2001. It was renewed in May of 2006 and again in 2011, and a decision about whether and how to renew again is scheduled for 2015. The Act gives federal officials greater authority to track and intercept communications, both for law enforcement and foreign intelligence-gathering purposes. It vests the Secretary of the Treasury with regulatory powers to combat corruption of U.S. financial institutions for foreign money laundering purposes. It seeks to further close our borders to foreign terrorists and to detain and remove those within our borders. It creates new crimes, new penalties, and new procedural efficiencies for use against domestic and international terrorists.

A portion of the Act addresses issues suggested originally in a Department of Justice proposal circulated in mid-September 2001. The first of its suggestions called for amendments to federal surveillance laws, which govern the capture and tracking of suspected terrorists' communications within the United States. Federal law features a three-tiered system, created for the dual purpose of protecting the confidentiality of private telephone, face-to-face, and computer communications while enabling authorities to identify and intercept criminal communications.

The USA PATRIOT Act consists of 10 titles that, in addition to other purposes:

- give federal law enforcement and intelligence officers increased short-term authority to gather and share evidence particularly with respect to wire and electronic communications;

- amend federal money laundering laws, with an emphasis on those involving overseas financial activities;

- incorporate acts of terrorism into new federal crimes, increase the penalties for existing federal crimes that relate to terrorism, and adjust existing federal criminal procedure to deal with the challenges of prosecuting terrorists;

- modify immigration law to prevent foreign terrorists from entering the United States, to detain foreign terrorist suspects at the borders, to deport foreign terrorists, and to provide immigration benefits to foreign victims of September 11; and

- authorize appropriations to enhance the capacity of immigration, law enforcement, and intelligence agencies to more effectively respond to the threats of terrorism.

Among other things, this legislation makes it a federal crime to:

- Hijack or destroy a foreign aircraft outside the United States and take refuge in the United States.

- Use violence against any passenger on board a civilian or government aircraft.

- Commit a crime against a federal official.

- Travel interstate or use foreign transportation to commit murder or assassination.

- Train foreign nationals in the use of firearms, munitions, or explosives.

- Murder a hostage.

- Kidnap, assault, or murder a United States citizen outside the country, if the suspect is returned to the United States.[4]

The U.S. Congress also passed the Public Health Security and Bioterrorism Preparedness and Response Act of 2002 (H.R. 3448), which placed greater controls on protection of food and water and enhanced controls on biological agents and toxic substances, and established new powers for several levels of government, including the Department of Agriculture and the Food and Drug Administration. There is no international convention on the prevention and suppression of terrorism as a whole, but conventions do exist to address related issues.

The federal government continues to pass new legislation designed to strengthen laws related to terrorism. Many other countries have also passed legislation related to terrorism that enables greater cooperation, communication, and intelligence gathering between nations.

Constraints on Intelligence-Gathering Activities

In an effort to curb the overzealous efforts of some investigative personnel, several United States Attorneys General issued guidelines to regulate domestic intelligence gathering. Some federal district courts entered judgment orders (consent decrees) for the same purpose. The fundamental concern is the threat to First Amendment rights posed by domestic intelligence operations. The problem is finding a way to separate those who are legitimately protesting or dissenting from those who go outside the law by carrying out the threat of violence or inciting others to do so. A "reasonable suspicion" standard is applied to determine whether an investigation may be undertaken to gather evidence concerning suspected criminal conduct that has occurred, is occurring, or is about to occur. Reasonable suspicion may be defined as "the belief of a reasonably prudent person, based on specific, articulate facts, that an investigation is justified to determine if 'probable cause' exists to issue a warrant, or to support some other appropriate police action."[5] By specifying the criteria used to select the targets of the investigation, criticism of proactive investigations can be softened or eliminated.

The USA PATRIOT Act authorized a broader approach to the interception of electronic information. Cases involving terrorism investigations permit disclosure of more non-content information than is permissible in other types of criminal investigations. The Act, which applies to Internet service providers (ISPs), "can force the disclosure of a subscriber's name; address; local and long distance telephone connection records, or records of session times and duration, length of service (including start date and types of service utilized); telephone or instrument number or other subscriber number or identity, including any temporary assigned network address; and means and source of payment for such service of a subscriber."[6]

Court Proceedings

Terrorist planning and tactics have become more sophisticated with regard to the American legal system, and both domestic and foreign terrorists have used the courts to further propaganda, as well as to use various legal strategies and disruption of proceedings to hamper prosecution efforts. For this reason it is extremely important that investigators pay particular attention to rules of evidence, maintenance of detailed records, and procedural requirements in case preparation.

William Dyson, a retired FBI supervisor, notes that:

> Investigators should be well prepared when they testify in court. They should not be surprised if they are asked about specific aspects of the Constitution or about their "oath of office." They should also not be taken aback if they are asked if they have committed any illegal activities during the course of the investigation...
>
> If an officer has functioned in an undercover capacity during the case, he will probably be questioned in detail about entrapment issues. Thorough documentation of the investigation can do much to support the investigator's testimony...[7]

In some cases, defendants refusing to accept the legal system have disrupted proceedings, frequently supported by followers; in others, they have filed civil actions against officers; and in others they have used the courts to gather information about investigative methods, undercover operatives or informants. A variety of legal tactics used as stalling procedures are not uncommon.

TERRORISM INVESTIGATIONS

As noted earlier, there are many similarities between terrorism and urban gang investigations, and a number of unique characteristics set them apart from more traditional investigations. Perhaps the most significant difference involves the utilization of task forces or teaming models that involve individuals from various organizations and jurisdictions. Investigators assigned to these types of investigations must be willing to work closely with other members of the team, setting aside personal loyalties to their own organization. The investigation of a terrorist cell in New York City in September 2009 was flawed, according to the media and informed sources, because of friction between two units within the New York Police Department (NYPD), as well as friction between the FBI and the NYPD.

Personnel assigned to such investigations must have a high tolerance for long stakeouts and surveillance, be mindful of minor details and seemingly insignificant information, and be willing to shun publicity. He or she must recognize the importance of teamwork and cooperation, be thoroughly familiar with technology and the use of computers, and have an appreciation for detail. Terrorist investigations are usually lengthy, and may involve months or even years of painstaking effort. William Dyson spent most of his career investigating terrorist movements. His book, *Terrorism: An Investigator's Handbook*, is one of the most comprehensive publications available to investigators.

The success of such investigations depends largely on intelligence and analysis. They are likely to involve numerous suspects operating over large geographic areas, who are usually suspicious by nature and watchful of surveillance. The investigator must take copious notes and keep detailed records, which may prove crucial not only in making a case but also in developing a successful prosecution. Unlike most criminal investigations, if at all possible, a case must be made *before* the criminal act is carried out. The successful investigation will result in charges of conspiracy (if more than one person is involved) and charges for an *attempted* crime, such as attempted murder. The point at which an arrest is made may well depend on circumstantial evidence, which will no doubt complicate prosecution. For this reason, physical evidence (e.g., explosives or receipts of purchase) and record keeping are important. The investigator must be able to explain why or how actions of a suspect can be linked to the crime charged. For example, the fact that a person says he wishes someone is dead, and then goes out and purchases bomb-making equipment, follows a potential victim or "cases" a location, and purchases a one-way ticket to Timbuktu may well establish a *prima facie* case.

In recent years, the number of local police assigned to joint federal investigation teams has increased dramatically. The FBI Joint Terrorism Task Forces (JTTF) number more than 100 groups throughout the country and are made up of federal, state, and local representatives from law enforcement, prosecutors, and other agencies. The NYPD, for example, has about 200 detectives assigned to the Task Force. A national JTTF was established in 2002 in Washington, DC. It includes representatives from nearly 30 different agencies. The Foreign Terrorist Tracking Task Force (FTTTF) and the Office of Law Enforcement Coordination were established in 2001 and also play significant roles in terrorist-related investigations.

When an investigation takes place *after* a crime has been committed, it is important to identify the group that is responsible right away. Frequently, there are a number of groups that take credit for an act, and efforts must be made to sort out prank calls or those of imposter groups. Incidents involving known groups or suspects necessitate reviewing all of the information that is available both in police files and from other sources. Many radical groups now have Internet web sites, and these should be monitored.

At the scene of a terrorist incident, care should be taken with regard to secondary devices that may be planted to explode after the police arrive in response to the first explosion or call. Crime scene investigators should also be aware that "booby traps" may be planted. Once a crime scene has been secured, it is important to conduct a thorough search. Because there is a high probability that there will be another incident, reconstructing the event may be very important. For example, one should ask: where was the explosive device planted, how was it delivered, was there a warning, and was it designed to inflict personal injury or property damage? Some terrorist groups will establish a "code word" or phrase that can be used in future communications to convince authorities that they are communicating with the actual perpetrators. Obviously, it is important to try to open and maintain communication in whatever form is possible. This may include the use of telephones, mail, the Internet, or even uninformed messengers.

The actual investigation of an incident will frequently include different agencies or organizations. Accordingly, a central command office should be established. Most large cities now have command and control facilities that are well equipped. Of particular importance is the availability of telephones, computers, and peripherals (e.g., scanners). Personnel trained in the use of databases and who are familiar with ways to draw information from computerized databanks should also be available. It is imperative that all information collected in the investigation be centralized in some manner. Because the investigation may involve more than one incident, it is also important to be able to conduct comparative data analyses.

Terrorist Suspects

The primary difference between terrorist-related investigations and more traditional investigations is in the use of intelligence. Because individuals involved in terrorist acts are likely to be part of a larger group, and their activities are more likely to range over large geographical areas (between states or even countries), there is a strong need for communication and coordination between organizations and governments. Thus, intelligence represents a key element in the investigative process.

Further, because different individuals may be involved in specific criminal acts of the group, the *modus operandi* associated with a particular crime may vary from act to act. For this reason, it becomes important to know about:

1. a group's stated goals;

2. its organizational structure;

3. its membership;

4. its tactical approach;

5. its means of communication;

6. its methods of raising funds;

7. its propensity for violence; and

8. its security procedures.

Obviously, it is important to know who is in the group. However, this can create special problems due to restrictions on keeping records concerning innocent people who may be supportive of the group's aims but who are opposed to criminal activity.

In order to develop a file on an individual or a group, it is generally necessary to establish a *prima facie* case establishing the probability that a crime has occurred or is about to occur, or that there is a conspiracy among specific individuals to commit a crime. An exception to this is when the investigative action is less restricted (for example, where there is reliable information on an activity, but it may be inconclusive with regard to who is involved).

Successful investigation of terrorist groups requires patience, skill, and cooperation. For this reason, the task force approach offers the highest probability of success. Teams working together can compile a considerable amount of information and, when aided by an analyst, can do much more than a single individual or a group of individuals acting independently because other agencies or organizations may have more information or expertise in a particular area. If a group has been identified as a criminal organization, every effort should be made to collect as much information as possible about the group and its members. A fine line must be observed. For example, a great many people are involved in the animal rights movement, yet only a few are committed to violence. How then does the investigator make a distinction between legitimate protest and criminal activity? First, one must be familiar with the aims and goals of the group and, even more importantly, with the tactics it espouses to carry out its aims. If the literature of the group calls for illegal acts, such as destruction of property or injury to persons, there are reasonable grounds to investigate further. One must keep in mind that it is not illegal to espouse the idea of overthrowing the government. It is, however, illegal to support and conspire to commit an illegal act in an attempt to carry out this goal.

Observing the behavior of individuals in a group can be productive. Rather than focusing on everyone in the group (an approach sometimes used in the past), attention should be given to individuals who go beyond mere protest and civil disobedience. Individuals involved in domestic terrorism in the United States will frequently display a pattern of activity that begins with protesting, moves on to civil disobedience, and escalates to committing assaults or other significant crimes, such as destruction of property. Often acting out of frustration with their inability to sway the political process, such individuals are likely to progress to more serious crimes. In many cases, this will mean more extensive destruction of property, usually without the intent to injure. In the final phase of their transition, they justify murder to accomplish their goals. The point at which a person moves beyond civil disobedience is the stage at which further investigation is warranted.

When an individual or group becomes the subject of an investigation, an effort must be made to understand the psychological dimensions involved. A background investigation can provide information on an individual's arrest history, psychological makeup, friends and acquaintances, technical skills (such as pilot training or experience with weapons or explosives), military service, prior experience or employment, geographical movement, and economic status. Observation of the individual will provide information of daily habits, contacts, employment, knowledge of the city or community, and commitment to the group or cause. As Neil Pollard notes:

> Terrorists transact, and these transactions create records and leave footprints in cyberspace. When terrorists decide to exploit an opportunity, they are consumers. They buy products and services, they travel, they communicate, they send or receive money, they apply for and present passports, they drive cars, they rent hotel rooms, and they conduct surveillance on their targets. In virtually all cases, terrorists have left detectable clues in transactions, generally found after the attack. The hypothesis underlying the use of data mining, aggregation and pattern recognition is that these transactional patterns, indicative of terrorist activity, can be identified and interdicted before an attack.[8]

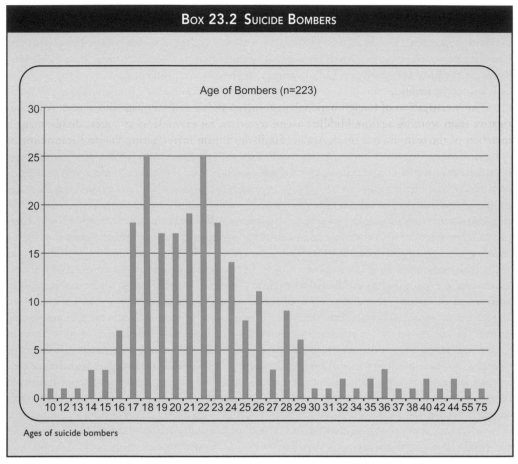

BOX 23.2 SUICIDE BOMBERS

Age of Bombers (n=223)

Ages of suicide bombers

Source: Vesna Markovic. Slide presentation for NATO Conference, University of New Haven (2012). Suicide bombers on the global level range in age from as young as 10 to as old as 72, but the vast majority are between 17 and 26.

Investigations involving foreign nationals may prove more difficult because the background of a foreign subject is more difficult to determine and, in the case of state-sponsored terrorists or those belonging to a known terrorist group, they may be trained to avoid detection. In such cases, the investigative team frequently must depend on information from the community, from other law enforcement agencies, or from informants or undercover operatives. Most immigrants and foreign nationals living in the United States have no desire to support terrorists. However, they may have a fear of cooperation with law enforcement because of negative experiences with police in their country of origin. Developing informants is thus an important but difficult task.

Although informants are helpful, the investigator should be aware that such individuals may have their own motives for cooperating. Paid informants may give false information in order to stay on the payroll; criminal informants may give false information to protect themselves or others.

Undercover operatives working in other areas, particularly narcotics, organized crime, or gunrunning, frequently will have information on potential terrorists. For this reason, it is important to maintain good contacts with other units within the local police organization, as well as with federal and state authorities working in this area. Drug Enforcement Administration (DEA) and Alcohol, Tobacco, Firearms, and Explosives (ATF) agents, customs officers, postal inspectors, and immigration officials can be helpful.

The investigation of foreign nationals also suffers because of language differences. An investigative team working against Middle Eastern terrorists, for example, is at a great disadvantage if members of the team do not speak Arabic. Similarly, a team investigating Puerto Rican terrorists will not be very effective if no team member understands Spanish. Information often comes from members of a specific ethnic community, most of whom are wary of police or do not have a strong command of the English language. When language skills are absent or poor, an effort should be made to identify individuals who can speak more than one language. Maintaining a department "skills index" is useful. A skills index involves recording the special training or other skills that individuals in the department or other agencies possess, such as scuba, sniper, computer, or hostage-negotiation training.

In addition to knowing the language spoken by an individual or group, the investigator should understand the culture of the individual or group under investigation. Although this may be obvious with regard to foreign nationals, it is important to recognize that there are a great many cultural differences in the United States that are not necessarily ethnically based. These range from regional differences, to neighborhood, racial, occupational, and educational differences.

Some international terrorist groups will cooperate with each other in matters such as recruit training and information sharing. Some will even join forces to carry out a particular deed, or one group may act on behalf of another. Similarly, effective action against international terrorism requires the coordinated efforts of the central governments of nations and the cooperation of law enforcement agencies in each country. They will be assisted by INTERPOL, the international, voluntary organization of police agencies headquartered in France. INTERPOL's purpose is to assist and improve police cooperation and the exchange of information between 190 member countries. With the capability of working in four official languages—French, English, Spanish, and Arabic—messages and inquiries are received and transmitted to the proper authorities, data is computerized, and text may be retrieved in English. INTERPOL routinely files requests for help in tracing passports; identifying weapons, explosives, and vehicles; and identifying persons, whether victims or criminals. Additional services include establishing links between cases; obtaining information about suspected terrorists, their criminal records, and proper identification; and circulating warning notices about suspects who have committed or are likely to commit terrorist activities.

Another potential source of information is the uniformed patrol force that works in the community every day. However, it is important to brief the beat officers on things to be aware of and watch for. A progressive training program will address the collection of information by the patrol force and other investigators.

When a terrorist event has taken place, the preliminary investigation should make every effort to identify potential witnesses, particularly people who may have been in the vicinity prior to the event. In many cases, the perpetrators of terrorist acts will survey the area prior to the incident. Their actions may have been observed by witnesses who may be located through a canvass of the neighborhood after the crime. Security cameras both inside and outside of buildings have become so commonplace that a canvass of such security devices in the vicinity should be made. They may have recorded the terrorists as they "cased" the target or even as they actually perpetrated the crime.

Physical Evidence

One of the most important components of terrorist-related investigations is the collection and preservation of physical evidence (see Figure 23.5). A terrorist attack necessitates careful analysis and examination not only of the immediate crime scene, but of the surrounding area and locations where the suspects may have conducted surveillance or that were used as hideouts or *safe houses* (rendezvous points free of surveillance that were used for illegal activities such as making bombs). Meticulous examination of the debris from the 1993 bombing of the World Trade Center resulted in the discovery of a piece of the rear frame rail that bore the vehicle identification number (VIN) of the suspect vehicle, which led to the first break in the case.

Because terrorist activities are usually carried out by more than one individual, it may prove important to establish each individual's activities or whereabouts through physical evidence. In some cases, one individual will carry a bomb or weapon to the scene, another may place the explosives or carry out the attack, and yet another may detonate the bomb or, if necessary, remove the weapon. Still another may leave the communiqué or otherwise make the claim. If it's a suicide bombing you may have a handler drive the bomber to the scene, and that person may also remotely detonate if the bomber backs out.

Most terrorist acts involve bombing, kidnapping (hostage-taking), or assassination. Each of these acts provides different forms of physical evidence. The collection of physical evidence is covered in Chapter 2, and various types of explosives, IEDs (improvised explosive devices), and military ordnance are covered in Chapter 21. Weapons of mass destruction represent another type of threat that will usually involve specialists in the identification and handling of hazardous materials.

AP Photo/John Kuntz, Pool

Figure 23.5
Investigators sift through the rubble on the ground at the Alfred P. Murrah Federal Building bombing site in Oklahoma City. The April 1995 truck bomb blast killed 168 people and injured 850. The destructive effects of this explosion were obvious. Less obvious was the meticulous detail and investigative expertise involved in bringing the perpetrators to justice.

Weapons of Mass Destruction

Nuclear: The prospect of a terrorist organization acquiring a nuclear device, or even radiological material, is one of the most frightening scenarios that law enforcement must consider and prepare for. Even a low-level nuclear attack (for instance, a 30-pound nuclear warhead detonated in a suitcase) would have yields as low as 50 tons (high explosive equivalent) to tens of kilotons, several times the size of the first nuclear weapons that were dropped on Hiroshima and Nagasaki.

In a nuclear terrorist event, the hazards are thermal radiation, blast or shock effect, and nuclear radiation. Obviously, the most protective measure is to be as far away from the blast or burst as possible. For nuclear radiation, both distance and shielding help mitigate the initial radiation, consisting of penetrating gamma and beta radiation. Residual nuclear radiation is commonly referred to as *fallout* and consists of particles dangerous to inhale or get on the skin (gamma, alpha, and beta particles). Individuals who survive the blast will be immediately affected by radiation poisoning and will experience the following symptoms: fever, nausea, vomiting, lack of appetite, bloody diarrhea, hair loss, subcutaneous bleeding, sores in their throat or mouth (nasopharyngeal ulcers), and decay and ulceration of the gums about the teeth (necrotic gingivitis). High rates of radiation exposure often result in death.

The likelihood of a terrorist organization employing nuclear terrorism is relatively low. This is because terrorists are generally rational actors that are seeking to accomplish a political goal rather than killing for the sake of killing. Further, the logistical support needed to acquire, transport, and detonate a nuclear device is substantial, and most terrorist organizations would be unable to accomplish this without a state sponsor. It is unlikely that a state would be willing to risk facing a full military reprisal if it supported a nuclear attack on the United States.

Biological: There are many advantages for terrorists who attempt to use biological weapons, namely, the availability of biological agents and the ease with which they can be transported. Unlike nuclear devices, the technical knowledge necessary to use biological agents is not difficult to obtain. There are no technical experts or high-technology laboratories required, and the costs would be minimal, although in some cases it is difficult to properly contain. Example: the 40 dead terrorists from the plague in an Algerian Al Qaeda camp where they were developing bio weapons.[9]

In October 2001, the United States was sent into near hysteria after letters containing anthrax were sent to five media outlets and two senators, resulting in the deaths of five and the infection of 23. The widespread panic and fear resulting from these letters shows how heightened responses from a coordinated biological weapons attack would increase the impact of the operation as well as the reputation of the terrorist organization.

Chemical: Although deadly chemical attacks have not been used in the United States, they do pose a threat. In 1995, a poison gas called Sarin was used in the Tokyo subway system, killing 11 people and injuring hundreds more. Sarin and Tabun are nerve agents that kill by short-circuiting the nervous system. Odorless and colorless, they enter the body by inhalation or through the skin. Symptoms include intense sweating, lung congestion, dimming of vision, vomiting, diarrhea, and convulsions. Death comes in minutes or hours, although an atropine sulfate injection can counter the respiratory paralysis of nerve gas. Similarly, butyric acid, which gives off a noxious odor and is difficult to remove, has been used in attacks on abortion clinics. Mustard gas causes sores on the skin and sears damp surfaces, eyes, lungs, and open sores. It can kill in a short period of time at very high doses, or can maim a victim.

BOX 23.3 TYPES OF BIOLOGICAL WEAPONS

- **Anthrax**—An acute infectious disease caused by the spore-forming bacterium *Bacillus anthracis.* Anthrax most commonly occurs in wild and domestic lower vertebrates (cattle, sheep, goats, camels, antelopes, and other herbivores), but it can also occur in humans when they are exposed to infected animals or tissue from infected animals.
- **Ricin**—Ricin is a poison that can be made from waste left over from processing castor beans. It can be in the form of a powder, a mist, or a pellet, or dissolved in water or weak acid. Death from ricin poisoning could occur within 36 to 48 hours of exposure, whether by inhalation, ingestion, or injection. Exposed people who live longer than five days without complications will probably survive.
- **Botulism**—There are three main kinds of botulism. Food-borne botulism is caused by eating foods that contain the botulism toxin. Wound botulism is caused by toxin produced from a wound infected with *Clostridium botulinum*. Infant botulism is caused by consuming the spores of the botulinum bacteria, which then grow in the intestines and release toxin. Infant botulism usually affects children between birth and one year. All forms of botulism can be fatal and are considered medical emergencies. Food-borne botulism can be especially dangerous because many people can be poisoned by eating contaminated food.
- **Smallpox**—Smallpox is contagious and sometimes fatal. A virus called *variola* causes smallpox. Smallpox spreads slowly, usually by face-to-face contact for an hour or more with a contagious person. Smallpox can be spread by contact with inanimate objects (such as clothing, towels, linens), but this is uncommon.

PROACTIVE INVESTIGATIONS

A proactive investigation focuses on the gathering of evidence that proves (or disproves) the involvement of a suspected perpetrator in a crime. In most proactive investigations, the subject has a criminal record with several convictions for the same crime that is less likely to be the case in the United States, although there are organizations whose members are capable of terrorist bombings. A major problem facing those directing a proactive investigation is trying to determine which group or which members or sympathizers should be the subjects of the investigation.

Information and Intelligence

Ultimately, the key to successful terrorism investigations is the use of information and intelligence. Information is the raw data that serves the intelligence function. For the most part, information is likely to come from local law enforcement and citizens. Great strides have been made in recent years to improve the intelligence function in the United States. The National Counter-Terrorism Center (NCTC) is the national intelligence collection and analysis agency, and combines representatives from a number of federal agencies, such as the FBI, the CIA, U.S. Immigration and Customs Enforcement (ICE), the Border Patrol, and other agencies under the Department of Homeland Security.

A number of educational, private, and state-supported operations are also involved in conducting research on terrorist groups, their goals, and their strategies. For example, the Institute for the Study

---

BOX 23.4 THE PSYCHOLOGICAL MOTIVES FOR TERRORISM

- A desire to be regarded as special is the most common and strong motive—the romantic view of the terrorist as special and having a unique mission.

- The desire to be known to the target audience is a strong motive—having a poster of one's image as a martyr posted on the walls of one's home town is titillating.

- The desire to be vicariously approved of by members of one's own reference group—activated into terrorist actions by favorable sentiments in one's own community.

- The desire to achieve personal congruence by aligning actions with ideological/religious convictions—not an expression of hatred.

- A desire to affiliate and be with others of a like mind; in recent cease-fire negotiations with Israel, the Hamas faction demanded to stop the killings of its leadership in order to protect its group integrity, instead of demanding other important political concessions over which they are supposedly fighting.

- The experience of social and psychological isolation resulting in little interface with other views—leading to preservation and hardening of opinions justifying terrorism.

- Vengeance for originally offended individuals who were perceived to have been unjustly treated by members/representatives of the target group—Eamon Collins testified that he joined the IRA in the mid-1970s following his brutal arrest and manhandling by British soldiers.

- Experience of an insult to the person's grandiose sense of self, but not necessarily a serious personal loss in the hands of the target group—Marwan Abu Uheida lost his sense of national dignity after American forces did not leave Iraq following the ousting of Saddam Hussein

---

Source: Adapted from Reuben Vaisman-Tzachor, "Psychological Profiles of Terrorists." *Forensic Examiner*, 15:2 (Summer 2006), 6.

of Violent Groups (ISVG) at the University of New Haven, supported by federal agencies, maintains one of the largest databases in the world on terrorist groups and tactics. More than 2,500 groups throughout the world are tracked.[10] The University of Maryland's National Consortium for the Study of Terrorism and Responses to Terrorism (START) also conducts research on terrorist incidents.[11] Analysis of data is developed using a broad range of statistical, geospatial, and linking formats.

In order to better understand the motivation of terrorists, greater attention should be given to psychological profiling. However, as Reuben Vaisman-Tzachor, a clinical psychologist familiar with counter-terrorism, notes, "... one must conclude that there are probably numerous profiles for numerous terrorist targets that vary along ideological lines, technical capacities, and group affiliations."[12] Box 23.4 focuses on the psychological motives for terrorism.

Conducting the Investigation

Because at least some members of a terrorist organization are likely to be known, painstaking surveillance can result in identifying others who may not be known. Accordingly, for this and other reasons, terrorists generally employ counter-surveillance measures—an activity generally unknown to (and certainly not practiced by) the average citizen. For example, terrorists may commit repeated traffic violations (going through a red light, driving the wrong way on a one way street, speeding, and so on) coupled with other counter-surveillance techniques (turning into a cul-de-sac) in order to detect surveillance. Such activity, combined with behavior such as using disguises or taking two hours to make a trip that should require less than 20 minutes, indicates that the subject under surveillance, as well as those people with whom he or she is in contact, is worth following. Observing other suspects engaged in similar conduct will aid in the construction of a terrorist group or cell profile.

A person who is close to the members of the suspected organization, or who has been arrested for terrorist activities or another crime, can sometimes be turned into an informant. This kind of person is often able to provide information that assists in further developing a profile of a terrorist bomber. By placing suspects who fit this profile under surveillance, it is possible that the investigator will finally be led to the safe house or bomb factory. If the location is an apartment building or other multi-party residence or building, further delicate investigation is required to determine which unit is being used without scaring the neighbors or warning the terrorist. The person who pays the rent and utility bills may serve in that capacity only, or may be involved somehow in constructing the bombs.

At some point in the investigation, it may be necessary to persuade a judge that there is probable cause to issue a warrant for placing a listening device in the suspected premises. Because terrorists engaged in making bombs have been known to pass written notes rather than speak to each other, it may become necessary to seek a warrant to install a video camera in the suspected premises (see Chapter 8 on surveillance). The evidence obtainable through such intrusion, of course, can be overwhelming and may provide the proof necessary for an arrest and ultimately a conviction.

REACTIVE INVESTIGATIONS

Traditionally, after-the-fact investigations of a bomb explosion focus on the site of the detonation in order to recover as many parts of the bomb or its carrier, such as a suicide bomber. Similarly, if a telephoned bomb threat is received and the bomb is discovered before it was set to go off (or if it was defective and failed to explode), considerable investigative effort is required. Following through on collecting and examining valuable evidence can yield important results:

1. A part or parts of the bomb may be traced to the source (manufacturer down to retailer). Similarly, a VIN from the vehicle used to carry explosives to a bomb site may be discovered following detonation by examining each piece of metal found at and near the scene.

2. If a series of bombings has occurred, they may be linked to show a common origin. Clues from each event then may be pooled to further the investigation.

3. Bomb parts recovered at the scene can be compared to similar parts or materials found in the bomb factory, if and when one is finally located.

4. Extensive research over the past decade on the characteristics and properties of different types of bombs has led to the creation of data banks designed to aid investigators. Much of this research has been carried out by the Energetic Materials Research and Testing Center (EMRTC) at New Mexico Institute of Mining and Technology (New Mexico Tech), which conducts counter-terrorism studies. Such research frequently makes it possible to determine the amounts and types of explosives used, their relationship to other physical evidence, and their origin.

Individuals who might possess useful information become known to the investigators through diverse sources.

1.   An organization may lay claim (through a telephone call or a letter distributed by the mass media) to having placed the bomb. The same organization is likely to be known to the police (whose presence at such events is necessary to preserve order) if it has been active in the past in any of the following ways: (1) disruptive picketing, (2) harassment of speakers who are discussing current social or political issues, or (3) distribution of inflammatory pamphlets supporting or opposing an issue.

2.   When an item of physical evidence is traced to the place where it was bought, an identification of the purchaser may result from a record of the transaction (sales slip, invoice, credit card slip, etc.). If the record bears no name or a fictitious name was used, but an organization has claimed responsibility or has been established by other means, photographs of its members can be shown to the salesperson to ascertain if a member of the group is recognized as the purchaser.

3.   An informant—especially an average citizen who reports observing some unusual, suspicious behavior to the police—can point to a suspect. A disaffected member of the terrorist group may also turn (or be turned) into an informant and provide very useful information.

Depending upon the facts developed during the investigation, interviews and surveillance can produce further information that must be followed up—ending either in interrogation or when an impasse is reached.

One of the longest investigations in a terrorism case involves the case of Ted Kaczynski (see Figure 23.6), known as the Unabomber, who eluded law enforcement for almost two decades. The break in the case came largely as a result of the release of the Unabomber's writings to the media, which resulted in recognition of the suspect's writing by a family member. The Federal Bureau of Investigation was able to tie to the suspect hundreds of small items of information and evidence collected over the years—including physical evidence, travel records, eyewitness reports, and writing samples. The investigation involved a suspect profile (which proved to be quite accurate), a study of the victims to determine relationships to each other as targets and how they might have been selected, reviews of various types of records of possible suspects, and the investigation of an estimated 10,000 suspects. Although the Unabomber was not classified as a terrorist by traditional definitions, his activities represented a new form of terrorism apparently carried out by a single individual.

Figure 23.6
Former University of California at Berkeley math professor Theodore John Kaczynski is escorted into the federal courthouse in Helena. Kaczynski was first charged with possessing the components of a bomb found in a search of his mountain cabin.

AP Photo/Elaine Thompson

Types of Terrorism and Violent Groups

There are three general categories of domestic terrorist groups: left-wing extremists, right-wing extremists, and single-issue or special interest groups.

As Dyson notes, "Left-wing extremists would like to see the creation of a nation in which the means of production will be commonly owned. Every person will receive what he or she needs, and every person will contribute what he or she can best provide. ... This is usually referred to as the 'Dictatorship of the Proletariat.'"[13] Not all left-wing extremists envision the same ideal state, though. Right-wing extremists generally foster any number of radical beliefs, and many groups foster a strong central government that espouses a "fascist state with all of its nationalist and supremacist philosophies."[14] However, the broad range of groups, from militant militias to the white supremacist groups such as the Ku Klux Klan, are representative of the more common right-wing groups.

So-called single-issue groups, which in many cases encompass legitimate protest movements, frequently involve fringe elements willing to use violence to achieve their ends.

Single Issue Groups

- Animal rights extremists
- Environmental or ecological radicals
- Anti-abortion activists
- Anti-genetic and other violent opponents of "scientific engineering," such as stem cell research
- Sovereign Citizens Movement

Supporters of Al-Qaeda

In his 1996 "Declaration for War," Osama bin Laden laid out his manifesto that espoused the use of violence as a means of changing the political order. The attacks on 9/11 were neither the beginning nor the end of a strategy that has developed as a lateral rather than a hierarchical model for carrying out what is today a global movement involving a loosely based network of operatives. "Functionalism stresses al-Qaeda's organizational form and capabilities above its ideology, leading to an explicit, succinct, grand strategy." It is estimated that between 10,000 to 110,000 recruits have "graduated" from al-Qaeda training camps in Afghanistan.[15]

In reviewing the most recent cases of conspiracy and other charges associated with the al-Qaeda movement in the United States, one finds that in some groups there were individuals trained overseas, and in others members that had no direct link other than an ideological connection, or in some cases an Internet observation of the rhetoric. Most domestic arrests by the FBI have been as the result of informants, tips from citizens, or wiretaps. Thus, understanding the so-called global Salafi Jihad (GSJ), a term coined by Marc Sageman,[16] as a worldwide revivalist movement is important because "understanding culture as an operational element also has implications for anti and counterterrorism policy:

- How does the GSJ's culture impact its choice of targets?

- How does the GSJ's culture impact Western countries' terrorism scenario design and development, such as the UK's "Atlantic Blue" or the U.S.'s Top Officials' Exercise (TOPOFF).

- Further, how can apprehending the nuances of the GSJ's culture and warfare, such as the disagreement over the brandishing of takfir (evidenced by the divergent voices within the culture of global jihad that call for the explicit targeting of Shi'a or other Sunni Muslims outside the pale of jihadi salafism), create avenues for exploitation."[17]

The investigator assigned to a counter-terrorism unit should be familiar with the many nuances associated with Middle Eastern-based extremism, as well as with the vast majority of the domestic community that rejects the so-called al-Qaeda philosophy.

Ecological Movements and Animal Rights Groups

Ecological terrorism, sometime called *ecotage* or *ecoterrorism*, involves efforts by groups to protect the environment. Driving spikes into trees to prevent lumbering, pouring sand into the gas tanks of vehicles, arson, and other forms of sabotage have been used, many resulting in severe injuries.

In recent years, law enforcement has increased its attention on animal rights activists. Activist group members sometimes progress to criminal activities. According to one FBI agent, groups like the Animal Liberation Front (ALF) are both deeply committed to their cause and difficult to trace: "There's no real leadership. Decisions are made by the group, which tends to be very loosely organized," he said. "Nobody really knows who else is in the organization."[18]

In a study of animal rights and ecology-based extremism, Hasan Arslan concluded that the vast majority of actions by the Animal Liberation Front and several other groups represent significantly more attacks than the ecology-based groups, such as the Earth Liberation Front (ELF) (see Figure 23.7). In most cases the attacks are less than lethal, amounting more to vandalism and property destruction in 1,762 incidents in the United States.[19] However, it is important to recognize that property and other damages have amounted to more than $50 million.

Agro-Terrorist Activities

Attacks on farms, ranches, and feedlots represent a threat because they are generally unprotected. Of particular concern is the introduction of foot-and-mouth disease into the food supply, a disease that is 20 times more infectious than smallpox. Although the disease is not dangerous to humans, the virus can be carried by them and be transmitted to animals. The economic impact of having to destroy animals could run into millions or even billions of dollars. In 2001, ranchers in England were required to eradicate more than four million cows.[20]

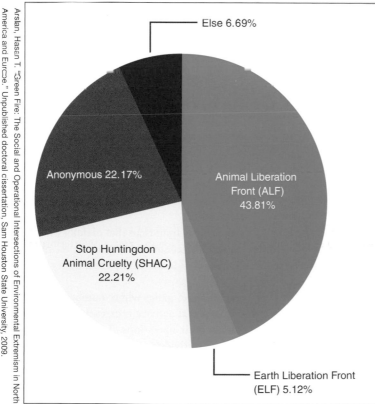

Arslan, Hasan T. "Green Fire: The Social and Operational Intersections of Environmental Extremism in North America and Europe." Unpublished doctoral dissertation, Sam Houston State University, 2009.

Else 6.69%

Anonymous 22.17%

Animal Liberation Front (ALF) 43.81%

Stop Huntingdon Animal Cruelty (SHAC) 22.21%

Earth Liberation Front (ELF) 5.12%

Figure 23.7
Actions by animal rights groups (ALF and SHAC) are significantly more frequent than those of the Earth Liberation Front (ELF).

AP Photo/Jeff Tuttle, Pool

Figure 23.8
Scott Roeder, center, leaves the courtroom in Wichita, Kansas, on January 29, 2010, after being found guilty of premeditated, first-degree murder in the shooting death of abortion provider Dr. George Tiller.

Anti-Abortion Violent Offenders

For the most part, the anti-abortion movement in the United States consists largely of individuals and groups operating peacefully and within the law to end legalized abortion, or to shut down medical practices where abortions are carried out. Most illegal activities consist of disorderly conduct, "staged" arrests, and letter campaigns identifying doctors who carry out abortions. In some extreme cases, abortion doctors have been targeted. For example, Dr. George Tiller was shot and killed in May 2009 (see Figure 23.8).

From an investigative standpoint, however, there continue to be individuals, many of whom are affiliated with legal groups, who choose to go beyond the group's limitations on violence and carry out bombings and assassinations.

URBAN VIOLENCE AND STREET GANG INVESTIGATIONS

The growth of urban violence, perpetrated in large part by major gangs operating across the country, many of which have international ties, represents an ongoing threat that frequently necessitates the employment of task forces and cooperative investigative arrangements. Although local gangs are generally within the jurisdiction of state and municipal law enforcement, the crossing of borders and specific types of criminal activity may come under the jurisdiction of a number of federal agencies.

The organizational structure of street gangs may be more transparent than that of domestic terrorist groups, at least at operational levels where the criminal acts are committed by younger members of the gang. Random violence, such as drive-by shootings, or intimidation of the community, may be orchestrated by a less visible leadership.

A disturbing trend has been the emergence of a variety of street gangs whose numbers can be extremely large and whose involvement in various forms of criminal activity is extensive. Many of them are involved in sophisticated drug-trafficking activities, their operations characterized by a high degree of violence. It has been estimated that the number of individuals involved in street gangs throughout the United States may surpass 200,000.

A number of the more notorious gangs are formed on the basis of ethnic or racial identity, and many of them recruit from prison populations. MS-13 (Mara Salvatrucha), for example, began as a Salvadoran gang in Los Angeles, but has grown to operate in as many as 42 states with a membership in the thousands. In Central America, the gang numbers more than 40,000, with as many as 10,500 in El Salvador, 36,000 in Honduras, and smaller numbers in Guatemala, Nicaragua, Costa

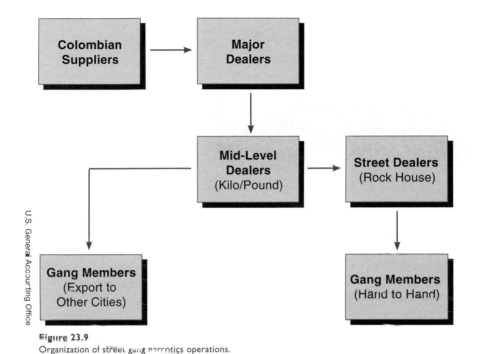

Figure 23.9
Organization of street gang narcotics operations.

Rica, Panama, and Belize. From an investigative standpoint, it is important to recognize that many immigrants, legal and illegal, are "controlled" by organized crime groups.[21]

Two of the most notorious street gangs that operate in many cities across the country are the Crips and the Bloods. Crips gangs are found in nearly every major city in the United States and have been identified in several foreign countries but they have no formal structure or head leader.

The Bloods are a rival gang created by the Piru Street Boys in 1972 to revolt against the Crips in Los Angeles. An east coast version was created in 1993 by African-American inmates at Rikers Island in New York. Although Blood gangs share the same name, there is no formal leadership structure that controls all Blood gangs.

Whereas the primary goal of the terrorist is focused largely on a political philosophy, the goal of the street gangs is on more traditional types of crimes aimed at illicit funding or dominance of a specific community by the use of force or the fear of force. However, in both instances the leadership seeks to thwart the public order and safety of the public.

Because gang leadership may appear to be amorphous, there are frequently close relationships between groups in other locations, and unwritten agreements relative to various types of criminal activity, such as drug trafficking, extortion, exploitation of women and children, and illegal immigration. See Figure 23.9 for a sample organizational chart of a street gang narcotics operation.

Membership in street gangs ranges from estimates of 100,000 to as many as 500,000 throughout the country. The activities of some of these groups are covered in more detail in Chapter 24 on enterprise and organized crime. However, the nature of gang investigations, particularly with regard to the leadership and mobility of suspects, does resemble terrorism investigations in many ways.

TYPES OF ATTACKS

Terrorists and gang members carry out a broad range of physical assaults and attacks as a means of instilling fear, including extortion and "warnings" to those who are outspoken against activities of groups. In addition to bombings, the investigation of which is discussed in Chapter 21 on Arson and Explosives, there are other types of assaults, including assassination, kidnapping, and random violence.

Assassination

Assassination attempts are often made through bomb attacks. In the United States, however, the trend in political assassination has involved firearms. When an attempt is made with a handgun and the perpetrator is apprehended immediately, the evidentiary requirements can be handled in a relatively routine fashion. Attacks using a rifle or automatic weapon represent a greater problem. Perhaps the most infamous assassination in the United States was the murder of President John F. Kennedy in Dallas, Texas.

Although the crime scene in the Texas Book Depository from which Lee Harvey Oswald fired was protected, a number of items were overlooked in the initial crime scene search. Perhaps more important was the failure to protect other potential sites where later speculation suggested there may have been a second or even a third gunman. The way in which this case was handled has created a national mystery that leaves unanswered questions in the minds of many Americans (see the Firearms section in Chapter 2). More recently assassinations and attempts involve disputes between rival gang members, or the elimination of witnesses. There have also been a number of attacks on police officers, although most involve random victims rather than focusing on specific individuals. The use of vehicles, in so-called drive-by attacks, has also been more common. Assassination attempts like the one above are frequently carried out by terrorist groups and are generally planned in advance. In almost every case, the scene has been analyzed, and avenues of escape have been plotted. The crime scene may actually be in several locations, and the investigator in making the initial assessment should take time to explore the various possibilities that may exist. The terrorist will frequently try to disguise or mislead in a variety of ways. This may involve the employment of a ruse or diversionary action, having more than one attack location, or even taking a hostage to gain access to a particular location. Tracing the activities of the suspects as soon as possible may lead to various locations and ultimately to additional physical evidence, but the investigator must take care not to form a hypothesis immediately or jump to conclusions.

Kidnapping

The investigation of kidnapping is difficult. Combined with a terrorist act, it becomes even more troublesome. The complexity of this type of investigation requires a thorough understanding of the use of the crime scene search to develop evidence that may lead to suspects and the location where the victim is being held. Most terrorist-related kidnappings involve a high degree of planning. At the outset, it is important to determine the reason for the kidnapping, which may be for monetary ransom, to force a political concession, or to bring a specific individual under the custody of the kidnappers for a "revolutionary trial." The initial crime scene will usually be the location where the person was kidnapped, followed by the location where he or she was held, but it may shift quickly to other locations as the case develops. Each individual location where it can be ascertained that any action took place should be treated as an individual crime scene. Some areas to consider are:

- Scene of the actual kidnapping
- Telephone booths
- Vehicles used
- Safe houses
- Locations where victim was held
- Victim's residence
- Victim's place of work

Beyond the normal evidence collected, some of which focuses on prosecutorial needs, the kidnapping scene may provide other information that will assist in the investigation. For example, dirt, clay, or other trace material that might adhere to shoes may, on occasion, offer a clue as to approximately where the offenders have been. Tire tracks may provide information on the type of vehicle or may link the vehicle to the scene. Items such as cigarettes, candy and chewing gum wrappers, articles of clothing, and other materials may help determine the number of perpetrators and even who they are. Bullets and shell casings may help determine if the weapon was used in another crime, which in turn may provide geographical information. Even books, magazines, and other reading materials may help identify potential suspects.

Evidentiary material collected at crime scenes should be compared with databases compiled for other intelligence purposes. Germany's Bundeskriminalamt (BKA) developed extensive profiles on individuals in the "Baader-Meinhof gang" (the Rote Armee Fraktion, a left-wing terrorist group active from 1970 to 1998) by means of such data-collection efforts, even though they did not know the exact identities of the individuals they were seeking. In one case, police knew that one of the male suspects always wore a raincoat, and that he would cut the pocket of the coat out so that he could reach for his weapon. This seemingly insignificant information not only saved the life of the police officer, but also made it possible to identify various locations where the suspect had been hiding out.

In addition, information regarding the names used to register for utilities or other services at safe houses made it possible to develop patterns for aliases. For example, many individuals will use their own first name or initials in selecting an alias. These names may appear on bills, letters, or other documents at a safe house. Maps obtained at safe houses should not be overlooked. They should be examined for marks on the document that identify targets, fingerprints, marking, or residue from handling certain parts of the map.

Regarding vehicles, careful attention should be given to the trunk (in which the victim may have been carried) and under the dashboard and seats (where weapons may have been stowed). Fragments of rope or fabric (including fibers) used to bind the victim may also prove valuable. The exterior parts of the vehicle must also be examined. Mud, dirt, or other debris located on the undercarriage may help identify locations where the vehicle has been. It is also not uncommon to use stolen plates on a vehicle. An examination of the vehicle from which the plates were stolen may provide latent prints. This is an avenue frequently overlooked by investigators.

When a victim has been found, he or she may have traces of evidence on clothing or body parts. It is important to ascertain whether the victim owns the clothing he or she is wearing when found.

Physical evidence can be extremely useful in kidnapping cases. The investigator should be aware of the value attached to such material and should work closely with evidence technicians and the crime laboratory. Additionally, MO may be important. For example, a serial kidnapper or a terrorist group may use similar tactics in carrying out kidnappings. In mass kidnappings by terrorist groups, large groups of people may be taken as part of an intimidation campaign. In one case, for example, the FARC came in military uniforms to a government building and told everyone to evacuate because there was a bomb threat. They loaded the hostages all on a bus and then unfurled their armbands and notified the people that they had all been kidnapped by the FARC.

Random Violence

Investigations of seemingly random violence can prove to be extremely difficult to investigate, largely because the victim or victims rarely know the attacker. These types of attacks include actions at riots and mob scenes (a common occurrence at sporting events or in the aftermath of an event), drive-by shootings, and acts by deranged individuals.

Kelly Dedel, in a study of drive-by shootings, notes that most such shootings do not result in death or injury, and where a person is killed there is usually significant media coverage. Many shootings involve multiple perpetrators and victims, and although gang involvement is frequent, non-gang-related attacks account for a significant number of attacks. Because there is no systematically collected national data, much of the research is based on local reports.[22]

STRATEGIC INITIATIVES

Because terrorist cases frequently involve more than one act and sometimes many individuals, the follow-up investigation requires particular care. Because these cases generally produce a large volume of paperwork, the use of computers as a means of storing, analyzing, comparing, and retrieving information should be considered. Several computer programs are available to assist in this effort. In a major case involving the Irish Republican Army (IRA), in which two soldiers had been killed at the funeral of an IRA member, the Royal Ulster Constabulary (RUC) put together an elaborate reconstruction of the crime by combining television coverage, surveillance films, and photographs. A computerized analysis made it possible to isolate virtually every one of the more than 100 persons at the scene. By analyzing the pictures from different angles it was possible to follow individual actions and determine who was actually responsible for the assault when a victim was dragged from his vehicle. The effort was also valuable in presenting what was a very complicated case to the court.

In another case, in which an individual attending another IRA funeral had thrown hand grenades at the mourners, the police were able to show that the individuals had ties to a "Loyalist" group. Although this appeared to be an isolated incident at first, a computer analysis of thousands of vehicle stop reports produced evidence that the suspect had been at another location months before with a known member of a Protestant terrorist group. This link furthered the investigation.

As noted, of singular importance is the timely use of intelligence and any other information collected. After a terrorist incident, the police may receive hundreds of anonymous phone calls from numerous sources. By entering this information into a computer it is possible to correlate variables that may make it possible to determine which calls are valid, and may even lead to identification of the caller.

Because terrorist investigations usually involve many investigators collecting large quantities of information, it is frequently difficult to correlate data without assistance. Crime analysis helps to identify the areas that require additional follow-up, the relationship between crimes and persons, and a wealth of other clues that heretofore might have been impossible to review and analyze. (See Chapter 12.)

In some cases, individuals involved in terrorist acts may have arrest records or have been involved in other confrontations with authority. For example, a few days prior to the World Trade Center bombing in 2011, one of the ringleaders, Mohammed Atta, was pulled over for speeding. Careful attention should be paid to records. Some areas that may prove valuable include:

1. arrest records;

2. reports of similar crimes or crimes that may have a link to the investigation, such as stolen vehicles, weapons, or explosives;

3. military records;

4. employment records, particularly of the victimized business or individual (for example, in "casing" the location for the crime, an individual may seek employment within an organization at that location; accordingly, employees who work for only a brief period that began shortly before and ended shortly after the crime should be investigated);

5. Driver's licenses; vehicle records of sales or rentals; VINS (e.g., the VIN on the demolished vehicle used to transport the explosive device to the New York World Trade Center attack in 1993 led to the individual who had rented the van in another state);

6. weapons and explosives dealers;

7. businesses that may have sold particular items;

8. school records;

9. bank records;

10. airline records;

11. car rental records;

12. credit bureau information;

13. applications for loans, credit cards, insurance, etc.

In addition, other law enforcement agencies may have specific information of value. The Secret Service maintains files on individuals who make threats against political leaders; customs records may provide information on imported goods; the Immigration and Naturalization Service (INS) can provide information on individuals entering and leaving the country; the Bureau of Alcohol, Tobacco, Firearms, and Explosives (ATF) maintains records on weapons; the U.S. Marshals Service maintains records on fugitives; the U.S. Postal Inspection Service may assist in matters related to the mail; and the Federal Bureau of Investigation (FBI) may have information because they have primary jurisdiction in terrorist-related cases. A 2012 report by the Aspen Institute Homeland Security Group, "Homeland Security and Intelligence: Next Steps in Evolving the Mission," stresses the need for DHS to expand its intelligence mission to focus on state and local first responders.[23] This shift would provide more national intelligence on investigations of gangs and other groups that operate across jurisdictions.

On the local level, police departments frequently maintain individual photo or "mug shot" files, alias files, business indexes, *modus operandi* (MO) files, victimization records, and crime pattern files. In addition, court records, probation and parole files, and other municipal or business records, such as for utilities, may prove valuable.

Surveillance and stakeouts are important components of terrorist investigations. These activities may require various forms of electronic surveillance, including wiretapping, eavesdropping, automobile locator systems, videotaping, and photography. Such efforts may require assistance from other agencies. The investigator should be familiar not only with the use of such equipment, but also with the laws surrounding their application. The investigator must know when a court order is necessary for the use of electronic surveillance. In no case should an investigator use extralegal means to secure information.

NOTES

[1]   Vesna Markovic, "Suicide Bombings and Lethality: A Statistical Analysis of Tactics, Techniques and Procedures." Unpublished dissertation, Sam Houston State University, 2009.

[2]   E.R. Bertolli, C.J. Forkiotis, D.R. Panone, and Hazel Dawkins, "Profiling Martyr Bombers: A Behavioral Optometric Perspective." *Journal of Counterterrorism and Homeland Security*, 12:2 (2006), 44–48.

[3]   *Report of the Vice President's Task Force on Terrorism* (Washington, DC: U.S. Government Printing Office), 1986, 2.

[4]   The USA PATRIOT Act, Pub. L. 107-56, 115 Sat 272 (effective October 26, 2001).

[5]   *Terry v. Ohio*, 392 U.S. 1 (1968).

[6]   Stephen W. Cogar, "Obtaining Admissible Evidence from Computers and Internet Service Providers." *FBI Law Enforcement Bulletin* (Washington, DC: U.S. Department of Justice, 2003), 15.

[7]   William E. Dyson, *Terrorism: An Investigator's Handbook*, 4th ed. (Boston: Elsevier/Anderson Publishing, 2012), 322.

[8]   Neil A. Pollard, "Competing With Terrorists in Cyberspace: Opportunities and Hurdles." In *Mapping Terrorism Research: State of the Art, Gaps and Future Direction*, edited by Magnus Ranstorp (New York: Routledge, 2006), 240.

[9]   See: http://www.telegraph.co.uk/news/worldnews/africaandindianocean/algeria/4294664/Al-Qaeda-cell-killed-by-Black-Death-was-developing-biological-weapons.html

[10]   Available at http://www.ISVG.org

[11]   Available at http://www.start.umd.edu

[12]   Reuben Vaisman-Tzachor, "Psychological Profiles of Terrorists." *Forensic Examiner*, 15:2 (2006), 6.

[13]   Dyson, op cit., 25–26.

[14]   Dyson, op cit., 26.

[15]   J.B. Cozzens, "Approaching Al-Qaeda's Warfare: Function, Culture and Grand Strategy." In *Mapping Terrorism Research: State of the Art, Gaps and Future Direction*. Edited by Magnus Ranstorp (London and New York: Routledge, 2007), 132–133.

[16]   Marc Sageman, *Understanding Terror Networks* (Philadelphia: University of Pennsylvania Press, 2004).

[17]   Cozzens, op. cit., 149.

[18]   James Osborn. "Animal Rights Terrorism on the Rise in the U.S." Fox News Online, June 3, 2009. Found at: http://www.foxnews.com/story/0,2933,525039,00.html

[19]   Hasan T. Arslan, "Green Fire: The Social and Operational Intersections of Environmental Extremism in North America and Europe." Unpublished dissertation, Sam Houston State University, 2009.

[20]   Glenn R. Schmitt. "Agro-Terrorism: The Role of Local Law Enforcement," *Sheriff* (May–June 2006). Also available at http://www.ojp.usdoj.gov/nij/topics/terrorism/agroterrorism.htm

[21]   Miriam Jordan. "Family Seeks U.S. Asylum After Fleeing Gang," *The Wall Street Journal*, (August 21, 2009), A3.

[22]   Kelly Dedel, *Drive-By Shootings*. Problem-Oriented Guides for Police, Problem-Specific Guide No. 47 (Washington, DC: U.S. Department of Justice, Office of Community Oriented Policing Services, 2007), 2–3. See http://www.cops.usdoj.gov/files/ric/Publications/e02072864.pdf

[23]   Hearing before the House Permanent Select Committee on Intelligence. *Homeland Security and Intelligence; Next Steps in Evolving the Mission*. January, 2012.

IMPORTANT CASE

Terry v. Ohio (1968)

DISCUSSION QUESTIONS

1. What is the USA PATRIOT Act?

2. What are some of the more commonly viewed forms of terrorism?

3. What are some of the more common types of criminal activity associated with terrorism?

4. What is stovepiping?

5. Investigations of terrorist groups should aim to ascertain what particulars about the group?

6. What does WMD refer to?

7. What is the NCTC?

8. What are the most common single-issue groups in the United States?

9. Why are street gangs considered to be a major threat in the United States?

SUPPLEMENTAL READINGS

Ambrose, S. M. (Ed.), *WMD terrorism: Science and policy choices*. Cambridge, MA: MIT Press.

Bullock, J., Haddow, G., & Coppola, D. (2013). *Introduction to homeland security: Principles of all-hazards risk management* (4th ed.). Boston: Elsevier/Butterworth-Heinemann.

Burke, R. J. (2007). *Counter-terrorism for emergency responders* (2nd ed.). Boca Raton, FL: CRC/Taylor & Francis.

Collins, P. A., Cordner, G. W., & Scarborough, K. E. (2006). *Contemporary issues in homeland security*. Newark, NJ: LexisNexis Matthew Bender.

Costigan, S. S., & Gold, D. (Eds.). (2007). *Terrornomics*. Burlington, VT: Ashgate.

Crank, J. P., & Patricia, G. (2005). *Counter-Terrorism after 9/11: Justice, security, and ethics reconsidered*. Newark, NJ: LexisNexis Matthew Bender.

Dyson, W. E. (2012). *Terrorism: An investigator's handbook* (4th ed.). Boston: Elsevier/Anderson Publishing.

Ekici, S., Ekici, A., McEntire, D. A., Ward, R. H., & Arlikatti, S. S. (Eds.), (2009). *Building terrorism resistant communities: Together against terrorism*. Amsterdam: IOS Press.

Haberfeld, M. R., King, J. F., & Lieberman, C. A. (2009). *Terrorism within comparative international context: The counter-terrorism response and preparedness*. New York: Springer.

Purpura, P. (2007). *Terrorism and homeland security: An introduction with applications*. Boston: Elsevier/Butterworth-Heinemann.

Schmid, A. P., & Albert, J. (2005). *Political terrorism: A new guide to actors, authors, concepts, data bases, theories, & literature* (2nd ed.). New Brunswick, NJ: Transaction.

Tompson, P. (2004). *The terror timeline: Year by year, day by day, minute by minute: A comprehensive chronicle of the road to 9/11—and America's response*. New York: Harper Collins.

White, J. R. (2011). *Terrorism and homeland security* (7th ed.). Belmont, CA: Wadsworth/Cengage Learning.

CHAPTER 24

ENTERPRISE CRIME

Organized, Economic, and White-Collar Crime

INTRODUCTION

The changing nature of organized crime prompted some criminologists to redefine, or at least bring under one heading, a phrase encompassing the broad range of crimes including but not limited to organized and white-collar crime, corruption and economic crime, organized drug trafficking, and other illicit activities of societal concern. Known as *enterprise crime*, this form of criminality includes a much broader range of criminal activity than what is commonly thought of as traditional organized crime; it is characterized by criminal networks and illegal relationships, and, more recently, by other types of white-collar criminal activity. The primary goals of individuals involved in enterprise criminality are: (1) propagation of a group, (2) financial or economic gain, and (3) the advancement of power and influence. Howard Abadinsky, an international authority on organized crime, notes that the changing global environment in terms of communications, trade, and travel has "given rise to massive opportunities for criminal organizations."[1]

> ### Attributes of Organized Crime
>
> - Absence of political goals
> - Is hierarchical
> - Has limited excusive membership
> - Constitutes a unique subculture
> - Perpetuates itself
> - Exhibits a willingness to use illegal violence
> - Is monopolistic
> - Is governed by explicit rules and regulations

Source: Howard Abadinsky. *Organized Crime*, 10th ed. Mason, OH: Cengage Learning, Wadsworth 2013.

Transnational criminal organizations have also exploited expanded financial markets and rapid technological developments.

The massive fraudulent activities carried out by Bernard Madoff, the former chairman of the NASDAQ stock exchange who duped investors out of more than a billion dollars, will go down in history as a reminder of the failure of government to adequately investigate a crime that was carried out over a span of more than 20 years.

THE ENTERPRISE CRIMINAL

Enterprise criminals differ from traditional lawbreakers in several ways. They represent a greater economic threat to society, are much more difficult to investigate and bring to trial and conviction,

Table 24.1
United Nations List of Transnational Crimes (by category)

PROVISION OF ILLICIT GOODS	PROVISION OF ILLICIT SERVICES	INFILTRATION OF BUSINESS
• Theft of art and cultural objects • Theft of intellectual property • Illicit arms trafficking • Sea piracy • Trade in human body parts • Illicit drug trafficking	• Money laundering • Trafficking in persons • Computer crime • Environmental crime	• Insurance fraud • Bankruptcy fraud • Computer crime • Infiltration of legal business • Corruption and bribery of public officials

Source: Jay S. Albanese, *Organized Crime in Our Times*, 7th ed. Boston: Elsevier/Anderson Publishing, 2011, p. 212.

and are usually self-perpetuating. The criminal groups are usually hierarchical in nature with an exclusive membership, and operate within their own code of behavior.

Definitions of transnational organized crime often differentiate between traditional crime organizations and more modern criminal networks. Traditional groups have a hierarchical structure that operates continuously or for an extended period. Newer networks, in contrast, are seen as having a more decentralized, often cell-like structure.[2]

Within this context we can identify numerous groups throughout the world, including the Mafia or *la Cosa Nostra* (traditional organized crime in the United States); Asian gangs in the United States (offshoots of the Triads in Hong Kong and Taiwan, and more recently in mainland China); the Yakuza in Japan; the United Bamboo Gang in Taiwan; drug cartels; and the drug "warlords" in Myanmar. Numerous other organizations are involved in enterprise crime, though they frequently are smaller and less well identified. Such newer groups are more likely to be involved in various aspects of white-collar and economic crime, and do not usually evidence the traditional organizational structure common to gangs. Nevertheless, their influence is pervasive and their danger to society can be immense. The growing influence of Russian enterprise criminality in the United States is notable and is carried out by well-organized and frequently violent groups.

Most of the 18 transnational crimes identified by the United Nations (see Table 24.1) are forms of organized crime. In 2000, the United Nations drafted the international Convention Against Transnational Organized Crime, which provides model law, policies, enforcement techniques, and prevention strategies against transnational criminal groups, money laundering, witness protection, and shielding organized crime figures. Countries that are party to the Convention must adopt laws that prohibit participation in organized criminal groups, money laundering, corruption, and obstruction of justice.[3]

INVESTIGATING ENTERPRISE CRIME

Investigation of the criminal activity associated with enterprise crime involves greater coordination and cooperation than for the more traditional forms of crimes. Experience has shown that all components of the criminal justice system—police, prosecution, courts, and corrections—must be well-trained and prepared to be flexible, innovative, and committed to joint efforts.

At the outset, one must recognize that not all investigations can be handled in the same manner, and that prosecution may require greater knowledge than currently exists within most investigative units. For example, it is difficult to investigate or prosecute computer fraud unless one knows something about how computers work (see Chapter 11). In cases in which a group is working transnationally, it is imperative that there be positive working relationships with investigators representing the other countries involved. Today, it is not uncommon for a criminal enterprise to plan a crime in one country, carry it out in another, escape to a third country, and keep the proceeds in a fourth country.

Enterprise crime, however, is not necessarily an international activity; most organized criminal activity of interest to the United States will occur within its borders. In some cases it will be necessary to pass new laws and develop new procedures for the control of enterprise crime, but this cannot be done without a full understanding of the problem. One of the most effective laws of recent origin involves *asset forfeiture*, which makes it possible for police to seize assets of criminals that are being used in criminal enterprises.

Investigating enterprise crime involves five primary areas of interest:

1. The organization and structure of the group.

2. The membership of the group.

3. The sphere of influence of individuals the group works with or controls.

4. The goals or purpose of the group.

5. The means by which the group attains its goals.

Organization and Structure

Not all groups are organized in the same way. Most groups are hierarchical, with individuals serving in the roles of leader, supervisors or managers, and workers. This is common in virtually all traditional organized crime groups. In some of the newer groups, however, investigators are finding shared leadership, sometimes involving a loose confederation of groups working together to commit crimes where particular expertise or contacts are necessary. For example, a group may be involved with one group for purposes of drug trafficking, another for prostitution, and so on.

Some of the newer international groups have committee structures similar to boards of directors, each with its own operating group. The cartels in Mexico and Colombia, for example, are known for their disparate structures.

Because law enforcement throughout the world has had some success in fighting enterprise crime, many groups have now introduced new "layers" of people to pass decisions on or carry out street-level activities. In the United States, for example, some states have passed laws imposing a mandatory life sentence on drug sellers; as a result, criminals have been recruiting children under the age of 15 (who as minors are not subject to such a sentence) to deliver drugs to customers.

In some criminal groups a person will be utilized between the leader and the criminal activity, so that the leader is not caught instructing someone to carry out a crime. Many big-time criminals use this approach today. In very large criminal enterprises the organization may be specialized for certain types of business, such as drugs, gambling, or prostitution. Regarding other groups, such as some Russian organizations, investigators are still learning about structures, one of which is marked by extensive use of the Internet and other forms of technology for communications.

Membership

In the more traditional groups, membership is strictly controlled; it may take years before an individual is fully trusted. Groups tend to develop elaborate recruiting procedures, including using young children as runners who "graduate" slowly to more difficult and challenging assignments. At the center or core of the leadership one usually finds old friends and frequently family members. Many of the newer groups are built around family relationships, which makes control much easier for the group and infiltration difficult for law enforcement.

In some criminal gangs, especially in the United States, new members are recruited from prisons. This lessens the possibility of infiltration and—because the person has a criminal record—ensures that his or her credibility is in question in the event he or she becomes an informant.

Most established criminal enterprises employ high-priced lawyers who are not actually members of the group but are paid well to represent them. The fact that they do not usually take part in criminal planning or other aspects of criminal activity means that they cannot be prosecuted. New laws in the United States attempt to discourage this by prohibiting illegal funds to be used to hire a lawyer. However, this has not been very successful because it is difficult to prove where the money comes from, especially in those groups that also run "legitimate" businesses.

Sphere of Influence

Most active enterprise crime groups could not survive without corrupt government officials. Corruption practices range from minor bribery of police officers to "look the other way" to paying off judges and high-ranking officials. The investigative team must have some idea of the dimensions of this type of activity.

It also should be noted that not all cooperative efforts are the result of bribery. In Colombia and Mexico, for example, drug cartels employ threats and other fear tactics to maintain power. Individuals who do not cooperate may find family members kidnapped or killed, or they themselves may be assaulted or killed.

Blackmail also is used frequently as a means of keeping people in line. Usually, a person is enticed into small illegal acts, the seriousness and number of which gradually increase. When the person reaches a point at which he or she refuses to cooperate, evidence of his or her misdeeds is used to coerce further cooperation.

There are also those who will "look the other way" because the activities of the illegal group benefit their interests. It is not uncommon, for example, for the police to overlook the criminal acts of one group in order to create competition with an established group, usually in the hope that it will drive the established group out of business or at least provide information on them. The problem with this approach is that innocent people are hurt and in the end there is usually little gain for the public.

Enterprise criminals are capable of finding ways to control people even at the highest levels of government; when this occurs, prosecution becomes extremely difficult. Knowing how these activities are carried out and who is involved is important during the preliminary phase of an investigation.

Goals and Means

The means by which a group attains its goals represent its *modus operandi*. Knowing how the group works provides the basis for building a criminal case. Enterprise criminals are likely to be very sophisticated. Generally, they would not have attained this level of criminal activity without some knowledge of how to avoid detection and prosecution. Illegal profits may be the goal, but the variety of schemes used is almost limitless.

In many cases the investigator may think he or she knows what is going on, but finds that his or her deductions are incorrect or that the criminals are creating a "smoke screen" to cover their real activities. A common problem for the investigator is the use of "go-betweens" or low-level persons to carry out the actual crimes. Drug traffickers frequently use well-paid "couriers" who are not part of the group, and are thus expendable to them.

Most white-collar crime transactions are recorded on paper or in a computer, but frequently it is difficult to trace the illegal movement of money or goods after the fact. The point at which a transaction becomes illegal may also vary; this makes the timing of the arrest very important. This is common in fraud cases.

Proper training, research, and recruiting of specialists are extremely important in combating enterprise crime. In fact, these means are the only way law enforcement personnel can prepare for the many types and methods of criminal activity they will encounter in this kind of investigation. Police departments in the United States have begun to recruit specialists in such areas as computer crime, business fraud, and the theft of technology.

From a research standpoint, efforts are now under way to help identify those areas in which new types of crime may begin, or in which they may increase. We know, for example, that international criminal activity has increased. With this in mind, the Justice Department has established an international section.

The National Institute of Justice, which funds research in the criminal justice area, also has sponsored studies of new ways to deal with enterprise crime. Much of this research is carried out at universities—away from the day-to-day problems of an operational setting with limited resources.

Some of the organized criminal groups operating in the United States include: the Mafia *(la Cosa Nostra)*; drug cartels; Jamaican Posses; Asian organized crime—ethnic Viet Ching (Vietnamese), Triads (Chinese), and Yakuza (Japanese); outlaw motorcycle gangs; and white-collar syndicates.

The Mafia

Although not the oldest form of organized crime in the United States, the Mafia—known also as *la Cosa Nostra* ("our thing"), the syndicate, or the mob—has managed to capture the imagination of the American people in a way that is nothing short of phenomenal. For many years the FBI refused to recognize the existence of the Mafia. It was not until a raid on a meeting of Mafia bosses in upstate New York in November of 1957 that people began to recognize the threat.

The Mafia has its roots in Sicily, a small Italian island that, to this day, spawns one of the most pernicious set of criminal enterprises in the world. Although there continues to be some relationship with the Sicilian Mafia, which in fact consists of several gangs who are frequently in conflict with one another, the American Mafia has its own unique and separate structure operating across the United States.

Although there has been some success in fighting the Mafia over the past two decades, the organization continues to be a powerful criminal cartel that operates almost with impunity in some parts of the United States. There are Mafia "families" in many cities in the United States, each with its own well-defined territory and loose agreements relative to the types of crime in which each is involved. See Figure 24.1.

Despite the perceived "romantic" images of brotherhood, a code of honor, and so-called family ties, the Mafia is a vicious, violent organization that preys largely on the failures of human nature. The Mafia is successful largely because of its ability to corrupt public officials and police, its emphasis on preying upon the weak, and its development of an organizational structure difficult for law enforcement to penetrate.

Some recent accounts in the media describe the Mafia as an aged organization that has lost most of its influence. Law enforcement officials who work in this area, however, contend that the Mafia is not only thriving but has become much more sophisticated as a purveyor of a variety of criminal activities—including drug trafficking, murder, loansharking, prostitution, penetration of legitimate businesses, and a broad range of other illegal activities.

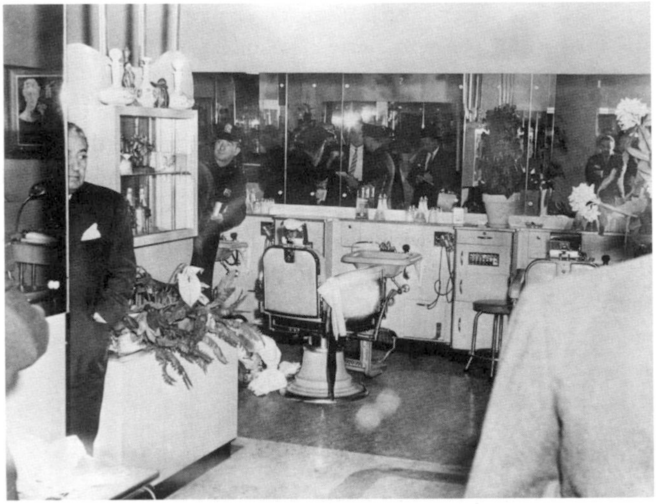

Figure 24.1
The body of Mafia boss Albert Anastasia lies on the floor of the barbershop at New York's Park Sheraton Hotel after his murder in October 1957. Anastasia's crime family was taken over by Carlo Gambino.

Figure 24.2
A wall with bullet holes is seen in an apartment in Cuernavaca, Mexico, in December 2009. Alleged drug cartel chief Arturo Beltran Leyva and three members of his cartel were said to be slain inside the apartment during a shootout with sailors.

Drug-Trafficking Organizations

America's fascination with drugs has spawned a series of international criminal organizations that span the world. Among the most notorious are the various drug cartels throughout the world who control the trafficking of heroin, cocaine, and designer drugs.

Drug cartels are characterized by extreme violence (see Figure 24.2), corruption of officials, and even the destabilization of governments. Thousands of people in Colombia, Mexico, Peru, and other countries have been murdered in drug wars, and the homicide rate in the United States is attributed in large measure to drug trafficking, use, and abuse.

It is estimated that drug networks now exist in every major American city. The DEA defines a Class I drug trafficker as a group with five or more members that smuggles at least four kilograms of cocaine or its equivalent into the United States in a one-month period. Outlaw motorcycle gangs are just one type of criminal group that has become involved in large-scale drug trafficking.[4] For instance, in 2006, the former president of the Chicago Hells Angels pleaded guilty to federal drug and racketeering charges.[5]

The extensive drug-trafficking networks provide high-priced lawyers, modern equipment (e.g., radios, cell phones, airplanes, helicopters), funds for bribing officials, and a broad range of weaponry. Cartels are noted for killing informants or "turnarounds" and will go to almost any length to protect the leadership.

A major concern with regard to cartel organization is the set of methods used for money "laundering" and moving funds to countries in the trafficking network. The sums, which are measured in billions of dollars, stagger the imagination. The introduction of new banking laws and other legislation designed to stop such illegal transactions has had relatively little impact; the cartels' sophisticated accountants have devised new ways to avoid detection.

Jamaican Posses

Jamaican Posses are thought to have as many as 10,000 members operating in the United States, Canada, Great Britain, and the Caribbean. They are involved primarily in drug dealing and firearms trafficking, and have been active in a wide variety of crimes, including burglaries, robberies, fraud, and auto theft.

The Posses originated in Kingston, Jamaica, and while they cooperate with one another at times, there is also some degree of rivalry and little loyalty among members. They are frequently confused with the Rastafarians, a Jamaican group whose members smoke marijuana as part of their religious practice. Although some Rastafarians are Posse members, there is not thought to be a strong linkage between the Rastafarians and the Posses. The two groups, however, use similar methods to smuggle marijuana. As the Posses became more sophisticated, their organizational structure developed along a traditional triangular model (see Figure 24.3).

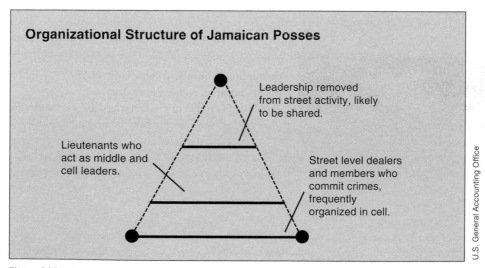

Figure 24.3
The triangular model representing the organizational structure of Jamaican Posses.

The Posses' leadership is generally not particularly stable, perhaps due to haphazard group organization and pressure from law enforcement. Leaders tend to be Jamaican nationals who have legal status in the United States, while many street-level members are illegal aliens. The Immigration and Naturalization Service (INS) reports that there has been no shortage of potential recruits in Jamaica who wish to join one of these groups.

The extensive network of the Posses has made it possible for them to secure forged documents and other certification to obtain passports and establish false identities. They have been known to move large quantities of illegal drugs, usually marijuana and crack cocaine, in rented trucks and trailers, storing the drugs in rented "safe" houses in various cities. Posse members also have been known to be heavily armed, with access to automatic weapons.

Asian Criminal Groups

The development of a number of independent criminal organizations representing various Asian groups has become a source of concern to law enforcement officials in the United States and abroad. Among these organizations are the Yakuza (a Japanese-based group), Chinese Triads and Tongs, and some Vietnamese-controlled groups. Among the more difficult aspects of investigating such groups are their international connections, the use of languages other than English, and a tightly knit structure that stresses individual discipline. Most of these gangs, according to Howard Abadinsky, a Chicago-based expert on organized crime, prey on victims from their own country, many of whom are fearful of cooperating with the police.[6]

Chinese Criminal Organizations

The expansion of American-based Chinese gangs, many with international connections, has resulted in efforts by law enforcement to learn more about their operations. Of particular concern has been the influence of Tongs, many of which are listed as social organizations and are frequently involved in legitimate as well as illegal operations. Tongs involved in illegal activity will usually be affiliated with a gang, which is likely to consist of younger members. Figure 24.4 illustrates the primary Tongs and their affiliated gangs that are operating in the United States. In recent years many of the gangs have begun to recruit Vietnamese immigrants, many of whom are in the country illegally.

Viet Ching and Vietnamese Gangs

During the 1980s, following the end of the Vietnam War, many Vietnamese immigrants migrated to the United States. Many of them were of Chinese ancestry, known as Viet Ching. A small number began to prey upon the Asian communities. From an investigative standpoint, very little is known about these groups.

Vietnamese gangs, which consist almost solely of immigrants from Vietnam and their offspring, are thought to be made up largely of former members of the Vietnamese armed forces and criminals from Vietnam. Adult gangs have a high propensity for violence, particularly within their own community, and are involved in extortion, murder, arson, and in a few cases, fraud. Vietnamese youth gangs have also emerged in several cities. They commit robberies, burglaries, and other street crimes,

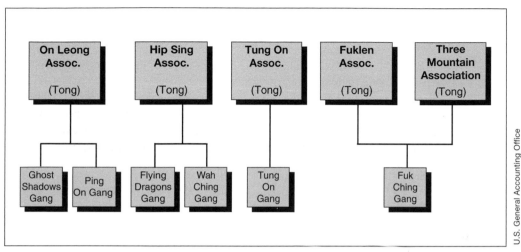

Figure 24.4
Primary Tongs and affiliated gangs in organized criminal activity.

U.S. General Accounting Office

and are likely to be armed with handguns and automatic weapons. Because the crimes are generally well-planned and executed, investigators believe that many of these gangs are led by an older member.

Triads

Triad societies have a long history in China, dating back more than 100 years. With the rise to power of the Chinese communists, many of the triads migrated to Taiwan and Hong Kong. Triads engage in a sophisticated set of rituals; the number three (3) represents an important symbol and source of identification and rituals. For example, each member is assigned a number, divisible by three. The term *triad* refers to the relationship between heaven, earth, and humankind.

Large Chinese Triads have been reported to be functioning in the United States and Canada, with estimates ranging in number from seven to 12 Triads, totaling more than 1,000 members.[7] Although there is relatively little Triad activity in the United States, their involvement in drug trafficking and forms of international crime leads some experts to believe that there is a growing relationship between Tongs and Triads.

GOVERNMENT CORRUPTION IN THE UNITED STATES

The growing number of corruption cases in federal, state, and local jurisdictions represents yet another area that is rarely covered in texts on criminal investigation. However, in today's society, in which the media, the Internet, electronic communication, and video capabilities abound, law enforcement is frequently made aware of any number of illegal activities, ranging anywhere from employee theft, graft, and fraud to abuses of authority.

The sensitivity of corruption complaints requires discretion on the part of an investigator because a false accusation may well negatively impact the career and personal life of a suspect. This does not mean that accusations or other information concerning illegal activities should not be investigated. One of the most difficult jobs in law enforcement is that of the internal affairs investigator. In policing, for instance, the so-called "blue wall" creates the perception by outsiders that the police are covering up for colleagues. One of the major tenets of a great police department is the willingness to investigate and remove those who operate outside the law or abuse their authority. In virtually every profession, there is a reluctance to testify or provide evidence against colleagues. Although the public may have a moral obligation to report corruption or illegal activity, law enforcement's obligation is to act according to the law.

In many cases, an investigator may be faced with a conflict of interest in which a friend, relative, or colleague is involved in an investigation. In others, there may be pressure from within or from an external source, further compounding the dilemma. Nevertheless, the failure to recognize that corruption and the abuse of authority will ultimately result in an irrevocable stain on those who are sworn to protect the public.

Corruption is by no means limited to law enforcement, and the illegal activities of municipal leaders, government officials, and those who are all too eager to provide payoffs or grant favors also set a tone that erodes public confidence. In his book on corruption in the New York City Police Department (NYPD), Leonard Levitt, a newspaper reporter and author, provides a sad commentary on many of the NYPD's leaders. There are, of course, other books about other police departments and their dark sides. What is most troubling is the impact on the thousands of police officers who have withstood the temptations that policing offers.[8]

Government corruption can be endemic, characterized by a growing number of individuals who become involved in a criminal enterprise. One case in New Jersey in 2009 involved a statewide investigation that resulted in the indictments and arrests of nearly 80 politicians, public officials, fixers, and businesspersons. In a three-stage FBI operation that began in 1999, the charges included: bribery, bid-rigging, extortion, mail fraud, bank fraud, and in one aspect of the case, human organ trafficking. The investigation involved as many as 2,000 FBI agents.[9]

Investigations of Government Corruption

The investigator faced with a case of corruption embarks on one of the more difficult assignments. Initially, a background check of those involved in the case should be undertaken. In addition to a financial assessment and record of assets, the suspect's personal characteristics, friends, and contacts, as well as his or her family situation should be conducted through media coverage, records and files, and other sources. The goal of such an approach should be to put together a composite verbal picture of the subject.

When the investigation is the subject of a complaint or other source, such as a newspaper article or a "whistleblower's" information, an interview should be conducted with the individual, following the guidelines in Chapter 6. The initial interview should begin with a clear statement of why an investigation is being conducted, omitting any reference to the background information unless it is designed to clarify those points that may be suspicious. Questions should be short and designed to elicit a specific response. For example, it is preferable to ask: "Can you tell me how much money you have in the bank?" rather than "I see that you have X amount of dollars in three bank accounts." The approach should be in line with assurances that you are just gathering information and that any help provided will be helpful.

Most individuals accused of wrongdoing will react angrily or in a hostile manner. This is not necessarily a sign of guilt, and the actions of the individual may also provide further leads. Care should be taken to advise the subject that you prefer not to interview people who may view the investigation in a negative way toward the subject. Unlike most investigations, the investigator may not be investigating an actual crime, but rather the allegation that a crime may have been committed. It is not required at this point to tell the subject who made the complaint or even who was previously interviewed.

Failure to provide specific details beyond the nature of the complaint may cause the subject to warn or threaten the investigator with statements such as: "You don't know who you're dealing with. I have friends in high places." An appropriate response may be: "If you'll give me their names, I'd be pleased to talk with them."

Keep in mind that the initial interview is not an interrogation. Every effort should be made to explain that there are no preconceived notions, but rather a desire to get at the truth. Care should be taken in keeping an accurate record of the interview, especially with regard to very specific details.

Some of the new and developing areas in which enterprise criminals operate include:

- Illegal drugs and drug trafficking—new forms

- Computer-related crime

- Theft of technology; industrial espionage

- Arms dealing

- Art and cultural object theft

- Dealing in body parts, such as kidneys and hearts

- "Kidnapping, slavery, and prostitution"—old crimes in new forms

- Mail fraud

- Investment fraud

These represent a few of the areas in which organized crime operates; they reflect the range of activity that, from an investigative standpoint, is creating an even greater need within the law enforcement community for specialization and subspecialization. In some police departments and federal agencies, individuals have developed a particular expertise over a long period of time; when they retire, the organization is likely to be faced with a "knowledge gap" of sizable proportion. Progressive organizations have begun to build into their organization an ability to pass on such knowledge through in-service training, partnering younger investigators with those experienced in specific areas, and using retired investigators as consultants. Ultimately, as the world becomes smaller and more complex, the need for greater subspecialization will continue to increase.

Fraud

The number of major fraud cases and media attention has placed a greater emphasis on forensic accounting, a subject that is gaining greater attention in investigative training as well as courses of study in higher education. George Manning, whose book, *Financial Investigation and Forensic Accounting*, is one of the most comprehensive in the field, notes that: "Forensic accounting can be defined as the science of gathering and presenting financial information in a form that that will be accepted by a court of jurisprudence against perpetrators of economic crimes."[10]

In major cases, the inclusion of a forensic accountant is of critical importance because the complexity of financial transactions in a world where sophisticated technology can be used for illegal purposes is a growing phenomenon. As Manning notes:

> Some of the largest bankruptcies have occurred during the last five years because management has been "cooking the books" to hide their skimming of huge amounts of funds from public corporations. This has resulted in many investors losing their life savings or retirement nest eggs...

> Individuals and businesses can easily understand the effect of crime in their everyday activities. However, most individuals and businesses have difficulty understanding the effect of crime on the community, national, and international levels.[11]

Organized Criminal Activities in the Public and Private Sector

Local industries:

- Prostitution
- Gambling
- Narcotics trafficking
- Auto theft and repairs
- Extortion
- Illegal liquor making or distribution
- Trafficking in tobacco

Local businesses in which organized crime likes to operate:

- Construction
- Waste removal
- Garment industry
- Food processing, distribution, and retailing
- Hotels
- Bars
- Banking
- Business and personals services
- Legalized gambling
- Liquor retailing and wholesaling
- Entertainment
- Motor vehicle sales and repairs
- Other cash-oriented businesses

Source: Manning, George. *Financial Investigation and Forensic Accounting.* (2nd edition). Boca Raton: Taylor & Francis, 2005.

Organized criminal groups also have a long history of involvement in a wide range of rackets that focus on legitimate business, vice operations, drug trafficking, and money laundering. Virtually all of these activities involve some form of financial transactions or record keeping.

Although the investigator may not be familiar with the more comprehensive aspects of accounting, he or she should have a basic knowledge of accounting and the types of activities in which illegal transactions are common. Fraud and identity theft complaints rose from 326,000 in 2001 to 1.8 million in 2011, with consumer fraud complaints increasing from less than 200,000 in 2001 to more than a million in 2011.[12]

Major fraud investigations involving international and other large corporations are beyond the scope of this text. Nevertheless, the average investigator is likely to handle fraud and identity theft cases. Fraud is defined as: "A deliberate deception practiced so as to secure unfair or unlawful gain." Some of the more common types of fraud are embezzlement, forgery, conspiracy, counterfeiting, and false statements. Many of these crimes are violations of federal statutes, and jurisdiction may fall under one of federal agencies, such as the Secret Service, the Federal Bureau of Investigation, the Postal Inspection service, or the Internal Revenue Service.

The Racketeer Influenced and Corrupt Organization statute, known as RICO, passed by Congress in 1970, which was used initially to focus on racketeering and organized crime groups, has been used in recent years to investigate private- and public-sector corruption. See more on RICO at the end of this chapter.

Investigating Fraud

At the outset in cases involving fraud, the investigator should be aware that the critical evidence for making a case involves records that may include ledgers, diaries, correspondence, contracts, telephonic transactions, e-mails, and other computerized files. Thus, it is important that suspects are not made aware that they are under investigation, at least not until a search warrant or wiretap can be obtained.

Allegations of fraud are most likely to come from a victim, a disgruntled employee, a bank or financial institution, or a *whistleblower*. Where an allegation is made, the investigator should conduct a thorough and in-depth interview that focuses on the specific details of the informant. In addition to determining who is involved, what the nature of illegal activity involves, how the illegal attacks are being carried out, where relevant information or items of evidence might be stored, and why the interviewee has come forward. Be aware that an allegation may be made as a form of retaliation against an employer or individual, and the veracity of the informant's motive may come into question at a later date, or if he or she is called upon as a witness in the case. Additionally, the investigator should ascertain the names of other individuals who might be willing to cooperate. This is particularly useful in developing witnesses who are not likely to be involved in the criminal activity. They include secretaries, administrative assistants, office workers, or individuals in other businesses who may be privy to incriminating information.

Of particular importance is the investigator's record keeping, which should be as detailed as possible, including dates, types of alleged transactions, the names and background information on all persons who may be involved (including suspects as well as uninformed employees), and business relationships. Background investigations should be conducted on suspects, including information on their financial holdings, indebtedness, marital status, travel, bank records, medical records, criminal record, lifestyle, credit and credit card activity, and major purchases. Although some of this information may require a search warrant, much can be obtained through open sources; observation or surveillance, credit reporting agencies such as Dun and Bradstreet, social media outlets, such as LinkedIn, Facebook, and Internet sources, such as Google and newspaper articles.

It is at this point that the investigator must prepare a detailed description of the suspected illegal activities, the list of informants or witnesses, and any evidentiary material that has been collected.

When a *prima facie* case has been made, it is advisable to secure one or more search warrants, or, where applicable, a wiretap authorization. Search warrants may be necessary to obtain information from other entities, such as banks, financial institutions, telephone records, computer activity, or other entities that are hesitant to cooperate.

Preplanning should address the strategy and tactics of the operation, including but not limited to who will do what and how it will be accomplished. If there is sufficient evidence to make one or more arrests, decisions must be made as to who will conduct interviews or interrogations, where they will take place, and what must be done to avoid individuals talking to each other. Where a suspect requests a lawyer, that individual should be moved from the scene, preferably to a police station where the suspect can meet with his or her lawyer. Interviewers on the scene should be prepared with a set of questions and responses recorded. A layout of the facility should be obtained in advance and investigators should determine locations where records are kept and computer systems are located, and where individuals can be held prior to conducting interviews in another location.

If a search warrant is to be executed, it should be at a point in time when the primary suspect(s) and employees are present, with a view toward surprise and the opportunity to conduct individual interviews. (See Chapters 6 and 10 on interviewing and interrogation.) These types of operations usually involve a number of officers, and in some cases a government prosecutor. In the preplanning stage, it should be determined who will be responsible for crime scene search. An investigator who is familiar with handling computer technology should be involved. In addition, keep in mind that securing a search warrant will necessitate *Miranda* warnings of principal suspects. These warnings should be given individually and, as noted, those requesting a lawyer should be taken from the scene.

If evidence, such as records or computers, is being removed, the objects' original locations should be recorded, and a chain of custody initiated. Most of these types of evidence will be examined later, and there should be a record of the persons responsible for the evidence. Care must be taken to protect the evidence, and it should be stored in a secure location. Examination of evidence is likely to open further avenues of investigation, and these should be pursued carefully. For example, evidence may identify others who may be involved, either as victims or suspects. During this phase, it is also important to record statements made by individuals, such as: "I told Mr. Smith that this would happen" or "I had nothing to do with this." These statements may be of value later in court testimony.

The US Code 18-1001, which is a federal crime and adopted by a number of states, makes it a crime to give false information to authorities:

> Whoever, in any manner within the jurisdiction of any department or agency of the United States and knowingly or willfully falsifies, conceals, or covers up by any trick, scheme, or device a material fact, or makes false, fictitious, or fraudulent statements or representations, or makes or uses any false writing or document knowing the same to contain any false, fictitious, or fraudulent statement or entry, shall be fined under this title or imprisoned not more than five years, or both.[13]

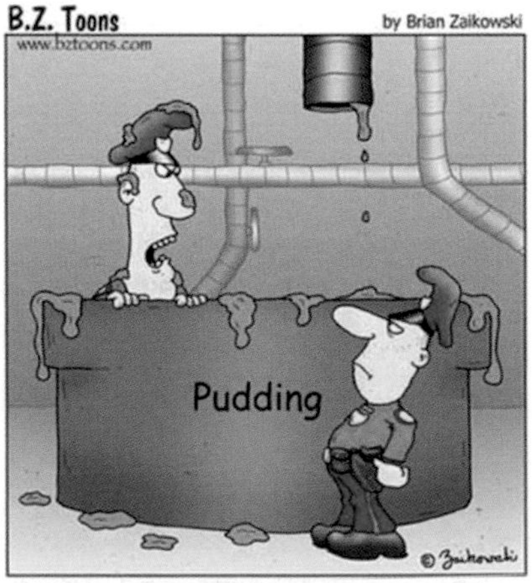
B.Z. Toons
by Brian Zaikowski
www.bztoons.com
Pudding
It's late, and we still don't have any proof. Are you going to get in here and help me or not?

Courtesy, Brian Zaikowski, http://www.bztoons.com/

Figure 24.5
Is the proof in the pudding?

Follow-up investigation will undoubtedly lead to further interviews as data is retrieved. For this reason it is also important to identify those individuals who have indicated a willingness to cooperate. In most cases, principle suspects will usually retain a lawyer, and may be possible to "turn" a suspect. A prosecutor should be present at these interviews.

Some mention should be made of cases involving organized crime activities or suspects who have criminal records. These types of fraud investigations are generally

Common Types of Fraudulent Activity

- Auto repair and maintenance
- Conspiracy
- Corporate fraud
- Counterfeiting
- Drug trafficking
- Extortion
- Forgery
- Identity theft
- Illegal credit card activities
- Illegal gambling
- Insurance claims
- International scams
- Medical-related – Medicare, Medicaid
- Money laundering

more difficult because suspects are likely to be more familiar with the criminal justice system, and may be less likely to be "turned." Nevertheless, a large number of cases have been solved in which an individual was willing to cooperate for a lesser charge. Here again, such decisions ultimately rest with the prosecutor and eventually the courts.

Investigators should be familiar with what is termed a *continuing criminal enterprise*. To establish this, a person must have committed and been "convicted of three or more felonies; be in a supervisory capacity; have five or more people working for him in some illegal capacity; and has acquired substantial assets or financial resources."[14]

Asset Recovery

One of the more important aspects of fraud investigation involves the recovery of assets. Sophisticated criminal networks as well as corporate-related criminal activity frequently involve the way in which funds are secreted. In addition to the use of offshore accounts, bank accounts held in another person's name, and the purchase of assets, such as real estate, money laundering has become an international phenomenon. The Stolen Asset Recovery Initiative (StAR) supported by the World Bank Group and the United Nations Office on Drugs and Crime (UNODC) provides a wealth of information on international asset recovery. Among their handbooks[15] for law enforcement are:

- *Asset Recovery Handbook*

- *A Good Practice Guide for Non-Conviction Based Asset Forfeiture*

- *The Puppet Masters: How the Corrupt Use Legal Structures to Hide Stolen Assets and What to Do About It*

- *Income and Asset Disclosure: Guide for Practitioners and Policy Makers*

- *Income and Asset Disclosure: Case Study Illustrations*

- *Illicit Enrichment Study*

- *Identification and Quantification of the Proceeds of Bribery – An OECD-StAR Analysis*

Established in 2007, the Stolen Asset Recovery Initiative (StAR) works to end safe havens for corrupt funds. StAR is a partnership between the World Bank and the UN Office on Drugs and Crime (UNODC). According to a StAR report, between 20 and 40 billion dollars are stolen from developing countries every year. Although, the primary efforts of this organization are focused on international crime, their reports will be of interest to investigators charged with the responsibility of conducting major corporate and corruption investigations.[16]

On the domestic level, the U.S. government has been successful in recovering the assets or initiating large fines from corporations and individuals who have been involved in large-scale fraud cases. Cooperation with a number of federal agencies, such as the FBI, the Secret Service, DEA, ICE, and the Postal Inspection Service, should be developed as a means of broadening investigative experience at the local levels of government.

Preparation for Court

Documentary evidence for presentation in court takes many forms and may include memoranda; records of acts or omissions; reports and materials maintained as part of the enterprise; transcripts and minutes; photographs relevant to the investigation (such as a meeting with co-conspirators); photostats; official records; and computer data relevant to the investigation, such as e-mails, news releases, and corporate actions. Generally, notes and records made by auditors may not be admissible.

The task of putting all of the direct evidence in perspective can be an exhausting and painstaking task, and will usually necessitate the assistance of one or more professional fraud examiners. Because the case must be prepared so that a jury will be able to understand what are frequently complex presentations, link charts or diagrams can be useful. Preparation for court presentations can be lengthy, and may take months. In many cases, the investigation may be handled by large numbers of investigators, forensic accountants, and prosecutors. A Task Force approach has been found to be the most successful method of developing and prosecuting fraud cases.

INVESTIGATING ILLEGAL DRUGS AND DRUG TRAFFICKING

Although drugs and drug trafficking have been around for several decades, the last part of the twentieth century saw some significant changes and trends. For the most part, drug-related cases have become a specialized form of investigation in the majority of departments and agencies.

Drugs are brought into the United States through many channels and by a variety of means. A key investigative activity is the development of information and intelligence relative to sources and methods of supply and the distribution networks within a city. Another important aspect of drug investigation involves tracking money. Most transactions occur in cash, but the large volume of currency, frequently in relatively small bills, makes concealing and "laundering" it extremely difficult. Drug dealers have adopted advanced methods of accounting, frequently using legitimate businesses and banks to help move funds through complicated transactions.

Most sophisticated drug dealers attempt to blend into the community. Their large expenditures, however, coupled with no visible means of support, may aid in detection. They are likely to use false credentials—driver's licenses or other forged documents—to maintain cover. Leads can be generated by developing informants among suppliers of such documents.

Generally, drug-related investigations involve five areas:

1. traditional investigations
2. surveillance
3. undercover and informant operations
4. cooperative inter-agency investigations
5. international investigations involving two or more countries.

Drugs

The discussion in this chapter centers on the activities of gangs and groups involved in drug trafficking, rather than on individual sellers ("pushers") and users. Nevertheless, it is important to be familiar with the various substances most likely to be marketed by criminal enterprises.

Cocaine is a powerful addictive stimulant that directly affects the brain. Cocaine has been labeled the drug of the 1980s and 1990s, because of its extensive popularity and use during this period. However, cocaine is not a new drug. In fact, it is one of the oldest known drugs. The pure chemical cocaine is a natural product derived from the leaves of the coca plant. A potent central nervous system stimulant and local anesthetic, it induces euphoria, confidence, and increased energy, and is accompanied physiologically by increased heart rate, dilated pupils, fever, and sweating. The "crash" following the "high" ranges from irritability and the desire for more drugs, to anxiety, hallucinations, and paranoia.[17]

Crack cocaine, sometimes referred to as rock cocaine, or free-base cocaine, is a pure form of cocaine that appears as a white crystal or cream-colored powder, sometimes in wet form, and frequently in a chunk or rock-like form. It is usually packaged in foil, although in recent years various forms of packaging have appeared. It is usually inhaled through a pipe, preferably a water pipe, with the high taking effect almost immediately and lasting for 10 to 20 minutes.[18] *Heroin* (diacetylmorphine) is a chemical derivative of morphine that is more potent and addictive than morphine. *Marijuana* is made from the dried leaves of the hemp plant. It is usually smoked for its intoxicating effect. *PCP* (phencyclidine), called "angel dust" on the street, is a very potent drug that causes hallucinations and flashbacks. *Methamphetamine*, known as crystal meth, is an addictive stimulant drug that dramatically affects the central nervous system. It is generally made in clandestine laboratories with relatively inexpensive over-the-counter ingredients. In addition to these commonly trafficked drugs, there is a large business in amphetamines (stimulants that affect the central nervous system), barbiturates (sedatives and hypnotics that depress the central nervous system), and a continually developing group known as "designer" drugs, which are created in illicit laboratories.

Virtually all cocaine is produced in South America, entering the United States through various ports of entry by a variety of illegal means. Southwest Asia continues to dominate the heroin market in terms of production and distribution. Most heroin seizures have taken place in Southwest Asia in the last decade.[19] Approximately 50 percent of heroin consumed in the United States originates in Southwest Asia, with a large proportion of the balance originating in Southeast Asia. Because drug sources and routes have begun to change as a result of pressures applied by the United States and cooperating countries, the reader should be aware that the most accurate assessment of the current situation can be obtained from the U.S. Drug Enforcement Administration (DEA).

Specialized criminal investigations require a well-planned, coordinated, step-by-step approach, usually involving more than one jurisdiction or agency. Penetration of drug rings is difficult and dangerous, and the investigative approach will frequently be determined by the type of gang under investigation. The use of undercover operatives has proved successful over the years, but the escalating caution exercised by gangs makes this tactic increasingly difficult. In recent years informants—frequently those who have been arrested and developed as "turnarounds"—have been used as an effective method for gaining permission to conduct wiretaps or other forms of electronic surveillance. This approach helps identify couriers and routes, as well as distribution points. Physical surveillance should be elaborately planned, and officers operating in teams offer the best probability of success.

When a gang has been identified, and the principals located, it is possible to monitor their activities and determine the means through which money is laundered or banked. A key aspect of the investigation is record keeping; every detail should be carefully documented for use in court. Frequently, a successful investigation will depend on the prosecution's ability to explain in minute detail (through an investigator's or informant's testimony) the means by which drugs are moved, who moved them, and who was responsible for the operation. Investigators should bear in mind that the actual handling of the drugs is usually left to relatively low-level members of the organization. The means by which these suspects pass information and money on to their leaders frequently forms the basis for a larger case. In this regard, even minute details are important, because acknowledgments are usually made in code, or through *cutouts* (individuals who know nothing other than the message being passed), and other forms of communication. The use of beepers, walkie-talkies, and cellular phones has become commonplace.

In one case, law enforcement officials reviewed the records of a paging company from which beepers had been rented, and were able to identify hundreds of contacts made between individuals. The code used was easily broken by the team conducting the investigation. For example, a specific number was used to indicate the quantity of drugs to be delivered, whether delivery was successful, and who was to carry the drugs. Although this appeared on the pager as something like "201054," the large volume of calls made it quite simple for investigators to decode meanings. Of course, the frequently called telephone numbers also proved of value, as a means of identifying both fixed locations and automobiles, through the use of a reverse directory. Where walkie-talkies are used, it may be possible to use a scanner to identify the frequencies being used by suspects. Tapping cellular phones is somewhat more difficult, but not impossible.

The investigator should constantly be aware of the importance of reaching higher up into the organization as the investigation progresses. The arrest of low-level dealers or suppliers has only minimal impact on a group's operations.

Traditional Investigations

Traditional investigations usually occur where there is a complainant, victim, or witness who provides information concerning a drug operation. Two aspects of such cases are somewhat different from those involving other forms of crime: (1) the need to secure evidence (illegal drugs usually are not sold to strangers), which establishes the *corpus delicti*; and (2) the frequent need to protect witnesses from the drug dealers.

In some cases the witness may also be a drug user, which can further complicate matters. Often there is also an ulterior motive for providing information, usually part of an effort to eliminate competition. In conducting such investigations it is important to make an effort to identify the drug network and the individuals within it. In today's society, it is relatively easy to arrest street-level pushers or locate "crack houses," but much more difficult to conduct successful investigations into the hierarchy of the criminal network. To do so requires patience, a willingness to explore and investigate a large number of possible clues, and usually a great deal of cooperation with other law enforcement personnel and agencies.

Surveillance

Surveillance, which makes up much of the work of drug investigators, represents the most effective means of collecting information in this area. Both electronic and visual surveillance have proved to be valuable tools. However, one of the pitfalls in such investigations is the inability, at least at the moment, to put together pieces of information in a way that makes sense. Many criminals have taken to using "code" words in conversations, which are designed to hinder eavesdropping efforts, while others move to other jurisdictions to conduct meetings. For this reason it is particularly important to record as many details as possible when working a surveillance. What may appear to be a casual meeting with a passerby, as well as the use of specific words—or even gestures—when communicating, may prove valuable as the investigation unfolds.

Undercover and Informant Operations

Undercover and informant operations represent an important means by which intelligence and information is collected; these techniques should be viewed in most cases as a feasible way to reach as high into the criminal enterprise as possible. Although some investigators in drug investigations concentrate on that which is before them, usually the point-of-sale, the identification of the seller's contacts and source of supply is of far greater importance. The user leads to the seller, who leads to a wholesaler, who leads to an organizational structure, which leads ultimately to the means by which drugs enter the country or are produced, i.e., the source of supply.

Surveillance and undercover investigations of organized criminal enterprises and global drug traffickers involve a degree of specialization and training beyond the scope of this text. However, it is important to recognize that these investigations are perhaps the most dangerous in police work today. See Chapter 8 for more information on general surveillance techniques.

The use of confidential informants in drug investigations also necessitates a high degree of care, both to protect the informant and to ensure that the information being provided is accurate and truthful. In drug-related cases, informants working for money have something to gain by providing information, even if it is false. Even those who have other reasons for informing are not likely to have humanitarian motives: they may provide information to keep the police off their backs, to eliminate the competition, or to settle an old score. Thus, it is important to ascertain an informant's motive for giving information.

Care should be taken when meeting informants, or when passing information, even over the telephone. If the information is used to make an arrest or conduct an investigation, every effort should be made to protect the source. This is easier said than done; a person who has been arrested, particularly when not for an obvious mistake, is generally looking and listening for a clue as to how he or she was "fingered." See Chapter 7 for more information on using and cultivating informants.

Cooperative Investigations

Cooperative investigations have become very commonplace, and the establishment of task forces and teams from several departments or agencies has proved to be an important part of successful drug investigation. At the outset, clear lines of responsibility and authority must be established. It is crucial that individuals recognize the importance of working as a team in every way.

A problem commonly suffered by multijurisdictional teams is a conflict over differences in policies and procedures. This can be resolved by instituting a joint training program. Individuals must be made aware of potential problems, and guidelines must be conceived of early on in the process—involving such things as who is to be notified when a case is implemented or an arrest made, what is the policy with regard to informants, what are the unit's weapons policies, and what is the chain of command. Some jurisdictions have experienced major problems with "leaks" of information, discordant positions on how an investigation should be conducted, and conflict over who is responsible for prosecution of a case. A successful drug investigation accomplishes a set of goals that is consistent with an organization's policy, aiming to bring into custody the highest individual involved who is within the scope of the law enforcement team's ability to investigate and produce a prosecutable case.

International Investigations

Investigations involving two or more countries have become commonplace in recent years, and are usually carried out by federal agencies. The Drug Enforcement Administration (DEA), the U.S. Customs Service, the Federal Bureau of Investigation, the U.S. Postal Inspection Service, and other agencies now have agents assigned to posts overseas, frequently working in cooperation with counterparts in other nations. Additionally, the Central Intelligence Agency and the U.S. military are also involved in assisting in international investigations involving organized crime and drug trafficking.

INTERPOL and EUROPOL serve as data-collection and information-exchange points, as well as intelligence sources for law enforcement agencies throughout the world. Local police can work through National Central Bureaus, which are established in countries belonging to each of these organizations. Although they do not have investigative powers, these organizations serve as important informational centers on individuals and groups. Often overlooked by investigators are the security operations of multinational corporations, which have operations throughout the world, and often can provide a wealth of information.

RICO and Asset Forfeiture

As noted earlier, one of the more effective tools used by law enforcement over the past decade has been what is known as *asset forfeiture*. It falls under the provisions of a federal law known as the RICO (Racketeer Influenced Corrupt Organizations) law, wherein civil remedies can be used against organized criminal activity. The RICO laws apply to a broad range of organized criminal activity. The government can seize property that has been used in violation of the law or bought with illicit money. In addition, property seized by a local law enforcement officer can be turned over to a federal agent, as if the seizure had been made by federal authorities.[20] The forfeiture does not require that an individual be convicted of a crime, but only that the person's property was used for or during the commission of a crime. Through asset forfeiture provisions the government has confiscated money, houses, cars, boats, airplanes, electronic equipment, and weapons. This has not only impacted on the specific criminals targeted, but in many jurisdictions has been used as a means for law enforcement to expand their own efforts.

Federal racketeering statutes were first enacted in 1934, but a major breakthrough in the law came in 1970 with the enactment of the Racketeer Influenced and Corrupt Organizations (RICO) Act, which amended existing statutes. The act prohibits four specific activities:

- Investing the proceeds of a pattern of racketeering activity in an enterprise that engages in interstate or foreign commerce;

- Acquiring or maintaining an interest in such an enterprise by means of a pattern of racketeering activity;

- Using a pattern of such activity in conducting the affairs of such an enterprise; or

- Conspiracy to do any of the above.[19]

RICO also provides a provision that makes it possible for lawyers and private citizens to sue if their property was part of a criminal act covered by the statute.

In order to strengthen drug laws, the Continuing Criminal Enterprise (CCE) statute was enacted to make it a crime if six or more persons acting in concert commit a continuing series of felonies under the 1970 Drug Abuse Prevention and Control Act. The courts have ruled that a "series" involves at least three related violations. This law provides for a mandatory 20-year sentence, a fine of not more than $2 million, and the forfeiture of profits and/or interests in the enterprise.

These laws provide the backbone of the government's efforts to combat organized and enterprise crime in the United States, and have been used against foreign nationals who are involved in illegal activities in the country.[20]

NOTES

[1] Abadinsky, Howard, *Organized Crime*, 10th ed. Wadsworth: Cengage Learning, U.S. 2013.

[2] John R. Wagley. "Transnational Organized Crime: Principal Threats and U.S. Responses" (CRS Report for Congress, March 20, 2006), 2. See http://fas.org/sgp/crs/natsec/RL33335.pdf

[3] Jay S. Albanese. *Organized Crime in Our Times*, 5th ed. (Boston: Elsevier/Anderson Publishing, 2011), 212–213.

[4] Thomas Barker, *Biker Gangs and Organized Crime* (Newark, NJ: LexisNexis Matthew Bender, 2007).

[5] Julian Sher. "Hell's Angels' Road Gets Rougher: The Outlaw Gang is Leaving a Trail of Death and Busts," *San Francisco Chronicle*, (May 7, 2006).

[6] Howard Abadinsky, *Organized Crime*, 3rd ed. Chicago: Nelson-Hall, 255.

[7] Albanese, op. cit., 218.

[8] Leonard Levitt, *NYPD Confidential: Power and Corruption in the Country's Greatest Police Force* (New York: St. Martin's Press, 2009).

[9] Suzanne Sataline. "New Jersey Corruption Bust Had Deep Roots," *The Wall Street Journal*, (August 27, 2009), A3.

[10] George Manning, *Financial Investigation and Forensic Accounting*, 3rd ed. CRC Press, 2010, p. v.

[11] Ibid., pp. v, 1.

[12] *Consumer Sentinel Network Databook*, Federal Trade Commission. February 2012.

[13] Manning, pp. 35–36.

[14] Manning, p. 24.

[15] Worldbank (http://www.worldbank.org/star)

[16] Stolen Asset Recovery (StAR) Initiative brochure.

[17] Karen Bellinir, ed., *Drug Abuse Sourcebook: Basic Consumer Health Information about Illicit Substances of Abuse and the Diversion of Prescription Medications* (Detroit: Omnigraphics, 2000).

[18] "What Is Crack," pamphlet published by Northeastern Metropolitan Enforcement Group.

[19] Kenneth Carlson and Peter Finn. "Prosecuting Criminal Enterprises," *Bureau of Justice Statistics*: *Special Report*, (Nov. 1993), 2.

[20] United Nations Office on Drugs and Crime, *Global Illicit Drug Trends 2003* (Vienna: UNODC, 2003).

DISCUSSION QUESTIONS

1. What is enterprise crime?

2. What are the characteristics of enterprise criminals?

3. What are some of the groups involved in enterprise or organized crime?

4. The investigation of enterprise crime involves what five primary areas of interest?

5. What political issue is common with regard to enterprise crime?

6. How does the DEA define Class I drug traffickers?

7. What are some of the new and developing areas of enterprise criminality?

8. What are the functions of INTERPOL and EUROPOL?

9. What is RICO?

SUPPLEMENTAL READINGS

Abadinsky, H. (2013). *Organized crime* (10th ed.). Wadsworth: Cengage Learning, U.S.

Albanese, J. S. (2011). *Organized crime in our times* (6th ed.). Boston: Elsevier/Anderson Publishing.

Barker, T. (2007). *Biker gangs and organized crime*. Newark, NJ: LexisNexis Matthew Bender.

Benson, M. L., & Cullen, F. T. (1998). *Combating corporate crime: Local prosecutors at work*. Boston: Northeastern University Press.

Booth, M. (1999). *The dragon syndicates: The global phenomenon of the triads*. New York: Doubleday.

Cullen, F. T., Maakestad, W. J., Cavender, Gray, & Benson, M. L. (2006). *Corporate crime under attack: The fight to criminalize business violence*. Newark, NJ: LexisNexis Matthew Bender.

Einstein, S., & Amir, M. (Eds.). (1999). *Organized crime: Uncertainties and dilemmas*. Chicago: Office of International Criminal Justice.

Finckenauer, J. O., & Waring, E. J. (1998). *The Russian Mafia in America: Immigration, culture, and crime*. Boston: Northeastern University Press.

Huston, P. (2001). *Tongs, gangs, and triads: Chinese crime groups in North America*. iUniverse.

Kelly, R. J. (1999). *The upperworld and the underworld: Case studies of racketeering and business infiltrations in the United States*. New York: Kluwer Academic/Plenum.

Kenney, D. J., & Finckenauer, J. O. (1995). *Organized crime in America*. Belmont, CA: Wadsworth.

Lyman, M. D., & Potter, G. W. (2011). *Drugs in society: Causes, concepts and control* (6th ed.). Boston: Elsevier/Anderson Publishing.

Madinger, J. (2011). *Money laundering: A guide for criminal investigators* (3rd ed.). Boca Raton, FL: CRC Press/Taylor & Francis.

Mahan, S., & O'Neil, K. (1998). *Beyond the Mafia: Organized crime in the Americas*. Thousand Oaks, CA: Sage.

Alvaro de Souza, P. (2006). *Narcoterrorism in Latin America: A brazilian perspective*. Hurlburt, FL: JSOU Press.

Schatzberg, R., & Kelly, R. J. (1997). *African-American organized crime: A social history*. New Brunswick, NJ: Rutgers University Press.

Serio, J. D. (2008). *Investigating the Russian Mafia: An introduction for students, law enforcement, and international business*. Durham, NC: Carolina Academic Press.

Williams, P. (1997). *Russian organized crime: The new threat?* Portland, OR: Frank Cass.

Glossary

A

a posteriori: reasoning from empirical facts or particulars (acquired through experience or experiment) to general principles; or, from effects to causes; see *induction*

a priori: from a known or assumed cause to a necessarily related effect; from a general law to a particular instance; valid independently of observation; see *deduction*

accelerant: a volatile organic liquid used to start a fire and help it spread more rapidly

accusation: a formal complaint of a crime or other questionable action

acquaintance rape: rape in which the offender is known to the victim

***ad hoc* agency**: a one-purpose agency established to deal with a particularly vexatious problem (e.g., in connection with sports such as horse-racing or boxing to control "fixing" the outcome of an event, or to deal with crime on the waterfront)

admission: an express or implied statement tending to support a suspect's involvement in a crime but insufficient by itself to prove guilt

AFIS: **A**utomated **F**ingerprint **I**dentification **S**ystem

agent provocateur: an individual hired to spy on the internal affairs of an organization or group, or one who is perceived as a betrayer

ALF: **A**nimal **L**iberation **F**ront

algorithm: a mathematical rule to solve a problem

alibi: a form of defense used in criminal procedure by which the accused attempts to prove that he or she was in some other place at the time the alleged offense was committed

allegation: a statement or document that accuses an individual or group of wrong doing

amplification technique: see *Polymerase Chain Reaction*

analysis: a process that starts with the whole (whether a material substance, thought, or impression) and then involves an effort to separate the whole into its constituent parts for individual study

antemortem statement: see *dying declaration*

arches: a *class characteristic* or general pattern (together with loops and whorls) used in classifying fingerprints

armed robbery: robbery involving the use of a weapon (also called *holdup, stickup, heist, hijacking*)

arson: the intentional and illegal starting of a fire

arson-for-profit: illegally starting a fire for insurance or other form of profit

artificial intelligence: a program designed to simulate human intelligence, with the capacity to perceive its environment and take actions that maximize its chances of success

asphyxiation: unconsciousness or death resulting from interference with the supply of oxygen to the lungs

asset forfeiture: an act allowed by recent law by which police may seize assets which are being used in criminal enterprises

associative evidence: physical evidence that links a suspect to a crime scene or victim; a nonlegal term

B

BAI: Behavior Analysis Interview

beacon: see *GPS device*

Bill of Rights: Constitutional protection of an individual's legal rights

blunt force wound: a wound which is the product of neither a penetrating nor a cutting instrument

BIOS: Basic Input/Output System

bit: a basic unit of computing represented by just two digits, 0 or 1

blog: a form of computer-related communication

blood splatter: the manner and direction in which blood strikes a floor, wall or other object

Bloods: a street gang

Bobby: nickname for a British police officer. The founder of the Metropolitan Police was Sir Robert Peel.

boot: start up a computer, i.e., load into memory a small program that enables it to load larger programs

break: the point in an interrogation when the investigator recognizes that the subject is about to confess

bug: a device used for such eavesdropping

bugging: eavesdropping by electronic means, such as a hidden microphone or radio transmitter;

burn the surveillance: when a surveillant's behavior causes the subject to surmise or know s/he is under surveillance

burned: when a subject's behavior signals suspicion

C

C-4: plastic explosive

CAD system: **C**omputer **A**ided **D**esign system

canvass: to ascertain information by systematically interviewing all people in a certain vicinity or area (in Britain called *intensive inquiry*)

career criminals: the select group of criminals responsible for an unduly large amount of crime in a particular area

carjacking: robbery of a person in a vehicle, and at times to steal the vehicle

case law: law created as a by-product of court decisions made in resolving unique disputes, as distinguished from statutory and constitutional law

case screening: the process by which investigative cases are removed (based on solvability factors) from the work load, making resources available for those holding greater promise of solution

cat burglar: a burglar who enters a residence at night, frequently when the occupants are present

certiorari: an original writ or action whereby a case is taken from an inferior to a superior court for review

chain of custody: a record of who handled evidence

chat room: a form of computer communication in which individuals can exchange dialog

child pornography: pornographic photos of minors, usually for distribution on the internet or between individuals

chop shop: a location, often an automobile repair shop or salvage yard, where a stolen car is stripped of its parts (radio, doors, trunk lid, engine, etc.); the remains are cut up and sold for scrap metal

circumstantial evidence: indirect proof from which the fact at issue may be inferred

class characteristics: the general patterns of a type of evidence (e.g., a Cat's Paw vs. an O'Sullivan heel impression, a loop vs. an arch in a fingerprint, a .22 caliber vs. a .38 caliber weapon, etc.)

classification: the systematic arrangement of objects into categories (groups or classes) based on shared traits or characteristics; see *identification*

clearance rate: the number and percentage of solved crimes as defined by the UCR

close surveillance: the subject is kept under constant surveillance, the aim of which is not to lose the subject even at the risk of being discovered (also called *tight surveillance*)

closed fracture: see *simple fracture*

cloud computing: the use of computing hardware and software delivered as a service over a network

CODIS: **Co**mbined **D**NA **I**ndex **S**ystem

cold case: an unsolved case that is usually reinvestigated

commercial burglary: burglary of a business establishment

composite images: the creation of an image of a suspect using a computer program

compound fracture: a fracture with the skin broken; an open wound—perhaps with the bone exposed (also called *open fracture*)

conditioned reflex: a response discovered by Pavlov stating that an artificial stimulus or signal could, by repeated association, be substituted for a natural stimulus to cause a physiological response

confession: an oral or written statement acknowledging guilt

contact wound: a wound that results when a small weapon is fired in contact with the skin (or up to a distance of approximately two or three inches from the body)

contusion: an injury to subsurface tissue caused by a blow from a blunt instrument that does not break the skin; a hemorrhage beneath the skin; a bruise

convoy: a countermeasure to detect a surveillance; a convoy, usually a person, is employed to determine whether or not a subject is under surveillance

corpus delicti: the proof that a crime has been committed—consisting of two components: (1) that each element of the crime be satisfied, and (2) that someone is responsible for inflicting the injury or loss sustained

cracker: a person who enters a computer system illegally to commit a crime such as sabotage or theft of information

crime mapping: a technique of crime analysis that maps, visualizes, and analyzes crime incident patterns

crime scene: the location or locations in which a crime was planned or carried out

Crimestoppers: a private organization that offers rewards for providing information on a crime to the police

crime suppression model: a model of the criminal justice system in which the role of the criminal justice process is, first and foremost, to suppress or control crime

criminal homicide: the unlawful taking of a human life

criminalistics: the branch of forensic science concerned with the scientific examination and interpretation of the minute details of physical evidence for the purpose of aiding the criminal investigator or a judge and jury during trial

Crips: a street gang

CSI effect: the way the exaggerated portrayal of forensic science on crime television shows such as "CSI" influences public perception

cutouts: individuals used by criminal enterprise organizations who know nothing about the operation other than the message being passed

cyanoacrylate fuming: a method of recovering latent fingerprints

cyberbullying: the use of the Internet to harm or threaten people in a deliberate, repeated, and hostile manner

cybercrime: the use of a computer or other form of technology to commit a crime

D

data mining: a method of examining various forms of information or records in which the goal is to discover patterns in large data sets

data set: a collection of related computer records

database: data arranged for retrieval

deduction: a process of reasoning that commences with a generalization or a premise and by means of careful, systematic thinking moves to a particular fact or consequence

demonstrative evidence: evidence in the form of a representation of an object (e.g., a chart, drawing, model, illustration, or experiment)

denature: the breaking apart of double-stranded DNA fragments by heat or chemical means, resulting in single-stranded fragments (these single strands can be combined, i.e., hybridized, with complementary single strands—called probes—to yield a DNA profile)

dermal nitrate test: an unreliable and discredited test formerly used to detect nitrates from gunpowder residue on the hand (also called *paraffin test*)

digital computing: computing that performs operations based on a series of digits

direct evidence: evidence that, in itself, proves or refutes the fact at issue (e.g., a confession)

discreet surveillance: see *loose surveillance*

distant discharge wound: a wound that results when a weapon is fired from a distance of at least 24 inches for handguns, or 36 inches for rifles

DNA fingerprinting: the information obtained through multilocus probe testing of DNA

due process model: a model of the criminal justice system in which the role of the criminal justice process is, first and foremost, to preserve liberty

dying declaration: a statement made just prior to death with the knowledge of impending death; though hearsay, dying declarations are allowed into evidence in homicide cases in certain jurisdictions (also called *antemortem statement*)

E

eavesdropping: refers to various forms of surveillance

ecotage: ecological terrorism; illegal (often violent) efforts by groups to protect the environment

electronic surveillance: the use of technology for surveillance

electronic tracking device: see *GPS device*

elements of a crime: the specific acts that, taken together, compose a crime

elimination prints: prints of known individuals who customarily inhabit the crime scene area; used to determine whether a latent crime scene print is that of a stranger or of someone who is customarily present

enterprise crime: the broad range of crime characterized by criminal networks and illegal relationships, including but not limited to organized drug trafficking, white-collar crime, corruption, economic crime, etc.

entomology: the branch of zoology dealing with insects

entrapment: an act by a governmental agent that lures an individual into committing a crime not otherwise contemplated, for the purpose of prosecuting him or her

excusable homicide: a killing in which one person kills another by accident (without gross negligence) and without intent to injure

exemplars: specimens of physical evidence of known origin (used for comparison with similar crime scene evidence)

***ex parte* order**: an order issued by a judge (and submitted to the appropriate federal or state judge for approval) authorizing the interception of a wire or oral communication

F

fallout: residual nuclear radiation

felony: a crime for which punishment exceeds one year in prison

fence: a person in the business of buying stolen goods, usually for resale; to buy or sell stolen goods

fingerprint: the impression of the friction ridges on the skin surface of the last joint of the fingers and thumb

file-based credit reporting bureau: a business that collects information from creditors on how bills are paid

finished sketch: a precise rendering of a crime scene with clean, straight lines and typeset or typewritten lettering; usually prepared after leaving the crime scene with information obtained from the original rough sketch, notes, and photographs taken at the crime scene

fixed surveillance: surveillance conducted from a stationary position, such as a parked van, or room facing the subject's residence or workplace, or by posing as a street vendor or utility worker; the aim is to allow the surveillant to remain inconspicuously in one locale (also called *stakeout, plant*)

flagrante delicto: in the very act of committing a misdeed

flat file: a file of data that has no internal hierarchy

flashover: a phenomenon that occurs when, in the growth of a fire, all the fuel in a room is ignited and flames flash over the entire area

fluoresce: to absorb ultraviolet radiation and immediately re-emit it in the visible region of the spectrum where it can be seen by the naked eye

forensic: pertaining to, connected with, or used in courts of law or public discussion and debate

forensic medicine: the use of medicine to determine the cause or time of death, or for other legal purposes (also called *legal medicine, medical jurisprudence*)

forensic nursing: a nursing specialty that entails caring for victims and perpetrators of crime while attempting to collect forensic evidence on the circumstances surrounding the incident

forensic odontology: the study of teeth, dentures, and bite marks for the purpose of obtaining criminal evidence, or identifying physical remains or the source of bite wounds

forensic pathology: pathology that goes beyond the normal concern for disease to the study of the causes of death—whether from natural, accidental, or criminal agency (see *pathology*)

forensic psychiatry: the study of a criminal's mental state and probable intent

forensic serology: the study of blood for the purpose of obtaining criminal evidence or for other legal purposes

forensics: a fairly new, all-encompassing term, it characterizes the scientific examination of evidence. Owing to television and motion picture shows, the term is now generic and part of the vocabulary of the average person (and, therefore, jurors)

fragmentation: in weaponry, the process by which the casing of an artillery shell, bomb, grenade, etc. is shattered by detonating highly explosive filling

Frame-by-Frame Analysis (FFA): the detailed analysis of a victim or suspect's statement that focuses on very specific details, as if watching a movie frame by frame

fracture: a break or crack of a bone, cartilage, or glass

fraud: an intentional misrepresentation or deception employed to deprive another of property or a legal right or to otherwise do him or her harm.

G

Galton details: see points of identification

galvanic skin response (GSR): the electrical conductance of the skin, one of the physiological responses measured by the polygraph or lie detector to ascertain whether a subject is telling the truth

garbageology: the study of trash

gel electrophoresis: a step in the DNA analysis process in which DNA fragments are broken apart by means of denaturing them

gene amplification: see Polymerase Chain Reaction

geographical information system (GIS): a system that captures, stores, analyzes, manages, and presents data that is linked to location

geospatial analysis: the use of mapping technology to provide an array of information on the locations of specific events

GPS device: a battery-operated device that emits radio signals that permit it to be tracked by a directional finder-receiver as it moves about (also called beeper, beacon, transponder, electronic tracking device)

grand jury: a panel of citizens with responsibility for determining whether an indictment for a crime, known as a true bill, can be issued

grounder: police jargon used to describe cases which are easily solved (also called *platter* or *meatball*)

H

hacker: a person who enters a computer system illegally or without permission

hearsay: statement(s) made out of court and offered in court to support the truth of the facts asserted in the statement

heist: see *armed robbery*

hematoma: a localized wound in which swelling is caused by the rupture of blood vessels

hesitation marks: slight, often superficial marks (usually cuts) that typify suicide and suicide attempts

hijacking: see *armed robbery*

holdup: see *armed robbery*

home invasion: entry of a residence to carry out a crime

homicide: the killing of one human being by another

hybridization: the process of recombining single DNA strands to form a double strand

hypnosis: a sleep-like mental state induced by a person whose suggestions are readily accepted by the subject; because it sometimes releases memories of traumatic events that are otherwise inaccessible, it is sometimes used to discover answers to significant questions, e.g., what was seen or heard during a criminal event

hypothesis: a conjecture that provisionally accounts for a set of facts; can be used as the basis for additional investigation and a guide in gathering further information

I

identification: an analytical and classification process by which an entity is placed in a predefined, limited, or restricted class (see *classification*)

identification parade: see *lineup*

identity: the result of continuing the process of classification (beyond identification) to the point at which an entity is in a class by itself

identity theft: the unauthorized use of personally identifying information, such as name, Social Security number, or credit card number, to commit fraud or other crimes

IED: improvised explosive device

in-between: a case which appears to have a solution but will require some effort

incest: sexual activity with a relative

incision: a relatively clean (not ragged) cut that results when a sharp instrument is applied to a small, limited area of skin tissue

indictment: see *grand jury*

individual characteristics: the details (noted by a criminalist) in physical evidence that make possible an inference concerning the common origin of some crime scene evidence and an exemplar (or comparison specimen of known origin)

individualized: put in a class of one, thereby establishing an identity (see *identity, individual characteristics, classification, identification*)

induction: a process of reasoning based on a set of experiences or observations (particulars) from which a conclusion or generalization based on those specifics is drawn; it moves from the specific to the general

informant: an individual who discloses information to an investigator

information: a finding by a grand jury that the crime is a misdemeanor

information technology (IT): all forms of technology that encompass the means for storing transmitting data

injury: a wound, especially one in which the skin is pierced, cut, torn, or otherwise broken

inner tracing: a subclassification of a whorl fingerprint pattern, delineated by tracing a ridge line from the left delta to the right delta of a whorl pattern (also called *inner whorl*)

inorganic substance: a substance that does not contain carbon (see *organic substance*)

in situ: in its original location

INTERPOL: **Inter**national **Pol**ice Organization

intensive inquiry: the British term for seeking information by canvass (see *canvass*)

interrogation: the questioning process used for a suspect, or a suspect's family, friends, or associates—people who are likely to withhold information or be deceptive

interview: the questioning process used for a victim or eyewitness—people who reasonably can be expected to disclose what they know

investigative credit reporting bureau: a business that gathers information on an individual's lifestyle and reputation

J

Jeffreys probe: a multilocus probe (see *multilocus probe test*)

judicial restraint: the application of a narrow interpretation of the constitution to issues raised in the enforcement of criminal law (also called *strict construction*)

justifiable homicide: the intentional but lawful killing of another human being (e.g., the execution of a convicted murderer)

K

kinesics: the study of the use of body movement and posture to convey meaning

"knockoffs": counterfeit consumer goods

L

laceration: a tearing of skin tissue, generally with ragged edges

LAN: Local Area Network; a network connecting several computers that are located close to one another, allowing them to share files and devices

larceny: the crime of taking another person's property without consent and with the intent of depriving the owner of the property

latent print: a fingerprint (left when a person touches an object or surface) which is not visible unless treated (developed) in some way; *latent* is derived from the Latin word for "hidden"

LEADS: Law Enforcement Agencies Data System

leakage: signals emitted in nonverbal communication

legal medicine: see *forensic medicine*

lettre de cachet: a letter bearing the seal of the sovereign, usually authorizing the imprisonment without trial of a named person

lie detector: see *polygraph*

ligature: anything that serves to bind or tie up (e.g., lamp or telephone cords, neckties, nylon hose, towels, or t-shirts are some of various ligatures used to commit homicide).

lineup: the practice of placing a suspect within a group of people lined up for the purpose of being viewed (and possibly identified as the perpetrator) by eyewitnesses (also called *identification parade*)

link chart: the depiction of linkages between variables, usually computer-generated

linkage: the production of a list of suspects based on *modus operandi* or through crime analysis patterns

livor mortis: see *postmortem lividity*

loiding: using plastic or celluloid to "slip" a lock

loops: a *class characteristic* or general pattern (together with whorls and arches) used in classifying fingerprints

loose surveillance: a cautious surveillance wherein the loss of the subject is preferred to possible exposure (also called *discreet surveillance*)

luminesce: to absorb illumination and re-emit it at a wavelength different from the incident light; akin to fluorescence, luminescence is useful to criminal investigation in that latent fingerprints become visible because organic solids in perspiration can be detected by lasers due to their luminescence

M

macro: with regard to computers, an instruction that stands for a sequence of simpler instructions

made: to be *made* is to be detected or suspected of being a surveillant by the subject

mail cover: the printing and writing on the outside of a piece of mail, copied by postal authorities

malice aforethought: premeditation

malum in se: an act that is wrong in itself whether or not prohibited by law, e.g., the deliberate killing of another human being

malum prohibitum: an act that is prohibited by law, but is not necessarily wrong in itself, e.g., a farmer's act in burning down his barn is not unlawful in itself, but becomes so if done to defraud an insurance company

malware: malicious software

manslaughter: the unlawful killing of another without intent—express or implied—to effect death; may be voluntary or involuntary

mass murder: the killing of more than one individual in a single instance

meatball: see *grounder*

medical jurisprudence: see *forensic medicine*

meet tracing: a subclassification of a whorl fingerprint pattern, delineated by tracing a ridge line from the left delta to the right delta of a whorl pattern (also called *meeting whorl*)

memory: the storage and retention of sensory stimuli that has been observed and encoded

mind-set: a way of thinking employing skepticism and doubt to provide foresight, and possible insight, to the creative investigator

minutiae: see *points of identification*

misdemeanor: a crime punishable by up to one year in jail or prison

modus operandi (MO): an offender's pattern of operation (method of preparing for and committing a crime)

Molotov cocktail: a homemade firebomb made with an empty bottle, flammable liquid, and a wick

morphology: the general structure and shape (or form) of an entity, constituting, in criminalistics, the details used in the study and comparison of physical evidence

motive: the reason why a person commits an act

moving surveillance: surveillance in which the surveillant moves about in order to follow the subject

mug shot file: a file of photographs of arrested individuals; usually includes full-face and profile photographs (mug shots) along with detailed physical description, age and place of birth, social security number, fingerprint classification, nicknames and aliases, *modus operandi*, etc. (also called *Rogues Gallery*)

mugging: see *strong-arm robbery*

multilocus probe (MLP) test: a test in which one probe simultaneously binds many DNA fragments from different chromosomes

murder: the unlawful killing of another human being with malice aforethought (premeditation); killing a person during the commission of a felony also constitutes murder—even when the killing is unintentional

muscle job: see *strong-arm robbery*

mustard plaster: a form of open surveillance in which the subject is followed so closely that surveillant and subject are almost in lock step; tantamount to protective custody

mystery: a case (usually a homicide) in which no apparent solution is readily perceived, and therefore, much time and effort are in order (also called *who-done-it*)

N

narco-terrorism: drug-related terrorism with the intent to achieve a political aim

near discharge wound: a wound that is the result of firing at a distance of approximately six to 24 inches for handguns, and six to 36 inches for rifles

neutron activation analysis (NAA): a test used to detect the level of metal residue (barium and antimony) left on the skin from the primer of a gun cartridge

nol-prossing: convincing the prosecutor to agree not to proceed any further with an action; derived from *nolle prosequi (nol. pros.)*, an entry made on the court record by which the prosecutor declares that s/he will proceed no further

nonverbal communication: messages unwittingly sent through changes in facial expressions, voice quality, body movements, and the distancing of one's self from the other speaker (see *kinesics, paralinguistics, proxemics*)

O

odontology: the study of dentistry

omerta: the Mafia code of silence; secrecy sworn to by oath

open fracture: see *compound fracture*

open surveillance: surveillance in which there is little or no attempt at concealment; the subject may be and most likely is aware of the surveillance, but must not be lost (also called *rough surveillance*)

organic substance: a substance that contains carbon; all other substances are inorganic

outer tracing: a subclassification of a whorl fingerprint, delineated by tracing a ridge line from the left delta to the right delta of a whorl pattern (also called *outer whorl*)

P

paraffin test: see *dermal nitrate test*

paralinguistics: the study of the variations in the quality of the voice (pitch, intonation, loudness, softness) and their effect on the meaning conveyed

pathology: the branch of medicine that studies diseases and trauma (their causes and consequences)

pen register: a device that records all numbers dialed in a telephone, generally installed at the telephone company's central office

perpetrator: an individual who commits a crime

per se **rule**: by itself, alone; an automatic rule of exclusion

perception: the interpretation, classification, and conversion of sensory stimuli into a more durable configuration for memory

peripheral device: a device that is connected to a host computer, but is not part of it

phishing: a computer scam in which a victim is contacted, usually by e-mail, and asked for his or her social security number or other sensitive information that can then be used to defraud the victim

petechiae: pinhead-sized (red) dots which are minute hemorrhages found inside the eyelids and the facial skin; considered by pathologists to be a sign of strangulation

photomacrograph: a photographic image that is larger than actual size

photomicrograph: a photographic image of an object as seen through the eyepiece of a microscope

plant: *in arson investigation*, an ignition device that ignites the first fuel, or assists the initial flame to build in intensity; it may include a timing mechanism; *in surveillance*, a technique in which the surveillant remains essentially in one position or locale (also called *stakeout, fixed surveillance*)

plastic print: a three-dimensional fingerprint impression

platter: see *grounder*

plea bargaining: the process whereby a suspect agrees to plead guilty for a lesser crime or punishment, usually in return for providing information of interest to law enforcement

points of identification: the individual characteristics found by a criminalist in physical evidence that provide the basis for establishing an identity; in a fingerprint they are called *Galton details, Galton minutiae, ridge characteristics, minutiae*; in firearms they are called *striations*

polygraph: see *lie detector*

polymerase: a DNA enzyme used to accomplish a chain reaction that amplifies certain DNA sequences in a specimen

Polymerase Chain Reaction (PCR): a procedure that uses a DNA enzyme (polymerase) to set in motion a chain reaction that increases the quantity of certain DNA sequences in a specimen so that it can be analyzed

portrait parlé: a verbal description of a perpetrator's physical characteristics and clothing provided by an eyewitness; loosely translated as "verbal picture"

postmortem lividity: the bluish-purple color that develops after death in the undermost parts of the body—those which have been facing downward (also called *livor mortis*)

precipitin test: a test for distinguishing human blood from animal blood

predictive policing: a law enforcement concept that integrates approaches such as crime analysis, crime-fighting technology, and intelligence-led policing to inform forward-thinking crime prevention strategies and tactics

presumptive test: a sensitive, simple field test using a chemical reagent that permits detection of the slightest residues of blood; such tests are not specific for blood, are only preliminary, and are of little value in court

prima facie: at first view; sufficient in itself to prevail

privileged communication: communication that is generally inadmissible in court, such as that between spouses, or legal counsel

proactive investigation: an investigation taken in anticipation of the commission of a crime in order to prevent it or to apprehend the offender

probable cause: a reasonable ground for suspicion, supported by circumstances sufficiently strong to justify the issuance of a search warrant or to make an arrest

probative value: the quality of evidence which serves to substantiate or help prove that a particular action took place

probe: a laboratory-tagged single-strand DNA molecule used to detect any complementary single strands of DNA obtained by denaturing the crime scene sample

profiling: the psychological assessment of a crime, in which the personality type of the perpetrator is surmised through the recognition and interpretation of visible or spoken evidence at the crime scene. See also racial profiling

procedural law: law dealing with how the state may proceed in the trial of an alleged offender

protective custody: the confinement or guardianship of an individual by law enforcement with the objective of preventing an assault or other crime against him or her

proxemics: the study of the physical distance individuals put between themselves and others, noting any shift from between an open posture and a protective one (as in folding the arms across the chest)

psychological autopsy: a technique whereby a consensus is developed by a team of experts as to the mental attitude or outlook of a deceased individual; usually used to determine whether or not a death is a suicide

psychological profile: see *profiling*.

pyromania: an irresistible impulse or compulsion to start a fire or set something on fire

pyrolysis: chemical decomposition brought about by the action of heat

Q

qualified expert: an individual about whom it is demonstrated to the court that s/he possesses specialized, relevant knowledge ordinarily not expected of the average layperson

query: in computing, a specific request for data from one or more databases

quid pro quo: something for something, as in making a deal, e.g., plea bargaining

R

racial profiling: taking a police action based solely on a person's race

radial loop: a fingerprint pattern in which the open end leads out to the thumb

reactive investigation: investigation of a crime after it has been committed (see *proactive investigation*)

Real Time Crime Center (RTCC): centralized technology center, the purpose of which is to give field officers and detectives instant and comprehensive information to help identify patterns and stop emerging crime

recall: to bring a previous event back from memory, usually as a verbal description of the previous event (a crime)

recognition: the act of remembering an event after some cue is provided that assists in its recollection, as when a mug shot is picked from a mug shot file or an individual from a lineup

record fingerprints: a set of an individual's fingerprints recorded in proper order on a fingerprint card using printer's ink

reliability: the extent to which an experiment, test, or measuring procedure yields consistent and reproducible results

res gestae: all of the things done or words spoken in the course of a transaction or event; a record of what was said or done in the first moments of an investigation

resolution: the capability of an optical device to separate into two or more objects (or points) what to the unaided eye appears to be one object (or point), thus yielding details not otherwise perceptible

Restriction Fragment Length Polymorphism (RFLP) analysis: DNA analysis that involves either single locus probes or multilocus probes

restriction site: a sequence of certain nucleotide combinations repeating themselves at random intervals throughout the length of the DNA chain; the term comes from the naturally occurring restriction enzymes obtained from certain bacteria

ridge characteristics: see *points of identification*

RICO: **R**acketeer **I**nfluenced and **C**orrupt **O**rganizations

rigor mortis: the stiffening of the body after death resulting from chemical changes within muscle tissue

Rogues Gallery: a file of photographs of arrested individuals; usually includes full-face and profile photographs (mug shots) along with detailed physical description, age and place of birth, social security number, fingerprint classification, nicknames and aliases, *modus operandi*, etc. (also called *mug shot file*)

root directory: the main directory of a computer disk, containing files and/or subdirectories

ROM: **R**ead-**O**nly **M**emory; memory in a computer that can be read by the computer, but cannot be used for storing data

roping: placing an undercover agent on a surveillance job (see *undercover*)

rough sketch: a relatively crude, freehand representation of all essential information (including measurements) at a crime scene; it is made while at the scene

rough surveillance: see *open surveillance*

RPG: **R**ocket-**P**ropelled **G**renade

S

safe house: a rendezvous thought to be free of surveillance that is used for illegal activities such as bomb-making by terrorists

scale drawing: a drawing by a skilled draftsperson in which all distances in the finished sketch are precise and proportional

search warrant: a written order of consent, issued by a court, that specifies the place where a search is to be made and the seizable property that is to be looked for, and directs that, when such property is found, it should be brought before the court (also see *seizable property*)

sebum: the semifluid, fatty substance secreted by the sebaceous glands at the base of the hair follicles

second-story job: a burglary in which the offenders come through a skylight or an opening made in the roof

seizable property: contraband, or the fruits or instruments of crime (e.g., a weapon, or other relevant evidence); its nature, as well as where it is to be discovered must be specified in a search warrant (see *search warrant*)

self-incrimination: a statement in which an offender gives evidence against himself or herself, or provides some other form of documentation that provides incriminating evidence.

serial murder: the killing of more than one individual in separate occurrences wherein the crimes are not usually linked by victims

SEMTEX: a type of explosive

shadow: to follow secretly; to place a person under surveillance

short tandem repeats (STRs): repeating sequences of 2–6 base pairs of DNA

show-up: a one-on-one confrontation wherein a suspect and eyewitness are brought together for identification purposes

single locus probe (SLP) test: a test that identifies a fragment of DNA whose sequence appears only once in a chromosome; several single locus tests can be performed using different probes

simple fracture: a fracture in which there is no break in the skin (also called *closed fracture*)

smart phone: a mobile phone built on a mobile operating system, with more advanced computing capability and connectivity than an ordinary cell phone

sniffer: *in arson investigation*, a catalytic combustion device employed to detect flammable vapors

social networking: the sharing of ideas, activities, events, and interests via Internet services, platforms, or sites (i.e., *social media*) that focuses on social relations (e.g., Twitter, Facebook, LinkedIn, etc.)

speaker kill switch: a switch on a personal computer that enables and disables the speaker

spoofing: efforts by criminals to obtain caller ID numbers for the victim's cell phone, which can then be used to obtain information about the victim's identity

stakeout: a surveillance technique in which the surveillant remains essentially in one position or locale; the term is derived from the practice of tethering animals to a stake, allowing them a short radius in which to move (also called *plant, fixed surveillance*)

statutory rape: illegal sexual intercourse with a minor as defined by state laws

stickup: see *armed robbery*

stipulation: an agreement between opposing litigants that certain facts are true

stop and frisk: a law that permits law enforcement officers in some jurisdictions to search an individual based upon reasonable suspicion that they are carrying a weapon

stovepiping: keeping information or intelligence data within an organization and not sharing with other agencies

strategy: the overall planning of operations; in original military sense, "the art of the commander-in-chief"

straw ownership: a situation in which the individual or business entity on record as the owner is a front for the real owner; straw ownership is lawful if not set up for illegal purposes, but generally implies shady or questionable business practices

streamer: see *trailer*

striations: a series of roughly parallel lines of varying width, depth, and separation; scratch marks caused by irregularities or a lack of microfine smoothness of the surface of a gun barrel or on the working edge of a jimmy

strict construction: see *judicial restraint*

strings: *with regard to computers*, groups of characters entered for computer searches

strong-arm robbery: robbery involving the use of physical force (also called *mugging, muscle job*)

sublimation: a phenomenon in which a crystalline substance has the capability of changing directly to a vapor from a solid state

substantive law: law specifying which acts are forbidden and the punishment to be inflicted when the law is broken

suicide: the taking of one's own life; not a crime, but considered a grave public wrong, in many cultures

superglue procedure: a procedure for developing latent fingerprints with cyanoacrylate fuming; named for the commercial product, Super Glue

Supreme Court: the highest court in the land, composed of nine justices appointed for life by the President of the United States

surveillance: the observation of a person, place, or thing—generally, but not necessarily, in an unobtrusive manner

surveillant: the person conducting a surveillance (see *surveillance*)

synthesis: the combining of separate parts or elements to provide a single entity

T

tactics: the means employed to secure an objective; in original military sense, the art or science of deploying in the military

tail: to follow and keep a person or vehicle under surveillance; a surveillance

tailgating: a form of open surveillance in which the subject's vehicle is closely followed

targeted investigation: an anticipatory (proactive) approach to solving crime, focusing on the small group of career criminals responsible for a large amount of crime in an area

taxonomy: the science of classification

technical surveillance: surveillance conducted by means of scientific devices which enhance hearing or seeing the subject's activities—may involve electronic eavesdropping devices (wiretaps, pen registers); electronic tracking devices (beepers), or assorted visual and infrared optical devices

terrorism: the use of force or the fear of force to achieve a political end

testimonial evidence: verbal statement given before the court or other judicial proceeding

theory: a somewhat verified hypothesis; a scheme of thought with assumptions chosen to fit empirical knowledge or observations

third degree: the use of excessive force or torture during an interrogation

tight surveillance: see *close surveillance*

timing device: a device used to "trigger" an action, such as detonate a bomb

toolmarks: particular marks made by a tool or other instrument

touch analysis: analysis in which samples are drawn from a location where a subject has touched an object

toxicology: the study of poisons: their origins and properties, their identification by chemical analysis, their action upon humans and animals, and the treatment of the conditions they produce

trace evidence: physical evidence so small (in size or forensic detail) that an examination requires a stereomicroscope, a polarized light microscope, or both

trajectory: the path or line of a bullet or other object from one location to another

transnational crime: crime that occurs across an international border

transponder: see *GPS device*

trailer: a device or substance used to spread a fire from one part of a structure to another (also called *streamer*)

trauma: an injury that is the result of any force—blunt, sharp, or penetrating

triangulation: a method of measurement to fix the location of an object or place

tweet: a text-based message of up to 140 characters, sent through the social networking service, Twitter

U

UCR: see *Uniform Crime Report*

ulnar loop: a fingerprint pattern in which the open end of the loop leads out to the little finger

unconscious transference: an individual's mistaken recollection of an incident; in criminal investigation, a witness may have a mistaken recollection about a crime that implicates an individual who was not involved

undercover: in secret; an undercover agent often gets to know or work alongside the subject under investigation; an undercover agent is said to *be planted*; a form of surveillance (see *roping*)

undocumented alien: an individual who does not have proper authorization to be in the country

unfounded case: a criminal allegation or report that cannot be proven

Uniform Crime Report (UCR): the annual report on crime published by the FBI

V

validity: the extent to which an experiment, test, or procedure accurately measures that which it is purported to measure (also called *accuracy*)

V pattern: a type of burn pattern

variable: categorization of information types

Vehicle Identification Number: See *VIN*

VICAP: **Vi**olent **C**rime **A**pprehension **P**rogram

victimology: the study of victims

VIN: Vehicle Identification Number. The serial number that car manufacturers stamp on several motor vehicle parts (many of which are inaccessible) for the purpose of tracing and identifying car ownership

virus: a software program that is attached illegally to a larger program and replicates itself by attaching to other programs and files, usually for the purpose of destroying or altering the primary program

voice polygraph: see *voice stress analysis*

voice stress analysis: the detection and analysis of voice changes caused by stress; alleged to be useful in determining whether someone is lying

W

waiving of rights: the willingness of an interviewee to forego civil rights, such as the right to have a lawyer, usually associated with the *Miranda* warnings

whistleblower: an individual who informs on illegal or other violations within an organization

White probe: a single locus probe

wiretap: an eavesdropping device usually attached to telephone wires to listen to private conversations

who-done-it: see *mystery*

whorls: a class characteristic or general pattern (together with loops and arches) used in classifying fingerprints

wire transfer: use of the Internet to transfer funds

wiretap: the interception of communication electronically that is illegal without a search warrant

WMD: weapons of mass destruction

wound: an injury resulting from a blunt force or sharp instrument

Index

Note: Page numbers followed by "*b*," "*f*," and "*t*" refer to boxes, figures, and tables, respectively.

O

P